Macmillan
Australian Primary

DICTIONARY

2ND EDITION

MACMILLAN

Published by Pan Macmillan Australia Pty Ltd
1 Market Street, Sydney, New South Wales, Australia, 2000

First edition published 2005 (revision 2010) by Macmillan Education Australia Pty Ltd
Second edition published 2015 by Pan Macmillan Australia Pty Ltd
Reprinted 2016, 2018, 2021, 2023

ISBN: 9781742619941

Cover design and illustration by Astred Hicks, Design Cherry
Typeset by MPS Limited, Bangalore, India
Printed in China

A Cataloguing-in-Publication entry is available from the National Library of Australia

CONTENTS

EXAMPLE
OF DICTIONARY ENTRIES

Headword
(the word you
are looking up)

Definition
(what the word means)

broad /say brawd / *adjective*
If something is **broad**, it is very wide. *The river is so broad, it would take a long time to swim across it. | To win on a quiz show, you have to have a very broad knowledge of all sorts of things.*

Word Building: **broaden**, *verb* If you make something more broad, you **broaden** it. –**breadth** /say bredth /, *noun*

Word Building
(other words made from
the headword)

Extra information
about the word

The opposite is **narrow**.

★ ***Spelling Tip:*** Remember the *oa* spelling for the 'aw' sound. Think of a 'broad board'. *Board* also has an *oa* spelling – in fact, it has all the same letters as **broad**, but with the *r* in a different position.

Spelling advice

How the ending
of the word
changes

broadcast *verb* (broadcasts, broadcasting, broadcast, has broadcast)
If sounds or pictures are **broadcast**, they are sent by radio or television. *The game will be broadcast later tonight, so let's stay up to watch it.*

broccoli /say **brok**-uh-lee, **brok**-uh-luy / *noun*
Broccoli is a green vegetable with small, hard flowers close together like a cauliflower.

Pronunciation
(how you say the
word)

★ ***Spelling Tip:*** Remember that there is a double *c* and only one *l* in **broccoli**. Also remember the *i* spelling for the 'ee' or 'uy' sound at the end. All of this is because **broccoli** comes from Italian.

Spelling advice

broken *adjective*
1. Something is **broken** if it has separated into pieces. *Sally picked up the bits of the broken cup from the floor.*
2. Something is **broken** if it is not able to work properly because something is wrong with one of the parts. *I don't know what time it is because my watch is broken.*

Part of speech
(the work the word
does in a sentence)

Two definitions
for two meanings

Example sentence

brolga *noun*
A **brolga** is a large, silver-grey bird with long legs. It is especially known for the beautiful movements that it does which look like a dance.

This word comes from an Aboriginal language of New South Wales called Kamilaroi.

Extra information
about the word

HOW TO USE
THE MACMILLAN AUSTRALIAN PRIMARY DICTIONARY

The *Macmillan Australian Primary Dictionary* gives you lots of information about words – their meanings, how to use them in sentences, word building, similar and opposite words, help with difficult spellings, and so on. Here is some guidance on how all this information is set out. Also look at the example of entries on the opposite page.

Finding the word you want to look up

The **headword** is the word you are looking up. You can find it easily because it is in large print and in the colour red.

The headwords are in alphabetical order. To help you find the word you are after, each page has a special guide word at the top of the page. You can use these to work out which words are on that page. The guide word matches the headword of the first entry on a left-hand page, and the headword of the last entry on a right-hand page.

If you are unsure of the spelling, get as close as you can to it by following the letters you are sure about, and then check several words until you find the one you're after. Check the *Spelling Guide* on page vii for help in finding words that might start with unusual spellings.

Saying the word

Sometimes it can be quite hard to work out how to say a word. Each headword that might be difficult has a **pronunciation** after it. Sometimes an easier word that rhymes with the headword will be given, or another word which has exactly the same sound. Usually, though, a special system has been used which will allow you to sound out each part of the word. Look at the *Pronunciation Guide* on page viii to find out more about this.

The work the word does in a sentence

The **part of speech** tells you how a word works in a sentence. For example, a word might be a *noun*, *verb*, *adjective*, *adverb* or *preposition*. This information comes after the headword or pronunciation. Then there are the meanings for that part of speech. Some words can work in different ways, so there may be another part of speech at the start of a new list of meanings.

Words that change their endings

Many words change their ending according to the work they are doing in a sentence. For example, most nouns can have an *s* added at the end to show that there is more than one of them (the plural form) and most verbs can have *ed* or *ing* added. When there is something unusual about the way the ending of the word changes, this is shown in brackets after the part of speech.

What the word means

The sentence telling you what the word means is called the **definition**. The definitions are written in simple language, using words that most people know so that they are easy to understand. If you do find a word that you don't know used in a definition, you will be able to look it up at its own headword in the dictionary.

Many words have more than one meaning. In this case, each definition is given a number. For example, a **hall** can be either a large building or room where a lot of people can meet (definition 1) or a passage inside the front door of a house (definition 2).

If a word has meanings that are very different, each meaning is given under a new headword. When this happens, the headwords themselves are given numbers. For example, look up **can¹** and **can²**.

How a word is used

Most definitions are followed by a sentence which uses the word. This will help you understand more about the word's meaning and how it is used.

Other words that are made from the headword

These are part of the headword's family and you will find them in a box with the heading **Word Building**, along with their meaning or an example sentence. For example, look up **accident**. At the end of this entry, there is information about the word **accidentally**.

Finding out extra information about the word

At the end of some entries, you will find a box giving extra information. This might be another way you can spell the word, a short form of the word, another word with a similar meaning, a word with the opposite meaning, information about where the word comes from, or extra guidance about how a word is used.

Spelling tips

A special feature of this dictionary is the guidance given on the spelling of difficult words. These tips have been written with the advice of education expert Dr Donna Gibbs. The tips suggest a variety of ways in which you can deal with spelling problems, for example:

- pointing out a common difficulty such as a silent letter in a word or a double letter spelling where you might expect a single letter
- reminding you of a spelling rule
- clearing up the confusion that can be caused by different spellings (and meanings) for words that have the same sound
- making a link with words that have the same spelling pattern
- explaining the word's history
- giving a humorous suggestion to jog your memory
- showing how you can break the word up into small parts that are easy to remember.

SPELLING GUIDE

This will help you find the word you are looking up if it starts with a letter that you don't hear when you say the word, or with a letter that is said in an unusual way.

Starting sound	Starting letters might be …	Example
f	ph	phone
g	gh	ghost
g	gu	guess
h	wh	who
j	g	gentle
k	ch	chemist
k	qu	quay
kw	qu	quite
n	gn	gnome
n	kn	knife
r	rh	rhinoceros
r	wr	wrap
s	c	certain
s	sc	scent
s	sw	sword
sh	s	sugar
sk	sch	school
t	tw	two
w	wh	wheel
z	x	xylophone

PRONUNCIATION GUIDE

This guide will help you understand the pronunciations that come after some headwords, following the word 'say'.

a sounds	*e* sounds	*i* sounds
a as in 'bat'	*e* as in 'get'	*i* as in 'bit'
ah as in 'cart'	*ee* as in 'sleep'	*uy* as in 'buy'
ay as in 'day'	*air* as in 'hair'	*ear* as in 'near'

o sounds	*u* sounds	*er* sounds
o as in 'dot'	*u* as in 'but'	*er* as in 'dirt'
oh as in 'coat'	*oo* as in 'book'	*uh* as in 'bett<u>er</u>'
aw as in 'saw'	*ooh* as in 'boot'	
ow as in 'now'		
oy as in 'boy'		

th as in 'thin'	*zh* as in 'trea<u>s</u>ure'	*g* as in 'girl'
dh as in 'then'	*ch* as in 'cheese'	*ng* as in 'ba<u>ng</u>'
sh as in 'shed'	*j* as in 'jam'	

Bold (thick) letters show the part of the word that is said with more stress than the other parts of the word.

anchor

abbreviate /*say* uh-**bree**-vee-ayt/ *verb*
(**abbreviates, abbreviating, abbreviated, has abbreviated**)
If you **abbreviate** a word, you make it shorter by leaving out some of the letters. *You can abbreviate 'Street' to 'St'.*

> **Word Building: abbreviation**, *noun* When you abbreviate a word, you get an **abbreviation**.

abdomen /*say* **ab**-duh-muhn/ *noun*
Your **abdomen** is the part of your body that has your stomach in it.

ability *noun* (*plural* **abilities**)
Ability is the power to do something. *Pui has the ability to swim across the pool.*

able *adjective*
If you are **able** to do something, you have enough power, knowledge or time to do it. *He will be able to come back to school in a few days.* | *'Are you able to come to my party?' 'I would love to but I will be away.'*

Aboriginal /*say* ab-uh-**rij**-uh-nuhl/ *adjective*
1. An **Aboriginal** person is someone related to the first people to live in Australia. *There were several Aboriginal actors in the film we saw.*
2. Something that is **Aboriginal** has to do with the first people to live in Australia. *We are learning an Aboriginal language.*
–*noun* **3.** An **Aboriginal** is an Aboriginal person.

> You can also say **Aborigine** for def. 3 but most Aboriginal people prefer the word **Aboriginal**.

Aborigine /*say* ab-uh-**rij**-uh-nee/ *noun*
Look up **Aboriginal**.

about *preposition, adverb*
1. You can use **about** in many different ways. Its main meanings are 'near' or 'having to do with'. Here are some examples. *We were walking about the place for hours.* | *I'll see you at about six o'clock.* | *Our class has about thirty students in it.* | *She wrote a composition about our beautiful*

beaches. | *I don't know what you are so happy about.*
2. about to, If you are **about to** do something, you are going to do it very soon. *Tom is getting dressed. He is about to go to school.*

above *preposition*
1. If something is **above** something else, it is over it or in a higher place than it. *Hold your hands above your head.* | *'Where do you want to sleep?' 'I want to sleep on the bunk above you.'*
2. If you use **above** before a number or amount, you mean more than that number. *It is very hot today. The temperature is above 30 degrees.*

> The opposite is **under** or **below**.

abrasion /*say* uh-**bray**-zhuhn/ *noun*
An **abrasion** is a wound or sore on your skin that is caused when your skin rubs hard against something rough.

abroad /*say* uh-**brawd**/ *adverb*
If you go **abroad**, you go out of your own country. *If I ever go abroad, I want to go to Africa to see the wild animals.*

absent *adjective*
If you are **absent**, you are not where you should be or where you normally are.

> The opposite is **present**.

accent /*say* **ak**-sent/ *noun*
Your **accent** is the way you say words.

accept /*say* uhk-**sept**/ *verb*
If you **accept** something that someone gives you, you take it or agree to take it. *Sarah accepted the invitation to the fancy-dress party but didn't know what to wear.* | *She felt proud as she accepted the prize.*

> The opposite is **reject** or **refuse**.

> ⭐ *Spelling Tip:* Remember that there is a double *c* in **accept** but that each *c* makes a

a b c d e f g h i j k l m n o p q r s t u v w x y z

different sound – the first has a 'k' sound and the second an 's' sound.

access /say **ak**-ses / noun
1. **Access** is a way of getting to some place. *If you need access to the back of the stage, go through that door.*
2. If someone has **access** to someone else, they have the chance to visit or go to see them. *The principal told the parents at the meeting that they could have access to her whenever they liked to discuss things about the school.*
–verb 3. If you **access** information stored on a computer, you are able to find it and use it. *Our first lesson in computers was about how to access the files.*

accident /say **ak**-suh-duhnt / noun
An **accident** is something bad that happens without being planned or expected. *Sam was hurt in a car accident.* | *I'm sorry I broke the window – it was an accident.*

> *Word Building:* **accidentally**, adverb If something happens that is an accident, it happens **accidentally**.

> 🕮 *Spelling Tip:* Remember that there is a double c in **accident** but each c makes a different sound – the first has a 'k' sound and the second an 's' sound.

according adverb **according to**,
You use **according to** before the name of someone who has told you something, or something that has given you information. *According to my grandfather, I look like my father did when he was young.*

account noun
1. An **account** is the money that you have in a bank or some place like that. *My mum started an account for me at the bank so that I can start saving.*
2. An **account** is a story telling the important things that have happened. *The police wanted us to give an account of everything that we had seen.*

accurate /say **ak**-yuh-ruht / adjective
If something is **accurate**, it is exactly right or correct. *The person who saw the crash gave an accurate account of how it had happened.*

> *Word Building:* **accurately**, adverb Something that is accurate has been done **accurately**. –**accuracy** /say **ak**-yuh-ruh-see /, noun

Something that is accurate shows a lot of **accuracy**.

accuse verb
If you **accuse** someone, you say that you blame them for doing something wrong. *Sarah accused Kylie of stealing the pencil case.*

> *Word Building:* **accusation**, noun When you accuse someone of doing something wrong, you make an **accusation**.

ace noun
1. An **ace** is a playing card with a single shape on it. *The ace of hearts has a single red heart on it.*
2. An **ace** is a serve in tennis so good that the other player cannot touch or hit the ball at all. *She served several aces during the game and won easily.*

ache /rhymes with cake / noun
1. An **ache** is a pain that goes on for a long time. It is usually not a strong pain. *Helen is in bed because she has an ache in her stomach.*
–verb 2. If part of your body **aches**, you feel a pain there that goes on for a long time. *I rode my bike very fast and now my legs are aching.*

> Also look up **headache**.

acknowledge /say uhk-**nol**-ij / verb
1. If you **acknowledge** something, you admit that it is real or true. *Sam acknowledged that winning the race would be difficult.*
2. When you **acknowledge** someone or something, you show that you recognise them or understand something important about them. *She saw him on the other side of the room and acknowledged him with a wave of her hand.*

> *Word Building:* **acknowledgement**, noun When you acknowledge something, you make an **acknowledgement** of it.

acknowledgement of country noun
An **acknowledgement of country** is a ceremony that takes place at the start of a public event in Australia in which someone makes a speech officially recognising the Indigenous people who first lived in the area where the event is taking place.

acrobat noun
An **acrobat** is someone who does all sorts of skilful physical tricks. **Acrobats** turn and roll their body in many difficult positions and keep their balance while walking on a rope high in the air.

across *preposition*
1. If something is **across** something, it goes from one side of it to the other side. *They are building a new bridge across the river.*
–adverb **2.** If you go **across**, you go from one side to another. *The road is very busy. Walk across at the traffic lights.*

act *noun*
1. An **act** is something that has been done or performed.
–verb **2.** If you **act** in a certain way, you do something in that way. *John acted quickly when he saw the rock falling.*
3. If someone **acts** in a play or a film, they play the part of a character in it. *He began acting in plays when he was young and now he is a famous film actor.*

action *noun*
1. An **action** is an act. It is something that someone or something does. *She was saved by her brother's quick action in pulling her out of the way.*
2. in action, When a machine is **in action**, it is turned on and is going. *Keep right away from the electric saw when it is in action.*
3. out of action, If a machine is **out of action**, it is not working. *The washing machine has been out of action for a week.*

active *adjective*
If you are **active**, you have a lot of energy and do lots of things.

activity *noun (plural* **activities***)*
An **activity** is something you do, often something that takes a lot of energy.

actor *noun*
An **actor** is someone who acts the part of a character in a play, in a film or on television.

An **actor** used to be only a man or a boy, but more and more people use the word to refer to anyone who acts, male or female. You can also say **actress** for a woman who acts.

actress *noun*
An **actress** is a girl or woman who acts the part of a character in a play, film or on television.

actual */say* **ak**-chooh-uhl */ adjective*
If something is **actual** it is real and not just in the mind. *I like films that are about actual events. | We were late for the football match. The clock said it was one o'clock but the actual time was three o'clock.*

Word Building: **actually**, *adverb: Please tell me what actually happened.*

✴ *Spelling Tip:* Remember that this word has *act* in it. This will remind you of the *t*. With the *u* following, it has a 'ch' sound and you might not hear the *t*.

adapt *verb*
If you **adapt** something, you change it in a way that makes it better or more useful. *She adapted her story so that it would be easy for kindergarten children to understand.*

Word Building: **adaptation**, *noun* When something has been adapted, an **adaptation** has taken place. When there has been an **adaptation** of a living thing, it has changed in a way that makes it easier for it to survive in its environment.

add *verb*
1. If you **add** something, you put it with something else to make it bigger. *Sam asked his mother to add a few more bags of chips and lollies to the picnic basket.*
2. If you **add** numbers, or **add up** numbers, you find how much they are all together. *'Add 9 and 7 and tell me the answer.' 'Is the answer 16?' 'Yes, you have added it up perfectly!'*

Word Building: **addition**, *noun* If something is added to something else, it is an **addition**. *They are building a new addition to the house.*

addict */say* **ad**-ikt */ noun*
An **addict** is someone who cannot do without something, especially drugs.

Word Building: **addicted** */say* uh-**dik**-tuhd /, *adjective* A person who is an addict is **addicted** to something. –**addiction**, *noun* A person who is an addict is suffering from an **addiction**.

address *noun*
1. Someone's **address** is the number of the house and the name of the street and town where they live. *Write the address clearly on the front of the letter.*
2. On a computer, an **address** is the group of letters and numbers that you key in to send an email to someone or to go to a particular place on the internet. *I want to send her an email but I don't know her address.*

adjective *noun*
An **adjective** is a type of word which describes a noun, such as 'cold' in *a cold wind*.

admiral *noun*
An **admiral** is the most important person in the navy.

admire *verb*
If you **admire** someone or something, you think they are very good. *We all admired the way our coach kept working with our team even though we kept losing.*

> *Word Building:* **admiration**, *noun* If you admire someone or something, then you feel **admiration** for them.

admit *verb* (**admits**, **admitting**, **admitted**, **has admitted**)
If you **admit** something, you say that you have done something wrong. *Samantha admitted that she had opened the chocolate biscuits and eaten almost all of them.*

> *Word Building:* **admission**, *noun* If you admit something, you make an **admission**.

adopted *adjective*
You are **adopted** if you were chosen by your family to belong to them after you were born.

> *Word Building:* **adoption**, *noun* **Adoption** is what happens when a child is adopted by a family.

adore *verb*
If you **adore** someone or something, you feel very strong love for them. *Victoria adored her little dog and wanted it to sleep in her bedroom.*

> *Word Building:* **adoration**, *noun* If you adore someone or something, then you feel **adoration** for them.

adult /*say* uh-**dult**, **ad**-ult/ *noun*
An **adult** is someone who has grown up and is not a child any more.

advance *verb*
1. If you **advance**, you move forwards. *The little dog was scared but advanced cautiously towards his new owner.*
–*noun* 2. **in advance**, If you do something **in advance**, you do it before something happens.

advantage *noun*
An **advantage** is something that puts you ahead of other people.

adventure /*say* uhd-**ven**-chuh/ *noun*
An **adventure** is something that you do which is exciting and perhaps a bit dangerous.

> *Word Building:* **adventurous**, *adjective* Someone who is **adventurous** likes to have adventures.

adverb *noun*
An **adverb** is a type of word which tells you something extra about a verb (such as 'quickly' in *She ran quickly*), an adjective (such as 'really' in *He is really clever*), or another adverb (such as 'very' in *He will arrive very soon*).

advertisement /*say* uhd-**vert**-uhs-muhnt/ *noun*
An **advertisement** is a notice that tells you that something is for sale or that something is going to happen.

> *Word Building:* **advertise** /*say* **ad**-vuh-tuyz/, *verb* You **advertise** something in an advertisement.

> This word is often shortened to **ad**.

> ✪ *Spelling Tip:* The word **advertisement** comes from the word **advertise**, although there is a change in the sound. This should remind you not to make the mistake of leaving out the *e* before the *ment* at the end.

advice /*say* uhd-**vuys**/ *noun*
If someone gives you **advice**, they tell you the best thing to do. *I need some advice about how to fix my bike.*

> ✪ *Spelling Tip:* Also look up **advise** and remember that the noun **advice** (the 'thing' word) ends with *ice* while the verb **advise** (the 'doing' or 'saying' word) ends with *ise*. This is the pattern with other pairs of words with these endings, for example *practice* (noun) and *practise* (verb). Try thinking that *ice* is a noun as a way to remember this.

advise /*say* uhd-**vuyz**/ *verb*
If someone **advises** you about something, they tell you the best thing to do. *My dad advises people on how to look after their money but he could not advise me on how to fix my bike.*

> ✪ *Spelling Tip:* Look up the note at **advice**.

aerobics /*say* air-**roh**-biks/ *noun*
When you do **aerobics**, you do exercises to improve your fitness, usually to music.

aeroplane *noun*
An **aeroplane** is a machine that can fly and which usually carries passengers.

> This word is often shortened to **plane**.

affect *verb*
If something **affects** something or someone, it changes them in some way. *He is such a sensible person that winning all that money has not affected him at all.*

> Don't confuse **affect** with **effect** which is something that happens because of something else. Look up **effect**.

affection /*say* uh-**fek**-shuhn/ *noun*
Affection is great liking for someone or something.

> **Word Building: affectionate** /*say* uh-**fek**-shuh-nuht/, *adjective* If you feel or show affection, you are **affectionate**.

afford *verb*
If you can **afford** something, you have enough money to pay for it. *They can afford to buy a car.*

afraid *adjective*
If you are **afraid**, you feel frightened. *He was afraid that he would fall over in the dark.* | *Our small dog Pip is afraid of very large dogs.*

after *preposition*
1. If something is **after** something else, it is later than it or behind it. *The carriage comes after the train.* | *Night comes after day.*
2. If someone does something **after** someone else, then they have their turn when that person has finished. *You can use the computer after me.*
3. after all, You use **after all** to say that something has happened or can happen when you had thought it might not happen. *The rain has stopped, so we can play tennis after all.*
—*adverb* **4.** If something comes **after**, it comes behind. *James went first and we all followed after.*
—*conjunction* **5.** You use **after** to show that something has happened later in time than something else. *The coach gave us oranges to eat after we had played the first half.*

afternoon *noun*
Afternoon is the time from the middle of the day until evening.

after-school care *noun*
After-school care is a place where you can go in the afternoon when school finishes, where people look after you before you go home.

again /*say* uh-**gen**, uh-**gayn**/ *adverb*
1. If something happens **again**, it has happened before and now is happening another time. *The television has stopped working again.*
2. again and again, If something happens **again and again**, it keeps on happening many times. *Max tried to grab the rope again and again, but he kept missing it.*
3. once again, If you do something **once again**, you do it one more time just as you have done it before. *The teacher asked us to try the song once again.*

against /*say* uh-**genst**, uh-**gaynst**/ *preposition*
1. If something is **against** something, it is touching it. *He leaned the piece of wood against the wall.*
2. If you are **against** something, you do not like it or think it is right. *I am against people being cruel to animals.*
3. If you play a game or sport **against** someone, they are on the other side and you are trying to beat them. *We played a tennis match against a team from another school.*

age *noun*
Your **age** is how many years you have been alive. It tells how old you are.

aggressive *adjective*
People or animals are **aggressive** if they feel like attacking you.

> **Word Building: aggression**, *noun* When someone is aggressive, they might show their **aggression** by shouting or pushing you.

ago *adverb*
1. If something happened a particular time **ago**, it happened that amount of time before now. *I arrived home two hours ago.*
2. long ago, If something happened **long ago**, it happened many, many years before now. *Long ago there were no cars or planes.*

agony *noun*
Agony is a lot of pain, almost too much for a person to deal with.

agree *verb*
1. If you **agree**, you say yes. *Dad asked me to help him paint the boat and I agreed to do it.*
2. If you **agree**, you think the same. *'I thought that film was good.' 'I agree. I thought it was very good.'* | *I agree with you that it is too late to go.* | *All the girls in the netball team agreed on Monday night for training.*

a b c d e f g h i j k l m n o p q r s t u v w x y z

Word Building: **agreement**, *noun* When you agree to do something, you make an **agreement**. *We made an agreement to meet at eight o'clock.*

The opposite is **disagree**.

agriculture /*say* **ag**-ruh-kul-chuh/ *noun*
Agriculture is the work of farming, for example growing plants or keeping animals for food.

ahead *adverb*
1. If you move or look **ahead**, you move forwards or look to the front of you. *I'll go ahead. You wait here.*
2. **go ahead**, If someone tells you to **go ahead**, they are allowing you to do something you want to do. *'Could I have a ride on your bike?' 'Yes, go ahead.'*

aid *noun*
1. **Aid** is help. *Our class is saving up to send some aid to children in famine areas.* | *When he fell over, I went to his aid.*
2. An **aid** is something or someone that helps. *This dictionary is an aid to spelling.* | *The teacher's aid helped me to read.*
–*verb* 3. If something or someone **aids** you, they help you. *Some old people use sticks to aid them in walking.*

AIDS /*say* aydz/ *noun*
AIDS is a very serious disease. If a person has AIDS their body is not able to fight other diseases and sicknesses that healthy bodies can fight.

aim *verb*
If you **aim** something, you point it towards something. *The soldier aimed the gun carefully.*

air *noun*
1. **Air** is what we breathe. It is all around us but we cannot see it. *This room doesn't have enough air. Please open the window.*
2. **Air** is the space above us and above the things of the world. *Look at the plane flying through the air.*

air conditioner *noun*
An **air conditioner** is a machine that makes a place cooler.

aircraft *noun* (*plural* **aircraft**)
An **aircraft** is a machine that can fly, such as a plane or helicopter.

air pollution *noun*
Air pollution is dirt in the air caused by smoke and gases from factories, cars, and other things.

airport *noun*
An **airport** is a place where aircraft arrive and leave.

alarm *noun*
1. An **alarm** is a sound or signal that is used to warn people.
–*verb* 2. If you **alarm** someone or something, you make them feel frightened. *Don't move too quickly – you'll alarm the horses.*

album *noun*
An **album** is a book with pages where you can keep things like photographs, pictures or stamps.

alert *adjective*
You are **alert** if you are watching very carefully, ready for action.

alive *adjective*
If someone is **alive**, they are living and not dead.

all *adjective*
1. You use **all** to mean the whole of something or the whole number or amount of something. *I would like to see all the world.* | *All the milk has been drunk.*
–*pronoun* 2. You use **all** to mean the whole lot of a group of things or people. *We have eaten all the apples.* | *'Are any of the children awake?' 'No, all of them are still sleeping.'*
3. **in all**, You use **in all** after a number of things or people to show that is the whole number. *When we added up the number of pets that people in our class had, we had 20 pets in all.*
–*adverb* 4. **all over**, If something is **all over** something else, it is on every part of it. *He had dirt all over his clothes.*

allergy /*say* **al**-uh-jee/ *noun* (*plural* **allergies**)
If someone has an **allergy**, their skin can become red or they get a sick feeling when they eat certain foods or go near certain plants or certain substances.

Word Building: **allergic** /*say* uh-**ler**-jik/, *adjective* Someone who has an allergy is **allergic** to something.

alley *noun* (*plural* **alleys**)
An **alley** is a rather narrow space between buildings where people can walk through.

alligator /*say* **al**-uh-gay-tuh/ *noun*
An **alligator** is a large animal from America. It is like a lizard with thick, hard skin and sharp teeth, and it lives near water. It has a wider nose than a crocodile.

allow *verb*
If you **allow** someone to do something, you say that they can do it. *Our teacher allowed us to go home early today.*

Another word with a similar meaning is **permit**.

all right *adjective*
1. If someone is **all right**, they are safe or not sick.
–*interjection* **2.** You can say **all right** when you agree to something and mean 'yes'. *'Can I visit you on Tuesday?' 'All right, come on Tuesday.'*

ally /*say* **al**-uy/ *noun* (*plural* **allies**)
An **ally** is a person or country who is your friend or supporter.

almost *adverb*
You use **almost** to mean 'nearly but not quite'. *She's almost ten – no more single numbers!*

alone *adjective*
If you are **alone**, there is no-one with you. You are by yourself. *She doesn't like being alone in the house at night.* | *My mum likes to be alone and have peace and quiet sometimes.*

Compare **alone** with **lonely**. If you are **lonely**, you feel sad because you are not with other people or because you do not have many friends. You might want to be **alone** but nobody likes to be **lonely**.

along *preposition*
If you go **along** something, you go from one end of it towards the other end. *We walked along the road.*

aloud *adverb*
If you say something **aloud**, you say it in an ordinary voice that people can hear. *Dad read the newspaper story aloud so that we all would know what had happened.*

alphabet /*say* **al**-fuh-bet/ *noun*
An **alphabet** is all the letters of a language put in order.

***Word Building:* alphabetical** /*say* al-fuh-**bet**-ik-uhl/, *adjective* When something has been arranged in the order of the alphabet, then it is in **alphabetical** order.

alps *noun*
Alps are high mountains.

***Word Building:* alpine**, *adjective* People go to the alps for **alpine** sports such as skiing.

already *adverb*
If something has happened **already**, it has happened before now. *My dad offered to try to fix my bike but my friend had already fixed it.*

✸ *Spelling Tip:* Remember that there is only one *l* in **already**. Although this word is made up of *all* and *ready*, the second *l* in *all* has been dropped.

also *adverb*
You use **also** to show that something is being added to what has already been mentioned. *I would like to invite Sarah and Yumiko to my party, and also Helen.*

altar /*say* **awl**-tuh/ *noun*
An **altar** is a special table in a church.

✸ *Spelling Tip:* Don't confuse the spelling of **altar** with **alter** which has the same sound but is spelt with an *e*.

alter /*say* **awl**-tuh/ *verb*
If something **alters**, it changes. *I will alter the drawing I have done of my father to make him look a bit thinner.*

***Word Building:* alteration**, *noun* When you alter something, you make an **alteration**.

✸ *Spelling Tip:* Don't confuse the spelling of **alter** with **altar** which has the same sound but is spelt with an *a*.

although /*say* awl-**dhoh**/ *conjunction*
1. If you do something **although** there is something that might stop you, you do it without taking notice of that thing. *Although my little sister is only six, she can read all the books that I am reading.*
2. If something happens **although** you might not expect it to, or **although** you try to stop it, it happens anyway. *Although it is winter, it's been very hot recently.* | *Although I go to bed early, I find it hard to wake up in the morning.*

✸ *Spelling Tip:* **Although** has been formed from *all* (remember that one *l* has been dropped) and *though*. Notice that in both **although** and *though* there is the spelling *ough* for the 'oh' sound.

altitude /*say* **al**-tuh-tyoohd/ *noun*
The **altitude** of something is how high it is above the level of the sea.

altogether *adverb*
You use **altogether** to show that you are talking about the total number of something. You are

a
b
c
d
e
f
g
h
i
j
k
l
m
n
o
p
q
r
s
t
u
v
w
x
y
z

including everything or everyone. *There are five fingers on each hand, so we have ten fingers altogether.*

> ✳ *Spelling Tip:* Remember that there is only one *l* in **altogether**. Although this word is made up of *all* and *together*, the second *l* in *all* has been dropped.

aluminium /*say* al-yuh-**min**-ee-uhm/ *noun*
Aluminium is a metal that is silver-grey in colour and is used to make things like containers for drinks.

always *adverb*
If something **always** happens, it happens every time. *I always go to school on the bus.*

amateur /*say* **am**-uh-tuh, **am**-uh-chuh/ *noun*
An **amateur** is someone who does something for fun and not for money. *Only amateurs used to be able to go in the Olympic Games.* | *My uncle makes furniture, but he is an amateur – he doesn't do it as a job.*

> The opposite is **professional**.

> ✳ *Spelling Tip:* Remember that the 'uh' sound in the middle of this word is spelt *a* and the final sound is spelt *eur*. The ending is spelt like this because **amateur** comes from French.

amaze *verb*
If you **amaze** someone, you surprise them a lot. *It would amaze my friends if I changed the colour of my hair to green.*

> *Word Building:* **amazement**, *noun* If you amaze someone, they might look at you in **amazement**.

ambassador /*say* am-**bas**-uh-duh/ *noun*
An **ambassador** is someone who is sent by their country to live in another country. Their job is to represent the government of their own country.

> ✳ *Spelling Tip:* Remember the double *s*, and the *or* (not *er*) ending.

ambition /*say* am-**bish**-uhn/ *noun*
If you have an **ambition**, it is what you want for your future. *His ambition is to sing in a rock band.*

> *Word Building:* **ambitious** /*say* am-**bish**-uhs/, *adjective* If you work hard towards your ambition and want to be successful, then you are **ambitious**.

ambulance /*say* **am**-byuh-luhns/ *noun*
An **ambulance** is a special vehicle that takes sick or injured people to hospital.

ambush *verb*
If you **ambush** someone, you hide and wait and then attack them suddenly. *The bushrangers were waiting in the hills to ambush the coach carrying the gold into town.*

ammunition /*say* am-yuh-**nish**-uhn/ *noun*
Ammunition is things like bullets that you fire from a gun or other weapon.

among *preposition*
If you are **among** a group of people or things, you are in the middle of them. They are all around you. *Helen is standing among her friends over there.*

> Look up **between**. You use **among** when you are talking about a group of more than two people or things. You use **between** when there are only two people or things. *Helen is standing between Mary and Sophie.*

amount *noun*
An **amount** of something is how much there is of it.

amuse *verb*
1. If something **amuses** you, it makes the time pass happily for you. *It was raining outside so we amused ourselves in the kitchen making a cake.*
2. If something **amuses** you, it makes you laugh or smile. *It really amused Vijay to see how funny the singers looked on television when he turned the sound down.*

> *Word Building:* **amusement**, *noun* If you are amused, you feel **amusement**.

ancestor /*say* **an**-ses-tuh/ *noun*
Your **ancestor** is someone related to you who lived a long time ago.

> ✳ *Spelling Tip:* Remember that there is a *c* (not an *s*), at the start of the second part of **ancestor**. Also notice that the ending is *or* (not *er*). Think *o* for old, because that is what **ancestors** are!

anchor /*say* **ang**-kuh/ *noun*
An **anchor** is something heavy tied to a boat that you drop into the water so that it lands on the bottom and stops the boat moving away.

> ✳ *Spelling Tip:* Remember that **anchor** is spelt with *ch* (for the 'k' sound). Think of

other words that you know that are like this, such as *Christmas*. Also notice that the ending is *or*.

ancient /*say* **ayn**-shuhnt / *adjective*
If something is **ancient**, it is very old.

and *conjunction*
You use **and** to join words or parts of sentences together. *Remember to bring your towel and sunscreen when we go to the beach.*

angel /*say* **ayn**-juhl / *noun*
In some religions, people believe that an **angel** is one of God's messengers. We usually draw them as humans with wings.

> ⭐ *Spelling Tip:* Don't confuse the spelling of **angel** with **angle** which is a pointed shape. Notice that the *g* in **angel** makes a soft 'j' sound and in **angle** it makes a hard 'g' sound.

anger *noun*
Anger is the strong feeling you have when you think that something wrong has been done to you or to other people.

angle /*say* **ang**-guhl / *noun*
An **angle** is the pointed shape that two straight lines make when they meet.

> ⭐ *Spelling Tip:* Don't confuse the spelling of **angle** with **angel** which is a messenger of God in some religions.

angry *adjective* (**angrier**, **angriest**)
If you are **angry**, you have a feeling of anger.

> *Word Building:* **angrily**, *adverb* If you do something in an angry way, you do it **angrily**.

animal *noun*
An **animal** is a living thing that is not a plant and is able to feel and move around. *Cats, dogs, elephants and mice are all animals.*

ankle *noun*
Your **ankle** is the part of your body where your foot joins your leg.

anniversary /*say* an-uh-**ver**-suh-ree / *noun* (*plural* **anniversaries**)
An **anniversary** is the time each year when you remember something that happened at the same time in an earlier year.

announce *verb*
If you **announce** something important, you tell a lot of people about it. *She announced the names of the winners.*

> *Word Building:* **announcement**, *noun* When you announce something, you make an **announcement**.

annoy *verb*
If someone or something **annoys** you, it makes you feel cross. *My mother was annoyed because we were all late for dinner.*

> *Word Building:* **annoyance**, *noun* Something that annoys you is an **annoyance**.

annual *adjective*
Something is **annual** if it happens once a year.

> *Word Building:* **annually**, *adverb* If something is annual, then it happens **annually**.

another *adjective*
1. You use **another** to mean one more thing or person.
–*pronoun* **2. Another** is one more thing or person. *'There are three planes in the sky.' 'Look, there's another. That makes four.'*
3. one after another, If a lot of people do something **one after another**, first one person does it and then another does it, and then another, and so on. *They all ran into the room one after another.*

answer /*say* **an**-suh / *noun*
1. An **answer** is what you say to someone after they have asked you something. *I asked her what food she liked. Her answer was that she liked ice-cream best.*
2. An **answer** is what you write or say when you are asked a question to test what you know. *We had a test today at school and I knew all the answers.*
–*verb* **3.** If you **answer**, you say something to someone after they have asked you a question. *She answered that she liked chocolate best.*
4. If you **answer** a letter or something like that, you write to the person who sent it to you. *She answered the email immediately.*

ant *noun*
An **ant** is a small insect without wings.

antelope *noun* (*plural* **antelope** *or* **antelopes**)
An **antelope** is an animal like a deer, which can run very fast. **Antelopes** live mainly in Asia and Africa.

anthem *noun*
An **anthem** is a song that you sing at important times or events. *Australia's national anthem is 'Advance Australia Fair'.*

a b c d e f g h i j k l m n o p q r s t u v w x y z

antibiotic /*say* an-tee-buy-**ot**-ik / *noun*
An **antibiotic** is a type of medicine that makes you better by fighting something in your body which is making you sick.

antique /*say* an-**teek** / *noun*
An **antique** is something made a long time ago, such as a piece of furniture or art.

anxious /*say* **ang**-shuhs / *adjective*
If you feel **anxious**, you are worried about something.

> **Word Building: anxiously**, *adverb* If you do something in an anxious way, you do it **anxiously.** –**anxiety** /*say* ang-**zuy**-uh-tee /, *noun* When you are anxious, you have a feeling of **anxiety**.

> ✳ *Spelling Tip:* The most difficult bit in spelling this word is remembering the *x* (which spells the 'sh' sound). Try thinking that if you are feeling **anxious**, it can make you act as if you are cross – and there is a cross in the form of an *x* in the word.

any /*say* **en**-ee / *adjective*
1. You use **any** in questions or after the word 'not' to mean 'some'. *'Have you got any money, Richard?' 'No, I have not got any money.' 'Sue, have you got any money?' 'Yes, I've got some money.'*
2. You can use **any** to mean 'no special one'. *You can sit on any chair. It doesn't matter which one.*
–*pronoun* 3. You use **any** in questions or after the word 'not' to mean 'some'. *There is plenty of food left. Do you want any?* | *He asked me for some money but I didn't have any.*

anyone *pronoun*
You use **anyone** when you are talking about people in general but not a particular person. *Anyone can learn to sing. Even my dad can sing.*

> You can also say **anybody**.

anything *pronoun*
You use **anything** when you are talking about something or some things in a general way. If you use **anything**, it means you are not talking about a particular thing or you do not think it is important to mention a particular thing. *Have you got something to wear to a fancy-dress party? Anything will do!*

anyway *adverb*
You use **anyway** to mean that something has happened or should happen even though there is something which you might expect to stop it happening. *I missed the bus, but I got to school on time anyway.*

> You can also say **anyhow**.

anywhere /*say* **en**-ee-wair / *adverb*
You use **anywhere** when you are talking about a place in general, not a particular place. *Did you go anywhere interesting on the weekend?*

Anzac *noun*
An **Anzac** is a soldier from Australia or New Zealand who fought during World War I.

> This name was made by joining the first letters of the words **Australian (and) New Zealand Army Corps**.

apart *adverb*
1. If things or people are **apart**, they are separated or not together. *For this game we need to keep the older children and the younger children apart.*
2. If something is taken **apart**, it is split up into pieces. *He took the clock apart to see how it worked.*

apartment *noun*
An **apartment** is a set of rooms for living in, usually on one floor, among others in a building.

> Another word with a similar meaning is **flat**.

ape *noun*
An **ape** is one of the large monkeys that do not have tails.

apologise /*say* uh-**pol**-uh-juyz / *verb*
If you **apologise**, you say that you are sorry. *She apologised for dropping the brick on his foot.*

> **Word Building: apology** /*say* uh-**pol**-uh-jee /, *noun* When you apologise, you make an **apology**. *Please accept my apology for dropping a brick on your foot.*

> Another spelling for this word is **apologize**.

app *noun*
An **app** is a digital product which you can download onto a smart phone or tablet.

appeal *noun*
An **appeal** is a call for help.

appear *verb*
If something **appears**, it comes to where you can see it. *Mum suddenly appeared from around the corner.*

appearance *noun*
1. When someone or something arrives or comes to where they can be seen, they make an **appearance**. *He didn't make an appearance until the party was nearly over.*
2. Your **appearance** is the way you look. *She is always thinking about her appearance. She likes to have nice clothes.*

appendix *noun* (*plural* **appendixes** *or* **appendices** /*say* uh-**pen**-duh-seez/)
1. An **appendix** is a small part like a tube inside your body near your stomach. If it gets bigger and becomes sore, you might need to have an operation to have your **appendix** removed. *Su Li has had her appendix taken out and won't be back at school for a week.*
2. An **appendix** is a section added at the back of a book to give extra information on things mentioned in the main part of the book. *At the back of my book on animals, there is an appendix with lists of animals and which countries they are found in.*

> The illness you have if your appendix becomes swollen and sore is called **appendicitis** /*say* uh-pen-duh-**suy**-tuhs/.

appetite /*say* **ap**-uh-tuyt/ *noun*
If you have an **appetite**, you have the feeling that you would like to eat.

> � **Spelling Tip:** Remember that there is a double *p* but the *t* is single both times it appears.

applaud /*say* uh-**plawd**/ *verb*
If you **applaud**, you show that you are pleased by clapping your hands. *Everybody applauded as she ran towards the finishing line.*

> **Word Building: applause**, *noun* If you applaud someone, then they get **applause**.

apple *noun*
An **apple** is a round fruit with thin red or green skin.

appointment *noun*
An **appointment** is a special time you have made to do something.

approach *verb*
If you **approach** something, you come near to it. *The plane was approaching the runway and we watched the flaps on the wings being raised.*

apricot *noun*
An **apricot** is a small, round, yellow fruit. It is soft and juicy with one large seed inside.

April /*say* **ay**-pruhl/ *noun*
April is the fourth month of the year, with 30 days. It comes between March and May.

apron *noun*
An **apron** is a piece of clothing you wear over your clothes to keep them clean when you are doing something that could make them dirty.

aquarium /*say* uh-**kwair**-ree-uhm/ *noun*
An **aquarium** is a container where you keep fish.

arch *noun* (*plural* **arches**)
An **arch** is a curved part which helps hold up a bridge or building, or forms the top part of a door.

architect /*say* **ah**-kuh-tekt/ *noun*
An **architect** is someone whose job is to plan buildings.

area *noun*
An **area** is a particular part of something, especially part of a city or of a country.

arena *noun*
An **arena** is a space that has been closed in for sports events and shows.

argue *verb*
If you **argue** with someone who does not agree with you, you talk to them about it in a loud or angry way. *Marco argued with Sam about who should have the ball.*

> **Word Building: argument**, *noun* When you are arguing, you are having an **argument**.

> ✲ **Spelling Tip:** Notice that you leave the *e* off the end of **argue** when you make the word **argument**.

arithmetic *noun*
Arithmetic is working things out using numbers.

arm *noun*
Your **arm** is one of the two parts of your body from your shoulders to your hands.

armour *noun*
1. **Armour** is the metal clothing that knights used to wear when they fought against each other. *In museums, you can still see the armour that knights wore.*
2. **Armour** is the metal coverings on planes and ships that protect them in a war. *The armour on the outside of the tank had been hit but the tank was not seriously damaged.*

> Another spelling for this word is **armor**.

a
b
c
d
e
f
g
h
i
j
k
l
m
n
o
p
q
r
s
t
u
v
w
x
y
z

arms *noun*

Arms are the guns, knives and other weapons people use to fight with.

army *noun* (*plural* **armies**)

A country's **army** is made up of a large number of soldiers who have been trained to fight on land.

around *adverb*

1. If you go **around**, you go from one place to another. *We walked around for a long time but we still couldn't find the station.*
2. If something like a wheel goes **around**, it moves in circles. *The wheels of my bike go around very fast.*
–*preposition* **3.** If something is **around** something, it is on all sides of it. *Dad built a fence around the garden.* | *He tied a rope around the tree trunk.*
4. If you go **around** something, you go in a circle around it or you go from place to place in it. *For exercise, the teacher made us run around the block.* | *We walked around the town, looking for a shop that sold chocolate ice-creams.*
5. If you use **around** before a time or a number, you mean close to that time or number but not exactly that time or number. *They arrived at around three o'clock.* | *I've eaten two apples so I think I have around four left.*

You can also say **round**.

arrange *verb*

If you **arrange** things, you put them in order. *She arranged her books neatly on the shelf.*

Word Building: arrangement, *noun* When you arrange something you make an **arrangement**.

arrest *verb*

If the police **arrest** someone, they take them prisoner because they have done something wrong. *The police have arrested someone in connection with the robbery.*

arrival *noun*

Your **arrival** at a place is when you get there. It is the act of arriving.

arrive *verb*

If you **arrive**, you come to a place. *They arrived at the oval early.*

arrow *noun*

An **arrow** is a thin pointed piece of wood that you shoot from string stretched between the ends of a piece of curved wood.

art *noun*

1. **Art** is the making of something beautiful, especially by painting or drawing. *Dhin is good at art. She paints pictures very well.*
2. **Art** can mean the many things made in this way. *We are going to look at a collection of modern art.*

artery *noun* (*plural* **arteries**)

An **artery** is one of the small tubes inside your body that carry blood from your heart.

The tubes that carry blood **to** your heart are **veins**.

article *noun*

1. An **article** is a thing. *His house was a jumble of things he had discovered on his travels – all sorts of unusual articles.*
2. An **article** is a special kind of word which comes before a noun. The word *a* (or *an*) is the **indefinite article** and *the* is the **definite article**.

artificial /*say* ah-tuh-**fish**-uhl / *adjective*

Something is **artificial** if it has been made by humans. *That strawberry drink has an artificial colour in it to make it pink – I don't think there are any strawberries in it at all!*

The opposite is **natural**.

artist *noun*

An **artist** is someone who paints or draws or makes other kinds of art.

Word Building: artistic, *adjective* If someone is **artistic**, they can make beautiful things.

as *conjunction*

1. If something happens **as** something else is happening, it happens at the same time. *As he was going out the door, the phone rang.*
2. You can use **as** to mean that something happens because of something else. *You cannot go and play, as you have not finished your homework yet.* | *As it is raining, we will not be able to play football.*
3. as … as, You use these words to compare things and say they are the same in amount or value. *His work is as good as hers.* | *Marco is as tall as Richard.*
4. not as … as, You use these words to compare things and say they are not the same in amount or value. *Marco is not as tall as his father.* | *Your bike is not as fast as mine.*
5. as if, You use **as if** to say that an event or situation makes you think of a reason for that event, but that is probably not the real reason.

He was shaking as if he was cold, but he was actually just very scared.

ascend /*say* uh-**send**/ *verb*
If you **ascend**, you climb or go up. *The poor old man ascended the stairs with a look of pain on his face.*

> **Word Building: ascent**, *noun* When you ascend, you make an **ascent**. *His ascent was slow because the stairs were steep.*

> The opposite is **descend**.

> ✳ *Spelling Tip:* Remember that there is a silent *c* after the *s* in **ascend**. The *c* is left over from the Latin beginnings of the word – *ad* (meaning 'towards') and *scandere* (meaning 'to climb'). Notice that the silent *c* also appears in the opposite word, **descend**, meaning 'to go down'. Going up or coming down, don't forget the *c*!

ash *noun*
Ash is the grey or black dust that is left after something has burnt.

ashamed *adjective*
If you are **ashamed**, you feel very sorry about something wrong you have done.

ask *verb*
1. If you **ask** someone something, you say or write a question that you want them to answer. *The teacher asked the new girl what country she came from.*
2. ask for, If you **ask** someone **for** something, you tell them you want them to give it to you. *She asked her father for some money to buy books.*

asleep *adjective*
1. If someone is **asleep**, they are sleeping.
–*adverb* **2. fall asleep**, If someone **falls asleep**, they start sleeping. *She went to bed and immediately fell asleep.*

assemble *verb*
1. If you **assemble** something, you put it together. *Sharmin assembled the model aeroplane and painted it green.*
2. If you **assemble**, you come together. *On our first day, we all had to assemble in the playground to be sorted into classes.*

assembly *noun* (*plural* **assemblies**)
An **assembly** is a group of people meeting for a special reason.

assist *verb*
If you **assist** someone, you give them some help. *The community got together to assist the family who had lost their home in the fire.*

> **Word Building: assistant**, *noun* If you assist someone, you are their **assistant**. –**assistance**, *noun* If you assist someone, you give them **assistance**.

asthma /*say* **as**-muh/ *noun*
Asthma is a sickness that sometimes makes it hard for you to breathe.

> ✳ *Spelling Tip:* Don't forget the silent letters *th*. Think about how you get a t<u>h</u>ick feeling in your chest when you have **asthma** and remember to add in the *th* when you spell it.

astonish *verb*
If something **astonishes** you, it surprises you very much. *The news that she had won the race astonished everyone because she hadn't practised at all.*

> **Word Building: astonishment**, *noun* When someone is astonished, they are full of **astonishment**.

astronaut /*say* **as**-truh-nawt/ *noun*
An **astronaut** is someone trained to travel in space.

> ✳ *Spelling Tip:* The spelling of **astronaut** will be easier if you see that it is made up of two parts: *astro* (from the Latin word meaning 'star') and *naut* (from the Latin word meaning 'sailor').

astronomy /*say* uh-**stron**-uh-mee/ *noun*
Astronomy is the study of the sun, moon, stars and planets.

> **Word Building: astronomer**, *noun* Someone whose job is astronomy is an **astronomer**.

at *preposition*
You can use **at** in many ways. Its main meanings have to do with where something is placed or is going, or with time. Here are some examples. *We are at school. | Dad is at home. | Look at the plane. | He threw a ball at the target. | The train leaves at three o'clock.*

athlete /*say* **ath**-leet/ *noun*
An **athlete** is someone who trains to be good at sports such as running and jumping.

> **Word Building: athletics** /*say* ath-**let**-iks/, *noun* An athlete takes part in **athletics**.

a b c d e f g h i j k l m n o p q r s t u v w x y z

—**athletic** /say ath-**let**-ik/, adjective An athlete needs to be very fit or **athletic**.

atlas noun

An **atlas** is a book of maps.

ATM noun

An **ATM** is a machine that you use to get your money from a bank by using a plastic card which has a special number so that only people who know the number can get money.

This stands for automatic teller machine.

atmosphere /say at-muhs-fear/ noun

1. The **atmosphere** is the air all around the earth. The most dangerous part of space travel is when the spaceship comes back into the earth's atmosphere.
2. The **atmosphere** of a place is the feeling that it has. I like visiting my cousins because there is always a happy atmosphere in their house.

atom noun

An **atom** is one of the very small bits that all things are made of.

attach verb

1. If you **attach** something, you fasten or join it to something else. Everyone had to attach a label with their name on it to their bag.
2. **attached to**, If you are **attached to** someone, you like or love them very much. Nei Lee is very attached to her grandmother.

> **Spelling Tip:** Remember that there are two *t*'s side by side, **attached** to each other, in the first part of this word. However, there is no *t* in the *ach* at the end (although it sounds like it could be spelt 'atch').

attack verb

If someone **attacks** someone, they begin to fight them or try to hurt them. The dog attacked the little girl and bit her leg.

attempt verb

1. If you **attempt** to do something, you try to do it. He attempted to swim across the beach but the current was too strong for him so he swam back to shore.
—noun **2.** An **attempt** is when you try to do something.

attend verb

If you **attend** an event, such as a meeting or a party, you go to it. Boris said that he wouldn't be able to attend the soccer meeting.

attendance noun

Your **attendance** is the number of times that you are present at a place.

attention /say uh-**ten**-shuhn/ noun

1. **Attention** is when you fix your thoughts on something and do not think about anything else. Our class gave all their attention to the man from the fire brigade.
2. **pay attention**, If you **pay attention**, you watch and listen carefully. Please pay attention while I tell you what to do.

> **Word Building: attentive**, adjective When you pay attention, you are being **attentive**.

> **Spelling Tip:** There are three *t*'s in this word – two drawing **attention** to themselves together near the beginning and one by itself before the *ion* at the end. The final spelling *tion* makes a 'shuhn' sound, as in many other words.

attic noun

An **attic** is a room or a space inside the roof of a building.

attract verb

If something or someone **attracts** you, they make you like them or feel interested in them. It is always the sharks at the aquarium that attract people most.

attractive adjective

1. Someone is **attractive** if they are pleasing to look at. Sophie thought she would be more attractive with blonde hair but her mother said her hair was fine.
2. Something is **attractive** if it makes you feel pleased and happy. The idea of travelling for a few months every year is a very attractive one.

auction /say **ok**-shuhn/ noun

An **auction** is a sale at which things like houses or paintings are sold to the person who offers the most money.

> **Word Building: auctioneer** /say ok-shuhn-**ear**/, noun Someone whose job is to sell things at an auction is an **auctioneer**.

audience /say **aw**-dee-uhns/ noun

An **audience** is a group of people who listen to or watch something like a play.

audio /say **aw**-dee-oh/ adjective

Something is **audio** if it has to do with sound or hearing.

August /*say* **aw**-guhst/ *noun*
August is the eighth month of the year, with 31 days. It comes between July and September.

aunt *noun*
Your **aunt** is the sister of your father or mother, or the wife of your uncle.

Australian Rules /*say* uhs-trayl-yuhn **roohlz**/ *noun*
Australian Rules is kind of football played by two teams of players, who kick an egg-shaped ball around a field. This game started in Australia.

> A short name for this is **Aussie Rules**.

author *noun*
An **author** is someone who writes books.

authority /*say* uh-**tho**-ruh-tee/ *noun*
If you have **authority**, you have the power to decide things, or to make people do as you think best.

> ***Word Building:*** **authorise** /*say* **aw**-thuh-ruyz/, *verb* If you have authority, then you are able to **authorise** things to happen.

autograph /*say* **aw**-tuh-graf, **aw**-tuh-grahf/ *noun*
Someone's **autograph** is their name in their own handwriting.

automatic /*say* aw-tuh-**mat**-ik/ *adjective*
1. Something is **automatic** if it can work or go all by itself.
–*noun* 2. An **automatic** is a car which changes speeds without the driver having to change the gears.

> ***Word Building:*** **automatically**, *adverb* If something is automatic, then it does things **automatically**.

autumn /*say* **aw**-tuhm/ *noun*
Autumn is the season of the year following summer and coming before winter.

> The other seasons of the year are **winter**, **spring** and **summer**.

> ✳ ***Spelling Tip:*** Don't forget the silent *n* at the end of **autumn**.

available *adjective*
Something or someone is **available** if they are ready or able to be used. *There is a computer available for you to use in the classroom.* | *Our teacher is always available to help us with our schoolwork.*

avalanche /*say* **av**-uh-lansh, **av**-uh-lahnsh/ *noun*
An **avalanche** is a large amount of snow falling suddenly down a mountain.

avenue *noun*
An **avenue** is a street or road, often with trees on both sides of it.

average /*say* **av**-rij/ *adjective*
1. If something is **average**, it is ordinary. It is not good and it is not bad.
–*noun* 2. You find out the **average** of a group of numbers by adding the numbers together and dividing them by how many numbers are in the group.

> ✳ ***Spelling Tip:*** Remember that there is an *e* in the middle of **average**, though you usually say it without this sound. Also remember the *age* spelling at the end of the word (although it sounds like 'ij'). If you think of finding the **average** age of your class, it might help to remind you how to spell the ending.

avocado /*say* av-uh-**kah**-doh/ *noun* (*plural* **avocados**)
An **avocado** is a green fruit shaped like a pear, with a green or black skin and a large stone in the centre. It is often used in salads.

avoid *verb*
If you **avoid** something or someone, you keep away from them. *My mother always tries to avoid the lady on the corner because she talks too much.*

awake *adjective*
If you are **awake**, you are not sleeping.

award *noun*
An **award** is a prize that you win for doing well.

aware *adjective*
If you are **aware** of something, you know about it or have a feeling about it.

away *adverb*
1. You use **away** to mean 'to or in another place'. *We're going away on holiday tomorrow.* | *Please put the cups and plates away.* | *Tom's away from school today because he's sick.*
2. **go away**, If you tell someone to **go away**, you mean that you do not want them to stay near you. *Go away – I'm trying to read and I can't concentrate with you bothering me all the time.*

awful *adjective*
Something that is **awful** is very bad or unpleasant.

a
b
c
d
e
f
g
h
i
j
k
l
m
n
o
p
q
r
s
t
u
v
w
x
y
z

⁂ *Spelling Tip:* The trick here is to remember that the first meaning of **awful** was 'full of awe' (*awe* is a word meaning 'a feeling that something is so good that you are almost afraid'). Then you can see that **awful** is made up of *awe* (without its *e*) and the word part *ful* (meaning 'full of'). Remember that *full* always loses an *l* when it is changed into the word part *ful* at the end of a word. Now it's not so **awful**!

awkward *adjective*

1. Someone who is **awkward** does not look comfortable in the way they move about. They might even knock into things. *She always had trouble doing sport because she was very awkward.*

2. Something that is **awkward** can cause you a lot of trouble. *The camp is awkward to find because there are so many tracks through the bush and you can get lost.*

⁂ *Spelling Tip:* The spelling of this word is **awkward** to remember, mainly because there are two *w*'s – one before the *k* and one after it. Remember that the last part of the word is the word part *ward*, the same as appears in words such as *forward* and *backward*.

axe *noun*

An **axe** is a tool with a metal end with a very sharp edge for cutting wood into pieces.

axle *noun*

An **axle** is the thin stick of metal or wood that goes through the middle of a wheel and joins it to something.

baby *noun* (*plural* **babies**)
A **baby** is a very young child or animal.

back *noun*
1. The **back** of something is the part of it that is farthest from the front. *Please take the chairs to the back of the room.*
2. Your **back** is the part of your body opposite your chest and stomach. *I like to carry my bag on my back so that both my hands are free.*
3. back to front, If something is **back to front**, it is the wrong way round, with the back part at the front. *You've put your shirt on back to front!*

backwards *adverb*
1. If something moves **backwards**, it moves with its back first instead of its front. *The car rolled backwards down the hill.*
2. If you look **backwards**, you look behind you. *She looked backwards at the old woman walking slowly behind her.*
3. If you do something **backwards**, you do it in the opposite way to usual. *Count backwards from one hundred to zero.*

You can also say **backward**.

bacon *noun*
Bacon is the meat from a pig, which has been treated with salt or smoke.

bad *adjective* (**worse**, **worst**)
1. If something is **bad**, it is not good. *We've just seen a really bad film. We didn't like it at all.*
2. An accident or mistake is **bad** if it is serious. *It's surprising you weren't hurt in such a bad accident.*
3. If food is **bad**, it is not good to eat because it is not fresh. *That bad meat smells terrible.*

badge *noun*
A **badge** is something made of metal or some other material that you attach to your clothes. It can tell people who you are, which group you belong to, or what sort of things you like.

badly *adverb*
If you do something **badly**, you do not do it well. *They painted the wall badly and now it looks awful.*

bag *noun*
A **bag** is something you use to carry things in.

baggage /*say* **bag**-ij / *noun*
Your **baggage** is all the bags you use to carry your things when you travel.

> ⭐ *Spelling Tip:* Remember the double *g* in the middle – think of the bag being very heavy with an extra *g*. Also remember that the ending is spelt *age* (although it sounds like 'ij').

bait *noun*
Bait is food you put on a fishing line to catch fish. You can also use **bait** to catch other animals.

bake *verb*
If you **bake** food, you cook it by putting it in an oven. *We like to bake bread on cold winter days.*

baker *noun*
A **baker** is someone whose job is to bake bread and cakes.

> *Word Building:* **bakery**, *noun* The place where the baker bakes the bread and cakes is a **bakery**.

balance *verb*
1. If you **balance** something, you keep it steady. *I can balance a tennis ball on top of a ruler.*
–*noun* **2.** Your **balance** is the steady position that your body has that allows you to stand and walk.

balcony /*say* **bal**-kuh-nee / *noun* (*plural* **balconies**)
A **balcony** is a small area which comes out from the wall of a building, usually up high, where you can stand or sit outside. It usually has rails around it for safety.

bald /*say* bawld / *adjective*
You are **bald** if you have only a little hair or no hair at all on your head.

> *Word Building:* **baldness**, *noun* Someone who is going bald is suffering from **baldness**. –**balding**, *adjective* Someone who is going bald is **balding**.

ball[1] *noun*
A **ball** is a round or egg-shaped object which you can throw or kick or hit and then catch in games.

ball[2] *noun*
A **ball** is a large, formal kind of party where people dance.

ballerina /*say* bal-uh-**ree**-nuh / *noun*
A **ballerina** is a girl or woman who dances in a ballet.

ballet /*say* **bal**-ay / *noun*
A **ballet** is a special sort of dancing with very controlled movements, done by a group of dancers who act out a story on a stage.

> ✷ *Spelling Tip:* Don't forget the silent *t* at the end of **ballet** – the *et* spelling makes an 'ay' sound. Other words with this ending are *bouquet* and *beret*. They all come from French.

balloon *noun*
A **balloon** is a small rubber bag which is filled with air and used as a toy.

bamboo *noun*
Bamboo is a plant with long, flat, green leaves and long, strong stems which are used for making things like furniture and fences.

banana *noun*
A **banana** is a long fruit with a yellow skin.

band[1] *noun*
A **band** is a group of people who play music together.

band[2] *noun*
1. A **band** is something you use for tying or fastening things. *I put a rubber band around my pencils to keep them all together.*
2. A **band** is a stripe. *The snake had bands of red around its belly.*

bandage *noun*
A **bandage** is a narrow piece of material which you wrap around a sore part of your body.

bandaid *noun*
A **bandaid** is a cover that you stick over a cut or a sore to protect it.

bandicoot *noun*
A **bandicoot** is a small Australian animal which has fur and a pointed nose, and digs for a lot of its food. The female carries her babies in a pouch.

bang *noun*
1. A **bang** is a sudden loud noise, like one heavy object striking another.
–*verb* **2.** If something **bangs** something else, it hits it in a noisy way. *Sandra was so angry that she walked out of the room and banged the door behind her.*

banish *verb*
If you **banish** someone, you send them away because they have done something wrong. *After he showed he could not be trusted, he was banished from the meetings.*

banjo *noun* (*plural* **banjos**)
A **banjo** is a musical instrument which you play by running your fingers across the strings and picking them with your nails to give a sharp sound. A **banjo** is smaller than a guitar and a slightly different shape.

bank[1] *noun*
1. A **bank** is a pile or mass of something. *The flowers were planted in a long bank of earth.*
2. The **bank** of a river is the land beside it. *They sat on the bank of the river, resting under a tree.*

bank[2] *noun*
A **bank** is a place where you keep your money and take it out again when you need it.

banksia *noun*
A **banksia** is an Australian plant that has hundreds of tiny flowers crowded together in yellow or orange long, round shapes.

> This plant was called after Joseph Banks, who studied the plants of Australia when he visited with Captain Cook in 1770.

banquet /*say* **bang**-kwuht / *noun*
A **banquet** is a big dinner party with many people.

> ✷ *Spelling Tip:* Remember that the sound in the middle of **banquet** is spelt *qu*. There are many words in which *qu* sounds like 'kw', such as *quiet* and *queen*. Think of 'a queen attending a banquet'. Remember also that there is only one *t* at the end.

baptism /*say* **bap**-tiz-uhm / *noun*
A **baptism** is a special ceremony in which someone has some water put on them as a sign

that they are a new member of the Christian church.

bar *noun*
1. A **bar** is a long piece of wood or metal or some other material. *The athlete ran up and jumped over the bar easily.*
2. A **bar** of something is a long, thin piece of it. *He bought two bars of chocolate.*
3. A **bar** is a long high table in a place like a hotel where drinks are served. *The man they were looking for was sitting at the bar.*

barbecue /*say* **bah**-buh-kyooh/ *noun*
1. A **barbecue** is a fire that you set in the outdoors, for cooking food on. *After we caught the fish, we cooked it on the barbecue.*
2. A **barbecue** is an outdoor party where the food is cooked over an open fire. *The people next door invited us to a barbecue at their place.*

Another way of spelling this is **barbeque**.

barber *noun*
A **barber** is someone whose job is to cut men's hair.

barcode *noun*
a printed code with a series of stripes that can be read by a special scanner connected to a computer. It is used to identify things, such as goods being sold in a shop or stored somewhere.

You can also write this as two words (**bar code**).

bare *adjective*
If something or someone is **bare**, they do not have any covering over them.

⭐ *Spelling Tip:* Don't confuse the spelling of **bare** with **bear** which has the same sound. A **bear** is a large animal. If you **bear** something, you carry it.

bargain /*say* **bah**-guhn/ *noun*
A **bargain** is something you buy for less than you expected to pay for it.

bark[1] *noun*
1. A **bark** is the noise a dog makes.
–*verb* 2. If a dog **barks**, it makes a sharp, hard noise. *I couldn't sleep because the dog barked all night.*

bark[2] *noun*
Bark is the outer covering on the trunk and branches of a tree.

bar mitzvah /*say* bah **mits**-vuh/ *noun*
A **bar mitzvah** is the special time when a Jewish boy turns 13, and becomes an adult member of the Jewish community.

barn *noun*
A **barn** is a building on a farm, used to store feed for animals or as a shelter for them.

barramundi /*say* ba-ruh-**mun**-dee/ *noun* (*plural* **barramundi** *or* **barramundis**)
A **barramundi** is a large, silver-grey coloured fish, which is good to eat.

This word comes from an Aboriginal language of Queensland.

barrel *noun*
A **barrel** is a large, rounded container made of narrow pieces of wood held in place by iron bands.

barrier *noun*
A **barrier** is something that blocks the way.

base *noun*
1. The **base** of something is the bottom part of it, which gives it support. *The base of the bridge was set into the rock.*
2. A **base** is the main place from where things are organised. *They had climbed as far they could in the terrible weather and returned to the base that night.*

baseball *noun*
Baseball is a ball game played by two teams in which a long, thin bat is used to hit a hard ball. Players must run around three points on the field.

basement *noun*
A **basement** is a room or space below the ground floor of a building.

bash *verb*
If you **bash** something, you hit it hard. *The kookaburra killed the snake by bashing it against the branch of a tree.*

basic /*say* **bay**-sik/ *adjective*
If something is **basic**, it is the main or most important thing. *Our basic problem was that we had brought no water with us.*

Word Building: **basically**, *adverb*: *Basically, our problem was a lack of water.*

basin *noun*
A **basin** is something you use to hold water in for washing.

basket *noun*
A **basket** is a woven container for storing or carrying things.

basketball *noun*
Basketball is a game played by two teams of players, who try to earn points by throwing a ball through a ring or basket on top of a tall post.

bat¹ *noun*
A **bat** is a specially shaped piece of wood that you use to hit the ball in games like cricket.

bat² *noun*
A **bat** is a small animal with fur and wings. It flies about at night to feed on fruit and insects, and in the day it sleeps hanging from tree branches.

bath *noun*
1. A **bath** is something for washing yourself in, which is large enough for you to sit or lie in. *Sarah filled the bath with warm water.*
2. A **bath** is a wash you have in this way. *You should have a bath before we go out.*

bathe /*say* baydh / *verb*
1. If you **bathe** in the sea or a pool, you go swimming. *There's no way I'd bathe there – it looks like crocodile country to me!*
2. If you **bathe** a part of your body, you wash it. *Bathe your eye in some warm water.*

bathroom *noun*
A **bathroom** is a room where you go to wash yourself. It usually has a shower or a bath, a place to wash your hands, and often a toilet.

bat mitzvah /*say* baht **mits**-vuh / *noun*
A **bat mitzvah** is the special time when a Jewish girl turns 12, and becomes an adult member of the Jewish community.

battery *noun* (*plural* **batteries**)
A **battery** is a container which stores electricity.

battle *noun*
1. A **battle** is a fight, usually between two armies. *Many people died in the battle.*
2. A **battle** can be any serious fight or struggle. *We have finally won the battle to have a pedestrian crossing built near the school.*
–*verb* **3.** If you **battle**, you fight or struggle. *The doctors battled to save his life.*

bay *noun*
A **bay** is a part in the line of the coast where the land curves in.

be *verb* You use **be** or one of its forms in many ways, for example: **1.** when you are describing someone or something. *You are late.* **2.** as part of another verb. *I am waiting.*

> The different forms of the verb **to be** are:
> ❖ *Present:* I **am**, you **are**, he/she/it **is**, we **are**, they **are**
> ❖ *Past:* I **was**, you **were**, he/she/it **was**, we **were**, they **were**
> ❖ I have **been**
> ❖ I am **being**

beach *noun* (*plural* **beaches**)
A **beach** is the land at the edge of a sea, lake or river. It is usually covered in sand, but can be covered in small rocks.

bead *noun*
A **bead** is a small, hard ball made of glass, plastic or wood, which has a hole through the middle so that you can thread it onto a string.

beak *noun*
A **beak** is the hard pointed part of a bird's mouth.

> A word which means almost the same is **bill**.

beam *noun*
1. A **beam** is a long, strong piece of wood, concrete or metal. *The beam was so heavy, a crane was brought in to lift it.*
2. A **beam** is a long straight line of light. *Suddenly, we saw a kangaroo in the beam of the car light.*

bean *noun*
A **bean** is a plant with small, smooth seeds growing in long seed cases called pods. You can eat the seeds and sometimes the pods as a vegetable.

> ✸ *Spelling Tip:* Don't confuse the spelling of **bean** with **been** which sounds the same, but is spelt with a double *e*. **Been** is a form of **be**: *I have been here before.*

bear¹ *noun*
A **bear** is a large heavy animal with short rough hair and a very short tail.

> ✸ *Spelling Tip:* Don't confuse the spelling of **bear** with **bare** which has the same sound. Something that is **bare** is not covered.

bear² *verb* (**bears**, **bearing**, **bore**, **has borne**)
1. If something **bears** something else, it holds it up or carries it. *Be careful! I don't think that branch is strong enough to bear your weight.*
2. If you cannot **bear** something, you really do not like it. *I can't bear pain. | I can't bear people who tell lies.*

3. If a woman **bears** children, she gives birth to them. If a plant **bears** something, it produces it. *My grandmother bore three sons and three daughters.* | *This tree bears oranges.*

beard *noun*
A **beard** is the hair that grows on the lower part of a man's face.

beast *noun*
1. A **beast** is any animal with four legs, like a cow or a dog, especially a large animal. *Some of the cattle that you see at the show are huge beasts, especially some of the bulls.*
2. A **beast** is a rough, cruel person. *He treated his family so badly that they described him as a beast.*

beat *verb* (**beats, beating, beat, has beaten**)
1. If you **beat** something or someone, you hit them again and again. *The angry child was lying on the floor, beating it with her hands.* | *The rain beat against the window.*
2. If something **beats**, it makes the same movement over and over again. *The bird was beating its wings.* | *My heart beat loudly.*
3. If you **beat** someone in a game or a race, you defeat them. *She swam so fast she beat everyone in her class.*
–*noun* **4.** A **beat** is a sound made over and over again. *Can you hear the beat of your heart?* | *I like dancing to music that has a strong beat.*

beautiful /*say* **byooh**-tuh-fuhl / *adjective*
1. If someone, especially a woman, is **beautiful**, they are very pleasant to look at. *She looked beautiful in her wedding dress.*
2. If something is **beautiful**, it is very pleasing and enjoyable to look at, touch, smell, taste or hear. *Thank you – those flowers are beautiful.*

> **Word Building: beautifully**, *adverb* If something is done in a beautiful way, it is done **beautifully**.

beauty /*say* **byooh**-tee / *noun*
Something has **beauty** if it is very pleasing and enjoyable to look at.

because *conjunction*
1. You use **because** when you want to give the reason for something happening. *We went by car because it was raining.*
–*preposition* **2. because of**, If something happens **because of** something else, it is caused by it. *We had to play inside because of the bad weather.*

become *verb* (**becomes, becoming, became, has become**)
If something or someone **becomes** something, they come to be it, or grow to be it. *The two boys became good friends during the holidays.* | *We had become very hungry after walking all morning.* | *The puppy has become quite big.*

bed *noun*
A **bed** is a place to sleep, especially a piece of furniture with covers to keep you comfortable and warm while you are sleeping.

bedroom *noun*
A **bedroom** is a room where you sleep and dress yourself, with a bed and places to put your clothes and other things.

bee *noun*
A **bee** is a flying insect which makes a special low sound as it flies. We can eat the honey that some **bees** make.

beef *noun*
Beef is the meat from cattle.

beer *noun*
Beer is a drink that some adults like. It is usually light brown in colour.

beetle *noun*
A **beetle** is a flying insect which has a hard covering over its wings.

before *adverb*
1. If something has happened **before**, it has already happened at an earlier time. *'Have you been here before?' 'No, this is the first time.'*
–*preposition* **2.** If something happens **before** something else, it happens earlier than it. *Let's go for a walk before lunch.*

before-school care *noun*
Before-school care is a place where you can go in the mornings, where people look after you before school starts.

beg *verb* (**begs, begging, begged, has begged**)
1. If someone **begs**, they ask for money or food because they do not have any. *The old man stood at the corner, begging for some money from the people passing by.*
2. If you **beg**, you ask for something in a very serious way. *They begged the police to help them find the lost child.*

> **Word Building: beggar**, *noun* Someone who needs to beg for money or food is a **beggar**.

begin verb (**begins**, **beginning**, **began**, **has begun**)
If you **begin**, you start or take the first step in something. *Please begin work now.*

> **Word Building: beginner,** *noun* When you are just beginning to learn something, you are a **beginner**. *This work is too hard for beginners.*

beginning noun
The **beginning** of something is the very first part.

behave /*say* buh-**hayv**/ verb
If you **behave** in a certain way, you act in that way. *'Did you behave well today?' 'Yes, I behaved well, but John behaved badly.'* | *She is only ten, but she behaves like an adult.*

> **Word Building: behaviour** /*say* buh-**hayv**-yuh/, *noun* The way you behave is your **behaviour**, which can be good or bad.

behind preposition
1. If something is **behind** something else, it is at the back of it. *Your coat is hanging behind the door.*
–*adverb* **2.** If you are **behind** in something, you are doing it more slowly or later than you expected to do it. *Our team is behind in the training we were going to do because of the weather.*

believe /*say* buh-**leev**/ verb
1. If you **believe** something, you think it. *I believe that it will rain today – there are lots of clouds.*
2. If you **believe** someone, you think that what they are saying is true. *I believe him – he always tells the truth.*

> **Word Building: belief** /*say* buh-**leef**/, *noun* Something that you believe is a **belief**.

> ✹ **Spelling Tip:** Remember that **believe** has *ie* (to spell the 'ee' sound) following the *l*. This follows the rule that *i* comes before *e* except after *c*.

bell noun
A **bell** is a piece of metal shaped like a cup turned over, which makes a ringing sound when you hit it. You usually ring a **bell** to let people know that something is going to happen, or to warn them about something.

bellow /*rhymes with* yellow/ verb
If you **bellow**, you call out with a loud, deep sound. *The cattle were bellowing in fright.*

belly noun (plural **bellies**)
Your **belly** is the front part of your body that has your stomach inside it.

> Another word that means nearly the same is **abdomen**.

belong verb
1. If something **belongs** to someone, they own it. *'Who does this book belong to?' 'It's mine. I must have dropped it.'*
2. If you **belong** to something, you are a part of it. *I belong to a swimming club.*

below preposition
1. If something is **below** something else, it is lower than it. *She cut her leg below the knee.*
–*adverb* **2.** If something is **below**, it is under something. *From the plane we could see all the towns below.*

belt noun
A **belt** is a narrow length of strong material, usually worn to hold up trousers.

> Also look up **seatbelt**.

bench noun (plural **benches**)
A **bench** is a seat which is long enough for several people to sit on.

bend verb (**bends**, **bending**, **bent**, **has bent**)
1. If you **bend** something, you force it so that it is no longer straight but at an angle. *He bent a piece of wire to try to get into the locked car.*
2. If you **bend** or **bend down**, you move your body forwards or down, often in order to reach something. *She bent to lift up the box.*
–*noun* **3.** A **bend** in something is where there is a turn in it.

beneath preposition
If something is **beneath** something else, it is under it. *The treasure is hidden somewhere beneath the sand.*

bent adjective
If something is **bent**, it has a bend in it and so is not straight.

beret /*say* be-ray/ noun
A **beret** is a soft round cap.

berry noun (plural **berries**)
A **berry** is a small fruit, often brightly coloured.

beside preposition
If something is **beside** something else, it is next to it. *There was a large tree beside the house.*

besides *preposition*
1. **Besides** means 'in addition to'. *Did anyone go to the meeting besides you?* | *How many classes besides your class are walking to the oval?*
2. **Besides** means 'other than'. *I have two other friends besides you.*
–*adverb* 3. You use **besides** if you are saying something extra about something you've already spoken about, especially to add strength to what you have said. *I haven't got enough money to go to the movies. Besides, I don't want to see that film.*

best *adjective*
1. Something is **best** if it is as good as possible and better than anything or anyone else.
–*adverb* 2. If you do something **best**, you do it most successfully. *Of all her friends she swims best.*
–*noun* 3. **the best**, If something or someone is **the best**, they are better than anything or anyone else.

betray *verb*
If you **betray** someone, you harm them by telling their secret when you are not supposed to. *'Please don't betray me', he whispered as I crept away from his secret hiding place.*

> *Word Building:* **betrayal**, *noun* When you betray someone, your action is a **betrayal**.

better *adjective*
1. If something is **better** than something else, it is of a higher standard. *The hamburgers at the little shop are better than the ones at the big shops.*
2. If you are **better**, you are well again after being sick. *Last week I was so sick I couldn't go to school, but I'm better now. I feel great!*
3. If you are **better**, you are becoming well again after being sick. *I still feel bad, but I'm a lot better than I was.*
–*adverb* 4. If you do something **better** than someone else, or than you have done in the past, you do it in a more excellent way. *You can swim better than me – you always beat me.*

bettong /*say* **bet**-ong / *noun*
A **bettong** is a very small kangaroo with a short nose. There are not many of these animals left.

> This word comes from an Aboriginal language of New South Wales called Dharug.

between *preposition*
1. If something is **between** two things, it is within the space, time or amount separating them. *We walked along the path between the houses.* | *We*
had a short rest between the games. | *There's a big difference between the prices of those two cars.*
2. If something is **between** two things, it connects them. *They are talking about making a better track between the camp and the river.*
3. If there is something like an agreement or a conversation **between** two people, they are the two taking part in it. *I could hear an angry discussion between my parents.*
4. If you do something **between** you and someone else, you do it together. *It was a difficult problem, but we worked it out between us.*

beware *verb*
If you tell someone to **beware**, you mean they should be careful of something or someone. *The sign said 'Beware of the dog'.*

bewilder /*say* buh-**wil**-duh / *verb*
If someone or something **bewilders** you, it makes you very confused. *When the new kids start at school, they are sometimes bewildered with all the new things they have to learn – but it gets easier.*

beyond *preposition*
If something is **beyond** something else, it is more distant than it. *We told the man that the station was beyond the shops.*

bicentenary /*say* buy-suhn-**teen**-uh-ree / *noun* (*plural* **bicentenaries**)
A **bicentenary** is a time when people remember something that happened 200 years ago.

> ✳ *Spelling Tip:* The spelling of **bicentenary** will be easier if you see that it contains two important word parts – *bi* (meaning 'two') and *cent* (which comes from Latin and appears in many words whose meaning has to do with 100, such as *cent* and *century*). Then you can concentrate on remembering the single *e* (for the 'ee' sound) and the single *n* in the last part of the word.

bicycle /*say* **buy**-sik-uhl / *noun*
A **bicycle** is something you ride on. It has two wheels which you move by pushing your feet down on special little bars. You change direction by turning the large bar which is connected to the front wheel.

> The short form is **bike**.

big *adjective* (**bigger**, **biggest**)
Something is **big** if it is greater in size than the usual.

a b c d e f g h i j k l m n o p q r s t u v w x y z

bike *noun*
Bike is a short word for a bicycle.

bike rack *noun*
A **bike rack** is a piece of equipment that you can lock bikes onto so they cannot be stolen.

bilby *noun* (*plural* **bilbies**)
A **bilby** is a type of bandicoot which has long ears and long, soft fur. **Bilbies** are not seen much now.

> This word comes from an Aboriginal language of New South Wales called Yuwaalaraay.

bill[1] *noun*
A **bill** is a written or printed note telling you how much money you owe for something.

bill[2] *noun*
A **bill** is the hard part of a bird's mouth.

> A word which means almost the same is **beak**.

billabong *noun*
A **billabong** is a section of water that was once part of a river.

> This word comes from an Aboriginal language of New South Wales called Wiradjuri.

billion *noun*, *adjective*
A **billion** is a very large number, a thousand times a million.

> *Word Building:* **billionth**, *adjective*: *No-one knows who the six billionth baby to be born was.*

> In the past a **billion** was a million times a million, and some people still use it to mean this amount.

billy *noun* (*plural* **billies**)
A **billy** is a can with a handle and a lid, that you use to boil water in over an open fire.

> This is also called a **billy can**.

billy goat *noun*
A **billy goat** is a male goat.

> You can also write this as one word (**billygoat**).

bin *noun*
A **bin** is a box or container used to keep things in, or put rubbish in.

bind *verb* (**binds**, **binding**, **bound**, **has bound**)
If you **bind** something, you tie it up. *The cloth that bound the body was maybe two thousand years old.*

bindi-eye /*say* **bin**-dee-uy / *noun*
A **bindi-eye** is a small plant that sometimes grows in grass. Its pointed seeds are tiny but hurt if you step on them with no shoes on.

> ❖ This word comes from Aboriginal languages of New South Wales called Yuwaalaraay and Kamilaroi.
> ❖ You can call this plant a **bindy** or **bindi** for short. The plant also has other names in some parts of Australia, such as **joey** and **jo-jo**.

binoculars /*say* buh-**nok**-yuh-luhz / *noun*
Binoculars are special glasses set in a piece of equipment which you hold to your eyes to make things that are a long way away seem much nearer.

> ❖ *Spelling Tip:* Remember that the first part of **binoculars** is spelt *bi*. This is a word part meaning 'two'. The next part of the word comes from the Latin *oculus* meaning 'eye'. Remember that there is not a *k* in sight.

biodegradable /*say* buy-oh-duh-**gray**-duh-buhl / *adjective*
If something is **biodegradable**, it is able to break down in the soil and not harm the environment.

biology /*say* buy-**ol**-uh-jee / *noun*
Biology is the science or study of all living things.

> *Word Building:* **biologist**, *noun* Someone whose work is biology is a **biologist**.

bird *noun*
A **bird** is an animal with wings, feathers and two legs. Birds lay eggs.

birth *noun*
1. A baby's **birth** is when it comes out of its mother's body at the start of its life. *There was a newspaper article about the birth of a baby gorilla at the zoo.*
2. A **birth** is the beginning of anything. *Each year we celebrate the birth of our nation.*

birthday *noun*
Your **birthday** is the date on which you were born.

birthplace *noun*
Your **birthplace** is the place you were born.

biscuit /*say* **bis**-kuht / *noun*
A **biscuit** is a small, flat piece of food, usually sweet, made from a mixture of flour and other things, which has been baked until it is quite hard.

a
b
c
d
e
f
g
h
i
j
k
l
m
n
o
p
q
r
s
t
u
v
w
x
y
z

⚡ *Spelling Tip:* Don't forget the *ui* spelling for the 'uh' sound. This is because **biscuit** comes from French.

bit[1] *noun*
A **bit** is a small piece or amount.

bit[2] *noun*
A **bit** is a small metal bar which goes into a horse's mouth and is attached to the reins.

bite *verb* (**bites, biting, bit, has bitten**)
1. If you **bite** a piece of food, you take a piece out of it with your teeth. *He bit the piece of fruit.*
2. If something like a dog **bites** you, it uses its teeth to hold you, sometimes cutting your skin. *A dog bit me on the leg last week.*
–*noun* 3. A **bite** is the amount of something that you take by biting. *She took a big bite of apple.*
4. A **bite** is a mark or sore made by something biting you. *His legs were covered with mosquito bites.*

bitter *adjective*
1. If something tastes **bitter**, it is sharp and unpleasant. *The fruits of some plants are too bitter to eat.*
2. If you are **bitter** about something, you are angry and hurt. *He felt bitter that his friend had been given the prize instead of him.*

black *adjective*
Something is **black** if it is completely dark in colour.

blackboard *noun*
A **blackboard** is a smooth dark board which is used for writing or drawing on with chalk.

blade *noun*
1. The **blade** of a knife is the flat metal part that you cut with. *We found the knife in the grass when we saw the blade glittering in the sun.*
2. You also use **blade** for something that has the same shape as a knife blade, like a leaf of grass. *A few blades of grass have appeared again after the fire.*

blame *verb*
If you **blame** someone for something bad, you say that it was their fault that it happened. *They blamed me for the broken window, but I was not even there at the time.*

blank *noun*
Something is **blank** if it has not been written or printed on.

blanket *noun*
A **blanket** is a large piece of wool or cotton material, used as a bed covering.

blast *noun*
1. A **blast** is a sudden strong rush of wind or air.
–*verb* 2. If something **blasts** something, they blow it hard or they blow it apart. *The explosion blasted the building to pieces.*

blaze *verb*
If something **blazes**, it burns strongly with a lot of flame. *A huge fire was blazing in the bush behind our house.*

blazer *noun*
A **blazer** is a short coat which people sometimes wear as part of a uniform.

bleach *verb*
If you **bleach** something, you put it in a special liquid to make it white or pale. *We had to bleach my white sports pants after I fell in the mud.*

bleak *adjective*
If the weather is **bleak**, it is so cold and grey that it makes you feel unhappy.

bleat *verb*
If a sheep **bleats**, it makes a noise like a soft cry. *We heard the lambs bleating in the paddock.*

bleed *verb* (**bleeds, bleeding, bled, has bled**)
If something **bleeds**, blood comes out of it. *I bumped my nose and it began to bleed.*

blend *verb*
If you **blend** things, you mix them together. *After school, we blended ourselves a fantastic mixture of all the fruit in the fridge and some ice-cream.*

Word Building: blender, *noun*
A small machine you use in the kitchen to blend things is a **blender**.

bless *verb*
If someone **blesses** someone, they ask that God will keep them safe and happy. *The priest went to the hospital to bless the sick child.*

blind *adjective*
1. Someone is **blind** if they are not able to see.
–*noun* 2. A **blind** is a cover over a window which keeps out light.

Word Building: blindness, *noun* If you are blind, you suffer from **blindness**.

blink *verb*
If you **blink**, you shut and open your eyes quickly. *It made me blink when the bright sunlight shone into my eyes.*

blister *noun*

A **blister** is a small swelling on your skin filled with a substance like water. *My new shoes are too tight and now I have blisters.*

block *noun*

1. A **block** is a solid piece of some hard material. *It had been a freezing night in the mountains and the water in the bucket was a solid block of ice.*
2. A **block** is a piece of land on which a house or other building may be built. *We haven't got a big garden because our house is on a small block.*
3. A **block** is a building with many different units or offices in it. *There are thirty families living in our block of flats.*
−*verb* 4. If something **blocks** something else, it gets in its way. *The accident blocked the traffic.*

blog *noun*

A **blog** is a kind of website that has information about a particular subject that people can comment on, often with links to other sites on the same subject.

> *Word Building:* **blogger**, *noun* When you write a blog, you are a **blogger**.

blond *adjective*

You are **blond** if you have fair hair.

> *Word Building:* **blonde**, *noun* A woman with blond hair is a **blonde**.

blood /*say* blud / *noun*

Your **blood** is the red liquid that is pushed through your body by your heart. It is a very important part of the way your body works.

bloom *verb*

If a plant **blooms**, it produces flowers. *Most plants bloom in summer.*

blossom *noun*

A **blossom** is the flower on a plant, especially one on a fruit tree.

> ✪ *Spelling Tip:* Remember that there is a double *s* in the middle and only one *m* at the end. Think of the related word *bloom* and put a double *s* between the two *o*'s.

blouse /*say* blowz / *noun*

A **blouse** is a kind of shirt worn by women and girls.

blow¹ *noun*

1. If someone gives you a **blow**, they hit you hard with their hand or with something held in it. *The last thing he remembered was getting a blow on his head – it felt like a piece of wood.*

2. If something is a **blow** to you, you feel shock when something bad happens that you have not been expecting. *The fire was a terrible blow to the family.*

blow² *verb* (**blows**, **blowing**, **blew**, **has blown**)

1. If the wind **blows**, it is moving along. *The wind was blowing so hard that it picked up her hat and carried it away.*
2. If you **blow**, you make air come out of your mouth. *He blew on the fire to make it stronger.*

blue *adjective* (**bluer**, **bluest**)

Something is **blue** if it is the colour of a clear sky on a sunny day.

bluebottle *noun*

A **bluebottle** is a small blue sea animal. Its body is like a small ball filled with air and it has long thin hanging parts which can sting you.

blue-tongue *noun*

A **blue-tongue** is a large Australian lizard with a blue tongue.

blunder *noun*

1. A **blunder** is a silly mistake.
−*verb* 2. If you **blunder**, you move in an awkward or careless way. *She blundered through the hall with tears pouring from her eyes.*

blunt *adjective*

If a thing is **blunt**, it is not sharp.

blush *verb*

If you **blush**, you go red in the face. *She was very shy and used to blush when anyone spoke to her.*

BMX *noun*

A **BMX** is a strongly built bicycle with smaller wheels and thicker tyres than other bikes. It is good for riding on dirt tracks.

board *noun*

1. A **board** is a long, thin piece of wood. *Peter always thought that there might be treasure hidden under the boards in his room.*
2. A **board** is a thin flat piece of material which is made for a certain purpose. Many different games are played on **boards**. *I've lost the Monopoly board, so we can't play.*
3. **on board**, If you are **on board** a ship, boat, plane, car, bus or train, you are on it, ready to travel. *The ship will leave when all the passengers are on board.*
−*verb* 4. If you **board** a train, bus, ship or plane, you get on it, usually to take a journey somewhere. *It always takes a long time to board a plane because there are so many things that have to be checked.*

5. If you **board** somewhere, you pay to sleep and eat there. *My cousins from the country go to school a long way from home and have to board at school.*

> **Word Building: boarder**, *noun* Someone who boards somewhere is a **boarder**. *There are forty boarders at their school.*

boast *verb*

If you **boast**, you speak in a way that shows you are too proud of yourself or things you own. *Jamie boasted so much about his bike that the other boys were sick of hearing about it.*

> **Word Building: boastful**, *adjective* Someone who boasts a lot is **boastful**.

boat *noun*

A **boat** is something you use to carry people and things across water.

body *noun* (*plural* **bodies**)

1. A **body** is all of a living person or animal. *It was freezing – he felt cold in every part of his body.*
2. A **body** is a dead person. *Seven bodies were found after the accident.*

boil *verb*

1. If you **boil** a liquid, you heat it so much that steam comes off it and it cannot get any hotter. *The first thing my dad does every morning is boil the water to make a cup of tea.*
2. If you **boil** food, you cook it in water that is boiling. *I know how to boil eggs but that is about all I can cook.*

bold *adjective*

If you do something that is **bold**, you do something that is dangerous or means taking a risk.

> **Word Building: boldness**, *noun* A bold person shows **boldness**. –**boldly**, *adverb* A bold person acts **boldly**.

bolt *noun*

1. A **bolt** is a bar which you slide to hold a door or gate shut. *Widya forgot to pull the bolt across and the animals got out.*
2. A **bolt** is a thick metal pin which you use to hold pieces of wood or metal together. *The bolts they used in the bridge were as thick as a man's thumb.*

bomb /*rhymes with* from/ *noun*

A **bomb** is something made so that it will explode and kill people and damage large areas.

bone *noun*

A **bone** is one of the very hard parts inside a body. **Bones** all join together to support the body and allow it to do things like stand and walk.

> **Word Building: bony**, *adjective* If someone is so thin that you can see the shape of their bones under their skin, they are **bony**.

bonfire *noun*

A **bonfire** is a large fire that you light outside in an open place to burn rubbish or to have a party around.

boogie board *noun*

A **boogie board** is a small, light and slightly curved board that you use in the water at the beach. You ride the board by lying on it.

book *noun*

1. A **book** is a number of pages fastened together with a cover, with words written or printed in it for you to read, or with empty pages for you to write on.
–*verb* **2.** If someone **books** a ticket to travel somewhere, or to see a show, they organise it early, to make sure that they will get it. You can also **book** rooms at hotels or places at restaurants. *My family has booked a house at the beach for the holidays.*

> **Word Building: booking**, *noun* If you book tickets, or a place at a hotel or restaurant, you make a **booking**.

bookcase *noun*

A **bookcase** is a piece of furniture with shelves, for storing books.

> You can also call this a **bookshelf**.

bookmark *noun*

A **bookmark** is a small length of paper, cloth, or something similar, which you place between the pages of a book to mark your place.

boomerang *noun*

A **boomerang** is a curved piece of wood used as a weapon by Aboriginal people. One kind comes back to you when you throw it.

> This word comes from an Aboriginal language of New South Wales called Dharug.

boot[1] *noun*

1. A **boot** is a kind of shoe which covers your foot and part of the lower part of your leg. *Anna's mother bought her a very smart pair of brown boots.*
2. A **boot** is a separate part at the back of a car for bags and other things. *The bags couldn't all fit in the boot so we put some on the back seat.*

boot² *verb*

When you **boot** or **boot up** a computer, you start it so that it gets ready to be used. *There is something wrong. The computer shut down while I was trying to boot it up.*

border *noun*

1. A **border** is the edge or side of anything. *My great-grandmother used to sew lace around the borders of her handkerchiefs.*
2. A **border** is a line that separates or divides one country or state from another. *There is a place called Cameron Corner where the borders of New South Wales, Queensland and South Australia meet.*

bore¹ *verb*

1. If a machine or something like that **bores**, it makes a round hole. *On farms, they have special diggers to bore holes in the ground for fence posts.*
–*noun* 2. A **bore** is an extremely deep hole you make in dry parts of a country to reach water that is under the ground.

bore² *verb*

1. If something **bores** you, you lose interest in it. You get tired of it. *I get bored cleaning my room up – I would much rather be outside.*
–*noun* 2. A **bore** is a person who bores you.

> **Word Building: boring**, *adjective* Things that bore you are **boring**. –**boredom**, *noun* Things that bore you fill you with feelings of **boredom**.

born *adjective*

When a baby is **born**, it comes out of its mother's body at the start of its life.

borrow *verb*

If you **borrow** something from someone, you take it to use, but you return it to them later. *I borrowed a hat from the lost property office because I had left mine at home.*

> The opposite is **lend**.

boss *noun*

A **boss** is someone who employs people and tells them what to do.

> **Word Building: bossy**, *adjective* If you are **bossy**, you like to tell other people what to do.

both *adjective*

1. You use **both** when you are talking about two things or people together.
–*pronoun* 2. You use **both** to mean 'the two' things or people. *Peter and Sally weren't sure* about going to the party, but now both have decided to go.

bother *verb*

1. If you **bother** someone, you annoy them. *Stop bothering me with questions – I'm trying to read.*
2. If you **bother** to do something, you take the time or trouble to do it. *He never bothers to clean up his room.*

bottle *noun*

A **bottle** is a glass or plastic container, usually narrow at the top, often used to keep liquids in.

bottlebrush *noun*

A **bottlebrush** is an Australian plant with red or pink flowers like round brushes.

bottom *noun*

1. The **bottom** of something is its lowest or deepest part. *We ran to the bottom of the hill.*
2. The **bottom** of something is the side or surface underneath it. *The mark on the bottom of the bottle tells you whether it can be recycled.*
3. Your **bottom** is the part of your body that you sit on. *The children slid down the hill on their bottoms.*

bough /*rhymes with* cow/ *noun*

A **bough** is one of the large branches of a tree.

> ✳ **Spelling Tip:** Remember the *ough* spelling for the 'ow' sound in **bough**. Don't confuse it with **bow** which means to bend over to show respect and has the same sound.

boulder /*say* **bohl**-duh/ *noun*

A **boulder** is a large, smooth rock.

bounce *verb*

1. If something **bounces**, it strikes against something and springs up or back. *The ball bounced right over the back fence.*
2. If you **bounce** something, you throw it against something, causing it to spring up or back. *He bounced the ball along the path.*

bound *noun*

A **bound** is a big jump from one place to another.

boundary /*say* **bown**-dree/ *noun* (*plural* **boundaries**)

A **boundary** is a line that divides one thing from another, or marks a limit.

bouquet /*say* booh-**kay**, boh-**kay**/ *noun*

A **bouquet** is a bunch of flowers.

> ✳ **Spelling Tip:** Don't forget the silent *t* at the end – the *et* spelling makes an 'ay' sound. Other words with this ending are *ballet* and

beret. They all come from French. Also remember the *qu* spelling for the 'k' sound in **bouquet**.

bow¹ /*rhymes with* cow/ *verb*
If you **bow**, you bend your head or your body forwards for a short time to show respect for someone. *At the beginning of the dance, the men bowed to the ladies.*

bow² /*rhymes with* so/ *noun*
1. A **bow** is a piece of wood bent by a string stretched from one end of it to the other. It is used to shoot arrows. *Evan was making a bow out of a length of bamboo.*
2. A **bow** is a tie that you make with two rounded pieces and two loose ends and which you can undo easily. *I'll tie this ribbon in a bow for your hair.*
3. A **bow** is the long thin piece of wood you use to play a musical instrument with strings. *Hamish put the violin and the bow on the desk.*

bowl¹ *noun*
A **bowl** is a deep round dish, usually used for holding food.

bowl² *verb*
If you **bowl** a ball, you throw it or roll it along the ground. *She bowled the ball towards me and I hit it hard.*

Word Building: bowler, *noun* Someone who bowls the ball in a game like cricket is a **bowler**.

box¹ *noun*
A **box** is a container, often made of wood or very hard, thick paper, usually with a cover.

box² *verb*
If you **box**, you fight using only your fists, usually while wearing special thick gloves. *Bruno is learning to box at a club he goes to.*

Word Building: boxing, *noun* If you box, you take part in the sport of **boxing**. –**boxer**, *noun* If your sport is boxing, then you are a **boxer**.

boy *noun*
A **boy** is a male child.

bracelet /*say* **brays**-luht/ *noun*
A **bracelet** is a chain or band worn on your arm as a decoration.

brain *noun*
Your **brain** is the part of your body, inside your head, which controls your movements, feelings and thoughts.

Word Building: brainy, *adjective* You call someone **brainy** if they are very clever.

brake *noun*
A **brake** is the part of a car or bike which stops it or makes it go slower.

⭐ **Spelling Tip:** Don't confuse the spelling of **brake** with **break** which has the same sound. When something **breaks** it separates into pieces.

branch *noun* (*plural* **branches**)
1. A **branch** is one of the large arm-like parts of a tree. *When we climbed up to one of the highest branches of the tree, we could see the whole town.*
2. A **branch** of a large organisation is one of the parts of it that is found in a different place from the main office. *Our bank has a branch in most suburbs.*

brand *noun*
A **brand** is a kind of thing that is made by a particular maker.

brass *noun*
Brass is a yellow metal that is made from copper.

brave *adjective*
If someone is **brave**, they are full of courage and do not show if they are afraid.

Word Building: bravely, *adverb* When you are brave, you do things **bravely**. –**bravery**, *noun* When you are brave, you show **bravery**.

Another word that means nearly the same is **courageous**.

bread *noun*
Bread is a food made by baking flour and water, usually together with something to make the mixture rise so that it is soft and light.

breadth /*say* bredth/ *noun*
The **breadth** of something is how far it is from one side to the other.

Another word that means nearly the same is **width**.

⭐ **Spelling Tip:** Don't forget the *ea* spelling (although it sounds like it would be spelt with just an *e*). The *bread* part of this word is not related to what you eat but is a form of the word *broad*. This may help you to remember the *a*. Then there is *th* added at the end.

break *verb* (**breaks**, **breaking**, **broke**, **has broken**)
1. If something **breaks**, or if you **break** it, it separates into pieces, usually because it has been dropped or hit. *The glass broke when I dropped it.*
2. If you **break** something like the law or a promise, you do not obey what it says you should do. *The teacher said if we broke the rules, we would be sorry.*
3. break down, If something **breaks down**, it stops working properly. *The machine broke down the first day we used it.*
4. break out, **a.** If something **breaks out**, it begins suddenly. *Fire broke out on the fifth floor of the building.* **b.** If someone **breaks out** of prison, they escape. *They had to stay inside their homes because two dangerous prisoners had broken out of jail.*
–*noun* **5.** If you have a **break** from something you are doing, you have a short rest.

Word Building: breakable, *adjective* If something can break, it is **breakable**.

✳ **Spelling Tip:** Don't confuse the spelling of **break** with **brake** which has the same sound. A **brake** makes a car go more slowly.

breakfast /*say* **brek**-fuhst / *noun*
Breakfast is the meal you eat when you wake up in the morning.

breast /*say* brest / *noun*
1. Breasts are the soft, rounded parts of a woman's body that make milk to feed babies. *The baby sucked at its mother's breast.*
2. Your **breast** is your chest. *He held the child to his breast.*

Breast in definition 2 is a rather old-fashioned word.

breath /*say* breth / *noun*
1. Your **breath** is the air you take into your body through your mouth or nose and let out again. *His warm breath melted the ice on the window.*
2. A **breath** is the act of breathing once. *You need to take a deep breath before swimming under water.*
3. hold your breath, If you **hold your breath**, you make yourself stop breathing. *Can you hold your breath until I count to 20?*
4. out of breath, If you are **out of breath**, you find it difficult to breathe, the way you sometimes do after doing exercise. *At the end of the race, we were completely out of breath.*

Word Building: breathless, *adjective* If you are out of breath, you are **breathless**.

✳ **Spelling Tip:** Remember that there is no *e* at the end of this word. Don't confuse it with the verb **breathe**.

breathe /*say* breedh / *verb*
When you **breathe**, you take air into your body through your mouth or nose and then let it out. *We breathe without thinking about it.*

✳ **Spelling Tip:** Remember to put an 'e' at the end of this word. Compare it with the noun **breath**.

breed *verb* (**breeds**, **breeding**, **bred**, **has bred**)
If you **breed** animals, you keep them so that they can produce young ones. *The farmer was breeding emus to sell for their oil.*

breeze *noun*
A **breeze** is a light wind.

brick *noun*
A **brick** is a small hard block of baked earth, used for building.

Word Building: bricklayer, *noun* Someone who builds with bricks is a **bricklayer**.

bride *noun*
A **bride** is a woman who is being married.

bridegroom *noun*
A **bridegroom** is a man who is being married.

The short form is **groom**.

bridesmaid *noun*
A **bridesmaid** is a woman or girl whose job is to help a bride on the day of her wedding.

bridge *noun*
A **bridge** is something built over a river, road or railway line, to provide a way of getting from one side to the other.

brief /*say* breef / *adjective*
If something is **brief**, it is short.

✳ **Spelling Tip:** Remember that **brief** is spelt with *ie* (to spell the 'ee' sound). This follows the rule that *i* comes before *e* except after *c*. Think of similar words such as *thief* and *chief*.

brigade *noun*
A **brigade** is a group of people trained to do a special job. These people usually wear a uniform.

bright /say bruyt/ adjective

1. Something is **bright** if it shines or gives out a strong light. *He held out a bright new coin.*
2. If a room is **bright**, it has plenty of light. *The big window in my room makes it very bright.*
3. Someone is **bright** if they are clever. *The teacher thinks the children in this class are very bright.*

Word Building: brighten, *verb* If something is bright, it **brightens** things up. –**brightly**, *adverb* Something that is bright shines **brightly**. –**brightness**, *noun* If something is bright, it has **brightness**.

brilliant adjective

1. Something is **brilliant** if it shines with a very bright light. *My teacher said it was a great day for a carnival – brilliant sunshine and a light breeze.*
2. If someone is **brilliant**, they are very, very clever. *One day, I would like to be a brilliant scientist.*
3. If something is **brilliant**, it is so good that it stands out from all the rest. *The film we saw last night was brilliant.*

Word Building: brilliance, *noun* Something or someone who is brilliant has **brilliance**.

brim noun

1. A **brim** is the top edge of something hollow like a cup or bowl. *I would like a mug filled to the brim with hot chocolate.*
2. A **brim** is the outer edge of a hat. *She pulled down the brim of her hat to keep the sun out of her eyes.*

bring verb (brings, bringing, brought /say brawt/, has brought)

1. If you **bring** something, you carry it with you. *I will bring the book this afternoon.*
2. **bring up, a.** If you **bring** someone **up**, you care for them while they are children. *Her grandmother brought her up after her parents were killed in an accident.* **b.** If you **bring** something **up**, you mention it in a conversation. *I'm glad you brought that up – I have been meaning to talk about it for a while.*

⚉ Spelling Tip: Remember the *ough* spelling for the 'aw' sound in the past form **brought**. Other words like this are *bought* and *thought*.

bristle /say bris-uhl/ noun

A **bristle** is a short, stiff hair or something like this. *My new hairbrush is red with lots of black bristles. | Our dad didn't shave when we* were on holidays, and his chin was covered with bristles.

⚉ Spelling Tip: Don't forget the *st* (not double *s*) spelling. The *t* is silent.

brittle adjective

Something is **brittle** if it is likely to break easily.

broad /say brawd/ adjective

If something is **broad**, it is very wide. *The river is so broad, it would take a long time to swim across it. | To win on a quiz show, you have to have a very broad knowledge of all sorts of things.*

Word Building: broaden, *verb* If you make something more broad, you **broaden** it. –**breadth** /say bredth/, *noun*

The opposite is **narrow**.

⚉ Spelling Tip: Remember the *oa* spelling for the 'aw' sound. Think of a 'broad board'. *Board* also has an *oa* spelling – in fact, it has all the same letters as **broad**, but with the *r* in a different position.

broadcast verb (broadcasts, broadcasting, broadcast, has broadcast)

If sounds or pictures are **broadcast**, they are sent by radio or television. *The game will be broadcast later tonight, so let's stay up to watch it.*

broccoli /say brok-uh-lee, brok-uh-luy/ noun

Broccoli is a green vegetable with small, hard flowers close together like a cauliflower.

⚉ Spelling Tip: Remember that there is a double *c* and only one *l* in **broccoli**. Also remember the *i* spelling for the 'ee' or 'uy' sound at the end. All of this is because **broccoli** comes from Italian.

broken adjective

1. Something is **broken** if it has separated into pieces. *Sally picked up the bits of the broken cup from the floor.*
2. Something is **broken** if it is not able to work properly because something is wrong with one of the parts. *I don't know what time it is because my watch is broken.*

brolga noun

A **brolga** is a large, silver-grey bird with long legs. It is especially known for the beautiful movements that it does which look like a dance.

a b c d e f g h i j k l m n o p q r s t u v w x y z

This word comes from an Aboriginal language of New South Wales called Kamilaroi.

bronze *noun*
Bronze is a brown metal which is made by mixing copper and tin.

brooch /*say* brohch / *noun* (*plural* **brooches**)
A **brooch** is a small piece of jewellery that you can fasten to your clothes with a pin.

⚡ *Spelling Tip:* Remember the double *o* spelling for the 'oh' sound. If you think of the two *o*'s as being like two little round jewels in a **brooch** you will remember this difficult part.

broom *noun*
A **broom** is a brush attached to a long handle, used for sweeping floors.

brother *noun*
Someone's **brother** is a man or boy who has the same parents as them.

brown *adjective*
If something is **brown**, it is the colour of earth, a mixture of red, yellow and black.

browser *noun*
A **browser** is a kind of computer program that helps you find information on the internet.

bruise /*say* broohz / *noun*
A **bruise** is a mark that appears on your skin if you have had a fall or been hit.

brush *noun*
A **brush** is a tool with hairs or things like hairs, which you can use to paint, to make your hair tidy or to clean.

bubble *noun*
A **bubble** is a small ball of air or gas.

bubblegum *noun*
Bubblegum is a thick kind of chewing gum that you can blow bubbles with.

bucket *noun*
A **bucket** is a round, open container made of metal or plastic with a flat bottom and a handle to hold it with.

buckle *noun*
A **buckle** is something made of metal or plastic you use to fasten something together. Some shoes have **buckles** on them.

Buddhism /*say* bood-iz-uhm / *noun*
Buddhism is a religion started by a special teacher called the Buddha who lived in India a very long time ago. This religion teaches that we

can be happy if we stop wanting more and more things and try to love instead of hate.

Word Building: **Buddhist** /*say* **bood**-uhst /, *noun* Someone whose religion is Buddhism is called a **Buddhist**.

budge *verb*
If someone or something **budges**, they move. *I won't budge from here until he comes.*

budgerigar /*say* **buj**-uh-ree-gah / *noun*
A **budgerigar** is a kind of small yellow, green or blue parrot. It is found in parts of Australia away from the coast but can be kept as a pet.

❖ This word is often shortened to **budgie**.
❖ This word comes from an Aboriginal language of New South Wales called Kamilaroi.

buffalo *noun* (*plural* **buffalos** or **buffaloes**)
A **buffalo** is a kind of wild cattle, sometimes kept by humans and used for pulling heavy loads.

⚡ *Spelling Tip:* Remember the double *f*'s (a bit like this animal's two curly horns), but only one *l*. Also note the *o* ending, which you see in many words which come from Italian, as **buffalo** does.

buffet /*say* **buf**-ay, **boo**-fay / *noun*
A **buffet** is a table or section in a restaurant holding a lot of food from which you can choose what you want for yourself.

build /*say* bild / *verb* (**builds**, **building**, **built**, **has built**)
If you **build** something, you make it by joining parts together. *They have started to build our new house.*

Word Building: **builder**, *noun* Someone whose job is to build houses is a **builder**.

building /*say* **bild**-ing / *noun*
A **building** is something with a roof and walls, built for people to live or work in.

bulb *noun*
1. A **bulb** is the round, white part of some plants which is under the ground. *Mum is very angry with the dog – he has dug up all her bulbs! She was looking forward to a lot of flowers next spring.*
2. A **bulb** is anything with a shape rather like that of a plant bulb. *The light bulb smashed when it hit the ground.*

bulge *verb*
If something **bulges**, it swells out. *Hugo had eaten so much that his stomach was bulging.*

bull *noun*
1. A **bull** is a large male member of the cattle family. *The bull was rather aggressive and was in a paddock by himself.*
2. A **bull** can also be a male elephant, whale or seal. *While we were watching the whales, a bull came up for air and we could see how big he was.*

The female is a **cow**.

bulldozer *noun*
A **bulldozer** is a heavy vehicle with a powerful motor which is used to move trees and rocks and to make land flat.

bullet *noun*
A **bullet** is a small piece of metal made to be shot from a gun.

bully *noun* (*plural* **bullies**)
1. A **bully** is someone who hurts or frightens people smaller or weaker than themselves.
–*verb* (**bullies**, **bullying**, **bullied**, **has bullied**)
2. If you **bully** someone, you behave as a bully towards them. *She bullied Jai by sending nasty messages about him to all their class-mates.*

bump *verb*
1. If you **bump** something, you knock against it by mistake. *Hector just couldn't help bumping into things all the time.*
–*noun* 2. A **bump** is a small swelling caused by a knock or hit. *She had a bump on her forehead from where she had fallen over.*
3. A **bump** is a small part raised higher than what is all around it. *Watch out for the bump in the road – you'll damage the car if you go too fast.*

Word Building: **bumpy**, *adjective* Something that has many bumps is **bumpy**.

bun *noun*
A **bun** is a kind of round bread roll which can be plain or sweet.

bunch *noun* (*plural* **bunches**)
A **bunch** of things is a group that are joined or have been gathered together.

bundle *noun*
A **bundle** is a group of things held together in a loose way.

bunk *noun*
1. A **bunk** is a narrow bed which looks a bit like a long shelf. These sorts of beds are seen on ships and places where lots of people have

to sleep. *The bunks in a submarine are really small.*
2. A **bunk** is one of two matching beds built one above the other. *I don't think it's fair that my brother always gets the top bunk.*

bunyip *noun*
A **bunyip** is a creature that is in many Aboriginal stories but that is not real.

This word comes from an Aboriginal language of Victoria called Wembawemba.

buoy /*say* boy / *noun*
A **buoy** is something that is made to sit in one place on the surface of the sea so that it can guide ships.

✿ *Spelling Tip:* Don't confuse the spelling of **buoy** with **boy** which has the same sound. Remember the extra letter *u* in **buoy**.

burden *noun*
A **burden** is a load that is very heavy to carry.

burger *noun*
A **burger** is a bread roll containing a flat, round piece of meat, and often other things like tomato, lettuce and cheese.

Burger is short for **hamburger**.

burglar *noun*
A **burglar** is someone who breaks into a building to steal things.

Word Building: **burgle**, *verb* If burglars steal things from buildings, they **burgle** them. –**burglary**, *noun* The crime of being a burglar is **burglary**.

burn *verb* (**burns**, **burning**, **burnt** *or* **burned**, **has burnt** *or* **has burned**)
1. If something **burns**, it is on fire. *The wood is burning now – we'll soon be warm.*
2. If you **burn** something, you set it on fire. *We'll burn this wood to make a fire.*
3. If something **burns** you, it hurts you by heat or fire. *Be careful! That hot soup will burn your mouth.*
–*noun* 4. A **burn** is a sore made by something hot.

burrow *noun*
A **burrow** is a hole in the ground that an animal digs to live in.

burst *verb* (**bursts**, **bursting**, **burst**, **has burst**)
1. If something **bursts**, it suddenly breaks open. *One of the school water pipes burst and we all got very wet.*

a
b
c
d
e
f
g
h
i
j
k
l
m
n
o
p
q
r
s
t
u
v
w
x
y
z

2. If you **burst** into a room, you suddenly rush into it. *The police burst into the building but the thief had escaped through a back window.*

bury /rhymes with very/ verb (**buries**, **burying**, **buried**, **has buried**)
If you **bury** something or someone, you put them in the ground and cover them with earth. *She asked to be buried near the sea when she died. | We can bury the kitchen scraps in the garden.*

> **Word Building:** burial /say **be**-ree-uhl/, noun
> If you bury a dead person, you give them a **burial**.

bus noun (plural **buses** or **busses**)
A **bus** is a road vehicle that many people can sit in to travel from one place to another.

bush noun
1. A **bush** is a plant like a small tree with many branches spreading out from near the ground. *We couldn't see the road through all the thick bushes in the garden.*
2. The **bush** is an area where a lot of native trees or bushes grow. *We had a picnic and then went for a walk in the bush. | We drove a long way through bush before we reached the farm.*
3. The **bush** is the Australian country, away from the cities. *We are going to visit our cousins who live in the bush.*

> **Word Building:** bushy, adjective Something that grows thickly like a bush is **bushy**. *The possum had a bushy tail.*

bushcare noun
When someone does **bushcare**, they look after the native plants in a particular area or they plant new native plants.

bushfire noun
A **bushfire** is a fire that spreads through an area of bush or forest.

bushranger noun
A **bushranger** was someone who hid in the bush and got money and food by stealing from travellers.

business /say **biz**-nuhs/ noun
1. Someone's **business** is the work they do to earn money. *Her business is making jewellery.*
2. A **business** is an organisation which buys and sells things or provides a service for people. *They own a building business.*
3. Your **business** is something which you have a right to know about. *My test result is my business, not yours!*

> **Word Building:** businessman, noun
> –**businesswoman**, noun

> ⚑ **Spelling Tip:** Don't forget the *i* in the middle of **business**. This will be easier to remember if you see that it is made up of *busy* (with the *y* changed to an *i*) and the word part *ness*.

busy /say **biz**-ee/ adjective (**busier**, **busiest**)
1. You are **busy** if you have plenty of things to do. *We were busy the whole weekend seeing friends.*
2. If you are **busy** with something, or **busy** doing something, you are doing it and nothing else. It is taking all your attention. *I was busy building a castle in the sand and didn't notice the crab until it climbed onto my foot.*
3. A certain time can be **busy** if there are many things happening. *Saturday morning is a busy time at the shops.*

> **Word Building:** busily, adverb If you are busy doing something, you are doing it **busily**.

but conjunction
1. You use **but** when you are saying something that is different to, or even opposite to what you have just said. *All my friends went, but I didn't.*
2. **But** means 'except' or 'apart from'. *We could do nothing but wait and see what happened.*
–preposition **3.** **But** means 'except'. *He drank nothing but water.*

butcher noun
A **butcher** is someone who prepares meat to sell.

> **Word Building:** butchery, noun The shop where a butcher sells meat is a **butchery**.

butter noun
Butter is a soft yellow food made from cream, which you spread on bread. It is also used in cooking.

butterfly noun (plural **butterflies**)
A **butterfly** is an insect with large wings which are often brightly coloured.

button noun
1. A **button** is a small, usually round, object sewn onto clothing to join two parts together. *Her new coat has five red buttons down the front.*
2. A **button** is a small round object that you press for some purpose, such as to ring a bell or to operate a television. *I pushed the button, but no-one came to the door.*

buy *verb* (**buys**, **buying**, **bought** /*say* bawt/, **has bought**)

If you **buy** something, you get it by paying money for it. *Our family bought a new car last week.*

> *Word Building:* **buyer**, *noun* Someone who buys something is a **buyer**.

> The opposite of **buy** is **sell**, and the opposite of **buyer** is **seller**.

> ❉ *Spelling Tip:* Remember the *ough* spelling for the 'aw' sound in the past form **bought**. Other words like this are *brought* and *thought*.

buzz *noun*

A **buzz** is a low continuous noise like the sound a bee makes.

by *preposition*

You can use **by** in many ways. Its main meanings have to with being near or going past something, or with how or by which person something is done. Here are some examples. *I live close by the school.* | *We drove by the school on our way home.* | *We went to the shops by train.* | *They were to arrive by air.* | *I like reading the Harry Potter books by JK Rowling.* | *She was given a beautiful present by her mother.* | *Be home by eight o'clock.*

bye *interjection*

Bye is a short way of saying goodbye. *Bye, everyone! I'll see you tomorrow!*

byte /*say* buyt/ *noun*

A **byte** is a unit of information stored by a computer.

> ❉ *Spelling Tip:* Notice the letter *y* in **byte**. Don't confuse it with **bite** which has the same sound. When you **bite**, you use your teeth to take a piece of food.

a b c d e f g h i j k l m n o p q r s t u v w x y z

cat

cab *noun*
Look up **taxi**.

cabbage *noun*
A **cabbage** is a large round vegetable with green leaves.

cabin *noun*
1. A **cabin** is a building like a small house. *The old man lived in a cabin in the bush.*
2. A **cabin** is a room in a ship where people sleep. *Our cabin on the ship is small but everything fits very neatly.*
3. A **cabin** is the space inside a plane where people sit. *My dad always wants to sit at the front of the cabin when he goes on a plane.*

cable *noun*
A **cable** is thick, strong rope or wire.

cactus *noun* (*plural* **cactuses** *or* **cacti** /*say* **kak**-tuy /)
A **cactus** is a plant with a lot of sharp points on it, which grows in hot, dry places. It can store water inside its stem.

cafe /*say* **kaf**-ay / *noun*
A **cafe** is a restaurant where you can have coffee and small meals.

> You can also write this as **café**, with a mark over the letter 'e' because it comes from French.

cage *noun*
A **cage** is a place or a box with wire or other material around it, for keeping animals or birds in.

cake *noun*
Cake is a sweet food, made by mixing flour, sugar, eggs and sometimes other things such as chocolate, and then baking it. *Do you like to eat cake? | Let's make a cake.*

calculator *noun*
A **calculator** is a small machine that you can use to do sums.

calendar *noun*
A **calendar** is a list that shows you the days and weeks of each month of the year.

calf[1] /*say* kahf / *noun* (*plural* **calves**)
1. A **calf** is a young cow or bull. *The old cow had just given birth to two calves.*
2. A **calf** is a young elephant, whale or seal. *The whale calf stayed close to its mother.*

> ❄ *Spelling Tip:* Don't forget the *l*. The *alf* spelling gives the 'ahf' sound.

calf[2] /*say* kahf / *noun* (*plural* **calves**)
Your **calf** is the back part of your leg, below your knee.

> ❄ *Spelling Tip:* Look up **calf**[1].

call *verb*
1. If you **call**, you say something in a loud voice so that someone can hear you. *Dad is calling from the garden. He must want me to help him.*
2. If you **call** a person or animal, you ask them to come. *She became very sick so her mother called a doctor.*
3. If you **call** someone, you ring them on the telephone. *Sam called me last night to talk about his homework.*
4. If you **call** someone a name, you give them that name, often when they are born. *Her parents called her Yumiko.*
5. If you **call** something a name, you use that name to describe it. *A very tall hill is called a mountain.*

calm /*say* kahm / *adjective*
1. If the sea or a lake is **calm**, the water is quite still, with no large waves. *We enjoyed the boat trip because the sea was very calm.*
2. If someone is **calm**, they are not excited or nervous. *He always stays calm when there is trouble.*

Word Building: **calmly,** *adverb* When you do something in a calm way, you do it **calmly.** *She sat calmly in spite of the noise around her.*

✱ *Spelling Tip:* Don't forget the *l*. The *alm* spelling gives the 'ahm' sound.

camel *noun*
A **camel** is a large animal with humps on its back. It is used to carry people and loads across the desert.

camera *noun*
A **camera** is a machine that you use to take photographs.

camouflage /*say* **kam**-uh-flahzh/ *verb*
If someone **camouflages** something, they hide it by changing the way it looks. *Soldiers camouflage themselves by wearing colours of the trees and grass they walk through.*

✱ *Spelling Tip:* Remember that the 'uh' sound in the middle of this word is spelt *ou*. Also remember the *age* spelling for the 'ahzh' sound at the end. This is because **camouflage** comes from French.

camp *noun*
1. A **camp** is a place where you live for a while, cooking your meals and sleeping in the open air or in tents.
–*verb* 2. If you **camp**, you live like this for a while. *We camped beside a river during our holidays.*

Word Building: **camper,** *noun* Someone who camps at a place while they are having a holiday is a **camper.**

can¹ *verb* (**could**)
1. If you **can** do something, you have the power, knowledge or time to do it. *I don't think I can lift that box.* | *He tried to lift the box but he could not move it.*
2. If someone says you **can** do something, they allow you to do it. They give you permission. *You can come and see me at three o'clock.* | *Can I have some more to eat, please?*

❖ **Can** is always used with another verb.
❖ When you use **can** with *not*, the two words join together to make **cannot.** *I'm sorry but I cannot come tonight.* The short form of **cannot** is **can't.**

can² *noun*
A **can** is a metal container for food or drink.

canal /*say* kuh-**nal**/ *noun*
A **canal** is a long line of water which has been made by cutting through land. It is used where there is no river for boats to carry people and goods.

canary /*say* kuh-**nair**-ree/ *noun* (*plural* **canaries**)
A **canary** is a small, yellow bird that sings sweetly. You can keep it as a pet.

cancel *verb* (**cancels, cancelling, cancelled, has cancelled**)
If you **cancel** something that you have arranged, you stop it from happening. *I'm afraid we'll have to cancel the game – it's raining.*

Word Building: **cancellation,** *noun* If you have to cancel something, you make a **cancellation.**

cancer *noun*
Cancer is a bad sickness that can make a lump grow in one part of your body and spread to other parts as well.

candle *noun*
A **candle** is a long stick of wax with a piece of thin string through it which you can burn to give light.

cane *noun*
Cane is the thin hard stem of some plants.

cannibal /*say* **kan**-uh-buhl/ *noun*
A **cannibal** is someone who eats other people.

cannon *noun*
A **cannon** is a large gun on wheels.

cannot *verb*
Cannot is a way of writing *can not*. *I cannot help you because I don't have enough time.*

canoe /*say* kuh-**nooh**/ *noun*
A **canoe** is a light narrow boat that you move by using a special kind of oar (a paddle).

✱ *Spelling Tip:* Remember that the ending is spelt *oe* (not *oo*). It might help if you think of a word you know well which has the same spelling for this sound, such as *shoe*.

canteen *noun*
A **canteen** is a place in a school that sells food.

Another word for this is **tuckshop.**

canvas *noun*
Canvas is strong cotton cloth used to make things like sails and tents.

a b c d e f g h i j k l m n o p q r s t u v w x y z

canyon *noun*

A **canyon** is a long deep valley with very steep rocky sides, often with water running along the bottom.

> ✸ *Spelling Tip:* Remember that the letter after the *y* is an *o*.

cap *noun*

A **cap** is a small, soft hat with a piece at the front.

capital *noun*

1. If a city is a **capital**, it is the most important city in a country because the government is there. *Canberra is the capital of Australia.*
2. If a letter is a **capital**, it is one of the set of larger letters of the alphabet which are used at the start of the names of particular people and places. *When you are writing, you have to start each sentence with a capital.*

> You can also say **capital city** for definition 1 and **capital letter** for definition 2.

> ✸ *Spelling Tip:* Remember that the end of **capital** is spelt *al* (not *le*). It might help if you think of other words which have the same spelling for this sound, such as *metal* and *total*.

capsize *verb*

If something **capsizes**, it turns over. *Look out! The boat is going to capsize.*

capsule /*say* **kap**-shoohl / *noun*

1. A **capsule** is a very small container that has medicine powder inside it. *The doctor gave my mum some capsules for her headaches.*
2. A **capsule** is the part of a spaceship where the astronauts sit while they are controlling it. *On television, we saw pictures of the inside of the space capsule as well as shots of the spaceship travelling through space.*

captain /*say* **kap**-tuhn / *noun*

1. A **captain** is someone who is in charge of a ship or plane, or who is in charge of a group of soldiers. *The captain gave the order to move forwards.*
2. A **captain** is a leader of a team of people. *He is the captain of the school football team.*

> ✸ *Spelling Tip:* Remember that the final part of this word is spelt *ain*. Think of other words with this spelling for an 'uhn' sound, such as *certain* and *curtain*.

capture /*say* **kap**-chuh / *verb*

If you **capture** someone or something, you catch them and do not let them get free. *After the robbery, the police captured two men running away from the bank.*

> *Word Building:* **captive**, *noun* Someone you capture is your **captive**.

car *noun*

A **car** is something you travel in on the road. It has a motor and four wheels.

caramel *noun*

Caramel is a light brown kind of sweet, made from sugar, butter and milk.

> ✸ *Spelling Tip:* There are no double letters in **caramel**: only one *r*, one *m* and one *l*.

caravan *noun*

A **caravan** is a vehicle with windows and a door, that is pulled along by a car. You can live in it when you are on holidays.

carbon *noun*

Carbon is a chemical substance found in living things and in things such as coal, petrol and diamonds. **Carbon dioxide** is a gas form of carbon and is found in the air you breathe out. It is also produced by factories using coal, by the burning of coal and oil to make electricity, by the using of petrol to make cars go, by the burning of forests, and so on. Too much carbon dioxide in the air can be harmful to the environment.

carbon footprint *noun*

The **carbon footprint** of a person or organisation is a measure of how much they hurt the environment by using or making things that give out carbon dioxide.

card *noun*

1. A **card** is a piece of folded thick paper, usually with a picture on the front and writing inside. *I chose a birthday card for my mother with a picture of flowers on the front.*
2. A **card** is one of a set of small pieces of thick paper with pictures on them, usually making up a set that you play games with. *Mum and I played a game of cards.*

cardboard *noun*

Cardboard is a thick stiff sort of paper.

cardigan *noun*

A **cardigan** is a warm piece of clothing for the top part of your body. It has buttons down the front.

care *noun*

1. If you do something with **care**, you give it your complete attention and do it as well as possible. *Make sure you do your work with care.*

2. take care of, If you **take care of** someone or something, you look after them and keep them safe. *Sally's grandmother takes care of her during the school holidays when her mother is working.* –*verb* **3.** If you **care** about something, you think it is important or worth worrying about. *He cares about sport more than school work.*

4. care for, If you **care for** someone, you look after them and do things for them that they are too old, too young or too sick to do themselves. *A nurse's job is to care for sick people.*

careful *adjective*

If you are **careful**, you do something with care.

The opposite is **careless**.

careless *adjective*

If you are **careless**, you do something without thinking about it enough.

The opposite is **careful**.

cargo *noun* (*plural* **cargoes**)

Cargo is the goods carried on a ship, plane, truck, and so on, from one place to another.

carnival *noun*

1. A **carnival** has sporting events held one after the other on a certain day. *I'm going to watch my sister race at the surf carnival on Saturday.*

2. A **carnival** is a special time when there are shows in the streets and parks and people like to join in with dancing and singing. *At the carnival there were some really funny clowns doing tricks as they danced down the road.*

carol *noun*

A **carol** is a special Christmas song.

carpenter *noun*

A **carpenter** is someone who makes things out of wood and puts up wooden parts of a building.

Word Building: **carpentry**, *noun* The work a carpenter does is **carpentry**.

carpet *noun*

Carpet is a thick covering for the floor.

carriage /*say* **ka**-rij / *noun*

1. A **carriage** is one of the parts of a train which is used to carry passengers. *I'll meet you in the third carriage.*

2. A **carriage** is a vehicle with wheels, pulled by a horse or horses. Carriages were used in the past to carry people about. *The queen was taken to the wedding in her golden carriage.*

carrot *noun*

A **carrot** is an orange-coloured, long, thin vegetable.

carry *verb* (**carries, carrying, carried, has carried**)

1. If you **carry** something, you hold it or support it and take it from one place to another. *She carried the baby in her arms.*

2. carry on, If you **carry on** doing something, you keep on doing it. *You can carry on playing after lunch until the bell goes.*

3. carry out, If you **carry out** something planned, you finish doing it. *I don't think we will be able to carry out our plan for a holiday this year.*

cart *noun*

A **cart** is something used for carrying things, with either two or four wheels, usually wooden and sometimes pulled by a horse.

carton *noun*

A **carton** is a box made of cardboard or plastic, often used for food.

cartoon *noun*

1. A **cartoon** is a funny drawing. *Did you see that cartoon in the paper?*

2. A **cartoon** is a film, usually funny, in which all the characters are drawn by an artist. *Bugs Bunny is a famous cartoon character.*

Word Building: **cartoonist**, *noun* Someone whose job is to draw cartoons is called a **cartoonist**.

carve *verb*

1. If you **carve** something that is hard, you cut it to give it a certain shape. *He was trying to carve the stone into the shape of an animal.*

2. If you **carve** meat, you cut it into pieces ready for eating. *Mum carved the meat before bringing it to the table.*

case *noun*

A **case** is a kind of container, usually quite small.

Also look up **suitcase**.

cash *noun*

Cash is money in paper notes or coins.

In a shop, the cash is stored and counted in a **cash register**.

a
b
c
d
e
f
g
h
i
j
k
l
m
n
o
p
q
r
s
t
u
v
w
x
y
z

cassette

40

cassette /*say* kuh-**set**/ *noun*
A **cassette** is the plastic container that holds the tape you use to record sound or film.

> You can use a **cassette** in a **cassette player** or a **cassette recorder**.

> ❋ *Spelling Tip:* Remember the double *s* and double *t* and remember that the ending is spelt *ette* (although it sounds like 'et' or 'ett'). It is spelt like this because it comes from French (meaning 'little box'). Another word with this ending is *serviette*.

cast *verb* (**casts**, **casting**, **cast**, **has cast**)
1. If you **cast** something, you throw it out or throw it to some place. *They cast the dead fish into the sea.*
–*noun* **2.** A **cast** is all the actors chosen to be in a play. *Almost all my friends were chosen to be in the cast of the school play.*
3. A **cast** is the material that sets hard around a broken arm or leg to help the broken bits join properly. *All my friends wrote on my cast after I broke my arm.*

castle /*say* **kah**-suhl/ *noun*
A **castle** is a large old building with very strong walls.

> ❋ *Spelling Tip:* Don't forget the *st* (not double *s*) spelling. The *t* is silent.

casual /*say* **kazh**-yooh-uhl/ *adjective*
1. Something is **casual** if it happens by chance. *It was just a casual meeting in the street but we talked for quite a while.*
2. Something you say is **casual** if you say it without thinking much about it. *My father got upset when I made a casual remark about the nasty smell in the kitchen.*
3. Clothes are **casual** if they are not meant for important occasions. *I wore my casual clothes to the beach.*

> *Word Building:* **casually**, *adverb* If you say or do something in a casual way, then you say or do it **casually**.

casualty /*say* **kazh**-yooh-uhl-tee/ *noun* (*plural* **casualties**)
1. A **casualty** is someone hurt or killed in an accident or war. *There were lots of casualties during the war.*
2. Casualty is the section of a hospital where very sick or injured people are taken to get treated

immediately. *The ambulance took the man who was hurt in the accident to casualty.*

> ❋ *Spelling Tip:* Remember that there is a *u* and an *a* in the middle of **casualty**. People often say this word as if there was an *a* only, which is why you have to especially remember the *u*. Try breaking the word up as *cas+u+al+ty*.

cat *noun*
A **cat** is a small furry animal which you can keep as a pet.

catch *verb* (**catches**, **catching**, **caught** /*say* kawt/, **has caught**)
1. If you **catch** someone or something, you take hold of them, especially when you have run after them. *Quick! Catch that man! He has taken my bag.*
2. If you **catch** something that has been thrown, you take it in your hands. *Can you catch this ball?*
3. If you **catch** a bus, train, or plane, you are in time to get on it before it leaves. *If you run, you will catch the bus that leaves at ten o'clock.*
4. catch up with, If you **catch up with** someone, you reach where they are. *Sam caught up with the other runners in the race.*

> ❋ *Spelling Tip:* Remember the spelling *augh* in the past form **caught** (although it sounds like 'aw'). It might help if you think of some other words which have the same spelling for this sound, such as *daughter* and *naughty*.

caterpillar /*say* **kat**-uh-pil-uh/ *noun*
A **caterpillar** is a grub that turns into a moth or a butterfly.

> ❋ *Spelling Tip:* Some **caterpillars** will sting you if you step on them, and there are certainly several prickly bits in its spelling. Try thinking of the words *cat* and *pill*. Put *er* in between these and *ar* at the end.

cathedral /*say* kuh-**thee**-druhl/ *noun*
A **cathedral** is a very big and important church.

cattle *noun*
Cattle are a kind of large animal often kept on a farm for their meat (called beef). The females are also often used for the milk they produce.

cauliflower /*say* **kol**-ee-flow-uh/ *noun*
A **cauliflower** is a vegetable with a large round part at the top of its stem, made up of hard white flowers.

> ❋ *Spelling Tip:* A **cauliflower** is actually the flower of a particular plant, which makes the

spelling of the last part of the word easy. The main thing to remember is that the first part is spelt *caul* (although it sounds like it could be spelt *col*).

cause *verb*

If something **causes** something, it makes it happen. *Fast driving causes many accidents.*

cautious /say **kaw**-shuhs / *adjective*

You are **cautious** if you take great care when there is danger.

> **Word Building: caution** /say **kaw**-shuhn/, *noun* If you are cautious, then you do things with **caution**.

> ❇ *Spelling Tip:* Remember the *au* spelling for the 'aw' sound. It might help if you think of some other words which have the same spelling for this sound, such as *audience*. Then, as in many other words, the ending *tious* is the spelling for a 'shuhs' sound.

cave *noun*

A **cave** is a large hole in a rocky place, such as under the ground or in the side of a mountain.

CD *noun*

A **CD** is a compact disc.

> A machine that you play CDs on is called a **CD player**.

CD-ROM /say see-dee-**rom** / *noun*

A **CD-ROM** is a compact disc containing writing, sound and pictures that can be displayed on a computer.

cease *verb*

If you **cease** doing something, you stop doing it. *If you don't cease that silly behaviour, I will get very angry.*

ceiling /say **see**-ling / *noun*

A **ceiling** is the top inside part of a room.

> ❇ *Spelling Tip:* Remember that **ceiling** begins with a *c* (with an 's' sound). Also remember the *ei* spelling for the 'ee' sound. This follows the rule that *i* comes before *e* except after *c*.

celebrant /say **sel**-uh-bruhnt / *noun*

A **celebrant** is a special person who leads a ceremony, such as a wedding.

celebrate /say **sel**-uh-brayt / *verb*

If you **celebrate** something, you do something to show that you are happy about it, such as have a party. *All the family went out to a restaurant to celebrate Dad's birthday.*

> **Word Building: celebration**, *noun* When you celebrate something, you have a **celebration**.

celery /say **sel**-uh-ree / *noun*

Celery is a vegetable with long, green stems that are good to eat.

> ❇ *Spelling Tip:* Remember that **celery** begins with a *c* (although it sounds like an 's'). Don't confuse it with **salary** (money that someone earns). Also notice that there are two separate *e*'s. Remind yourself that *e* is for *eat* which is what you do with **celery**.

cell *noun*

1. A **cell** is a small room in a prison. *The prisoner was kept in the cell for four days.*
2. A **cell** is one of the very tiny parts of everything that is alive. A cell is so small that you need a microscope to see one. *Even something as tiny as an ant has thousands of cells in its body.*

cellar *noun*

A **cellar** is a room under the ground which is used for storing things like wine.

Celsius /say **sel**-see-uhs / *noun*

Celsius is a way to measure how hot something is, using 0° as the point where ice melts and 100° as the point where water boils.

> The sign for **Celsius** is **C**, so *30°C* means *30 degrees Celsius*.

cement /say suh-**ment** / *noun*

Cement is the grey powder you use for making concrete.

cemetery /say **sem**-uh-tree / *noun* (plural **cemeteries**)

A **cemetery** is a place for burying dead people.

> ❇ *Spelling Tip:* Remember that **cemetery** begins with a *c* (with an 's' sound). Also remember that there are three *e*'s buried in **cemetery**.

cent *noun*

A **cent** is a small piece of money used in some countries. There are 100 **cents** in a dollar.

centenary /say sen-**teen**-uh-ree / *noun* (plural **centenaries**)

A **centenary** is a time when people remember something that happened 100 years ago.

a b c d e f g h i j k l m n o p q r s t u v w x y z

⚙ *Spelling Tip:* You can see that **centenary** begins with the word *cent* (from the Latin word for 'a hundred'). Then you have to remember the single *e* in the middle and the *ary* ending.

centimetre /say **sen**-tuh-mee-tuh/ noun
A **centimetre** is a measurement of length. It is a small length. There are 100 **centimetres** in a metre.

The short way of writing this is **cm**.

centipede /say **sen**-tuh-peed/ noun
A **centipede** is a small animal with a long, thin body and many pairs of legs.

⚙ *Spelling Tip:* The spelling of **centipede** will be easier if you see that it is made up of *centi* (which comes from the Latin word for 'hundred', just like *cent* does) and *pede* (from the Latin word for 'foot'). So the idea is that a **centipede** has a hundred feet – more or less!

central adjective
If something is **central**, it is in the centre or middle of something.

centre noun
The **centre** of something is its middle part.

century /say **sen**-chuh-ree/ noun (plural centuries)
A **century** is a period of 100 years.

cereal /say **sear**-ree-uhl/ noun
1. A **cereal** is a grain plant such as wheat or rice that farmers grow for food. *Many cereals are used to make food for farm animals.*
2. **Cereal** is a food made from grain, especially the food you eat in the morning with milk. *We always have to eat our cereal before we go to school.*

cerebral palsy /say se-ruh-bruhl **pawl**-zee/ noun
A person who has **cerebral palsy** has had some sort of injury to their brain and they do not have complete control over the movements of their arms and legs.

ceremony /say **se**-ruh-muh-nee/ noun (plural ceremonies)
People often have a **ceremony** to mark an important event in their life. There are usually other people there to watch.

⚙ *Spelling Tip:* Remember that the beginning of **ceremony** is spelt with a *c* (although it

sounds like an 's'). Also remember that the letter before the *m* is an *e* (not an *i*), and that the ending is spelt *mony* (although the *o* gives a 'u' sound). Try breaking the word up as *ce + re + mon + y*.

certain /say **ser**-tuhn/ adjective
If you are **certain** about something, you do not think you could be wrong about it. You do not have any doubts.

Another word with a similar meaning is **sure**. Also look up **certainly**.

⚙ *Spelling Tip:* Remember that **certain** begins with a *c* (with an 's' sound) and that the final part is spelt *ain*. Think of other words with this spelling for an 'uhn' sound, such as *captain* and *curtain*. But be sure not to confuse **certain** with **curtain** (something you hang over a window).

certainly adverb
1. You use **certainly** to show that something is certain and there is not any doubt about it. *I don't know where she is, but she certainly isn't with me.*
2. You can use **certainly** as a polite way of saying that you agree to do something. It means 'yes'. *'May I borrow your book?' 'Certainly. Please keep it for as long as you like.'*

For definition 2, you can also say **sure** but this is more informal. You might use **sure** when you are talking with your friends.

certificate /say suh-**tif**-uh-kuht/ noun
A **certificate** is a piece of paper that says in writing some important things about you.

chain noun
A **chain** is something made of a lot of metal rings joined together. *Sally tied up her dog with a long chain. | She wore a pretty chain around her neck.*

chair noun
A **chair** is a piece of furniture that you sit on, with a back and often with arms.

chalk /rhymes with fork/ noun
Chalk is a kind of soft white rock, often made into sticks used for drawing or writing on blackboards.

challenge /say **chal**-uhnj/ verb
If you **challenge** someone, you ask them to see if they can do better than you at something. *The new boy wants to challenge you to a game of chess.*

Word Building: challenger, *noun* If you challenge someone, then you are the **challenger.**

champion *noun*
A **champion** is someone who is the best at a sport or in a competition.

chance *noun*
1. If something happens by **chance**, it happens without being planned. It seems to happen without any reason. *'Were you planning to meet your friend today?' 'No, we met by chance at the shops.'*
2. If you have a **chance** to do something, it is a good time for you to be able to do it. *He's sitting by himself. Now is your chance to have a talk with him.*

change /say chaynj/ *verb*
1. If you **change** something, you make it different. *I would like to change the colour of the walls in my bedroom.*
2. If someone or something **changes**, they become different. *She has changed a lot in the last year. | Mum says this town hasn't changed since she was a child.*
3. change into, If something **changes into** something else, it becomes the other thing. *Water changes into ice when it freezes.*
—noun **4.** A **change** is what happens when something or someone becomes different. *I would like my room to be a different colour. I feel like a change. | Have you noticed the change in her lately? She used to be sad and now she is always happy.*

Word Building: changeable /say **chayn**-juh-buhl/, *adjective* If something changes often, it is **changeable**. *The weather has been changeable recently; sometimes it's hot and sometimes it's cold.*

channel *noun*
1. A **channel** is a narrow way in the ground for water to flow along. *The farmer dug a channel to allow the flood water to flow away.*
2. A **channel** is a narrow piece of water joining two seas. *The channel is too narrow to be used by big ships.*
3. A **channel** is a TV station. *My mother and I often disagree about which channel to watch.*

✲ Spelling Tip: Remember that there is a double *n* in the middle and only one *l* at the end of **channel**.

chant *verb*
If you **chant** something, you say words over and over again so that they sound like music. *At the athletics carnival, everyone was chanting Tom's name to encourage him in the race.*

chapter *noun*
A **chapter** is a part of a book, usually with a number and a title.

character /say **ka**-ruhk-tuh/ *noun*
1. A **character** is someone in a story. *Wayang's favourite character in the book was the one who tried to be a detective and solve crimes.*
2. Your **character** is the special things about you that make you different from other people. *He's quiet and thoughtful, with a character not at all like his noisy cousin.*

charge *verb*
1. If someone **charges** an amount of money for something, that is what you have to pay to buy it. *How much would you charge to fix my bike?*
—noun **2. in charge,** If you are **in charge**, you are the leader or the one who tells people what to do. *Who is in charge here? | I want to speak to the person in charge.*
3. in charge of, If you are **in charge of** something or someone, it is your job to look after them or have control over them. *Who is in charge of giving out the books? | The coach is in charge of the football team.*

charity /say **cha**-ruh-tee/ *noun* (plural **charities**)
1. If you do something for **charity**, you do it to help people who need it. *Our school is holding a concert for charity – the money we raise will be spent on toys for sick children.*
2. A **charity** is a group which gives money, clothes and food to people who need it. *Our class is raising money for several charities.*

Word Building: charitable /say **cha**-ruh-tuh-buhl/, *adjective* When a person or group gives charity to someone who needs help, then they are doing a **charitable** thing.

charm *verb*
1. If you **charm** someone, you please them or make them feel happy. *My baby brother's smile charms everyone.*
—noun **2.** If something or someone has **charm**, they have something which pleases and attracts

chart 44

you. *My mum and dad said that the old stone cottage had a charm of its own.*
3. In stories, a **charm** is an act that shows that someone or something has special powers. *The magician put a charm on the boy to make him go to sleep.*
4. A **charm** is a small object worn on a piece of jewellery. *Carlotta has lots of charms on her bracelet.*

> **Word Building: charming**, *adjective* Someone or something with the ability to charm is **charming**.

chart *noun*
A **chart** is a map or plan.

chase *verb*
If you **chase** someone or something, you run or drive after them because you want to catch them. *The police chased the man who stole the money.*

chat *verb* (**chats**, **chatting**, **chatted**, **has chatted**)
If you **chat**, you talk in a friendly way. *Ann and Sophie chatted about what they did on their holidays.*

chatter *verb*
If you **chatter**, you talk quickly and noisily and sometimes too much. *The children at the party were chattering happily to each other.*

> **Word Building: chatterbox**, *noun* Someone who chatters a lot is sometimes called a **chatterbox**.

cheap *adjective*
If something is **cheap**, you do not have to pay very much to buy it. It has a low price.

> Some words with the opposite meaning are **expensive**, **dear** and **costly**.

cheat *verb*
1. If you **cheat**, you act secretly in a way that is not honest. *Did you try to cheat in the test by looking at my work?*
2. If you **cheat** someone, you trick them. *Don't let anyone cheat you out of your money.*
–*noun* **3.** A **cheat** is someone who breaks the rules or tries to trick you in a way that is not honest.

check *verb*
If you **check** something, you look at it to make sure it is right. *The teacher checked that everyone was in the classroom.*

> Also look up **cheque**.

cheek *noun*
Your **cheek** is one of the two parts of your face, on either side of your nose and below your eyes.

cheeky *adjective* (**cheekier**, **cheekiest**)
Someone who is **cheeky** is rude, and without respect.

> **Word Building: cheekily**, *adverb* You are cheeky if you behave **cheekily**. –**cheekiness**, *noun*: *Richard was punished for his cheekiness in class.*

cheer *verb*
1. If you **cheer**, you shout to show that you like or admire someone or something. *Everyone cheered when the winner came onto the stage.*
2. cheer up, If you **cheer up**, you begin to feel happier. *We cheered up when we heard that Dad was coming home from hospital.*
–*noun* **3.** A **cheer** is a shout showing that you like or admire someone or something.

> **Word Building: cheerful**, *adjective* Someone who is **cheerful** is happy.

cheer squad *noun*
A **cheer squad** is a small group of people who cheer a person or a team that is competing, usually in sports.

cheese *noun*
Cheese is a food made from milk, usually yellow and quite hard.

chemist /*say* **kem**-uhst/ *noun*
1. A **chemist** is a shop where medicines are made and sold. *She asked Sarah to go to the chemist and buy something for her headache.*
2. A **chemist** is someone whose job is to make and sell medicines. *The chemist sold Sarah a new medicine for headaches.*

chemistry /*say* **kem**-uhs-tree/ *noun*
Chemistry is a part of science in which you study what things are made of and the way they change.

cheque /*say* chek/ *noun*
A **cheque** is a special piece of paper which you write on, telling a bank to pay an amount of your money to a particular person.

> ✴ *Spelling Tip:* Notice that **cheque** sounds the same as the word *check* (which is the spelling used for this word in America). The spelling we use comes from French, which is why the letters *que* make the sound of 'k'.

cherry *noun* (*plural* **cherries**)
A **cherry** is a small, round, red fruit with a hard stone in the centre.

chess *noun*
Chess is a game played by two people, each with 16 pieces, on a board.

chest *noun*
Your **chest** is the front part of your body from your neck to your stomach.

chew *verb*
If you **chew** something, you bite and crush it with your teeth. *He was always chewing lollies and got very bad tooth decay.*

chewing gum *noun*
Chewing gum is a type of sweet that you only crush with your teeth and do not swallow.

chicken *noun*
A **chicken** is a kind of bird that people keep to get eggs from or to use for food. *Look at the little yellow chickens with the mother hen. | We are having chicken for dinner.*

chickenpox *noun*
Chickenpox is a sickness that makes you feel hot and gives you red spots that you want to scratch.

chickpea *noun*
A **chickpea** is a small, round, yellow vegetable.

chief /*say* cheef / *noun*
1. A **chief** is the leading person in a group.
–*adjective* **2.** If something is the **chief** thing, it is the most important or main thing.

> ❄ *Spelling Tip:* Remember the *ie* spelling for the 'ee' sound. This follows the rule that *i* comes before *e* except after *c*.

child *noun* (*plural* **children**)
You are a **child** from the time you are born until you are almost an adult.

> *Word Building:* **childhood**, *noun* The time you spend as a child is your **childhood**. –**childish**, *adjective* Someone who behaves like a silly child is behaving in a **childish** way.

chill *verb*
1. If you **chill** something, you make it colder. *Put those bottles of drink in the tub of ice to chill them for the party.*
–*noun* **2.** A **chill** is a feeling of cold. *Winter must be on the way – there's a chill in the air.*
3. A **chill** is a sickness like a cold that makes you shake as if you are cold and feel hot at the same time. *Ajay caught a chill when he walked home in the rain.*

> *Word Building:* **chilly**, *adjective* When there is a chill in the air, the day feels **chilly**.

chilli *noun* (*plural* **chillies**)
A **chilli** is a small green or red vegetable that tastes hot, and is used in cooking.

chimney *noun* (*plural* **chimneys**)
A **chimney** is the part of a house that takes smoke from a fire up through the roof to the outside.

chimpanzee *noun*
A **chimpanzee** is a kind of ape from Africa which spends much of its life in the trees.

chin *noun*
Your **chin** is the part of your face below your mouth.

chip *noun*
1. A **chip** is a small piece cut or split off from something larger. *There were small chips of wood on the ground where they had chopped down the tree.*
2. **Chips** are small pieces of potato that are cooked in oil. *Dad gave us the money to buy a bag of chips each.*
–*verb* (**chips**, **chipping**, **chipped**, **has chipped**)
3. If you **chip** something, you cut or break a small piece off something larger. *We chipped a bit of bark off the tree.*

chocolate /*say* **chok**-luht / *noun*
1. **Chocolate** is a brown-coloured sweet food. *I like the taste of chocolate.*
2. **Hot chocolate** is a hot drink made from chocolate and milk. *It is good to have a cup of hot chocolate on a cold winter's night.*

> ❄ *Spelling Tip:* The main thing to remember about **chocolate** is that it has an *o* in the middle, even though you don't hear this sound when you say it. The last three letters make the word *ate* which is what happens to **chocolate** – it gets eaten all too quickly.

choice *noun*
When you make a **choice**, you choose something.

choir /*say* **kwuy**-uh / *noun*
A **choir** is a group of people who sing together.

> ❄ *Spelling Tip:* Remember that **choir** starts with *ch* (with a 'k' sound as in the similar word *chorus*). But the most unusual thing about the word *choir* is its *oir* ending. Remember there is no *w* in the spelling although you hear its sound.

choose *verb* (**chooses, choosing, chose, has chosen**)
If you **choose**, you decide which one you want out of a group. *'Which book did you choose?' 'I chose the one about animals.'*

> Other words with a similar meaning are **select** and **pick**.

chop *noun*
1. A **chop** is a fairly thick piece of meat with the bone in it.
−*verb* (**chops, chopping, chopped, has chopped**)
2. If you **chop** something, you cut it up by hitting it hard and quickly with a sharp tool. *We need to chop the wood for our fire.*

chopsticks *noun*
A pair of **chopsticks** is two thin sticks, usually made of wood or plastic. You use them to lift food when you are eating Asian food.

chorus /*say* **kaw**-ruhs/ *noun*
A **chorus** is the words that are repeated after each verse of some songs or poems.

christen /*say* **kris**-uhn/ *verb*
If a baby is **christened**, they are given a name, usually in a ceremony in a church. *The family took their new daughter to the church to be christened. They christened her Sarah.*

> *Word Building:* **christening**, *noun* When a baby is christened, the ceremony is called a **christening**.

> ✴ *Spelling Tip:* Don't forget the *st* (not double *s*) spelling. The *t* is silent. Remember that this word comes from *Christ*, who started *Christianity*. You can hear the *t* in these words.

Christianity /*say* kris-tee-**an**-uh-tee/ *noun*
Christianity is a religion started by a special teacher called Jesus Christ who lived a long time ago. This religion teaches that Jesus Christ is the Son of God.

> *Word Building:* **Christian** /*say* **kris**-chuhn/, *noun* Someone whose religion is Christianity is a **Christian**.

chuckle *verb*
1. If you **chuckle**, you laugh quietly. *Alice was chuckling as she was reading. It was a very funny book.*
−*noun* 2. A **chuckle** is a quiet laugh.

church *noun* (*plural* **churches**)
A **church** is a special building where people meet to learn about God or speak to God.

churinga /*say* chuh-**ring**-guh/ *noun*
A **churinga** is an object made by Aboriginal people which represents an important being or thing in their religion.

> This word comes from an Aboriginal language of the Northern Territory called Arrernte.

cicada /*say* suh-**kah**-duh, suh-**kay**-duh/ *noun*
A **cicada** is a large flying insect which is found in the trees in summer. It makes a loud high noise that goes on and on.

cigarette *noun*
A **cigarette** is a roll of tobacco for smoking, wrapped up in very thin paper.

cinema /*say* **sin**-uh-muh/ *noun*
A **cinema** is a place where you go to watch films.

circle /*say* **ser**-kuhl/ *noun*
A **circle** is a completely round shape, like a wheel.

> *Word Building:* **circular** /*say* **ser**-kyuh-luh/, *adjective* If something is shaped like a circle, it is **circular**.

circus *noun*
A **circus** is a show in a big tent with clowns, acrobats and sometimes animals such as lions and elephants.

citizen /*say* **sit**-uh-zuhn/ *noun*
A **citizen** is someone who belongs to a particular country by law.

city *noun* (*plural* **cities**)
A **city** is a large or important town.

claim *verb*
1. If you **claim** something, you say that it belongs to you. *When explorers reached new lands, they claimed them for their country.*
2. If you **claim** something, you say that it is true or that it is the case. *My mum claims that she can walk two kilometres in half an hour.*

clamp *verb*
1. If you **clamp** things, you use something to hold them together tightly. *Put glue on both pieces, and then clamp them together while it sets.*
−*noun* 2. A **clamp** is a tool which holds something tightly.

clap *verb* (**claps, clapping, clapped, has clapped**)
If you **clap**, you hit your hands together in a noisy way, to show that you think someone or something is good. *Everyone clapped for a long time as the singer left the stage.*

class *noun*
A **class** is a group of people who are taught together. They have lessons together.

classmate *noun*
A **classmate** is someone who is in your class at school.

classroom *noun*
A **classroom** is a room in a school where you have lessons.

claw *noun*
A **claw** is the hard, sharp, curved nail on the foot of a bird or animal.

clay *noun*
Clay is thick, sticky soil which is used to make pots and bricks. You make it into the shape you want and then dry or bake it until it is hard.

clean *adjective*
1. If something is **clean**, it has no dirt on it.
–*verb* 2. If you **clean** something, you take dirt from it by washing, sweeping, or rubbing. *Sue cleaned the table with a cloth.*

> **Word Building: cleaner**, *noun* Someone whose job is to clean is a **cleaner**.

clear *adjective*
1. If something like glass or water is **clear**, you can see through it. *The water was so clear they could see some coins lying at the bottom.*
2. If what someone says or writes is **clear**, you can hear it or understand it easily. *The teacher explained how to do the maths problem until it was clear to everyone. | Please speak in a clear voice.*
3. If a place is **clear**, it has nothing on it that can get in the way or stop you going along it. *We got there quickly because the road was clear.*
4. If a day is **clear**, there are no clouds or not many clouds. It is bright. *Yesterday was a clear sunny day.*
–*verb* 5. If you **clear** something, you take away something from it that is blocking it or stopping it being used. *Ben helped his mother clear the table after dinner.*

clearly *adverb*
If something is done **clearly**, it is done in a way that is easy to see, hear or understand. *We couldn't see the mountain clearly once the sun went down.*

clerk /*rhymes with* bark/ *noun*
A **clerk** is someone who works in an office, doing things like keeping records, opening letters and sending out bills to people who owe money.

> **Word Building: clerical** /*say* **kle**-rik-uhl/, *adjective* The work that a clerk does is **clerical** work.

clever *adjective*
Someone who is **clever** is good at thinking and is able to learn quickly.

> **Word Building: cleverly**, *adverb* If you are clever at something, you do it **cleverly**.

click *noun*
1. A **click** is a short, sharp noise, sometimes made with your fingers.
–*verb* 2. If you **click** when you are using a computer, you press a button on the mouse. *We clicked twice to open the program.*

cliff *noun*
A **cliff** is a very steep, rocky slope, sometimes at the edge of the sea.

climate /*say* **kluy**-muht/ *noun*
Climate is the usual weather in a place.

climate change *noun*
Climate change is a change in weather conditions that goes on for a long time, such as when the temperature becomes warmer or colder than it used to be and stays like that.

> Also look up **global warming**.

climb /*rhymes with* time/ *verb*
1. If something **climbs**, it moves upwards. *The plane climbed slowly into the sky.*
2. If you **climb** something, you move up it. *The old man slowly climbed the stairs.*

cling *verb* (**clings, clinging, clung, has clung**)
If you **cling** to something, you hold onto it very tightly. *My little brother clung to Mum – he didn't want her to go to work.*

clinic *noun*
A **clinic** is a place where you can go to see a doctor or have tests or treatment when you are sick or hurt.

clock *noun*
A **clock** is an instrument that shows you what the time is.

a b c d e f g h i j k l m n o p q r s t u v w x y z

close¹ /say klohz/ verb
1. If you **close** something, you shut it. You move it so that it is not open. *She closed the window because of the cold wind.*
2. If something **closes**, it stops being open. *This shop closes at seven o'clock.*

close² /say klohs/ adjective
If something is **close**, it is near.

> **Word Building: closely**, *adverb*: *He went ahead and she followed closely behind.*

cloth noun
Cloth is material used for clothes and other things such as curtains and furniture coverings.

> Look up **clothes. Clothes** is not the plural of **cloth**.

clothes /say klohdhz/ noun
Clothes are the things you wear on your body.

clothing /say **klohdh**-ing/ noun
Clothing is what you wear on your body.

cloud noun
1. A **cloud** is a white or grey mass of small drops of water that hangs in the sky and stops the sun shining through it. Sometimes it turns into rain, which falls to the ground. *It was sunny this morning but now there are a lot of clouds.*
2. the cloud, On the internet, **the cloud** is a place where you can store files so that they don't take up space on your computer and make it run slowly.

> **Word Building: cloudy**, *adjective* If there are a lot of clouds in the sky, it is **cloudy**.

clover /say **kloh**-vuh/ noun
Clover is a small plant which has leaves with three round parts. Some people say that if you find a clover leaf with four round parts, you will have good luck.

clown noun
A **clown** is someone who wears funny clothes, has a painted face and makes people laugh.

club noun
A **club** is a group of people who have joined together because they like doing the same thing.

clue noun
A **clue** is something that might give you the answer to a puzzle.

clumsy /say **klum**-zee/ adjective (**clumsier, clumsiest**)
You are **clumsy** if you often drop things or walk into things without meaning to.

clutch verb
If you **clutch** something, you take hold of it suddenly and hold it tightly. *Amber clutched her mother's arm because she was so scared.*

coach noun (plural **coaches**)
1. A **coach** is a large, comfortable bus, usually for long trips. *The coach our family travelled in to go to north Queensland showed good movies.*
2. A **coach** is a vehicle pulled by horses, used in the past to carry people. *The princess rode to her wedding in a gold coach.*
3. A **coach** is someone whose job is to train people in a sport, such as swimming or football. *There is a swimming coach at the local pool that a lot of the kids go to.*

coal noun
Coal is a black or dark brown rock that you can burn to make heat.

coast noun
The **coast** is the part of the land that is beside the sea.

> **Word Building: coastal**, *adjective* If a town is on the coast, it is a **coastal** town.

coat noun
A **coat** is a piece of clothing for the top part of the body, which you wear over other clothes.

cobweb noun
A **cobweb** is a thin, sticky thread which a spider makes and uses to catch insects.

cock noun
A **cock** is a male chicken.

cockatiel /say kok-uh-**teel**/ noun
A **cockatiel** is a bird with a long tail and feathers that stand up on the top of its head.

cockatoo noun
A **cockatoo** is an Australian bird with a loud call. A cockatoo can make the feathers on the top of its head stand up.

coconut noun
1. A **coconut** is a large brown nut with a hard, hairy outside and a slightly sweet white food and kind of milk inside. *Be careful a coconut does not fall down from the tree and hit you!*
2. Coconut is the sweet white food that comes from the inside of a coconut. *I like the taste of coconut.*

cocoon /say kuh-**koohn** / noun

A **cocoon** is the soft outer covering that animals like silkworms make from thin threads. They make it to cover themselves before they begin to grow and change into adult insects.

code noun

A **code** is the special signs, letters or words you use to send messages.

coffee noun

Coffee is a hot drink made from the seeds of a special plant.

coffin noun

A **coffin** is a long box in which a dead body is put.

coin noun

A **coin** is a piece of money made of metal.

cold adjective

1. If something is **cold**, it has a low temperature and does not give out warmth or heat. *I would like a cold drink.*
2. If the weather is **cold**, it has a low temperature that you find is uncomfortable. *It's a cold day so you will need to wear a heavy coat.*
3. If you are **cold**, you feel uncomfortable because of the weather being cold. *She was so cold that she was shaking.*
−*noun* **4.** A **cold** is a sickness in which your nose is blocked and you cough. *A cold can make you feel very sick.*
5. catch a cold, If you **catch a cold** or **catch cold**, you become sick with a cold. *I got wet in the rain and caught a cold.*

Also look up **cool** which has a similar meaning to definitions 1 and 2.

collapse /say kuh-**laps** / verb

If someone or something **collapses**, they fall down suddenly. *His illness was so severe that it made him collapse.*

collar noun

A **collar** is the part of a shirt, a dress or a coat that fits around your neck.

⭐ *Spelling Tip:* Remember that the ending is spelt *ar* (not *er*).

collect verb

1. If you **collect** things, you gather them together or bring them all together. *Please collect all the books from the desks.*
2. If you **collect** something, you go and get it from somewhere. *I will collect the book from the library tomorrow.*

Word Building: **collection**, *noun* If you collect things, you have a **collection**. *Our class has the best insect collection in the whole school.*

college noun

A **college** is a place where you can go to learn after you have finished school. It is like a university.

collision /say kuh-**lizh**-uhn / noun

A **collision** is a crashing together of two things.

Word Building: **collide**, *verb* If two things have a collision, they **collide**.

colony /say **kol**-uh-nee / noun (plural **colonies**)

1. A **colony** is a group of people who take over land in a new country, away from their home country, and live there. They are still governed by their home country. *The whole colony was hungry until they learned to farm the land.*
2. A **colony** is a place which has been taken over by people from another country. *The people who first lived in the country were forced further and further away from the new colony.*

colour noun

1. The **colour** of something is the special look it has which we call by names such as *red*, *orange*, *yellow*, *green*, *blue* and *brown*.
−*verb* **2.** If you **colour** something, you put colour on to it. *Tapan drew a picture of a tree. He coloured the branches brown and the leaves green.*

Word Building: **colourful**, *adjective* If something has bright or strong colours, it is **colourful**.

Another spelling for this word is **color**.

comb /rhymes with home / noun

1. A **comb** is a piece of plastic or metal with a row of very thin pointed pieces, which you use to make your hair tidy.
−*verb* **2.** If you **comb** your hair, you use a comb to tidy it. *He combed his hair and cleaned his teeth before leaving for school.*

⭐ *Spelling Tip:* Don't forget the silent *b* at the end.

come verb (**comes, coming, came, has come**)

1. If you **come** towards a person or place, you move towards them. *Please come here immediately.* | *The teacher asked Henry to come to the front of the classroom.* | *Can you come to the shops with me?*

2. If someone or something **comes** to a place, they arrive there. *I arrived at two o'clock but John didn't come until three o'clock.* | *What time does the train come?* | *The train came into the station on time.*

3. If something **comes** at a certain time, it happens then. *Christmas comes in December each year.* | *I hope my turn will come soon.*

4. come from, If you **come from** a country or a town, you were born there or you usually live there. *'Where does Sam's family come from?' 'They come from Malaysia.'*

5. come out, If something or someone **comes out**, they come to a position where you can see them. *The stars come out at night.* | *I told my little brother to come out because I could see where he was hiding.*

comet *noun*
A **comet** is an object in space that moves around the sun. It has a bright centre with a long cloudy part behind it like a tail.

comfort /*say* **kum**-fuht / *verb*
If you **comfort** someone, you try to make them feel less sad or worried. *When Helen started to cry, her father comforted her by putting his arm around her.*

comfortable /*say* **kumf**-tuh-buhl / *adjective*
If something is **comfortable**, it makes your body feel pleasant.

The opposite is **uncomfortable**.

⭐ *Spelling Tip:* The spelling of **comfort** is really quite easy, as long as you remember that it is made up of the word *comfort* and *able*, even though you say the *comfort* part in a short way. Remember that the letter after the *c* is *o*, although it gives a 'u' sound.

comic *noun*
A **comic** is a magazine with funny or exciting stories told in words and pictures.

command *verb*
1. If you **command** someone, you tell them that they have to do something. *'I command you to attack the enemy', said the general.*
–*noun* **2.** A **command** is an instruction, telling someone what they have to do. *He gave the command to move forward and the soldiers immediately obeyed.*
3. A **command** is an instruction to a computer to do a particular thing. It is part of a program. *Do you know what the command is to print a file?*

commercial /*say* kuh-**mer**-shuhl / *noun*
A **commercial** is an advertisement on radio or television.

common *adjective*
Something is **common** if you often see or find it, or if it happens a lot.

commonwealth /*say* **kom**-uhn-welth / *noun*
A **commonwealth** is a country made up of several states. There is one government for the whole country and each state has its own government as well. *The Commonwealth of Australia was formed over 100 years ago.*

communication /*say* kuh-myooh-nuh-**kay**-shuhn / *noun*
1. Communication is the sharing of thoughts, ideas or information with someone. *There was no communication between them for years.*
2. Communications are ways of passing on information, such as computers, telephone, radio, and television. *Modern communications, like the internet, mean that many people can do their work at home.*

Word Building: **communicate**, *verb* When there is communication between people, they **communicate**.

community /*say* kuh-**myooh**-nuh-tee / *noun* (*plural* **communities**)
A **community** is a group of people who live in one area or are connected in some way.

compact disc *noun*
A **compact disc** is a small, round, flat piece of plastic with music or other information on it that you can hear or read by putting it into a special machine or into a computer.

You can also say **CD** which is short for **compact disc**.

⭐ *Spelling Tip:* Also look up **disk**. Remember that, though the spelling **disk** is usually used when it has to do with computers, **compact disc** is usually spelt with a *c*.

companion *noun*
Your **companion** is someone who goes somewhere with you.

company /*say* **kum**-puh-nee / *noun* (*plural* **companies**)
A **company** is a business organisation.

compare /*say* kuhm-**pair** / *verb*
1. If you **compare** things, you look at them or think about them to see if they are similar or

different. *Ann and Helen compared their work and found that Ann had got more answers right than Helen.*

2. compare with, If you **compare** something **with** something else or **to** something else, you think about whether it is similar to or different from that other thing. *Ann compared her work with Helen's and found that she had got more answers right.*

> **Word Building: comparison** /*say* kuhm-**pa**-ruh-suhn/, *noun* When you compare things, you make a **comparison**.

compass /*say* **kum**-puhs / *noun*
A **compass** is an instrument with a needle that points to the north. You use it to find out which way to go.

competition /*say* kom-puh-**tish**-uhn / *noun*
A **competition** is a test between two or more people to see who is the best at something, or who will win.

> **Word Building: compete**, *verb* If you take part in a competition, then you **compete** with other people. –**competitor** /*say* kuhm-**pet**-uh-tuh /, *adjective* If you take part in a competition, then you are a **competitor**.

complain *verb*
If you **complain** to someone, you tell them about all the things you don't like, or that make you unhappy. *My dad said if I complained about his cooking once more, I could have toast for dinner instead.*

> **Word Building: complaint**, *noun* If you complain about something, then you make a **complaint**.

complete *adjective*
1. If something is **complete**, it has all its parts. Nothing is missing.
–*verb* **2.** If you **complete** something, you finish it. *'Have you completed your work?' 'No, I have a bit more to do.'*

completely *adverb*
You use **completely** to make what you are saying stronger and to show that something is true in every way. *I completely forgot that I said I would meet you after school. | I am completely full – I could not eat anything more.*

complicated /*say* **kom**-pluh-kay-tuhd / *adjective*
Something is **complicated** if it is has a lot of parts to it and so is difficult or hard to understand. *Murray found the new dance they were learning*

at school very complicated – there were too many steps to remember.

compliment /*say* **kom**-pluh-muhnt / *noun*
A **compliment** is something nice you say to tell someone that they look good, or that they have done something well.

composer *noun*
A **composer** is someone who writes music.

composition *noun*
A **composition** is a short piece of writing which you do as part of school work.

compost *noun*
Compost is a mixture of bits of food, leaves and other things that fall apart after a while and become good food for gardens. It is often added to the soil to help plants grow.

computer *noun*
A **computer** is a machine which does mathematical sums very quickly, and which stores and gives out information. You need a computer to get information on the internet.

computer game *noun*
A **computer game** is a game that is designed to be played on a computer.

concentrate /*say* **kon**-suhn-trayt / *verb*
If you **concentrate**, you think very hard about one thing. *Just concentrate on watching the ball and you'll be able to catch it.*

> **Word Building: concentration**, *noun* If you concentrate on something, you give it your **concentration**.

concert /*say* **kon**-suht / *noun*
A **concert** is a performance of music for people to come and listen to.

concrete *noun*
Concrete is a mixture of cement, sand, water and gravel, used for building. It goes hard as it dries.

> ✵ *Spelling Tip:* Remember that the final part of **concrete** is spelt *ete* (not *eet*). It might help if you think of some other familiar words that have the same spelling for this sound, such as *complete* and *compete*.

condition *noun*
The **condition** of someone or something is the way they are, good or bad. *My mum goes to the gym to keep her body in good condition. | The bike was old and in very bad condition so my dad decided not to buy it.*

a b c d e f g h i j k l m n o p q r s t u v w x y z

conduct *noun* /say **kon**-dukt/

1. Your **conduct** is the way you behave or act. –*verb* /say kuhn-**dukt**/ **2.** If you **conduct** people who are playing instruments or singing, you lead them and control the way they play or sing. *It's your turn to conduct the band, so don't forget to show each group of players when to start.*

conductor *noun*

A **conductor** is the person who directs the playing or singing of people in a music group.

> **Spelling Tip:** Remember that the last part of **conductor** is spelt *or* (not *er*).

cone *noun*

1. A **cone** is a shape with a flat round bottom and sides that meet in a point at the top. *A wizard's hat is in the shape of a cone.*
2. A **cone** is the hard fruit with pointed pieces on its sides that comes from some trees. *We collected the pine cones that were lying under the trees.*

confess *verb*

If you **confess**, you say that you have done something wrong. *Anna confessed that she had broken the plate.*

> **Word Building: confession**, *noun* If you confess to something, then you make a **confession**.

confident *adjective*

You are **confident** if you feel sure about something.

> **Word Building: confidence**, *noun* If you're confident, then you have a feeling of **confidence**.

confuse *verb*

1. If something or someone **confuses** you, they make you feel not certain or not sure. *All these instructions for the game have confused me.*
2. If you **confuse** things, you mistake one for the other. *I often confuse him with his brother – they look almost the same.*

> **Word Building: confusion**, *noun* If something confuses you, then you're filled with **confusion**.

congratulate /say kuhn-**grach**-uh-layt/ *verb*

If you **congratulate** someone, you tell them that you're happy that something good has happened to them. *We all congratulated Wayang on running so well in the race.*

congratulations /say kuhn-grach-uh-**lay**-shuhnz/ *interjection*

Congratulations is a word that you use when you want to tell someone that you are happy about something good that has happened to them. *Congratulations! You ran a very good race.*

conjunction *noun*

A **conjunction** is a type of word which joins parts of a sentence together, such as 'and' in *He sat down and started to eat* and 'because' in *We went home because it was raining*.

connect *verb*

If you **connect** things, you join them together. *They built a road to connect two cities.* | *You can print by connecting this machine to the computer.*

> **Word Building: connection**, *noun* When you connect things, you make a **connection**.

conquer /say **kong**-kuh/ *verb*

If you **conquer** an enemy, you beat them. *Tim was playing a computer game, trying to conquer the strange hairy creatures from outer space.*

> **Word Building: conqueror** /say **kong**-kuh-ruh/, *noun* If you conquer an enemy, then you are the **conqueror**. –**conquest** /say **kon**-kwest/, *noun* If you conquer an enemy, you have made a **conquest**.

> **Spelling Tip:** Remember the *qu* spelling for the 'k' sound in the middle and the *er* ending, and you will have **conquered** this word.

conscious /say **kon**-shuhs/ *adjective*

You are **conscious** if you know what is happening around you.

> The opposite is **unconscious**.

> **Spelling Tip:** Remember that there is an *sc* in this word, spelling the 'sh' sound. Like the word *science*, it comes from the Latin word for 'knowledge'. If you think about the *sc* spelling in *science*, it will help you to spell **conscious**. Remember also the silent *i* before the *ous* ending.

conservation /say kon-suh-**vay**-shuhn/ *noun*

Conservation is taking care of the air we breathe, our water, our plants and our animals, so that no-one damages or hurts them.

consider *verb*

1. If you **consider** something, you think about it carefully. *It looked as though it was going to rain*

and the teacher considered whether the class should stay inside for lunch.
2. considered to be, If someone is **considered to be** something, people think about them in that way. *Jack is considered to be the best footballer in the class.*

consist *verb*
If something **consists** of particular things, it is made up of them. *The furniture in the room consisted of just a few old chairs.*

consonant /*say* **kon**-suh-nuhnt/ *noun*
A **consonant** is any letter of the alphabet which is not *a, e, i, o* or *u*.

> Look up **vowel**.

construct *verb*
If you **construct** something, you build it. *How many years did it take to construct that long bridge?*

> **Word Building: construction**, *noun* A **construction** is something that has been constructed, usually a building. *What's the new construction being built near the school?*

contain *verb*
If something **contains** something, it has it inside itself. *This bottle contains milk.*

container *noun*
A **container** is something that you can put things in. Boxes, bags, bottles and cans are all **containers**.

container ship *noun*
A **container ship** is a ship that carries goods from one part of the world to another in very large containers.

content /*say* kuhn-**tent**/ *adjective*
If you are **content**, you feel pleased or you feel happy about something.

> **Word Building: contentment**, *noun* If you are content, you have a feeling of **contentment**.

contents /*say* **kon**-tents/ *noun*
The **contents** of something are whatever is inside or contained in it.

contest /*say* **kon**-test/ *noun*
A **contest** is a competition to see who is the best at something.

> **Word Building: contestant** /*say* kuhn-**tes**-tuhnt/, *noun* If you enter a contest, then you are a **contestant**.

continent *noun*
A **continent** is one of the main areas of land in the world.

> There are seven **continents** in all: North America, South America, Africa, Europe, Asia, Australia, and Antarctica. Australia is the smallest continent.

continue *verb*
1. If you **continue** doing something, you do not stop doing it. You keep on doing it. *Zac and Ben continued to jump on the jumping castle even though it was raining.*
2. If something **continues**, it does not stop. *Rain will continue all day.*

> **Word Building: continuous**, *adjective* Something that continues is **continuous**. *There was continuous rain all day.*

contract /*say* **kon**-trakt/ *noun*
A **contract** is a piece of paper you sign, which says that you agree to do something.

contrast *verb* /*say* kuhn-**trahst**/
1. If something **contrasts** with something else, it looks different beside it. *The red and white of our team contrasted with the green and black of their team.*
–*noun* /*say* **kon**-trahst/ **2.** A **contrast** is a strong difference.

contribute /*say* kuhn-**trib**-yooht/ *verb*
If you **contribute** to something, you give your share to it. *Will you contribute to Sally's birthday present?*

> **Word Building: contribution** /*say* kon-truh-**byooh**-shuhn/, *noun* If you contribute something, then you make a **contribution**.

control *verb* (**controls, controlling, controlled, has controlled**)
1. If you **control** someone or something, you are in charge of them. It is your job to make them do what you think should be done. *My mother runs the canteen at school and she controls the food that is ordered.*
2. If you are able to **control** something, you can keep it held back or make it do what you want. *Kylie was trying to control her feelings but then she started to cry.*

> ✳ **Spelling Tip:** Remember that there is only one *l* at the end of **control**. However, when you add *ed* or *ing*, the *l* is doubled.

a b c d e f g h i j k l m n o p q r s t u v w x y z

convenient /*say* kuhn-**vee**-nee-uhnt/ *adjective*
If something is **convenient**, it is good or easy because it fits in with what you want or need. *That house would not be convenient for my grand-mother because it is too far away from the bus stop.* | *My sister worked out a convenient time to meet her friend.*

⭐ *Spelling Tip:* Remember that the 'ee' sound after the *v* is spelt with only one *e*.

conversation /*say* kon-vuh-**say**-shuhn/ *noun*
A **conversation** is a talk among people.

convict /*say* **kon**-vikt/ *noun*
A **convict** is someone who has done something wrong and has been put in prison. *He was sent from England to Australia as a convict in 1798.*

This word was used more often in the past.

cooee /*say* **koo**-ee/ *noun*
A **cooee** is a long, loud call used to signal someone, especially when you are in the bush.

This word comes from an Aboriginal language of New South Wales called Dharug.

cook *verb*
1. If you **cook** food, you make it ready for eating in a way that uses heat. *There are many ways to cook potatoes.*
–*noun* 2. A **cook** is someone who cooks or prepares food.

cool *adjective*
1. If something is **cool** or the weather is **cool**, it has a low temperature but is not very cold. *It was a bit cool in the morning but not cold enough for a jumper.*
2. You can say that something is **cool** when it is attractive or fashionable. *Anna has some really cool new jeans.*

Also look up **cold** which has a similar meaning to definition 1.

coolibah /*say* **kooh**-luh-bah/ *noun*
A **coolibah** is a sort of gum tree with short branches, which grows where there is water or where water is sometimes found.

This word comes from an Aboriginal language of New South Wales called Yuwaalaraay.

copper *noun*
Copper is a metal with a red-brown colour.

copy *noun* (*plural* **copies**)
1. A **copy** is something which is made the same as something else. *The secretary made extra copies of the letter for other people to read.*
–*verb* (**copies**, **copying**, **copied**, **has copied**)
2. If you **copy** something you make something that is the same as it. If you **copy** someone, you do something in the same way as they are doing it. *Copy these maths problems from the board.* | *If you don't know how to do the dance, just copy me.*

copyright /*say* **kop**-ee-ruyt/ *noun*
If a person has **copyright** in writing, drawings or music, it means that it is against the law for other people to use it unless they have permission.

coral *noun*
Coral is the hard material in many different shapes that is formed from the bones of small sea animals. You can find it in many beautiful colours in places like the Great Barrier Reef.

corn *noun*
Corn is a kind of grain plant that you can eat as a vegetable, use in cooking, or use to make flour.

corner *noun*
A **corner** is a place where two lines or edges meet.

corpse /*say* kawps/ *noun*
A **corpse** is the body of a dead person.

correct *adjective*
If something is **correct**, it does not have any mistakes.

❖ Another word with a similar meaning is **right**.
❖ Words with the opposite meaning are **incor-rect** and **wrong**.

corridor *noun*
A **corridor** is a part of a building that is long and narrow and leads from one room to another.

⭐ *Spelling Tip:* Remember that the letter after the double *r* is an *i*. Also, don't forget the *or* ending (not *ore*).

corroboree /*say* kuh-**rob**-uh-ree/ *noun*
A **corroboree** is an Aboriginal dance ceremony which includes singing and music. Many people come together for the ceremony in which the dancers paint themselves in traditional designs.

This word comes from an Aboriginal language of New South Wales called Dharug.

cost *noun*
1. The **cost** of something is how much you have to pay for it. *The cost of a bus ride is much more than it used to be.*
–*verb* (**costs, costing, cost, has cost**)
2. If something **costs** a particular amount of money, or **costs** you an amount of money, that is how much you have to pay for it. *How much does it cost to get a bus from here to the city? | These books cost my dad more than $40.*

costly *adjective* (**costlier, costliest**)
If something is **costly**, it costs a lot to buy it.

Other words with a similar meaning are **expensive** and **dear**.

costume *noun*
A **costume** is the special clothes you wear for going on the stage or when you want to dress to make you appear like someone else.

Also look up **swimming costume**.

cosy *adjective* (**cosier, cosiest**)
Something is **cosy** if it has a comfortable and pleasant feel.

cot *noun*
A **cot** is a bed with high sides around it, for a baby or a young child.

cottage *noun*
A **cottage** is a small house.

cotton *noun*
1. **Cotton** is a light material made from part of a plant. *Clothes made of cotton are comfortable to wear when it is very hot.*
2. **Cotton** is a thread used for sewing. *We didn't have the right colour cotton to fix up my skirt.*

couch *noun* (*plural* **couches**)
A **couch** is a long, comfortable seat with sides and a back, for two or more people.

Other words that mean the same are **sofa** and **lounge**.

cough /*rhymes with* off/ *verb*
1. When you **cough**, you send out air from your mouth suddenly and noisily, the way you do when you are sick with a cold or when you have breathed in something bad. *Ann felt very sick and coughed all night.*
–*noun* 2. A **cough** is the loud sudden noise you make when you cough.

🌟 *Spelling Tip:* Remember that there is no *f* in **cough** – the spelling *ough* gives the 'off' sound.

could /*rhymes with* good/ *verb*
Look up **can**[1].

council /*say* **kown**-suhl/ *noun*
A **council** is a group of people who meet often to talk about things and to decide things.

Word Building: **councillor** /*say* **kown**-suh-luh/, *noun* If someone is a member of a council, such as a city council, then he or she is a **councillor**.

count *verb*
If you **count**, you use numbers to find the total amount of a group of things. *Sam counted the trucks as they passed. He counted 41 trucks.*

counter *noun*
A **counter** is a long shelf in a shop where you can stand and pay for the things you want to buy. The person selling the things stands on the other side.

country /*say* **kun**-tree/ *noun* (*plural* **countries**)
1. A **country** is an area of land separated from other areas by having its own government. *In our school, there are kids from lots of different countries.*
2. When Australian Indigenous people talk about **country**, it is the land where they have traditionally lived, with everything about it the same as it came to them from the Dreaming.
3. **the country**, **The country** is the land away from cities and towns, especially when it is used for farming. *Sue likes living in the city but still likes to visit her grandmother in the country.*

Another word with a similar meaning to definition 1 is **nation**.

couple /*say* **kup**-uhl/ *noun*
1. Two people make a **couple**, especially if they are married. *I heard my grandmother say that my mother and father were a very happy couple.*
2. **a couple of**, If you say **a couple of** something, you mean two of those things. *There were a couple of horses in the field.*

courage /*say* **ku**-rij/ *noun*
Courage is the strength a person has inside them to do something they find frightening.

Word Building: **courageous** /*say* kuh-**ray**-juhs/, *adjective* If you have courage, you are **courageous**.

a b c d e f g h i j k l m n o p q r s t u v w x y z

course /rhymes with horse/ noun
1. A **course** is the ground or water on which you have a race. *The course for the race was a pretty hard one with lots of hills.*
2. A **course** is one part of a meal. *We had meat and vegetables for the main course and then we had some ice-cream and fruit.*
3. **of course**, You say **of course** to show that something is usual or is what you would expect and doesn't need to be talked about any more. *She arrived late, of course.*

court /rhymes with short/ noun
1. A **court** is the hard ground where games such as tennis are played. *The players walked onto the court for the start of the game.*
2. A **court** is the place where decisions are made about who is responsible for a crime and how they should be punished. *Everyone has to stand up when the judge enters the court.*
3. A **court** is the place where a king or queen lives and the people who live or work there. *The play was about a murder that took place at the court of the king.*

courteous /say **ker**-tee-uhs/ adjective
If you are **courteous**, you are polite. *The teacher reminded them to be very courteous to the visitors.*

> **Word Building: courtesy** /say **ker**-tuh-see/, *noun* If you are courteous, then you do things with **courtesy**.

> ❄ *Spelling Tip:* Don't forget that the first part of **courteous** is spelt *court* (although it sounds like it could be spelt *curt*). In fact, the meaning of this word is related to a *court* in the sense of the special behaviour used at the court of a king or queen in the past.

courtyard noun
A **courtyard** is an open area that is part of a house or building and has walls or buildings all around it.

cousin /say **kuz**-uhn/ noun
Your **cousin** is the son or daughter of your uncle or aunt.

cover verb
1. If something **covers** something, it lies over it or is placed over it. *Clouds covered the sun.*
2. If you **cover** something, you place something over it. *He covered his face with his hands.*
–noun 3. A **cover** is something you use to put over something, usually to keep it safe or clean.

> **Word Building: covering**, *noun* Something that covers something else is a **covering**.

cow noun
1. A **cow** is a large female animal of the cattle family, often kept on farms to give milk. *My favourite cows are the soft brown ones with big brown eyes.*
2. You can also use the word **cow** for the female of other animal families, like whales, seals and elephants. *We were lucky enough to see some whales – a cow and her calf came very close to the ship.*

> The male is a **bull**.

coward /say **kow**-uhd/ noun
A **coward** is someone who runs away from the things that make them afraid.

> **Word Building: cowardice** /say **kow**-uh-duhs/, *noun* The behaviour of a coward is called **cowardice**. –**cowardly**, *adjective* A coward does **cowardly** things.

crab noun
A **crab** is a sea animal with a hard, flat outer covering, eight legs and two large claws at the front of its body.

crack verb
1. If something **cracks**, it breaks or splits with a sharp sound. *The branch of the tree cracked as it fell.*
–noun 2. A **crack** is the line that you can see when something has a split or a break in it.

cradle noun
A **cradle** is a small bed for a baby, which you can rock.

craft noun
A **craft** is an activity where you have to use your hands in a skilful way to make something.

crafty adjective (**craftier**, **craftiest**)
Someone who is **crafty** is clever at finding ways to trick people.

cramp noun
A **cramp** is a sudden pain in your arms, your legs or your stomach.

crane noun
1. A **crane** is a large bird with long legs, a long neck and a long bill. It moves around near the edges of water looking for food. *We saw two cranes down at the lake.*

2. A **crane** is a machine with a long arm for lifting and moving heavy things around. *We watched the crane carrying huge pieces of steel to the top of the building.*

cranky *adjective* (**crankier**, **crankiest**)
You are **cranky** when you are angry and people can tell that you are not pleased.

crash *verb*
1. If something **crashes** into something, it hits it with a lot of force and noise. *The plane fell from the sky and crashed into the ground.*
–*noun* 2. A **crash** is an accident in which two things hit each other hard, usually causing a lot of damage.

crater *noun*
1. A **crater** is the opening at the top of a volcano. *Hot lava was pouring out of the crater.*
2. A **crater** is a round hole in the ground made by a meteor or a bomb. *In the centre of Australia, there are craters as big as football fields caused by meteors that fell centuries ago from far away in outer space.*

crawl *verb*
1. If you **crawl**, you move along on your hands and knees. *My baby brother is learning to crawl.*
2. If you **crawl**, you go very slowly. *The traffic had to crawl around the accident which blocked the road.*

crayfish *noun* (*plural* **crayfish**)
A **crayfish** is an animal with a hard outer covering. It lives in creeks and rivers.

crayon *noun*
A **crayon** is a stick of coloured material that you use for drawing or colouring.

crazy *adjective* (**crazier**, **craziest**)
1. If someone is **crazy**, they are likely to do very silly things. *You must be crazy to think about going out without a coat when it is so cold.*
2. If an idea is **crazy**, it is very silly. *It is crazy to go out without a coat when it is so cold.*

creak *verb*
If something **creaks**, it makes the kind of sound that wood makes when it is bent. *The boards in my room creak when you walk on them.*

> ***Word Building:*** **creaky**, *adjective* Things that creak are **creaky**.

> ***Spelling Tip:*** Don't confuse the spelling of **creak** with **creek** which has the same sound but is spelt with a double *e*.

cream *noun*
Cream is the thick part at the top of milk, sometimes eaten with sweet food at the end of a meal.

create /*say* kree-**ayt**/ *verb*
When you **create** something, you make it or invent it. *Sarah created a beautiful work of art.*

> ***Word Building:*** **creative**, *adjective* If you are good at creating things, you are **creative**. –**creation**, *noun* Something that has been created is a **creation**. –**creator**, *noun* Someone who creates something is its **creator**.

creature /*say* **kree**-chuh/ *noun*
A **creature** is any animal.

credit card *noun*
A **credit card** is a plastic card which is used to make a record of what someone owes when they buy something but do not pay in money.

creek *noun*
A **creek** is a small stream.

> ***Spelling Tip:*** Don't confuse the spelling of **creek** with **creak**.

creep *verb* (**creeps**, **creeping**, **crept**, **has crept**)
1. If you **creep** somewhere, you go there as slowly and quietly as you can. *We crept through the house as quietly as mice.*
–*noun* 2. **the creeps**, If something gives you **the creeps**, it makes you feel frightened.

> **The creeps** is an informal phrase that you might use when talking to your friends.

crew *noun*
A **crew** is all the people who work on a ship or plane.

cricket[1] *noun*
A **cricket** is an insect with large back legs for jumping. It makes a loud noise by rubbing its wings together.

cricket[2] *noun*
Cricket is a game for two teams where players have to run between two points after hitting the ball with a bat.

> ***Word Building:*** **cricketer**, *noun* If you play cricket regularly, you are a **cricketer**.

criminal *noun*
A **criminal** is someone who has done a bad thing that the law says you must not do.

> ***Word Building:*** **crime**, *noun* A criminal is guilty of a **crime**.

crisp adjective
Food is **crisp** if it is firm and fresh.

croak verb
If something **croaks**, it makes a low, rough sound. *Listen to the frogs croaking in the pond.*

> **Word Building: croaky**, *adjective* If you have a cold and you can only croak, then your voice is **croaky**.

crocodile noun
A **crocodile** is an animal with a long body and thick skin that lives in the rivers or seas of some hot countries.

> ✦ **Spelling Tip:** Remember the *o* spelling (not *a*) in the middle. Also remember that there is no *k* in **crocodile**. After that, you won't have any problems with this beast.

crooked /say **krook**-uhd / adjective
If something is **crooked**, it is not straight.

crop noun
Crops are the plants, like wheat or potatoes, that a farmer grows for food.

cross noun
1. A **cross** is anything in the shape made by two lines going through each other, such as '+' or '×'. *The teacher put a cross next to the answer that was wrong.*
–*verb* 2. If you **cross** something, you go from one side of it to the other side. *We crossed the main road at the lights.* | *The bridge crosses the river.*
–*adjective* 3. If you are **cross**, you are feeling angry or not happy about something. *'Why are you cross with me?' 'I'm cross because you ate all the chocolate biscuits.'*

crossing noun
A **crossing** is a place where you can go from one side of something to the other side.

crouch verb
If you **crouch**, you bend your knees and lean forward and down. *If we crouch behind the bush they won't see us.*

crow[1] noun
A **crow** is a big, black bird with shiny feathers.

crow[2] verb (crows, crowing, crew, has crowed)
When a rooster **crows**, it makes a loud, important-sounding noise. It is usually very early in the morning. *The rooster was crowing too early in the morning and waking the neighbours.*

crowd noun
A **crowd** is a lot of people all in one place.

crowded adjective
If a place is **crowded**, there are a lot of people in it.

crown noun
A **crown** is the circle of gold or silver, often set with jewels, that a king or queen wears on their head.

cruel /say **krooh**-uhl / adjective
If someone is **cruel**, they like to hurt other people or animals or make them unhappy.

> **Word Building: cruelty**, *noun* If someone does cruel things it shows their **cruelty**.

> The opposite is **kind**.

cruise /say kroohz / noun
A **cruise** is a holiday on a ship.

> ✦ **Spelling Tip:** Remember the *ui* for the 'ooh' sound, and the *se* giving the 'z' sound.

crumb /rhymes with sum / noun
A **crumb** is a small piece of bread, cake or some other food like that.

> ✦ **Spelling Tip:** Don't forget the silent *b* at the end (think of *b* for *breadcrumb*).

crumble /say **krum**-buhl / verb
If you **crumble** something, you break it into little pieces. *Mum crumbled the bread into bits and sprinkled it on top of the dish.*

crunch verb
If you **crunch** food, you break it into little pieces with your teeth. *I like the noise hard biscuits make when I crunch them.*

crush verb
If you **crush** something, you press it hard until it breaks it into little pieces. *The huge machine crushed the rocks in no time.*

crust noun
The **crust** is the hard outside part of something, especially the hard part on the outside of bread.

> The outside layer of the earth is also called the **crust**.

crutch noun (plural crutches)
A **crutch** is a stick which fits under your arm and helps you to walk if you have a sore leg.

cry verb (cries, crying, cried, has cried)
When you **cry**, tears come out of your eyes because you are sad or because you have been

hurt. *Sophie is crying because her grandmother has died.*

cube *noun*
A **cube** is a shape with six square sides which are all the same size.

cuddle *verb*
If you **cuddle** someone, you put your arms around them in a loving way. *My mum cuddled me after I fell over and I felt heaps better.*

> **Word Building: cuddly,** *adjective* If people or things are nice to cuddle, then they are **cuddly**.

culprit /*say* **kul**-pruht/ *noun*
A **culprit** is someone who has done something wrong.

culture /*say* **kul**-chuh/ *noun*
A **culture** is a way of life, especially the know-ledge, beliefs and customs that belong to a nation or people.

> **Word Building: cultural,** *adjective* If some-thing has to do with a culture, it is **cultural**.

cunning *adjective*
You are **cunning** if you are good at thinking of clever plans or at tricking people. *Our dog is very cunning – he always manages to find a way to escape. | Kate had worked out a cunning way to open the biscuit packet without anybody knowing.*

cup *noun*
A **cup** is a small, round, open container that you drink from. It usually has a special part for holding it on the side. You often have hot drinks, such as tea, coffee or soup, in a **cup**.

cupboard /*say* **kub**-uhd/ *noun*
A **cupboard** is a piece of furniture with doors and often with shelves, used for keeping things in.

cure *verb*
If someone or something **cures** you, they make you well again after you have been sick. *The doctor said that he could cure my mother. | That medicine cured my cold quickly.*

curious /*say* **kyooh**-ree-uhs/ *adjective*
If you are **curious**, you want to learn and find out about things.

> **Word Building: curiosity** /*say* kyooh-ree-**os**-uh-tee/, *noun* If you are curious, you have feelings of **curiosity**.

curl *verb*
1. If you **curl** something, you turn it so that it is not going in a straight direction. You curve it. *When I read, I always curl my legs up under me.* –*noun* 2. A **curl** is some hair that turns in a loose curve or a tight circle.

> **Word Building: curly,** *adjective* If you have curls, then your hair is **curly**.

currant *noun*
A **currant** is a small grape with no seeds, dried until it is very sweet and quite strong in taste.

> ✴ **Spelling Tip:** Don't confuse the spelling of **currant** with **current** which has the same sound but is spelt with an *e*. Remember, you eat *a* curr**a**nt.

current *noun*
A **current** is a flow or movement of water, air or electricity in one direction.

> ✴ **Spelling Tip:** Don't confuse the spelling of **current** with **currant** which has the same sound but is spelt with an *a*.

curry *noun* (*plural* **curries**)
A **curry** is food such as meat, fish or vegetables, cooked with spices which make it taste good and sometimes extremely hot.

curse *noun*
A **curse** is a strong wish that something bad will happen to someone. In fairy stories, the curse can come true.

cursor /*say* **ker**-suh/ *noun*
The **cursor** on a computer screen is the small moving sign to show you where the writing will start when you type.

curtain /*say* **ker**-tuhn/ *noun*
A **curtain** is a piece of material that hangs over a window.

> ✴ **Spelling Tip:** Remember that the final part of **curtain** is spelt *ain*. Think of other words with this spelling for an 'uhn' sound, such as *captain* and *certain*. But be careful not to confuse **curtain** with **certain** (meaning 'sure').

curve *noun*
A **curve** is a line that bends, or a shape with no pointed corners.

> **Word Building: curved,** *adjective* Something with the shape of a curve is **curved**.

cushion /*say* **koosh**-uhn/ *noun*
> A **cushion** is a kind of bag filled with something soft that you sit on or lean against, especially on a chair.

custard /*say* **kus**-tuhd/ *noun*
> **Custard** is a soft food you make from milk, eggs and sugar, and eat after the main course in a meal.

custodian /*say* kus-**toh**-dee-uhn/ *noun*
> **1.** A **custodian** is someone who looks after or guards something. *He works at the museum as the custodian of the Egyptian section.*
> **2.** A **traditional custodian** is an Australian Indigenous person who has special knowledge about the secret ceremonies that connect his or her people to the land and to its history going back to the Dreaming.

custom *noun*
> A **custom** is something that people usually do. *It's the custom to give presents to someone when it is their birthday.*

customer *noun*
> A **customer** is someone who buys something from another person.

cut *verb* (**cuts**, **cutting**, **cut**, **has cut**)
> **1.** If you **cut** something, you make an opening in it with something sharp. *Oh no! I've cut my finger with the knife.*

2. If you **cut** something, you break it into two or more pieces with something sharp. *Could you lend me your scissors so that I can cut this string?*
> **3. cut off**, If you **cut** something **off**, you use something sharp to take it away from what it is joined to. *Dad is cutting some branches off the tree.*

cyber /*say* **suy**-buh/ *adjective*
> Something **cyber** has to do with the internet.

cyber safety *noun*
> **Cyber safety** is doing things to protect yourself from being tricked or bullied when on the internet.

cycle /*say* **suy**-kuhl/ *verb*
> If you **cycle**, you ride a bicycle. *Carlotta cycled into town to get some bread and milk.*

> ***Word Building:*** **cyclist** /*say* **suyk**-luhst/, *noun* Someone who cycles is a **cyclist**.

cyclone /*say* **suy**-klohn/ *noun*
> A **cyclone** is a storm with very strong winds.

cylinder /*say* **sil**-uhn-duh/ *noun*
> A **cylinder** is something that has the shape of a tube with flat round ends.

> �֎ ***Spelling Tip:*** Remember that the first part is spelt *cyl* (not *sil*). As with many words that start *cy*, **cylinder** comes from Greek.

Dd

dad *noun*
1. Your **dad** is your father. *My dad works as a police officer.*
2. **Dad**, You can use **Dad** as a name for your father when you talk to him. *Hurry up, Dad, or we'll be late!*

Some children also say **daddy**.

daffodil /*say* **daf**-uh-dil/ *noun*
A **daffodil** is a yellow flower which grows from a bulb.

> ✱ *Spelling Tip:* Remember that there is only one *l* at the end, but a double *f* in the middle.

dagger *noun*
A **dagger** is a short, pointed sword.

daily *adjective*
1. If something is described as **daily**, it happens every day.
–*adverb* 2. If something happens **daily**, it happens every day. *This newspaper is printed daily.*

dainty *adjective* (**daintier**, **daintiest**)
If something is **dainty** it is small and beautifully made.

dairy /*say* **dair**-ree/ *adjective*
1. **Dairy** foods are milk and other foods that come from milk, like cheese, cream and yoghurt.
–*noun* (*plural* **dairies**)
2. A **dairy** is a place on a farm where you milk cows.

daisy *noun* (*plural* **daisies**)
A **daisy** is a flower which has a yellow centre and lots of white or coloured petals.

dam *noun*
1. A **dam** is a strong wall built across a river to hold back water, so that there is a supply of water for people and animals to drink, and for farmers to use on their land. *When the dam was built, a valley was flooded.*
2. A **dam** is the lake created when a river is blocked. *During the flood, the dam was almost empty.*
3. A **dam** on a farm is a big hole dug in the ground which fills with water from rain. *The cows were all drinking at the dam.*

damage *verb*
1. If something **damages** something, it hurts it or makes it not as good as it was. *Eating too much sweet food can damage your teeth.*
–*noun* 2. **Damage** is the hurt that is done to something when something damages it.

> ✱ *Spelling Tip:* The tricky bit is remembering how to spell the last part of this word. You might remember that things sometimes get damaged because of their age – the spelling of *age* gives you the last three letters of the word **damage**.

damp *adjective*
If something is **damp**, it is a bit wet but not very wet.

> *Word Building:* **dampness**, *noun* When something is damp, it has a feeling of **dampness**.

damper *noun*
Damper is a kind of bread that you cook over a fire when you are outdoors.

dance *verb*
1. When you **dance**, you move your feet and body in time with music. *After the wedding, everyone danced until midnight.*
–*noun* 2. A **dance** is a set of steps and movements you do usually with music.

> *Word Building:* **dancer**, *noun* Someone whose job is to dance is a **dancer**.

dandelion /*say* **dan**-duh-luy-uhn/ *noun*
A **dandelion** is a plant with bright yellow flowers that turn into soft balls of seeds which are blown by the wind.

danger noun

1. Danger is a situation in which something might hurt you. *Peter didn't think about the danger when he ran across the road.*
2. A **danger** is something that might hurt you. *A careless driver is a danger on the road.*

dangerous adjective

If something is **dangerous**, it might hurt you.

The opposite is **safe**.

⭐ *Spelling Tip:* The **dangerous** part in spelling this word is to remember that there is an *e* in it, although you sometimes do not pronounce it. This will be easier if you think about the meaning of the word and can see that it is made up of *danger* and the ending *ous* (meaning 'full of').

dare /rhymes with pair/ verb

If you **dare** to do something dangerous or exciting, you are brave enough to do it. *No-one dared to go swimming. The waves were too big.*

Word Building: **daring**, *adjective* Someone who dares to do exciting things and likes adventures is **daring**.

dark adjective

1. If a place is **dark**, it has no light or not much light.
—*noun* **2. Dark** is the time when it is night.

Word Building: **darkness**, *noun* When there is no light or not much light, there is **darkness**.

dash verb

If you **dash** somewhere, you move there very quickly. *Mum had to dash inside to answer the phone.*

data /say day-tuh, dah-tuh/ noun

Data is facts and information.

date noun

A **date** is a particular day or year and the numbers that show you this day or year.

daughter /say daw-tuh/ noun

If someone has a **daughter**, they have a female child. She may be a girl or she may have grown up to be a woman.

⭐ *Spelling Tip:* Remember the *augh* spelling in the first part of this word (which sounds like 'aw'). It might help if you think of other words with the same spelling for this sound, such as *naughty* and *caught*.

dawn noun

Dawn is the time of day when it begins to get light.

day noun

1. A **day** is the time between when it gets light and when it gets dark, when people are awake and doing things. *It is a cold, rainy day.*
2. A **day** is a period of 24 hours. *There are seven days in a week.*
3. the other day, If something happened **the other day**, it happened a few days ago. *We visited our grandmother the other day.*

Word Building: **daytime**, *noun* If something happens during the time when it is day, it happens in the **daytime**.

dazed adjective

If you are **dazed**, you cannot think properly because something has happened to you.

dead adjective

If a person, an animal or a plant is **dead**, they have stopped living.

Word Building: **deadly**, *adjective* If something can make a person or animal die, it is **deadly**.

deaf /say def/ adjective

If you are **deaf**, you are not able to hear properly or you are not able to hear at all.

Word Building: **deafness**, *noun* If you are deaf, you suffer from **deafness**.

deal verb (deals, dealing, dealt, has dealt)

1. If you **deal** something, such as cards during a game, you give some to each person in a group. *My big sister always deals the cards when she plays with her friends.*
2. deal with, If you **deal with** something, you do what is needed to look after it or get it done. *Mum asked me to deal with getting the drinks ready, while she dealt with the food for the party.*
—*noun* **3. a good deal of**, If there is **a good deal** or **a great deal of** something, there is a lot of it.

dear adjective

1. If someone is **dear** to you, you love them. *A very dear friend of my mother has come to stay.*
2. If something is **dear**, it costs a lot. *Sam had trouble buying Christmas presents for everyone because things were so dear.*
3. Dear, You use **Dear** at the beginning of a letter before the name of the person you are writing to. It is the polite way to start a letter. *Dear Amber, I am writing to thank you for your invitation.*

Other words with a similar meaning to **dear** (definition 2) are **expensive** and **costly**. The opposite is **cheap**.

✹ *Spelling Tip:* Don't confuse the spelling of **dear** with **deer** which sounds the same. A **deer** is a type of animal.

death /*say* deth/ *noun*
Someone's **death** is when they die. It is the ending of their life.

debate *noun*
A **debate** is a competition between two teams in which each side has to argue about a subject.

debt /*say* det/ *noun*
A **debt** is something, usually money, that you owe someone.

✹ *Spelling Tip:* Don't forget the silent *b* before the *t*.

decade /*say* **dek**-ayd/ *noun*
A **decade** is ten years.

decay /*say* duh-**kay**/ *verb*
1. If something **decays** it slowly falls apart because it is old or dead or has something wrong with it. It goes bad. *This bridge is not safe because the wood has begun to decay.*
–*noun* **2. Decay** is when something is going bad.

deceive /*say* duh-**seev**/ *verb*
If you **deceive** someone, you trick them or tell them lies. *She tried to deceive them by saying she was very poor – but she really just wanted to get their money.*

✹ *Spelling Tip:* Remember the *ei* spelling for the 'ee' sound. This follows the rule that *i* comes before *e* except after *c*.

December /*say* duh-**sem**-buh/ *noun*
December is the last month of the year, with 31 days. It comes after November.

decide /*say* duh-**suyd**/ *verb*
If you **decide** to do something, you say in your mind that you are going to do it. *Bella decided to get a torch for her brother for his birthday.*

decimal /*say* **des**-uh-muhl/ *noun*
A **decimal** is a number or fraction written in a special way that uses the number ten, for example, for $\frac{1}{10}$ we write 0.1, for $\frac{1}{2}$ we write 0.5, and for $1\frac{3}{10}$ we write 1.3.

decision /*say* duh-**sizh**-uhn/ *noun*
If you make a **decision**, you decide to do something.

deck *noun*
A **deck** is the floor of a ship.

declare /*say* duh-**klair**/ *verb*
If you **declare** something, you say it in a very clear way that shows you really mean it and want people to know it. *In a loud and angry voice, she declared that she had not stolen the bag.*

decorate /*say* **dek**-uh-rayt/ *verb*
If you **decorate** something, you make it bright and pretty by adding things. *Let's decorate the classroom with balloons for the teacher's birthday.*

Word Building: **decorative** /*say* **dek**-uh-ruh-tiv/, *adjective* If you decorate something, you make it look **decorative**. –**decoration** /*say* dek-uh-**ray**-shuhn/, *noun* If you decorate something, you use a **decoration**.

decrease /*say* duh-**krees**/ *verb*
If something **decreases**, it gets smaller. *The number of fish you can catch in this lake is decreasing every year.*

The opposite is **increase**.

deed *noun*
A **deed** is an action. It is something that someone does.

This is an old-fashioned word except when you use it in a phrase such as **a good deed**: *Sue did a good deed when she helped the old lady cross the road.*

deep *adjective*
If something is **deep**, it goes a long way down or a long way in. *The swimming pool is very deep at one end.* | *The knife made a deep cut in John's leg.*

❖ Look up **depth**.
❖ The opposite of **deep** is **shallow**.

deer *noun* (*plural* **deer**)
A **deer** is a wild animal that moves quickly and usually travels in groups. Male **deer** have horns on their heads.

The male is a **buck** or a **stag**; the female is a **doe**; the young is a **fawn**.

✹ *Spelling Tip:* Don't confuse the spelling of **deer** with **dear** which sounds the same.

a b c d e f g h i j k l m n o p q r s t u v w x y z

> **Dear** describes someone who is loved: *a dear friend*.

defeat *verb*

1. If you **defeat** someone, you win a game or a fight against them. *Our football team defeated the team from the other school.*
–*noun* 2. If you suffer a **defeat**, someone else wins in a game or a fight against you.

defence *noun*

A **defence** is something that gives you protection when you might be attacked or hurt.

> **Defence** comes from the verb **defend**.

defend *verb*

If you **defend** something or someone, you fight to protect them from someone or something. *The soldiers defended the city against the enemy.*

define *verb*

When you **define** a word, you explain what it means. *Writers of dictionaries have to define many words.*

> **Word Building: definition**, *noun*: *Dictionaries are full of definitions.*

definite /*say* **def**-uh-nuht/ *adjective*

If you are **definite**, you are very sure.

> ✳ *Spelling Tip:* Remember that there are two separate *i*'s in this word – one in the middle and one in the *ite* ending. Many people get this wrong, especially by putting *ate* at the end – but this word definitely has nothing to do with eating. Instead **definite** includes the word *finite* which means 'having limits or boundaries'.

defy /*say* duh-**fuy**/ *verb* (**defies, defying, defied, has defied**)

If you **defy** someone, you do something that you have been told not to do. *The girl tried to defy her mother by sneaking out the back door after she had been sent to her room.*

degree *noun*

A **degree** is a measurement of temperature. It tells how hot or cold something is.

> We use the mark ° to mean **degrees**, so **30°** means **thirty degrees**.

delay *verb*

1. If something **delays** you, it makes you late. *We were late because the traffic delayed us.*

2. If you **delay** something, you decide to do it at a later time than was planned. *We delayed our holiday because of the bad weather.*
–*noun* 3. If there is a **delay**, something happens at a later time than it should have.

delicate /*say* **del**-uh-kuht/ *adjective*

Something is **delicate** if it can easily be damaged.

delicatessen /*say* del-uh-kuh-**tes**-uhn/ *noun*

A **delicatessen** is a shop which sells foods like different kinds of cheese and cold meat.

> The short form of this, used in informal language, is **deli**.

> ✳ *Spelling Tip:* A **delicatessen** sells delicious foods for you to eat. Inside this long word you can see two shorter words – *delicate* and *essen* (a German word meaning 'eat'). When they are put together, *essen* eats up the letter *e* at the end of *delicate*, making **delicatessen**.

delicious /*say* duh-**lish**-uhs/ *adjective*

If something is **delicious**, it tastes very good.

delight /*say* duh-**luyt**/ *verb*

If something **delights** you, it pleases you very much. It makes you feel very happy. *My mum told me that the school concert delighted all the parents.*

> **Word Building: delighted**, *adjective* If something delights you, you are **delighted** with it. *Helen was delighted with her birthday presents.* –**delightful**, *adjective* Something that delights you is **delightful**.

> ✳ *Spelling Tip:* Remember that the end of **delight** is spelt *ight* (although it sounds like 'uyt'). It might help if you think of a word you know well which has the same spelling for this sound, such as *light*, *bright* and *sight*.

deliver *verb*

If you **deliver** something, you take it to where it should go. *The postman's job is to deliver the mail to everyone's houses.*

> **Word Building: delivery**, *noun* When you deliver something, you make a **delivery**.

demand *verb*

If you **demand** something, you say strongly that you must have it or that it must happen. *Mum demanded her money back from the bicycle shop. She said that the bike had not been fixed properly.*

demolish /say duh-**mol**-ish/ verb
If someone **demolishes** something, they knock it down. *My dad is going to demolish the old garage and try to build a new one himself.*

demonstration /say dem-uhn-**stray**-shuhn/ noun
1. A **demonstration** is what happens when someone shows and tells people how to do a particular thing. *The teacher gave us a demonstration of how to use the computer.*
2. A **demonstration** is a meeting or a march through the streets by a lot of people to show everyone what they think about something. *There were hundreds of people at the demonstration and many of them were carrying signs saying how angry they were.*

> *Word Building:* **demonstrate**, *verb* When you give a demonstration, you **demonstrate** something.

dense adjective
If something is **dense**, it is very thick.

dent noun
When something has a **dent**, that part of it goes in because something has hit it there.

dentist noun
A **dentist** is someone whose job is to keep your teeth healthy.

deny /say duh-**nuy**/ verb (**denies**, **denying**, **denied**, **has denied**)
If you **deny** something, you say that it is not true. *Anna denied that she was the one who drew on the teacher's desk.*

> *Word Building:* **denial** /say duh-**nuy**-uhl/, *noun* When you deny something, you make a **denial**.

depart /say duh-**paht**/ verb
If you **depart** from a place you go away or leave it. *We decided to meet at the station and depart from there.*

> *Word Building:* **departure** /say duh-**pah**-chuh/, *noun* When you depart from somewhere, you make a **departure**. *I was surprised by their sudden departure.*

department noun
A **department** is one of the parts of a large organisation such as a government, a university, or a big shop.

department store noun
A **department store** is a very large shop, with many parts to it, where you can buy many different kinds of things.

depend verb
If you **depend** on someone or something, you trust them to be there when you need them to help you. *My grandmother depends on my mother to do her shopping and cleaning.*

deposit /say duh-**poz**-uht/ noun
A **deposit** is a sum of money that you put into your bank account.

depth noun
The **depth** of something is a measurement of how deep it is.

> **Depth** comes from the adjective **deep**.

deputy /say **dep**-yuh-tee/ noun (plural **deputies**)
A **deputy** is the person who is second in charge and who takes control when the person in charge is away.

descend /say duh-**send**/ verb
If someone or something **descends**, they go down. *She descended the stairs slowly.*

> *Word Building:* **descent**, *noun* When you descend, you make a **descent**.

> The opposite is **ascend**.

> ⭐ *Spelling Tip:* Remember that there is a silent *c* after the *s*. This is left over from its Latin beginnings – *de* (meaning 'down') and *scandere* (meaning 'to climb'). Notice that the silent *c* also appears in the opposite word **ascend**, which means 'go up'. Going up or coming down, don't forget the *c*!

describe verb
If you **describe** something or someone, you say what they look like or what kind of thing they are. You use words to give a picture of them. *We knew the lady was Giuseppe's mother because Giuseppe had described her so well.*

> ⭐ *Spelling Tip:* The spelling of **describe** will be easier if you see that it is made up of *scribe* (someone in the past whose job was to write or copy things in words) and the word part *de*.

description noun
1. A **description** of something or someone is a picture of them in words. It describes something

or someone. *Can you give the police a description of the driver of the car?*
2. If you write a **description**, you do a piece of writing that describes a person, animal, thing, or event. *We all had to write a description of the person sitting next to us.*

desert[1] /*say* **dez**-uht / *noun*

A **desert** is very dry place where not many plants grow because there is not enough rain.

> ⚡ *Spelling Tip:* Don't confuse the spelling with **dessert** (which has a double *s*). A **dessert** is sweet food eaten at the end of a meal.

desert[2] /*say* duh-**zert** / *verb*

If someone **deserts** someone, they leave when they should stay. They go away and do not plan to come back. *He deserted his friends when they needed his help.*

> *Word Building:* **deserted** /*say* duh-**zert**-uhd /, *adjective* If a place is **deserted**, there are no people there. *The city streets are deserted in the middle of the night.*

> ⚡ *Spelling Tip:* Don't confuse the spelling with **dessert**.

deserve *verb*

If you **deserve** something, you receive a reward if you have done something good or a punishment if you have done something bad. *She deserved to win the race because she trained so hard.* | *The criminal deserved to go to jail for stealing.*

design /*say* duh-**zuyn** / *verb*

1. If you **design** something, you draw a plan of how it should look or how it should be made. *My aunt's job is to design office buildings.*
–*noun* **2.** A **design** of something is a drawing or a plan showing how it should be made or built.

> ⚡ *Spelling Tip:* Remember the *g* in this word. The letter group *ign* gives the 'uyn' sound, as in the word *sign*.

desire *verb*

If you **desire** something, you want it very much. *What she desired more than anything was the chance to show that she could run as well as the others.*

desk *noun*

A **desk** is a table that you use when you are writing, or working on a computer. It often has drawers for things such as papers and pens.

despair *noun*

Despair is a feeling of great sadness because you think there is no hope.

> ⚡ *Spelling Tip:* The difficulty in spelling **despair** is remembering that the last part is spelt *air*. Try thinking that if you had no air to breathe, you would be sure to be full of **despair**.

dessert /*say* duh-**zert** / *noun*

Dessert is the fruit or sweets you eat at the end of your meal.

> ⚡ *Spelling Tip:* Remember the double *s* in **dessert**. Don't confuse it with **desert** (a dry area of land) or **desert** (to leave someone or something). Think of the double *s* in **dessert** standing for an extra helping of <u>s</u>ugar.

destroy *verb*

If something **destroys** something else, it damages it so much it cannot be used any more or it is completely gone. *Look at my shoes! The dog has completely destroyed them.*

detail *noun*

A **detail** is one of many small parts or happenings that go to make up a whole thing.

detective *noun*

A **detective** is someone whose job is to try to work out the people who are guilty of crimes.

determined /*say* duh-**ter**-muhnd / *adjective*

If someone is **determined** to do something, they have their mind set on doing it. They have very clearly decided to do it.

detour /*say* **dee**-toouh / *noun*

A **detour** is a road or path which you have to use when the way you wanted to go is closed.

develop /*say* duh-**vel**-uhp / *verb*

If something or someone **develops**, they grow larger or stronger. *They could see that the colour of the baby rosella was changing as it developed into an adult bird.*

development /*say* duh-**vel**-uhp-muhnt / *noun*

1. Development is what happens when someone or something develops. *We watched the development of a plant on a video at school – all the way from a seed to a flower.*
2. A **development** is something new that happens. *There have been many developments in medicine in the last 100 years.*

devil *noun*

In some religions, the **devil** is the power of evil or the most powerful evil spirit.

devoted *adjective*
If you are **devoted** to someone, you love them very much.

dew *noun*
Dew is the tiny drops of water that you find on things outside in the early morning.

> ✳ *Spelling Tip:* Don't confuse the spelling of **dew** with **due** which sounds the same. **Due** means 'expected': *The train is due at 10 o'clock.*

diabesity /*say* duy-uh-**bee**-suh-tee / *noun*
If someone has **diabesity**, they weigh more than is healthy and they also have diabetes.

> ✳ *Spelling Tip:* The spelling of **diabesity** will be easier if you see that it is a combination of the words *dia*(*betes*) and (*o*)*besity*.

diabetes /*say* duy-uh-**bee**-teez / *noun*
Diabetes is a disease where your body finds it difficult to use sugar and passes it out in your urine.

> *Word Building:* **diabetic** /*say* duy-uh-**bet**-ik /, *noun* Someone who has diabetes is a **diabetic**. –**diabetic** /*say* duy-uh-**bet**-ik /, *adjective*: *The doctor has a number of diabetic patients.*

> ✳ *Spelling Tip:* This word has an unusual spelling because it comes from Greek where it means 'a passing through'. The most difficult part to spell is the final part, *betes*. Remember that a single *e* turns up twice in this word part (each time giving the sound 'ee').

diagnosis /*say* duy-uhg-**noh**-suhs / *noun* (*plural* **diagnoses** /*say* duy-uhg-**noh**-seez /)
A **diagnosis** is the decision reached from working out what disease a patient has.

> *Word Building:* **diagnose**, *verb* If a doctor **diagnoses** you, they work out what is wrong with you.

diagonal /*say* duy-**ag**-uh-nuhl / *noun*
A **diagonal** is a sloping line which goes from one corner to the opposite corner of a square or rectangle.

diagram /*say* **duy**-uh-gram / *noun*
A **diagram** is a drawing or plan which shows you how something works.

dial *noun*
A **dial** is the part of a clock, telephone, radio or measuring instrument that has numbers or letters on it.

diameter /*say* duy-**am**-uh-tuh / *noun*
A **diameter** is a straight line which goes across a circle from one side to the other side, passing through the centre.

diamond /*say* **duy**-muhnd / *noun*
A **diamond** is a very hard stone which is clear like glass and is used in jewellery.

> ✳ *Spelling Tip:* Don't forget the silent *a* after the *i*.

diarrhoea /*say* duy-uh-**ree**-uh / *noun*
Diarrhoea is a sickness that gives you pains in the stomach and makes you go to the toilet a lot.

> ✳ *Spelling Tip:* This word comes from Greek and there is no way you could guess the spelling, so you have to make sure you remember some special things about it. There is a double *r* in the middle, followed by a silent *h*. Worst of all, the 'ee-uh' sound at the end is spelt by the letters *oea*. **Diarrhoea** is not nice to have, and it is certainly not nice to spell!

diary /*say* **duy**-uh-ree / *noun* (*plural* **diaries**)
A **diary** is a book in which you write down what happens each day or what you are thinking each day.

dice *noun*
Dice are small square-shaped objects with six sides that you use in games. Each side has a different number of spots, from one to six.

dictator *noun*
A **dictator** is someone who has all the power in ruling a country.

dictionary /*say* **dik**-shuhn-ree / *noun* (*plural* **dictionaries**)
A **dictionary** is a book which tells you what words mean. You can also find out how to spell words and how to say them.

> ✳ *Spelling Tip:* The spelling of **dictionary** will be easier if you see that it begins with *dictio*, which is Latin for 'word'.

didjeridu /*say* dij-uh-ree-**dooh** / *noun*
A **didjeridu** is an Aboriginal musical instrument. It is a long wooden tube that you blow through.

> Another spelling for this word is **didgeridoo**.

die *verb* (**dies**, **dying**, **died**, **has died**)
When a person, an animal or a plant **dies**, they stop living. Their life comes to an end. *My grandmother died last year. She died of old age.*

Look up **dead** and **death**.

⚡ **Spelling Tip:** Don't confuse the spelling of **die** with **dye** which has the same sound but is spelt with a *y*. **Dye** is a liquid that you use to colour things with.

diet *noun*
1. Your **diet** is the sort of foods that you eat. *Her diet is full of sugar and her face is full of pimples.*
2. A **diet** is a plan of eating foods that people follow when they want to lose weight. *My big sister is always going on diets but it seems to be only between meals.*

differ *verb*
1. If you **differ** from someone, you are not the same. *My brother differs from my sister in what they like eating – my brother loves meat and my sister is a vegetarian.*
2. If you and someone else **differ** about something, you disagree. *If my brother and I differ about which television program to watch, we have to ask Mum to decide.*

difference *noun*
The **difference** between people or between things is the way that they are different from each other. It is the way they are not the same.

different *adjective*
If people or things are **different**, they are not like each other.

⚡ **Spelling Tip:** Remember the double *f*.

difficult *adjective*
If something is **difficult**, it is not easy to do or understand. *Learning a new language is very difficult. | The walk through the bush to the camping place was difficult. | That book is too difficult for me – it has too many long words.*

Another word with a similar meaning is **hard**.

difficulty *noun (plural **difficulties**)*
1. A **difficulty** is something that is difficult. It is a problem. *I thought it would be easy to change the furniture in my room but there were many difficulties. For example, the cupboard was too heavy to me to move.*
2. If you have **difficulty** doing something, you cannot do it easily. It is hard for you to do. *Ann has difficulty learning maths.*

dig *verb (**digs**, **digging**, **dug**, **has dug**)*
If you **dig**, you make a hole in the ground by moving the soil with a special tool or with your

hands. *Dad spent the day digging in the garden and planting new flowers.*

digger *noun*
A **digger** is an Australian soldier, especially one from World War I.

digital /*say* **dij**-uh-tuhl/ *adjective*
1. If something, such as a television, radio or camera, is **digital**, it works by storing information in a similar way to a computer. *Have you got digital TV yet?*
2. If something, such as a clock, is **digital**, it uses numbers rather than hands to show the time. *Many people have digital watches these days.*

dillybag *noun*
A **dillybag** is a small bag made out of string or something like this, that you use to carry food or other things.

This word comes from an Aboriginal language of Queensland called Yagara.

dim *noun*
If light is **dim**, it is not bright.

dimple *noun*
A **dimple** is a small hollow place in your cheek, which gets deeper when you smile.

dine *verb*
If you **dine**, you have dinner. *The hotel manager said people normally dined at 8 o'clock.*

dinghy /*say* **ding**-gee/ *noun (plural **dinghies**)*
A **dinghy** is a small boat that you row.

⚡ **Spelling Tip:** Don't forget the silent *h* between the *g* and the *y*. This word is unusual because it comes from the Indian language Hindi. Remember the <u>h</u> for <u>H</u>indi in **din<u>gh</u>y**.

dingo *noun (plural **dingoes** or **dingos**)*
A **dingo** is an Australian wild dog. It has brown-yellow hair, a bushy tail and pointed ears.

This word comes from an Aboriginal language of New South Wales called Dharug.

dining room *noun*
A **dining room** is the room in a house where you have meals.

dinner *noun*
Dinner is the main meal that you eat every day, usually in the evening.

dinosaur /*say* **duy**-nuh-saw/ *noun*
A **dinosaur** is an animal like an extremely large lizard, which lived millions of years ago.

> ✳ **Spelling Tip:** Remember that the sound in the middle is spelt *o*. Remember also that the last part of **dinosaur** is spelt *saur* (although it sounds like it might be spelt *sore*). This comes from the Latin word *saurus* meaning 'lizard'. The word parts *saur* or *saurus* appear in the names of many kinds of **dinosaur**, such as *brontosaurus*.

dip *verb* (**dips**, **dipping**, **dipped**, **has dipped**)
   1. If you **dip** something into a liquid, you put it there for a short time. *I dipped my brush into the paint.*
   2. If the ground **dips**, it slopes down. *I almost fell off my bike when the road suddenly dipped.*

direct *verb*
   If you **direct** someone, you show or tell them the way to where they want to go. *'Can you direct me to the station?' 'Yes, it is around the corner on the left.'*

direction *noun*
   The **direction** of something is the way you go if you want to get to it.

director *noun*
   A **director** is the person in charge of a business organisation, or in charge of the making of a film or some other kind of work.

dirt *noun*
   1. **Dirt** is loose bits of soil. *The dog was digging through the dirt looking for his bone.*
   2. **Dirt** is anything that makes something not clean. *There was dirt all over the car and Dad thought he should wash it before he went out.*

dirty *adjective* (**dirtier**, **dirtiest**)
   If something is **dirty**, it has dirt on it and so is not clean.

disagree *verb*
   If you **disagree** with someone, you do not think the same as them. You do not agree with them. *Rata and her mother disagreed about what clothes Rata should wear to the party.*

> **Word Building: disagreement**, *noun* When you disagree with someone, you have a **disagreement** with them.

disappear *verb*
   If someone or something **disappears**, they go where you cannot see them any more. *I asked Mum a question but she had suddenly disappeared from the room.*

disappoint /*say* dis-uh-**poynt**/ *verb*
   If something or someone **disappoints** you, they make you feel unhappy because what you hoped would happen has not happened. *Joe disappointed his coach when he missed training again.*

> **Word Building: disappointed**, *adjective* When something disappoints you, you are **disappointed**. *Su Li felt very disappointed when she didn't get a new bike for her birthday.* –**disappointing**, *adjective* If something disappoints people, it is **disappointing**. *It was a disappointing visit to the museum – many of the rooms were closed.* –**disappointment**, *noun* When something disappoints you, you have a feeling of **disappointment**.

> ✳ **Spelling Tip:** The spelling of **disappoint** will be easier if you remember that it starts with the word part *dis* (which means 'not' or 'without', and is often used at the beginning of words whose meanings have to do with things not happening). Also, don't forget the two *p*'s in the middle – or you'll be doubly disappointed.

disaster /*say* duh-**zah**-stuh/ *noun*
   A **disaster** is something terrible that happens suddenly.

> **Word Building: disastrous** /*say* duh-**zah**-struhs/, *adjective* Something that causes a disaster is **disastrous**.

> ✳ **Spelling Tip:** The spelling of **disaster** will be easier if you remember that it comes from the idea of not having a lucky star, and can see that it is made up of *aster* (which comes from the Italian word for 'star') and the word part *dis* (meaning 'not' or 'without').

disc *noun*
   A **disc** is something that is flat and round in shape. *The full moon looked like a silver disc in the sky.*

> ✳ **Spelling Tip:** When you are talking about computers, you usually use the spelling **disk**. Look up **disk** and **compact disc**.

disco *noun* (*plural* **discos**)
   A **disco** is a place or club in which you dance to music.

> **Disco** is short for **discotheque** /*say* **dis**-kuh-tek/.

discover *verb*
   If you **discover** something, you find it or find out about it for the first time. *Vijay discovered some*

old coins buried under the ground. | *I have just discovered that Sophie used to live in England. Did you know that?*

discovery *noun* (*plural* **discoveries**)
If you make a **discovery**, you discover something. You find it or find out about it for the first time.

discuss *verb*
If you **discuss** something, you talk about it with other people, usually for quite a long time. Often when you **discuss** things, it is because you are trying to decide something. *My parents were discussing where we would go for our next holiday.*

discussion *noun*
1. If people have a **discussion** about something, they talk about it and give their opinions about it, usually for quite a long time. *My parents had a discussion about where we would go for our next holiday.*
2. If you write a **discussion**, you do a piece of writing about the different opinions that people might have about something. *We had to write a discussion on whether or not school children should have to wear uniforms.*

> ✪ *Spelling Tip:* Remember that the letter *s* really wants to be heard in a **discussion**. It turns up three times – the first time by itself, the second time in company with another *s*.

disease /*say* duh-**zeez**/ *noun*
A **disease** is a sickness in your body.

> ✪ *Spelling Tip:* The spelling of **disease** will be easier if you see that it is made up of the word *ease* (what you feel when you are comfortable) and the word part *dis* (meaning 'not' or 'without'). This adds up to **disease** – something that always makes you feel uncomfortable.

disguise /*say* duhs-**guyz**/ *noun*
A **disguise** is the clothes that you put on so that you will not look like yourself.

disgust *verb*
If something **disgusts** you, it gives you a strong feeling of anger and annoyance. *She was disgusted by the way he left the house – there was mess all over the floor and the whole place smelt of rotten food.*

> *Word Building:* **disgusting**, *adjective* Something that disgusts you is **disgusting**.

dish *noun*
A **dish** is a container for cooking food or for putting food on when it is ready to be eaten. A **dish** is open at the top and not very deep.

dishwasher *noun*
A **dishwasher** is a machine for washing things you use for eating and cooking, such as plates, cups, pans and knives.

disk *noun*
A **disk** is a flat, thin, round part of a computer that stores information.

> Also look up **compact disc**.

dislike *verb*
If you **dislike** something or someone, you do not like them. *I dislike the way he is often rude to people.*

dismal /*say* **diz**-muhl/ *adjective*
If something is **dismal**, it makes you feel sad. *It was a dismal, grey day – we didn't feel like going out.*

dismiss *verb*
If you **dismiss** someone, you tell them to leave. *The teacher dismisses the class when the bell goes.*

disobedient /*say* dis-uh-**bee**-dee-uhnt/ *adjective*
You are **disobedient** if you refuse to do something that you have been told to do. *Our dog is still disobedient, even though we have taken her to special classes.*

> *Word Building:* **disobey** /*say* dis-uh-**bay**/, *verb* If you are disobedient, you **disobey**. –**disobedience**, *noun* If you're disobedient, you show **disobedience**.

display *verb*
If you **display** something, you show it, especially so that people can have a good look at it. *The teacher put our paintings on the wall to display them for our parents.*

disqualify /*say* dis-**kwol**-uh-fuy/ *verb*
(**disqualifies, disqualifying, disqualified, has disqualified**)
If you **disqualify** someone, you put them out of a competition because they have broken a rule. *The judges will disqualify you if you start running before the whistle blows.*

distance *noun*
1. The **distance** between two places or things is the length of the space between them. *'What is*

the distance between your house and your school?' 'It is about one kilometre. It takes me about 20 minutes to walk.'
2. in the distance, If something is **in the distance**, it is in a place far away from where you are. *If you listen carefully, you can hear a train in the distance.*

distant *adjective*
If something is **distant**, it is far away from where you are.

distress *noun*
Distress is the feeling you have when you have a lot of sadness, worry or pain.

district *noun*
A **district** is a particular part of a country, town or city.

disturb *verb*
If you **disturb** someone, you interrupt what they are doing or you stop them feeling quiet and peaceful. *Jane doesn't like to be disturbed when she is doing her homework.*

ditch *noun (plural **ditches**)*
A **ditch** is a long, narrow hole dug in the ground.

dive *verb*
If you **dive**, you jump into water with your arms and head first. *The boys dived into the swimming pool.*

> **Word Building: diver**, *noun* Someone who dives for a sport or for their job is a **diver**.

divide /*say* duh-**vuyd** / *verb*
1. If you **divide** something, you cut it or separate it into parts. *If we divide this cake into ten pieces, there will be enough for everyone.*
2. When you **divide** in maths, you find out how many times a particular number goes into a particular bigger number. *When you divide 10 by 2, you get 5.*

> **Word Building: division** /*say* duh-**vizh**-uhn /, *noun* When you divide something, you make a **division**. When you divide in maths, you do a **division**. *The teacher made a division of the class into three teams.*

divorce *noun*
If a husband and wife do not want to be together any more, they can end their marriage by getting a **divorce** from a court.

dizzy *adjective (**dizzier**, **dizziest**)*
You are **dizzy** if you feel as if your head is going around in circles.

do *verb (**does**, **doing**, **did**, **has done**)*
If you **do** something, you perform an action or carry out a job. *She did that painting very well.*

> When you use **do** with *not*, the words are sometimes joined together and made into the short form **don't**.

dock *noun*
A **dock** is the place where the goods that a ship is carrying are put on or taken off it.

docket *noun*
A **docket** is a piece of paper that shows that you have bought something.

> ✸ *Spelling Tip:* Put your **docket** in your *pocket* – these two words have the same spelling, except for the first letter. Remember that there is only one *t* at the end.

doctor *noun*
A **doctor** is someone whose job is to try and make sick people better.

dodge *verb*
If you **dodge** something, you move quickly out of the way of it. *Every time I got close enough to grab him, he would dodge past me.*

doe *noun*
A **doe** is a female deer.

> The male is a **buck** or a **stag**.

> ✸ *Spelling Tip:* Don't confuse the spelling of **doe** with **dough** which sounds the same. **Dough** is a mixture of flour and water or milk which is baked to make bread or pastry.

dog *noun*
A **dog** is an animal with four legs which eats meat and which many people keep as a pet.

doll *noun*
A **doll** is a child's toy which is made to look like a person.

dollar *noun*
A **dollar** is the money that is used in some countries, including Australia. There are 100 cents in a **dollar**.

> You can write $ before an amount of money instead of 'dollars', as in *$300*.

dolphin /*say* **dol**-fuhn / *noun*
A **dolphin** is an animal which lives in the sea and which has a long, pointed nose.

a b c d e f g h i j k l m n o p q r s t u v w x y z

domino /say **dom**-uh-noh/ noun (plural **dominoes**)

A **domino** is a small, flat, rectangular piece of wood or plastic with a number of dots on it, that you use to play a game.

donkey noun

A **donkey** is an animal with a body like a small horse and long ears. In some countries, **donkeys** are used on farms to carry things.

door noun

1. A **door** is a large piece of wood, metal or other material, which can be moved to open or close the opening to something, such as a house, room, cupboard or car. *The teacher asked me to close the door of the classroom.*
2. A **door** is the opening of a room or building. *She jumped up and ran out the door.*

You can also say **doorway** for definition 2.

dose noun

A **dose** is the amount of medicine that you take at one time.

dot noun

A **dot** is a very small round mark.

double /say **dub**-uhl/ adjective

1. If something is **double**, it is two times as big or as many as usual.
–verb **2.** If you **double** something, you make it two times as much. *If you double 4, you get 8.*

doubt /rhymes with out/ verb

If you **doubt** something, you are not sure about it. You do not think it is likely to happen or to be the truth. *The boy was not a very fast runner and the teacher doubted that he would win the race. | I have always doubted her story. I think she is making it up.*

Word Building: doubtful, adjective When you doubt something, you are **doubtful** about it.

⚒ *Spelling Tip:* Don't forget the silent *b*. The *b* is left behind from the Latin word it first came from – *dubitare*.

dough /rhymes with slow/ noun

Dough is a mixture of flour and water that you can bake to make bread. You make different sorts of dough to make things like pizza or scones.

⚒ *Spelling Tip:* Don't confuse the spelling of **dough** with **doe** which sounds the same. A **doe** is a female deer.

down adverb

1. If someone or something moves **down**, they move to a lower place. *Climb down from that tree immediately!*
–preposition **2.** If you go **down** something, you go to a lower part of it. *They walked down the stairs.*

download verb

If you **download** information, pictures, or music, you copy it from one computer to another, or from the internet to a computer, USB drive, or disk. *I need to download some articles about Aboriginal art for my school project.*

downstairs adverb

1. If you go **downstairs**, you go to a lower floor in a building. *I'll run downstairs and see what Mum is doing.*
–adjective **2.** If something is **downstairs**, it is on a lower floor on the bottom floor of a building.

downwards adverb

If something goes **downwards**, it goes towards a lower place. *The road goes downwards from here.*

You can also say **downward**.

dozen /say **duz**-uhn/ noun (plural **dozen** or **dozens**)

A **dozen** is a group of 12.

draft noun

A **draft** is a rough drawing or piece of writing. *I did a quick draft of my story and then I wrote it out properly.*

drag verb (**drags**, **dragging**, **dragged**, **has dragged**)

If you **drag** something, you pull it along slowly. *Can you drag that box of books over here?*

dragon noun

A **dragon** is a creature in stories that breathes out fire and looks like a very large lizard with wings.

dragonfly noun (plural **dragonflies**)

A **dragonfly** is a large insect which lives near water. It has a long, thin body and four long, clear wings.

drain noun

A **drain** is a pipe for taking away water, or a place in the ground shaped for taking away water.

drake noun

A **drake** is a male duck.

The female is a **duck**.

drama /say **drah**-muh / noun

1. A **drama** is an exciting, sad or serious play acted on stage, radio or television. *My parents always choose a drama to watch on television but we kids like cartoons much better.*
2. Drama is any exciting event or series of events. *There was quite a lot of drama in our team's football game – players getting injured, fights, and all sorts of things.*

> **Word Building: dramatic** /say druh-**mat**-ik/, *adjective* If something is full of drama, it is **dramatic**.

draught /rhymes with craft / noun

A **draught** is air that blows into a room.

> **Word Building: draughty**, *adjective* If there is a draught in the room, then the room is **draughty**.

> ✖ *Spelling Tip:* Remember that the middle sound in **draught** is spelt *augh* (although it sounds like 'ahf'). It might help if you think of a word you know well which has the same spelling for this sound, such as *laugh*. The spelling of **draught** can be confusing because it is sometimes spelt **draft**, especially in American English. However, in Australian English, the spelling **draft** is used where the meaning is an outline of a story (look up **draft**). **Draught** continues to be the main spelling in Australian English for air blowing through a room.

draw verb (draws, drawing, drew, has drawn)

If you **draw** something, you make a picture of it with a pencil or pen. *Eleni has drawn a map of her suburb.*

drawer /say draw/ noun

A **drawer** is a container shaped like a box that slides in and out of a piece of furniture such as a cupboard or desk.

> ✖ *Spelling Tip:* **Drawer** sounds the same as *draw*, but remember that it has a silent *er* added at the end.

drawing noun

A **drawing** is a picture that someone has drawn with a pencil or pen.

dreadful /say **dred**-fuhl / adjective

If something is **dreadful**, it is very bad.

dream noun

1. Your **dreams** are the thoughts and pictures that pass through your mind when you are sleeping.

–*verb* (**dreams, dreaming, dreamed** *or* **dreamt, has dreamed** *or* **has dreamt**)
2. When you **dream**, you have thoughts and pictures in your mind while you are sleeping. *Last night I dreamed that I was flying in a plane.*

Dreaming noun

The **Dreaming** is the special time when the world began, which Aboriginal people tell about in stories.

> You can also say **the Dreamtime** for this word.

dress noun

1. A **dress** is a piece of clothing for a woman or girl, which goes from the shoulders to part way down the legs.
–*verb* **2.** If you **dress** someone you put clothes on them. *Wait while I dress the baby.*

dribble verb

1. If you **dribble**, you let a little bit of spit come out of your mouth. *Babies dribble a lot when their teeth are starting to come through their gums.*
2. If you **dribble** a ball, you move it along the ground with little kicks or pushes. *Andrew was dribbling the ball along the ground and wouldn't let Tim have it.*

drift verb

If something **drifts**, it moves slowly along in water or in air. *We dropped sticks into the river and watched them drift away.*

drill noun

A **drill** is a tool for making holes in something hard such as wood.

drink verb (drinks, drinking, drank, has drunk)

1. When you **drink**, you take in liquid through your mouth. *I was so thirsty that I drank two glasses of water.*
–*noun* **2.** A **drink** is the liquid that you take in.

drip verb (drips, dripping, dripped, has dripped)

If a liquid **drips**, it falls in drops. *Water was dripping from the trees after the storm.*

drive verb (drives, driving, drove, has driven)

1. If someone **drives** a car or other kind of vehicle, they control the movement of it and make it go in a particular direction. *How old do you have to be to drive a car?*
–*noun* **2.** A **drive** is a trip in a car.

driver noun

The **driver** of a car, bus, or other vehicle is the person who controls its movement.

droop *verb*
If something **droops**, it hangs down. *The plants were beginning to droop in the heat.*

drop *noun*
1. A **drop** is a small round amount of liquid which falls.
–verb (**drops**, **dropping**, **dropped**, **has dropped**)
2. If you **drop** something, you let it fall when you did not mean to. *Oh no! I dropped the glass and it has broken.*
3. If something **drops**, it falls. *The glass just dropped from my hand.*

drought /*rhymes with* out/ *noun*
A **drought** is very dry weather which lasts for a long time.

> ✴ *Spelling Tip:* Remember the *ough* spelling in **drought** (which sounds like 'ow'). Other words like this are *plough* and *bough*.

drover *noun*
A **drover** is someone who is in charge of cattle or sheep when they are being taken to market or to other places to feed.

> *Word Building:* **droving**, *noun* A drover's job is **droving**.

drown *verb*
If a person or animal **drowns**, they die because they have been under water for so long that they cannot breathe. *During the flood some animals drowned in the river.*

drug *noun*
1. A **drug** is something that you take into your body to make you better when you are sick. It is a medicine. *She was given a new kind of drug that stops pain while she was in hospital.*
2. A **drug** is something like this which people sometimes use because it gives them a good feeling. Sometimes they cannot stop themselves using it. It is often against the law to use this kind of drug. *The police are looking for him because they think he sells drugs.*

drum *noun*
A **drum** is a hollow musical instrument that makes a deep sound when you hit it.

> *Word Building:* **drummer**, *noun* If you play the drum, then you are a **drummer**.

drunk *adjective*
If someone is **drunk**, they have had too much of a drink like beer or wine.

dry *adjective* (**drier**, **driest**)
1. If something is **dry**, it has not got water or other liquid on it or in it. *The clothes have been out in the sun all day so they should be dry now.*
2. If the weather is **dry**, there is not much rain. *In the country, it has been so dry that there is not much grass in the paddocks.*
–verb (**dries**, **drying**, **dried**, **has dried**)
3. If you **dry** something, you stop it being wet or you take liquid out of it. *He hung the washing out to dry.*

drycleaner *noun*
A **drycleaner** is someone who cleans clothes with special substances, not with water.

duck[1] *noun*
A **duck** is a bird with short legs and flat feet which it uses to swim in the water. It is often used for food. *Look at the ducks swimming across the lake. | We are having duck for dinner.*

> *Word Building:* **duckling**, *noun* A young duck is a **duckling**.

> The male of this bird is a **drake**.

duck[2] *verb*
If you **duck**, you act quickly to get your head down out of the way of something. *If you don't duck now, you'll be hit by the ball.*

due *adjective*
1. If something is **due** at a particular time, it is expected to be ready or to arrive then. *The train is due in ten minutes but Tom can't find his shoes.*
2. **due to**, If something is **due to** something else, it has been caused by that thing or event. *The accident was due to the bad weather.*

> ✴ *Spelling Tip:* Don't confuse the spelling of **due** with **dew** which sounds the same. **Dew** is the tiny drops of water that you find on things outside in the early morning.

duel /*say* **dyooh**-uhl/ *noun*
A long time ago a **duel** was a fight between two people to settle some problem between them and where they both use the same sort of weapon.

duet /*say* dyooh-**et**/ *noun*
A **duet** is a piece of music for two people.

dull *adjective*
If something, such as a book or film, is **dull**, it is not interesting.

dumb /*rhymes with* sum/ *adjective*
1. People who are not able to speak used to be called **dumb**.

2. You can use **dumb** to mean that you cannot talk for a short time for a special reason. *She was dumb with fear.*

3. You sometimes call someone or something **dumb** if they are stupid or silly. *He gave such a dumb answer because he wasn't thinking about what the teacher had asked him.*

✤ Definition 1 is not used very much these days and may upset people. It is better to use another term such as **speech-impaired**.

✤ **Dumb** in definition 3 is an informal word that you might use when talking to your friends.

✦ *Spelling Tip:* Don't forget the silent *b* at the end.

dummy *noun* (*plural* **dummies**)
1. A **dummy** is a piece of rubber attached to a piece of specially shaped plastic that you give a baby to suck. *To stop the baby crying, we put a dummy in his mouth.*
2. A **dummy** is a model of a person. You use it to show how clothes look. *The dummy in the shop had fallen over and an arm had dropped off.*

dump *verb*
1. If you **dump** something, you throw it down in a careless way. *Don't just dump your clothes in a pile on the floor.*
–*noun* **2.** A **dump** is a place where you throw things you do not need.

dungeon /*say* **dun**-juhn/ *noun*
A **dungeon** is a small dark prison, usually under the ground. In the past, castles often had a **dungeon** underneath them.

dunnart /*say* **dun**-aht/ *noun*
A **dunnart** is a small animal about the size of a mouse which is found only in Australia.

This word comes from an Aboriginal language of Western Australia called Nyungar.

during /*say* **dyooh**-ring/ *preposition*
If something happens **during** a particular period of time, it happens all through that period or at some time within that period. *During the morning, we set up camp and went down to the beach to swim for a few hours.*

dusk *noun*
Dusk is the time at the end of the day when it is starting to get dark.

dust *noun*
Dust is very, very small bits of soil, or other material, that are like powder.

Word Building: **dusty**, *adjective* Something that is covered in dust is **dusty**.

duty *noun* (*plural* **duties**)
1. Your **duty** is what you should do. It is what you feel is the right thing to do. *The teacher said it was our duty to look after our little brothers and sisters when they first started at school.*
2. A **duty** is what you have to do because of your job or position. *The leader of the team has many duties. One of them is to tell everyone the date of the next game.*

DVD *noun*
1. A **DVD** is a special kind of disc which stores information such as film, music and computer games. *You can get that film on DVD now.*
2. A **DVD** is a film or other entertainment on this kind of disc. *We watched two DVDs over the weekend.*

This stands for *digital video disc.*

dwarf /*say* dwawf/ *noun* (*plural* **dwarfs** *or* **dwarves**)
A **dwarf** is a person, an animal or a plant much shorter than usual.

✦ *Spelling Tip:* Remember the *ar* spelling for the 'aw' sound. Another word with this sound and spelling pattern is *wharf.*

dye /*rhymes with* my/ *noun*
A **dye** is a liquid like paint. You use it to colour cloth, your hair and other things as well.

✦ *Spelling Tip:* Don't confuse the spelling of **dye** with **die** which has the same sound but is spelt with an *i.* **Die** means 'to stop living'.

dynamite /*say* **duy**-nuh-muyt/ *noun*
Dynamite is material that explodes when you light it. It can cause a lot of damage.

✦ *Spelling Tip:* Remember that the beginning of **dynamite** is spelt *dyn* (although it sounds as if it might be spelt 'dine'). Like many words with a *y* spelling, **dynamite** comes from Greek.

egg

each *adjective*
1. You use **each** when you are thinking of things or people in a group one by one.
–*pronoun* 2. You use **each** to stand for a thing or person when you are thinking of them one by one. *I'm going to give each of you a pen.*

eager *adjective*
If you are **eager** to do or have something, you want very much to do it or have it.

> **Word Building: eagerly,** *adverb* If you are eager, you wait for something or do something **eagerly.** –**eagerness,** *noun* If you are eager, you are full of **eagerness.**

eagle *noun*
An **eagle** is a large bird which hunts small animals for food, seeing them from a long way up in the air and quickly going down to get them.

ear *noun*
Your **ear** is one of two parts of the body you use to hear, one on each side of your head.

early *adverb*
1. If something happens **early**, it happens before the usual time or before the time it should happen. *Because it was so hot, the teacher let us go home from sport early.*
–*adjective* 2. If something is **early**, it happens before the usual or proper time.

> The opposite is **late.**

earn *verb*
When you **earn** money, you get it for the work you do. *Film actors earn a lot of money.*

earth *noun*
1. The **earth** is the world we all live in. *The earth goes around the sun.*
2. **Earth** is soil from the ground, not rocks or sand. *Dad dug up a lot of earth to make a garden.*

> You can also spell definition 1 with a capital letter. *The Earth has existed for millions of years.*

earthquake *noun*
An **earthquake** is a violent shaking of the ground, which can cause a lot of damage.

east *noun*
1. The **east** is the direction from which the sun rises.
–*adjective* 2. If something is **east**, it is in or towards the east.
–*adverb* 3. If something goes **east**, it goes towards the east. *We had to drive east for 100 kilometres to get there.*

> **Word Building: eastern,** *adjective* If something is in the east, it is **eastern.** *Sydney is on the eastern coast of Australia.*

> The opposite direction is **west.** The other directions are **north** and **south.**

easy *adjective* (**easier, easiest**)
If something is **easy**, you can do it or understand it without a lot of trouble. *My little sister always gets to do the easy jobs in the house. | I think maths is easy.*

> **Word Building: easily,** *adverb* If something is easy to do, you can do it **easily.**

> The opposite is **difficult** or **hard.**

eat *verb* (**eats, eating, ate, has eaten**)
When you **eat** food, you take it into your body through your mouth. *My mother says you should eat some orange and green vegetables every day.*

ebb *verb*
If something **ebbs**, it flows back or away as the sea does. *We watched as the tide ebbed and flowed.*

eccentric /*say* uhk-**sen**-trik / *adjective*
Someone is **eccentric** if they do things in a strange or unusual way.

echidna /*say* uh-**kid**-nuh / *noun*
An **echidna** is a small Australian animal which is covered in long sharp spines and which eats

ants. It lays eggs and feeds its babies with its own milk.

> **Spelling Tip:** The word **echidna** comes from Greek (meaning 'snake') which is why it has the spelling *ch* to make the 'k' sound.

echo /*say* **ek**-oh/ *noun* (*plural* **echoes**)
An **echo** is a sound that comes back to you after you have made it.

eclipse /*say* uh-**klips**/ *noun*
1. An **eclipse** is the darkness that comes when the moon is between the sun and the earth and blocks the sun's light. This is called a **solar eclipse**. *You must never look at the sun during an eclipse.*
2. An **eclipse** is also the darkness that comes over the moon when the earth is between the moon and the light of the sun. This is called a **lunar eclipse**. *The moon turned a funny red colour during the eclipse.*

eco-friendly /*say* **eek**-oh-frend-lee/ *adjective*
If something is **eco-friendly**, it does not harm the environment or it harms the environment less than other types of the same thing.

ecology /*say* uh-**kol**-uh-jee/ *noun*
Ecology is the science or study of the relationship of living things to each other and to their environment.

> ***Word Building:*** **ecologist**, *noun* Someone whose work is ecology is an **ecologist**.

economy /*say* uh-**kon**-uh-mee/ *noun*
Economy is looking after your money, your food, and anything else that is yours, in a careful way.

> ***Word Building:*** **economical** /*say* ek-uh-**nom**-ik-uhl/, *adjective* If you use **economy** and don't waste things, then you're **economical**.

ecosystem /*say* **ee**-koh-sis-tuhm/ *noun*
An **ecosystem** is a group of living things that live in a particular environment and the environment that they all live in.

edge *noun*
The **edge** of something is the part of it that is furthest away from its centre. It is the part or line where something stops or comes to an end.

educate /*say* **ej**-uh-kayt/ *verb*
When someone **educates** you, they teach you and give you knowledge. *A teacher's job is to educate children.*

> ***Word Building:*** **educated**, *adjective* When someone educates you, they make you **educated**.

education *noun*
Your **education** is the learning you do at school or university or places like that. It is what you are taught at those places.

> ***Word Building:*** **educational**, *adjective* Something that helps in someone's education is **educational**.

effect *noun*
An **effect** of something is what it causes to happen.

> Don't confuse **effect** with **affect** which means 'to make something different'. Look up **affect**.

effort *noun*
1. Effort is when you have to use a lot of your body's strength. *It takes a lot of effort to push a car.*
2. An **effort** is when you try hard to do something. It is a serious attempt. *If you made an effort, you could be a better player.*

EFTPOS /*say* **eft**-pos/ *noun*
EFTPOS is a way of paying for things at the shops, using a plastic card.

egg *noun*
1. An **egg** is something which a female bird produces and which a baby bird grows inside. It has an oval shape and has a thin shell. The **eggs** laid by hens are often used as food. *There were three eggs in the nest. | We had eggs and toast for breakfast.*
2. An **egg** is one of the similar things that some other animals, such as snakes or insects, develop inside. *We found some lizard eggs under a rock in the garden.*

eight /*say* ayt/ *noun*, *adjective*
Eight is a number which you can write as 8.

> ***Word Building:*** **eighth**, *adjective*: *This is the eighth time I have read this book – I really love it.*

> **Spelling Tip:** Remember the *eigh* spelling for the 'ay' sound. Some other words which have an *eigh* spelling for the same sound are *neigh* and *weigh*. Also remember that when you add *th* to make **eighth**, you drop the *t* so that **eighth** has only one *t*.

eighteen /say ay-**teen**/ noun, adjective
Eighteen is a number, which you can write as 18.

> **Word Building: eighteenth**, adjective: Today is the eighteenth day of the month.

eighty /say **ay**-tee/ noun, adjective
Eighty is a number which you can write as 80.

> **Word Building: eightieth** /say **ay**-tee-uhth/, adjective: Today is my grandfather's eightieth birthday.

either /say **uy**-dhuh, **ee**-dhuh/ adjective
1. You use **either** to mean one or the other out of two things or people. Mum said we could have either a chocolate biscuit or a lamington, but not both.
2. You can use **either** to mean both one and the other out of two things or people. There were trees on either side of the road.

elastic adjective
Something is **elastic** if you can stretch it and then let it go back into shape again.

elbow noun
Your **elbow** is the middle part of your arm where the top half joins the bottom half.

elder adjective
1. An **elder** brother or an **elder** sister is a brother or sister who is older.
–noun 2. An **elder** is a person who is older than you, whether or not they are in the same family as you. My dad never stops telling me to listen to my elders.
3. An **elder** is an important person in an Indigenous community, especially someone who knows all about the traditional language and culture.

> **Word Building: elderly**, adjective A person who is quite old is **elderly**.

eldest noun
Someone who is the **eldest** is the oldest or the one born first.

elect verb
If you **elect** someone, you choose them by voting for them. My mum hopes they will elect her to be on the school council.

> **Word Building: election**, noun The person you elect to do a job has won an **election**.

electric adjective
If something is **electric**, it is produced by electricity or needs electricity to make it work.

> **Word Building: electrical**, adjective Something to do with electricity is **electrical**.

> **Electric** and **electrical** are similar words but they are used differently. **Electric** is used mainly to describe machines that work by electricity. He bought a new electric guitar. **Electrical** is used to describe something else that has to do with electricity.

electrician /say uh-lek-**trish**-uhn/ noun
An **electrician** is someone whose job is to put electrical connections in houses and to fix them when they are not working properly.

> �֍ **Spelling Tip:** Remember that the ending of **electrician** is spelt ician. Many other words have this spelling for an 'ishuhn' sound, such as magician and musician.

electricity /say uh-lek-**tris**-uh-tee/ noun
Electricity is energy or power that we use for lighting and heating, and to make machines work. It is carried along in wires.

elegant adjective
You are **elegant** if you dress and move in a way that appears very beautiful and suitable for any occasion.

> **Word Building: elegance**, noun If you're elegant, then you have **elegance**.

elephant /say **el**-uh-fuhnt/ noun
An **elephant** is a very large animal that comes from Africa or India, with a thick, grey skin and a long nose (called a trunk) that it uses to pick things up.

elevator /say **el**-uh-vay-tuh/ noun
An **elevator** is something shaped like a large box for carrying people up and down inside tall buildings.

> Another word for this is **lift**.

eleven noun, adjective
Eleven is a number which you can write as 11.

> **Word Building: eleventh**, adjective: The eleventh player came onto the field.

elf noun (plural **elves**)
An **elf** is a tiny person in fairy stories who can do special things that normal people cannot do and who often plays tricks on people.

eliminate /*say* uh-**lim**-uh-nayt/ *verb*
If you **eliminate** someone or something, you get rid of them. *Our team was eliminated from the competition because we were coming last.*

> **Word Building: elimination**, *noun* If you eliminate something, then you make an **elimination**.

else *adverb*
1. You use **else** to mean someone or something instead of or different from the person or the thing mentioned. *Would you like a book for a present or would you like something else?*
2. You use **else** to mean someone or something added to the other people or things mentioned. *We have five people in the team already. Who else wants to play?*

email *noun*
1. **Email** is a way of sending messages from one computer to another. *Email makes it easy to communicate with people a long way away.*
2. An **email** is a message sent by computer, from one person to another person. *My friend sent me a really funny joke in an email so I've sent it on to my other friends.*
–*verb* 3. If you **email** someone, you send them a message by email. *I emailed invitations to all my friends.*

> ✤ This is short for **electronic mail**.
> ✤ You can also spell this word **e-mail**.

embarrass /*say* em-**ba**-ruhs/ *verb*
If you **embarrass** someone, you make them feel silly in front of other people. *It embarrassed everybody in the class when we had to show our baby photos.*

> **Word Building: embarrassment**, *noun* Things that embarrass you fill you with **embarrassment**.

> ✳ **Spelling Tip:** Remember that there are two double letters in **embarrass** – a double *r* and a double *s*.

embassy /*say* em-buh-see/ *noun* (*plural* **embassies**)
An **embassy** is the place in your country where an ambassador from another country works or lives.

embrace *verb*
If you **embrace** someone, you hold them close to you. *My grandmother embraces us in a big warm hug whenever we visit her.*

emerald /*say* **em**-ruhld/ *noun*
An **emerald** is a valuable, bright green jewel.

emergency /*say* uh-**mer**-juhn-see/ *noun* (*plural* **emergencies**)
An **emergency** is something serious that happens when it is not expected and that you have to do something about at once.

emotion *noun*
Emotion is a feeling you have, such as love, hate, happiness, sadness or anger.

> **Word Building: emotional**, *adjective* When you have a strong emotion, you're **emotional**.

empire *noun*
An **empire** is a group of countries ruled over by one very powerful country. *Australia used to be part of the British Empire.*

employ *verb*
If someone **employs** someone, they give them work to do, and they pay them for it. *The factory employs hundreds of people.*

> **Word Building: employment**, *noun* If someone employs people, they give them **employment**. –**employer**, *noun* Someone who employs someone else is an **employer**. –**employee**, *noun* Someone who is employed by someone else is an **employee**.

empty *adjective* (**emptier**, **emptiest**)
If something is **empty**, it has nothing inside it.

> **Word Building: emptiness**, *noun* When something is empty, you can talk about its **emptiness**.

> The opposite is **full**.

emu *noun*
An **emu** is a large Australian bird which is not able to fly.

encourage /*say* en-**ku**-rij/ *verb*
If you **encourage** someone, you give them help and support, often to make them feel that they can do something. *Wayang's mother encouraged him to go in the race by telling him that he was a very good runner.*

> **Word Building: encouragement**, *noun* When you encourage someone, you give them **encouragement**.

a
b
c
d
e
f
g
h
i
j
k
l
m
n
o
p
q
r
s
t
u
v
w
x
y
z

encyclopedia /say en-suy-kluh-**pee**-dee-uh/ noun

An **encyclopedia** is a book that has information which is arranged by letters of the alphabet. It is often in many separate books because there is so much information that one book is not enough.

> ✵ *Spelling Tip:* Another spelling for this word is **encyclopaedia** but this is not used very much these days. The most important thing to remember is the *cyc* spelling. Think of the word *cycle* to remind yourself of this. **Encyclopedia** is from a Greek word meaning 'a cycle (or course) of learning'.

end noun

1. The **end** of something is when it stops.
–verb 2. If something **ends**, it stops and does not continue. *I hope this film ends soon. It is boring.*

> *Word Building:* **ending**, noun The last part of something is its **ending**. *The ending of the film was very sad.*

> ✤ The opposite of definition 1 is **beginning** or **start**.
> ✤ The opposite of definition 2 is **begin** or **start**.

endanger verb

If you **endanger** someone or something, you cause them to be in danger or at risk. *You seriously endanger your life if you walk too close to big bears.*

> *Word Building:* **endangered species**, noun A group of animals or plants which is in danger of becoming extinct is called an **endangered species**. *Australia has many endangered species.*

endeavour /say en-**dev**-uh/ verb

If you **endeavour** to do something, you try or attempt to do it. *They were endeavouring to reach home before night.*

> Another spelling for this word is **endeavor**.

endless adjective

If something is **endless**, it does not finish. It goes on for ever, or seems to go on for ever.

enemy noun (plural **enemies**)

1. Someone's **enemy** is a person who hates them, or wishes to harm them or something that is important to them. *The politician wanted to save the endangered whales but he had enemies who tried to stop his efforts.*

2. The **enemy** is a country and its soldiers which are fighting against your country. *Many people died when our soldiers were attacked by the enemy.*

energy /say **en**-uh-jee/ noun

1. **Energy** is the power to be strong and very active. If you have a lot of **energy**, you feel like doing work and playing games. *We didn't have any energy left after walking three kilometres.*

2. **Energy** is the power which is taken from things in nature like sun or water or wind to be used to do all sorts of work. *The teacher told us that the dam was used to make enough energy to make electricity for millions of people.*

> *Word Building:* **energetic** /say en-uh-**jet**-ik/, adjective If you have a lot of energy, you are **energetic**.

engaged adjective

1. If someone or something is **engaged**, they are busy or already being used or doing something else. *Her telephone is engaged so I'll ring again later.*

2. You are **engaged** if you are going to be married. *Now that my aunt is engaged, she is busy planning her wedding.*

> *Word Building:* **engagement**, noun If you're engaged, then you've told everyone of your **engagement**.

engine /say **en**-juhn/ noun

1. The **engine** of a car, bus, ship or of a machine is the part of it that produces the power to make it move *Our car stopped because the engine had become too hot.*

2. The **engine** of a train is the front part that pulls the rest along. *The driver sits in the train's engine.*

> Another word with a similar meaning to definition 1 is **motor**.

engineer /say en-juh-**near**/ noun

An **engineer** is someone whose job is designing and building things such as roads, bridges and machines.

> *Word Building:* **engineering**, noun The work that an engineer does is **engineering**.

> ✵ *Spelling Tip:* If you know the spelling of *engine* (with a soft *g*, not a *j*), you will be all right with **engineer** which has the basic meaning of 'someone who makes engines'.

enjoy verb
If you **enjoy** something, you are happy while you are doing it. *Did you enjoy your holiday?*

> **Word Building: enjoyment**, *noun* If you enjoy something, it gives you **enjoyment**.

enjoyable adjective
If something is **enjoyable**, you enjoy it.

enormous adjective
If something is **enormous**, it is much bigger than usual.

enough /say uh-**nuf**/ adjective
1. If something is **enough**, there is as much of it as you want or need.
–adverb 2. You use **enough** to mean as much as is necessary. *Hurry up! You're not walking fast enough.*
–pronoun 3. **Enough** is as much of something as you want or need. *'Do you want some more food?' 'No, thank you, I've had enough.'*

> ✴ **Spelling Tip:** Remember that there is no *f* in **enough** – the spelling *ough* gives the 'uf' sound, as it does in some other words like *rough* and *tough*.

enter verb
If you **enter** a place, you come or go into it. *We all stood up when the principal entered the room.*

entertain verb
If you **entertain** someone, you interest and amuse them. *Ari entertained us by balancing a spoon and a fork on a cup.*

> **Word Building: entertainer**, *noun* Someone whose job is to entertain you is an **entertainer**. –**entertainment**, *noun* Something that entertains you, like a film or a show, is an **entertainment**.

enthusiastic /say en-thooh-zee-**as**-tik/ adjective
If someone is **enthusiastic**, they have a strong interest in something.

> **Word Building: enthusiasm** /say en-**thooh**-zee-az-uhm/, *noun* If you are enthusiastic about something, then you have **enthusiasm** for it.

entire adjective
You use **entire** to make it clear that you mean all of something or the whole of something.

entrance noun
The **entrance** to a place is the way into it.

entry noun (plural **entries**)
1. An **entry** is coming in or going in. *Everyone turned and looked when the bride made her entry into the church.*
2. An **entry** is the way in. *The entry to our drive was blocked by a van.*

envelope /say **en**-vuh-lohp, **on**-vuh-lohp/ noun
An **envelope** is a folded paper cover that you put a letter in.

environment /say en-**vuy**-ruhn-muhnt/ noun
1. An **environment** is everything around someone in their daily life. *Because we live in the city, we have got used to an environment full of buildings, cars and lots of noise.*
2. The **environment** is everything in nature, such as plants, animals, land, rivers and the sea. *Many people think we should do more to protect the environment.*

envy noun
Envy is the feeling of wanting what someone else has, or the feeling that you would like to have a life like theirs.

> **Word Building: envious**, *adjective* When you have a feeling of envy, you are **envious**.

equal /say **ee**-kwuhl/ adjective
1. If something is **equal** to something else, there is the same amount of it, or it has the same value. *We will have equal shares of the food.* | *Ann and Susan got equal marks in the test. They both got 8 out of 10.*
–verb (**equals**, **equalling**, **equalled**, **has equalled**)
2. If something **equals** something else, it has the same amount or value as it. *Five and five equals ten.*

> **Word Building: equally**, *adverb*: *John and Henry are equally hungry – they both think they could eat a horse!* –**equality** /say ee-**kwol**-uh-tee/, *noun* If two things are equal, they have **equality**. You talk about people having **equality** when they all have the same rights.

> The opposite of **equal** is **unequal**, and the opposite of **equality** is **inequality**.

equator /say uh-**kway**-tuh/ noun
The **equator** is the circle we imagine all the way around the middle part of the earth. *The weather in countries that are near the equator is usually very hot.*

a b c d e f g h i j k l m n o p q r s t u v w x y z

equip /say uh-**kwip**/ verb (**equips**, **equipping**, **equipped**, **has equipped**)
If you **equip** someone, you give them all the things they need to do something. *Dad went to the camping shop to equip us for our trip.*

equipment /say uh-**kwip**-muhnt/ noun
Equipment is the things you need for a particular job, such as tools, or the things you need to do something like play sport.

eraser noun
An **eraser** is a small piece of soft rubber used to rub out pencil marks.

> A more usual word for this is **rubber**.

erosion /say uh-**roh**-zhuhn/ noun
Erosion is damage to the land caused when soil has been washed or blown away, usually by the weather.

> **Word Building: erode**, *verb* Erosion happens when wind or water **erodes** the soil.

errand /say **e**-ruhnd/ noun
An **errand** is a small job or task.

error noun
An **error** is a mistake.

escalator /say **es**-kuh-lay-tuh/ noun
An **escalator** is a set of moving stairs that take people up or down.

> ⚙ *Spelling Tip:* Remember the *ala* spelling in the middle of this word. This is because **escalator** comes from *scala*, the Italian word for 'steps'. Also remember that the ending is *or* (not *er*).

escape /say uhs-**kayp**/ verb
If you **escape**, you get free from somewhere or from someone who is trying to catch you or keep you as a prisoner. *He escaped from prison.*

> **Word Building: escapee** /say es-kuh-**pee**/, *noun* Someone who has escaped from prison is an **escapee**.

especially /say uh-**spesh**-uh-lee/ adverb
1. You use **especially** to mean more than usually. *Please be especially careful!*
2. You use **especially** to show that what you are saying has to do with one person or thing more than others. *He played all sports well, especially tennis.*

estimate /say **es**-tuh-mayt/ verb
If you **estimate** the price, amount or size of something, you try to guess or judge it. *We tried to estimate how long it would take someone to walk across Australia.*

etc. /say et-**set**-ruh/ You use **etc.** at the end of a list to show you mean the list to include more things of the same kind, but you do not want to say or write all of them. *Bring all your school things with you – books, pens, pencils, paper, etc.*

> **Etc.** is short for the Latin words *et cetera* which mean 'and others'. This explains the way it is said.

ethnic adjective
Something is **ethnic** if it has to do with a group of people who are all similar in their language or their customs, because they all come from a particular part of the world.

eucalypt /say **yooh**-kuh-lipt/ noun
An **eucalypt** is a gum tree.

euro[1] /say **yooh**-roh/ noun (plural **euros**)
A **euro** is a type of wallaroo with red-coloured, short hair.

> This word comes from an Aboriginal language of South Australia called Adnyamathanha.

euro[2] /say **yooh**-roh/ noun (plural **euros**)
A **euro** is the money used in many European countries, such as France, Germany, Italy, Greece, and Spain.

evaporate /say uh-**vap**-uh-rayt/ verb
If something **evaporates**, it dries up and disappears. *There is water in that puddle now, but it will probably evaporate during the day.*

eve noun
The **eve** is the day before an important day or event.

even adjective
1. If a number is **even**, you can divide it by two. *Four, six, eight and ten are even numbers.*
2. If things are **even**, they are equal in size. *We cut the cake into even pieces because we all wanted the same amount.*
3. If a surface is **even**, it is smooth and flat. *Michiko fell over because the ground was not even.*
–adverb 4. You use **even** to make the word after it stronger. *Our netball team is playing even better now that we are training twice a week.*
5. You use **even** to show that something is surprising. *Even my noisy friends were quiet when the police walked in.*

> ❖ The opposite of definition 1 is **odd**.
> ❖ The opposite of definitions 2 and 3 is **uneven**.

evening *noun*
The **evening** is the early part of the night.

event *noun*
An **event** is something which happens.

ever *adverb*
You use **ever** to mean 'at any time'. *'Have you ever seen him before?' 'No, I have never seen him.'*

every *adjective*
1. You use **every** to show that you are talking about all members of a group or all parts of something. *Every student in the school must wear this uniform.*
2. You use **every** to say that something happens regularly and you are talking about how often it happens. *We go swimming every day.*

everyday *adjective*
If something is **everyday**, you use it or do it or say it in ordinary situations, rather than formal situations. *'Okay' is part of everyday language. | You can wear your everyday clothes when you come to dinner. We are just inviting a few friends.*

When you write this as two words (**every day**), it has a different meaning. It means 'on all days'. *We go for a walk every day.*

everyone *pronoun*
Everyone is all people, or every person in a group. *Could everyone at the back of the room stand up, please.*

You can also say **everybody**.

everything *pronoun*
Everything is all things. *Bring everything you have with you – don't leave anything behind.*

everywhere /*say* **ev**-ree-wair/ *adverb*
If something happens or is done **everywhere**, it happens or is done in all places. *I have looked everywhere for those missing jigsaw pieces but I can't find them.*

evil *adjective*
Someone is **evil** if they do extremely bad things to hurt people.

evolution /*say* ev-uh-**looh**-shuhn/ *noun*
Evolution is the slow change of plants, animals and humans over millions of years. They change and develop as the environment changes.

evolve /*say* uh-**volv**/ *verb*
When plants, animals or humans **evolve**, they change slowly over time as the environment changes. *Many scientists think that land animals evolved from sea animals.*

ewe /*say* yooh/ *noun*
A **ewe** is a female sheep.

The male is a **ram**.

exact *adjective*
If something is **exact**, it is completely correct in all ways. *She gave an exact description of the animal she saw in the bush. | He told me the exact amount of money he had in the bank.*

exactly *adverb*
1. You use **exactly** to say that information you are giving or asking for is completely correct with nothing left out. *The train leaves at exactly 10.15 in the morning.*
2. You use **exactly** to say that something is completely as you describe it, not just close to it. *This book is exactly what I wanted.*

exaggerate /*say* uhg-**zaj**-uh-rayt/ *verb*
If you **exaggerate**, you say more about something than is true. *We'll have to exaggerate the story – instead of saying you were a bit sick, we'll say you nearly died.*

Word Building: **exaggeration**, *noun* If you exaggerate, then you make an **exaggeration**.

⚡ *Spelling Tip:* Remember the double *g* in the middle – in other words **exaggerate** the *g*.

examination /*say* uhg-zam-uh-**nay**-shuhn/ *noun*
1. An **examination** of something is when someone looks at it very carefully. *The doctor made a careful examination of my foot and said I had broken a bone in my little toe.*
2. An **examination** is a test of how much you know in a particular subject. *She did very well in the examination at the end of the year.*

The short form of definition 2 is **exam**.

examine /*say* uhg-**zam**-uhn/ *verb*
If you **examine** something, you look at it carefully. *The doctor examined my arm to see if it was broken.*

example *noun*
1. An **example** is a member of a group or a part of something which shows you what the rest is like. *The teacher showed our class an example of the kind of work she wanted.*
2. for example, You say **for example** when you are using something as an example to make what

you are saying easy to understand. *My mother said there were many ways of saving money. For example, I could stop buying lollies after school every day.*

When you write **for example**, you often use the short form **e.g.** *This shop sells women's clothes, e.g., skirts and dresses.*

excellent /*say* **ek**-suh-luhnt/ *adjective*
If something is **excellent**, it is very, very good.

Word Building: **excellently**, *adverb*: *Donna plays the piano excellently.*

except /*say* uhk-**sept**/ *preposition*
If you talk about everything **except** one particular thing or person, what you are saying does not include that person or thing. *All the class went to the museum except Allie who had a broken leg.*

Don't confuse **except** with **accept** which means 'to agree to take something'.

exchange *verb*
If you **exchange**, you give one thing and get another thing in return. *Sally's mother was a bit sorry that Sally had got mice at the pet shop and wanted her to exchange them for a dog.*

excite /*say* uhk-**suyt**/ *verb*
If something **excites** you, or you are **excited**, you feel very strongly about it, often in a way that makes you not want to stay still. *The girls were so excited about getting into the finals of the netball.*

Word Building: **excitement**, *noun* If you are excited, you are full of **excitement**. –**exciting**, *adjective* If something excites you, it is **exciting**.

exclaim /*say* uhks-**klaym**/ *verb*
If you **exclaim**, you cry out suddenly because you are pleased or frightened. *'Is that really for me?' she exclaimed happily.*

Word Building: **exclamation** /*say* eks-kluh-**may**-shuhn/, *noun* When you exclaim, you make an **exclamation**.

⚙ *Spelling Tip:* Notice that when you make the word **exclamation** from **exclaim**, you leave out the *i* and the way you say it changes.

excursion /*say* uhk-**sker**-zhuhn/ *noun*
An **excursion** is a short trip you take for a special reason.

excuse *verb* /*rhymes with* choose/
1. If you **excuse** someone, you forgive them when they have done something wrong. You say

it does not matter. *The teacher excused Daniel for being late, because she knew his mother was sick.*
2. excuse me, **a.** You say **excuse me** when you want to interrupt someone or ask someone to move out of your way. *Excuse me, I need to get to the back of the bus to get off.* **b.** You use **excuse me** when you want to say you are sorry for doing something rude or for something you have done by accident. *Excuse me. I didn't mean to bump you when I walked past.*
–*noun* /*rhymes with* goose/ **3.** An **excuse** is a reason why you should be forgiven for doing something wrong.

execute /*say* **eks**-uh-kyooht/ *verb*
If someone **executes** someone, they kill them because they believe they have done something wrong. *In some countries they execute people who sell drugs.*

Word Building: **execution**, *noun* When people execute someone, there is an **execution**.

exercise /*say* **eks**-uh-suyz/ *noun*
Exercise is what you do to make your body strong and healthy.

exhausted /*say* uhg-**zaws**-tuhd/ *adjective*
If you are **exhausted**, you are extremely tired.

Word Building: **exhaustion** /*say* uhg-**zaws**-chuhn/, *noun* When you are exhausted, you feel **exhaustion**.

exhibition /*say* eks-uh-**bish**-uhn/ *noun*
An **exhibition** is a show or display of something that a lot of people can go to and see.

Word Building: **exhibit** /*say* eg-**zib**-uht/, *verb* When there is an exhibition, people **exhibit** things.

exist *verb*
1. If something **exists**, it is in the world as a real thing. *The earth has existed for millions of years.*
2. If living things **exist**, they continue to live. *People and animals cannot exist without water.*

Word Building: **existence**, *noun* If something or someone exists, they have **existence**.

exit *noun*
1. An **exit** is the way out.
–*verb* (**exits**, **exiting**, **exited**, **has exited**)
2. If you **exit**, you leave. *Please exit through the side door.*

expand *verb*
1. If something **expands**, it gets bigger. *As our family expanded, Dad built more rooms to fit us in.*
2. If you **expand** something, you make it bigger or develop it. *Dad expanded the house by building another two bedrooms on.*

expect *verb*
1. If you **expect** something to happen, you think that it will happen. *We expect that it will get colder soon because winter is coming.*
2. If you **expect** something or someone, you think that they will arrive soon or at a particular time. *We're expecting visitors at seven o'clock.*

expedition /*say* eks-puh-**dish**-uhn/ *noun*
An **expedition** is a journey you make for a special reason.

expensive *adjective*
If something is **expensive**, it costs a lot of money to buy it.

> Other words with a similar meaning to **expensive** are **dear** and **costly**. The opposite is **cheap**.

experience /*say* uhk-**spear**-ree-uhns/ *noun*
1. An **experience** is something that happens to you. *We had fantastic experiences when Dad took us camping.*
2. **Experience** is the knowledge that you get from doing things over a long time. *Delivering the paper gives you great experience in dealing with dogs.*

experiment /*say* uhk-**spe**-ruh-muhnt/ *noun*
An **experiment** is a test which you do to try to find out something.

expert *noun*
An **expert** is someone who knows a lot about a particular thing.

explain *verb*
If you **explain** something, you make it clear or easy to understand. *We have a really good book that explains all about keeping a worm farm.*

explanation /*say* eks-pluh-**nay**-shuhn/ *noun*
1. If you give an **explanation**, you say how or why something happens. *He couldn't give an explanation for why he was late.*
2. If you write an **explanation**, you do a piece of writing which tells how or why something happens. *He wrote an explanation about how a baby bird is born.*

explode /*say* uhks-**plohd**/ *verb*
If something **explodes**, it bursts into pieces with a loud noise. *The fireworks exploded* over the water and made a beautiful display of colours.

> **Word Building: explosion** /*say* uhks-**ploh**-zhuhn/, *noun* When something explodes, there is an **explosion**.

explore *verb*
If you **explore** a place that you have never been to before, you look around it and find out what is there. *Are you coming with us to explore the island?*

> **Word Building: explorer**, *noun* If you go to places that are not known and that are a long way away to explore them, you are an **explorer**. –**exploration**, *noun* If you are an explorer, your job is **exploration**.

exposition /*say* eks-puh-**zish**-uhn/ *noun*
If you write an **exposition**, you do a piece of writing that only gives one opinion on something.

express *verb*
1. If you **express** your thoughts or feelings, you put them into words. You say what you are thinking or feeling. *At the football meeting, we all had to express an opinion as to why we weren't playing so well.*
–*adjective* 2. An **express** train or an **express** bus is one that travels very fast, without stopping.

expression *noun*
1. An **expression** is a group of words that have a particular meaning. It is a way of saying something. *The expression 'Let sleeping dogs lie' means that if things are okay, you should not change them.*
2. An **expression** is a look on someone's face. *Something must be wrong. Look at Mum's angry expression.*

expressway *noun*
Look up **freeway**.

extend *verb*
If you **extend** something, you pull or stretch it out. *The lifesavers extended the rope as far as they could to rescue the swimmer.*

> **Word Building: extent**, *noun* How far something extends is its **extent**.

exterior /*say* uhks-**tear**-ree-uh/ *noun*
Something is **exterior** if it is on the outside of a place or building.

> The opposite is **interior**.

a b c d e f g h i j k l m n o p q r s t u v w x y z

external *adjective*
If something is **external**, it is on the outside.

The opposite is **internal**.

extinct /*say* uhks-**tingkt**/ *adjective*
1. An **extinct** animal or plant is one that no longer exists. *A dinosaur is an extinct type of reptile.*
2. A volcano that is **extinct** no longer has gases and rocks coming out of it. *That mountain is really an extinct volcano.*

Word Building: extinction /*say* uhks-**tingk**-shuhn/, *noun* When something is extinct, it is in a state of **extinction**.

extinguish /*say* uhks-**ting**-gwish/ *verb*
If you **extinguish** a light or a fire, you put it out. *We always made sure we extinguished the fire at our camp before we left.*

Word Building: extinguisher, *noun* You can extinguish a fire with an **extinguisher**.

extra *adjective*
1. If something is **extra**, it is more than usual. *We are having visitors so we need to put extra plates on the table.*
2. If something is **extra**, it is more than you need. *'We haven't brought any food.' 'Don't worry. We have brought extra food, so you can have some of ours.'*

extraordinary /*say* uhk-**straw**-duhn-ree/ *adjective*
Something that is **extraordinary** is so unusual that you cannot help noticing it. *Did you see that extraordinary hat in the shape of a banana?*

extreme *adjective*
If something is **extreme**, it is very great.

Word Building: extremely, *adverb* If you feel extreme happiness, then you are **extremely** happy.

eye *noun*
Your **eye** is one of the two parts of your face that you see with.

flower

fable *noun*

A **fable** is a short story that teaches people about how they should behave.

face *noun*

1. Your **face** is the front of your head, where your mouth, nose and eyes are. *Everyone has a different face – yours is broad and mine is thin.*

2. The **face** of something is its surface. *The clock had a black face with gold numbers.*

3. **face to face**, If you are **face to face** with someone, you have met with them and can look at them. *Mum said it was too important to talk about on the telephone – she wanted to talk to an officer face to face.*

–*verb* 4. If something or someone **faces** something, they have their front towards it. *The house faces the sea.*

fact *noun*

1. A **fact** is something that is true or real. *It is a fact that leaves grow on trees.*

2. **in fact**, You use **in fact** when you want to say what really is the truth. *Maria said it was an accident, but, in fact, she pushed me.*

factory *noun* (*plural* **factories**)

A **factory** is a building or group of buildings where machines are used to make things which are then sold.

fade *verb*

If something **fades**, it loses its colour or strength. *My big sister left her jeans out in the sun so they would fade. | When she ate some fruit, her hunger faded.*

fail /*say* fayl/ *verb*

If you **fail**, you do not succeed in something you are trying to do. *He failed his driving test three times.*

> *Word Building:* **failure** /*say* **fayl**-yuh/, *noun* If you fail something, you have had a **failure**.

faint *verb*

1. If you **faint**, you feel weak, your head feels as though it is going round and round and you fall over and everything goes black. *We knew that something must be wrong when Yusef fainted and fell to the floor.*

–*adjective* 2. If something you see or hear is **faint**, it is weak or distant. *We could just hear a faint sound coming from the bushes. | High up in the clouds, we could see a faint object which was probably an eagle.*

fair *adjective*

1. If someone is **fair**, they treat people equally, making certain that they do the same for each person. *He was a fair umpire and both the teams thought he did a really good job.*

2. If something is **fair**, it seems to people to be right, and everyone is treated equally. *It's not fair that I have to do all the cooking when all four of us are having dinner.*

3. If someone has **fair** hair or skin, it is quite pale in colour. *With your fair skin, you should not stay in this hot sun for too long.*

fairly *adverb*

1. If you act **fairly**, you treat people equally. *Sport works best when everybody plays fairly on the field.*

2. You can use **fairly** to make the next word less strong and show that it is a bit true but not completely true. *The book I am reading is fairly good but it gets a bit boring sometimes.*

fairy *noun* (*plural* **fairies**)

A **fairy** is a tiny person who is not real but who is written about in some stories. **Fairies** have wings and special powers, and can do things that ordinary people cannot do.

fairytale *noun*

A **fairytale** is a story in which things happen that could not happen in real life.

faith *noun*

If you have **faith** in someone or something, you have complete trust in them.

faithful *adjective*
You are **faithful** if you can be trusted and always do what you have said.

fake *noun*
A **fake** is something which is not real that you use to trick people.

fall *verb* (**falls**, **falling**, **fell**, **has fallen**)
1. If something **falls**, it drops suddenly from a higher to a lower place. *The bowl fell from the shelf and broke.*
2. **fall apart**, If something **falls apart**, it breaks into pieces, usually because it is old or weak, or it has not been made well. *The chair fell apart when I sat on it.*

false /*say* fawls, fols / *adjective*
1. If something is **false**, it is not true or correct. *No-one believed him, because we knew what he said had to be false.*
2. If something is **false**, it is not real or natural. *My grandmother has false teeth and takes them out every night.*

familiar /*say* fuh-**mil**-yuh / *adjective*
Something is **familiar** if you are used to seeing, doing or hearing it.

> ✿ *Spelling Tip:* Remember that the ending of **familiar** is spelt *iar* (not *ier*). Try breaking the word up as *fam+ il+ i+ ar*.

family *noun* (*plural* **families**)
Someone's **family** is their parents, their brothers and sisters, their husband or wife, their children, and sometimes other relations such as grandmothers and grandfathers.

famine /*say* **fam**-uhn / *noun*
A **famine** is a time when there is very little food.

famous *adjective*
Someone is **famous** if everyone knows who they are.

> *Word Building:* **fame**, *noun* If you are famous, you have **fame**.

fan[1] *noun*
A **fan** is something which moves the air and makes you feel cooler.

fan[2] *noun*
A **fan** is someone who is a strong supporter of a sport or a team or a person.

fancy *adjective*
If something is **fancy**, it is decorative.

> When you dress up in special clothes and pretend to be someone else, you are in **fancy dress**.

fang *noun*
A **fang** is a long, pointed tooth. Animals such as dogs and some snakes have them.

fantastic *adjective*
Something that is **fantastic** is very good.

far *adverb* (**further** *or* **farther**, **furthest** *or* **farthest**)
1. If someone or something is **far** or goes **far**, they are a long distance away or go a long distance. *Our grandfather lives far away from us.* | *Rebecca hit the ball so far it went over the fence.* | *John can hit the ball further than Sam.*
2. **so far**, If you use **so far**, you are saying that something has been true up until now. *So far, things are going well, but I don't know what will happen in the future.*
—*adjective* (**further** *or* **farther**, **furthest** *or* **farthest**)
3. You use **far** to describe something that is the greatest distance away. *They walked to the far end of the road.*

fare /*rhymes with* pair / *noun*
A **fare** is the money that you pay to travel on a bus, train, boat or plane.

farm *noun*
A **farm** is an area of land used for growing things to eat or keeping animals for food.

> *Word Building:* **farming**, *noun* The work on a farm is called **farming**.

farmer *noun*
A **farmer** is someone who works on a farm, growing plants and keeping animals for food.

fashion /*say* **fash**-uhn / *noun*
Fashion is a particular way of dressing that a lot of people follow at a particular time and that other people copy.

fast[1] *adjective*
1. If you are **fast**, you are able to move quickly. *He is a fast runner.*
2. If a clock or watch is **fast**, the time it shows is ahead of the correct time. *I'm early because my watch is five minutes fast.*
—*adverb* 3. If you do something **fast**, you do it quickly. *Sue works fast – she always finishes her work early.*
4. If you hold **fast** to something, you hold it firmly. *Hold fast to that rope.*

The opposite of definitions 1 and 2 is **slow**. The opposite of definition 3 is **slowly**.

fast² *verb*
If you **fast**, you go without food, usually for a special reason. *Our class is fasting for 12 hours to raise money for famine victims in Africa.*

fasten /*say* **fah**-suhn/ *verb*
If you **fasten** something, you close it or firmly fix it in place. *The first thing you have to do when you get into a car is fasten your seatbelt.*

✷ *Spelling Tip:* Don't forget the *st* (not double *s*) spelling. The *t* is silent. Remember that this word comes from *fast* meaning 'firm' (as in 'hold fast'), where you can hear the *t*.

fat *adjective* (**fatter**, **fattest**)
If someone is **fat**, they weigh a lot more than they should.

The opposite is **thin**.

fatal /*say* **fay**-tuhl/ *adjective*
Something is **fatal** if it makes someone die.

fate *noun*
Some people think that things happen because of **fate**, something outside your control that seems to control the things that happen to you.

✷ *Spelling Tip:* Don't confuse the spelling of **fate** with **fete** which sounds the same. A **fete** is an event for selling things at a school.

father *noun*
Your **father** is your male parent.

fault /*say* fawlt, folt/ *noun*
1. If it is your **fault** that something bad has happened, you have caused it to happen. *It was my fault that the video didn't record, because I pressed the pause button.*
2. A **fault** is something wrong with something, caused by a mistake when it was being made. *My mum's mobile phone has a fault in it – the display screen keeps disappearing.*

Word Building: **faulty**, *adjective* When something has a fault, it is **faulty**.

✷ *Spelling Tip:* Remember the *au* spelling (although you say it as either 'aw' or 'o').

favour *noun*
If you do someone a **favour**, you do something kind for them that helps them in some way.

Another spelling for this word is **favor**.

favourite *adjective*
You use **favourite** to describe a thing or person in a group that you like more than all the others in that group.

Another spelling for this word is **favorite**.

fawn *noun*
1. A **fawn** is a young deer.
–*adjective* 2. If something is coloured **fawn**, it is yellow-brown.

fax *noun*
1. If you send a page of writing or a picture by **fax**, you use a method that sends it along a telephone line. *If you want to get a message there fast, it's better to send it by fax than by mail.*
2. A **fax** is a piece of writing or a picture sent in this way. *My mum's first job in the morning is to check the faxes that have come in.*

This word is short for **facsimile** /*say* fak-**sim**-uh-lee/ which means 'an exact copy'. The first part of the word was chosen and the spelling was changed to match how you say it.

fear *noun*
Fear is the feeling you have when you think that something bad might happen to you.

feast *noun*
A **feast** is a large meal for a lot of people.

feather /*say* **fedh**-uh/ *noun*
A **feather** is one of the light, soft things that cover a bird's body.

February /*say* **feb**-yooh-uh-ree, **feb**-rooh-uh-ree/ *noun*
February is the second month of the year. It usually has 28 days, but every fourth year has 29 days. It comes between January and March.

✷ *Spelling Tip:* Remember the *r* after the *b* in **February**. Many people don't say the sound of the *r*, but it is always there when you spell it. Try breaking the word up as as *Feb+ru+a+ry*.

feeble *adjective*
If something is **feeble**, it is weak.

feed *verb* (**feeds**, **feeding**, **fed**, **has fed**)
If you **feed** someone, you give them food to eat. *She is feeding the baby.*

a b c d e f g h i j k l m n o p q r s t u v w x y z

feel *verb* (**feels, feeling, felt, has felt**)
1. If you **feel** something, you touch it with your hands to find out what it is like. *Feel this wool – it's very soft.*
2. If you **feel** a certain way, that is the way you are inside yourself. *He felt such happiness when he got into the team.*

feeling *noun*
If you have a **feeling** of some kind, you have a certain state in your mind or body.

feet *noun*
Look up **foot**.

felt *verb*
1. Look up **feel**.
–*noun* **2.** **Felt** is a thick, smooth cloth made of wool, fur or hair.

felt pen *noun*
A **felt pen** is a thick, brightly coloured pen that is used for drawing or writing.

This is sometimes called a **texta**.

female *noun*
A **female** is a person or animal that can have babies.

The opposite is **male**.

fence *noun*
A **fence** is something that is built to separate one area from another, usually made of wood, stone or wire.

fern *noun*
A **fern** is a green plant with no flowers which needs to be around water if more of these plants are to grow. **Ferns** do not grow from seeds and so are different to other plants.

ferry *noun* (*plural* **ferries**)
A **ferry** is a boat that carries people and sometimes cars.

fertile *adjective*
Ground is **fertile** if it can grow plants easily.

festival *noun*
1. A **festival** is a special time when people do things, such as dance or march, to celebrate something. *Some country towns have festivals to celebrate the start of spring.*
2. A **festival** is a time when a lot of people do the same activity at the same time. *My parents have bought tickets to the film festival.*

fetch *verb*
If you **fetch** something, you go and get it from somewhere and bring it back. *The dog fetched the ball.*

fete /*say* fayt/ *noun*
A **fete** is an event where people sell things in order to make money for a school, church or some other group.

⚜ *Spelling Tip:* Don't confuse the spelling of **fete** with **fate** which sounds the same. Your **fate** is what happens to you. **Fete** is spelt and sounds this way because it came first from French. This is why it is sometimes spelt with a mark on the first *e*: **fête**.

fever /*say* **fee**-vuh/ *noun*
If you have a **fever**, you have a sickness which causes your body to get too hot.

few *adjective* (**fewer, fewest**)
1. If there are **few** things or people, there are not many.
–*pronoun* **2.** A **few** is a small number of things or people. *Only a few in our class offered to help clean up the playground.*

fiction *noun*
Fiction is stories about people and events that someone has made up.

fiddle *verb*
If you **fiddle** with something, you play around with it. *Whenever Hamish fiddles with the computer, something goes wrong.*

fidget /*say* **fij**-uht/ *verb*
If you **fidget**, you keep moving about. *Don't fidget while I'm trying to explain this to you!*

field /*say* feeld/ *noun*
A **field** is an area of ground where people grow plants or keep animals, or where you can play sport.

⚜ *Spelling Tip:* Remember the *ie* spelling for the 'ee' sound. This follows the rule that *i* comes before *e* except after *c*.

fierce *adjective*
If an animal or person is **fierce**, they are wild, strong and angry.

⚜ *Spelling Tip:* Remember the *ie* spelling (for the 'ee' sound). This follows the rule that when the sound is 'ee', *i* comes before *e* except after *c*. Also don't forget the *ce* ending.

fifteen *noun, adjective*

Fifteen is a number which you can write as 15.

> *Word Building:* **fifteenth**, *adjective: She is the fifteenth student from our school to win the prize.*

fifth *adjective*

If something is the **fifth**, it is the one you count as number five.

fifty *noun, adjective*

Fifty is a number which you can write as 50.

> *Word Building:* **fiftieth**, *adjective: This is the school's fiftieth year.*

fig *noun*

A **fig** is a soft fruit shaped like a small pear, with a lot of small seeds inside.

fight /*say* fuyt / *noun*

1. A **fight** is when two or more people struggle with each other, usually hitting and kicking each other. *The boys had a fight in the street.*
2. A **fight** is an argument. *I always have a fight with my sister about who will clear the table.*
–*verb* (**fights**, **fighting**, **fought** /*say* fawt /, **has fought**)
3. If people **fight**, they struggle with each other, usually hitting and kicking each other. *As soon as their parents left the room, the boys started fighting.*
4. If people **fight**, they have an argument. *We were fighting about clearing the table so Mum told us to keep quiet.*
5. If soldiers **fight**, they take part in a war that their country is having with another country. *My grandfather has fought in two wars.*

figure /*say* **fig**-uh / *noun*

1. A **figure** is a sign that you use for a number. *The figure 3 stands for the number three.*
2. Your **figure** is the shape of your body. *My aunt has a great figure and looks good in anything she wears.*

file[1] *noun*

1. A **file** is a collection of information, either papers kept together in a cover, or information stored on a disk. *I am going to set up a file called 'Emails' so I can copy all my old emails and keep them there.*
2. A **file** is a line of people. *The teacher made us walk into the hall in file.*

file[2] *noun*

A **file** is a flat tool with a rough surface that you rub against things to make them smooth.

fill *verb*

If you **fill** something, you put as much into it as it will hold. *She filled her glass with water.*

film *noun*

1. **Film** is thin, specially treated plastic which you put in your camera to record pictures. *We don't need to buy film now that we have a digital camera.*
2. A **film** is a moving picture which tells a story and is often shown in a cinema. *I'd like to go and see an exciting film tonight.*

> You can also say **movie** for definition 2.

filthy *adjective* (**filthier**, **filthiest**)

If something is **filthy**, it is very dirty.

> *Word Building:* **filth**, *noun* If something is filthy, then it's covered with or full of **filth**.

fin *noun*

A **fin** is one of the thin, flat parts that come out from a fish's body and help it to swim and balance.

final *adjective*

1. If something is **final**, it is the last thing, coming right at the end.
–*noun* 2. A **final** is a race or part of a competition which comes at the end.

> *Word Building:* **finally**, *adverb* If something happens **finally**, it happens after a long time.

finalist *noun*

A **finalist** is a person who is in the last part of a competition.

find *verb* (**finds**, **finding**, **found**, **has found**)

1. If you **find** something which has been lost, you discover it again, usually after searching for it. *Our dog disappeared last week, but we found him this morning near the river.*
2. If you **find** something, you discover it by accident or when you are not expecting it. *I found a gold ring lying on the road.*

fine[1] *adjective*

1. If you are **fine**, you are feeling well or healthy. *I'm fine now that I've recovered from my cold.*
2. If the weather is **fine**, it is sunny, or it is not raining. *If it's a fine day tomorrow, we'll walk along the beach.*
3. If something is **fine**, it is very thin. *This cloth is so fine you can almost see through it.*
4. You can use **fine** to describe something that is excellent or someone that does something very well. *She's a fine trumpet player.*

a
b
c
d
e
f
g
h
i
j
k
l
m
n
o
p
q
r
s
t
u
v
w
x
y
z

fine² *noun*

A **fine** is money that you have to pay for doing something wrong.

finger *noun*

Your **finger** is one of the five long end parts of your hand.

finish *verb*

1. If something **finishes**, or if you **finish** it, it comes to an end. *When the sad film finished, we were all crying.*
−*noun* 2. The **finish** of something is its end.

fir *noun*

A **fir** is a tree with long, thin leaves or stems like needles. **Firs** produce seed in hard fruits called cones.

fire *noun*

1. **Fire** is the heat and light produced by burning. *Most animals are afraid of fire.*
2. A **fire** is a mass of burning material that you have made to keep warm or to cook something. *It was so cold that we had to light a fire.*
−*verb* 3. If someone **fires** using a weapon, they use it to shoot. *The policeman grabbed his gun and fired at the escaping prisoner.*

fireworks *noun*

Fireworks are containers filled with a powder that burns and produces brightly coloured lights that entertain people. They sometimes make a loud noise.

firm¹ *adjective*

1. If something is **firm**, it is solid and hard, or does not move easily. *After being on the boat all day, it was good to stand on firm land again.*
2. If someone is **firm**, they are strong in the way they think and they show that they will not change their ideas. *She is very firm about her decision to stay at home.*

> *Word Building:* **firmly**, *adverb*: *He held her arm firmly.* | *She answered firmly that she would stay at home.*

firm² *noun*

A **firm** is a group of people joined together in a company to do business.

first *adjective*

1. If something or someone is **first**, they are before all others.
−*adverb* 2. If someone does something **first**, they do it before anyone or anything else. *Su Li stood up first and soon everyone else was standing.*

−*noun* 3. The **first** is someone or something that comes before all others.

first aid *noun*

First aid is help that you give quickly to someone who is hurt, before a doctor arrives.

fish *noun* (*plural* **fish** *or* **fishes**)

A **fish** is an animal which lives and breathes under the water. It is often used for food.

> *Word Building:* **fishing**, *noun* The work or sport of catching fish is called **fishing**.

fist *noun*

Your **fist** is your hand when the fingers are rolled in tightly.

fit *adjective* (**fitter**, **fittest**)

1. You are **fit** if you are healthy and strong.
−*verb* (**fits**, **fitting**, **fitted**, **has fitted**)
2. If something **fits** you, it is the right size or shape for you. *This uniform fits me well.*

> *Word Building:* **fitness**, *noun* If someone is fit, they have a certain amount of **fitness**.

five *noun*, *adjective*

Five is a number which you can write as 5.

> *Word Building:* **fifth**, *adjective*

fix *verb*

If you **fix** something, you repair it. *My camera isn't working properly. Can you fix it?*

fizzy *adjective* (**fizzier**, **fizziest**)

If something is **fizzy**, it is full of tiny bubbles.

flag *noun*

A **flag** is a piece of cloth with a special design which shows that it belongs to one country or group, or that it has a certain meaning.

flake *noun*

A **flake** is a small, flat, thin piece of something.

flame *noun*

The **flame** is the hot, yellow light of a fire that moves in the air above something that is burning.

flammable *adjective*

If something is **flammable**, it is likely to burn easily.

> The opposite is **nonflammable**.

flap *verb* (**flaps**, **flapping**, **flapped**, **has flapped**)

1. If something **flaps**, it moves up and down. *The bird flapped its wings and flew away.*
−*noun* 2. A **flap** is something flat and thin that is joined to something else along one edge.

flash *noun*

A **flash** is a sudden burst of bright light.

A flood that happens quickly when you do not expect it is a **flash flood**.

flask *noun*

A **flask** is a bottle that you put drink into.

flat[1] *adjective*

1. If something is **flat**, it is smooth and level. *It is easier to run on flat ground.*

2. If a tyre is **flat**, there is no air in it, or not enough air. *We got to the concert late because we had to change a flat tyre.*

Word Building: flatten, *verb* If you make something flat, you **flatten** it.

flat[2] *noun*

A **flat** is a set of rooms for living in, usually on one level in a building. A number of other **flats** will be in the same building.

flavour *noun*

The **flavour** of something is its taste.

Another spelling for this word is **flavor**.

flea *noun*

A **flea** is a small insect without wings, which sucks blood from animals like cats and dogs, and moves by jumping.

⚡ *Spelling Tip:* Don't confuse the spelling of **flea** with **flee** which has the same sound but is spelt with a double *e* at the end.

flee *verb* (**flees, fleeing, fled, has fled**)

If you **flee** from something or someone, you run away from them. *We fled from the old house when we heard the strange noise.*

⚡ *Spelling Tip:* Don't confuse the spelling of **flee** with **flea**.

fleece *noun*

A **fleece** is the wool that covers a sheep.

fleet *noun*

A **fleet** is a group of ships sailing together.

flesh *noun*

Flesh is the soft part of a person's or animal's body, between the skin and the bone.

flicker *verb*

If something **flickers**, it burns brightly and then weakly, so that the light keeps on changing and is not regular. *The wind made the candle flicker.*

flight /*say* fluyt/ *noun*

1. A **flight** is a movement or journey through the air. *Some birds make a flight of hundreds of kilometres to go to where they find food in winter.*

2. A **flight** of stairs is a set of stairs. *Maria was in such a hurry that she ran up three flights of stairs in less than a minute.*

3. **take flight**, If you **take flight**, you run away. *The cat took flight when the dog appeared.*

flight attendant *noun*

A **flight attendant** is a person who works on a plane and looks after the passengers.

fling *verb* (**flings, flinging, flung, has flung**)

If you **fling** something, you throw it away from you. *She was so angry that she flung the telephone onto the floor.*

flipper *noun*

1. A **flipper** is the broad flat part at the side of an animal such as a seal or whale that is used for swimming. *Dolphins use their flippers to swim very fast.*

2. A **flipper** is one of a pair of pieces of rubber that you wear on your feet to help in swimming. *She swam faster than me because she was wearing flippers.*

float *verb*

If something **floats**, it rests or moves lightly on the top of a liquid. *The leaves were floating on the surface of the pool.*

flock *noun*

A **flock** is a group of animals, like birds or sheep.

flood /*say* flud/ *noun*

A **flood** is a great flow of water over land which is usually dry.

floor *noun*

1. The **floor** is the lowest flat part of a room. *Don't drop food on the floor! I've just swept it.*

2. You can use **floor** to mean the lowest part of some other places, such as the sea. *The ship sank to the ocean floor.*

3. A **floor** is one of the different levels of a building. *That office building has thirty floors.*

floppy disk *noun*

A **floppy disk** is a computer disk that is made of plastic and stores a certain amount of information. These are now less popular than other types of storage items such as USB drives, which can store much more information.

a b c d e f g h i j k l m n o p q r s t u v w x y z

flour *noun*
Flour is a fine powder made from wheat or other grain and used in cooking.

> ⭐ *Spelling Tip:* Don't confuse the spelling of **flour** with **flower** which has the same sound.

flow *verb*
1. If a liquid **flows**, it moves smoothly along in one direction. *The river flows out to the sea.*
2. If people or things **flow**, they move along continuously and smoothly. *Hundreds of people flowed into the football ground as soon as the gates were opened. | Thoughts flowed into her mind more quickly than she could write them down.*

flower *noun*
A **flower** is the part of many plants which contains the seed and which often has a bright colour and pleasant smell.

> ⭐ *Spelling Tip:* Don't confuse the spelling of **flower** with **flour.**

flu *noun*
Flu is a sickness that makes you feel sore in parts of your body, get hot, and feel as though you have a very bad cold.

> This word has been shortened from **influenza.**

fluff *noun*
Fluff is soft light bits that come from wool or cotton.

> *Word Building:* **fluffy**, *adjective* (**fluffier, fluffiest**) Something that is soft and light like a piece of fluff is **fluffy.**

fluoro /*say* **flooh**-roh/ *adjective*
If something is **fluoro**, it is an extremely bright colour. *If I could choose the colour for our school uniform, I would pick fluoro orange.*

> This is short for **fluorescent** /*say* flooh-**res**-ent/.

flute *noun*
A **flute** is a musical instrument that you play by blowing across a hole near the top.

flutter *verb*
If something **flutters**, it moves with small quick movements. *Watch the butterfly flutter by.*

fly[1] *verb* (**flies, flying, flew, has flown**)
1. If something **flies**, it moves through the air with the help of wings, the wind or some other force. *The bird flew from the fence to the top of the tree.*

2. If you **fly**, you travel in a plane. *My uncle flew to London yesterday.*

fly[2] *noun* (*plural* **flies**)
A **fly** is a small insect with two wings.

foal *noun*
A **foal** is a young horse.

foam *noun*
Foam is a lot of bubbles on top of water or some other liquid.

fog *noun*
Fog is a layer of wet air near the ground. It looks like a cloud and is difficult to see through.

> *Word Building:* **foggy**, *adjective* When there is a lot of fog, then it is **foggy.**

fold *verb*
If you **fold** something, you turn one part of it over another part. *You'll need to fold that letter to fit it in the envelope.*

folder *noun*
1. A **folder** is a cardboard cover for keeping your papers in. *I have a folder for Christmas present ideas.*
2. A computer **folder** is a space for storing files that are about the same thing. *On our computer at home we have football information for me in one folder and tennis information for my brother in another one.*

foliage /*say* **foh**-lee-ij/ *noun*
Foliage is the leaves of a plant.

follow *verb*
1. If you **follow** someone or something, you go after them. *I had a feeling that someone was following me.*
2. If you **follow** a road or something similar, you move along it. *We followed a track through the bush and at last we came to the river.*

fond *adjective*
If you are **fond** of someone or something, you like them a lot. *He is very fond of his grandfather. | My brother is fond of soccer.*

font *noun*
A **font** is a style of printing type. You can choose between different **fonts** when you use a computer.

food *noun*
Food is what people and animals eat to keep them alive.

food chain *noun*

The **food chain** is all plants and animals connected by the way in which they eat each other to survive. Something higher on the food chain eats something lower on the food chain.

foolish *adjective*

Someone is **foolish** if they are not sensible.

> **Word Building: fool**, *noun* Someone who does foolish things is a **fool**.

foot *noun* (*plural* **feet**)

1. Your **foot** is the part of your body at the end of your leg, which you use for standing and walking. *It is difficult to find shoes to fit my feet.*
2. A **foot** is a unit of length, equal to about 30 centimetres. It used to be used in Australia, and is still used in some countries such as America. *The Empire State Building in New York is 1250 feet high. It used to be the tallest building in the world.*

> **Word Building: footprint**, *noun* If your foot makes a mark somewhere, it is a **footprint**.

football *noun*

1. **Football** is a game played between two teams of players who try to get a ball into a certain area of the field (the goal). *Mario looks forward to playing football each weekend.*
2. A **football** is the ball used in these games. *We've lost our football so we can't play this afternoon.*

> **Word Building: footballer**, *noun* If someone plays football, they are a **footballer**.

> There are different types of football played in Australia, all with different rules. The main ones are **Australian Rules**, **Rugby League**, **Rugby Union** and **soccer**.

for *preposition*

You can use **for** in many ways. Its main meanings have to do with who uses something, or the purpose or reason for something. You also use it to show a connection or when you are talking about time or distance. Here are some examples. *This is a very good book for children. | She had a gift for me in her hand. | She has a deep love for her country. | The black horse is good for children to ride. | We went outside for a walk. | His reason for going was not clear. | We are really hoping for good weather. | We have lived here for a long time. | Could you wait for five minutes? | They walked through the bush for 20 kilometres.*

forbid *verb* (**forbids, forbidding, forbade, has forbidden**)

If you **forbid** someone to do something, you tell them that they are not allowed to do it. *I forbid you to tell anyone what you have just heard.*

force *noun*

1. **Force** is strength or power.
–*verb* 2. If you **force** someone to do something they do not want to do, you make them do it, often by using your strength, or by saying you will do something bad if they don't. *The man pointed the gun at them and forced them to give him their money.*
3. If you **force** something, you use your strength to get it to do something. *The door was locked but he forced it open.*

forecast /*say* **faw**-kahst/ *verb* (**forecasts, forecasting, forecast, has forecast**)

If you **forecast** something, you tell what might happen in the future. *Did they forecast that there will be rain tomorrow?*

forehead /*say* **fo**-ruhd/ *noun*

Your **forehead** is the top part of your face under the place where your hair starts.

foreign /*say* **fo**-ruhn/ *adjective*

Someone or something from a country other than your own is **foreign**. *She is foreign and so she might not understand our language. | Can you speak any foreign languages?*

> **Word Building: foreigner**, *noun* Someone who is foreign is a **foreigner**.

> ✴ *Spelling Tip:* Remember that the ending is spelt *eign* (not *in* or *en*). The *g* is silent.

forest *noun*

A **forest** is an area of land covered with trees.

> ✴ *Spelling Tip:* Remember that there is only one *r* in **forest**.

forever *adverb*

If something lasts **forever**, it keeps on going, without ending. *This road seems to go on forever.*

forge /*say* fawj/ *verb*

If you **forge** something, you make a copy of it and use it to trick someone. *Sally was in big trouble because she forged her mother's signature on a note.*

> **Word Building: forgery** /*say* **faw**-juh-ree/, *noun* Something that someone forges is a **forgery**.

forget *verb* (**forgets**, **forgetting**, **forgot**, **has forgotten**)
If you **forget** to do something or **forget** to bring something, you do not remember to do or take that thing. *I forgot to clean my teeth.* | *The barbecue started late because we had forgotten the sausages.*

Word Building: forgetful, *adjective* If you forget things a lot, you are **forgetful**.

forgive *verb* (**forgives**, **forgiving**, **forgave**, **has forgiven**)
If you **forgive** someone who has done something wrong, you stop feeling angry with them. *He will forgive you if you say you are sorry.*

fork *noun*
A **fork** is something with several long, thin pointed parts which you can use for lifting food when you are eating.

form *noun*
1. The **form** of something is its shape. *The teacher got us to make cards in the form of an 'M' for Mother's Day.* | *I could just make out her form in the distance.*
2. A **form** is a type or kind. *Soccer is my favourite form of sport.*
3. A **form** is a printed piece of paper with spaces you have to write in. *To be in the game, you need to fill in this form.*
—*verb* 4. If you **form** something, you make, build or produce it. *We formed a tennis club at school last year.* | *We used clay to form the shapes of our pets.*

formal *adjective*
If something is **formal**, it is not part of your usual or normal life. It has to do with a situation where everything has to be done in a special, proper way, such as an important event.

The opposite is **informal**.

format *noun*
The **format** of something is its shape, plan or style.

fort *noun*
A **fort** is a strong building which is used to protect soldiers or other people by being difficult for an enemy to get into.

fortnight /*say* **fawt**-nuyt/ *noun*
A **fortnight** is two weeks, or 14 days and nights.

Word Building: fortnightly, *adverb* If something happens every fortnight, it happens **fortnightly**.

fortunate /*say* **faw**-chuh-nuht/ *adjective*
If you are **fortunate**, you are lucky.

fortunately *adverb*
You use **fortunately** when you want to say that it is lucky that something has happened. *Fortunately, the bottle didn't break when I dropped it.*

fortune *noun*
1. A **fortune** is a very large amount of money. *My aunt is hoping to make a fortune in her new restaurant.*
2. If you have good **fortune**, you have good luck. *We had the good fortune to have fine weather for the picnic.*
3. Some people say that your **fortune** is what is going to happen to you in your life. *No-one really knows what their fortune is.*

forty *noun*, *adjective*
Forty is a number which you can write as 40.

Word Building: fortieth, *adjective*: *The fortieth person to get on the bus sat behind the driver.*

forwards *adverb*
If someone or something moves **forwards**, they move ahead, in the direction that is in front of them. *They pushed forwards, to the front of the crowd.*

You can also say **forward**.

fossil *noun*
A **fossil** is an animal or plant that lived long ago and which has become as hard as rock.

fossil fuel *noun*
Fossil fuel is fuel, such as coal and oil, made from what is left, deep within the earth, of plants and animals that lived long ago.

foul *adjective*
1. If something is **foul**, it is very dirty.
—*noun* 2. A **foul** in sport is something that breaks the rules or is not allowed in a game.

Spelling Tip: Don't confuse the spelling of **foul** with **fowl** which has the same sound but is spelt with a *w*. A **fowl** is a bird which is kept for eating, like a chicken.

found *verb*
Look up **find**.

foundations *noun*
Foundations are the base on which a building stands.

fountain /*say* **fown**-tuhn/ *noun*
A **fountain** is something which has been built, usually in a pool, making water shoot up or flow down. They are made because they look and sound attractive.

> ✽ *Spelling Tip:* Remember that the ending is spelt *ain* (although it sounds like 'uhn' or sometimes as if there is nothing between the *t* and the *n*). The word *mountain* has a similar pattern.

four *noun, adjective*
Four is a number which you can write as 4.

> *Word Building:* **fourth**, *adjective*: *This is the fourth time we have tried to climb the mountain.*

fourteen *noun, adjective*
Fourteen is a number which you can write as 14.

> *Word Building:* **fourteenth**, *adjective*: *She was the fourteenth person to arrive at the party.*

fowl *noun*
A **fowl** is a bird, especially one that people use for its meat or eggs.

> ✽ *Spelling Tip:* Don't confuse the spelling of **fowl** with **foul** which has the same sound but is spelt with a *u*. Something that is **foul** is very dirty.

fox *noun*
A **fox** is a small wild dog with red-brown fur, a long bushy tail and pointed ears. Foxes are found all over the world.

fraction *noun*
A **fraction** is a part of a whole number, such as $\frac{1}{2}$, $\frac{3}{4}$ and $\frac{5}{8}$.

fragile /*say* **fraj**-uyl/ *adjective*
If something is **fragile**, it is easily damaged or broken.

fragment *noun*
A **fragment** is a piece that has come off something.

frame *noun*
1. A **frame** is the part which goes around a picture or a pair of glasses. *This photo would look good in a silver frame.*
2. A **frame** is the part which holds something up and which gives it its shape. *When they started to build the house, they put up a wooden frame and then put bricks around it.*

fraud /*say* frawd/ *noun*
1. A **fraud** is a crime where people are tricked out of their money by people who are not acting honestly. *The bank manager was sent to jail for fraud after the bank discovered how he had changed the records in order to steal thousands of dollars.*
2. A **fraud** is someone who tries to trick you by pretending to be someone else. *I don't believe a word he says – I think he's a fraud.*

> ✽ *Spelling Tip:* The trick in **fraud** is to remember the *au* spelling (although it sounds like 'aw'). Think of some other words you know well which have the same spelling for this sound, such as *cause* and *sauce*.

freak *noun*
A **freak** is someone or something that is very strange or different from usual. *Everybody thought the new boy was a bit of a freak because he was always looking at books on insects.*

freckle *noun*
A **freckle** is a small brown spot on your skin.

free *adjective* (**freer**, **freest**)
1. Something is **free** if you do not have to pay any money for it. It costs nothing. *We were given free tickets to the new film.*
2. Someone or something is **free** if they are able to choose where to go and what to do. *The bird flew out of his hand and was free.*
3. Someone is **free** if they are not busy and have time to do something. *I'll be free in a minute – I'll help you then.*
4. Something is **free** if it is not being used. *The room is free now – you can start your meeting.*

freedom *noun*
If you have **freedom**, you are able to choose where to go and what to do. You can act and speak as you wish.

> ✽ *Spelling Tip:* The spelling of **freedom** will be easier if you see that it contains *free* and the word part *dom* (meaning 'general condition'). Think of other words with this ending such as *kingdom* and *wisdom*.

free-range *adjective*
1. If animals are **free-range**, they can walk around and feed freely, rather than being kept in a cage. *We only eat eggs from free-range chickens.*

2. If food is **free-range**, it is produced by free-range animals. *We asked the shopkeeper for free-range eggs.*

freeway *noun*
A **freeway** is a large road people use if they want to drive fast, without stopping for anything.

> Other names for a **freeway** are **motorway** and **expressway**.

freeze *verb* (**freezes, freezing, froze, has frozen**)
1. When a liquid **freezes**, it turns to ice. *In very cold places, the water can freeze in the pipes.*
2. If you say that you are **freezing**, you are feeling very cold. *'Are you warm enough without a fire?' 'No! I'm freezing!'*
3. If you **freeze** food, you put it in a place where the temperature is very low so that it becomes solid like ice. You do this so that you can keep the food for a longer time. *My mum buys meat once a fortnight and freezes it.*

> **Word Building: frozen**, *adjective* If you freeze something, it is **frozen**.

frequent /*say* **free**-kwuhnt/ *adjective*
Something is **frequent** if it happens often.

> ✴ **Spelling Tip:** Notice that the first part of **frequent** is spelt just *fre* (although it sounds like 'free'). The *qu* spelling in the middle gives a 'kw', as it does in many other words.

frequently /*say* **free**-kwuhnt-lee/ *adverb*
If something happens **frequently**, it happens often. *We frequently go shopping at the supermarket.*

fresh *adjective*
1. If food is **fresh**, it has not been frozen or put in a can. *In summer we eat fresh peaches, but in winter we eat peaches from tins.*
2. If food is **fresh**, it has only recently been picked or made, so it has not gone bad. *'Is that fruit fresh?' 'Yes. It was just picked from the tree this morning.'* | *We love eating warm, fresh bread.*
3. If something is **fresh**, it is new. *Use a fresh piece of paper for the test.*

Friday *noun*
Friday is a day of the week. It comes after Thursday and before Saturday.

fridge *noun*
Fridge is a short word for a refrigerator.

friend /*rhymes with* bend/ *noun*
A **friend** is someone you know well and like, and who likes you.

friendly *adjective* (**friendlier, friendliest**)
If someone is **friendly**, they behave in a pleasant, kind and interested way towards you.

friendship *noun*
A **friendship** is a relationship between friends.

fright /*say* fruyt/ *noun*
A **fright** is when you are suddenly frightened or get a shock.

frighten /*say* **fruy**-tuhn/ *verb*
If something or someone **frightens** you, you are afraid of them. *Please stop shouting – you're frightening me.*

> **Word Building: frightening**, *adjective* Something that frightens you is **frightening**. *I didn't like the film. It was too frightening.* –**frightened**, *adjective* When something or someone frightens you, you are **frightened**. *I could hear a strange noise outside and I was too frightened to come out of my bedroom.*

frill *noun*
A **frill** is a length of material gathered up and put on curtains or clothes to make them look pretty.

fringe *noun*
1. A **fringe** is loose threads hanging from the ends of clothing or some other kind of cloth. *The curtains on the stage were deep red with a gold fringe running along the bottom.*
2. If you have a **fringe**, your hair is cut so that it comes across the top part of your face. *Alison made a bit of a mess trying to cut her own fringe.*

frog *noun*
A **frog** is a small animal which lives in water or on land. It has smooth skin, long back legs for jumping and no tail.

from *preposition*
You can use **from** in many ways. Its main meanings have to do with where someone was before, or where something was made. You also use it when talking about direction or time, or the difference between things. Here are some examples. *Sarah is from Hong Kong.* | *I got the idea from my friend.* | *These shoes are from France.* | *The road runs west from the sea.* | *She jumped from the car and ran home as fast as she could.* | *From that moment on he knew she was his friend.* | *Can you tell black from white?*

front /rhymes with blunt/ noun
The **front** of something is the part or surface that faces forward or that you see most of the time.

frost noun
Frost is the tiny bits of ice that cover the ground on a very cold morning.

froth noun
Froth is the small bubbles which come to the top of water when it is shaken up, or which is on the top of some drinks.

> **Word Building: frothy**, adjective If a liquid has froth on top, then it's **frothy**.

frown verb
If you **frown**, lines come onto the top part of your face because you are cross or worried. Mum frowned when I told her I'd lost my jumper again.

fruit noun
Fruit is a type of food which is the part of a tree or other plant that contains a seed or seeds. **Fruit** is usually juicy, with a sweet taste.

fry verb (**fries**, **frying**, **fried**, **has fried**)
If you **fry** food, you cook it in a pan, usually using oil. We caught a fish and fried it in a pan over the fire.

> **Word Building: fried**, adjective Food you fry is **fried**.

fuel /say **fyooh**-uhl/ noun
Fuel is anything which is burnt to give heat or to make an engine work. This wood will be good fuel for the fire. | We had to stop and buy some fuel for the car.

full adjective
1. If a container is **full**, it has as much in it as it will hold. Don't put any more lemonade into the glass – it's already full.
2. If someone says that they are **full**, they mean that they have had enough to eat and cannot eat anything more. I can't eat those vegetables – I'm full.
3. If something is **full**, it is whole or complete. He has finally got a full set of the cards he has been collecting.

> The opposite of definition 1 is **empty**.

fun noun
1. If you have **fun**, you enjoy yourself. We had great fun at the party.
2. **make fun of**, If you **make fun of** someone, you make cruel jokes about them, making other people laugh at them. They all made fun of me when I fell down the stairs.

funeral /say **fyoohn**-ruhl/ noun
A **funeral** is a ceremony held before the body of a dead person is burnt or buried.

fungus /say **fung**-guhs/ noun (plural **fungi** /say **fung**-gee/ or **funguses**)
A **fungus** is a type of plant which does not grow from seeds and also does not have a green stem or green leaves. Mushrooms are one type of **fungus**.

> ✪ **Spelling Tip:** Remember that the ending is spelt us (not ous). **Fungus** comes from Latin (meaning 'mushroom'). The us ending is mainly found in words like this that have come straight from Latin.

funnel noun
1. A **funnel** is the part of a ship or a steam engine that takes smoke or steam from the engine to the outside. Thick smoke was coming out of the ship's funnel.
2. A **funnel** is an object that has a large round top leading down to a thin tube at its bottom which you use for pouring liquids into bottles or other small holes. She used a funnel to pour oil into the car engine.

> ✪ **Spelling Tip:** Remember that there is a double n in the middle and only one l at the end of **funnel**. However, when you add ed or ing, the l is doubled.

funny adjective (**funnier**, **funniest**)
1. If something is **funny**, it makes you laugh. We thought our dog looked so funny when he had to wear a bucket on his head.
2. If something is **funny**, it is strange. Seeing the old houses in our street being pulled down gave us all a funny feeling.

fun run noun
A **fun run** is a long running race, often used to raise money.

fur noun
Fur is the short soft hair of some animals, such as cats.

> **Word Building: furry**, adjective (**furrier**, **furriest**) An animal with fur is **furry**.

furious /say **fyooh**-ree-uhs/ adjective
If you are **furious**, you are very angry.

Word Building: **fury**, *noun* If you're furious, you are full of **fury**.

furniture /say **fer**-nich-uh/ *noun*
Furniture is the chairs, beds, tables and other things that you use in a room or house for sitting or lying on, or for putting things on.

⚡ *Spelling Tip:* Remember that **furniture** has nothing to do with ferns, and so the first part is spelt with *ur* (not *er*). Other things to remember are the *i* spelling for the middle sound and the *ture* ending (although it sounds like 'chuh'). Many other words end with this spelling and sound, such as *creature* and *picture*.

further *adverb*
1. If something goes **further**, it goes to a greater distance than something or someone else. *I ran further than you.*
–*adjective* **2.** You use **further** to mean 'more'.

❖ You can also say **farther** for definition 1.

❖ The word in definition 1 is part of the set **far, further, furthest**. Look up **far**.

⚡ *Spelling Tip:* Remember that the first part of **further** is spelt with *ur* (not *er*) – you can remind yourself that *u* is further along in the alphabet than *e*. However, *er* is used for the sound at the end of the word.

fuse *noun*
1. A **fuse** is the thread or tube containing material which will burn and that you light to set off something that explodes. *He lit the fuse of the firework and then ran for cover.*
2. A **fuse** is a bit of wire that melts and stops electricity from passing through it when something is wrong with your power. *Dad had to change the fuse after the storm.*

fuss *noun*
Fuss is too much worry and attention given to things that are not important.

Word Building: **fussy**, *adjective* Someone who makes a fuss about little things is **fussy**.

future /say **fyooh**-chuh/ *noun*
The **future** is the time which has not yet come.

Also look up **present**[1] and **past**.

fuzzy *adjective* (**fuzzier, fuzziest**)
1. If something is **fuzzy**, it is covered with a light, soft covering. *The new baby had a little red face and short, fuzzy brown hair on its head.*
2. Something is **fuzzy** if you cannot see or hear it clearly. *I can't tell if that person is me because the photo is too fuzzy.* | *It was an old video and the sound was fuzzy so we couldn't hear what they were saying.*

Word Building: **fuzziness**, *noun* If something is fuzzy, then it has a lot of **fuzziness**.

give

gadget /say **gaj**-uht/ noun
A **gadget** is a small tool or machine that you use to do a particular job.

gag verb (**gags**, **gagging**, **gagged**, **has gagged**)
If you **gag** someone, you cover their mouth to stop them from speaking or from making any noise. *They gagged the poor woman with her own scarf.*

gaily adverb
If you do something **gaily**, you do it in a way that shows you are happy and not worried. *We could hear her singing gaily while she had a shower.*

gain verb
If you **gain** something, you get or win it. *We gained an extra player when Anika joined our team. | The student who gained first prize would be given a trip.*

galah /say guh-**lah**/ noun
A **galah** is an Australian parrot with pink and grey feathers.

This word comes from an Aboriginal language of New South Wales called Yuwaalaraay.

gale noun
A **gale** is a very strong wind.

gallery noun (plural **galleries**)
A **gallery** is a room or a building where you can go to see paintings and other types of art.

⚙ **Spelling Tip:** Remember the double *l* in the middle. Also remember that the ending is spelt *ery* (not *ary*).

gallop verb
If a horse **gallops**, it is moving as fast as it can go. *The wild horses galloped through the valley trying to escape the fire.*

gamble verb
If someone **gambles**, they play a game or take a risk in the hope of winning some money. *He lost a lot of his family's money because he couldn't stop gambling.*

Word Building: **gambler**, noun A person who gambles is a **gambler**. –**gambling**, noun A person who gambles does a lot of **gambling**.

game noun
A **game** is something you play, usually according to rules.

gander noun
A **gander** is a male goose.

The female is a **goose**.

gang noun
A **gang** is a group of people who do things together.

gaol /say jayl/ noun
Look up **jail**.

garage noun
1. A **garage** is a building or part of a house for keeping a car. *People keep all sorts of things in their garages.*
2. A **garage** is a place where petrol is sold and sometimes cars and trucks are repaired. *Mum drove to the garage to buy some petrol.*

You can also say **petrol station** or **service station** for definition 2.

garbage noun
Garbage is the rubbish that people throw away.

garden noun
1. A **garden** is an area of ground where particular types of plants like flowers or vegetables are grown. *My grandmother has a rose garden behind her house.*
2. A **garden** is an area, usually with trees and plants, where you can play or sit. *Let's play cricket in the garden.*

Word Building: **gardener**, noun Someone who works in a garden is a **gardener**.

⚙ **Spelling Tip:** When you are spelling **gardener**, remember that it is made up of *garden* with the word part *er* added. This will help you to remember the *e* before the *ner*, although you often don't hear this sound when people say this word.

garlic *noun*
Garlic is a plant with a white bulb that you use in cooking to give food a strong taste.

garment *noun*
A **garment** is any of the clothes you wear, such as a dress or a shirt.

gas *noun* (*plural* **gases**)
1. A **gas** is anything like air that is able to fill up whatever space it is in. *What sort of gas is in the hot air balloons that people can ride in?*
2. A **gas** is the fuel which is like air, that we get from burning coal or that we find under the ground. *Turn on the gas and I'll heat the water.*

Think about how a **gas** is different from a **liquid** and a **solid**.

gate *noun*
A **gate** is a kind of door, often made of wood or metal, in an outside wall or fence.

gather *verb*
1. If you **gather** things or people, you bring them together. *After the carnival, we gathered our things and got on the bus.*
2. If people **gather**, they come together. *A crowd gathered to see the fire.*

Word Building: **gathering**, *noun* When people gather, they form a **gathering**. *There was a big gathering in the hall.*

gaze *verb*
If you **gaze** at someone or something, you look at them for a long time without taking your eyes from them. *They sat gazing at the fire until it burnt down.*

gear *noun*
1. A **gear** is a part of a machine such as a car or a bicycle. You use the gears to make it easier to keep the wheels going at the speed you want. *Mum put the car into a very low gear going down the mountain so that it didn't go too fast.*
2. Gear is all the special things you need for something. *Have you got your bats, balls and all the rest of the gear you need for the game?*

gelato /*say* juh-**lah**-toh/ *noun* (*plural* **gelatos** *or* **gelati** /*say* juh-**lah**-tee/)
Gelato is a kind of ice-cream.

gem *noun*
A **gem** is a beautiful stone you use to make jewellery.

gene /*say* jeen/ *noun*
Your **genes** are the units in your body by which certain things about the way you look and the way your body works have been passed on to you from your parents, for example, the colour of the eyes, hair, and so on.

Word Building: **genetic** /*say* juh-**net**-ik/, *adjective* Something that has to do with genes is **genetic**.

general *adjective*
1. If something is **general**, it affects most people. *The teacher said she hoped there was a general understanding about the rules of the road.*
2. If something is **general**, it is not special or particular. *She began with a general talk about animals and then moved on to talk about her favourite one, the koala.*
–*noun* **3.** A **general** is an important army officer.

generally *adverb*
You use **generally** when you are talking about what is true most of the time or what most people do. *People are generally taller now than 100 years ago.*

generation /*say* jen-uh-**ray**-shuhn/ *noun*
A **generation** is all of the people born at a similar time.

generous /*say* **jen**-uh-ruhs/ *adjective*
If you are **generous**, you are ready to give what you have to other people.

Word Building: **generosity** /*say* jen-uh-**ros**-uh-tee/, *noun* A generous person is full of **generosity**.

genius /*say* **jee**-nee-uhs/ *noun* (*plural* **geniuses**)
A **genius** is an extremely clever person. *I wish I was a genius in maths so I could do my homework quickly.*

gentle *adjective*
1. If someone is **gentle**, they are calm and kind. They are not rough in the way they treat people or animals. *He was very gentle with the old horse.*
2. Something is **gentle** if it is not rough, but pleasant and calm. *A gentle wind blew through the window. | I felt her gentle touch on my shoulder.*

Word Building: **gently**, *adverb*: *He touched her gently on the shoulder. | The boat rocked gently on the water.*

gentleman *noun* (*plural* **gentlemen**)
You use **gentleman** when you are talking politely about a man.

genuine /*say* **jen**-yooh-uhn/ *adjective*
If something is **genuine**, it is real or true. *Can you tell the difference between a fake diamond and a genuine one?* | *I knew her story was genuine.*

> ✴ *Spelling Tip:* Don't forget the *e* at the end of **genuine**. Think of other words which have an *ine* spelling for an ending that sounds like 'uhn', such as *engine* and *imagine*.

geography /*say* jee-**og**-ruh-fee/ *noun*
If you study **geography**, you learn about the earth, including such things as mountains and seas, different countries, the weather, soil and plants, and how people live with and use these things.

geometry /*say* jee-**om**-uh-tree/ *noun*
Geometry is the part of maths that has to do with shapes and lines.

germ /*say* jerm/ *noun*
A **germ** is a very small living thing that can make you sick. *If you really want to see germs, you will have to look through a microscope.*

get *verb* (**gets**, **getting**, **got**, **has got**)
1. If you **get** something, you go and collect it, or buy it, or someone gives it to you. *Could you please run over to your house and get the book we need?* | *I got a new pair of jeans yesterday.*
2. If you **get** what someone has said, you hear or understand them. *'Did you get that?' 'No. Could you repeat it please?'*
3. If you **get** to a place, you reach it. *We should get to Queensland tomorrow.*
4. If you **get** something done, you cause it to happen. *I must get the car fixed.*
5. If you **get** a certain way, you become or grow like that. *I am getting tired.* | *She got angry when the children ran away.*

ghost /*say* gohst/ *noun*
A **ghost** is the spirit of a dead person, that some people think comes back to earth and can be seen.

> *Word Building:* **ghostly**, *adjective*: *We were frightened by the ghostly shapes of the dead trees.*

> ✴ *Spelling Tip:* Don't forget that a ghostly *h* has slipped silently in after the *g* in **ghost**.

giant /*say* **juy**-uhnt/ *noun*
1. A **giant** is someone in stories who looks like a man but who is much bigger and stronger.
–*adjective* **2.** Something that is **giant** is very, very large.

> *Word Building:* **gigantic** /*say* juy-**gan**-tik/, *adjective* If you're a giant, you're **gigantic** in size.

gift *noun*
A **gift** is something you give to someone, usually for a special reason.

giggle *verb*
If you **giggle**, you laugh in a silly way. *I made faces at my friend and he started to giggle.*

> *Word Building:* **giggly**, *adjective* If you giggle a lot, you're **giggly**.

gill *noun*
A **gill** is the part of the body that fish and other sea animals use for breathing.

ginger *noun*
1. **Ginger** is the root of a plant, which you use in some kinds of cooking to give flavour to food.
–*adjective* **2.** Something that is **ginger** is red-brown in colour.

giraffe /*say* juh-**rahf**/ *noun*
A **giraffe** is an extremely tall African animal with spots on its body, a very long neck and long legs.

> ✴ *Spelling Tip:* If you remember the sentence 'Giraffes indeed reach all fresh food easily' and put the first letter of each word together you have **giraffe** with its one *r* and two *f*'s.

girl *noun*
A **girl** is a female child or a young woman.

give *verb* (**gives**, **giving**, **gave**, **has given**)
1. If you **give** something you own or have bought to someone, you hand it over to them, so that they now own it. *My parents are going to give me a cricket bat if I do well in the test.*
2. If you **give** something to someone, you place it in their hands. *Could you give me that book, please?*
3. give up, If you **give up** something , you stop doing it. *My mum is trying to give up drinking coffee.*

given name *noun*
the name that you have been given, separate from your surname.

> You can also say **Christian name**.

glacier /say **glay**-see-uh/ noun

A **glacier** is a large mass of ice which has formed from snow over many years and which moves slowly, sometimes like a frozen river, down from high mountains.

glad adjective (**gladder**, **gladdest**)

If you are **glad**, you are happy about something.

> **Word Building: gladly**, adverb If you are glad, you do things **gladly**. –**gladness**, noun If you are glad, you are full of **gladness**.

glance verb

If you **glance** at something or someone, you look quickly at them. *Billy glanced at the referee to see if he had noticed what had happened.*

glass noun

1. **Glass** is a hard material that you can see through, and that breaks quite easily. It is used for such things as windows and bottles. *Vijay cut himself on a piece of broken glass.*
2. A **glass** is a container that you drink from, made of glass. *Pass me two glasses, please.*

glasses noun

Glasses are something you wear over your eyes to help you see more clearly. They are specially made for you from two pieces of curved glass held in place by wire or plastic that fits over your nose and goes behind your ears.

gleam verb

If something **gleams**, it shines with a soft light. *Dad polished our car until it gleamed.*

glide verb

If something **glides**, it moves along smoothly. *See how the swans glide through the water.*

glider noun

1. A **glider** is a plane without an engine that flies by using wind and currents of air. *We watched the glider from the beach.*
2. A **glider** is a possum with thick skin stretched between its front and back legs to help it fly smoothly through the air. *We are hoping to see gliders in the bush at night.*

glisten /say **glis**-uhn/ verb

If something **glistens**, it shines with the soft light that you see on water. *Tears glistened on her cheeks.*

> ✸ **Spelling Tip:** Don't forget the *st* (not double *s*) spelling. The *t* is silent.

glitter verb

If something **glitters**, it shines with bright sharp points of light that seem to move. *We looked down from the plane and could see the lights of the city glittering in the dark below.*

global warming noun

Global warming is a rise in the earth's temperature that is so great that it can have a bad effect on the environment. Many people think that this is caused by there being too many greenhouse gases let out into the earth's atmosphere by things humans do, such as using petrol to drive cars and using coal and oil to make electricity.

> Also look up **greenhouse effect**.

globe noun

1. A **globe** is a ball-shaped object with a map of the world on it. *Can you point to where France is on the globe?*
2. The **globe** is the whole world. *They have travelled to most parts of the globe.*

> **Word Building: global**, adjective If something has to do with the whole world, it is **global**. *The internet has made global communication a lot easier.*

glory noun

Glory is the admiration of other people.

> **Word Building: glorious**, adjective If something gives you glory, it is **glorious**.

glove noun

A **glove** is a covering for your hand with a separate part for each finger.

glow verb

If something **glows**, it gives out light and heat without any flame. *I blew on the ashes and they began to glow.*

glue noun

Glue is a sticky substance which sets hard, which you use to stick things together.

gnome /say nohm/ noun

A **gnome** is a little old person in some stories. They are not real.

> ✸ **Spelling Tip:** Don't forget the silent *g* at the start of this word.

go verb (**goes**, **going**, **went**, **has gone**)

1. If you **go**, you leave or move away from somewhere. *Where are you going?*
2. If you **go** somewhere, you move yourself towards that place. *It's time to go home.*

3. If something **goes**, it works properly. *'What's wrong?' 'The car won't go!'*
4. If someone or something **goes** a certain way, they get to be like that. *She went red with anger.*
5. If something like a road **goes** somewhere, it reaches that place. *That road goes to the river.*
6. If something **goes** somewhere, it belongs or has a place there. *Where do the plates go?*
7. You can use **go** to talk about doing something, such as a sport. *We go fishing and swimming in summer, and we go skiing in winter.*

goal /*say* gohl/ *noun*
1. A **goal** is an area, basket or something similar at which you aim the ball in sports such as football. You get points when you succeed. *Dad put a netball ring up on a tree for a goal so that we could practise.*
2. A **goal** is something you aim towards. *Our goal is to cover all the classroom walls with paintings for our parents to see.*

goanna /*say* goh-**an**-uh/ *noun*
A **goanna** is a large Australian lizard.

goat *noun*
A **goat** is an animal which is able to live in rocky mountain areas and is used as a farm animal all over the world.

gobble *verb*
If you **gobble** your food, you eat it quickly in large bits. *The dog was gobbling up the food as fast as I was giving it to him.*

goblin *noun*
A **goblin** is a small, ugly man in some stories who makes bad things happen to people. They are not real.

god *noun*
1. A **god** is a spirit, sometimes thought to be like a person, who is believed to have power to control what happens to people or nature. *Some people believe in many gods, and others believe in just one.*
2. **God**, For people who believe in only one god, **God** is the one who makes and rules the world. *'I will ask God for help',* she said.

goddess *noun*
A **goddess** is a female person or thing that is worshipped. *Athena was the Greek goddess of war and so you often see her in pictures with a bow and arrow.*

goggles *noun*
Goggles are special glasses with pieces at the side. You use them to keep wind, dust, water or bright light out of your eyes. *I have to wear goggles when I swim at the pool because the water hurts my eyes.*

gold *noun*
Gold is a very valuable yellow metal.

golden *adjective*
1. If something is **golden**, it is made of gold. *She wears a lot of golden jewellery.*
2. If something is **golden**, it is the colour of gold. *The leaves of some trees turn golden in autumn.*

good *adjective* (**better**, **best**)
1. If something is **good**, it is of a high standard. *We've just seen a very good film.*
2. If someone is **good**, they behave kindly towards other people, and try to help them. *She is a really good woman – she doesn't deserve such bad luck.*
3. If a child is being **good**, they are behaving well. *The teacher told us that we had been very good during the long concert.*
4. If something is **good**, it is enjoyable or pleasant. *Did you have a good holiday?*

Word Building: **goodness**, *noun* If you are good, you are full of **goodness**.

goodbye *interjection*
Goodbye is a word you use when you are leaving someone, or they are leaving you. *Goodbye. I'll see you tomorrow.*

goods *noun*
1. **Goods** are things you can buy. *The shops along this street sell very expensive goods.*
2. Your **goods** are the things you own. *We have to lock up all our goods when we go away.*

goose *noun* (*plural* **geese**)
A **goose** is a large bird with a long neck and feet that are good for swimming. They are kept for their meat and their feathers.

The male of this bird is a **gander**. A young one is a **gosling**.

gorilla *noun*
A **gorilla** is the largest kind of ape.

⚙ *Spelling Tip:* This word has only one *r* but a double *l*. Think of 'an ill gorilla' to remind yourself of the double *l*.

gossip *noun*
Gossip is silly talk about other people that is not kind.

government *noun*

A **government** is the group of people who rule a country or state.

> *Word Building:* **govern**, *verb* When a government rules a country, they **govern** it.

governor *noun*

A **governor** is someone who represents the Queen in one of the states of Australia.

> The person who is the actual leader of the government in a state of Australia is the **premier**.

> ✸ *Spelling Tip:* The difficulty with this word is remembering the *or* ending. There are two common word parts that are used to show that someone does something – *er* and *or*. In **governor**, it is the *or* ending that has been added to the word *govern* which means 'to rule'.

gown *noun*

A **gown** is a flowing dress or kind of coat someone wears to a special place or at an important time. *She wore a bright pink gown to the end-of-school dance.* | *The judge wore a wig and gown at the trial.*

grab *verb* (**grabs**, **grabbing**, **grabbed**, **has grabbed**)

If you **grab** someone or something, you take hold of them suddenly. *Sali grabbed her mother's hand in fear when the loud noise started.*

grade *noun*

A **grade** is a division of a school, made up of a class or group of classes for students of about the same age.

gradual *adjective*

Something is **gradual** if it happens a little bit at a time. *The weather report said that the early part of the day would be sunny but there would be a gradual change.*

gradually *adverb*

If you do something **gradually**, you do it little by little. *At swimming lessons, all the kids who are scared gradually get used to jumping into the water.*

graduate /*say* **graj**-ooh-ayt/ *verb*

If you **graduate** from a university, you succeed in completing your studies there. *After my aunt graduated in nursing, she got a job in a hospital.*

graduation *noun*

Your **graduation** is when you have completed your studies at university and you are given papers at a special ceremony to say that you have been successful.

grain *noun*

1. A **grain** is a small, hard seed of a plant like rice or wheat, which is used for making food. *The farmer was packing up bags of grain.*
2. A **grain** is any small, hard bit of something. *My eye is sore. I think I have a grain of sand in it.*

gram *noun*

A **gram** is a very small measure of what something weighs. There are 1000 grams in a kilogram.

> The short way of writing this is **g**.

grammar *noun*

Grammar is the way the words in a language go together to form larger units like sentences.

> *Word Building:* **grammatical**, *adjective* If something has to do with grammar, it is **grammatical**.

> ✸ *Spelling Tip:* There is a double *m* in this word but the part most people get wrong is the *ar* (not *er*) ending. Remember you have to put an *a* from the <u>a</u>lphabet into **grammar** and you will get it right.

grand *adjective*

Something is **grand** if it is large and looks important.

grandchild *noun* (*plural* **grandchildren**)

Someone's **grandchild** is the child of that person's son or daughter.

granddaughter /*say* **gran**-daw-tuh/ *noun*

Someone's **granddaughter** is the daughter of that person's son or daughter.

grandfather *noun*

Your **grandfather** is the father of your mother or father.

grandmother *noun*

Your **grandmother** is the mother of your father or mother.

grandparent *noun*

Your **grandparents** are the mother and father of either your mother or your father.

grandson *noun*

Someone's **grandson** is the son of that person's daughter or son.

grape *noun*

A **grape** is a small, round, green or purple fruit which is used for eating or making wine.

graph /say graf, grahf/ noun
A **graph** is a picture which shows different measurements.

grass noun
Grass is a plant with thin, green leaves, growing close to the ground, and often cut short.

grasshopper noun
A **grasshopper** is an insect which has large back legs for jumping and which eats plants.

grateful noun
You are **grateful** if you feel like thanking someone for something they have done.

grave[1] noun
A **grave** is a hole in the earth where a dead person is buried.

grave[2] adjective
1. You look **grave** when you are thinking serious thoughts and you do not feel like joking. *Dad looked very grave and we wondered if we were in trouble.*
2. If a situation is **grave**, it is very serious or full of danger. *Patrick's condition is grave and he may die.*

gravel /say **grav**-uhl/ noun
Gravel is small stones, sometimes mixed with sand.

gravity /say **grav**-uh-tee/ noun
Gravity is the strong force that pulls things or that makes them fall towards the earth.

gravy /say **gray**-vee/ noun
Gravy is a hot, brown sauce you make to pour over meat before you eat it.

graze[1] verb
If an animal **grazes**, it eats grass that is growing. *We'll move the cows over to the other paddock to graze because there is more grass there.*

graze[2] verb
If you **graze** yourself, you rub or scratch the skin from part of your body. *I grazed my knee when I fell over running down the track.*

grazier /say **gray**-zee-uh/ noun
A **grazier** is a farmer with lots of land for keeping cattle or sheep.

grease noun
Grease is thick sticky oil.

great adjective
1. Something is **great** if it is large. *A great crowd of people were at the airport to see the film star arrive.*
2. If someone is **great**, they are known for having done something important in their special field. *He was one of the great artists of the 20th century.*

greedy adjective (**greedier**, **greediest**)
Someone who is **greedy** has a strong wish to have more things like money and food than is fair.

Word Building: **greed**, noun People who are greedy are full of **greed**. –**greediness**, noun People who are greedy show **greediness**.

green adjective
Something is **green** if it is the colour of growing grass.

greenhouse noun
A **greenhouse** is a glass house which gets very warm inside, used for growing plants that like warm weather.

greenhouse effect noun
The **greenhouse effect** is a condition when the weather gets hotter around the world because the air surrounding the earth keeps in the heat from the sun, in the same way that the glass of a greenhouse does.

greet verb
If you **greet** someone, you welcome them, usually with friendly words. *If you had to greet the prime minister you would have to be very polite.*

Word Building: **greeting**, noun When you greet someone, you give them a **greeting**.

grey adjective
Something is **grey** if it is a colour between black and white.

grief /say greef/ noun
Grief is the sad feeling you have when someone you love dies.

Word Building: **grieve** /say greev/, verb If you feel grief, then you **grieve**.

Spelling Tip: Remember that the letters *ie* spell the 'ee' sound. This follows the rule that *i* comes before *e* except after *c*.

grill verb
If you **grill** food, you cook it by putting it on top of a pan that you slide under heat. *Mum grilled some sausages for our dinner.*

grin verb (**grins**, **grinning**, **grinned**, **has grinned**)
If you **grin**, you give a big smile. *Jack grinned when he saw what the dog had brought home.*

grind *verb* (**grinds**, **grinding**, **ground**, **has ground**)
If you **grind** something, you crush it into a powder. *These machines grind the wheat to make flour.*

grip *verb* (**grips**, **gripping**, **gripped**, **has gripped**)
If you **grip** something, you hold it tightly. *Grip my hand – I won't let you fall.*

groan *noun*
1. A **groan** is the low, sad sound you make if you are in pain or if you feel very sad.
–*verb* **2.** If you **groan**, you make this kind of sound. *The sick man groaned all night.*

grocer *noun*
A **grocer** is a person who sells food, drinks and other things for the house.

> *Word Building:* **grocery**, *noun* A grocer works in a **grocery**. –**groceries**, *noun* Things that you buy from a grocer are called **groceries**.

grommet /*say* **grom**-uht/ *noun*
A **grommet** is a small tube put into a person's ear by a doctor to help carry away the material that makes their ear feel bad.

groom *noun*
1. A **groom** is someone who looks after horses. *The groom was rubbing down the horse's coat.*
2. Look up **bridegroom**.

groove *noun*
A **groove** is a long, narrow cut you make with a tool.

ground *noun*
1. The **ground** is the solid surface of the earth. It is dry land. *He fell to the ground with a cry of pain.*
2. A **ground** is a piece of land used for a special purpose. *There was a long line of people waiting to get into the football ground.*
–*adjective* **3. ground floor**, The **ground floor** of a building is the level that you walk into from the street.

group *noun*
A **group** is a number of people or things gathered together or connected in some way.

grow *verb* (**grows**, **growing**, **grew**, **has grown**)
1. If something **grows**, it increases in size or amount. *The pile continued to grow as we added more wood. | The more we saw stick insects, the more our interest in them grew.*
2. If you **grow** a plant, you put it in the ground and look after it so that it gets bigger. *Uncle Joe grows vegetables in the garden behind his house.*

3. If you **grow** to be a certain way, you get to be like that. *We are all growing older.*

> *Word Building:* **growth**, *noun* Something that grows has **growth**.

growl *verb*
If something or someone **growls**, they make a deep, angry sound. *When the dog saw me it started to growl.*

grub *noun*
A **grub** is a small creature, like a worm, that will turn into an insect.

grumble *verb*
If you **grumble**, you keep on saying in an annoyed way that you are not happy about something. *My brother always grumbles about having to eat his pumpkin.*

grunt *verb*
If an animal or person **grunts**, they make a short, rough sound like a pig. *Instead of answering my question, he just grunted and went on reading the paper.*

guard /*say* gahd/ *verb*
If you **guard** someone or something, you protect them or keep them safe from being attacked or hurt. *Our dog guards our house even though he is little.*

> ✸ *Spelling Tip:* Don't forget the silent *u* after the *g*.

guess /*say* ges/ *verb*
If you **guess**, you try to give an answer but you are not sure that it is right. *We had to guess what the teacher was holding behind her back.*

guest /*say* gest/ *noun*
A **guest** is someone you invite to visit you.

guide /*say* guyd/ *verb*
1. If someone or something **guides** you, they show you the way. *She guided the old man to the bus stop.*
–*noun* **2.** A **guide** is someone who helps you find your way, especially someone employed to show travellers and visitors around a place. *Aunt Helen had a job in the holidays as a guide in the mountains.*
3. A **Guide** is a member of a club for girls that organises interesting activities. *The Guides were in the bush putting up tents.*

> *Word Building:* **guidance**, *noun* If you guide someone, you give them **guidance**.

guilty /say **gil**-tee/ adjective (**guiltier**, **guiltiest**)
1. You are **guilty** if you have done something that is wrong. *The police thought he was probably guilty because he was seen near the house at the time of the robbery.*
2. If you feel **guilty**, you feel bad because of doing something that you know was wrong. *James felt so guilty about hiding his sister's pet mice that he put them back in their cage again.*

> **Word Building: guilt**, *noun* If you feel bad because you know you are guilty of something, you feel **guilt**.

> ✽ **Spelling Tip:** Don't forget the silent *u* after the *g*.

guinea pig /say **gin**-ee pig/ noun
A **guinea pig** is a small animal with short fur, short ears, and short legs.

guitar /say guh-**tah**/ noun
A **guitar** is something you can play music on. It has strings that you move your fingers across.

> **Word Building: guitarist**, *noun* Someone who plays a guitar is a **guitarist**.

> ✽ **Spelling Tip:** Don't forget the silent *u* after the *g*.

gully noun (plural **gullies**)
A **gully** is a low area of land dug out by water running through it.

gulp verb
If you **gulp** something, you swallow it quickly. *Rakesh gulped down his meal as fast as he could so he could get to cricket training on time.*

gum[1] noun
Gum is a sticky substance.

gum[2] noun
Your **gum** is the part of your mouth that your teeth grow out of.

gum tree noun
A **gum tree** is an Australian tree that makes a thick, sticky liquid which you can sometimes see on its trunk.

Another name for this tree is **eucalypt**.

gun noun
A **gun** is something used for killing and hurting people and animals. It shoots out small metal balls at high speed.

gutter noun
1. A **gutter** is the part along the side of the road that carries away water. *Don't step in the gutter – it's full of dirty water.*
2. A **gutter** is a long, open pipe along the edge of your roof that carries away water from rain. *There was too much water for our gutters and it was pouring off the roof.*

gym /say jim/ noun
A **gym** is a room or building where you do exercises to make your body to be strong and healthy.

> ✽ **Spelling Tip:** Remember that this word has nothing to do with the boy's name Jim! It is spelt *gym* because it comes from Greek. *Gym* is short for *gymnasium* which comes from the Greek word for 'naked' (in ancient times, athletes were naked when they trained). *Gym* can also be short for the following word *gymnastics*.

gymnastics /say jim-**nas**-tiks/ noun
Gymnastics is a sport in which you do difficult exercises that need your body to be strong and to move and bend easily.

> **Word Building: gymnast** /say **jim**-nuhst/, *noun* Someone who is very good at doing gymnastics is called a **gymnast**.

> ✽ **Spelling Tip:** Look up **gym**.

gypsy /say **jip**-see/ noun (plural **gypsies**)
A **gypsy** is one of a group of people who travel about from place to place and who often live in caravans.

You can also spell this **gipsy**.

hair

habit *noun*

A **habit** is your particular and usual way of behaving. Your **habits** are things you do often without thinking and which you do in your own special way.

habitat /*say* **hab**-uh-tat/ *noun*

The **habitat** of a plant or animal is the place where it naturally lives or grows.

hack *verb*

1. To **hack** into something is to cut or chop it with rough, heavy blows.
2. **hack into**, If you **hack into** a computer, you secretly access the information on it without having permission.

> *Word Building:* **hacker**, *noun* Someone who hacks into computers is a **hacker**.

hail *noun*

Hail is balls of ice that fall from the clouds like frozen rain.

hair *noun*

1. **Hair** is what grows on your head and on the body of animals. *Makiko has beautiful hair.*
2. A **hair** is a single piece of hair, long and fine. *She's got a few grey hairs now that she is getting older.*

> *Word Building:* **hairy**, *adjective* If someone or something is covered with a lot of hair, they are **hairy**.

> ✳ *Spelling Tip:* Don't confuse the spelling of **hair** with **hare** which has the same sound. A **hare** is an animal like a rabbit.

haircut *noun*

If you have a **haircut**, someone cuts your hair to make it tidy or look good.

hairdresser *noun*

A **hairdresser** is someone whose job it is to wash hair, cut it, and sometimes arrange it in a special way.

half /*say* hahf/ *noun* (*plural* **halves**)

A **half** of something is one of two equal parts into which it has been divided.

> ✳ *Spelling Tip:* Don't forget the *l*. The *alf* spelling gives the 'ahf' sound.

hall *noun*

1. A **hall** is a large building or room where a lot of people can meet. *All the parents came to a meeting in the school hall.*
2. A **hall** is a passage inside the front door of a house, from which you can get to the other rooms. *To get to the living room, go down the hall and through the second door on the left.*

Halloween /*say* hal-uh-**ween**/ *noun*

Halloween is the night of 31 October, when children dress up and ask people for sweets. If they don't get them, then they play a trick.

halo /*say* **hay**-loh/ *noun* (*plural* **haloes**)

A **halo** is a circle of light which shines around something.

halt *verb*

If someone or something **halts**, they stop. *The teacher told all of us to halt when we we got to the corner.*

ham *noun*

Ham is a kind of meat that comes from a pig, usually eaten cold.

hamburger *noun*

Look up **burger**.

hammer *noun*

A **hammer** is a tool made of a wooden handle with a heavy metal part at the end. It is used for hitting nails into wood.

hammock *noun*

A **hammock** is a hanging bed made from strong cloth or net.

hand *noun*

1. Your **hand** is the part of your body at the end of each of your arms, used for touching and holding things.
–verb **2.** If you **hand** something to someone, you give it to them with your hand. *Hand me a pen, please.*

handbag *noun*

A **handbag** is a small bag, held in the hand or worn hanging from the shoulder, which is used for carrying money, keys and other things.

handkerchief /*say* **hang**-kuh-cheef/ *noun*

A **handkerchief** is a small piece of cloth that you use to blow your nose.

You often say **hanky** for short.

⚡ *Spelling Tip:* Don't forget the *d* after the *n*. It will help if you see that **handkerchief** contains the word *hand*. The other part is *kerchief* (an old word meaning 'a cloth worn or carried on your body'), so the meaning of the whole word is 'a cloth that you carry in your hand'.

handle *noun*

A **handle** is a part which is put onto something to hold it with or to open it with.

handlebars *noun*

The **handlebars** on your bike are the metal bar with rubber-covered ends which you hold to guide a bike.

handsome /*say* **han**-suhm/ *adjective*

If a man is **handsome**, he is good to look at.

⚡ *Spelling Tip:* Don't forget the *d* after the *n*. Also remember that the ending is spelt *some* (although it sounds like 'suhm'). The original meaning of the word was 'easy to handle' and it was formed by putting *hand* and *some* together.

hang *verb* (**hangs, hanging, hung, has hung**)

1. If you **hang** something, you fix it at the top but not at the bottom. *Mum hung a rope from a high tree in our yard so she could make us a swing.*
2. If something **hangs**, it is fixed at the top and not at the bottom. *The rope is very safe – it is hanging from a strong branch.*

happen *verb*

If there is an event of any kind, you say that it **happens**. It takes place or exists. *Where did the accident happen?*

Word Building: **happening**, *noun* Something that happens is a **happening**. *There was a strange happening at school today.*

happy *adjective* (**happier, happiest**)

If you are **happy**, you have a good feeling of being pleased. You feel like smiling or laughing.

Word Building: **happily**, *adverb* If you do something in a happy way, you do it **happily**. *–***happiness**, *noun* If you are happy, you have a feeling of **happiness**.

The opposite is **unhappy** or **sad**.

harbour *noun*

A **harbour** is a part of the sea near the coast where the water is deep and calm and ships are safe from the wind and from big waves.

Another spelling for this word is **harbor**.

hard[1] *adjective*

If something is **hard**, it does not change shape when you push it or press it. It is solid and firm when you touch it.

Word Building: **harden**, *verb* If you make something hard, then you **harden** it. If it gets hard, it **hardens**.

The opposite is **soft**.

hard[2] *adjective*

1. If something is **hard**, you have to make a lot of effort to do or understand it. *Walking to the top of the hill was hard but we got there.* | *This maths is very hard.*
–adverb **2.** If you work **hard** or try **hard**, you do as much as you can, with a lot of effort. *He has done well because he has worked hard all through the year.*

The opposite of definition 1 is **easy**.

hard disk *noun*

A **hard disk** is a computer disk that is built into the computer and is not easily removed. *You have to keep your hard disk organised so that you know where to find your files.*

hardly *adverb*

If you can **hardly** do something, you can almost not do it at all. You can only just do it. *The smoke was so thick, we could hardly see.*

a
b
c
d
e
f
g
h
i
j
k
l
m
n
o
p
q
r
s
t
u
v
w
x
y
z

hardworking *adjective*
If you are **hardworking**, you work hard and you do your work in a careful way.

hare *noun*
A **hare** is an animal like a large rabbit. It has long back legs and can move very quickly.

> ⭐ *Spelling Tip:* Don't confuse the spelling of **hare** with **hair** which has the same sound. Your **hair** grows on your head.

harm *verb*
If you **harm** someone or something, you hurt or damage them. *That gentle old dog would never harm anyone.*

harp *noun*
A **harp** is a musical instrument. It has a large frame shaped like a triangle, with strings stretched across that you pick or move over with your fingers.

harvest *noun*
The **harvest** is when fruit, vegetables or grain grown on a farm are gathered or picked.

hat *noun*
A **hat** is a covering for the head, which you usually wear when you are outside.

hatch *verb*
If something **hatches**, it breaks out of an egg. *I would love to see an emu hatch out of its egg.*

hate /*say* hayt/ *verb*
If you **hate** something or someone, you have a very strong feeling of not liking them. *Sally says she hates Sue, but I don't believe her. It's just because they have had a fight.*

> *Word Building:* **hatred** /*say* **hay**-truhd/, *noun* If you hate something or someone, you have a feeling of **hatred** for them.

haul *verb*
If you **haul** something, you pull it hard. *It was not easy to haul the heavy canoe out of the river.*

haunt *verb*
If people say that a ghost **haunts** a place, it means that they believe that a ghost goes there often. *The old house scared us so much that we thought maybe it was haunted by ghosts.*

have *verb* (**has**, **having**, **had**, **has had**)
1. If you **have** something, it is yours. You own it or it is one of the things that make you look the way you do. *I have a new bike.* | *I have brown hair.*
2. If you **have** a particular experience, that experience happens to you. *We had a good time at the party.* | *I have had a pain in my leg for two days.*
3. If you **have** food or drink, you eat or drink it. *I need to have a glass of water.*
4. If something **has** something, it contains or includes it. *Each hand has five fingers.* | *This box has toys in it.* | *All your books should have your name on them.*
5. You also use **have** or one of its forms as part of another verb when you are talking about an action that is finished. *I have eaten dinner already.* | *Have you ever visited Perth?* | *She has fallen asleep.*

> **Have** is often shortened to **'ve**: *I've been here too long.* **Has** is often shortened to **'s**: *He's just left.* **Had** is often shortened to **'d**: *He'd just left when she arrived.*

hawk *noun*
A **hawk** is a bird that looks like an eagle and hunts for small animals to eat.

hay *noun*
Hay is dry grass that is used to feed animals when there is no fresh feed around.

hazard /*say* **haz**-uhd/ *noun*
A **hazard** is something that might be a danger to you.

> ⭐ *Spelling Tip:* Remember that there is only one *z* in **hazard**. Also remember that the ending is spelt *ard* (not *erd*). Some other words which have the same spelling for this sound are *lizard* and *wizard*.

he *pronoun*
You use **he** to stand for a man or boy or male animal. *He is my father.*

> Also look up **him** and **his**.

head *noun*
1. Your **head** is the top part of your body containing your brain, eyes, ears, nose and mouth. *Babies' heads often look too big for their bodies.*
2. The **head** of something is the top or front part of it. *Sarah is at the head of the queue so she won't have long to wait.*

headache /*say* **hed**-ayk/ *noun*
A **headache** is a pain in your head.

head lice *noun*
Look up **lice**.

heal *verb*
1. If you **heal** someone, you make them well again. *A doctor's job is to heal sick people.*

2. If something **heals**, it gets better. *You must stop scratching that sore so that it can heal.*

health /*say* helth/ *noun*
1. Your **health** is the general condition of your body. *My grandmother worries a lot about her health.*
2. Health can also mean the condition of your body when you have good health and are not sick. *She says it is more important to have health than wealth.*

healthy /*say* **helth**-ee/ *adjective* (**healthier**, **healthier**)
If a person or animal is **healthy**, they have good health. They are not sick very often.

The opposite is **unhealthy**.

heap *noun*
A **heap** is a lot of things lying one on top of the other.

hear *verb* (**hears**, **hearing**, **heard** /*say* herd/, **has heard**)
When you **hear** a sound, the sound comes to your ears and you know that it is there. *If nobody is there to hear a tree fall down, does it still make a noise?*

Word Building: hearing, *noun*: *People can lose part of their hearing if they work with noisy machines.*

Spelling Tip: Don't confuse the spelling of **hear** with **here** which has the same sound. **Here** means 'in this place'.

heart /*say* haht/ *noun*
1. Your **heart** is the inside part of your body that makes your blood keep moving through your body. *My grandfather had to have an operation on his heart.*
2. by heart, If you learn or know something **by heart**, you have every bit of it clearly in your memory. *I have learned my speech by heart.*

heat *noun*
1. Heat is the warm feeling that comes from something hot.
–*verb* **2.** If you **heat** something, you make it get hot or warm. *We heated up some lasagne for dinner.*

Word Building: heater, *noun* A **heater** is a machine that you use to make a room warm.

heaven /*say* **hev**-uhn/ *noun*
Some people believe that **heaven** is a place outside the world where God lives and where good people go when they die.

heavy /*say* **hev**-ee/ *adjective* (**heavier**, **heaviest**)
If something is **heavy**, it has a lot of weight which makes it hard to lift or carry.

The opposite is **light**.

hedge *noun*
A **hedge** is a row of bushes planted close together to make a fence.

heel *noun*
1. Your **heel** is the back part of the underneath of your foot. *Jules has a sore on his heel because his new shoes are too tight.*
2. A **heel** is the back part of a shoe or something else you wear on your feet. *Ella had holes in the heels of her socks.*

height /*rhymes with* kite/ *noun*
1. The **height** of something is how high it is. *The height of Mount Kosciuszko is 2228 metres.*
2. Your **height** is how tall you are. It is what you measure from the bottom of your feet to the top of your head. *My little sister and I measure our height next to the door and make a mark to show how tall we are each time.*

Spelling Tip: The word **height** comes from *high* and it sounds like *high* with a *t* added on. However, you have to remember that there is an *e* following the *h*.

heir /*sounds like* air/ *noun*
A person's **heir** is someone who will get what belongs to that person when he or she dies.

Spelling Tip: Don't confuse **heir** with the **air** that you breathe, which has the same sound. **Heir** is connected to other words such as *inherit* whose meaning has to do with the handing down of things from the older to the younger generation through time. All these words come from *heres*, the Latin word for an 'heir'. Think that 'humans eventually inherit riches' to help you remember the *h* at the beginning and the *eir* spelling.

helicopter *noun*
A **helicopter** is a flying machine without wings. Its power to fly comes from the propeller on top (which goes round and round).

hello *interjection*

Hello is the word you say to someone when you meet them. *Hello Shamim, where have you been?*

help *verb*

1. If you **help**, you do something to make what someone else is doing easier. *Can you help me with this computer problem, please?*
2. help yourself to, If you **help yourself to** something, you take it for yourself. *His mother was angry because he had helped himself to the biscuits without asking.*
—*noun* **3. Help** is what you do when you help someone.

helpful *adjective*

If you are **helpful**, you do something to help someone.

hen *noun*

A **hen** is a female bird, especially the kind that people keep to get eggs from.

The male of this is a **rooster**.

her *pronoun*

1. You use **her** to stand for a woman or girl or female animal. *I saw her yesterday.*
2. You also use **her** to show that a woman or girl owns something. *Give that book to Helen. It is her book.*

herb *noun*

A **herb** is a plant that you can add to food to make it taste better, or sometimes use to make medicines.

herd *noun*

A **herd** is a large group of animals.

here *adverb*

If something is **here** or happens **here**, it happens in the place where you are. **Here** means 'in this place' or 'to this place'. *No matter how often I tell my dog to come here, he goes somewhere else!*

The opposite is **there**.

hermit *noun*

A **hermit** is someone who chooses to live alone and who stays away from other people.

hero /*say* **hear**-roh/ *noun* (*plural* **heroes**)

A **hero** is someone who has done something very brave and who people admire.

Word Building: **heroic** /*say* huh-**roh**-ik/, *adjective* A hero does **heroic** things.

hers *pronoun*

You use **hers** to say that something belongs to a woman or girl. *Give that book to Susan. It's hers.*

herself *pronoun*

You use **herself** to mean 'her and no-one else'. *She cut herself when she was chopping up meat for cooking.* | *Lyn is making herself a sandwich for lunch.* | *She carried the bags herself. She did not need anyone to help.*

hiccup *noun*

A **hiccup** is a sudden movement in your chest that you cannot stop and which makes you give a short, sharp sound like a cough.

hide *verb* (**hides**, **hiding**, **hid**, **has hidden**)

1. If you **hide** something, you stop it being seen. You put it in a place where people can't see it. *Mum used to hide the Christmas presents under the bed until we found them.*
2. If you **hide**, you go to a place where people cannot see you. *We couldn't find Tom because he was hiding in a cupboard.*

high /*rhymes with* my/ *adjective*

1. If something is **high**, the top of it is a long way above the ground. *Some of the buildings in the city are so high, you can hardly see the top of them from the street.*
2. The measurement of something from bottom to top is how **high** it is. *He built a wall two metres high.*
3. If an amount or measurement is **high**, it is more than usual. *The temperature is very high today. It must be more than 35 degrees.*

Look up **height**.

highlighter /*say* **huy**-luy-tuh/ *noun*

A **highlighter** is a thick pen that you use to put colour over special words or pictures that you want to be noticed.

highway /*say* **huy**-way/ *noun*

A **highway** is a main road.

hike *noun*
A **hike** is a long walk in the country that you do for enjoyment.
> *Word Building:* **hiker**, *noun* Someone who goes on a hike is a **hiker**.

hill *noun*
A **hill** is a high part of the land, smaller than a mountain.
> *Word Building:* **hilly**, *adjective* An area that has a lot of hills is **hilly**.

him *pronoun*
You use **him** to stand for a man or boy or male animal. *'Have you seen John recently?' 'Yes, I saw him yesterday.'*

himself *pronoun*
You use **himself** to mean 'him and no-one else'. *He hurt himself when he fell off the fence. | Peter is old enough to dress himself now. | Dad painted the room himself. He did not want to pay someone else to do it.*

hind *adjective*
The **hind** legs of an animal are their back legs.

Hinduism /*say* **hin**-dooh-iz-uhm/ *noun*
Hinduism is the main religion of India. In this religion, many gods are worshipped.
> *Word Building:* **Hindu**, *noun* Someone whose religion is Hinduism is a **Hindu**.

hint *noun*
A **hint** is a small piece of information that helps you to work something out.

hip *noun*
Your **hip** is one of the bony parts on each side of your body, just below your waist.

hippopotamus /*say* hip-uh-**pot**-uh-muhs/ *noun* (*plural* **hippopotamuses** or **hippopotami** /*say* hip-uh-**pot**-uh-muy/)
A **hippopotamus** is a large, heavy animal with short legs, that lives near lakes and rivers in Africa.
> ✳ *Spelling Tip:* The word **hippopotamus** comes from Greek words meaning 'horse of the river'. If you think of it in five parts – *hip* + *po* + *pot* + *a* + *mus* – you should get the double *p* in the right place!

hire *verb*
If you **hire** something, you pay money so that you can use it for a while. *Our family hired a boat and went up the river.*

his *pronoun*
You use **his** to show that a man or boy owns something. *'Does this book belong to Andrew?' 'Yes, it is his book.'*

hiss *verb*
If something or someone **hisses**, they make the sound 'sss', like a snake. *The geese hissed at us whenever we went near them.*

history *noun* (*plural* **histories**)
History is all the events which have happened in the past, or the events that have happened in the past in a particular place or period of time.
> *Word Building:* **historic** /*say* his-**tor**-ik/, *adjective* Something that is important in history is **historic**.

hit *verb* (**hits, hitting, hit, has hit**)
1. If you **hit** someone, you strike them with your hand or with something else because you want to hurt them. *James hit Sam and then they had a fight.*
2. If you **hit** something, you strike it with something. *She hit the ball well.*

hive *noun*
A **hive** is a place that bees live in.

hoarse /*say* haws/ *adjective*
If your voice is **hoarse**, it has a low, rough sound. *Our voices were hoarse from cheering for our team all afternoon.*

hoax *noun*
A **hoax** is something that is done to trick people.

hobby *noun* (*plural* **hobbies**)
A **hobby** is something interesting that you enjoy doing in your own time.

hockey *noun*
Hockey is a game played on a field or on ice in which two teams try to hit a ball into a goal using a stick with a curved end.

hold *verb* (**holds, holding, held, has held**)
1. If you **hold** someone or something, you have them in your arms or hands. *You have to be careful when you're holding a baby.*
2. If a container **holds** a particular amount, that is how much can fit into it. *This bag is just big enough to hold all my books.*

hole *noun*
A **hole** is an opening that goes through or into something. *The dog is digging a hole in the ground. | Oh no, I've got a hole in my new shirt!*

holiday *noun*

1. A **holiday** is a time away from school or work, often because it is a special day or time of year. *There is a holiday next Monday for Australia Day.*
2. A **holiday** is a time away from school or work, spent in a place that is not your home or travelling from place to place. *We are going camping for two weeks for our holiday.*

> ✴ *Spelling Tip:* Remember that there is only one *l*. This is because **holiday** comes from 'holy day', but with the *y* changed to an *i*.

hollow *adjective*

1. Something is **hollow** if it is empty inside. *My grandmother has a big hollow emu egg sitting in her lounge room.*
2. A **hollow** is where the surface of something is slightly pressed in. *Make a hollow in the clay with your finger.*

holy *adjective* (**holier**, **holiest**)

If something is **holy**, it is special because it has to do with God or religion.

home *noun*

Your **home** is where you live.

home page *noun*

The **home page** of a website on the internet tells you what sort of information you can find there. You can click on words or signs on the **home page** to go to the page with the information you want.

homework *noun*

Your **homework** is school work that a teacher expects you to do at home, not in class.

honest /*say* **on**-uhst / *adjective*

If someone is **honest**, they always tell the truth and they do not do things such as stealing from people.

> *Word Building:* **honestly**, *adverb*: *I have answered all your questions honestly.* –**honesty**, *noun* An honest person shows **honesty**.

honey /*rhymes with* funny / *noun*

Honey is a sweet, sticky food that is made by bees.

honour /*say* **on**-uh / *noun*

1. Honour is what a person or group of people has when they behave in an honest and good way that makes people respect them. *She behaved with honour and didn't cheat the way others did.*
2. An **honour** is something that someone gives you or asks you to do which you feel very special

about. *Jodie thought it was a great honour to be asked to give a speech in front of the whole school.*

> Another spelling for this word is **honor**.

hood *noun*

A **hood** is a soft covering for your head and neck, which is usually attached to a coat.

hoof *noun* (*plural* **hoofs** *or* **hooves**)

A **hoof** is the hard part that covers the feet of animals, like horses and cows.

hook *noun*

A **hook** is a piece of curved metal for hanging things on or for catching hold of things. *Hang your coat on this hook.* | *People who work on wharves use big hooks to lift cargo.*

hop *verb* (**hops**, **hopping**, **hopped**, **has hopped**)

If you **hop**, you jump up and down on one leg only. *Can you hop all the way to school?*

hope *verb*

If you **hope** for something or **hope** that something will happen, you wish that it will happen because it is something good. *We are hoping for a sunny day for the party.*

> *Word Building:* **hopeful**, *adjective* If you hope for something and you think it will happen, you are **hopeful**. *The clouds are going away so we are hopeful that the rain will stop soon.*

hopeless *adjective*

If a situation is **hopeless**, it is not possible for it to turn out well or to be successful. *My grandfather's doctor said that the situation was hopeless. They could not make him better.* | *It is hopeless trying to read when there is so much noise.*

hopscotch *noun*

Hopscotch is a game in which you throw a stone onto one of a pattern of squares drawn on the ground, and then hop on the other squares.

horizon /*say* huh-**ruy**-zuhn / *noun*

A **horizon** is the line where the land or the sea seems to meet the sky.

horizontal /*say* ho-ruh-**zon**-tuhl / *adjective*

If something is **horizontal**, it is level or lying in a line that is flat like the ground.

> Think about how this is different from **vertical**.

horn *noun*

1. A **horn** is a pointed bone that grows on the head of animals like cattle and sheep. *It would be very uncomfortable to get too close to a bull's horns.*

2. A **horn** is a musical instrument that you blow. *Andrew will be playing the horn at the school concert.*

3. A **horn** is something that makes a sound to warn you or attract your attention. *The driver blew the horn when I started to walk in front of the car.*

horrible *adjective*
Something that is **horrible** is very unpleasant. It affects you badly.

horror *noun*
If you feel **horror**, you have a feeling of very great fear.

horse *noun*
A **horse** is a large animal which you can ride on or which can be trained to pull loads.

hose *noun*
A **hose** is a long tube made of rubber or plastic so it can bend, which is made to carry water from a tap to where it is needed.

hospital *noun*
A **hospital** is a building where sick people or people who have been hurt are looked after by doctors and nurses.

hot *adjective*
1. If something is **hot**, it has a high temperature and gives out a lot of heat. *Don't touch the iron. It is very hot.*

2. If the weather is **hot**, it reaches such a high temperature that it can make you uncomfortable. *It was such a hot day that we didn't feel like running around.*

3. If you are **hot**, you feel uncomfortable because you have too many clothes on, or because the weather is too hot, or because you have a sickness that gives you a high temperature. *She was so hot that she felt sick.*

Also look up **warm**.

hot dog *noun*
A **hot dog** is a food made of a kind of sausage inside a bread roll.

hotel *noun*
A **hotel** is a building with rooms which people can pay to sleep in when they are away from home.

hour /*sounds like* our/ *noun*
An **hour** is a period of time. There are 24 **hours** in a day and there are 60 minutes in an **hour**.

house *noun*
A **house** is a building where a family or other people live.

housework *noun*
Housework is the work of looking after a home by keeping it clean and tidy.

hovercraft /*say* **hov**-uh-krahft/ *noun* (*plural* **hovercraft**)
A **hovercraft** is a vehicle without wheels that can travel quickly on land and water.

how *adverb, conjunction*
You use **how** to mean 'in what way' or 'in what state'. *How do you open this cupboard?* | *How did the accident happen?* | *How are you feeling today?* | *She didn't know how to get to the station.*

however *adverb*
1. You use **however** to show that it does not matter how far, how much or how strong something is. *However hard he tries, he'll never win.*

2. You use **however** to join two ideas when it is surprising that they go together. You mean that the second thing happens without taking notice of the first thing. *We know it's cold. However, we still want to go swimming.*

howl *noun*
A **howl** is a long, loud cry, like a dog in pain.

huddle *verb*
If people or animals **huddle** together, they gather very close together. *We all had to huddle under one umbrella.*

huge *adjective*
If something is **huge**, it is very, very big.

hum *verb* (**hums**, **humming**, **hummed**, **has hummed**)
1. If you **hum**, you make a tune with your lips closed. *I don't know the words of the song but I can hum the tune.*

–noun **2.** A **hum** is a low, continuous sound, like the one a bee makes. *There is a hum in the garden from all the bees flying around.* | *There was a hum of conversation coming from the teachers' room.*

human /*say* **hyooh**-muhn/ *noun*
1. A **human** is a person like you or me, not another kind of animal, or plant, or object.

–adjective **2.** If something is **human**, it has to do with humans.

You can also say **human being** for definition 1.

humankind *noun*
Humankind is all humans.

Other words to use are **humanity** and **mankind**. Because **mankind** begins with the word *man*, some people think it should not be used to talk about all humans (women and men).

humble *adjective*
You are **humble** if you do not speak too proudly of yourself or your situation.

hummus /*say* **hoom**-uhs, **hom**-uhs/ *noun*
Hummus is a food made from chickpeas and oil.

Another spelling is **hommos**.

humorous *adjective*
If something is **humorous**, it is funny.

Word Building: humour, *noun* Something that is humorous is full of **humour**.

⚜ *Spelling Tip:* This word is made up of *humour* and the ending *ous* (meaning 'full of'). However, you have to remember that the *u* in *humour* has been left out.

hump *noun*
A **hump** is a big raised mass on the back of an animal, like the camel, or on a person. *We rode on camels and sat behind their humps.* | *The old lady had a hump on her back.*

hundred *noun, adjective*
A **hundred** is a number which you can write as 100.

Word Building: hundredth, *adjective: She is a very old woman, in the hundredth year of her life.*

hunger *noun*
Hunger is the uncomfortable feeling you have when you need food.

hungry *adjective* (**hungrier, hungriest**)
If you are **hungry**, you have the uncomfortable feeling of needing to eat food.

hunt *verb*
1. If an animal **hunts** another animal, or a person **hunts** an animal, they chase it because they want to kill it for food or sport. *Owls hunt mice at night.*
2. If you **hunt** for someone or something, you look for them. *He spent about half an hour hunting for his other sock.*

hurry *verb* (**hurries, hurrying, hurried, has hurried**)
If you **hurry**, you move or act quickly because there is not much time. *We had to hurry or we would have missed the train.*

hurt *verb*
1. If you **hurt** someone or something, you make them feel pain. *Tom hurt me when he hit me on the arm.*
2. If a part of your body **hurts**, you feel pain in that part. *My leg hurts.*

husband *noun*
A woman's **husband** is the man she is married to.

hydrofoil /*say* **huy**-druh-foyl/ *noun*
A **hydrofoil** is a boat with special parts underneath it that help it travel very fast along the surface of the water.

hymn /*sounds like* him/ *noun*
A **hymn** is a song that praises God.

⚜ *Spelling Tip:* Don't confuse **hymn** with the pronoun **him**, which has the same sound. Remember the *y* spelling for the 'i' sound in **hymn** and the silent *n* at the end.

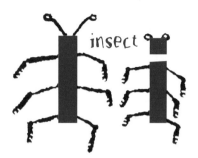

insect

I *pronoun*
You use **I** when you are talking about yourself. *'Tell me about yourself.' 'I am eight years old. My name is Sam.'*

Also look up **me**, **my** and **mine**[1].

ice *noun*
Ice is water that has frozen and become hard.

iceberg *noun*
An **iceberg** is a very large piece of ice in the sea.

ice-cream *noun*
Ice-cream is a sweet food made with cream or milk that has been frozen.

ice skate *noun*
An **ice skate** is a shoe like a boot which underneath has a long sharp piece of metal which you wear to move smoothly over ice.

Word Building: **ice skating**, *noun: Anna loves ice skating.*

icicle /*say* **uy**-sik-uhl / *noun*
An **icicle** is a piece of ice that is made when drops of water freeze. It hangs down from something and has a pointed shape.

⭐ *Spelling Tip:* Remember that **icicles** are made of *ice*. So the first part of **icicle** is spelt *ic* – you drop the *e*. Then you have to remember to add another *ic*, like another little drop of *ic(e)*, and end with *le* (not *al*).

icing *noun*
Icing is a sweet layer put over the top of a cake, made from sugar and water mixed together.

icon /*say* **uy**-kon / *noun*
An **icon** is a small picture on a computer screen that stands for something, such as an instruction to open a program. You can click on the **icon** to make the instruction work.

idea *noun*
An **idea** is something like a plan or a picture that you think of or see in your mind.

identical *adjective*
People or things are **identical** if they are the same as each other in every way.

idiot /*say* **id**-ee-uht / *noun*
An **idiot** is a very stupid person.

Word Building: **idiotic** /*say* id-ee-**ot**-ik /, *adjective* An idiot is likely to do **idiotic** things.

igloo *noun*
An **igloo** is the shelter that the Inuit people build out of blocks of hard snow.

ignorant *adjective*
Someone is **ignorant** if they do not know very much.

Word Building: **ignorance**, *noun* If someone is ignorant, you talk about their **ignorance**.

ignore *verb*
If you **ignore** what someone says, you take no notice of it. *My little sister ignored my mother when she told her to tidy her room – and now she is in big trouble.*

ill *adjective*
If you are **ill**, you are not well in your body.

illness *noun*
If you have an **illness**, you are sick. You are not well in your body.

illustration *noun*
An **illustration** is a picture in a book.

Word Building: **illustrate**, *verb* If you draw illustrations to go with something, you **illustrate** it.

⭐ *Spelling Tip:* Remember the double *l* and notice that the next letter is a *u*.

imagination /*say* i-maj-uh-**nay**-shuhn / *noun*
Your **imagination** is the ability you have to make pictures in your mind or to think of interesting stories.

Word Building: imaginative /say i-**maj**-uh-nuh-tiv /, *adjective* If you are good at using your imagination, then you're **imaginative**.

imagine /say i-**maj**-uhn / *verb*
If you **imagine** something, you make a picture of it in your mind. *Close your eyes and imagine that you are going around the earth in a rocket. How exciting that would be!*

immediately /say i-**mee**-dee-uht-lee / *adverb*
If something happens **immediately**, it happens now or straight after something else. *As soon as they get our email, they will answer immediately.*

⭐ **Spelling Tip:** Remember the double *m* and the *ate* spelling for the 'uht' sound. Try breaking the word up as *im + me + di + ate + ly*.

immune *adjective*
If you are **immune** to a disease, you are protected from it.

Word Building: immunity, *noun* If you have **immunity** to something, you are safe from it.

impatient /say im-**pay**-shuhnt / *adjective*
You are **impatient** if you want to do something right now and if you do not want to wait.

Word Building: impatience, *noun* If you are impatient, then you are filled with **impatience**.

important *adjective*
1. If something is **important**, it matters a lot to you or to people in general. It is something that you must have or know about, or it is something that makes a difference to people's lives. *We had a talk at school today about how important education is.*
2. If someone is **important**, they are in charge of other people or have some kind of power. *The prime minister is one of the most important people in the country.*

Word Building: importance, *noun* If something is important, you talk about its **importance**.

impossible *adjective*
If something is **impossible**, it cannot be done.

The opposite is **possible**.

improve /say im-**proohv** / *verb*
1. If you **improve** something, you make it better than it was. *I'm trying to improve my school work by studying hard.*

2. If something **improves**, it becomes better than it was. *My school work is beginning to improve.*

Word Building: improvement, *noun* If you improve something or it improves, there is an **improvement**.

in *preposition*
If something is **in** something else, it has that thing all around it: *The books are in that box.* This is the basic meaning of **in** but you can use it many ways, for example. *They are swimming in the pool.* | *Mum works in an office in the city.* | *Cars were invented in the 20th century.* | *The train will arrive in ten minutes.*

You use **in** to talk about travelling in some things, but you use **on** for others. You travel *in a car*, *in a boat* and *in a helicopter*, but you travel *on a ship*. You can travel *in* or *on a bus* and you can travel *in* or *on a plane*.

inch *noun* (*plural* **inches**)
An **inch** is a measurement of length. It used to be used in Australia, and still is used in some countries, such as America. It is a small length, equal to 2.54 centimetres.

include *verb*
If something **includes** something, it has it as a part of itself. *This book is mainly about electric trains, but also includes some information about steam trains.*

Word Building: including, *preposition* When an amount is **including** something, it is counting that thing as part of the total. *There are ten kids going to the game, including four from another class.*

income *noun*
Someone's **income** is the money they get from working and which they use to pay for the things they need.

increase /say in-**krees** / *verb*
1. If you **increase** something, you make it bigger or more in number or amount. *If you increase the amount of honey you put into the recipe, the cake will be sweeter.*
2. If something **increases**, it becomes bigger or more in number. *Because of the increasing number of cars on the road, pollution has increased.*

The opposite is **decrease**.

incredible *adjective*
If something is **incredible**, it is very hard to believe.

indeed *adverb*
1. You use **indeed** to make the word 'very' stronger. *I liked the new ride at the show very much indeed – it was the best!*
2. You use **indeed** to show that something actually happened. *She said she would arrive at nine o'clock and indeed she did.*

index *noun*
An **index** is a list of all the things that are in a book and where you can find them.

indicate /*say* **in**-duh-kayt/ *verb*
1. If someone or something **indicates** something, they point to it. *Can you indicate your house as we're passing?*
2. If a situation **indicates** something, it is a sign of it or it tells you that it is the case. *The fact that the phone hasn't been answered indicates they have probably gone out.*

indigenous /*say* in-**dij**-uh-nuhs/ *adjective*
1. Someone who is **indigenous** to a place belongs to a group of people who were the first people in that place. *Australia's Indigenous people are the Aboriginal and Torres Strait Islander people.*
2. An **indigenous** plant or animal grows or lives naturally in a place and has not been brought there from somewhere else. *Kangaroos are indigenous to Australia but horses are not.*

When you are writing about Aboriginal and Torres Strait Islander people, or something to do with them, you usually use a capital letter: *There are hundreds of Indigenous languages.*

indoors *adverb*
Indoors is inside a house. *It was rainy so we decided to have my party indoors.*

industry /*say* **in**-duhs-tree/ *noun* (*plural* **industries**)
An **industry** is a kind of business in which things are made in a factory and sold to people.

Word Building: industrial /*say* in-**dus**-tree-uhl/, *adjective* If something has to do with industry, or has a lot of industries, it is **industrial**.

infant *noun*
An **infant** is a baby or a very young child.

infect /*say* in-**fekt**/ *verb*
If you **infect** someone with a sickness, you pass it on to other people. *Cover your mouth when you cough or you'll infect the whole family with your cold.*

Word Building: infection, *noun* If you have an **infection**, you can infect people. –**infectious** /*say* in-**fek**-shuhs/, *adjective* If a sickness can pass from person to person, it is **infectious**. If you can infect people, you are **infectious**. *A cold is an infectious illness.*

inferior /*say* in-**fear**-ree-uh/ *adjective*
If something is **inferior**, it is not as good as something else.

The opposite is **superior**.

inferno *noun* (*plural* **infernos**)
An **inferno** is a fire where the heat and flames are so extreme that people cannot stand to be near it.

inflammable *adjective*
If something is **inflammable**, it is likely to burn easily.

This word looks like it is the opposite of **flammable** (also meaning 'likely to burn easily') but it actually means the same. Because this confusion could be dangerous, **inflammable** is not used much any more and the usual word is **flammable**. The opposite is **nonflammable** (meaning 'not likely to burn easily').

inflate *verb*
To **inflate** something is to fill it up with gas or air. *My job at the party is to inflate the balloons.*

informal *adjective*
If something is **informal**, it has to do with situations when you are relaxed. **Informal** language is what you use when you are talking to your friends or people you know well. You do not usually use this kind of language in writing.

The opposite is **formal**.

information *noun*
Information is knowledge about something that someone has told you, or which you can find in a book, on television, on the internet, and so on.

information report *noun*
An **information report** is a piece of writing which gives facts on something.

ingredient *noun*
An **ingredient** is one of the parts of a whole thing. *We had all the ingredients for the cake except for the chocolate chips.*

⭐ *Spelling Tip:* Remember that there is only one e before the *d* in **ingredient** (although it sounds like 'ee'). If you notice the word *red* hidden inside **ingredient** that will remind you. Also remember that the ending is spelt with another e – *ient* (not *iant*).

inhabit *verb*
If you **inhabit** a place, you live in it. *People and animals who inhabit desert areas have to use clever ways to find their water.*

Word Building: **inhabitant**, *noun* Someone who inhabits a place is an **inhabitant** of it.

inherit *verb*
If you **inherit** something, you receive it from someone who has died. *When my grandmother died, my mother inherited her house.*

Word Building: **inheritance**, *noun* What you inherit is your **inheritance**.

initial /*say* i-**nish**-uhl / *noun*
An **initial** is the first letter of a word or of your name.

⭐ *Spelling Tip:* Remember that **initial** has *ti* in the middle, making a 'sh' sound.

injection *noun*
You have an **injection** when a doctor or nurse uses a special hollow needle to put medicine into your body.

Word Building: **inject**, *verb* When you have an injection, the doctor or nurse **injects** you with a needle.

injure /*say* in-juh/ *verb*
If something **injures** you, it hurts you. *Lara was injured badly when she fell between the rocks at the end of the beach.*

Word Building: **injury**, *noun* When something injures you, you get an **injury**.

ink *noun*
Ink is a coloured liquid used for writing or printing.

inland *adjective*
A place is **inland** if it is in the middle of a country, a long way from the sea.

inner *adjective*
If something is **inner**, it is in the inside area of something, rather than near the outside.

innocent /*say* in-uh-suhnt/ *adjective*
You are **innocent** if you have not done anything wrong. *We knew Pete had to be innocent*

because he wasn't even there at the time the bag was stolen.

Word Building: **innocence**, *noun* If someone is innocent, then you talk about their **innocence**.

insect *noun*
An **insect** is a small living creature with three parts to its body, six legs and usually with two pairs of wings to fly.

inside *preposition*
1. If something is **inside** something, it is contained in it. *Let's open the box and see what's inside it.* | *Everyone should stand inside the circle.*
–*noun* **2.** The **inside** of something is the part near the middle of it or the side of it that is in it, not out of it. *The inside of an orange is juicy.*
–*adverb* **3.** If you go **inside**, you go into a house or other building. *It's starting to rain. Let's go inside.*

insist *verb*
If you **insist** that someone does something, you say strongly that they must do it. *We wanted to keep on playing the game, but Mum insisted that we come inside and have dinner.*

inspect *verb*
If you **inspect** something, you look over it in a very careful way. *Can I inspect your ticket please?*

Word Building: **inspection**, *noun* If your job is to inspect, then you make **inspections**. –**inspector**, *noun* If your job is to inspect, then you are an **inspector**.

instant *noun*
1. An **instant** is a very short time.
–*adjective* **2.** Something that is **instant** is in a form that makes preparation quick and easy.

instead *preposition*
1. If you do something **instead** of someone, you do it and the other person does not do it. *Julie was sick so I played the part instead of her.*
2. If you do something **instead** of something else, you do that thing and not the other thing. *We went to the movies instead of the beach because it was raining.* | *The local shop was shut so we went to the supermarket instead.*

instinct *noun*
An **instinct** is the strong wish or need that people and animals are born with to behave in certain

ways. *Some types of whales know by instinct to travel far north to breed.*

instruct *verb*
If someone **instructs** you, they teach you. *The teacher instructed us on how to look for information on the computer.*

Word Building: instructor, *noun* If you instruct someone in something like swimming or driving, then you are an **instructor**.

instruction *noun*
If you give someone an **instruction**, you tell them what to do or how to do something.

instrument */say* in-struh-muhnt */ noun*
1. An **instrument** is any tool or machine that helps you to do a job. *The doctor had an instrument which found out how much sound went into each ear.*
2. An **instrument** is something you use to make a musical sound. *Some of the violins and other instruments in the school orchestra need to be replaced.*

insult *verb /say* in-**sult** /
1. If someone **insults** you, they behave or speak to you rudely. *Sam tried to insult me by calling me a baby.*
—*noun /say* **in**-sult / 2. An **insult** is a rude action or rude thing that someone says or does to another person.

intend *verb*
If you **intend** to do something, you have it in your mind to do it, but you have not done it yet. *I have been intending to tidy my room for about a week now.*

Word Building: intention, *noun* If you intend to do something, then it is your **intention** to do it.

interest *verb*
1. If something **interests** you, it holds your attention and makes you want to know more about it or see more of it. *Stories about space do not interest me much.*
—*noun* 2. **Interest** is the feeling you have when something interests you.

interested *adjective*
1. If you are **interested**, you are thinking about or looking at something that interests you. It is keeping your attention. *Everyone in the class was interested when I showed them my mouse.*
2. If you are **interested** in something, you want to know more about it, or you like doing it. *My dad*

is much more interested in cooking than my mum so he makes most of our dinners.*

interesting *adjective*
If something is **interesting**, it keeps your attention. It interests you.

interfere */say* in-tuh-**fear** / *verb*
If you **interfere** in something that has to do with other people, you say or do things that have to do with it, although they do not want you to. *We would have finished this work already if you hadn't interfered.*

Word Building: interference */say* in-tuh-**fear**-ruhns /, *noun* If something or someone interferes then what they do is an **interference**.

interior */say* int-**ear**-ree-uh / *noun*
The **interior** is the inside of something.

The opposite is **exterior**.

interjection *noun*
An **interjection** is a type of word which you can use by itself, without a normal sentence. Some examples are 'hello', 'yes', 'okay', and 'sorry'.

internal *adjective*
If something is **internal**, it is on the inside.

The opposite is **external**.

international *adjective*
If something is **international**, it has to do with two or more countries.

This word comes from *inter* which means 'between' and **nation** which is another word for **country**.

internet *noun*
The **internet** is the way in which millions of computers around the world are connected so that people can send emails, look at websites, and find information about many things.

You can also spell this word with a capital letter: **the Internet**. It is often shortened to **the Net**.

interrupt *verb*
If you **interrupt**, you do or say something that makes someone stop speaking, or stop what they are doing. *I can't answer the question if you keep on interrupting.*

Word Building: interruption, *noun* If someone or something **interrupts** then what they do is an **interruption**.

> ✱ *Spelling Tip:* Remember that **interrupt** begins with the word part *inter* (meaning 'between'). It is followed by the word part *rupt* (meaning 'broken') and so has a double *r*.

intersection *noun*
An **intersection** is a place where streets cross each other.

interval *noun*
An **interval** is a short break during a film, play or concert.

into *preposition*
If something or someone goes **into** something else, they go inside it: *She ran into the kitchen.* This is the basic meaning of **into** but you can use it in many ways, for example: *I'm well into the book now.* | *The grub turned into a butterfly.* | *Two into ten equals five.*

introduce *verb*
If you **introduce** someone to another person who does not know them, you make them known to each other by saying their names and sometimes telling them something about each other. *The teacher introduced the new boy to our class and asked me to show him around the school.*

> *Word Building:* **introduction**, *noun* When you introduce one person to another, you make an **introduction**.

invade *verb*
If a country **invades** another country, it goes into it with an army and attacks it. *A war starts when one country invades another.*

invalid /*say* in-vuh-lid / *noun*
An **invalid** is someone who is sick, or someone who needs someone to look after them after a sickness.

invaluable /*say* in-**val**-yuh-buhl / *adjective*
If something is **invaluable**, it is worth more than you can measure. *He used to play cricket for Australia, so his advice on how to improve our game was invaluable.*

invent *verb*
If someone **invents** something, they make or design something new that has not been made before. *Humans invented the wheel thousands of years ago.*

> *Word Building:* **invention**, *noun* When you invent something, it is an **invention**.

investigate *verb*
If you **investigate** a problem or a situation, you look into it with a lot of care. *There was a loud crash from the bedroom and we all ran in to investigate.*

> *Word Building:* **investigation**, *noun* When you investigate, you make an **investigation**.

invisible /*say* in-**viz**-uh-buhl / *adjective*
Something is **invisible** if no-one can see it.

invite *verb*
If you **invite** someone to come to a meal, a party or any occasion, you ask them to come to it. You say that you would like them to come. *Mum invited my friend to dinner at our house.*

> *Word Building:* **invitation**, *noun* When you invite someone to something, you give them an **invitation**.

iron /*say* **uy**-uhn / *noun*
1. Iron is a strong metal used for making tools, machines and parts of buildings. *The house was surrounded by a brick wall and a heavy iron gate.*
2. An **iron** is an electric tool which you can heat and use to press clothes flat. *Dad burnt himself with the iron.*
–*verb* **3.** When you **iron** clothes, you use an iron to press them flat. *Dad ironed his shirt before he went out.*

irrigate *verb*
If someone **irrigates** land, they supply water to the ground for growing plants by sending it along pipes or specially dug areas. *You can always tell where land has been irrigated because it is greener.*

irritate *verb*
If you **irritate** someone, you make them cross or angry. *My little sister always irritates me by wanting to play when I want to read magazines.*

> *Word Building:* **irritation**, *noun* Things that irritate you cause **irritation**.

> ✱ *Spelling Tip:* You might think of the phrase 'irritated people <u>r</u>un <u>r</u>apidly' to remind you of the double *r*.

Islam /*say* **iz**-lam, **iz**-lahm / *noun*
Islam is a religion started by a special teacher called Mohammed who lived a long time ago. This religion teaches that we should do what Allah (God) wants us to do.

> Someone whose religion is Islam is a **Muslim**.

island /*say* **uy**-luhnd/ *noun*

An **island** is a piece of land that has water all around it.

isolate *verb*

If you **isolate** people or things, you keep them all alone or all by themselves. *They had to isolate the prisoner to stop him hurting the others.*

> **Word Building: isolation**, *noun* If you isolate people or things, you keep them in **isolation**.

> ✳ *Spelling Tip:* Remember that there is only one *s*. Also remember that the next letter is *o*. Though not connected to the meaning, it will help if you notice that **isolate** contains the words *is* and *late* with an *o* **isolated** between them.

it *pronoun*

You use **it** in many ways, such as when you are talking about a thing, or a baby or animal when you do not know if they are male or female. *The book is on the desk. Please get it for me.*

> Also look up **its**.

itch *verb*

If you **itch**, you have a feeling on your skin which makes you want to scratch. *After she touched the plant, Sophie's hand was itching so badly, she thought she would go mad.*

> **Word Building: itchy**, *adjective* When your skin starts to itch, it is **itchy**.

item /*say* **uy**-tuhm/ *noun*

An **item** is one thing from a list.

its *pronoun*

You use **its** to show that something belongs to something, or that something belongs to a baby or animal when you do not know if they are male or female. *The chair is getting old. One of its legs is broken.*

> Remember that **its** is not the same as **it's**, which is the short form of *it is* or *it has*, as in *It's time to go* or *It's been a long time*.

itself *pronoun*

1. You use **itself** when you are saying that a thing or animal does something and that it, rather than something else, is affected by it. *The cat cleaned itself with its tongue.*
2. by itself, If something does something **by itself**, it does it without anyone having to help or do something. *You don't have to turn that light on. It comes on by itself when it gets dark.*

ivory /*say* **uy**-vuh-ree/ *noun*

Ivory is the hard white material that the tusks of elephants are made of. It is used to be used for things like the white keys of pianos.

ivy *noun*

Ivy is a plant with shiny, green leaves. As it grows, it climbs higher by holding onto walls or by twisting around branches.

a
b
c
d
e
f
g
h
i
j
k
l
m
n
o
p
q
r
s
t
u
v
w
x
y
z

jar

jabiru /say jab-uh-**rooh**/ noun

A **jabiru** is a large white and green Australian bird with a green-black head, neck and tail and long red legs. It has a long black beak and it catches fish.

jackaroo noun

A **jackaroo** is a young man who is working on a cattle or sheep station, usually to gain experience in the skills needed to own or manage a station.

A young woman working on a cattle or sheep station is called a **jillaroo**.

jacket noun

A **jacket** is a short coat.

jackpot noun

A **jackpot** is the very biggest prize that you can win in some competitions or games.

jagged /say **jag**-uhd/ adjective

If something is **jagged**, it has very sharp edges.

jail noun

A **jail** is the place where prisoners are kept.

Another spelling is **gaol** which you say with the same sound.

jam¹ verb (jams, jamming, jammed, has jammed)

1. If something **jams**, it becomes stuck so that it will not move. *I can't open the door. It's jammed.* –noun **2.** A **jam** is a lot of people or things crowded together so that they cannot move much.

jam² noun

Jam is a sweet food made of fruit and sugar which you spread on bread.

January /say **jan**-yooh-uh-ree/ noun

January is the first month of the year, with 31 days. It comes before February.

jar noun

A **jar** is a glass container which you use for keeping food in.

jarrah /say **ja**-ruh/ noun

A **jarrah** is a tall gum tree with dark red wood.

This word comes from an Aboriginal language of Western Australia called Nyungar.

✳ **Spelling Tip:** Remember that this word has a double *r*. Also remember the *ah* ending. Several other words that come from Aboriginal languages, such as *galah*, have this spelling pattern.

jaw noun

A **jaw** is one of the two bones that form the frame of your mouth and that your teeth grow in.

jazz noun

Jazz is a type of music with a strong beat, first played by African-Americans.

jealous /say **jel**-uhs/ adjective

You are **jealous** of someone if you want something they have.

***Word Building:* jealousy,** *noun* When you are jealous, you feel **jealousy**.

jeans noun

Jeans are trousers made of a special strong material, usually blue.

You can also say **a pair of jeans**, but then you speak about them as though they are one thing: *This pair of trousers is my favourite.*

jeer verb

If you **jeer** at someone, you make fun of them or say mean things about them. *She was upset because some of the other children jeered at the clothes she was wearing.*

jelly noun (plural jellies)

A **jelly** is a soft food made of fruit, sugar and water. It shakes when you move it.

jerk noun

1. A **jerk** is a sudden, quick movement. –verb **2.** If you **jerk** something, you pull it suddenly. *She jerked the line when she felt a fish bite.*

Word Building: **jerky**, *adjective* If you move with jerks, then your movements are **jerky**. –**jerkiness**, *noun* If you move with jerks, then your movements have a lot of **jerkiness**.

jet *noun*
1. A **jet** is a stream of water or gas that shoots out of a small opening. *A jet of steam burst out of the pipe.*
2. A **jet** is a very fast plane. *We had to stop talking because of the noise of the jet above us.*

jetty *noun* (*plural* **jetties**)
A **jetty** is a long platform that has been built to go out from the land into a river or into the sea. You can tie boats or ships to it.

Jew *noun*
A **Jew** is someone whose religion is Judaism.

Word Building: **Jewish**, *adjective* A Jew is a **Jewish** person.

jewel /*say* **jooh**-uhl / *noun*
A **jewel** is a stone that has been cut and polished and is worth a lot of money.

Word Building: **jewellery**, *noun* Jewels that have been made into beautiful things to wear around your neck or on your arm are called **jewellery**.

⭐ *Spelling Tip:* This word is not spelt as you might expect. It has an unusual group of letters *ewe* making the 'ooh' sound. Remember this and put a *j* and *l* either side to spell **jewel**.

jigsaw *noun*
A **jigsaw** is a puzzle made up of many different pieces which fit together to make a picture.

jillaroo *noun*
a **jillaroo** is a young woman who is working on a cattle or sheep station, usually to gain experience in the skills needed to own or manage a station.

A young man working on a cattle or sheep station is called a **jackaroo**.

jingle *verb*
If something **jingles**, it makes a sound like small bells ringing. *My keys jingled as I ran along.*

job *noun*
1. A **job** is a particular piece of work which you do for someone. *My job is to clear the table and my brother's job is to dry up.*
2. Someone's **job** is the work they do for money. *When I grow up, I would like a job as a pilot.*

jockey *noun*
A **jockey** is someone who rides horses in races.

joey *noun*
A **joey** is a baby kangaroo.

jog *verb* (**jogs**, **jogging**, **jogged**, **has jogged**)
If you **jog**, you run along slowly. *My grandmother jogs around the park every morning.*

Word Building: **jogger**, *noun* If you jog for exercise, then you're a **jogger**.

join *verb*
1. If you **join** two or more things, you put them together so that they touch or make one thing. *Janie tried to join the pieces of the broken chair together before her mother came home.* | *Mum made her dress longer by joining some new material to it.*
2. If things **join**, they come together so that they touch or become one thing. *Your funny bone is where your two arm bones join – if you knock it, it really hurts!*
3. If you **join** a club or any other group of people, you become a member of that group. *I'm going to join our school netball team.*

joke *noun*
1. A **joke** is something which you say or do to make people laugh, especially a little story with a funny ending.
–*verb* 2. If you **joke** about something, you speak about it in a funny way. *We were joking about how funny it would be to have elephants sitting in the classroom.*

journey /*say* **jer**-nee / *noun*
A **journey** is a trip you make from one place to another.

Also look up **voyage** which is a journey made in a ship.

⭐ *Spelling Tip:* This word comes from the idea of a trip made in a day. If you think of this, and can see that it contains *jour*, the French word for 'day', the spelling will be easier. Also remember the *ey* ending.

joy *noun*
Joy is a feeling of great happiness.

Word Building: **joyful**, *adjective* If you have a feeling of joy, you are **joyful**.

Judaism /*say* **jooh**-day-iz-uhm / *noun*
Judaism is a religion which began a very long

time ago and that teaches that there is only one God.

Someone whose religion is Judaism is a **Jew**.

judge *noun*
A **judge** is someone whose job it is to make decisions in a law court, especially to decide how to punish someone who is guilty of doing something that is against the law.

judo *noun*
Judo is a sport which comes from the Japanese way of protecting yourself without using weapons.

juggle *verb*
If you **juggle** things, you throw them in the air and keep them moving without dropping any. *When I can juggle two balls, then I'll move up to three.*

Word Building: **juggler**, *noun* Someone who juggles is a **juggler**.

juice /*say* joohs/ *noun*
Juice is the liquid that comes from fruit, often used as a drink.

Word Building: **juicy**, *adjective* (**juicier**, **juiciest**) If a piece of fruit has a lot of juice, then it is **juicy**.

July *noun*
July is the seventh month of the year, with 31 days. It comes between June and August.

jumble *verb*
If you **jumble** things, you mix them up so that they are not organised at all. *Dad said my room was a mess because I had jumbled everything up looking for my other red sock.*

jumbo *adjective*
1. You can use **jumbo** to describe a plane that is very large, or something else that is much larger than usual.
–*noun* (*plural* **jumbos**) **2.** A **jumbo** is a very large plane.

jump *verb*
If you **jump**, you move upwards with both your feet off the ground. *Show me how high you can jump.*

jumper *noun*
A **jumper** is a piece of warm clothing which you wear on the top half of your body, usually over other clothes.

June *noun*
June is the sixth month of the year, with 30 days. It comes between May and July.

jungle *noun*
A **jungle** is a place where trees and other plants grow thickly. You find jungles in parts of the world where it is very warm and rains a lot, such as parts of Africa and Asia.

junior *adjective*
Someone who is **junior** is younger or smaller than the others.

junk *noun*
Junk is old things that no-one wants any more.

junk food *noun*
Junk food is food that is not healthy.

jury /*say* **jooh**-ree/ *noun* (*plural* **juries**)
A **jury** is the group of people who have to try and decide if someone is guilty or not guilty in a law court. There are usually 12 people in a **jury**.

Word Building: **juror** /*say* **jooh**-ruh/, *noun* A member of a jury is a **juror**.

just *adverb* You can use **just** in many ways, for example:
1. to show that something happened a very little time before now. *Wayang is not here. He has just left.*
2. to say that you are doing something now or will do it very soon. *You've come at a good time. We are just starting to play a game.*
3. to mean that something or someone is the same or almost the same as someone or something else. *He looks just like his father.*
–*adjective* **4.** If something is **just**, it is right and fair. It is what should happen.

Word Building: **justice**, *noun* If decisions are just, then there is **justice**.

kite

kangaroo *noun*
A **kangaroo** is an Australian animal that uses its large tail and strong back legs for jumping. The female carries her babies in a pouch at the front of her body.

This word comes from an Aboriginal language of Queensland called Guugu Yimidhirr.

karaoke /*say* ka-ree-**oh**-kee / *noun*
Karaoke is singing along to a video of a song. The singer reads the words to the song shown on a video screen and follows the music that the video is playing.

✳ *Spelling Tip:* Remember that there is no *i* or *y* in this word. That sound is spelt by the second *a*. The word **karaoke** comes from two Japanese words – *kara* meaning 'absent' and *oke* meaning 'orchestra'. Try breaking the word up as *ka+ra+o+ke*.

karate /*say* kuh-**rah**-tee / *noun*
Karate is a sport which comes from the Japanese way of protecting yourself without using weapons.

kebab /*say* kuh-**bab** / *noun*
A **kebab** is a kind of food made of pieces of meat and sometimes vegetables on a thin stick, cooked close to a flame.

keel *noun*
A **keel** is a long piece of wood or metal put along the bottom of a ship to hold it together. On a yacht, it goes very deep and is very heavy, to stop the yacht from going over.

keen *adjective*
You are **keen** if you want to do something very much.

keep *verb* (**keeps, keeping, kept, has kept**)
1. If you **keep** something in a particular state, you make sure that it is always like that. *Mum wants me to keep my bedroom tidy.*
2. If you **keep** something, you have it as your own and do not give it back to someone. *You can have this book for a few days but you can't keep it.*

kelpie *noun*
A **kelpie** is an Australian sheep dog.

kennel *noun*
A **kennel** is a small building for keeping a dog warm and dry.

kerb *noun*
The **kerb** is the raised row of stones or concrete at the edge of a street.

kettle *noun*
A **kettle** is a pot for boiling water in. It has a handle and a specially shaped opening for pouring the boiling water out.

key¹ *noun*
A **key** is a small piece of metal with a special shape that can open a lock.

key² *noun*
1. A **key** is one of a row of flat, narrow, black or white pieces on an instrument like a piano which you press down to make the instrument play. *The piano keys were not white any more because the piano was so old.*
2. A **key** is one of the small pieces in rows which you use to type words into the computer. *She spelt the word wrongly because she hit the wrong key accidentally.*
–*verb* **3.** When you **key** in something on a computer, you type information into it. *To log on, you must key in your name.*

Word Building: **keyboard**, *noun* The keys of an instrument or a computer are on a **keyboard**. –**keyer**, *noun* Someone employed to key information into a computer is a **keyer**.

kick *verb*
If you **kick** someone or something, you hit them with your foot or make them move with your foot. *Don't walk behind the horse. It might kick you.*

kid¹ *noun*
1. A **kid** is a baby goat. *The mother goat had twin kids.*

2. A **kid** is a child. *Ann wanted to go and join the kids who were playing in the park.*

Although people often use **kid** to mean 'a child' (as in definition 2), remember that it is an informal word. You use it when talking to your friends, but not when you are writing in a very formal way.

kid[2] *verb* (**kids, kidding, kidded, has kidded**)
If you **kid** someone, you try to trick them as a joke. *Don't be upset – he was only kidding when he said you couldn't come with us.*

kill *verb*
If someone or something **kills** someone, they make them die. *He was put in prison because he killed a woman.*

kilogram *noun*
A **kilogram** is a measurement of weight.

The short form is **kilo**. A short way of writing **kilogram** is **kg**.

⭐ *Spelling Tip:* The middle sound is spelt *o*. Learn the word part *kilo* (which means 'thousand') and you will be able to spell not only **kilogram** but other words which include it, such as *kilometre*.

kilometre /*say* **kil**-uh-mee-tuh, kuh-**lom**-uh-tuh/ *noun*
A **kilometre** is a measurement of length. It is a long length, equal to 1000 metres.

The short way of writing this is **km**.

kind[1] *adjective*
If you are **kind**, you are friendly and want to help other people or animals.

Word Building: **kindly**, *adjective* If you have a kind nature then you are **kindly**. –**kindness**, *noun* If you are kind, you show **kindness**.

The opposite is **unkind** or **cruel**.

kind[2] *noun*
A **kind** is a group of people or things that are similar in some way.

Other words with a similar meaning are **type** and **sort**.

kindergarten *noun*
A **kindergarten** is a school for very young children.

⭐ *Spelling Tip:* Remember the *er* spelling in the middle. This is because the first part of the word is *kinder*, the German word for 'children' (in German *er* makes the plural of some words). Added to it is *garten*, the German word for 'garden'. Don't get confused and put a *d* instead of the *t*.

king *noun*
In some countries, the **king** is a man who is the leader of the country or the most important person in the country. He becomes the king because of the special family he is born into.

kingdom *noun*
A **kingdom** is a country that has a king or a queen as its leader.

kiosk /*say* **kee**-osk/ *noun*
A **kiosk** is a small shop which sells things like newspapers, drinks and things to eat.

⭐ *Spelling Tip:* The most difficult part is the *ki* opening (giving a 'kee' sound). This word is unusual because it comes from Turkish.

kiss *verb*
If you **kiss** someone, you touch their face or lips with your lips, especially as a way of saying hello or goodbye or to show that you like them very much. *Peter was crying so his mother put her arms around him and kissed him.*

kitchen *noun*
A **kitchen** is the room in a house where you cook food and get it ready for eating.

kite *noun*
A **kite** is a toy made of paper or cloth stretched over a light frame and tied to a long string. You hold the end of the string while the wind makes the **kite** fly.

kitten *noun*
A **kitten** is a baby cat.

kiwi /*say* **kee**-wee/ *noun* (*plural* **kiwis**)
A **kiwi** is a New Zealand bird that cannot fly. It has a large rounded body, thick legs and a long, thin beak.

knee /*say* nee/ *noun*
Your **knee** is the middle part of your leg where the top part joins the bottom part.

kneel /*say* neel/ *verb* (**kneels, kneeling, knelt, has knelt**)
If you **kneel**, you lower your body and go down on your knees. *Mum knelt down and looked under the furniture for the missing book.*

knife /say nuyf / noun (plural **knives**)

A **knife** is a tool with a sharp part along one side for cutting things, especially food.

knight /say nuyt / noun

1. A **knight** is a man who has the special name 'Sir' given to him by a queen or king. *He was made a knight at a special ceremony.*
2. In times long ago, a **knight** was a man who fought on a horse to help the king. *I have read about knights like Sir Galahad and Lohengrin.*

knit /say nit / verb (**knits, knitting, knitted, has knitted**)

If you **knit**, you make clothes by weaving lengths of wool or some other material together with two long needles. *I am going to knit a scarf in the colours of my favourite football team.*

knob /say nob / noun

A **knob** is a round handle on a door or a drawer.

knock /say nok / verb

1. If you **knock**, you hit something, usually a door, with your hand so that it makes a noise and people know you are there. *We knocked at the door and waited to see who would come.*
2. If you **knock** something, you hit it hard. *She knocked the chair as she walked past and it fell over.*
–noun 3. A **knock** is the sound made when someone knocks.

knot /say not / noun

1. A **knot** is the part where something long and thin, like a piece of rope or string, has been tied tightly to make a fastening. *I tied my shoe laces in a knot so they wouldn't come undone while I was in the race.*
2. A **knot** is the part where something long and thin has accidentally got tied up in a way which is hard to undo. *The fishing line was tangled and we had to cut out the knot because we couldn't undo it.*

know /say noh / verb (**knows, knowing, knew, has known**)

1. If you **know** something or how to do something, you feel certain about it being right because you have learned and understood it or you have done it before. *Our teacher wants us to know all the major rivers in our state before we finish this year.* | *I know how to ride a bike but my little sister has not learned yet.*
2. If you **know** someone, you have met them, usually many times. *I have known Sam ever since kindergarten.*

knowledge /say **nol**-ij / noun

Knowledge is what someone knows.

knuckle /say **nuk**-uhl / noun

Your **knuckle** is the place in your finger where it bends or where it meets the rest of your hand.

koala /say koh-**ah**-luh / noun

A **koala** is an Australian animal with grey fur and no tail. **Koalas** eat the leaves of gum trees. The females carry their babies in a pouch.

This word comes from an Aboriginal language of New South Wales called Dharug.

kookaburra noun

A **kookaburra** is an Australian bird with a call that sounds like someone laughing.

This word comes from an Aboriginal language of New South Wales called Wiradjuri.

✺ *Spelling Tip:* Remember that there are two *o*'s and two *r*'s in **kookaburra**. There are also two separate *k*'s but no *c*. No-one would want to *cook* a nice bird like a kookaburra!

kowari /say kuh-**wah**-ree / noun

A **kowari** is a small, yellow-brown animal with a black bushy tail that lives in the Australian desert. There are not many of these animals left.

This word comes from an Aboriginal language of South Australia called Diyari.

kurrajong noun

A **kurrajong** is a tree growing mainly in the eastern part of Australia.

This word comes from an Aboriginal language of New South Wales called Dharug.

lifesaver

laboratory /say luh-**bo**-ruh-tree/ noun

A **laboratory** is a special room or building where scientists work.

> You can also say **lab**, which is a short word for a **laboratory**. It is a rather informal word that you might use when speaking rather than writing.

> ✷ *Spelling Tip:* The original meaning of **laboratory** was a workshop. This can help you remember that the first part of the word is spelt *labor* (a form of the word *labour* meaning 'work'). Also remember that the ending is *ory* although you don't hear the *or* when the word is said. Try breaking the word up as *lab+or+ a+tor+y*.

label noun

A **label** is a piece of paper put on something to tell you what it is, who it belongs to or where it is going.

> ✷ *Spelling Tip:* Remember that the ending of **label** is spelt *el* (not *le*). The more common ending is *le* but there are a lot of *el* words, such as *angel*, *camel* and *kennel*.

labour noun

1. Labour is hard or tiring work.
–verb **2.** If you **labour**, you work hard at some-thing. *The builders laboured all morning in the sun.*

> *Word Building:* **labourer**, *noun* A **labourer** is someone who works at a job which uses strength and effort rather than special skill or training.

> Another spelling for this word is **labor**.

lace noun

1. Lace is a net-like material with patterns made of fine threads with holes in between. *Shona's new dress has very pretty lace around the collar.*

2. A **lace** is a piece of strong, thin material that you use to tie up your shoe. *My lace broke right before the race so I ran without shoes.*

lack noun

1. If there is a **lack** of something, there is none of it at all, or there is not enough of it.
–verb **2.** If you **lack** something, you are without it, or you do not have much of it. *We lacked the right equipment to do the hard bush walk, and decided on the easier one.*

ladder noun

A **ladder** is a piece of equipment that you use if you need to climb up or down. It is made from two long pieces of wood, metal or rope, with steps between them.

lady noun (plural ladies)

You use **lady** when you are talking in a polite or respectful way about a woman.

ladybird noun

A **ladybird** is a small beetle which has an orange back with black spots on it.

lagoon noun

A **lagoon** is a large area of calm water cut off from a larger body of water like the sea.

lake noun

A **lake** is a large area of water with land all around it.

lamb /rhymes with dam/ noun

1. A **lamb** is a young sheep. *It was spring and we saw lots of new lambs.*
2. Lamb is the meat from a young sheep. *My favourite dinner is roast lamb with gravy.*

lame adjective

If you are **lame**, you have something wrong with your foot or your leg that stops you walking properly.

lamington noun

A **lamington** is a piece of light cake in a square shape, covered in chocolate and coconut.

lamp *noun*
A **lamp** is a type of light, often one which has a cover of some kind.

land *noun*
1. **Land** is the part of the earth's surface not covered by water. *After being on the boat all day, it was good to be back on dry land again.*
2. **Land** is a particular area of the surface of the earth, especially when you are talking about who owns it, what it looks like or what it is used for. *Her uncle owns the land right down to the river. | This is good land for growing vegetables.*
–*verb* 3. If something **lands** somewhere, they come to rest there, after being in the air. *What time does the plane land? | The ball landed in a bad place – over the neighbours' fence!*

landing *noun*
When a plane ends its journey, it makes a **landing** on the ground.

lane *noun*
1. A **lane** is a narrow road, or a narrow way between houses or fences. *The car entry to the shop was through a lane around the back.*
2. A **lane** is part of a wide road for one line of traffic to travel along. *The driver moved over into the right lane, because he was about to make a right-hand turn.*
3. A **lane** is a part of a running track or of a swimming pool that has been marked out as the space for one person. *It was exciting watching her move further and further ahead in her lane.*

language /*say* **lang**-gwij/ *noun*
A **language** is the set of words you use when you speak and write, and the way they are put together to mean something. Different **languages** can be used by different countries and groups of people.

> ✸ *Spelling Tip:* The *gu* spelling for the 'gw' sound in the middle is the difficult bit here. It might help if you remember that **language** comes from *langue* (the French word for 'tongue' or 'language'). The *e* has been dropped and the word part *age* added.

lap¹ *noun*
Your **lap** is the front part of your body, from your waist to your knees, when you are sitting down.

lap² *noun*
A **lap** is one complete length of a racing track or a swimming pool.

laptop *noun*
A **laptop** is a small computer that can be carried around easily and used anywhere. You can put it on a desk or you can use it while it is sitting on your lap.

large *adjective*
Something is **large** if it is greater in size or number than the usual. *An elephant is a very large animal. | There was a large crowd of people at the concert.*

lasagne /*say* luh-**sahn**-yuh/ *noun*
Lasagne is a kind of Italian food made from flat sheets of pasta, meat, tomato and cheese.

lash *noun*
A **lash** is one of the short, curved hairs that grow around the edges of your eye.

> **Lash** is the short form of **eyelash**.

last¹ *adjective*
1. If something or someone is **last**, they come after everything else in time, order or place. *Because my name starts with 'Z', I'm always last on every list. | She missed the last train and had to get a taxi home.*
2. You use **last** to describe something that is the most recent. *We went to a concert last night.*
–*adverb* 3. If you do something **last**, you do it after all the others. *He came last in the race.*

last² *verb*
If something **lasts**, it goes on or continues. *After-school care lasts for two hours.*

late *adjective*
1. Something is **late** if it happens after it usually does, or after it should happen. *We had a late lunch at school today because the boy who rang the bell forgot.*
2. You use **late** when you are talking about something happening near the end of a period of time. *We all met at the beach in the late afternoon to watch the sunset.*

> The opposite is **early**.

lately *adverb*
If something has happened **lately**, it has happened during the period of time that is close to now. *Our netball team has been playing much better lately.*

later *adverb*
1. If something happens **later**, it happens some time after something else. *At Marco's birthday party, we had the food first and the clown came later.*
–*adjective* 2. If something is **later** than something else, it happens at some time after it.

a
b
c
d
e
f
g
h
i
j
k
l
m
n
o
p
q
r
s
t
u
v
w
x
y
z

laugh /say lahf/ verb
1. If you **laugh**, you make sounds that show that you are happy, or that you have found something funny. *We all laughed when Ann told us a funny story about her dog.*
2. Sometimes, if you **laugh at** someone, you laugh and make jokes about them in a way that is not kind. *Everyone laughed at me when I fell over during the concert.*
–noun **3.** A **laugh** is a sound made by someone when they are happy or think something is funny.

> **Word Building: laughter** /say **lahf**-tuh/, noun When you laugh, people can hear your **laughter**.

laundry /say **lawn**-dree/ noun (plural **laundries**)
A **laundry** is the room in your house for washing dirty clothes.

> ✪ **Spelling Tip:** Remember the *au* spelling for the 'aw' sound. You will also notice that the last three letters spell the word *dry* – very suitable for a **laundry**.

lava /say **lah**-vuh/ noun
Lava is the very hot, melted rock that flows out of a volcano.

law noun
A **law** is a rule or set of rules, especially those that everyone in a country must obey.

lawn noun
A **lawn** is the part of a garden with grass that has been cut very short.

lawyer /say **law**-yuh, **loy**-yuh/ noun
A **lawyer** is someone whose job it is to give advice about the law or argue for you before a judge.

> ✪ **Spelling Tip:** To get this spelling right you have to remember that a **lawyer** knows about the *law*. This will give you the first three letters (which some people say more like the sound 'loy'). Then add *yer* and you're there.

lay¹ verb (**lays**, **laying**, **laid**, **has laid**)
1. If you **lay** something somewhere, you put it down or place it there. *She is going to lay the paintings on the table so that we can all see them.*
2. If a bird or animal **lays** an egg, it produces it, usually pushing it out of its body. *One of our hens had found a secret place under a bush to lay her eggs.*

> Don't confuse **lay** with **lie**. **Lie** means 'to be in a flat position', while **lay** means 'to put something

somewhere'. It can be confusing because the words have a similar meaning. To make things even more confusing, **lay** is also the form of **lie** that you use when the lying down action was in the past: *I lay on the bed for the whole of the afternoon.* As you can see from the above example, the form of **lay** that you use when you are talking about something that has already happened is **laid**: *She laid the plates on the table.*

lay² verb
Look up **lie¹**.

layer noun
A **layer** is a single thickness of something. *Rata's birthday cake had three layers.* | *This wall needs a new layer of paint.*

lazy /say **lay**-zee/ adjective (**lazier**, **laziest**)
If someone is **lazy**, they do not like work or effort. *We don't have any lazy students in our class this year – everyone tries hard.* | *He is so lazy he won't even walk down to the shop on the corner.*

> **Word Building: lazily**, adverb If you are lazy, you do things **lazily**. –**laziness**, noun If someone is lazy, you talk about their **laziness**.

> ✪ **Spelling Tip:** Remember that the letter *a* alone spells the 'ay' sound.

lead¹ /say leed/ verb (**leads**, **leading**, **led** /say led/, **has led**)
1. If someone or something **leads** you, they guide you, often in a particular direction or to a particular place. *We led them to the place where we had found the money.*
2. If you are **leading** a group which is moving somewhere, you are in the front of the other people. *We had a special guide to lead us around the zoo.*
3. If someone **leads** a group of people, like an army or a country, they are in charge of them. *He led the government for 20 years.*
–noun **4.** A **lead** is a long piece of leather, chain or rope for holding an animal.

> **Word Building: leader**, noun Someone who leads is a **leader**.

lead² /say led/ noun
Lead is a heavy blue-grey metal.

> **Word Building: leaded**, adjective If petrol has lead in it, is is **leaded**. Most petrol these days does not have lead in it and so is **unleaded**.

leaf *noun* (*plural* **leaves**)
A **leaf** is one of the thin, flat, usually green parts of a plant.

league /*say* leeg/ *noun*
A **league** is a group of people, countries or organisations who have joined together for a particular purpose.

leak *noun*
1. A **leak** is a small hole or split in something that lets liquid or a gas out when it is not supposed to get out.
–*verb* 2. If liquid or gas **leaks**, it comes out of a place where it is not supposed to. *You can hear the air leaking out of my bike tyre.*

lean *verb* (**leans**, **leaning**, **leaned** *or* **leant** /*say* lent/, **has leaned** *or* **has leant**)
If you **lean**, you bend or curve your body towards or against something. *Lean over here and I'll whisper a secret in your ear.*

> ✱ *Spelling Tip:* Remember that the past form **leant** keeps the spelling *lean* (with *t* added), even though the sound changes to 'lent'.

leap *verb* (**leaps**, **leaping**, **leapt** /*say* lept) *or* **leaped**, **has leapt** *or* **has leaped**)
If you **leap**, you jump or move quickly. *We leapt into the car and Mum drove us to the station.*

> ✱ *Spelling Tip:* Remember that the past form **leapt** keeps the spelling *leap* (with *t* added), even though the sound changes to 'lept'.

learn *verb* (**learns**, **learning**, **learned** *or* **learnt**, **has learned** *or* **has learnt**)
If you **learn** something, you come to have knowledge of it, or skill in doing it. *We are learning about multiplication at school.*

> *Word Building:* **learner**, *noun* Someone who is learning something is a **learner**.

least *adverb*
1. You use **least** when you are talking about something which is the smallest in size or amount. *We didn't have much money so we bought the least expensive socks in the shop.*
2. **at least**, **a.** You use **at least** to show that something is equal to or greater than the amount you are saying. *There must have been at least a hundred kids on the oval for the fun run.* **b.** You use **at least** when you want to point out something that is the one good part of something

bad. *I feel very sick, but at least I don't have to go to school.*

> The opposite is **most**.

leather /*say* ledh-uh/ *noun*
Leather is the skin of animals that has been specially prepared so that it can be used to make such things as shoes and bags.

> ✱ *Spelling Tip:* Remember the *ea* spelling for the 'e' sound.

leave *verb* (**leaves**, **leaving**, **left**, **has left**)
1. If you **leave** a place or a person, you go away from them. *We had to leave home straight after breakfast to catch the train.*
2. If you **leave** something in a particular way, you let it stay or remain like that. *He left the door open.*
3. **leave out**, If you **leave out** something, you do not include it. *If you leave out the sugar, the cake won't be any good.*

lecture /*say* lek-chuh/ *noun*
A **lecture** is a speech that someone gives to a group of people, often students, in order to teach them or give them information.

left[1] *adjective*
1. The **left** side of your body is where your heart is.
–*noun* 2. The **left** is the direction to the left side of your body.

> The opposite is **right**.

left[2] *verb*
1. Look up **leave**.
–*adjective* 2. If something is **left**, it remains after others like it have gone or been used.

leg *noun*
1. A **leg** is one of the parts of a person or animal's body which is used for support and for walking. *The hard part in jumping heights is getting your second leg over.*
2. The **leg** of a piece of furniture is one of the parts which supports it. *My desk has a wobbly leg.*

legend /*say* lej-uhnd/ *noun*
A **legend** is a story that comes from long ago in the past. At least part of the story is probably true.

> Also look up **myth**.

lemon *noun*
A **lemon** is a yellow fruit with a sour taste.

lemonade *noun*
Lemonade is a sweet drink full of tiny bubbles of gas.

lend *verb* (**lends**, **lending**, **lent**, **has lent**)
If you **lend** something to someone, you allow them to take it, knowing that they must return it to you. *I'll lend you my bike, but I will need to have it back tomorrow.*

The opposite is **borrow**. If you lend someone something, they are borrowing it from you.

When you lend someone something, you give them a **loan** of it.

length *noun*
The **length** of something is how long it is from one end to the other.

Word Building: **lengthen**, *verb* If you give something more length, you **lengthen** it.

Spelling Tip: Remember **length** is formed from *long* and so it has a *g* in it.

leopard /*say* **lep**-uhd/ *noun*
A **leopard** is a large member of the cat family that has yellow fur with black spots. **Leopards** live in Africa and Asia.

Spelling Tip: Remember the *eo* spelling for the 'e' sound in the first part of the word. This is because the word comes from *leo*, the Latin word for 'lion'. Also remember there is an *r* in the last part.

less *adjective*
1. You use **less** when you are describing something smaller in size or amount than something else.
–*adverb* **2.** You use **less** when you are describing something not as big or as much as another sort. *Choose a less expensive present.*

The opposite is **more**.

lesson *noun*
1. A **lesson** is the time during which a student or a class is taught one subject. *Our first lesson on Mondays is always spelling.*
2. A **lesson** can be anything that you learn, or from which you learn how to behave in the future. *Leaving my bag on the train was a lesson to me not to be thinking about too many things at once.*

let *verb* (**lets**, **letting**, **let**, **has let**)
1. If you **let** someone do something, you allow them to do it. *She let us leave early.*
2. let down, If you **let** someone **down**, you disappoint them. *You will let us down if you don't come.*
3. let out, If you **let** something or someone **out**, you allow them to leave a place where they have been locked up. *We let the dog out of the house and now we can't find it.*

letter *noun*
1. A **letter** is a message in writing or print that you send to someone. *We don't send so many letters now that we have email.*
2. A **letter** is one of the signs used in writing and print to stand for a sound you make in speech. *'A' is the first letter of the alphabet.*

letterbox *noun*
A **letterbox** is a box outside your home where your letters are delivered.

lettuce *noun*
A **lettuce** is a plant with big, green leaves that you eat in salads.

Spelling Tip: Notice the ending is *uce* (not *ice*).

level *adjective*
1. If a surface is **level**, it is even. No part of it is higher than another part. *Tennis courts have to be level or the balls would bounce all over the place.*
2. If two or more things are **level**, they are equal. *I bent down so I was level with my little brother.*
–*noun* **3.** The **level** of water in a river or lake, or of a liquid in a container, is how high its surface is. *The level of the water in the river is so low that we can't swim.*
4. A **level** is a flat surface that is either higher or lower than another flat surface. *You get the best view from the top level, but some of us were so tired that we couldn't climb all the stairs.*

lever /*say* **lee**-vuh/ *noun*
A **lever** is a handle that you push or pull to make a machine work.

liar *noun*
A **liar** is someone who doesn't tell the truth.

liberate /*say* **lib**-uh-rayt/ *verb*
If you **liberate** someone, you set them free. *After the war, the army liberated all the prisoners.*

Word Building: **liberation**, *noun*: *Everyone celebrated the prisoners' liberation.*

librarian /*say* luy-**brair**-ree-uhn/ *noun*
A **librarian** is someone who looks after the books in a library.

library /say **luy**-bree/ noun (plural **libraries**)

A **library** is a room or building where books and other study materials are kept for people to use.

⭐ **Spelling Tip:** Don't forget that the ending of **library** is *ary* although the *ar* is usually not said. Think of 'r̲elax a̲nd r̲ead' to remind you of *a* between the two *r*'s in this word.

lice noun

Lice are very small insects that can live in your hair.

Another name is **head lice**. For one of these insects we use the word **louse**.

licence noun

A **licence** is a printed form that says you can do, use or own something.

lick verb

If you **lick** something, you move your tongue over it. *Lick the back of the stamp and stick it on the envelope.*

licorice /say **lik**-uh-rish/ noun

Licorice is a sweet, black food made from the root of a plant.

Another spelling for this word is **liquorice**.

lid noun

A **lid** is a movable top for covering a container.

lie[1] verb (**lies**, **lying**, **lay**, **has lain**)

If you **lie** somewhere, your body is stretched out flat. *She lay under the tree and went to sleep.*

Don't confuse **lie** with **lay**. **Lay** means 'to put something somewhere', while **lie** means 'to be in a flat position'. It can be confusing because the words have a similar meaning. To make things even more confusing, **lay** is also the form of **lie** that you use when the lying down action was in the past: *I lay on the bed for the whole afternoon.* So you have to be careful about which **lay** you are using.

lie[2] noun

1. A **lie** is something you say that you know is not true.

–verb (**lies**, **lying**, **lied**, **has lied**)

2. If you **lie**, you say something that you know is not true. *My grandfather lied about his age so he could join the army.*

life noun (plural **lives**)

1. **Life** is the condition that makes animals and plants different from dead things and from other objects such as rocks, liquids and machines. *The man lying on the road showed no sign of life.*

2. Your **life** is the time you are alive, from your birth to your death, or from your birth up to the present time. *He had only a short life. He died when he was 30.*

3. You can use **life** when you are talking about the way someone lives. *Life in a big city is so different from life in the desert.*

lifesaver noun

A **lifesaver** is someone who watches people swimming at the beach and helps them if they are having trouble in the water.

Another word for this is **lifeguard**, particularly for someone who looks after the safety of people swimming in a pool.

lifetime noun

Your **lifetime** is the length of time you are alive.

lift verb

1. If you **lift** something, you move it to a higher position. *We lifted up the mat and what do you think we found underneath?*

–noun **2.** A **lift** is something shaped like a small room which you get into to travel from one level of a building to another.

Another word for definition 2 is **elevator**.

light[1] /say luyt/ noun

1. **Light** is what allows you to see things. The light of the day comes from the sun, but light can also come from other things such as a lamp or a fire. *The light from the sun is too bright – it's hurting my eyes.*

2. A **light** is something that produces light so you can see when it is dark. *It's too dark in here – turn on the light.*

–adjective **3.** If a place is **light**, it has a lot of light in it. *My bedroom is a nice, light room. It gets a lot of sun.*

4. If a colour is **light**, it is pale. *She was wearing a light blue dress.*

–verb (**lights**, **lighting**, **lit** or **lighted**, **has lit** or **has lighted**)

5. If you **light** something, you make it start to burn. *It was so cold we lit a fire.*

The opposite of definitions 3 and 4 is **dark**.

light[2] /say luyt/ adjective

1. If something is **light**, it does not weigh very much. It is easy to lift or carry. *These boxes are very light – we won't need any help to carry them.*

2. If something is **light**, it is small in amount or force. *We always have something light to eat after*

a b c d e f g h i j k l m n o p q r s t u v w x y z

school when we get home. | *It was only light rain so we kept playing.*

> **Word Building: lightly,** *adverb*: *She touched her hair lightly.*

> The opposite is **heavy**.

lightning /*say* **luyt**-ning/ *noun*
Lightning is a sudden burst of light in the sky caused by electricity in the air during a storm.

like¹ *preposition*
1. If something is **like** something else, it is similar to it in some way. *Our school uniform is like the one they have at the school down the road – the only difference is they have a hat and we don't.*
2. If you say that some behaviour is **like** someone, you mean that it is the sort of thing they usually do. *She swept into the room like a princess.*
3. You can use **like** when you are giving examples of something. *My favourite foods are sweet things, like chocolate, jelly and ice-cream.*

like² *verb*
If you **like** something, you find it pleasant. You enjoy it. You can **like** people as well as things. *I like having a pet, especially when it's a dog.*

> **Word Building: liking,** *noun* When you like something, you have a **liking** for it.

likely *adjective*
If you say that something is **likely**, you mean that it is probably going to happen.

limb /*rhymes with* dim/ *noun*
1. Your **limbs** are your arms and legs. *Swimming is good exercise for your limbs, which is why swimmers have such big muscles in their legs and arms.*
2. A **limb** is the branch of a tree. *The council is going to cut off the limb that hangs over the building.*

> ✴ **Spelling Tip:** Don't forget the silent *b* at the end.

limerick /*say* **lim**-uh-rik/ *noun*
A **limerick** is a poem with five lines, intended to make you laugh.

limit *noun*
A **limit** is an amount or level that you cannot or should not go beyond.

line *noun*
1. A **line** is a long thin mark made on paper, wood or some other surface. *The teacher asked us to draw three lines across the paper.*
2. A **line** is a group of things placed one after the other. *There was a long line of people waiting to buy tickets to the game.*
–*verb* **3. line up,** If people **line up**, they wait one behind the other. *We had to line up for two hours before we could get into the game.*

link *noun*
1. A **link** is one of the rings in a chain.
2. When you click on a **link** on the internet, it takes you to another website.
–*verb* **3.** If you **link** one thing to another, you make them join together, like the rings in a chain. *For the dance, we all had to link arms and make a circle.*
4. If something **links up with** something, or is **linked to** something, these things are connected so that they can work together. *The company Mum works for is linked to a bigger company in another country.*

lion *noun*
A **lion** is a large, wild animal in the cat family, with yellow-brown fur. Lions live in Africa and southern Asia.

> The female is a **lioness**.

lip *noun*
Your **lip** is one of the two soft edges of your mouth.

liquid /*say* **lik**-wuhd/ *noun*
A **liquid** is anything that can flow like water. It is different from air and it is different from something that is solid. *You need to drink a lot of liquid when the weather is very hot.*

liquid paper *noun*
Liquid paper is a thin white paint that is used to cover written mistakes on paper.

> Another word for this is **white-out**.

list *noun*
A **list** is a set of things written down one under the other.

listen /*say* **lis**-uhn/ *verb*
If you **listen** to something, you pay attention so that you are able to hear it. *We weren't listening and we didn't have a clue where we were supposed to go.*

> ✴ **Spelling Tip:** Don't forget the *st* (not double *s*) spelling. The *t* is silent.

litre /*say* **lee**-tuh/ *noun*
A **litre** is a measure of liquid.

> The short way of writing **litre** is **L** or **l**.

litter *noun*

1. **Litter** is things that people have thrown away, lying all over the place, especially in a public place. *The football oval was covered with litter after the game.*

2. A **litter** is a group of baby animals that are born at the same time. *Our cat had a litter of six kittens.*

little *adjective*

1. (**littler, littlest**) If something is **little**, it is small in size. *Our baby has little feet, and even littler toes.*

2. **Little** can mean 'not much'. *My dad said there was little reason to go to the football oval because it was pouring.*

live¹ /rhymes with give/ *verb*

1. If you **live**, you are alive. People, animals and plants **live**. *I want to live until I'm a hundred years old so I can do lots of things.*

2. If you **live** somewhere, you have your home there. *We live in a house near the river.*

live² /rhymes with dive/ *adjective*

1. **Live** animals and plants are living or alive. *That snake eats live mice.*

2. Something is **live** if it is on radio or television at the same time as it is happening. *We listened to a live broadcast of the game.*

3. Something is **live** if it has electricity running through it. *Be careful! That's a live wire!*

lively /say **luyv**-lee/ *adjective* (**livelier, liveliest**) If someone or something is **lively**, they are full of energy.

living *adjective*

A **living** person, animal or plant is one that is alive.

living room *noun*

A **living room** is a room in a home where people can sit and be together. It usually has things like comfortable chairs and a television.

Another word for this is **lounge room**.

lizard /say **liz**-uhd/ *noun*

A **lizard** is an animal with a long, thin body, four short legs, a long tail and skin like a snake.

load *noun*

1. A **load** is something that you carry. *That truck is carrying a heavy load.*

2. A **load** is also the quantity carried. *It had a full load of coal.*

−*verb* 3. If you **load** something, you put things in or on it for it to carry somewhere. *They loaded the truck with coal.*

loaf¹ *noun* (*plural* **loaves**)

A **loaf** is a piece of bread or cake baked in a particular shape.

loaf² *verb*

If you **loaf**, you do nothing. *The teacher was really angry because we had been loafing instead of working.*

loan *noun*

Someone gives you a **loan** when they lend you something and expect you to return it.

lobster *noun*

A **lobster** is an animal with a hard shell that lives in the sea. The first two of its ten legs are like big claws.

local *adjective*

Something is **local** if it belongs to a place, like your town or area.

lock¹ *noun*

1. A **lock** is something used to keep a door, gate, drawer or box shut. It needs a key to open it.

−*verb* 2. If you **lock** something like a door, you fasten it, usually with a key. *Please remember to lock the door when you leave.*

The opposite of definition 2 is **unlock**.

lock² *noun*

A **lock** is a piece of hair.

locust /say **loh**-kuhst/ *noun*

A **locust** is a kind of grasshopper. They fly about in very large numbers and can cause great damage by eating all the things that are growing in a place.

log¹ *noun*

A **log** is a large branch or the trunk of a tree which has fallen or been cut down.

log² *verb* (**logs, logging, logged, has logged**)

1. When you **log on** to a computer system, you start working on it, usually by putting in your name and password. *The first thing we learned in the computer lesson was how to log on.*

2. When you **log off**, you leave the computer system that you have been working in. *We logged off by clicking on the icon at the top of the screen.*

lolly *noun* (*plural* **lollies**)

A **lolly** is a sweet thing that you suck or eat.

lonely *adjective* (**lonelier, loneliest**)

1. If someone is **lonely**, they are unhappy because they are not with their friends or family. *The old man was lonely when his wife died.*

a b c d e f g h i j k l m n o p q r s t u v w x y z

2. A place is **lonely** if it is far away from where people are. *We travelled all night along a lonely road without seeing another car.*

Word Building: loneliness, *noun* If you are lonely, you have a feeling of **loneliness**.

Compare **lonely** with **alone**.

long[1] *adjective* (**longer**, **longest**)
1. Something is **long** if it measures a lot from one end to the other. *It is a long way from Melbourne to Darwin.*
2. Something is **long** if it lasts for a great amount of time. *I hope you didn't have a long wait in the rain.*

Look up **length**.

The opposite is **short**.

long[2] *verb*
If you **long** for something, you want it very much. *We were very hungry and longed for some food.*

look *verb*
1. When you **look**, you use your eyes to see. *I looked through the window and couldn't believe my eyes!*
2. If someone or something **looks** a particular way, they appear or seem to be that way. *He looked happy, but we all knew he was really feeling sad.*
3. look after, If you **look after** someone or something, you take care of them. *It was fun looking after my friend's pet mice while he was on holidays.*

loom[1] *noun*
A **loom** is a machine for weaving threads into cloth.

loom[2] *verb*
If something **looms**, it appears suddenly, usually in a way that frightens you. *I had a terrible dream that a huge monster was looming out of the darkness.*

loop *noun*
A **loop** is a length of something like a piece of string made into a circle shape.

loose /*say* loohs/ *adjective*
1. If something is **loose** it is not tied up or fastened. *Her loose hair blew in the wind.*
2. If something is **loose**, it does not fit tightly. *My grandmother is rather big and wears large, loose clothes.*

✸ Spelling Tip: Don't confuse the spelling of **loose** with **lose** (which has only one *o* and which you say *loohz*). If you **lose** something, you can't find it.

lord *noun*
1. In Britain, a **lord** is a man with an especially high position in society. The word **Lord** is also used in the man's title.
2. In Australia, **Lord** is used as part of the title of some important positions. *The Lord Mayor of Sydney was at the ceremony.*

lorikeet *noun*
A **lorikeet** is a small, brightly coloured parrot.

lose /*say* loohz/ *verb* (**loses**, **losing**, **lost**, **has lost**)
1. If you **lose** something, you are without it because you cannot find it. *Sam lost his ticket and had to pay for another one.*
2. If you **lose** a race or a game, someone else does better than you and wins. *We lost the boat race again this year.*

✸ Spelling Tip: Don't confuse the spelling of **lose** with **loose** (which has a double *o* and which you say *loohs*). **Loose** means 'not tight'.

loss *noun*
If you lose something, you talk about the **loss** of it.

lost *adjective*
1. If something is **lost**, you cannot find it. *When our dog was lost, we put signs everywhere to try to find him.*
2. If you are **lost**, you do not know where you are or you cannot find your way. *We took the wrong bush track and before long we realised we were lost.*

lot *noun*
1. a lot, You use **a lot** when you are talking about a large number or amount. *Bruce had such a lot of food I thought he would share it with us.*
2. the lot, **The lot** is the whole of something. *I asked Bruce if I could have some of his food, but he had eaten the lot.*

loud *adjective*
If something is **loud**, it makes a lot of sound.

Word Building: loudly, *adverb*: *She spoke loudly into the phone.*

The opposite is **quiet** or **soft**.

lounge *noun*
   1. A **lounge** is a long, comfortable seat with sides and a back, for two or more people. *Mum and Dad always sit on the lounge while they watch television.*
   2. A **lounge** is a room in your home with comfortable chairs in it. *My grandmother takes her most important visitors into the lounge and gives them tea and cakes.*

> Other words that mean the same as definition 1 are **sofa** and **couch**.

> You can also say **lounge room** for definition 2.

louse /rhymes with house/ *noun* (*plural* **lice**)
   Look up **lice**.

love *verb*
   1. If you **love** someone, you have a strong feeling of liking them very much. *She loved her children and would do anything to protect them.*
   –noun **2.** **Love** is a strong feeling that you have for someone that you like very much.

lovely *adjective* (**lovelier**, **loveliest**)
   1. If someone is **lovely**, they are beautiful to look at. *The actress in that new film is really lovely.*
   2. If something is **lovely**, it is very pleasant. *It was a lovely day, so we decided to go to the beach.*

low *adjective*
   1. If something is **low**, it is near to the ground or floor. *There was a low table in the centre of the room.*
   2. If something is **low**, it is small in amount. *Her mother's income was very low.*
   3. If a sound is **low**, it is quiet. *His voice was so low that we couldn't hear him.*

lower *verb*
   If you **lower** something, you make it go down. *We lowered the microphone so that the young children could speak into it.*

> The opposite is **raise**.

loyal *adjective*
   You are **loyal** if you are true to your friends and they can trust you.

> **Word Building: loyalty**, *noun* Someone who is loyal is full of **loyalty**.

> Another word with a similar meaning is **faithful**.

luck *noun*
   Luck is something which happens to you in a way that has not been planned. Usually **luck** means something good, but you can also have bad **luck**. *It was just luck that we got to the canteen as the lasagne was coming out of the oven.*

lucky *adjective* (**luckier**, **luckiest**)
   If someone is **lucky**, they have good luck. Something good has happened to them which was not planned or expected.

> **Word Building: luckily**, *adverb*: *Luckily, the sun came out on the day of the swimming carnival.*

luggage *noun*
   Your **luggage** is the bags that you carry your clothes and other things in when you travel.

> A word with a similar meaning is **baggage**.

> ✳ *Spelling Tip:* Remember the double g. **Luggage** comes from the word *lug* meaning 'to drag' so think of yourself 'lugging around luggage' and you will remember the double g.

lullaby *noun* (*plural* **lullabies**)
   A **lullaby** is a song sung to put a baby to sleep.

lump *noun*
   1. A **lump** is a piece of something with no special shape. *The art teacher took a lump of clay and made it into a bowl.*
   2. A **lump** is a swelling. *I have a lump on my head from where I fell over. It is going purple.*

lunar /say **looh**-nuh/ *adjective*
   Something is **lunar** if it has something to do with the moon.

lunch *noun* (*plural* **lunches**)
   Lunch is a meal you have in the middle of the day.

lung *noun*
   A **lung** is one of the two parts inside your chest that you use for breathing air in and out.

lunge /say lunj/ *verb*
   If you **lunge**, you jump or push forward suddenly towards something or someone. *The policeman lunged towards the thief as he tried to escape through the window.*

luxury /say **luk**-shuh-ree/ *noun* (*plural* **luxuries**)
   1. **Luxury** is extreme comfort in a rich and beautiful place. *When I leave school, I would like to live a life of luxury on a yacht and sail around the world.*

2. A **luxury** is something that you enjoy a lot, but that you do not really need. *My father says it is a luxury to have two bathrooms and we should be very grateful.*

lyrebird /*say* **luy**-uh-berd/ *noun*
A **lyrebird** is an Australian bird that builds its nest on the ground and can copy the sounds of other birds and animals. The male has a long beautiful tail which he spreads open when he is dancing for the female.

⚡ *Spelling Tip:* This bird can make all sorts of sounds, but it is not a *liar*. Remember that the first part of its name is the word *lyre*. It was given this name because people thought the lovely feathers of the male bird looked like the ancient Greek instrument.

  mask

machine /say muh-**sheen**/ noun
A **machine** is something that is made up of moving parts and is often run by electricity. People use **machines** to do work for them.

mad adjective
1. If someone is **mad**, they are sick in their mind. *The shock was so great that she went mad.*
2. If an action is **mad** or the person doing it is **mad**, it is very silly. *You're mad to want to go outside when it's raining.*

madam /say **mad**-uhm/ noun
Madam is a very polite word which you use when you are talking to a woman you do not know well or who is in a high position.

> The word you use for a man is **sir**.

magazine noun
A **magazine** is a kind of newspaper with stories and colour pictures in it. You can usually buy a new one of a particular **magazine** once a week or once a month.

magic /say **maj**-ik/ noun
Magic is the power to do things that no-one can explain. Most people do not believe that **magic** is real.

> **Word Building: magic trick**, noun A **magic trick** is a clever trick that seems to be impossible.

magician /say muh-**jish**-uhn/ noun
A **magician** is someone who can do magic tricks.

> ✸ **Spelling Tip:** Remember that this word comes from *magic* even though the sound of the *c* has changed. The ending *ian* (meaning 'having to do with') has been added. A word with a similar pattern is *musician* (from *music*).

magnet noun
A **magnet** is a piece of iron or steel that can pull other metal things towards it.

magnify /say **mag**-nuh-fuy/ verb (**magnifies, magnifying, magnified, has magnified**)
If something **magnifies** something, it makes it look larger. *My grandfather loves reading but he needs glasses to magnify the print.*

magpie noun
A **magpie** is a black and white bird, very common in Australia.

maid noun
A **maid** is a woman who is paid to live in a house or a hotel and to help look after it.

mail noun
1. **The mail** is letters and other things sent by post.
−verb 2. If you **mail** something, you send it by post. *I mailed my answer to the competition on Monday.*

> ✸ **Spelling Tip:** Don't confuse the spelling of **mail** with **male** which sounds the same. **Male** describes a man or boy.

main adjective
The **main** thing is the most important or biggest thing. *You can get there by staying on the main road. | We did some shopping, but the main reason we went to the city was to see a film.*

mainly adverb
You use **mainly** to say that something is true most of the time but not all the time. You also use it to say that something is true about the largest part of a group but not all of the group. *Our team mainly plays on the local oval but sometimes we have to go to other suburbs. | There are mainly boys in the team, but there are some girls.*

major adjective
If something is **major**, it is very important, especially when compared with something less important.

> The opposite is **minor**.

majority /say muh-**jo**-ruh-tee / noun
The **majority** of something is the greater number of it, or more than half of it.

> The opposite is **minority**.

make verb (**makes, making, made, has made**)
1. If you **make** something, you do something so that a new thing exists. *I will show you how to make rabbit ears with a handkerchief. | The government makes the laws.*
2. If something **makes** you a certain way, it has that effect on you. *Strange people make me nervous. | The rain has made the road dangerous to drive on.*
3. If someone **makes** you do something, they force you to do it. *Dad made me clean my room before I went out.*
4. If numbers **make** an amount, they add up to that amount. *3 and 3 make 6.*
5. make up, a. If you **make up** something, you put parts of it together to make it complete. *If we get three more players, we can make up a full team. | The word 'cupboard' is made up of two other words – 'cup' and 'board'.* **b.** If you **make up** a story, you imagine it. You invent it in your mind. *I did not know if what he said was true, or if he had made it up.*

male adjective
1. A **male** person or animal is of the kind that does not have babies.
–noun **2.** A **male** is a person or animal of the kind that does not have babies.

> The opposite is **female**.

> ✳ *Spelling Tip:* Don't confuse the spelling of **male** with **mail** which sounds the same. **Mail** is letters you get by post.

mall /say mawl, mal / noun
A **mall** is an open area for walking, surrounded by shops.

mammal noun
A **mammal** is an animal which feeds its babies with its own milk.

man noun (plural **men**)
A **man** is an adult male human.

> An adult female human is a **woman**.

manage verb
1. If you **manage** to do something, especially something difficult, you are able to do it. *He managed to feed himself even though he had a broken arm.*

2. If someone **manages** a place of work or an organisation, they are in charge of it. *My mother manages a large office.*
3. If you can **manage** someone or something, you are able to control them. *It's impossible to manage that dog without the lead!*

manager noun
The **manager** of an organisation is the person in charge of it, who tells people working there what to do, and makes sure it runs properly.

mane noun
A **mane** is the long hair on the head of a lion or along the neck of a horse.

mango noun (plural **mangoes** or **mangos**)
A **mango** is a sweet yellow fruit from a tree that grows in hot countries.

mankind noun
Look up **humankind**.

mansion /say **man**-shuhn / noun
A **mansion** is a very big house.

manual adjective
1. If something is **manual**, it has to do with using the hands. For example, a **manual** car is a car that has gears which the driver changes by hand. –noun **2.** A **manual** is a book that tells you how to do something.

manufacture /say man-yuh-**fak**-chuh / verb
If someone **manufactures** things, they make lots of them, usually with machines. *He works in a factory that manufactures washing machines and refrigerators.*

> ✳ *Spelling Tip:* The original meaning of **manufacture** was the making of things by hand. The spelling will be easier if you can see that is made up of *manu* (the Latin word for 'by hand') and *facture* (from the Latin word for 'make'). Another word coming from the same Latin word is *factory*.

many adjective (**more, most**)
1. You use **many** when you are talking about a large number of something.
–pronoun **2. Many** is a large number of something. *I have read many of the books in the library but there are too many for me to read all of them.*

> You use **many** for things that can be counted (*too many potatoes*). You use **much** when you are talking about something that is a mass and cannot be counted (*too much sugar*).

map *noun*
A **map** is a drawing of an area showing where certain things are, such as towns, roads and mountains, and where the borders between countries are.

marble *noun*
1. **Marble** is a sort of smooth, hard stone that you use in buildings or to make statues. *The office steps were made of marble and looked very grand.*
2. A **marble** is a small glass ball you use to play a game. *I have the best collection of marbles in the class.*

march *verb*
If you **march**, you walk like a soldier, with even steps and your arms swinging. *All the little kids love marching to music.*

March *noun*
March is the third month of the year, with 31 days. It comes between February and April.

mare /*rhymes with* hair/ *noun*
A **mare** is a female horse.

The male is a **stallion**.

margarine /*say* mah-juh-**reen**/ *noun*
Margarine is a food like butter, that you can spread on bread or use for cooking. It is made from vegetable oil.

margin /*say* **mah**-juhn/ *noun*
A **margin** is the space between the edge of a page and where the writing starts.

marine /*say* muh-**reen**/ *adjective*
A **marine** creature is one that lives in the sea.

mark *noun*
1. A **mark** is something, like a line or a small coloured or dirty part, that should not be on something. *The dog put marks all over the white carpet when it came inside.*
2. A **mark** is a written shape that gives information. *When you write a question, you put a question mark at the end of it. A question mark looks like this: ?*
3. A **mark** is a number or letter used to show how well or badly you have done a piece of school work or a test. *I was very pleased because I got nine marks out of ten.*

market *noun*
A **market** is a place where things are bought and sold, often at many different small shops.

marmalade *noun*
Marmalade is a jam made with oranges or other fruit like this.

✵ *Spelling Tip:* Remember that the middle sound is spelt *a* – in fact, you need three *a*'s to make **marmalade** properly. Apart from this, you should have no trouble with this word, especially if you divide it up into its parts: *mar + ma + lade*.

marriage /*say* **ma**-rij/ *noun*
1. A **marriage** is the time that two people live together as husband and wife. *My grandparents have had a very happy marriage.*
2. A **marriage** is a ceremony for joining together a man and woman as husband and wife, and the celebrations or party that follows. *My uncle says there is a lot of work to do to get ready for his marriage next month.*

Another word with a similar meaning to definition 2 is **wedding**.

✵ *Spelling Tip:* Notice that there is an *i* in the spelling of **marriage**, although you do not hear it when you say the word. It will help if you remember that **marriage** comes from the word *marry*. The *y* at the end has changed to an *i* before the adding of the final word part *age*.

marry *verb* (**marries, marrying, married, has married**)
When you **marry** someone, you take them as the special person you are going to live with. When a woman and a man **marry**, they become wife and husband. *My parents had a lot of photos taken the day they were married.*

marsh *noun*
A **marsh** is low, wet land.

Word Building: **marshy**, *adjective* Land that is a marsh is **marshy**.

Another word that means nearly the same is **swamp**.

marsupial /*say* mah-**sooh**-pee-uhl/ *noun*
A **marsupial** is an animal which keeps and feeds its babies in a pouch for a few months after they are born.

mask *noun*
A **mask** is something you can wear over your face to change the way you look or to protect it.

a b c d e f g h i j k l m n o p q r s t u v w x y z

mass *noun*
A **mass** is an amount of something with no particular shape or size.

massive *adjective*
If something is **massive**, it is very, very big.

mast *noun*
A **mast** is a tall pole that goes upwards from the floor of a ship to hold its sails up.

master *noun*
A **master** is a man who is in charge of someone or something.

mat *noun*
A **mat** is a piece of material of some kind used to cover the floor or part of the floor.

match[1] *noun* (*plural* **matches**)
A **match** is a short thin piece of wood with a special material on its top part that makes fire when you strike it against a surface that has been treated with a special substance.

match[2] *noun* (*plural* **matches**)
1. A **match** is a game between two or more people or teams.
–verb **2.** If two things **match**, they are similar in some way and this makes them look good together. *Don't wear those trousers and that shirt together. They don't match.*

material /*say* muh-**tear**-ree-uhl / *noun*
1. A **material** is anything you use to make something. *Wood and stone are good building materials.*
2. Material is cloth. *The material in our uniform is made of a mixture of wool and cotton.*

maths *noun*
Maths is learning to use numbers and to know sizes and shapes.

This word is short for **mathematics**. If you are describing something to do with maths, you say it is **mathematical**.

matter *verb*
If something **matters**, it is important. *'Does it matter if I don't come?' 'Yes it does. Everyone wants you to be there.'*

mattress *noun*
A **mattress** is the comfortable, thick part of a bed that you lie on.

maximum *noun*
The **maximum** is the most you can have.

The opposite is **minimum**.

may *verb*
1. You use **may** when you are asking for or giving permission to do something. *May I have the last piece of cake?* | *You may go now.*
2. You use **may** to show that it is possible something will happen. *The rain is stopping so we may go outside.*

May *noun*
May is the fifth month of the year, with 31 days. It comes between April and June.

maybe *adverb*
You use **maybe** to say that something might happen or it might not happen. *'Are you going to the party?' 'Maybe, I'm not sure yet.'*

Another word with a similar meaning is **perhaps**.

mayor /*say* mair / *noun*
A **mayor** is the person in charge of a city or town council.

me *pronoun*
You use **me** when you are talking about yourself. *Please give me the ball – it's my turn to have it.*

meal *noun*
A **meal** is food that you eat at certain times of the day.

mean[1] *verb* (**means**, **meaning**, **meant** /*say* ment/, **has meant**)
1. What something spoken or written **means** is what it says or expresses. *If you say you are angry, you mean you are very cross.*
2. What an action or event **means** is what it shows. *The way my father is looking at me means that I have to do my homework before I do anything else.* | *Does the rainy weather mean we can't play tennis?*
3. If you **mean** to do something, you have it in your mind to do it. *I meant to hurt him. It was not an accident.*

�֍ *Spelling Tip:* Remember that the past form **meant** keeps the spelling *mean* (with *t* added), even though the sound changes to 'ment'.

mean[2] *adjective*
Someone who is **mean** does not like to spend money or to give any of their things away unless it is completely necessary.

meaning *noun*
The **meaning** of what someone says or writes or of something that happens is what it means, or what it tells you.

meanwhile /say **meen**-wuyl / adverb
You use **meanwhile** to talk about the time until something happens. *The television will be fixed in a little while. Meanwhile, why don't we play cards?*

measles noun
Measles is a disease that gives you a temperature and red spots on your skin. You can easily catch it from someone else who has it.

measure /say **mezh**-uh / verb
If you **measure** something, you work out how big or little it is, or how much of it there is, usually by using a special tool. *We measured the dog kennel to see if it was big enough for our dog.*

> **Word Building: measurement**, noun When you measure something, you find out its **measurement**.

> ✳ **Spelling Tip:** Remember the *ea* for the 'e' sound in the first part of the word. Also remember the *sure* ending which sounds like 'zhuh'. Think of other words with this spelling and sound, such as *pleasure* and *treasure*.

meat noun
Meat is the flesh of an animal's body used for food.

> ✳ **Spelling Tip:** Don't confuse the spelling of **meat** with **meet** which sounds the same, but is spelt with a double *e*. When you **meet** someone, you come together with them.

mechanical /say muh-**kan**-ik-uhl / noun
Something is **mechanical** if it works because of some sort of machine.

> **Word Building: mechanic**, noun Something mechanical, like a car, needs a **mechanic** to look after it or fix it.

medal noun
A **medal** is a flat piece of metal, often with writing or a design on it, which people win for being brave, or get as a prize.

medallion /say muh-**dal**-yuhn / noun
A **medallion** is a large medal, especially one given as a prize.

meddle verb
If you **meddle**, you take part in someone else's business when it has nothing to do with you. *Stop meddling! We can work out how to get it going on our own.*

Another word with a similar meaning is **interfere**.

medical adjective
If something is **medical**, it has to do with treating diseases, or with doctors or hospitals.

medicine /say **med**-uh-suhn / noun
Medicine is something that a doctor gives you to drink or swallow to make you better when you are sick.

medium adjective
If something is **medium** in size, it is not very big and not very small.

meet verb (**meets, meeting, met, has met**)
1. If you **meet** someone, you come together with them, by planning or by accident. *Let's meet at the station at four o'clock. | Guess who I met at the shops!*
2. If things **meet**, they join together. *The paths meet near the river.*

> ✳ **Spelling Tip:** Don't confuse the spelling of **meet** with **meat** which sounds the same, but is spelt with *ea*. **Meat** is the flesh of an animal used as food.

meeting noun
A **meeting** is when people meet for a particular reason, usually to discuss something.

melody /say **mel**-uh-dee / noun (plural **melodies**)
A **melody** is made up of musical sounds that come one after another, making a pleasant pattern.

Another word with a similar meaning is **tune**.

melon noun
A **melon** is a large fruit with a lot of juice and with a thick skin.

melt verb
If something **melts** or is **melted**, it becomes soft and flowing when it is heated. *My ice-cream was melting in the sun.*

member noun
A **member** of an organisation is someone who belongs to that group.

memorial noun
A **memorial** is something that helps people remember a person or a special event. *This statue is a memorial to the soldiers who died fighting for their country.*

a b c d e f g h i j k l m n o p q r s t u v w x y z

memorise *verb*
If you **memorise** something, you put it into your mind so that you remember it well. You put it into your memory. *The teacher asked us to memorise all of the poem.*

Another spelling for this word is **memorize**.

memory *noun* (*plural* **memories**)
1. Your **memory** is the part of your mind that allows you to keep ideas and knowledge and remember them when you need to. *Larissa has a good memory – she never forgets anything.*
2. A **memory** is something you remember. *The older you get, the more memories you have.*
3. The **memory** of a computer is the part of it in which information is stored until needed. *Our new computer has a lot of memory.*

✸ *Spelling Tip:* Remember that the ending is *ory* (not *ary*). It might help if you think of *ory* being part of the word *story* – a memory is like a story from the past.

memory stick *noun*
Look up **USB drive**.

mend *verb*
If you **mend** something, you fix it when it has been broken or torn. You make it work properly again. *I hope the shop will be able to mend my bike.* | *He mended the bag by sewing up the hole.*

mental *adjective*
If something is **mental**, it has to do with a person's mind.

mention *verb*
If you **mention** something, you say or write something about it, usually in a very short way. *My mother mentioned to me that it was Dad's birthday so I would remember to say something when he came home.*

menu *noun*
1. A **menu** is a list of the dishes that you can choose to eat at a place like a restaurant. *I hope there will be ice-cream on the menu.*
2. On a computer, a **menu** is a list of possible things to do. *If you click on 'File', you will get a menu where you can choose to open a new file or save your file.*

mercy /*say* **mer**-see/ *noun*
Mercy is the kindness someone shows when they decide not to punish a person for what they have done.

Word Building: **merciful** /*say* **mer**-suh-fuhl/, *adjective* If someone shows mercy, then they are **merciful**.

meringue /*say* muh-**rang**/ *noun*
A **meringue** is a sweet, white food you make with sugar and the white parts of eggs.

merino /*say* muh-**ree**-noh/ *noun* (*plural* **merinos**)
A **merino** is a kind of sheep that has very fine wool.

mermaid *noun*
A **mermaid** is a sea creature in stories who looks like a woman from the waist up but like a fish from the waist down.

merry *adjective*
1. If someone is **merry**, they are happy and having fun. *Everyone at the party was merry and they were singing lots of funny songs.*
2. Merry Christmas, People say **Merry Christmas!** to each other when it is Christmas. It means 'I hope you enjoy Christmas and have a happy time'.

mess *noun*
A **mess** is something that is dirty or untidy.

message /*say* **mes**-ij/ *noun*
A **message** is important information or news that someone sends to another person.

Word Building: **messenger** /*say* **mes**-uhn-juh/, *noun* Someone who carries a message from one person to another is a **messenger**.

Also look up **text message**.

metal *noun*
A **metal** is a hard, shiny material, which can be bent when it is hot and made into something, or which can be used to carry electricity. Iron and tin are examples of **metals**.

meteor /*say* **mee**-tee-aw/ *noun*
A **meteor** is a small rock from outer space which often burns brightly across the sky as it falls towards the earth.

meter *noun*
A **meter** is an instrument that measures how much has passed through it, like a gas meter or a water meter.

method *noun*
A **method** of doing something is a way of doing it.

metre /say **mee**-tuh/ noun
A **metre** is a measurement of length. It is about as far as you can go in a very long step.

mice noun
Look up **mouse**.

microphone /say **muy**-kruh-fohn/ noun
A **microphone** is a instrument which you use when you want to make sounds louder or record them.

microscope noun
A **microscope** is an instrument you look into that makes very tiny things big enough for you to see.

microwave noun
A **microwave** is a type of oven that heats and cooks food very quickly.

This is short for **microwave oven**.

midday noun
Midday is the time in the middle of the day when it is 12 o'clock.

Another word for this is **noon**.

middle noun
The **middle** of something is the part of it half the way between its two sides or half the way though it.

midnight /say **mid**-nuyt/ noun
Midnight is the time in the middle of the night when it is 12 o'clock.

might[1] /say muyt/
You use **might** to show it is possible that something will happen but it is not certain. *We might win but it all depends on who will be playing.*

might[2] /say muyt/ noun
Might is power or strength.

mighty /say **muy**-tee/ adjective (**mightier**, **mightiest**)
1. If something is **mighty**, it is very powerful. *The mighty army had no trouble defeating their enemy.*
2. If something is **mighty**, it is very big. *The mighty wall of water completely covered the small boat.*

migrant /say **muy**-gruhnt/ noun
A **migrant** is someone who leaves their own country to go and live in another country.

mild noun
Something that is **mild** is soft, light or not strong.

mile noun
A **mile** is a measurement of length used in some countries, such as America. It is a long length, equal to about 1.6 kilometres.

Miles used to be used as a measurement in Australia, but now we use **kilometres**.

milk noun
1. **Milk** is the white liquid produced by female animals to feed their babies. People use the **milk** from some animals, such as cows, as food.
–verb 2. When farmers **milk** cows, they use machines or their hands to get milk from them. *The farmer was in the dairy milking his cows.*

mill noun
A **mill** is a building with machines for crushing grain into flour.

Word Building: **miller**, noun Someone in charge of a flour mill is a **miller**.

millimetre /say **mil**-uh-mee-tuh/ noun
A **millimetre** is a very small measurement of length. There are 1000 **millimetres** in a metre.

million noun, adjective
A **million** is a very large number which you can write as 1 000 000. It is made up of a thousand lots of a thousand (1000 x 1000).

mime verb
If you **mime** something, you act it without using any words. *We had to mime how we would look if we found a thousand dollars.*

mimic /say **mim**-ik/ verb (**mimics**, **mimicking**, **mimicked**, **has mimicked**)
If you **mimic** someone, you copy the way that they move and speak. *Adrian was really good at mimicking all the cartoon characters.*

mind noun
1. Your **mind** is the part of you that thinks and feels, and makes you able to decide things and remember things. *The scene of the whales coming up on to the beach will always stay in my mind. | Her mind was full of so many good ideas that she didn't know which to describe first.*
2. **make up your mind**, When you **make up your mind**, you decide something. *I've made up my mind to do my homework as soon as I get home.*
–verb 3. If you **mind** someone or something, you look after them and keep them safe because they cannot look after themselves. *We are minding our neighbour's cat while she is away.*
4. If you **mind** something, you do not like it or it makes you feel bad. *I hate hot weather but I don't mind the cold weather. | I try not to mind when he makes jokes about me.*

a b c d e f g h i j k l m n o p q r s t u v w x y z

5. never mind, You say **never mind** to show someone that you are not worried by something that has happened and that they should not worry either. *'I'm sorry, I've broken the glass.' 'Never mind, I'll get you another one.'*

mine¹ *pronoun*

You use **mine** to show that something belongs to you. *'Is this your pen?' 'Yes, it is mine.'*

mine² *noun*

1. A **mine** is a large hole people dig in the earth for taking out things like coal or gold. *We went down into a mine on our holiday.*

2. A **mine** is a bomb put under the ground or in the sea, which explodes when something touches it. *Farming is dangerous in some countries that have mines left in the fields from when there was a war.*

> *Word Building:* **miner**, *noun* Someone who works in a mine (definition 1) is a **miner**.

> ✹ *Spelling Tip:* Don't confuse the spelling of **miner** with **minor** which has the same sound. Something that is **minor** is less important than something else.

minimum *noun*

A **minimum** is the least you can have.

> The opposite is **maximum**.

> ✹ *Spelling Tip:* **Minimum** comes from the Latin word *minimus* which means 'least' or 'smallest'. Just think of a 'mini mum' and you won't go wrong.

minister *noun*

A **minister** is someone whose job is to be in charge of a church and guide and teach the people who come to the church.

minor *adjective*

If something is **minor**, it is not very important, especially when compared with something else.

> The opposite is **major**.

> ✹ *Spelling Tip:* Don't confuse the spelling of **minor** with **miner** which has the same sound. A **miner** is someone whose job is to dig in the ground. Look up **mine²**

minority /*say* muh-**no**-ruh-tee/ *noun*

A **minority** is the smaller number of something, or less than half of it.

> The opposite is **majority**.

mint¹ *noun*

1. Mint is a plant with leaves you can use for cooking. *We made a sauce from the mint in the garden.*

2. A **mint** is a sort of sweet. *Mints are very good to eat on long trips in the car.*

mint² *noun*

A **mint** is a place where the government makes money for us to use.

minus *preposition*

Minus means 'take away'. *5 minus 3 leaves 2.*

> The opposite is **plus**.

minute¹ /*say* **min**-uht/ *noun*

1. A **minute** is a small measure of time, 60 seconds long. There are 60 minutes in an hour. *I like my eggs boiled for exactly three minutes.*

2. A **minute** is any short amount of time. *Wait a minute – I'm not ready yet.*

minute² /*say* muy-**nyooht**/ *adjective*

If something is **minute**, it is very, very small.

miracle /*say* **mi**-ruh-kuhl/ *noun*

A **miracle** is a very good thing that happens which no-one can explain.

mirage /*say* muh-**rahzh**/ *noun*

A **mirage** is something you see in the distance that isn't really there at all. People often see **mirages** of water in the desert.

mirror *noun*

A **mirror** is a piece of glass that has been made so that you can see yourself in it.

mischief /*say* **mis**-chuhf/ *noun*

Mischief is a way of behaving that can make people annoyed or get you into trouble.

mischievous /*say* **mis**-chuh-vuhs/ *adjective*

You are **mischievous** if you like to do naughty things.

> ✹ *Spelling Tip:* Remember the *ie* spelling, just as in *mischief* from which this word is formed. Remember also that the ending of **mischievous** is *vous* – without an *i*, although some people say the word wrongly by adding in an 'ee' sound.

miserable /*say* **miz**-ruh-buhl/ *adjective*

If you are **miserable**, you are very unhappy or not comfortable.

> *Word Building:* **misery** /*say* **miz**-uh-ree/, *noun* When you are miserable, you're full of **misery**.

⚙ *Spelling Tip:* Don't forget the *e* in the middle, although you don't hear it when the word is said. It will help if you remember that this word comes from *misery* (meaning 'great sadness'), where you can hear the middle part with the *e* spelling.

miss *verb*
1. If you **miss** a train, bus or plane, you are too late to get on it before it leaves. *Hurry up, we are going to miss the bus!*
2. If you **miss** something such as a ball, you try to catch it or hit it but you are not able to. *I sometimes miss the ball when I play tennis.*
3. If you **miss** someone, you feel sad that they are not with you. *When my best friend moved to another state, I really missed her.*

Miss *noun*
You use **Miss** before the last name of a girl or a woman who is not married when you are talking about her or to her in a polite way.

You use **Mrs** before the name of a woman who is married. Some women like to use **Ms** instead of either **Miss** or **Mrs**. This does not show whether or not the woman is married.

missile /*say* **mis**-uyl/ *noun*
A **missile** is a weapon or anything like this that people can throw or shoot.

mist *noun*
Mist is a cloud of tiny drops of water which is hard to see through.

mistake *noun*
1. A **mistake** is something which someone has done wrongly. *I only made one mistake in the test.*
2. A **mistake** is thinking something is true when it isn't. *I made a mistake when I thought I saw Sam – it wasn't Sam at all, just someone who looked like him.*

Another word that means the same is **error**.

mitten *noun*
A **mitten** is a kind of glove with one part for your thumb and one part for your four fingers together.

mix /*say* miks/ *verb*
If you **mix** things, you put them together. *She mixed flour, sugar and eggs to make a cake.*

Word Building: **mixture** /*say* **miks**-chuh/, *noun* When you mix things together, you make a **mixture**.

moan *noun*
1. A **moan** is a long, low sound you make when you feel sad or when you are in pain.
–*verb* 2. If you **moan**, you let out a low, sad sound because you are in pain or very sad or upset. *She was moaning from the pain of her broken leg.*

moat *noun*
A **moat** is a deep, wide area which people in the past dug around a town or a building to keep out enemies. They usually filled it with water.

mobile /*say* **moh**-buyl/ *adjective*
1. If something is **mobile**, it is able to be moved.
–*noun* 2. A **mobile** is a hanging decoration made up of movable parts. *I made my baby cousin a mobile of coloured fish.*
3. Look up **mobile phone**.

mobile phone *noun*
A **mobile phone** is a telephone that you can take anywhere.

The short form is **mobile**.

mock *verb*
If someone **mocks** you, they make fun of you. *Sally was crying because someone had mocked the clothes she was wearing.*

model *noun*
1. A **model** is something that you can use as an example for you to copy. *The teacher used Jane's drawing as a model for the rest of us to copy.*
2. A **model** is a copy of something that is much smaller than the real thing. *Wayang is making a model of an old sailing ship.*
3. If someone is a **model**, their job is to wear new clothes to show people what they look like. *Models are lucky – they can wear all the new fashions.*

⚙ *Spelling Tip:* Remember the *el* ending (not *le*).

modem /*say* **moh**-dem/ *noun*
A **modem** is a machine that changes information from a computer into a form that can be sent by telephone to another computer.

modern *adjective*
If something is **modern**, it belongs to or has been made in the present time.

moist /*say* moyst/ *adjective*
If something is **moist**, it is a bit wet.

Word Building: **moisture** /*say* **moys**-chuh/, *noun* Something that is moist has some moisture in it.

moment *noun*

1. A **moment** is a very short amount of time. *It will only take a moment for me to get ready.*
2. the moment, You can talk about the present or another particular time as **the moment**. *I can't help you at the moment.*

Another word with a similar meaning is **minute**.

monarch /*say* **mon**-uhk/ *noun* (*plural* **monarchs**)

A **monarch** is a king or queen.

Monday *noun*

Monday is one of the days of the week. It comes after Sunday and before Tuesday. In most countries, **Monday** is the first day of the school and working week.

money *noun*

Money is the coins and pieces of paper which you use to pay for the things you buy.

monitor *noun*

1. A **monitor** is the part of a computer where you can see the information. *Your eyes will get tired if you stare at the monitor for too long.*
2. A **monitor** is a pupil in a class who has particular jobs to help the teacher. *The teacher asked the library monitor to collect the books.*

monk /*rhymes with* sunk/ *noun*

A **monk** is one of a group of men who choose to live away from the people and give their lives in service to God.

monkey *noun* (*plural* **monkeys**)

A **monkey** is a kind of animal that has a long tail and lives in trees in some hot countries.

monorail *noun*

A **monorail** is a train that runs on one rail.

monotreme /*say* **mon**-uh-treem/ *noun*

A **monotreme** is a special kind of mammal found only in Australia. **Monotremes** lay eggs and also feed their young with milk.

⭐ *Spelling Tip:* **Monotremes** are *extremely* unusual and interesting animals. The *treme* in *extreme* might help you to remember the spelling of the end of **monotreme**. In fact the word is made up of *mono* (meaning 'one') and *treme* (a form of *trema*, the Greek word for 'hole') – a **monotreme** has only one opening

for getting rid of waste stuff from its body and for making babies.

monster *noun*

A **monster** is someone or something that frightens you because it is so big, ugly or cruel.

month *noun*

1. A **month** is one of the 12 parts into which the year is divided. *Which month is your birthday in?*
2. A **month** is any period of about four weeks, or 30 days. *They have been away for three months.*

The months of the year are: **January, February, March, April, May, June, July, August, September, October, November, December**.

monument *noun*

A **monument** is something built, often in stone, that people make to remember a person or something important that has happened.

mood *noun*

Your **mood** is the way you feel. *We were all in a good mood because it was Friday afternoon.*

moon *noun*

The **moon** is the round object that you can see as a light in the sky at night. The **moon** is in space and moves around the earth in a circle every four weeks.

Word Building: **new moon**, *noun* At some time in the four weeks, the moon cannot be seen and then becomes a thin shape which slowly gets larger. While it is very thin, it is called a **new moon**.

mop *noun*

1. A **mop** is a long stick with some soft material at one end that you use for washing floors.
–*verb* (**mops**, **mopping**, **mopped**, **has mopped**)
2. If you **mop** something, you clean it with a mop. *She is mopping the floor.*

more *adjective*

1. You use **more** to talk about a greater amount or number of something. *We need more food for all these people.* | *There are more children in Sam's class than in Henry's.* | *There are more cars on the road every year.*
–*adverb* **2.** You use **more** to talk about a greater degree. *It rains more often in summer than in winter.* | *Please speak more slowly. I can't understand you.*

3. You use **more** to compare things or people. *This book is more interesting than the one I read last week.*
–*pronoun* **4. More** is a greater or extra amount or number of something. *Have you had enough to eat or do you want more? | We need more of these books in the library.*

The opposite is **less**.

morning *noun*
1. The **morning** is the first part of the day, from when it gets light to 12 o'clock. *We go to school in the morning and come home in the afternoon.*
2. Morning is also the period of the day from the middle of the night until the middle of the day. *Someone knocked on the door at one o'clock in the morning and woke us all up.*

mosque /*say* mosk/ *noun*
A **mosque** is a special building where Muslims worship.

✲ *Spelling Tip:* Don't forget the *que* spelling for the 'k' sound. **Mosque** is spelt in this way because it has come into English from French.

mosquito /*say* muhs-**kee**-toh/ *noun* (*plural* **mosquitoes**)
A **mosquito** is a small insect that sucks blood from people or animals.

✲ *Spelling Tip:* Remember the *qu* for the 'k' sound. This word comes from Spanish where the *ito* can mean 'small'. The meaning of this word in Spanish is 'small fly'.

moss *noun*
Moss is a plant with very small leaves. It grows in wet places.

most *adjective*
1. You use **most** to talk about the greatest amount or number of something.
–*adverb* **2.** You use **most** to talk about the greatest degree. *It was the most difficult thing I'd ever done.*
–*pronoun* **3.** The **most** is the greatest number, amount or degree. *Everyone at the party ate a lot of food but Fred ate the most.*

Word Building: **mostly**, *adverb*: *Tomorrow will be mostly fine.*

The opposite is **least**.

moth *noun*
A **moth** is an insect like a butterfly but it flies around at night or just before night.

mother *noun*
Someone's **mother** is their female parent.

motor *noun*
A **motor** is the part of a machine that gives it the power to work or go. You especially use this word when you are talking about something like a car, bus or boat.

motorbike *noun*
A **motorbike** is a large heavy bicycle with an engine.

motorway *noun*
Look up **freeway**.

mountain *noun*
A **mountain** is a very high part of the earth.

Word Building: **mountainous**, *adjective* An area that has a lot of mountains is **mountainous**.

Another word for **mountain** is **mount**, which is used especially in a name, such as *Mount Kosciuszko*.

✲ *Spelling Tip:* Remember that the ending is spelt *ain* (although it sounds like 'uhn' or sometimes as if there is nothing between the *t* and the *n*). The word *fountain* has a similar pattern.

mouse *noun* (*plural* **mice** *for definition 1*, **mouses** *for definition 2*)
1. A **mouse** is a small, furry animal with sharp teeth and a long tail, usually coloured brown, white or grey. *There were some mice living under the house which sometimes came into the kitchen for food.*
2. A **mouse** is a small object which you hold and press to get to a certain position in the information you can see on a computer. *You can use the mouse to move to where you want to start typing.*

moustache /*say* muh-**stahsh**/ *noun*
A **moustache** is the hair that grows on the top lip of a man.

✲ *Spelling Tip:* Remember the *ou* in the first part of the word. Another difficult part is the *ache* spelling for the 'ahsh' sound at the end. **Moustache** is spelt in this way because it comes from French.

mouth *noun*
Your **mouth** is the opening in your face which you use for eating, drinking and talking.

move *verb*

1. If someone or something **moves**, they change from one place or position to another. *I am too tired to move.*
2. If you **move** something, you make it change place or position. *Help me move this chair closer to the wall.*

Word Building: **movable**, *adjective*: *We made toys with movable parts.*

movement *noun*

A **movement** is the action of moving or changing from one place or position to another.

movie *noun*

1. a film. *Mum and Dad have gone out to see a movie.*
2. the movies, If you go to **the movies**, you go to see a film at a cinema. *Mum said that she would take us to the movies on Saturday.*

Mr /*say* **mis**-tuh / *noun*

You use **Mr** before the last name of a man when you are talking about him or to him in a polite way.

Mr is short for **Mister**, which is never written in full before a name any more.

Mrs /*say* **mis**-uhz / *noun*

You use **Mrs** before the last name of a woman who is married when you are talking about her or to her in a polite way.

✤ **Mrs** is short for **Mistress**, which is never written in full before a name any more.
✤ Some women like to use **Ms** instead. This does not show whether or not the woman is married.

Ms /*say* muhz / *noun*

You use **Ms** before the last name of a woman when you are talking about her or to her in a polite way.

Ms does not show if a woman is married or not. Many women prefer this to **Miss** or **Mrs**.

much *adjective* (**more**, **most**)

1. You use **much** when you are talking about a great amount of something.
–*pronoun* **2. Much** of something is a great amount of it. *Much of what Josh told us was true.*

You use **much** when you are talking about something that is a mass and cannot be counted (*too much sugar*). You use **many** for things that can be counted (*too many potatoes*).

mud *noun*

Mud is wet, soft, sticky earth.

Word Building: **muddy**, *adjective* When something is covered with mud, it is **muddy**.

mug *noun*

A **mug** is a large cup.

mule *noun*

A **mule** is an animal whose mother is a horse and whose father is a donkey.

mulga *noun*

A **mulga** is a tree with grey leaves that grows in dry parts of Australia. Cows like to eat its leaves.

This word comes from Aboriginal languages of New South Wales called Yuwaalaraay and Kamilaroi.

mulgara /*say* mul-**gah**-ruh / *noun*

A **mulgara** is a small marsupial that looks like a red-brown mouse with black hairs on the top side of its tail. It lives in the Australian desert.

This word comes from an Aboriginal language of South Australia called Wangganguru.

multiply /*say* **mul**-tuh-pluy / *verb* (**multiplies**, **multiplying**, **multiplied**, **has multiplied**)

If you **multiply**, you add a number to itself a number of times. *If you multiply 4 by 2, you get 8.*

Word Building: **multiplication** /*say* mul-tuh-pluh-**kay**-shuhn /, *noun* If you have to multiply in a sum, then you are doing **multiplication**.

mum *noun*

1. Your **mum** is your mother. *I walked home from school with my mum.*
2. Mum, You can use **Mum** as a name for your mother when you talk to her. *Can I go out and play, Mum?*

Some children say **mummy**.

mumps *noun*

Mumps is a sickness which makes your neck and face swell up and feel very sore.

munch *verb*

If you **munch** food, you crush it with your teeth in a noisy way. *Olaf was munching a piece of celery while we were trying to watch television and it was very annoying.*

murder *noun*

1. Murder is killing someone and meaning to kill that person.

–*verb* **2.** If someone **murders** someone, they kill that person and mean to do so. *She murdered the old man so that she could get his money.*

Word Building: **murderer**, *noun* Someone who murders someone is a **murderer**.

muscle /*say* **mus**-uhl / *noun*
A **muscle** is one of the pieces of flesh attached to the bones in your body that helps to make your body move.

museum /*say* myooh-**zee**-uhm / *noun*
A **museum** is a building where old, unusual or interesting things are kept for people to go and see them.

mushroom *noun*
A **mushroom** is a plant. Many **mushrooms** can be eaten.

See how this is different from a **toadstool**.

music /*say* **myooh**-zik / *noun*
Music is the pleasant sound that people make when they play an instrument or sing. It usually expresses ideas or feelings.

musical *adjective*
1. If something is **musical**, it has to do with music. *A piano is a musical instrument.*
2. If someone is **musical**, they are good at making music. *My father is very musical – he plays several instruments.*

Muslim /*say* **mooz**-luhm / *noun*
A **Muslim** is someone whose religion is Islam.

must *verb*
1. You use **must** when you mean that it is necessary to do something. *You must clean your teeth to keep them healthy.*
2. You use **must** to show that something is very likely to be true. *My great grandmother must be nearly 90.*

mustard /*say* **mus**-tuhd / *noun*
Mustard is a brown or yellow food which is used to make other food taste good. You usually eat it with meat.

mutiny /*say* **myooh**-tuh-nee / *noun* (*plural* **mutinies**)
A **mutiny** happens when soldiers or sailors refuse to obey the orders of the officers who are in charge.

mutter *verb*
If you **mutter**, you speak or complain in a quiet voice that is hard to hear. *Halimah was muttering something that we couldn't hear.*

my *pronoun*
You use **my** to show that you own something. *That is my hat.*

myself *pronoun*
You use **myself** to mean 'me and no-one else'. *I hurt myself when I fell over.*

mystery /*say* **mis**-tree / *noun*
A **mystery** is a strange thing that no-one can understand or explain.

Word Building: **mysterious** /*say* mis-**tear**-ree-uhs /, *adjective* Something that is a mystery is **mysterious**.

✸ *Spelling Tip:* Remember the *y* (not *i*) spelling in the first part of this word. Many words that come from Greek have this kind of *y* spelling. Also remember that there is another *y* (not *ey*) spelling the 'ee' sound at the end. This *y* changes to an *i* in the adjective **mysterious**.

myth /*say* mith / *noun*
A **myth** is a traditional story about gods and people, the world they lived in and what they did. **Myths** were told to explain natural things like why it rains or why the sun goes down every night.

Also look up **legend**.

✸ *Spelling Tip:* Remember the *y* (not *i*) spelling. Many words that come from Greek have this kind of *y* spelling. **Myth** comes from the Greek word meaning 'legend', 'story' or 'word'.

net

N n

nag *verb* (**nags**, **nagging**, **nagged**, **has nagged**)
If you **nag**, you keep on annoying someone or complaining to them about something. *Simon knew if he kept on nagging his mother, she would take him to the movies.*

nail *noun*
1. A **nail** is a small, thin piece of metal that is sharp at one end, with the other end flat, used to fasten wooden things together. *We need to put some nails in this table or it will fall apart.*
2. Your **nail** is one of the hard parts that grow at the end of your fingers and toes. *Ow! You've hurt my arm with your sharp nails.*

naked /*say* **nay**-kuhd / *adjective*
If you are **naked**, you do not have any clothes on.

Another word that means the same is **nude**.

name *noun*
A **name** is what someone or something is called.

nanny goat *noun*
A **nanny goat** is a female goat.

narrate *verb*
If you **narrate** a story, you tell what happens in it. *The teacher is going to narrate the story to us.*

Word Building: narrator, *noun* Someone who narrates a story is a **narrator**.

narrative /*say* **na**-ruh-tiv / *noun*
If you write a **narrative**, you do a piece of writing that tells a story.

narrow *adjective*
If something is **narrow**, it is only a small distance from one side to the other.

The opposite is **wide**.

nasty /*say* **nah**-stee / *adjective* (**nastier**, **nastiest**)
1. Something that is **nasty** is not pleasant. *I got a nasty fright when the big dog rushed at me.*
2. If someone is **nasty**, they are cruel or make other people unhappy. *She was so nasty to me that I felt like crying.*

nation *noun*
1. A **nation** is a large group of people living in one country under one government. *The leaders of most of the world's nations went to the meeting on climate change.*
2. A **nation** can be a group of people who have the same customs, history, and language, even though they may not have their own government. *The ceremony was opened by an elder of the Arrernte nation.*

national *adjective*
If something is **national**, it belongs to or is part of a nation.

nationality /*say* nash-uh-**nal**-uh-tee / *noun* (*plural* **nationalities**)
Your **nationality** is when you officially belong to a particular country, because you were born there, or because the government has made you a member of the country.

national park *noun*
A **national park** is an area of nature that is protected by the government so that its environment is not harmed and so that people can visit it.

native *noun*
1. You are a **native** of a place if you were born there. *My grandmother was a native of Ireland.*
2. A plant or animal is a **native** of a place if it first came from there. *This flower is a native of southern Africa but you see it a lot in Australia.*

natural *adjective*
1. If something is **natural**, it is found in or formed by nature. It has not been made by people or machines. *Natural materials like wool and cotton are comfortable to wear.*
2. Something, like a skill, is **natural** if you were born with it. *I wish I had his natural ability with a ball – he seems to be able to hit it exactly where he wants every time.*

Word Building: naturally, *adverb* If something is natural, it happens **naturally**.

The opposite of definition 1 is **artificial**.

nature /say **nay**-chuh/ noun
1. **Nature** is the world around us, made up of earth, sky, sea, the weather, and plant and animal life. *My dad said we should go outside to really experience nature instead of watching programs about it on television.*
2. Your **nature** is the way you really are inside. *She has a kind nature.*

naughty /say **naw**-tee/ adjective (**naughtier**, **naughtiest**)
You are **naughty** when you are not behaving well.

> ✵ *Spelling Tip:* Remember that the letters *augh* spell the 'aw' sound. Think of other words with the same spelling for this sound, such as *caught* and *daughter*.

navy noun (plural **navies**)
The **navy** is the part of a country's fighting forces that goes to war at sea.

> *Word Building:* **naval**, *adjective* Something to do with the navy is **naval**.

near adjective
1. If something is **near**, it is only a short distance away. *The shops are quite near, so we can walk.*
2. If something is **near**, it is going to happen soon. *The holidays are near.*
–preposition 3. If something is **near** something else, it is close to it. *We live near the school.*

nearby adjective
If something is **nearby**, it is close. It is not far away.

nearly adverb
Nearly means 'almost'. *We nearly reached the top of the mountain but had to come down because the weather got very bad.*

neat adjective
If something is **neat**, it is tidy and ordered.

> *Word Building:* **neatly**, *adverb* If you are neat, you do things **neatly**. –**neatness**, *noun* If something is neat, it shows **neatness**.

necessary /say **nes**-uh-se-ree/ adjective
If something is **necessary**, you really need it. You must have it.

> *Word Building:* **necessity** /say nuh-**ses**-uh-tee/, *noun* If something is necessary, it is a **necessity**.

> ✵ *Spelling Tip:* Remember that there is one *c* but two *s*'s in this word. Think that 'in the classroom school socks are **necessary**' to remind you of this.

neck noun
Your **neck** is the part of your body which joins the head to the rest of you.

nectar /say **nek**-tuh/ noun
Nectar is the sweet, sticky stuff that bees collect from flowers to turn into honey.

need verb
1. If you **need** something or **need** to do something, it is important that you get it or do it. *I need new shoes – these ones have holes. | We need to buy some milk. There is none left.*
–noun 2. If you are are in **need** of something, you must have it or it is necessary. *Many people who have lost their homes in the fire are in need of food and water. | The teacher said there was a need for us to be more understanding and helpful with the kindergarten kids.*

needle noun
1. A **needle** is a small, thin piece of metal with a very sharp point at one end and a hole at the other end that you put thread through. You use it for sewing. *Have you got a needle and thread? My shirt has a hole in it.*
2. A **needle** is something doctors use to put medicine straight into your body rather than putting it in your mouth. The medicine is pushed through a thin piece of metal which has been placed under your skin. *The baby has to have a needle to stop her getting sick.*

negative adjective
If something is **negative**, it says or means 'no'.

The opposite is **positive**.

neglect verb
1. If you **neglect** something or someone, you fail to look after them properly. *Mum said I had been neglecting my guinea pig and didn't deserve to have a pet.*
2. If you **neglect** to do something, you fail to do it. *We neglected to give them our address and so they couldn't write to us.*
–noun 3. **Neglect** is failing to look after something or failing to do something that you should.

neigh /say nay/ noun
A **neigh** is the sound that a horse makes.

Spelling Tip: Remember that the letters *eigh* spell the 'ay' sound. Think of other words with the same spelling for this sound, such as *eight* and *weigh*.

neighbour /*say* **nay**-buh / *noun*
A **neighbour** is someone who lives near you.

Word Building: **neighbourhood**, *noun* You and your neighbours live in your **neighbourhood**.

Another spelling for this word is **neighbor**.

Spelling Tip: Most **neighbours** talk, rather than *neigh* like a horse. However, *neigh* makes up the first part of this word. In this case, it comes from the Old English word meaning 'near'.

neither /*say* **nuy**-dhuh, **nee**-dhuh / *adjective*
1. You use **neither** to mean not one or the other. –*conjunction* **2. neither ... nor ...**, You use this phrase when you are saying that not one of the choices mentioned is true or possible. *Neither Sandra nor I wanted to help with washing the car – we both wanted to take the dog for a walk instead.*

Spelling Tip: There are two ways of saying **neither**, but only one way of spelling it. Remember the *ei* part, whether you say it as 'uy' or 'ee'.

nephew /*say* **nef**-yooh / *noun*
Someone's **nephew** is the son of their brother or sister.

nervous *adjective*
If you are **nervous**, you are afraid or excited.

nest *noun*
A **nest** is a shelter that birds and some other small animals make for their babies.

net *noun*
1. A **net** is something made of a material which has pieces of thread or rope tied together. The material can be very fine with small holes between the threads, or thick with large holes. Some **nets** are attached to long thin pieces of wood or plastic and used for things like catching fish. *Bring your net down to the river and we'll see what we can catch.*
2. the Net, Look up **internet**.

netball *noun*
Netball is a ball game played by two teams. Players try to gain points for their team by throwing the ball into a ring set at a certain height.

network *noun*
A **network** is a group of things or people who are connected with each other, especially a group of many computers connected to each other.

never *adverb*
If something **never** happens or has **never** happened, it does not happen and has not happened at any time. *The bus never comes on time.*

new *adjective*
1. If something is **new**, it has just been bought or made. *She had been shopping all day and had lots of new clothes.* | *We went to see the new film that we had read about.*
2. Something is **new** if you did not know it before. *We have just discovered a new way to school.*

The opposite is **old**.

news *noun*
News is information about something that has just happened. *Have you heard the news? Our team won the match!* | *Mum and Dad watch the world news on television every night before we have dinner.*

newsagency /*say* **nyoohz**-ay-juhn-see / *noun*
A **newsagency** is a shop where you can buy newspapers, pens, magazines and books.

Word Building: **newsagent**, *noun* Someone who runs a newsagency is a **newsagent**.

newspaper *noun*
A **newspaper** is something that you read to get news and other information. **Newspapers** are produced on large sheets of paper, and are usually printed every day.

New Year *noun*
New Year is the time at the beginning of the year, when people celebrate the end of one year and the beginning of the next.

next *adjective*
1. You use **next** when you are talking about something which is immediately following something else. *The letter arrived the next day.*
2. Next can mean 'nearest'. *We could hear noises from the next room.*

nibble *verb*
If you **nibble** something, you take a little bit of food at a time, like a mouse does. *Sali nibbled at the chocolate until there was nothing left.*

nice *adjective*
1. Something is **nice** if it is pleasant or enjoyable. *It was a nice day so we walked to school.*
2. If someone is **nice**, they are kind or easy to be friendly with. *The lady who answered the phone seemed very nice and gave me all the information I needed.*

nickname *noun*
A **nickname** is a name that people who know you sometimes use instead of your real name.

niece /*say* nees/ *noun*
Someone's **niece** is the daughter of their brother or sister.

> ✸ *Spelling Tip:* Remember that *ie* spells the 'ee' sound. This follows the rule that *i* comes before *e* except after *c*. Another word with this spelling pattern is *piece* (meaning a 'bit').

night /*say* nuyt/ *noun*
Night is the time of darkness after the sun sets and before it rises again.

> *Word Building:* **nightly**, *adjective* If something happens every night, it happens **nightly**.

nil *noun*
Nil is nothing.

nine *noun, adjective*
Nine is a number which you can write as 9.

> *Word Building:* **ninth**, *adjective*: *We live in the ninth house on the left.*

nineteen *noun, adjective*
Nineteen is a number which you can write as 19.

> *Word Building:* **nineteenth**, *adjective*: *You are the nineteenth person to come into the shop today.*

ninety *noun, adjective*
Ninety is a number which you can write as 90.

> *Word Building:* **ninetieth**, *adjective*: *It's the ninetieth year since the war ended.*

nit *noun*
1. **Nits** are the eggs of insects such as lice. They can stick to your hair. *Mum had to work hard to get all the nits out of my hair.*
2. **Nits** are the young lice when they come out of the eggs. *The nits made my head very itchy.*

no *interjection*
1. **No** is a word that you use when you are answering a question if you want to say that something is not correct, or that you do not agree to something you have been asked to do, or that you do not want something that you have been offered. *'I like the look of that book. Is it any good?' 'No, it's quite boring.'*
–*adjective* 2. You can use **no** to mean 'not any'.

> The opposite of definition 1 is **yes**.

noble *adjective*
If someone is **noble**, they behave in a way that is good or brave, and other people admire them.

nobody *pronoun*
Nobody means 'no person'. *There was nobody in the room.*

nocturnal /*say* nok-**ter**-nuhl/ *adjective*
An animal is **nocturnal** if it is active at night and asleep in the day.

nod *verb* (**nods, nodding, nodded, has nodded**)
If you **nod**, you move your head up and down in short quick movements, especially if you are agreeing with something. *We all nodded when the teacher asked if we would like to leave early.*

noise *noun*
A **noise** is any kind of sound, especially a sound which is too loud or which you do not like.

noisy *adjective* (**noisier, noisiest**)
If something or someone is **noisy**, they are making a lot of noise.

> *Word Building:* **noisily**, *adverb*: *The chairs scraped noisily on the floor.*

none *pronoun*
1. **None** means 'not one'. *None of the neighbours did anything about the alarm ringing.*
2. **None** means 'not any'. *That is none of your business.*

nonfiction *noun*
Nonfiction is stories about people and things which are real.

nonsense *noun*
Nonsense is words that are silly or that do not mean anything.

noodles *noun*
Noodles are a type of food made from flour and eggs, cut in long thin pieces, often served in soups or with a sauce.

noon *noun*
Noon is 12 o'clock in the day.

> Another word for this is **midday**.

a b c d e f g h i j k l m n o p q r s t u v w x y z

no-one *pronoun*
No-one means 'no person'. *There was no-one in the room.*

noose *noun*
A **noose** is a circle you make in a rope, that is tied so that it slides along and makes the circle smaller when you pull the rope.

nor *conjunction*
You use **nor**, usually with **neither**, when you are saying that not one of the choices mentioned is true or possible. *He could neither read nor write.*

normal *adjective*
If something is **normal**, it is ordinary or usual. It is the way it commonly happens.

> **Word Building: normally**, *adverb* If something is normal, it is what **normally** happens.

north *noun*
1. The **north** is the direction which is on your right when you face the west, that is, where the sun goes down.
–*adjective* 2. If something is **north**, it is in or towards the north.
–*adverb* 3. If someone or something goes **north**, they go towards the north. *We are going to go north for our holidays.*

> **Word Building: northern**, *adjective* If something is in the north, it is **northern**.

> The opposite direction is **south**. The other directions are **east** and **west**.

nose *noun*
Your **nose** is the part of your face you use for smelling and breathing. It sticks out above your mouth.

nostril *noun*
Your **nostril** is one of the two openings of your nose.

not *adverb*
You use **not** when you are saying 'no' about something, or when you are making a word or group of words mean the opposite of their usual meaning. *You must not dive into water until you know how deep it is.*

> **Not** is often joined on to another word and shortened to **n't**: *You shouldn't do that.*

note *noun*
1. If you write a **note**, you write something down to make you remember it. *We wrote a note on the calendar so we would remember her birthday.*

2. A **note** is a short letter. *Tapan sent a note to his grandmother when she was sick.*
3. A **note** is a piece of paper money. *The machine took notes but all we had were coins.*
4. A **note** is a musical sound, or the sign you use to write it down on paper. *The trumpets in the school band weren't very good on some of the high notes.*

notebook *noun*
A **notebook** is a book in which you write notes so that you will remember things.

nothing *noun*
Nothing means 'not anything'. *Say nothing about the party – it's a surprise.*

notice *noun*
1. A **notice** is a sign or note giving a warning or some information.
–*verb* 2. If you **notice** something, you know about it because you have seen, heard, smelt or felt it. *I didn't notice the letter that had been pushed under the door.*

nought /*rhymes with* fort/ *noun*
A **nought** is the sign '0' that we use for zero.

noun *noun*
A **noun** is a type of word which names something. There are **proper nouns** like *Harry Potter* or *Australia*, and **common nouns** like *elephant* or *mystery*.

novel *noun*
A **novel** is a story someone makes up that is so long it fills a whole book.

November *noun*
November is the eleventh month of the year, with 30 days. It comes between October and December.

now *adverb*
1. You use **now** when you are talking about the present time. *Jamie didn't like school when he first started but he does now.*
2. You use **now** when you are talking about the present moment. It means 'immediately'. *The bus is leaving now and anyone who isn't on it will miss the swimming carnival.*

nowadays *adverb*
If something happens **nowadays**, it happens in the time that you are living in, not in the past. *There used to be dinosaurs on the planet but nowadays the biggest animal you can see is a whale.*

nowhere /say **noh**-wair / adverb
Nowhere means 'not anywhere'. *My friends were nowhere to be seen.*

nuclear /say **nyooh**-klee-uh / adjective
If something is **nuclear** it has to do with the very strong energy given out when an atom is split. **Nuclear** energy can do things with great force and power.

nude adjective
If you are **nude**, you do not have any clothes on.

> Another word that means the same is **naked**.

nuisance /say **nyooh**-suhns / noun
If something or someone is a **nuisance**, they make you feel annoyed or give you trouble. *Our noisy new neighbours are a real nuisance!*

> ★ *Spelling Tip:* Remember the *ui* spelling for the 'yooh' sound. You could remind yourself that someone who is a **nuisance** is <u>u</u>nusually irritating.

nulla-nulla noun
A **nulla-nulla** is a heavy wooden stick that was used by Aboriginal people in fighting and hunting.

> This word comes from an Aboriginal language of New South Wales called Dharug.

numb /rhymes with sum / adjective
You are **numb** if you cannot feel anything.

> ★ *Spelling Tip:* Don't forget the *b* at the end.

numbat noun
A **numbat** is a small Australian marsupial that eats termites. It has red and brown fur, and white stripes on its back, a long, bushy tail, and a long, pointed nose.

> This word comes from an Aboriginal language of Western Australia called Nyungar.

number noun
A **number** is a word or a sign that you use to count.

nun noun
A **nun** is one of a group of women who choose to live a life of service to God by helping people who are poor or sick, or teaching young children.

nurse noun
1. A **nurse** is someone whose job is to look after sick people, usually in a hospital.
–verb 2. If someone **nurses** a child, they hold him or her in their arms. *Mum nursed the baby all the way to the city.*

nursery noun
1. A **nursery** is a room or place for children. *My aunt was very excited about having a baby and had the nursery decorated even before it was born.*
2. A **nursery** is a place where plants are grown. *Mum bought a gum tree from the nursery. We are going to plant it at the end of the garden.*

nut noun
1. A **nut** is a dry fruit with a hard shell. The part you eat is inside the shell. *We had to break the shells with a hammer to get to the nuts inside.*
2. A **nut** is a small piece of metal that you turn around on the end of a long piece of metal (called a 'bolt'). You use a **nut** and bolt to join things together. *My new bed was in pieces when it arrived from the shop. There was a bag of nuts and bolts with it so that we could put it together.*

nylon /say **nuy**-lon / noun
Nylon is a strong material which is used to make clothes or things like the short thin hairs on some brushes.

> ★ *Spelling Tip:* Remember that the second letter is *y*, giving an 'uy' sound.

a
b
c
d
e
f
g
h
i
j
k
l
m
n
o
p
q
r
s
t
u
v
w
x
y
z

Octopus

oak *noun*
An **oak** is a large tree with very hard wood.

oar /*rhymes with* for/ *noun*
An **oar** is a long pole that is wide and flat at one end. You use two **oars** for rowing a boat.

oasis /*say* oh-**ay**-suhs/ *noun* (*plural* **oases** /*say* oh-**ay**-seez/)
An **oasis** is a place in a desert where there is water and plants.

obedient /*say* uh-**bee**-dee-uhnt/ *adjective*
You are **obedient** if you do the things you are told to do.

The opposite is **disobedient**.

⭐ *Spelling Tip:* Notice that the sound in the second part of this word is spelt with a single *e* (although you say it as 'ee'). This is because **obedient** has been formed from the word *obey*.

obese /*say* oh-**bees**/ *adjective*
If you are **obese**, you are extremely fat.

Word Building: **obesity**, *noun* **Obesity** is a medical condition in which too much body fat affects the person's health.

obey *verb*
1. When you **obey**, you do what someone tells you to do. *Ann's dad is very strict – he expects her to obey whatever he says.*
2. When you **obey** someone, you do what that person tells you to do. *Ajay's mother is angry with him because he did not obey her.*
3. If you **obey** rules or **obey** the law, you do what the rules or the law say is the right thing to do. *When people don't obey the rules of the road, accidents happen.*

The opposite is **disobey**.

object *noun* /*say* **ob**-jekt/
1. An **object** is any thing which can be seen or felt and that is not alive.

–*verb* /*say* uhb-**jekt**/ **2.** If you **object**, or if you **object to** something, you do not agree with it and do not think it should happen. *We objected when they kept talking through the picture.*

Word Building: **objection**, *noun* If you object to something, you have an **objection** to it.

oblong *noun*
An **oblong** is a shape with two long sides and two short sides like a door has.

Also look up **rectangle**.

observation *noun*
1. When you make an **observation**, you watch something or someone carefully. *After his observation of the classroom, he decided that more tables and chairs were needed.*
2. If you write an **observation**, you do a piece of writing about something that has actually happened and tell how you feel about it. *She wrote an observation about an event in her early childhood.*

observe *verb*
If you **observe** something or someone, you watch them carefully. *When I am a detective, I am going to observe everybody very carefully just in case they turn out to be criminals.*

obstacle /*say* **ob**-stuh-kuhl/ *noun*
An **obstacle** is something that is in your way.

obtain *verb*
If you **obtain** something, you get it. *Mum managed to obtain tickets for the show on the last day.*

obvious /*say* **ob**-vee-uhs/ *adjective*
Something is **obvious** if it is easy to see or to understand.

occasion /*say* uh-**kay**-zhuhn/ *noun*
An **occasion** is a special time or event.

⭐ *Spelling Tip:* Remember that there is a double *c* but only one *s*. Also remember that there is a single *a* following the double *c* (although you say it as 'ay').

occur *verb* (**occurs, occurring, occurred, has occurred**)

If something **occurs**, it happens. *The accident occurred at three o'clock yesterday.*

Occur is a more formal word than **happen**. You usually say **happen**.

⚡ *Spelling Tip:* Remember that there is a double *c* but only one *r* at the end. However, when you add *ed* or *ing*, the *r* is doubled.

ocean /*say* **oh**-shuhn/ *noun*

An **ocean** is one of the large areas of water in the world, such as the Atlantic Ocean or the Pacific Ocean.

ocean liner *noun*

An **ocean liner** is a large ship that carries people or goods long distances.

o'clock *adverb*

You say **o'clock** after a number when you are saying what the time is. It means 'of or by the clock'. *It will be 12 o'clock in five minutes.*

October *noun*

October is the tenth month of the year and has 31 days. It comes between September and November.

octopus *noun* (*plural* **octopuses**)

An **octopus** is a sea animal with eight long arms.

odd *adjective*

1. Someone or something is **odd** if they are unusual or strange. *There was an odd little man with a very long beard sitting in the yard.*
2. A number is **odd** if you cannot divide it by two. *Three, five, seven and nine are odd numbers.*
3. A thing is **odd** if it is made into a pair that does not match. *I had to wear odd socks because I couldn't find two the same.*

The opposite of definition 2 is **even**.

odour *noun*

An **odour** is a smell.

of *preposition*

You can use **of** in many ways. Its main meaning has to do with owning or being included in something. You also use it to show what you are measuring. Here are some examples. *He is the prime minister of Australia.*

off *adverb, preposition*

1. You use **off** when you are talking about something being away or separate. Here are some examples. *He ran off before the police could catch him. | Where do we get off? | He fell off the horse. | We got off the bus. | Our house is not far off. | My birthday is only a week off.*
–*adjective* **2.** A machine that is **off** or is turned **off** is not going. *This room is very cold. The heater must be off. | Remember to turn the lights off before you go to bed.*

offer *verb*

1. If you **offer** something to someone, you hold it out for them to take if they want to. *I offered my jumper to Donna because she was cold.*
2. If you **offer** someone something, you say you are willing to give it to them or get it for them. *The coach offered me a place in the team.*
3. If you **offer** to do something, you say that you are willing to do it. *She offered to drive us home.*

office *noun*

An **office** is a place where people work at desks, writing and making telephone calls, or working on computers.

officer *noun*

An **officer** is someone who has an important position in an organisation, especially in an organisation like the army, navy, air force or police force.

official /*say* uh-**fish**-uhl/ *noun*

1. An **official** is someone who has an important job in an organisation. –*adjective*
2. If something is **official**, it has been arranged or agreed to by the government or by someone with the power to agree to it.

Word Building: **officially**, *adverb* If something is done following official rules, it is done **officially**.

often /*say* **of**-uhn, **of**-tuhn/ *adverb*

1. If someone or something does something **often**, they do it many times. *Sam often walks to school with Joe.*
2. If something happens **often**, it happens many times. It is usual. *It often rains in summer.*

⚡ *Spelling Tip:* Don't forget that in one of the ways of saying this word, there is a silent *t* after the *f*. If you think 'of ten' **often**, you will never forget!

oil *noun*

1. Oil is a rather thick liquid made from an animal or vegetable, which you use for cooking.

Dad heated the oil in the pan and added the vegetables.

2. Oil is a thick liquid used in machines to make them run smoothly. *Mum checked the oil in the car because she thought it might be low.*

Word Building: oily, *adjective* If something is covered with oil, it is **oily**.

ointment *noun*

Ointment is a smooth thick substance that you put on cuts and sores to help them get better.

okay *adjective*

1. If someone is **okay**, they are not hurt or sick.
–interjection **2.** You can say **okay** when you agree to something and mean 'yes'. *'Can I come with you?' 'Okay, you can come if you like.'*

Okay is an informal word that you might use when talking to your friends.

You can also write **OK**.

old *adjective*

1. If someone or something is **old**, they have lived or existed for a long time. *My grandfather is an old man.*
2. You use **old** when you are talking about someone's age. *'How old is Giuseppe?' 'He is 12 years old.'*
3. You can say something is **old** when you have had it for a while. *I don't like these old clothes. I would like to get some new ones.*

The opposite of definition 1 is **young**; the opposite of definition 3 is **new**.

old-fashioned *adjective*

If something is **old-fashioned**, it comes from an earlier time and is different from things that are made now.

The opposite is **modern**.

olive *noun*

Olives are the small round fruits from a tree which can be eaten or crushed for their oil.

Olympic Games *noun*

The **Olympic Games** are competitions in many sports such as running, swimming, jumping, shooting, and so on, between most countries of the world, taking place over a period of several weeks. They are held every four years, each time in a different country.

omelette /*say* **om**-luht/ *noun*

An **omelette** is a food you make by mixing eggs together and cooking them in a pan, sometimes with other food added.

omit *verb* (**omits**, **omitting**, **omitted**, **has omitted**)

If you **omit** something, you leave it out. *We omitted to put our address on the competition form so we can't win.*

on *preposition, adverb*

1. If something is *on* something else, it is in a higher position than it and touching it: *'Where are my books?' 'They are on the table.'* This is the basic meaning of **on**, but you can use it in many ways, for example: *There are two pictures on the wall.* | *She has a mark on her face.* | *Go through the door on the left.* | *They talked on the phone for a long time.* | *We came on foot.* | *They will arrive on Saturday.* | *The holidays start on the first day of June.* | *Have you got any books on animals?* | *He gave a talk on ants.* | *Put your coat on. It's cold.* | *The bus is ready to leave. We should get on now.*
–adjective **2.** A **machine** that is **on** or is turned **on** is going. *Is the computer on?* | *Turn the TV on – it's almost time for the film.*

once *adverb*

1. You use **once** to talk about a time in the past. *We once lived in the country but then we moved to the city.*
2. You use **once** to talk about one single time. *I'm only going to say this once, so listen carefully.*
3. at once, a. You use **at once** to mean 'now' or 'immediately'. *Come here at once!* **b.** You also use **at once** to mean 'at the same time'. *The teacher said she couldn't understand us if we all spoke at once.*
4. once upon a time, The phrase **once upon a time** is sometimes used at the beginning of a story about something that happened in the past. *Once upon a time, a beautiful girl became lost in a forest.*

one *noun*

1. One is a number which you can write as 1. It is the first number after zero (0) and stands for a single thing.
–pronoun **2. One** is a single person or thing. *After the nine green bottles had fallen off the wall, there was only one left.*
3. You can use **one** instead of repeating the name of a thing or person. *You have seen lots of animals today. Which one did you like the best?*

–*adjective* **4.** If there is **one** person or thing, there is a single person or thing only.

Also look up **first**.

onion /*say* **un**-yuhn/ *noun*
An **onion** is a round white vegetable that grows under the ground and has a very strong smell and taste.

⚡ *Spelling Tip:* An **onion** is a rather ordinary vegetable, but it has a difficult spelling, particularly as it does not sound as if it begins with an *o*. You could try thinking of it as being made up of two lots of *on* joined by an *i* in the middle.

online *adjective*
1. If a piece of equipment is **online**, it is connected to a computer. *Once the modem is online, we will be able to send emails.*
2. Your computer is **online** if it is connected to the internet. *I can't surf on the internet at home yet because we're still not online.*
3. If something like a business is **online**, it has a site on the internet. *We found a really interesting site online which told us how French people raise snails for eating.*

only *adverb*
1. You use **only** to describe a single person or thing. *Nanda is the only kid in our class from India.*
2. You use **only** to make it clear that something, especially an amount or number, is quite small. *There are only 20 people in our class today. Everyone has the flu. | He was here only a minute ago – you just missed him.*
3. You use **only** to make it clear that you mean that thing or that action and nothing more. *I was only joking. I didn't mean to upset you. | I have only come to watch. I don't want to play.*

Another word with a similar meaning to definitions 2 and 3 is **just**.

onto *preposition*
You use **onto** when you are talking about moving an object to a place or position on something. *I'll put the book back onto the shelf.*

ooze *verb*
If a liquid **oozes**, it moves or flows slowly as though it is coming out of a small opening. *There was oil oozing from the broken bottle.*

open *adjective*
1. If something such a door or window is **open**, people or things can go through it. It is not shut or locked. *The dog was able to run away because the gate was open.*
2. If a shop is **open**, it is doing business. You can go in and buy things. *I hope the shop will be open when we get there. Do you know what time it closes?*
–*verb* **3.** If you **open** something, you make it open. *Open the window – there is an awful smell in here.*
4. If a shop **opens**, it starts doing business. *The fruit shop opens at nine o'clock but the news-agency opens at about seven.*

opening *noun*
1. An **opening** is a hole or a space that people or things can go through. *The dog got out through an opening in the fence.*
2. The **opening** of a shop or a building is when it opens, especially when it opens for the first time. *There were lots of people there for the opening of the new library.*

opera *noun*
An **opera** is a play that is put to music, with the actors singing most of the words.

operate *verb*
1. If someone **operates** a machine, they make it work or run. *His job is to operate the printing machine.*
2. If a doctor **operates** on part of your body, he or she cuts that part open to try to make you better when you are sick or hurt. *The doctor will have to operate on her leg.*

operation *noun*
1. An **operation** is an activity that is planned and which has a lot of people taking part in it. *The rescue operation was very complicated but everyone on the plane was saved.*
2. An **operation** is what a doctor does when he or she cuts part of your body open to try to make you better. *My grandfather had to have an operation on his heart.*
3. in operation, If something is **in operation** it is working and able to be used. *This public phone isn't in operation at present.*

opinion /*say* uh-**pin**-yuhn/ *noun*
Your **opinion** is what you think or decide about something.

⚡ *Spelling Tip:* Remember that there is only one *p* in this word. Also remember that there is no *y*. The 'y' sound is spelt by the *i* in the *ion* ending.

opponent /say uh-**poh**-nuhnt/ noun
An **opponent** is someone who is on the opposite side to you in a competition.

opposite /say **op**-uh-suht/ adjective
1. If something is **opposite** to something else of the same kind, it is as different as it is possible to be. *White is the opposite colour to black.* | *She turned and walked away in the opposite direction.*
2. If something is **opposite** something else, it is in a position on the other side and across from it. *Jack lives in the house opposite to Tran.* | *I sit on the side of the classroom near the windows and Sophia sits on the opposite side.* –noun
3. The **opposite** of something or someone is a person or thing that is as different from them as it is possible to be. *Black is the opposite of white.* | *Right and left are opposites.* | *My opinion is the opposite of yours.*

> ✸ **Spelling Tip:** Remember that there is a double *p* but only one *s* in this word. Try thinking of **opposite** as being 'the perfect position for the other side'.

or conjunction
1. You use **or** to join words, phrases, or parts of sentences when you want to show that you can choose between them. You are showing that one may be chosen instead of another, or that one thing may happen and the other thing not happen. *Would you like a glass of lemonade or orange juice?*
2. or so, You use **or so** when you are talking about a number or amount that is not exact. It may be a bit more. *The trip will take 20 minutes or so.*

orange noun
1. An **orange** is a round, juicy fruit with a colour between red and yellow.
–adjective **2.** If something is **orange**, it has a colour between red and yellow.

orbit noun
An **orbit** is the curved path or line that something in space follows as it is moving around the earth or the sun.

orchard /say **aw**-chuhd/ noun
An **orchard** is a garden or farm where fruit trees are grown.

orchestra /say **aw**-kuhs-truh/ noun
An **orchestra** is a big group of people who play musical instruments together.

order verb
1. If someone **orders** you to do something, they say you have to do it. Usually they have the power to say you have to do it. *I can order the dog to sit down now that he has been to classes.*
2. If you **order** something from a shop or a restaurant, you ask for it to be given to you or made for you. *We ordered a large bag of chips.*
–noun **3.** An **order** is what someone says when they tell you that you must do something. *When I give you an order, I expect you to obey it.*
4. Order is how things are placed together, especially when they are placed together in an organised way. *We had to put the letters into alphabetical order.*
5. out of order, If something, such as a machine, is **out of order**, it is not working properly. *The public telephone is out of order again.*

ordinary adjective
If something is **ordinary**, it is usual or normal. It is not special in any way.

ore noun
Ore is a rock in the ground that contains a valuable metal.

organ noun
1. An **organ** is a musical instrument with black and white keys like a piano, as well as pedals that you press with your feet and pipes that the music comes through. *The music from the organ in the town hall filled the air.*
2. An **organ** is a part of your body which has a particular job. *The heart is a very important organ because it pumps your blood around your body.*

organisation /say aw-guh-nuy-**zay**-shuhn/ noun
An **organisation** is a group of people who work together or meet together for a particular reason.

> Another spelling for this word is **organization**.

organise verb
1. If you **organise** something, you plan how it will happen or how it will be run. *Dad is organising a holiday for us all.*
2. If you **organise** things, you place them tidily together. *I'm going to organise my books better.*

> Another spelling for this word is **organize**.

original /say uh-**rij**-uh-nuhl/ adjective
1. If something is **original**, it is the first or earliest. *All the original students at our school are being invited back to see the new buildings.*
2. If something is **original**, it has been invented and is not copied from something else. *The teacher asked us to write an original poem about our family.*

> ⚂ *Spelling Tip:* The main thing to remember is the *g* giving the 'j' sound in the middle.

orphan /*say* **aw**-fuhn/ *noun*
An **orphan** is a child whose parents are dead.

ostrich *noun* (*plural* **ostriches**)
An **ostrich** is a large bird with long legs, that lives in Africa. It can run fast, but it cannot fly.

other *adjective*
1. You use **other** to talk about a person or thing which is in addition to what you have already mentioned. *When we got to the oval, there was only one other person there.*
2. You use **other** to talk about a person or thing that is of the same kind as someone or something but is not that one. *It wasn't me you saw at the movies – it must have been some other girl with long hair.*
–*pronoun* **3.** You use **the other** to talk about the second of the two people or things when you have already mentioned the first one. *I have found one of my socks but I don't know where the other is.*
4. You use **the others** to talk about people or things that are more than or different to what you have already mentioned. *Tom and Jane have arrived already. Where are the others?*

otherwise *adverb*
You use **otherwise** to mean in all ways except for what you have just said. *Tuesday did not start off well when I missed the bus, but otherwise it was a very good day.*

> ⚂ *Spelling Tip:* The spelling of this word will be quite easy if you see that it is made up of *other* with the word part *wise*. This does not mean 'knowing the best thing to do', but is a form of *ways* used in words having to do with direction or the way something is done.

ought /*say* awt/ *verb*
1. If you **ought** to do something, there is a strong reason for you to do it. For example, it is your duty to do it or it would be kind to someone else to do it. *We ought to help Mum with the cleaning.*
2. You can use **ought** to mean that something is probably true. *One large bag of chips ought to be enough for us.*

> ⚂ *Spelling Tip:* Remember the *ough* spelling for the 'aw' sound. This letter group occurs in many other words, such as *bought* and *fought*.

our *pronoun*
You use **our** to show that something belongs to you all. *That's our house.*

ours *pronoun*
You use **ours** to show that something belongs to you all. *That white house over there is ours.*

ourselves *pronoun*
You use **ourselves** to mean 'us and no-one else'. *We enjoyed ourselves fishing from the wharf.*

out *adverb*, *preposition*
1. If someone or something is **out** or goes **out**, they are not inside any more. *When he came in, she went out.* | *Is it time to take out the pizza yet?* | *They went out for a walk.* | *He walked out of the room.* | *Dad took the pizza out of the oven.*
2. If something, such as a fire, goes **out**, it is no longer burning or giving light. *The lamp went out.*
3. out of, If something is made **out of** a material, that is the material that forms it. *My chess set is made out of wood.*
–*adjective* **4.** If someone is **out**, they are not in their home or in the place where they work. *I went around to see Makiko but she was out.*

outback *noun*
The **outback** is the part of the Australian country that is far away from the cities and from the sea.

outdoors *adverb*
If you go **outdoors** or do something **outdoors**, you go out of a building, or you do it somewhere that is not in a building. *As soon as it stopped raining we went outdoors to play in the puddles.*

> *Word Building:* **outdoor**, *adjective* You use **outdoor** to describe something that is placed out of a building or that you do out of a building. *I like outdoor games.*

outer *adjective*
If something is **outer**, it has to do with the furthest outside part.

outline *noun*
An **outline** is a line that shows the shape of something.

outside *noun*
1. The **outside** of something is the part or side that is not in it.
–*adverb* **2.** If you go **outside** or do something **outside**, you go out of a building, or you do it somewhere that is not in a building. *Isabella went outside while it was raining and got very wet.*

a b c d e f g h i j k l m n o p q r s t u v w x y z

oval *adjective*
1. If something is **oval**, it is shaped like an egg.
–*noun* 2. An **oval** is a field for playing sport on.

oven /*say* **uv**-uhn / *noun*
An **oven** is the part of a stove where you bake food.

over *preposition*, *adverb*
1. If something is **over** or goes **over** something else, it is higher than it or goes across it. *The plane flew over our house.*
2. If you use **over** before a number or amount, you mean more than that number. *Our school is over a kilometre away.*
3. If something falls **over** or you knock something **over**, it falls down. It is not straight up as it should be any more. *Dad knocked over the garbage bin with the car.*
4. **over and over**, If you do something **over and over**, you do it many times. *I had to play that piano piece over and over before I could remember it.*
–*adjective* 5. If something is **over**, it is finished or has come to an end.

overalls *noun*
Overalls are a type of loose trousers attached to either a shirt or a covering for just the front part of your body. You wear **overalls** over your other clothes.

> ✵ *Spelling Tip:* The spelling of this word will be quite easy if you see that it is simply made up of *over* and *all* joined together, with an *s* added at the end.

overcoat *noun*
An **overcoat** is a thick coat that is long enough to cover most or all of your clothes.

overtake *verb* (**overtakes**, **overtaking**, **overtook**, **has overtaken**)
If you **overtake** someone, you catch up with them and go past them. *If you run as fast as you can, you can overtake the leader.*

owe *verb*
1. If you **owe** someone some money, they have lent you that money and you have to pay it back to them. *I haven't forgotten that I owe you $2. I will pay it back tomorrow.*
2. If you **owe** an amount of money, that is the amount you have to pay back to someone. *Sasha has been lending me money and altogether I owe $5 now.*

owl *noun*
An **owl** is a bird with large eyes, that hunts for small animals at night.

own *verb*
1. If you **own** something, it belongs to you. It is yours. *I don't own a bike but I am hoping I will after my birthday.*
–*adjective* 2. You use **own** to describe something that belongs to you and not anyone else.
–*pronoun* 3. **on your own**, a. If you are **on your own**, you are alone. *My grandmother lives on her own now that my grandfather has died.* b. If you do something **on your own**, you do it without any help. *I can lift my little brother on my own.*

> *Word Building:* **owner**, *noun* If you own something, then you are the **owner**.

ox *noun* (*plural* **oxen**)
An **ox** is a large farm animal that is often used to pull loads. It is a kind of cattle.

oyster *noun*
An **oyster** is a sea animal you can eat. It lives inside a pair of shells which you often find joined to rocks.

ozone layer *noun*
The **ozone layer** is the outer area of the earth's atmosphere which protects the earth from the sun.

> ✵ *Spelling Tip:* You can think of **ozone** as being made up of *o* plus *zone* which will make the spelling easier. In fact, it comes from *ozein*, the Greek word for 'smell'.

parrot

pace *noun*
1. A **pace** is one walking step. *It was only about six paces from the car to the building but we still got wet in the rain.*
2. **Pace** is the speed at which something moves. *The car was going at such a pace that it spun out of control around the corner.*

pack *noun*
1. A **pack** is a bag that you use to carry things on your back. *We made sure we put plenty of water in our packs for the bush walk.*
2. A **pack** of something is a group of things that go together or that you can buy together. *He bought a pack of envelopes.*
3. A **pack** can also be the container that holds a group of things. *The information about the contents is on the back of the pack.*
– *verb* 4. If you **pack** things, you put them into a bag or box, because you want to take them with you or move them away. *Mum helped me pack for the school camp.*
5. If people or things **pack** together, there are a lot of them pressed close to each other. *We all packed into the hall to watch the play.*

package *noun*
A **package** is something wrapped up in paper or other material so that it can be sent somewhere.

packet *noun*
1. A **packet** is a group of things that are put together in a small container. *Jemma bought a packet of peanuts.*
2. A **packet** is also the container itself. *'Are there any peanuts left?' 'Sorry, the packet is empty.'*

pad *noun*
1. A **pad** is sheets of writing paper joined together at one edge. *We took a writing pad on our excursion to write down all the things we saw.*
2. A **pad** is a soft, thick piece of material that you use to protect something. *Mum put a pad of material on the hard chair so it would be more comfortable to sit on.*

paddle¹ *noun*
A **paddle** is a short oar that you use to make a canoe move through water.

paddle² *verb*
If you **paddle**, you walk in water that is not very deep. *It was too cold to go in so we just paddled at the edge of the beach.*

paddock *noun*
A **paddock** is a large area of land with a fence around it and grass growing on it for sheep or cattle to eat.

> ✷ *Spelling Tip:* Remember the double *d*. To remind you of this and the spelling of the end of the word, you can try thinking of it being made up of *pad* and *dock* though these words are not connected to the meaning.

padlock *noun*
A **padlock** is a lock with a curved bar that you can shut to join two things together. You open a **padlock** with a key.

page *noun*
1. A **page** is one of the pieces of paper that are a part of a book, magazine or letter. *Ben tore a page out of his book to write a note.*
2. A **page** is one side of one of these pieces of paper. *He wrote a poem at the top of the page and did a drawing underneath it.*

pain *noun*
Pain is a very uncomfortable feeling in your body that you have when you are hurt or when part of your body is sick.

> ✷ *Spelling Tip:* Don't confuse the spelling of **pain** with **pane** which has the same sound. A **pane** is the piece of glass in a window.

painful *adjective*
If something is **painful**, it gives you pain.

paint *noun*
1. **Paint** is a coloured liquid that you can put on a surface to give it colour, usually using a brush.

–*verb* **2.** If you **paint** something, you cover it with paint to give it colour. *They painted the fence blue.*

3. If you **paint** something or someone, you make a picture of them using paint. *Ella painted a picture of her mother for Mother's Day.*

> *Word Building:* **painter**, *noun* Someone whose job is to paint or who makes pictures by painting is a **painter**.

painting *noun*
A **painting** is a picture of something done with paint.

pair *noun*
1. A **pair** is two things of the same kind that go together because you need two of them, not one. You talk about **a pair of** these things. *My grandmother gave me a pair of pink socks for my birthday.*

2. A **pair** can be a single thing that is made of two parts that have been joined together. *Do you have a pair of scissors? | We had to find a pair of black pants to wear for the school concert.*

palace /*say* **pal**-uhs/ *noun*
A **palace** is a very large building which is the official home of a king, queen, or the ruler of some countries.

pale *adjective*
1. If something is **pale** it does not have much colour or is close to white in colour. *Anita's face is pale. She must be sick.*

2. If a colour is **pale**, it is not very bright. It is closer to white than a dark kind of that colour. *The wall was painted pale yellow.*

palm[1] /*say* pahm/ *noun*
Your **palm** is the inside of your hand, from your wrist to where your fingers start.

> ✣ *Spelling Tip:* Don't forget the *l*. The *alm* spelling gives the 'ahm' sound.

palm[2] /*say* pahm/ *noun*
A **palm** is a tall plant with large leaves and no branches.

> ✣ *Spelling Tip:* Look up **palm**[1].

pan *noun*
A **pan** is a wide dish, open at the top, which is used for cooking.

pancake *noun*
A **pancake** is a thin, flat piece of food made from flour, eggs and milk and cooked in a pan. You often put sugar or something else that is sweet on them.

pane *noun*
A **pane** is one sheet of glass in a window.

> ✣ *Spelling Tip:* Don't confuse the spelling of **pane** with **pain** which has the same sound. **Pain** is when your body hurts.

panic *noun*
Panic is sudden fear that is so strong it makes you do things without thinking.

pants *noun*
1. Pants are a piece of clothing for the lower part of the body, divided into two parts for the legs. *My brother's legs have suddenly grown, so he has to get new pants.*

2. Pants are a piece of clothing worn under other clothing, covering from the middle of the body to the top of the legs. *Mum always puts out my singlet and pants for me to put on in the morning.*

> ✤ Another word for definition 1 is **trousers**.
>
> ✤ Although the word **pants** means one piece of clothing, you speak or write about them as though they are two because they are made of two parts joined together. So you say: *Your pants are just like mine.* But if you are speaking or writing about **a pair of pants** you treat them as though they are one and say.

paper *noun*
1. Paper is a material that usually comes in thin pieces for writing or printing on, or wrapping things in. *Have you got a piece of paper to wrap the present in?*

2. A **paper** is a newspaper. *Mum likes to read the paper every morning before she goes to work.*

parachute /*say* pa-ruh-shooht/ *noun*
A **parachute** is a large piece of light, strong cloth tied to someone's back that opens out and makes their fall not as fast when they jump out of a plane.

parade *noun*
A **parade** is a group of people moving along the street for some special occasion with a crowd watching them go past.

paragraph /*say* pa-ruh-graf, pa-ruh-grahf/ *noun*
A **paragraph** is a short division in a piece of writing. You start a new **paragraph** when you are writing about a new idea or subject. Each new **paragraph** starts on a new line.

parallel /say **pa**-ruh-lel/ noun
Lines are **parallel** if they are the same distance from each other all the way along.

> ✸ **Spelling Tip:** Remember only one *r*, then a double *l*, then a single *l* at the end. Think: single – double – single.

paralysed /say **pa**-ruh-luyzd/ adjective
If some part of a person's body is **paralysed**, they are not able to move that part.

> **Word Building:** paralysis /say puh-**ral**-uh-suhs/, noun If you're paralysed, you suffer from **paralysis**.

> ✸ **Spelling Tip:** Remember that *y* (not *i*) spells the sound following the *l*.

parcel noun
A **parcel** is something wrapped up in paper, ready for posting or giving to someone.

> ✸ **Spelling Tip:** Remember that *c* spells the 's' sound in the middle, and that there is only one *l* at the end.

pardon verb
1. If someone **pardons** someone else, they forgive them and do not punish them. *The king decided to pardon the prisoners.*
–noun in the phrase 2. **I beg your pardon**, You use this phrase as a polite way of saying you are sorry for something you have done by accident or a polite way of asking someone to repeat what they have said because you didn't hear them. *I beg your pardon – I didn't mean to tread on your foot. | I beg your pardon – did you say you wanted a meal or a wheel?*

parent noun
A **parent** is a father or a mother.

park noun
1. A **park** is an area of land, usually with grass and trees, for people to walk, sit and play in.
–verb 2. When you **park** a car or a bike, you put it in a particular place, such as at the side of the road, and leave it there for a while. *Dad managed to park our car just outside the school.*

parliament /say **pah**-luh-muhnt/ noun
Parliament is the group of people we choose to represent us and make our laws.

> ✸ **Spelling Tip:** Don't forget the *i* before the middle *a*, although you don't hear the *i* when

you say the word. Try breaking the word up as *parl + i + a + ment*.

parrot noun
A **parrot** is a bird with brightly coloured feathers and a curved beak. You can teach some **parrots** to talk.

parsley noun
Parsley is a plant used in cooking.

part noun
1. A **part** is one of the pieces that make up the whole thing. *We had to colour in the part of the map where we lived.*
2. **take part**, If you **take part** in an activity or something that other people are doing, you do what the other people are doing. *We can all take part in the swimming carnival – it doesn't matter if you're not a great swimmer.*

particular /say puh-**tik**-yuh-luh/ adjective
1. You use **particular** when you are talking about a single or special one of a kind, rather than all of them. *I am looking for a particular book about guinea pigs. It's the one with the pictures of their babies on the front.*
2. You use **particular** to mean 'more than usual'. *Aaron had to take particular care of the book because it had been in the family for nearly a century.*
3. **in particular**, You use **in particular** when you are saying that one thing in a number of things is more important. *My parents said I had to be careful with my new bike. In particular, I wasn't allowed to take it on the road.*

> **Word Building:** particularly, adverb: *I want you to be particularly careful.*

partly adverb
You use **partly** to show that something has not happened completely. *The food was only partly eaten. There's still some left. | The house is made partly of stone and partly of wood.*

partner noun
A **partner** is someone who shares or does something with you.

party noun (plural **parties**)
1. A **party** is a gathering together of people to enjoy themselves, often to celebrate something. *At my brother's party, the kids were all were dressed up as clowns.*
2. A **party** is an organisation of people who have the same ideas about how the government of a country should be run. Members of a particular

party often make up the government of a country. *People vote for the party they think has the best ideas.*

pass *verb*

1. If you **pass** someone or something, you go by them or beyond them. *We pass the fire station on the way to school.* | *At the very last minute of the race, Grace passed Rachel and won.*
2. If you **pass** a test, you do it successfully. You do it as well as you have to do. *Tapan didn't get a very high mark in his violin test but he passed it.*
3. If you **pass** something to someone, you put it into their hand or give it to them. *Could you pass me the sugar, please.* | *Could you pass the message to the person in charge.*

passage *noun*

A **passage** is a way of going from one place or one room to another. It is sometimes rather long and narrow.

passenger *noun*

A **passenger** is someone who travels on a bus, train, ship or plane.

> �֍ *Spelling Tip:* Remember the double *s* and the *er* ending.

passer-by *noun* (*plural* **passers-by**)

A **passer-by** is someone who goes by something or someone on their way to somewhere else.

passionfruit /*say* pash-uhn-frooht/ *noun*

A **passionfruit** is a small fruit with purple skin. It has a soft yellow part inside and black seeds that you can eat.

password *noun*

A **password** is a secret group of letters or numbers you use to show who you are when you are doing something like starting to use your computer.

past *noun*

1. If something happened or existed in the **past**, it happened or existed in the time before now.
–*adverb* **2.** If someone or something goes **past**, they go by and beyond something. *We all watched as the parade went past.*

> Also look up **present**[1] and **future**.

pasta /*say* pas-tuh, pahs-tuh/ *noun*

Pasta is a food made from flour, water and sometimes egg as well. Spaghetti is a kind of pasta.

paste *noun*

1. A **paste** is a smooth wet material used for sticking paper onto things. *Anna made paste out*

of flour and water and stuck all of her pictures into a book.
2. A **paste** is a mixture that is soft and smooth like toothpaste and can be spread easily. *We mixed the paints up into pastes for the face painting at the fete.*

pastry *noun*

Pastry is a mixture of flour, water and fat that is cooked and used as the outside part of pies and tarts.

pasture /*say* pahs-chuh/ *noun*

Pasture is grass or other plants for feeding cows or sheep.

patch *noun* (*plural* **patches**)

1. A **patch** is anything you use to fix a hole or a weak part of something. *Mum sewed a patch on my jeans.*
2. A **patch** is a small piece of something. *In the corner of the yard, Makiko had a little patch of garden that was just for her.*

patent /*say* pay-tuhnt/ *noun*

A **patent** is permission given by the government to someone so they are the only person allowed to make or sell an invention.

path *noun*

A **path** is a narrow way for walking.

patient /*say* pay-shuhnt/ *noun*

1. A **patient** is someone who is being treated by a doctor or who is in a hospital.
–*adjective* **2.** If someone is **patient**, they can wait for a long time without getting angry.

> *Word Building:* **patience**, *noun* If you are patient, you have a lot of **patience**. –**patiently**, *adverb* If you are patient, you wait **patiently**.

> The opposite is **impatient**.

> ✤ *Spelling Tip:* Remember the *ti* spelling in the middle. These letters together make the 'sh' sound.

patio /*say* pat-ee-oh, pay-shee-oh/ *noun* (*plural* **patios**)

A **patio** is a part without a roof that joins onto a house, where people can can do things like eat in the fresh air or sit in the sun.

> ✤ *Spelling Tip:* Notice that there are two ways of saying this word. If you say it in the first way, you should have no trouble with the spelling. If you say it in the second way, you will

have to remember the *ti* spelling for the 'sh' sound.

patrol /*say* puh-**trohl**/ *verb* (**patrols, patrolling, patrolled, has patrolled**)
If someone **patrols** a place, they go around it at special times to make sure there is no trouble. *The police patrol this street several times each night.*

pattern *noun*
A **pattern** is a design that has the same shapes repeated over and over again.

> **Spelling Tip:** Remember the double *t* in the middle, and the *r* in the last part of this word, which you do not hear when you say the word.

pause *noun*
A **pause** is a short rest or stop.

pavlova *noun*
A **pavlova** is a sweet food made of a large, round meringue filled with cream, and usually with fruit on top.

paw *noun*
A **paw** is the foot of an animal.

pay *verb* (**pays, paying, paid, has paid**)
1. When you **pay**, you give money to someone in return for something they give you or do for you. *Dad pays a man to help in the garden. | How much did you pay for that new dress?*
2. **pay back**, When you **pay** someone **back**, you give them money that they have lent you. *If you lend me $2, I will pay you back tomorrow.*
–*noun* 3. Someone's **pay** is the money they are paid for the work they do as their job. *My mum's pay goes straight into her bank account.*

> **Word Building: payment**, *noun* When you pay for something, you make a **payment**.

PE *noun*
PE is sport and exercises for your body that you do at school.

> **PE** is short for **physical education**.

pea *noun*
A **pea** is a small, round, green vegetable. **Peas** grow in a pod.

peace *noun*
1. When there is **peace**, there is no war. *After many years of fighting, everyone wanted peace.*
2. **Peace** is a time when everything is quiet and still. *There is never any peace in our house because there are five people and a dog.*

> **Spelling Tip:** Don't confuse the spelling of **peace** with **piece** which has the same sound. A **piece** is a bit of something.

peaceful *adjective*
When it is **peaceful**, everything is quiet and still.

> **Word Building: peacefully**, *adverb*: *The baby is sleeping peacefully.*

peach *noun* (*plural* **peaches**)
A **peach** is a round sweet fruit with soft skin and with one large seed (which is called a stone) inside.

peacock *noun*
A **peacock** is a large male bird with long, brightly coloured feathers in its tail.

> **Word Building: peahen**, *noun* The female is a **peahen**.

peanut *noun*
A **peanut** is a small nut that you can eat.

pear *noun*
A **pear** is a pale green or brown fruit with a thin skin, round at one end and growing smaller towards the other end.

pearl /*rhymes with* curl/ *noun*
A **pearl** is a hard, shiny, white ball that grows inside the shells of some oysters and is used as a jewel.

pebble *noun*
A **pebble** is a small, smooth, round stone.

peculiar /*say* puh-**kyooh**-lee-uh/ *adjective*
If something is **peculiar**, it is strange or unusual.

> **Spelling Tip:** Remember the *iar* (not *ier*) ending. Another word with this ending is *familiar*. If you remember that, you should feel familiar with this spelling.

pedal *noun*
1. A **pedal** is a part of a vehicle, such as a bike or car, that you push with your foot to make is go faster or to stop it.
–*verb* (**pedals, pedalling, pedalled, has pedalled**)
2. If you **pedal** a bike, you push the pedals with your feet. *I had to pedal hard to get to the top of the hill.*

pedestrian /*say* puh-**des**-tree-uhn/ *noun*
A **pedestrian** is someone who walks somewhere in a town or city.

★ *Spelling Tip:* Remember that there is only one *d*. **Pedestrian** comes from *pedes*, the Latin word for 'feet'.

peep *verb*
If you **peep**, you look quickly from the place where you are hiding or you look through a small hole. *Graeme peeped out from behind the bush, but no-one had come looking for him yet.*

pelican *noun*
A **pelican** is a large bird with a bag of skin hanging under its bill for holding the fish it catches.

pen *noun*
A **pen** is something that you write with. It has ink inside it.

penalty /*say* **pen**-uhl-tee/ *noun* (*plural* **penalties**)
A **penalty** is what you have to pay for doing something wrong.

pencil *noun*
A **pencil** is something you use for writing or drawing. It is a thin pointed piece of wood with lead or another special coloured material inside it.

penguin /*say* **pen**-gwuhn/ *noun*
A **penguin** is a type of bird that lives in cold areas in the southern part of the world. *Penguins swim in the sea but cannot fly.*

penny *noun* (*plural* **pennies** *or* **pence**)
A **penny** is a coin worth only a small amount, used in Britain and some other countries.

people /*say* **pee**-puhl/ *noun*
1. You use **people** when you are talking about humans in general, not any particular person. *People usually have two legs and animals generally have four.*
2. You use **people** when you are talking about more than one person. *There were two people in the room.*

pepper *noun*
Pepper is a black or a white powder with a hot taste, that you use in cooking or to put on your food.

per cent /*say* puh **sent**/ *adverb*
Per cent means 'as part of a hundred'. You use it when you are showing how big a certain amount is compared to the whole amount. *About fifty per cent of the kids in our school are girls and fifty per cent are boys.*

You can also write this as one word (**percent**) or you can write the sign % after a number. *50% of 600 is 300.*

perch *noun* (*plural* **perches**)
A **perch** is a piece of thin wood for birds to rest on.

perfect *adjective*
If something is **perfect**, it is as good as it is possible to be. There is nothing wrong with it.

Word Building: **perfectly**, *adverb* If the work you do is perfect, you do it **perfectly**. **perfection**, *noun* If something is perfect, it is in a state of **perfection**.

perform *verb*
1. If you **perform**, you do something in front of a group of people, such as play a piece of music or act in a play. *Our dance group is performing at the school concert.*
2. If you **perform** a piece of music or a play, you present that music or play to a group of people. *We are going to perform the Frog Ballet.*

Word Building: **performer**, *noun* If you perform, you are a **performer**. **performance**, *noun* When you perform, you give a **performance**.

perfume *noun*
A **perfume** is a liquid with a sweet smell.

perhaps *adverb*
You use **perhaps** to say that something might happen or it might not happen. *Perhaps the teacher won't notice what we have done.*

period *noun*
1. A **period** is any part or division of time. *I was sick for a period of about two weeks.*
2. A **period** can be a particular division of time or history. *I like hearing about the period of history when new countries were being discovered.*

permanent *adjective*
Something is **permanent** if it lasts for a very long time or all the time.

The opposite is **temporary**.

★ *Spelling Tip:* The sound in the middle is spelt with an *a*. Try thinking that there is a *mane* in this word. This will also help you remember the *ent* ending.

permission *noun*
When someone gives you **permission** to do something, they say that you can do it.

permit *verb* /*say* puh-**mit**/ (**permits, permitting, permitted, has permitted**)
1. If you **permit** someone to do something, you let them do it. *The school does not permit us to come to school wearing anything we like. We have to wear our uniforms.*
–*noun* /*say* **per**-mit/ **2.** A **permit** is a special piece of paper that allows you to do something.

Another word with a similar meaning to definition 1 is **allow**. **Permit** is more formal than **allow**.

persist *verb*
If you **persist** in doing something, you keep doing it even though it may be difficult. *I am determined to persist with this sum until I get it right.*

Word Building: persistence, *noun* If you persist, then you have a lot of **persistence**.
–**persistent**, *adjective* If you persist, then you are **persistent**.

person *noun*
A **person** is a human being, like you and me.

personal *adjective*
If something is **personal**, it has to do with one particular person.

personal best *noun*
the best performance you have ever done in a sport or other activity.

The short form of this is **PB**.

persuade /*say* puh-**swayd**/ *verb*
If you **persuade** someone to do something, you make them do it by telling them a good reason for it. *We tried to persuade Victoria to come to tennis with us so there would be four people to play.*

Word Building: persuasion /*say* puh-**sway**-zhuhn/, *noun*: *She finally gave in to our persuasion and agreed to come.*

⭐ **Spelling Tip:** Remember that there is no *w* in **persuade**. The letters *su* spell the 'sw' sound.

pest *noun*
1. A **pest** is an insect or animal that attacks food that is growing. *Farmers have to know how to control pests that can destroy their crops.*
2. A **pest** is someone or something that annoys or hurts you. *My brother is a little pest whenever I have to look after him.*

pet *noun*
A **pet** is an animal that you keep in your home because you like to have it, not because it is useful like a farm animal is.

petal *noun*
A **petal** is any of the soft, coloured parts of a flower.

⭐ **Spelling Tip:** Remember that the ending is *al*.

petrol *noun*
Petrol is the liquid made from oil that is used to make car engines work.

Word Building: petrol station, *noun* The place where you buy petrol is called a **petrol station**.

pew *noun*
A **pew** is a long, wooden seat in a church.

phone /*say* fohn/ *noun*
1. A **phone** is an instrument you use to speak to someone who is a long way from you.
–*verb* **2.** If you **phone** someone, you call them or speak to them on a phone. *What's the best time to phone you?*

Phone is the short form of **telephone**.

photo /*say* **foh**-toh/ *noun* (*plural* **photos**)
A **photo** is a photograph.

photograph /*say* **foh**-tuh-graf, **foh**-tuh-grahf/ *noun*
A **photograph** is a picture you take with a camera.

The short form is **photo**.

phrase /*say* frayz/ *noun*
A **phrase** is a small group of words that go together, but do not make a complete sentence.

physical /*say* **fiz**-ik-uhl/ *adjective*
Something is **physical** if it has to do with your body.

physics /*say* **fiz**-iks/ *noun*
Physics is the part of science where you study things like heat, light, electricity and other forms of energy in the world.

piano *noun* (*plural* **pianos**)
A **piano** is a large musical instrument which has a row of white and black pieces called keys. You play it by pressing on the keys with your fingers.

pick *verb*
1. If you **pick** something or someone out of a group, you say you want that one. *We went to a*

place where they keep stray dogs and we had to pick the one that we wanted.
2. If you **pick** flowers or fruit, you take them from the plant they are growing on and gather them together. *We picked the apples from our neighbour's apple tree.*

picnic *noun*
A **picnic** is a meal that you eat outside, usually in a park or at a beach.

pictogram *noun*
A **pictogram** is a simple drawing that represents something.

picture /*say* pik-chuh/ *noun*
1. A **picture** is a drawing, painting or photo. *I gave my dad a Father's Day card with a picture of a boat on it.*
2. the pictures, If you go to **the pictures**, you go to see a film at a cinema. *Let's go to the pictures on Saturday.*

pie *noun*
A **pie** is a kind of food, with an outside part made of pastry filled with sweet things like fruit, or with meat or vegetables.

piece *noun*
A **piece** is one part of something, not all of it.

> ✵ *Spelling Tip:* Don't confuse the spelling of **piece** with **peace** which has the same sound. **Peace** is when there is no fighting.

pierce *verb*
If a thing **pierces** something, it goes into it or through it with a point. *The needle pierced her finger.*

> ✵ *Spelling Tip:* Remember the *ier* spelling for the 'ear' sound. This follows the rule that *i* comes before *e* except after *c*.

pig *noun*
A **pig** is a farm animal with short legs, a heavy body, a flat nose and a short curly tail, often with pink or sometimes black skin.

> The male is a **boar**; the female is a **sow**; the young is a **piglet**.

pigeon /*say* pij-uhn/ *noun*
A **pigeon** is a kind of bird that is usually grey and lives in towns or cities.

> ✵ *Spelling Tip:* Remember that there is a *pig* in this word, but with the *g* giving a 'j' sound which you might think would be spelt *dg*. Also remember the silent *e* before the *on* ending.

pile *noun*
A **pile** of things is a group of them lying on top of each other.

pillar *noun*
A **pillar** is a tall, solid support for holding up part of a building.

> ✵ *Spelling Tip:* Remember the *ar* (not *er*) ending. Think of other words with this ending, such as *collar* and *dollar*.

pillow *noun*
A **pillow** is a case filled with feathers or some other soft material that you rest your head on when you are in bed.

pilot *noun*
A **pilot** is someone whose job is to fly an aircraft.

pimple *noun*
A **pimple** is a small red spot on someone's skin.

pin *noun*
1. A **pin** is a small, thin piece of metal with a sharp, pointed end, used to fasten things like paper or pieces of cloth together.
–*verb* (**pins**, **pinning**, **pinned**, **has pinned**)
2. If you **pin** something, you fasten it with a pin or something similar. *I stood still while Mum pinned my dress up to the right length.*

pinch *verb*
1. If you **pinch** someone, you hold their skin so tightly between your finger and thumb that you hurt them. *Stop pinching my arm!*
2. If someone **pinches** something, they steal it. *Somebody must have pinched my bag – it was sitting there a moment ago and now it is gone!*

> **Pinch** (as in definition 2) is an informal word that you might use when talking to your friends.

pine[1] *noun*
A **pine** is a tree with leaves that are like green needles. **Pines** have cones instead of flowers.

pine[2] *verb*
If you **pine for** something, you want it very much and are sad because you do not have it. *They hadn't been home for weeks and they were pining for their families.*

pineapple *noun*
A **pineapple** is a large, yellow fruit which grows in hot places. It is sweet and juicy inside and has a thick rough skin on the outside.

ping-pong *noun*

Ping-pong is a game for two or four people which you play by hitting a small white ball over a net which divides the table in half.

Another name for **ping-pong** is **table tennis.**

pink *adjective*

If something is **pink**, it has a colour which is a mixture of red and white.

pioneer /*say* puy-uh-**near** / *noun*

A **pioneer** is someone who goes and lives in an area before other people do, or who does something that other people copy.

pipe *noun*

1. A **pipe** is a long, round tube which is empty on the inside so that liquid or gas can go through it. This is how water or gas is carried to a house from the outside, and how waste water is carried away from a house. *The plumber had to come because our pipes were blocked.*
2. A **pipe** is a tube with a small bowl at one end that people can put tobacco in and smoke. *My grandfather likes to smoke a pipe. He doesn't like cigarettes.*

pirate *noun*

A **pirate** is someone who attacks ships at sea and steals their goods.

pistol *noun*

A **pistol** is a small gun that can be fired with one hand.

pitch *verb*

1. If you **pitch** something, you throw it. *We pitched our bags into the back of the car.*
–*noun* (*plural* **pitches**)
2. A **pitch** is a piece of ground marked out for a ball game.

pity *noun*

1. **Pity** is the sympathetic feeling you have for someone who is very sad, very poor or who has had something very bad happen to them.
–*verb* (**pities**, **pitying**, **pitied**, **has pitied**)
2. If you **pity** someone, you feel sympathy for them because they are suffering in some way. *We pitied the families who were waiting to hear news of their lost children.*

pizza /*say* **peet**-suh / *noun*

A **pizza** is a kind of food, made of a piece of round, flat dough covered with tomato and cheese and often other foods, and baked in an oven.

place *noun*

1. A **place** is anywhere that someone or something can be. It is an area or part of space. *This is a nice place to be in a storm.*
2. take place, If something **takes place**, it happens. *A bad accident took place outside our house yesterday.*
–*verb* **3.** If you **place** something somewhere, you put it there. *We placed our shoes next to the fence.*

plague /*say* playg / *noun*

1. A **plague** is a sickness which spreads very quickly and can kill people. *Many people died in a terrible plague in the early 20th century.*
2. A **plague** is very large numbers of insects or mice that arrive at the same time. *A plague of mice was eating all the crops.*

> ✳ *Spelling Tip:* Remember the *ague* spelling for the 'ayg' sound at the end of this word. Think of a word you know with the same sound and ending, such as *vague*.

plain *adjective*

1. If a situation is **plain**, it is easy to understand or know about. *Dad made it quite plain that we couldn't watch television at all that night.*
2. If something is **plain**, it is simple and ordinary, without anything extra. *I had been sick and Mum said I should have just a plain piece of toast.*
–*noun* **3.** A **plain** is a large area of flat land.

> *Word Building:* **plainly**, *adverb* If you say that something is **plainly** the case, you mean that it is clear and that it is true.

> ✳ *Spelling Tip:* Don't confuse the spelling of **plain** with **plane** which sounds the same.

plait /*rhymes with* mat / *verb*

1. If you **plait** something like hair or rope, you take three or more pieces together and weave them so that they cross over and under each other. *Will you plait my hair for me?*
–*noun* **2.** A **plait** is a length of something that has been woven in that way.

> ✳ *Spelling Tip:* Remember the *ai* spelling for the 'a' sound. The *i* is there because this word once was said 'playt'. The way you say it has changed, but the spelling has not!

plan *noun*

1. A **plan** is an idea of doing something and an idea of how to do it. *Richard had a plan for how to get his bike home with a flat tyre.*

2. A **plan** is a drawing of how something should be made. *Mum showed the builder the plans for the new kitchen.*
–*verb* (**plans**, **planning**, **planned**, **has planned**)
3. If you **plan** something, or **plan** to do something, you decide to do it and make a plan for how to do it. *We are planning to give our teacher a going-away present.*

plane¹ *noun*
A **plane** is a machine that can fly and which usually carries passengers.

This word is short for **aeroplane**.

✳ *Spelling Tip:* Don't confuse the spelling of **plane** with **plain** which sounds the same.

plane² *noun*
A **plane** is a tool you use to make wood smooth.

planet *noun*
A **planet** is any of the very large objects in space that move around the sun. The earth is one of the **planets**.

plant *noun*
1. A **plant** is a living thing which grows in the ground and which cannot move around.
–*verb* **2.** If you **plant** something, you put it in the ground to grow. *Our class planted some daffodils near the canteen.*

plasma *noun*
1. Plasma is the liquid part of blood which contains the blood cells.
2. Plasma is a type of gas which can be used to display light on some types of television screens.

plaster *noun*
Plaster is a mixture of water, sand and white powder, which is soft when you spread it but which goes hard as it dries. It is used to cover walls and ceilings of buildings. The same sort of material is used around an arm or a leg to hold in place a broken bone.

plastic *noun*
Plastic is a material used in factories to make many different kinds of things, like bags, furniture, tools, bottles, and clothes that rain cannot get through. Things made of some kinds of **plastic** are hard to break.

Word Building: **plastic**, *adjective*: *We'll take plastic plates for the barbecue.*

plate *noun*
A **plate** is a flat round dish that you serve food on.

platform *noun*
A **platform** is a place to stand or sit that is made higher than the rest of the floor or ground.

platypus /*say* **plat**-uh-poos/ *noun* (*plural* **platypuses**)
A **platypus** is an Australian animal with fur and with feet and a bill like a duck's. The mother platypus lays eggs and feeds its babies with its own milk.

✳ *Spelling Tip:* Remember that the sound in the middle is spelt with a *y*. Also remember that there is a single *s* only at the end of the word. The final word part, *pus*, has nothing to do with a cat, but comes from *pous*, the Greek word for 'foot'. The first part comes from *platus*, Greek for 'flat'. So the name that was given to this animal means 'flat-footed'.

play *verb*
1. When you **play**, you have fun and enjoy yourself. *We played on the beach all afternoon.*
2. If you **play** a game or a sport, you take part in that game. *Let's play tennis this afternoon.*
3. If you **play** a musical instrument, you touch it or blow it so that it makes musical sounds. *John is at the back of the orchestra playing the trumpet.*
4. If you **play** a piece of music, you perform it on a musical instrument. *John is learning to play some Christmas carols.*
5. If you **play** a tape or CD, you make it produce the music or other sound that has been recorded onto it. *I will play my new CD for you.*
–*noun* **6.** A **play** is a story which can be performed by actors in a theatre.

Word Building: **playful**, *adjective* If a person or an animal plays and has fun a lot of the time, they are **playful**.

player *noun*
A **player** is someone who plays a game or sport, or who plays a musical instrument.

playground *noun*
1. A **playground** is a public place for children to play in, often with equipment especially for playing. *The swings in the playground can go really high if someone pushes you.*
2. A **playground** is an open area around school buildings, for playing or eating meals in between lessons. *We are not allowed to play any ball games in the playground unless we are a long way from the windows.*

playmate *noun*
Your **playmate** is another child that you play with.

pleasant /say **plez**-uhnt/ adjective

If something is **pleasant**, you enjoy it.

The opposite is **unpleasant**.

⚡ **Spelling Tip:** Remember the *ea* for the 'e' sound in the first part of the word. This will be easy if you remember that **pleasant** things are things that *please* you.

please verb

1. If something **pleases** you, it makes you feel happy or satisfied. *Davey did everything he could to please his dad so that he would be taken to the football game.*
–*interjection* **2. Please** is a polite word you use when you are asking someone to do something or to give you something. *Could I have something to drink, please?*

Word Building: pleasing, *adjective* Something that makes you happy, or that you like, is **pleasing**.

pleased adjective

If you are **pleased**, you feel happy or satisfied.

pleasure /say **plezh**-uh/ noun

Pleasure is a feeling of enjoyment or happiness.

⚡ **Spelling Tip:** Remember the *ea* spelling for the 'e' sound in the first part of the word. As with *pleasant*, remember that **pleasure** comes from things that *please* you. Also remember the *sure* ending which sounds like 'zhuh'. Think of other words with this spelling and sound, such as *measure* and *treasure*.

plenty pronoun

If you have **plenty**, you have an amount which is large or more than enough. *Take some of our chips – we have plenty.*

plough /rhymes with now/ noun

A **plough** is a machine that a farmer uses to dig the soil to make it ready for planting things.

⚡ **Spelling Tip:** Remember the *ough* spelling for the 'ow' sound (as in some other words, such as *bough*). This word is actually spelt **plow** in American English, but in Australian English the spelling **plough** is the most common so this is the one you should learn.

pluck verb

If you **pluck** the strings of a musical instrument, like a guitar, you make sounds by pulling at them with your fingers and then letting them go.

She plucked the notes of 'Happy Birthday' on her guitar.

plug noun

1. A **plug** is a thick circle of rubber or plastic you use to stop the water from running out of the hole in a bath or basin. *You can't have a bath because the plug is lost.*
2. A **plug** is the part at the end of an electric wire that fits into the special connecting place on the wall so that electricity goes through it. *Of course the iron isn't working – you haven't put the plug into the wall.*

plum noun

A **plum** is a soft fruit with a smooth skin and one hard seed inside.

plumber /say **plum**-uh/ noun

A **plumber** is someone whose job is to put in the pipes that carry water around a building and who comes to fix them when something goes wrong.

⚡ **Spelling Tip:** Don't forget the silent *b* following the single *m*. Think of a burst pipe to remind you of the *b*.

plump adjective

If someone or something is **plump**, they are rather fat, with a round body.

plunge /say plunj/ verb

If someone **plunges** into water, they throw themselves into it suddenly. *It was so hot that Rata couldn't wait to plunge into the pool.*

plus preposition

Plus means 'add'. *9 plus 1 is 10.*

The opposite is **minus**.

pocket noun

A **pocket** is a small piece of cloth sewn on your clothes to make a small bag with an opening so that you can put things into it.

pocket money noun

Pocket money is a small amount of money that some parents give their children each week, sometimes in return for doing jobs in the house.

pod noun

A **pod** is the long, thin part of some plants which holds the seeds.

poem noun

A **poem** is a piece of writing that is set out in a special way. **Poems** often have lines that have almost the same length, and some lines end with words which have a similar sound.

poet *noun*
A **poet** is someone who writes poetry.

poetry *noun*
Poetry is poems.

point *noun*
1. A **point** is a sharp end of something. *The point of the fishing hook was caught in Dimity's shorts.*
2. A **point** is a particular place. *From this point, it should only take an hour to get to the coast.*
3. A **point** is a kind of number you use to score in a game. *You get two points each time you get the ball over the line. | They need five more points to win.*
–*verb* **4.** If you **point**, you show where something or someone is by holding out your finger towards it. *I pointed to the top of my arm to show the doctor where it hurt most. | I asked her which boy was her brother and she pointed at the one with the red curly hair.*
5. point out, **a.** If you **point out** something, you show it to someone with your finger. *We pointed out the way to the people who were lost.* **b.** If you **point out** a fact, you say it in a way that makes it clear to someone. *Sam pointed out that he was there first.*

> *Word Building:* **pointed**, *adjective* Something that has a sharp end is **pointed**. *I don't like the shape of my nose. It is too pointed.*

poison *noun*
Poison is something that can kill you or make you very sick if you swallow it.

> *Word Building:* **poisonous**, *adjective* Anything that contains poison is **poisonous**.

poke *verb*
If you **poke** something, you push it quite hard with your finger or with a stick. *Dhin was upset because Mario poked her in the arm.*

pole[1] *noun*
A **pole** is a long, thin, post of wood or other material.

pole[2] *noun*
A **pole** is one of the two ends of the earth. The **North Pole** is at the furthest point north and the **South Pole** is at the furthest point south.

> *Word Building:* **polar**, *adjective* Anything to do with one of the Poles is **polar**.

police *noun*
The **police** are the group of people whose job is stop people breaking the laws of a country and to protect people and the things they own.

polish *verb*
If you **polish** something, you make it shiny by rubbing it, often with a substance like a liquid. *Mum polished the car with a special new wax until it gleamed.*

polite *adjective*
If you are **polite**, you speak and behave in a way that shows you respect other people and want to please them.

> *Word Building:* **politely**, *adverb* If you act in a polite way, you act **politely**. –**politeness**, *noun* When you are polite, you show **politeness**.

> The opposite is **impolite** or **rude**.

politician /*say* pol-uh-**tish**-uhn / *noun*
A **politician** is someone whose job is to represent people by being a member of the parliament and voting on the laws in the country. Some **politicians** are chosen to be members of the government.

> ❋ *Spelling Tip:* Remember that the ending of **politician** is spelt *ician*. Many other words have this spelling for an 'ishuhn' sound, such as *electrician* and *musician*.

politics *noun*
Politics has to do with the work of the government of a country or with how the people in the government or in the parliament are chosen.

> *Word Building:* **political**, *adjective* **Political** matters have to do with politics.

pollen *noun*
Pollen is the yellow seed dust in flowers.

pollute *verb*
When something **pollutes** the environment, it makes the air, rivers, seas, or the water that people drink dirty, and sometimes harmful to people and animals. *The rubbish from some factories pollutes the harbour.*

> *Word Building:* **pollution**, *noun: Pollution from all the traffic in the tunnel has turned the*

walls black. –**polluted**, *adjective: The polluted water was unsafe to drink.*

pond *noun*
A **pond** is an area of water that is smaller than a lake. A **pond** is often built by people, rather than being natural like a lake.

pool *noun*
A **pool** is a small area of water, especially one that people swim in.

poor *adjective*
1. If someone is **poor**, they do not have much money. *When people are poor, they do not have money to buy enough food.*
2. You can use **poor** when you are talking about a person or animal you feel sorry for. *Poor Clive, he always misses the bus!*
3. If something is **poor**, it is not good in quality. *Dad said the workers had done a very poor job and that was why the tiles were coming off.*

The opposite of definition 1 is **rich** or **wealthy**.

pop *noun*
Pop is a kind of music which is very popular at a certain time, especially among young people.

popular *adjective*
If someone or something is **popular**, a lot of people like them.

population /*say* pop-yuh-**lay**-shuhn/ *noun*
The **population** of a place is all the people who live there.

pop-up *adjective*
1. If something like a book or card is **pop-up**, it has parts that appear suddenly.
2. If something like a shop or restaurant is **pop-up**, it only opens for a brief time.

porch *noun* (*plural* **porches**)
A **porch** is the covered part at the door of a building.

pork *noun*
Pork is the meat from a pig.

porridge *noun*
Porridge is a hot food that some people eat in the morning, made from a grain (called 'oats') and cooked in water or milk.

✵ *Spelling Tip:* Remember the *idge* spelling at the end (not *age* or *ige*). You could think of making a *ridge* in your **porridge** with a spoon to remind you of this spelling.

port *noun*
A **port** is a town or city beside the sea, where there is a place to load things on the ships or take them off.

portrait /*say* **pawt**-ruht/ *noun*
A **portrait** is a picture of someone. It can be a painting, a drawing or even a photograph.

position *noun*
1. A **position** is a place. *These flowers need to be planted in a sunny position.*
2. A **position** is a way in which you have put your body. *I can't get into a comfortable position on this hard seat.*

positive *adjective*
If you are **positive** about something, you are very sure or certain.

possess *verb*
If you **possess** something, you have or own it. *All she possessed in the whole world was her cat and an old black bag.*

possession *noun*
A **possession** is something you own.

possible *adjective*
1. If something is **possible**, it is able to happen or it can be done. *Is it possible for you to help me with this?* | *This piano won't go through the front door – it's just not possible.*
2. If you say that something is **possible**, you mean it might happen or might be true, but you do not know for sure. *It's possible that there will be some rain later.*

The opposite of definition 1 is **impossible**.

possibly *adverb*
You use **possibly** when you want to say you may be able to do something or something may happen, but it is not certain. *The teacher said we could possibly get the afternoon off but she wasn't sure.*

possum *noun*
A **possum** is an Australian animal with a long tail, that lives in trees and feeds at night. The female has a pouch to carry her babies.

post¹ *noun*
A **post** is a long, thin piece of wood or metal that stands up with one end in the ground and is used as a support.

post² *noun*
1. The **post** is the way you send letters and packages to people. You pay by putting a stamp on the letter which you take to a special box. It is

a b c d e f g h i j k l m n o p q r s t u v w x y z

then taken to the person whose name you have written on it. *We can't get to Joshua's party so we will send a present by post.*

2. The **post** is things like letters that are sent by post. *Has the post arrived yet?*

–*verb* **3.** If you **post** a letter, you put it in special box so that it can be sent by post. *We posted Mum's letters on the way to school.*

4. If you **post** something on the internet you send a message to a site.

> ***Word Building: postman**, adjective* A man who delivers the post is the **postman**.

> Another word for **post** (definitions 1–3) is **mail**.

postbox *noun*
A **postbox** is a large box in the street where you can put letters and other things to be sent by post.

postcard *noun*
A **postcard** is a card you can send to someone by post, usually with a photograph or picture of a place on one side and space for writing on the other side. You usually send **postcards** to people when you are away on holidays.

poster *noun*
A **poster** is a large picture or notice printed on paper and put on a place like a wall where people can see it.

post office *noun*
A **post office** is a building where you can go to to buy stamps and other things you need in order to send letters and packages.

postpone *verb*
If you **postpone** something, you put it off until a later time. *We will have to postpone the sports day if it rains.*

pot *noun*
A **pot** is a deep, round container used for cooking.

potato *noun* (*plural* **potatoes**)
A **potato** is a vegetable which grows under the ground, is white inside and can be cooked in lots of different ways.

potoroo /*say* pot-uh-**rooh** / *noun*
A **potoroo** is a small Australian animal with a long nose and a pointed head. It lives in thick grass, and sleeps during the day and comes out at night. *We were lucky to see a potoroo in the bush because they are becoming rare.*

> This word comes from the Dharug language of New South Wales.

pouch *noun* (*plural* **pouches**)
1. A **pouch** is a small bag. *Yumiko decided to keep her new bracelet in a little cotton pouch.*

2. A **pouch** is a pocket of skin that some animals have on their bodies. Female kangaroos and other marsupials have a **pouch** to carry their babies. *The joey was getting too big for its mother's pouch.*

poultry /*say* **pohl**-tree / *noun*
Poultry is birds that are kept for their eggs or meat, such as chickens.

> ✷ ***Spelling Tip:*** Remember the *ou* spelling for the 'oh' sound.

pounce *noun*
If you **pounce** on someone or something, you jump on them suddenly.

pound *noun*
1. A **pound** is a measurement of weight used in some countries such as America. It is equal to just under half a kilogram. *Mum was following an old recipe that was written in pounds so she had to keep translating into kilograms.*

2. A **pound** is the money used in Britain and some other countries. *My uncle bought an old car in England for about three thousand pounds so he could travel around the country.*

> For definition 1, you can also write the sign **lb** after a number (*3lbs of rice*).

> For definition 2, you can also write the sign **£** before a number (*£1000*).

pour *verb*
1. If you **pour** a liquid, you make it flow out of its container into something else. *We poured orange juice into the glasses for everybody at the party.*

2. If a liquid **pours**, a lot of it flows from somewhere. *She laughed and laughed and tears poured from her eyes.*

3. If it is **pouring**, it is raining very hard. *Salim had to cancel the hockey because it was pouring.*

powder *noun*
Powder is a substance made up of very small loose bits of something dry.

power *noun*
1. If someone has **power** to do something, they are able to do it because of the special position and special rights that they have. *The government has the power to change some laws.*

2. Your **powers** are the things your body can do, such as see, hear and speak. *She was so* surprised that she lost her power of speech for a while.

3. Power is strength or force. *The car hit the pole with such power that it broke in two.*

powerful *adjective*

If someone or something is **powerful**, they are strong. They have a lot of power. *Salim's family has a new car with a powerful motor.* | *You can tell from the size of the man that he would be very powerful.* | *The USA is one of the most powerful countries in the world.*

practical *adjective*

1. If something is **practical**, it has to do with actually doing things, rather than with ideas. *You need practical skills like typing to do this job.*
2. If someone is **practical**, they are good at doing useful work and thinking of sensible answers to problems. *She is a good person to have around when things go wrong because she is so practical.*

practice /*say* prak-tuhs/ *noun*

1. Practice is actual action, rather than ideas. *His idea seemed good but it didn't work in practice.*
2. Practice is an action or performance that you do many times so that you get better at doing it. *Beth does her piano practice every morning.*

> ❇ *Spelling Tip:* Also look up **practise** and remember that the noun **practice** (the 'thing' word) ends with *ice* while the verb **practise** (the 'doing' word) ends with *ise*. This is the pattern with other pairs of words with these endings, for example *advice* (noun) and *advise* (verb). Try thinking that *ice* is a noun as a way to remember that the noun form of these words ends with *ice*.

practise /*say* prak-tuhs/ *verb*

If you **practise** something, you do it or perform it many times so that you get better at doing it. *He is practising what he has to say in the play.*

> ❇ *Spelling Tip:* Look up the note at **practice**.

praise *verb*

If you **praise** someone or something, you say that you think they are very good. *The teacher praised us for being well-behaved on the excursion.*

prance *verb*

If you **prance**, you move or jump around excitedly like a young animal playing. *All the kindergarten kids were prancing around waiting for the excursion bus to come.*

prawn *noun*

A **prawn** is a small sea animal that you can eat. Its body is covered by a soft shell.

pray /*say* pray/ *verb*

When someone **prays**, they talk to their god. *The people in the church had their eyes shut while they were praying.*

> **Word Building: prayer** /*say* prair/, *noun* When you pray, you are saying a **prayer**.

preach *verb*

When a person **preaches**, they talk to people, often about how they can do good in their lives and usually in a church. *The priest preached for more than an hour.*

precious /*say* **presh**-uhs/ *adjective*

If something is **precious**, it is very special to you. *This letter is very precious because my grandmother gave it to me just before she died.*

predict *verb*

When someone **predicts** something, they say what they think will happen in the future. *The radio report predicted a storm so we should take an umbrella with us.*

> **Word Building: prediction,** *noun* If you predict something, then you make a **prediction.** −**predictable,** *adjective* If it is easy to see what will happen, it is **predictable.**

prefer /*say* pruh-**fer**/ *verb* (**prefers, preferring, preferred, has preferred**)

If you **prefer** one thing to another, you like the first thing better. *I prefer strawberry ice-cream to vanilla.*

pregnant *adjective*

A female is **pregnant** if she is going to have a baby.

prehistoric /*say* pree-his-**to**-rik/ *adjective*

If something is **prehistoric**, it is from a time before history was written down.

premier /*say* **prem**-ee-uh/ *adjective*

1. Something that is **premier** is the first or best. −*noun* **2.** The **premier** is the leader of an Australian state's government.

premiere /*say* prem-ee-**air**/ *noun*

A **premiere** is the first time something is shown or done.

prepare *verb*

1. If you **prepare** something, you make it ready. *Mum is preparing the spare room for my grandmother who is coming to stay.*

2. If you **prepare for** something, you get ready for it. *We are preparing for our big hike by practising walking at the oval.*
3. be prepared for, If you are **prepared for** something, you are expecting it and are ready for it. *Sam is prepared for the race – he has been training for weeks.*
4. be prepared to, If you are **prepared to** do something, you say that you will do it. *We were lucky – the teacher said she was prepared to give us a second chance.*

> *Word Building:* **preparation**, *noun* When you prepare for something, you make **preparations**.

preposition *noun*
A **preposition** is a type of word which you use with a noun or a pronoun to show its relation to other words in the sentence, such as 'to' in *We walked to the beach* and 'from' in *He took some paper from me.*

preschool /*say* **pre**-skool / *noun*
A **preschool** is a place some young children go for a year or so before they start going to primary school.

prescription /*say* pruh-**skrip**-shuhn / *noun*
A **prescription** is the instructions that a doctor writes about the medicine that someone has to take when they are sick.

present[1] *noun*
1. The **present** is the time now. *The coach said that for the present we will concentrate on passing the ball.*
2. at present, You use **at present** to mean 'now'. *At present, it is really quiet in our classroom but it won't be when the bell goes.*
– *adjective* **3.** If someone is **present** at a place or at a meeting, they are there.

> Also look up **future** and **past**.

> The opposite of definition 3 is **absent**.

present[2] *noun*
A **present** is something that someone gives to someone else, often for special occasions.

preserve *verb*
1. If you **preserve** something, you keep it safe. *The council wants to preserve the bush that is near the oval.*
2. If you **preserve** food, you treat it a special way to stop it going bad. *In summer, my grandmother preserves peaches and plums in bottles.*

president *noun*
The **president** is the leader of the government in some countries.

press *verb*
1. If you **press** something, you push on it, sometimes with force. *Nadia pressed the button to make the bell ring.*
2. If you **press** clothes, you use an iron to make them flat and smooth. *Mum pressed our school clothes before we put them on.*

pressure /*say* **presh**-uh / *noun*
Pressure is the force that you use to press down or onto something.

pretend *verb*
If you **pretend** to do something, you make yourself look as though you are doing it but you are not really. *We all pretended we had forgotten Penny's birthday and then we gave her a big surprise.*

pretty *adjective* (**prettier**, **prettiest**)
If someone or something is **pretty**, they are pleasant to look at.

prevent *verb*
If you **prevent** something from happening, you stop it happening. You do not let it happen. *The farmer fixed the fence to prevent the sheep getting out.*

preview /*say* **pree**-vyooh / *noun*
If you see a **preview** of something, you see it before everyone else.

prey /*rhymes with* may / *noun*
1. **Prey** is any animal that is hunted and eaten by another animal or a human.
– *verb* **2.** If an animal **preys on** another one, it hunts it for food. *Many farmers think that foxes prey on their sheep.*

price *noun*
The **price** of something is the amount of money which you must pay to buy it.

prick *verb*
If you **prick** something, you make a small hole with an object that has a sharp point. *Sally accidentally pricked her finger with a needle.*

prickle *noun*
A **prickle** is something with a sharp point, like some grass seeds.

> *Word Building:* **prickly**, *adjective* Something that has prickles is **prickly**.

pride *noun*
Pride is the feeling of satisfaction you have about something that you have done well or something special that you own.

Look up **proud**.

priest /*say* preest / *noun*
A **priest** is someone whose job is to lead religious ceremonies and to teach people about God.

⭐ *Spelling Tip:* Remember the *ie* spelling for the 'ee' sound. This follows the rule that *i* comes before *e* except after *c*.

primary *adjective*
Something is **primary** if it is first. A **primary school** is the first school you go to, until you are about 12. Then you go to secondary school.

prime minister *noun*
A **prime minister** is the leader of the government in some countries, including Australia.

prince *noun*
A **prince** is the son of a king or queen.

princess *noun*
A **princess** is the daughter of a king or queen.

principal /*say* prin-suh-puhl / *adjective*
1. You use **principal** to describe something that is the main or most important thing or person. *The principal reason we do sport is to keep fit. | She is now the principal violin player in the orchestra.* –*noun* **2.** A **principal** is the person in charge of a school. *We are getting a new principal at our school next term.*

⭐ *Spelling Tip:* Don't confuse the spelling of **principal** with **principle** which has the same sound but is spelt *le* at the end.

principle /*say* prin-suh-puhl / *noun*
A **principle** is a rule.

⭐ *Spelling Tip:* Don't confuse the spelling of **principle** with **principal**.

print *verb*
1. If someone **prints** things like books and papers, they make copies of them by putting ink onto paper or other material. *Thousands of newspapers are printed every day.*
2. If you **print** something, you write it in separate letters rather than in letters joined together. *We printed our name and address on the competition form.*
–*noun* **3.** **Print** is words that have been printed.

printer *noun*
A **printer** is a machine that is attached to your computer and prints what you can see on your computer screen so that you can read it on paper.

prison *noun*
A **prison** is a place where people who have done something that is very wrong and against the law are kept locked up as punishment.

prisoner *noun*
1. A **prisoner** is someone who is kept in a prison as a punishment for breaking the law. *Three prisoners climbed over the high wall and escaped.*
2. A **prisoner** is someone who has been caught by someone else and is not free to leave. *The soldiers were kept as prisoners by the enemy.*

private /*say* **pruy**-vuht / *adjective*
Something is **private** if it belongs to someone in particular and not to everyone.

prize *noun*
A **prize** is what you get for winning something, such as a race, or for doing very well in your work or in a test.

probably *adverb*
If you say that something will **probably** happen, you mean it is likely or that you expect it to happen. *We will probably miss the bus, but if we run fast we might just catch it.*

Word Building: **probable**, *adjective* If something is **probable**, then it will probably happen.

problem *noun*
1. A **problem** is something that makes you worried because it is difficult to do or to fix. *We have a problem in our house because everyone always wants to use the phone at the same time.*
2. A **problem** is a difficult question which you have to answer as part of your school work. *The teacher has given us some maths problems to do.*

procedure /*say* pruh-**see**-juh / *noun*
1. A **procedure** is a way of doing something. *This is the procedure for fixing the video.*
2. If you write a **procedure**, you do a piece of writing which tells how to do or make something step by step. *Our class discussed how we would write a procedure about how to cross the road safely.*

⭐ *Spelling Tip:* Notice that the sound in the middle of this word is spelt with a single *e* (although it sounds like 'ee'). This word comes from *proceed* but you have to remember that one of the *e*'s has been dropped.

a b c d e f g h i j k l m n o p q r s t u v w x y z

proceed *verb*

If you **proceed**, you go on. *Mei proceeded along the road until she finally reached the sea.*

procession /*say* pruh-**sesh**-uhn/ *noun*

A **procession** is a group of people or cars moving along in a line, usually as part of a celebration.

> ✴ *Spelling Tip:* Notice that **procession** has one *c* (giving an 's' sound) and double *s*. You can remember the *c* spelling by reminding yourself that this word has nothing to do with a session.

prod *verb* (**prods, prodding, prodded, has prodded**)

If you **prod** someone or something, you push them with a finger or something pointed. *Mum prodded me under the table to tell me to be quiet.*

produce *verb*

1. If someone or something **produces** something, they make it. *Our class has produced some really good pictures to hang on the wall. | Bees produce honey.*
2. If someone **produces** something, they show it. *The magician suddenly produced a coin from behind my ear.*

> *Word Building:* **production,** *noun: The factory decided to increase its production of cheap cars.*

professor *noun*

A **professor** is someone whose job is at the highest level of teaching in a university.

> ✴ *Spelling Tip:* Remember that **professor** has one *f* and a double *s*. Also notice the *or* (not *er*) ending.

profit *noun*

Profit is the extra money that you get when you sell something for more than it cost you to make or to buy.

program *noun*

1. A **program** is a show on television or radio. *We have to clear the table before we can watch our favourite program.*
2. A **program** is a list that tells you what is going to happen at a concert or other performance, or what shows are on television or radio. *My job at the school concert was to give out the programs at the door.*
3. A **program** is a set of stored instructions inside a computer that tells the computer how to do things. *There was something wrong with the program and the computer kept stopping.*

> *Word Building:* **programmer,** *noun* Someone whose job it is to write programs for a computer is called a **programmer**.

> Another spelling for definitions 1 and 2 is **programme**.

progress *noun* /*say* **proh**-gres/

1. Progress is moving forward in a way that makes an improvement.
–*verb* /*say* pruh-**gres**/ **2.** If you **progress**, you move forward or move to a further or better level. *When we were in kindergarten, learning was easy. Now we have progressed to harder work.*

prohibit /*say* pruh-**hib**-uht/ *verb*

If someone **prohibits** something, they say that it must not be done. *There is a law to prohibit people from smoking on trains.*

project *noun*

A **project** is a special piece of work that you do for school where you find out as much as you can about something.

projector *noun*

A **projector** is a machine used for showing pictures or written information on a large screen.

> ✴ *Spelling Tip:* Remember the *or* (not *er*) ending. You could think of *o* for 'on screen' to remind you.

promise /*say* **prom**-uhs/ *noun*

1. A **promise** is what you say when you tell someone in a serious way that you will do something or stop doing something. *We made a promise to the teacher to get to the concert on time.*
2. break your promise, If you **break your promise** you do what you have promised not to do. You also **break your promise** if you do not do what you promised to do. *Yaeli broke her promise and looked through the door after she had promised her mother she wouldn't.*
–*verb* **3.** When you **promise** to do or to not do something, you say in a serious way that you will or will not do it. *Mum promised not to laugh when the boys were doing their dance.*

pronoun *noun*

A **pronoun** is a type of word which stands for a noun, such as 'he' in *He lives nearby*, 'them' in *The teacher told them to sit down*, 'herself' in *Sally cooked the meal herself*, and 'who' in *Who is coming tonight?*

pronounce *verb*
When you **pronounce** a word, you make the sound of it. *Do you know how to pronounce 'physics'?*

pronunciation /*say* pruh-nun-see-**ay**-shuhn/ *noun*
The **pronunciation** of a word is the way you say its sound.

> **Pronunciation** comes from the verb **pronounce**.

proof *noun*
Proof is something that shows you that a thing is true or real.

> **Proof** comes from the verb **prove**.

propeller *noun*
A **propeller** is a piece of equipment that makes a boat move through water or an aircraft move through air. **Propellers** are made of flat pieces set in a circle that go around very quickly.

> ✪ **Spelling Tip:** Remember that the second *p* is single, but the *l* is double. Also notice the *er* (not *or*) ending.

proper *adjective*
If something is **proper**, it is right or suitable.

> **Word Building: properly**, *adverb*: *She tried to do her work properly.*

property *noun* (*plural* **properties**)
1. **Property** is something that is owned by someone. *Among our books, we found a few that were the property of the library so we took them back straight away.*
2. A **property** is land or buildings owned by someone. *I live on a sheep property.*

prophecy /*say* **prof**-uh-see/ *noun* (*plural* **prophecies**)
If someone makes a **prophecy**, they say what they believe will happen in the future.

> ✪ **Spelling Tip:** Remember the *ph* spelling for the 'f' sound and the *ecy* ending. Don't confuse this noun ('thing' word) with the verb ('doing' word) **prophesy**.

prophesy /*say* **prof**-uh-suy/ *verb* (**prophesies**, **prophesying**, **prophesied**, **has prophesied**)
If someone **prophesies** something, they say that they believe that thing will happen in the future. *She prophesied that her daughter would be home by Christmas.*

> ✪ **Spelling Tip:** Remember the *ph* spelling for the 'f' sound and the *esy* ending. Don't confuse this verb ('doing' word) with the noun ('thing' word), **prophecy**.

prophet /*say* **prof**-uht/ *noun*
1. A **prophet** is someone who speaks for a god.
2. A **prophet** is someone who tells the future.

prosecute /*say* **pros**-uh-kyooht/ *verb*
If the police **prosecute** someone, they make that person go to a court of law because they believe that they have done something wrong.

prosperous *adjective*
If someone is **prosperous**, they are rich and successful.

protect *verb*
If you **protect** someone or something, you keep them safe and stop them being hurt or lost. *In summer, we have to wear our school hats to protect us from the sun.*

> **Word Building: protection**, *noun* If something protects someone or something, it gives **protection**.

protest *verb* /*say* pruh-**test**/
1. If you **protest**, you say or show that you are unhappy about something and want to complain about it. *Many people gathered to protest about the plan to widen the road.*
–*noun* /*say* **proh**-test/ 2. When you make a **protest**, you tell someone what are unhappy about or what you think is wrong with someone.

proud *adjective*
If you feel **proud**, you feel pleased or satisfied about something.

> **Word Building: proudly**, *adverb*: *The team smiled proudly when Vanessa went up to get the competition cup.*

> Look up **pride**.

prove /*say* proohv/ *verb* (**proves**, **proving**, **proved**, **has proven**)
If you **prove** something, you show that it is certainly true or real. *He used a photograph to prove that he was there at the time.*

> Look up **proof**.

> ✪ **Spelling Tip:** Remember that there is no double *o* in this word. The spelling *ove* makes the 'oohv' sound, as it does in other words such as *move*.

provide *verb*
If someone **provides** something that is needed, they give it or supply it. *The girls in the class brought the drinks for the picnic and the boys provided the food.*

prowl *verb*
If you **prowl**, you move about quietly, like an animal hunting. *Sam prowled around the whole yard, looking for his ball.*

prune[1] *noun*
A **prune** is a dried plum.

prune[2] *verb*
If you **prune** a tree or bush, you cut branches from it to make it grow better. *These trees produce more fruit when they have been pruned.*

public *adjective*
1. If something is **public**, it has to do with or is for the use of everyone who lives in a place.
–*noun* 2. You use the phrase **the public** to talk about people in general. *The film will not be shown to the public until next month.*
3. **in public**, If you do something **in public**, you do it in front of other people. *I like to sing when I'm in the shower, but I would never sing in public.*

> **Word Building: publicly**, *adverb*: *Our team manager said publicly that we would win the competition – I hope he's right!*

publish *verb*
If someone **publishes** a book, magazine or newspaper, they prepare and print it to be sold to the public. *My mum works for a company that publishes sports magazines.*

pudding /*say* **pood**-ing/ *noun*
A **pudding** is a soft, sweet food that people eat after the main part of their meal.

puddle *noun*
A **puddle** is a small pool of water.

puff *noun*
A **puff** is a small amount of air or smoke.

pull *verb*
If you **pull** something or someone, you move them so that they come after you or towards you. *The train engine was strong enough to pull more than 20 carriages.*

pulse *noun*
A **pulse** is the beat that you can feel when you put your fingers on your wrist. It is made by your heart pushing blood around your body.

pump *noun*
1. A **pump** is a machine that forces a liquid or air in or out of something.
–*verb* 2. If you **pump** liquid or air, you move it by using a pump. *They saved the houses by pumping water from the river.*

pumpkin *noun*
A **pumpkin** is a large round vegetable with a hard skin. The part you eat is orange but the skin is often green.

punch *verb*
If you **punch** someone or something, you hit them hard with your fist. *Some of the children were punching each other and we had to call the teacher.*

punctual /*say* **punk**-chooh-uhl/ *adjective*
You are **punctual** if you are exactly on time.

> ✱ *Spelling Tip:* Remember the *t* in this word. With the *u* following it has a 'ch' sound and you might not hear the *t*. Try breaking the word up as *punc+tu+al*.

punctuation /*say* punk-chooh-**ay**-shuhn/ *noun*
Punctuation is the marks you put next to some words when you write. They show things such as where a sentence ends or if someone is speaking.

puncture /*say* **punk**-chuh/ *noun*
A **puncture** is a small hole made in something.

punish *verb*
If someone **punishes** someone else, they make them suffer in some way because they have done something wrong. *The thief was punished by being sent to prison.*

> **Word Building: punishment**, *noun* Something that is done to punish someone is their **punishment**.

pupil[1] *noun*
A **pupil** is someone who is being taught.

pupil[2] *noun*
Your **pupil** is the small, dark spot in the middle of your eye.

puppet *noun*
A **puppet** is a toy figure with strings on its arms and legs that you can pull to make it move, or which is made in the shape of a glove that you can move with your fingers.

puppy *noun* (*plural* **puppies**)
A **puppy** is a young dog.

> You can also say **pup**.

pure *adjective*
If something is **pure**, it has nothing mixed with it, especially anything which might spoil it.

purple *adjective*
If something is **purple**, it has a dark red-blue colour.

purpose /*say* **per**-puhs / *noun*
1. The **purpose** of something is the reason it is done or made. *The purpose of the talk was to tell us all about water safety.*
2. **on purpose**, If you do something **on purpose**, you mean to do it. *Ann hit James on purpose.*

purr *verb*
When a cat **purrs**, it makes a special low sound which shows that it is happy. *My cat always purrs when she lies in front of the fire.*

purse *noun*
A **purse** is a small bag for carrying money, mainly used by women and girls.

pursue /*say* puh-**syooh** / *verb*
If you **pursue** someone, you chase them. *The police pursued the robbers through the town for two hours.*

> *Word Building:* **pursuit** /*say* puh-**syooht**/, *noun* When you pursue something, you are in **pursuit** of it.

> ✹ *Spelling Tip:* Remember that the beginning is *pur* (not *per*). Also notice the *sue* and remember that this changes to *suit* when the noun **pursuit** is formed (the same spelling as for a set of clothes).

push *verb*
1. If you **push** something or someone, you move them in a direction away from you by pressing or leaning against them. *Dad got some people to help him push the car off the road.*
2. If you **push** something into a container or place where there is not enough room for it, you force it in there. *Danny pushed all the books onto one shelf so that there was plenty of room on the other shelf for his cricket gear.*

put *verb* (**puts, putting, put, has put**)
1. If you **put** something somewhere, you move it so that it goes in that place. *It was my job to put the knives and forks on the table.*
2. **put up with**, If you **put up with** something you don't like, you allow it to go on without becoming angry. *The teacher said that she wouldn't put up with any more talking during the lesson.*

puzzle *noun*
1. A **puzzle** is a game or question that is fun to do but that you must think hard about before you work it out. *Can you work out this puzzle? You have to separate the two rings that are joined together.*
2. A **puzzle** is something that is difficult to understand. *We don't know why Jamie stopped playing with us – it's a real puzzle.*

pygmy /*say* **pig**-mee / *noun*
A **pygmy** is a person, animal or plant that belongs to a special kind that is very small.

> Another spelling is **pigmy**.

pyjamas /*say* puh-**jah**-muhz / *noun*
Your **pyjamas** are the loose pants and shirt that you wear to bed.

> ✹ *Spelling Tip:* Remember that the second letter is a *y*. The spelling with an *a* (**pajamas**) is used in American English but **pyjamas** is the main spelling that we use in Australian English. The word is unusual because it comes from the Hindi (a language of India) words for 'leg' and 'clothing'.

pylon /*say* **puy**-lon / *noun*
A **pylon** is a strong tall thing built to support something.

pyramid /*say* **pi**-ruh-mid / *noun*
A **pyramid** is a shape with a square bottom with sides that go up from the square to join together in a point at the top. The Egyptians long ago used to build pyramids out of stone blocks to hold the body of a dead king or queen.

> ✹ *Spelling Tip:* Remember that the second letter is a *y*. Like many words with a *y* spelling, **pyramid** comes from Greek.

python /*say* **puy**-thuhn / *noun*
A **python** is a very large, very strong snake that crushes another animal by closing its body tightly around it.

> ✹ *Spelling Tip:* Remember that the second letter is a *y*. Also remember that the ending is *on* (not *en*) – try thinking that **pythons** can kill a small animal by wrapping themselves *on* to it! Like many words with a *y* spelling, **python** comes from Greek. In an ancient Greek myth, the *Python* was a huge snake killed by the god Apollo.

a
b
c
d
e
f
g
h
i
j
k
l
m
n
o
p
q
r
s
t
u
v
w
x
y
z

quicksand

quack *noun*
A **quack** is the sound a duck makes.

quail *noun*
A **quail** is a small bird that builds its nest on the ground. It is sometimes used as food.

quality /*say* **kwol**-uh-tee / *noun*
Quality is how good a thing is.

quantity /*say* **kwon**-tuh-tee / *noun* (*plural* **quantities**)
A **quantity** is an amount or measure of something.

quarrel /*say* **kwo**-ruhl / *verb* (**quarrels, quarrelling, quarrelled, has quarrelled**)
If people **quarrel**, they talk in an angry way about something they do not agree about. *Tom has been quarrelling with James all morning. Tom says that James hit him on purpose and James says it was an accident.*

> ✳ **Spelling Tip:** Remember that there is a double *r* in this word but only one *l* at the end. Remember that the *l* is doubled when you add *ed* or *ing*.

quarter /*say* **kwaw**-tuh / *noun*
If you divide something into four equal parts, each one of the parts is a **quarter**.

quay /*say* kee / *noun*
A **quay** is a place where you can get on or off a ship.

> ✳ **Spelling Tip:** Notice that the letters *ay* spell the 'ee' sound. Don't confuse **quay** with **key** which has the same sound. A **key** is most often a small piece of metal that can open a lock or a piece on a piano or computer keyboard.

queen *noun*
A **queen** is a woman who, because of the special family she is born into, is the ruler of a country. Usually, in modern times, the country is actually ruled by the government, but the queen is still an important person.

queer *adjective*
If something is **queer**, it is strange or not usual.

question *noun*
A **question** is the thing you say or write when you ask someone something.

> ✳ **Spelling Tip:** Remember that the *s* is followed by a *tion* ending. There is no *ch* although you can sometimes hear that sound when people say the word.

queue /*say* kyooh / *noun*
A **queue** is a line of people or cars who are waiting to get something or go somewhere.

> ✳ **Spelling Tip:** Remember the *qu* spelling at the start for the 'k' sound and, even more unusual, the letter group *eue* making the 'yooh' sound. This is because **queue** comes from French. (It came from the Latin word for 'tail' – because of the shape of a **queue**).

quick *adjective*
If something is **quick**, it happens or is done in a short time.

> ***Word Building:*** **quickly**, *adverb*: *Grace ran to the shops quickly.* –**quickness**, *noun*: *We were surprised at the quickness of the mice at getting out of the box.*

> The opposite is **slow**.

quicksand *noun*
Quicksand is wet sand which is so soft and loose that if a person or animal falls into it, it is very difficult for them to escape.

quiet *adjective*
1. If a place is **quiet**, there is no noise or sound in it. *The room was completely quiet after the bad news was announced.*
2. If someone is **quiet**, they are not speaking or making any noise. *Ally stayed quiet even though she was frightened.*

3. If a sound is **quiet**, it is soft. *We could hear them having a quiet conversation.*

4. If a period of time is **quiet**, not much happens. *We had a quiet holiday.*

> *Word Building:* **quietly**, *adverb* If you do something in a quiet way, you do it **quietly**.

> The opposite of definition 1 is **noisy**. The opposite of definition 3 is **loud**.

> ✵ *Spelling Tip:* Don't confuse the spelling of **quiet** with **quite**.

quilt *noun*
A **quilt** is a light, warm cover for a bed.

quit *verb* (**quits**, **quitting**, **quit**, **has quit**)
If you **quit** something, you stop or leave it. *Zac wanted to quit learning the trumpet but his parents talked him into having lessons for a bit longer.*

quite *adverb*
1. You use **quite** to make the next word stronger and show that it is completely true. *Belinda was quite right.*
2. You can also use **quite** in another way, to make the next word less strong. You mean that something is a bit true but not completely true. *The film was quite interesting but I like the one we saw last week better.*

> ✵ *Spelling Tip:* Don't confuse the spelling of **quite** with **quiet**.

quiver *verb*
If you **quiver**, you shake with small movements of your body. *The kitten began to quiver with fear when I picked it up.*

quiz *noun* (*plural* **quizzes**)
A **quiz** is a test, often one that is question and answer out loud.

> ✵ *Spelling Tip:* Remember that there is only one *z* at the end. However, remember that the *z* is doubled when you make the plural **quizzes**.

quokka /*say* **kwok**-uh/ *noun*
A **quokka** is a small animal found in parts of Western Australia. It is a kind of wallaby.

> This word comes from an Aboriginal language of Western Australia called Nyungar.

quoll *noun*
A **quoll** is an Australian marsupial, about the size of a cat, with a long tail and spots.

> This word comes from an Aboriginal language of Queensland called Guugu Yimidhirr.

quotation /*say* kwoh-**tay**-shuhn/ *noun*
A **quotation** is a part of a book or of a speech that someone copies and repeats somewhere else.

> *Word Building:* **quote**, *verb* If someone uses a quotation, then they **quote** what another person has said.

> Another word for **quotation** is **quote**.

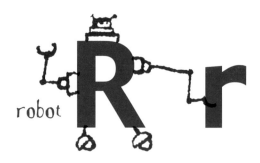

robot

rabbi /*say* **rab**-uy / *noun*

A **rabbi** is a priest of the Jewish religion.

> ✳ *Spelling Tip:* Remember the double *b*. Also notice that the ending is a simple *i*. This word comes from Hebrew.

rabbit *noun*

A **rabbit** is a small animal with long ears, that lives in a hole in the ground (called a burrow).

race¹ *noun*

1. A **race** is a kind of competition in which the winner is the person or animal who goes fastest and gets to a certain place first.
–*verb* **2.** If people or animals **race**, they compete with each other to see who can do the best. *Who wants to race around the oval?*

race² *noun*

1. A **race** is a very large group of people who are all similar in some way, for example, people who have the same skin colour. *Scientists have found that it is not important to divide people into races. What is the same about all people is more important.*
2. the human race, The **human race** is every person or human being. *This discovery is important for the whole human race.*

rack *noun*

A **rack** is a metal frame or set of bars to put things on or lock things onto.

racket *noun*

A **racket** is loud, mixed-up noise.

> There is another word **racket** which is a bat you use in tennis. Look up **racquet**.

racquet /*say* **rak**-uht / *noun*

A **racquet** is a kind of bat with a long handle and with strings stretched across a frame that you use to hit a ball in tennis.

> Another spelling for this word is **racket**. Look up **racket** as this also has another meaning.

> ✳ *Spelling Tip:* Notice that you can spell this word in two ways. The main one is the more difficult to remember because it uses *qu* following the *c* for the 'k' sound. This is because it comes from French.

radar *noun*

A **radar** is a machine that can tell where things like ships or planes are and how far away they are. The machine does this by sending out signals and seeing how long they take to come back.

radiator *noun*

1. A **radiator** is a heater with one or two round bars which are heated up by electricity and used to warm a room. *It was such a cold night that the whole family was huddled around the radiator.*
2. A **radiator** is the part of a car which is filled with water to keep the engine cool. *Dad said there was a hole in the radiator and that was why the engine had suddenly got too hot.*

radio *noun* (*plural* **radios**)

A **radio** is a machine which you turn on to hear news, entertainment or music.

radius /*say* **ray**-dee-uhs / *noun* (*plural* **radii** /*say* **ray**-dee-uy /)

A **radius** is a straight line going from the centre of a circle to its edge.

raft *noun*

A **raft** is one piece of wood or a number of pieces tied together, for carrying people or things over the water.

rage *noun*

Rage is very great anger.

raid *noun*

A **raid** is a sudden attack that nobody is expecting.

rail *noun*

1. A **rail** is a bar used to hold something up, or to hold something in or keep something out. *We rested our bikes on the rail that surrounded the garden.*

2. A **rail** is one of the long steel lengths that a train runs on. *Some of the rails had bent in the heat.*

railway *noun*
1. A **railway** is a set of metal tracks on the ground for trains to run on. *They have built a new bridge so that cars can pass over the railway.*
2. The **railway** is all these tracks and the trains that run on them. *Our city has a good railway. There are lots of trains and they are usually on time.*

rain *noun*
1. **Rain** is the water that falls from the sky in drops.
−*verb* **2.** When it **rains**, water comes down from the sky in drops. *It rained every day for a week.*

> **Word Building: rainy**, *adjective* (**rainier, rainiest**) When it rains, the weather is **rainy**. *It's been a rainy day.*

rainbow *noun*
A **rainbow** is the curved line of colours that you sometimes see in the sky when the sun starts shining after rain.

raincoat *noun*
A **raincoat** is a special coat that you wear when it is raining that stops the rain getting through to your clothes.

rainforest *noun*
A **rainforest** is the thick forest that grows in places where it rains a lot.

raise *verb*
If you **raise** something or someone, you lift them up to a higher place. *A huge crane raised the heavy steel bar to the top of the building.*

> Compare **raise** with **rise**. Remember that you **raise** something or someone, but that when something or someone **rises**, they get up or go upwards by themselves.

raisin *noun*
A **raisin** is a sweet grape that has been dried.

> ✖ *Spelling Tip:* Remember that the ending is *in* (not *on*). Try thinking of the word *raising* (lifting up) and leave off the *g*.

rake *noun*
A **rake** is a garden tool with a long handle that you use for gathering grass and leaves into a pile.

ram *noun*
1. A **ram** is a male sheep.
−*verb* (**rams, ramming, rammed, has rammed**)

2. If you **ram** into something, you hit it very hard. *The driver of the car lost control and it rammed into a brick wall.*

> For definition 1, the female is a **ewe**.

ranger *noun*
A **ranger** is someone who looks after one of the large parks owned by the government.

rank *noun*
1. A **rank** is the level of importance that someone reaches in their job. *My aunt has reached the rank of professor at the university where she works.*
2. A **rank** is a row or line of people. *The soldiers stood in rank.*

rap *noun*
1. A **rap** is the sound you make when you knock on a door.
−*verb* (**raps, rapping, rapped, has rapping**)
2. If you **rap**, you hit or knock something lightly, usually making a regular, repeated sound. *James rapped on the door.*

rapid *adjective*
If something is **rapid**, it is fast or quick. *It was hard to swim against the rapid movement of the river.*

> **Word Building: rapidly**, *adverb* If something is rapid, it happens **rapidly**.

rare *adjective*
If something is **rare**, it is not very common. You do not see it or find it very often.

rash *noun*
A **rash** is a place on your skin where there are red marks.

rat *noun*
A **rat** is an animal with a long tail, similar to, but larger than, a mouse.

rather *adverb*
1. You use **rather** to make the word that follows less strong. It is almost true but not completely true. *He is rather handsome, don't you think?*
2. If you say you would like to have or do one thing **rather** than another, you mean you would like to have or do it instead of the other thing. *Could I have water rather than orange juice, please.*

rattle *verb*
1. If something **rattles**, it makes short, sharp noises like things knocking together. *The windows started to rattle as the wind blew harder.*
−*noun* **2.** A **rattle** is a baby's toy which makes a noise when it is shaken.

raw *adjective*
If something is **raw**, it is not cooked at all.

ray *noun*
A **ray** is a line of light.

reach *verb*
1. If you **reach** a place, you get there. *We reached the museum just as the doors opened for the day.*
2. If you can **reach** something or a certain place, you can touch it, especially by stretching out your arm. *Mum has put the chocolate biscuits on a very high shelf so we can't reach them.*

read /*say* reed/ *verb* (**reads**, **reading**, **read** /*say* red/, **has read** /*say* red/)
1. If you **read** something written, you look at the words and understand them. *Hamish loves reading mystery stories.*
2. If you **read** something written to someone, you look at it and say the words aloud. *We had to read out our stories to the class.*

> *Word Building:* **reading**, *noun*: *We have a special time for reading after lunch.*

> ✷ *Spelling Tip:* Remember that the past form keeps the same spelling, **read**, even though the sound changes to 'red'.

ready *adjective*
1. If you are **ready**, you can do something immediately because you have done what you need to do first. *Once Larissa had cleaned her teeth, she was ready to go.*
2. If something is **ready**, you can use it immediately. *James went to the bike shop hoping that his bike was ready.*

real *adjective*
1. If something is **real** it actually exists or it is true. It is not just in someone's mind. *This story is even more exciting because you know it happened in real life.* | *You are not telling me the truth. Tell me the real reason you are late.*
2. If something is **real**, it is the actual thing, not a copy. *This ring is made of real gold.*

> ✷ *Spelling Tip:* Don't confuse the spelling of **real** with **reel** which sounds the same, but is spelt with a double *e*. A **reel** is a round thing with something wound on to it.

realise *verb*
If you **realise** something, you understand it when you did not understand it before. *We realised we had stayed too long when we saw how dark it was getting.*

> Another spelling for this word is **realize**.

really *adverb*
1. If something **really** happens, it actually happens. It does not just exist in someone's mind. *Jodie knew that she would have to tell the truth and say what really happened.*
2. You use **really** to make the word that follows stronger. It means 'very'. *I am really tired.*

rear[1] *noun*
The **rear** of something is the back of it.

rear[2] *verb*
1. If someone **rears** a child or young animal, they look after them until they are big enough to take care of themselves. *The mother sheep had died and the farmer was trying to rear its lamb by giving it milk every few hours.*
2. If an animal **rears**, it stands up on its back legs. *The horse reared when it saw the snake.*

reason *noun*
1. The **reason** for something happening is what has made it happen. *There were a few reasons why our team lost – mostly it was because the other team was better.*
2. The **reason** that someone does something explains why they did it. *The reason Zac left early was that he felt sick.*

receipt /*say* ruh-**seet**/ *noun*
A **receipt** is a piece of paper which shows that you have paid for something.

> ✷ *Spelling Tip:* Don't forget the *p* before the final *t*. It is there because the word comes from *recipere*, the Latin word for 'receive'. Also notice the *ei* spelling for the 'ee' sound. This follows the rule that *i* comes before *e*, except after *c*.

receive /*say* ruh-**seev**/ *verb*
If you **receive** something, you get it or you are given it. *I received some good presents for my birthday.*

> ✷ *Spelling Tip:* Remember the *ei* spelling for the 'ee' sound. This follows the rule that *i* comes before *e*, except after *c*.

recent *adjective*
If something is **recent**, it happened or was made not long ago. *In some of our recent games, we haven't even kicked a goal.* | *This is a recent photo of my family.*

recipe /*say* **res**-uh-pee/ *noun*
A **recipe** is a list of all the things you need for cooking something, and instructions telling you how to use them.

> ✴ *Spelling Tip:* The main thing to notice is the single *e* at the end giving the 'ee' sound. Also remember the *c* spelling for the 's' sound. It will help if you know that **recipe** comes from the Latin word *recipere*, meaning 'to receive'. The original use of the word **recipe** was as the instruction 'Receive!' written on medical prescriptions.

recite *verb*
If you **recite** something, you say the words from memory. *Ben wrote a poem about cats and recited it to the class.*

reckon *verb*
If you say that you **reckon** something is true, you mean that you think it is true. *I reckon that it will rain later today.*

recognise /*say* **rek**-uhg-nuyz/ *verb*
If you **recognise** someone or something you have seen before, you have the feeling of knowing them when you see them again. *We hardly recognised her because she had put a different colour in her hair.*

Another spelling for this word is **recognize**.

record *verb* /*say* ruh-**kawd**/
1. If you **record** information, you write it down so that other people can read it later. *My mother had to record what everybody said at the meeting.*
2. If you **record** music or a television show, you use a machine to put it on a special tape so that you can listen to it or watch it later. *We recorded our favourite television program because we were going to be out when it was on.*
–*noun* /*say* **rek**-awd/ **3.** A **record** is something that has been recorded in writing or print. *Mum had to read out the record of the last meeting.*
4. A **record** is a round flat piece of black plastic which was once used to record music. *Dad loves listening to old records.*
5. A **record** in a sport is the best performance in it by anyone so far. *Kylie holds the record in our school for running.*

recorder *noun*
1. A **recorder** is a machine for recording sound or film. It is recorded on a special tape so that you can watch it or listen to it later. A recorder for sound is often called a **tape recorder** and a recorder for film is often called a **video recorder**. *We don't use our tape recorder to listen to music very much now because we have a CD player.*
2. A **recorder** is a kind of musical instrument made of wood or plastic that you play by blowing into it. *The whole class is learning to play the recorder.*

recount /*say* **ree**-kownt/ *noun*
If you write a **recount**, you do a piece of writing which explains exactly how things happened.

recover *verb*
When you **recover**, you get well again after you have been sick. *The doctor said Jeremy would recover once he started taking the medicine.*

> *Word Building:* **recovery**, *noun* When you recover, you make a **recovery**.

recreation /*say* rek-ree-**ay**-shuhn/ *noun*
Recreation is what you do when you want to relax.

> ✴ *Spelling Tip:* Notice the *c* (not *ck*) spelling. In spite of the way you say this word, it begins with the word part *re* (meaning 'again'). It comes from the Latin word *recreare* meaning 'to make new again' (in the sense of making yourself feel good again, which is what **recreation** does for you).

rectangle *noun*
A **rectangle** is a shape with four straight sides.

> *Word Building:* **rectangular**, *adjective* Something in the shape of a rectangle is **rectangular**.

A **rectangle** can have two sides that are long and two sides that are shorter. Another word for this is **oblong**. A **rectangle** can also have four sides that are all the same length. This kind of rectangle is a **square**.

recycle /*say* ree-**suy**-kuhl/ *verb*
If you **recycle** something, you use it again, usually in a different way. *There is a company that recycles newspaper and makes it into cardboard boxes.*

red *adjective*
If something is **red**, it has the colour of blood or a similar colour.

reduce *verb*

If you **reduce** something, you make it smaller or less in amount. *The sign told drivers to reduce speed so Mum went slower.*

The opposite is **increase**.

reed *noun*

A **reed** is a kind of tall grass that grows in wet places.

reef *noun*

A **reef** is a section of rock, sand or coral above or just below the surface of the sea.

reel *noun*

A **reel** is a round piece of wood or metal that you can wind something onto.

> ✵ *Spelling Tip:* Don't confuse the spelling of **reel** with **real** which sounds the same, but is spelt with *ea*. Something that is **real** actually happens.

refer /*say* ruh-**fer** / *verb* (**refers, referring, referred, has referred**)

If you **refer** to something, you talk or write about in a short way. You mention it. *In assembly, the principal referred to the money our class had raised for charity.*

referee *noun*

A **referee** is someone in charge of some kinds of games and who makes sure they are played according to the rules.

> ✵ *Spelling Tip:* Remember that there is only one *f* in **referee**, but a double *ee* at the end. This will be easier to remember if you see that **referee** is made up of the word *refer* and the word ending *ee* (which is from French and is used in words for a person who receives something, or, as in this word, does something).

reference /*say* **ref**-ruhns / *noun*

1. If you make **reference** to something, you mention it. *She gets upset if anyone makes reference to the way she looks.*
2. A **reference** is a place in a book or other writing that tells you where to look to find information. *For our project on kangaroos, we looked up references on Australian animals and marsupials.*
3. reference book, A **reference book** is a book that contains information, such as a dictionary, encyclopedia, or atlas. *The reference books are kept in a special section of the library, separate from the novels.*

> ✵ *Spelling Tip:* Don't forget that there are four *e*'s in **reference**. Be careful about the second one, because you usually do not hear it when you say the word. This will be easier to remember if you see that it is made up of *refer* and the word ending *ence*. Try breaking the word up as *ref+ er+ ence*.

reflect *verb*

1. If something **reflects** light or heat, it sends the light or heat back from a shiny surface.
2. If a surface, such as glass or water, **reflects** something, it shows a kind of picture of that thing. *The clouds were reflected in the still water of the lake.*

> *Word Building:* **reflection**, *noun* When something is reflected, you see a **reflection**.

refresh *verb*

If something **refreshes** someone who is tired, it makes them feel strong and full of energy again. *Jumping into the lake refreshed all of us after the long walk.*

> *Word Building:* **refreshment**, *noun* Something that refreshes is a **refreshment**.

refrigerator /*say* ruh-**frij**-uh-ray-tuh / *noun*

A **refrigerator** is a large container that is kept cool inside with electricity and is used for keeping food and drink cold.

The short form is **fridge**.

> ✵ *Spelling Tip:* Remember that there is no *d* in this word (although there is in the short form *fridge*). In **refrigerator**, the *g* alone makes the 'j' sound. Also notice that the ending is *or* (not *er*).

refugee /*say* ref-yooh-**jee** / *noun*

A **refugee** is a person who has left the country they lived in because of danger, especially someone who has gone to a new country and hopes to be able to live there.

refund /*say* ruh-**fund** / *verb*

If someone **refunds** money, they pay it back to another person. *We asked the shop to refund our $5 when we found the mechanical croaking frog didn't croak.*

refuse *verb*

1. If you **refuse** to do something, you say you will not do it. *We asked Sophie to help but she refused.*

2. If you **refuse** something, you do not accept or take it. *We had to refuse an invitation to the football because we were going to our grandmother's place.*

regard *verb*
If you **regard** someone in a certain way, you think about them in that way. *I regard Sophie as my best friend.*

regret *verb* (**regrets, regretting, regretted, has regretted**)
If you **regret** something that you have done, you feel sorry or sad about it. *We regretted that we had forgotten to say happy birthday to our friend.*

regular *adjective*
1. If you say something is **regular**, you mean that it is usual or normal. *I want the regular size of drink, please.*
2. Something that is **regular** happens at particular times with the same amount of time in between. *You should eat regular meals.*

> **Word Building: regularly**, *adverb* If something happens again and again with the same amount of time in between, it happens **regularly**. *We could hear the clock ticking regularly.*

rehearse /*say* ruh-**hers**/ *verb*
If you **rehearse** something, you do it many times to make sure it is ready for other people to see or hear. *Our school choir has been rehearsing for the concert every afternoon.*

> **Word Building: rehearsal**, *noun* When you rehearse something, you have a **rehearsal**.

> ✷ **Spelling Tip:** Don't forget that there is an *a* in **rehearse**. Think of other words in which the letter group *ear* makes an 'er' sound, such as *earn* or *learn*.

reign /*sounds like* rain/ *verb*
When a king or queen rules over a country and its people, you say that they **reign**. *Queen Victoria reigned in Britain for 64 years.*

rein /*say* rayn/ *noun*
Reins are the long, thin lengths of leather that a rider uses to guide a horse.

reindeer /*say* **rayn**-dear/ *noun* (*plural* **reindeer**)
A **reindeer** is a kind of deer that lives in cold countries in northern parts of Europe and Asia.

> ✷ **Spelling Tip:** Although it might rain a lot where **reindeers** come from, this has nothing to do with the spelling of the word. The *rein* part comes from the original language, Old Norse

(the old language of Scandinavia). However, it might help to think of the word *rein* (a strap a rider uses to guide a horse) and imagine Santa Claus in his sleigh, guiding his **reindeers** with reins.

reject /*say* ruh-**jekt**/ *verb*
If you **reject** something, you say that you will not take it or use it. *A lady sitting near us in the restaurant rejected her meal – she sent it back to the kitchen because it was cold.*

> The opposite is **accept**.

rejoice *verb*
If someone **rejoices**, they are extremely pleased about something. *All the farmers were rejoicing because at last it was raining again.*

relation *noun*
1. The **relation** between people or things is the way that they are connected. *There was no relation between the pink on the colour chart and the pink that we painted on my wall.*
2. A **relation** is someone who is part of your family. *My aunt invited all her friends and relations to her wedding.*

> **Word Building: related**, *adjective* If people are relations or part of the same family, they are **related**. They are **related to** each other. *They look so similar I think they must be related.*

> For definition 2 you can also say **relative**.

relationship *noun*
The **relationship** between people is how they feel about each other.

relax *verb*
If someone **relaxes**, they rest and make themselves comfortable. *We made ourselves comfortable with cushions on the floor and relaxed in front of the television.*

> **Word Building: relaxation**, *noun* When you relax, you're in a state of **relaxation**.

release *verb*
If someone **releases** a person or an animal, they let them go free. *We caught a possum in the roof and released it into the bush.*

reliable /*say* ruh-**luy**-uh-buhl/ *adjective*
You are **reliable** if people can trust you to do things.

relief /*say* ruh-**leef**/ *noun*
If you have been feeling worried or upset and those feelings go away, you feel **relief**.

a b c d e f g h i j k l m n o p q r s t u v w x y z

Word Building: **relieved** /*say* ruh-**leevd**/, *adjective* When you feel relief you are **relieved**.

✳ *Spelling Tip:* Remember the *ie* spelling for the 'ee' sound. This follows the rule that *i* comes before *e*, except after *c*.

religion /*say* ruh-**lij**-uhn/ *noun*
Religion is the beliefs that people have about a god or gods.

Word Building: **religious** /*say* ruh-**lij**-uhs/, *adjective* Something that has to do with religion is **religious**.

remain *verb*
1. If you **remain** somewhere, you stay there. *Everyone else went to the party but I was sick and remained at home.*
2. If something **remains**, it is still there. *Some food remained after the party.*
3. If you **remain** a certain way, you stay like that. *We tried to make her happy but she remained sad.*

remark *verb*
When you **remark**, you say what you notice about something. *My mother remarked to my dad that it was a long time since we had had a holiday.*

remember *verb*
1. If you **remember** something, you keep it in your mind or you are able to bring it back into your mind. *Peter couldn't remember the answer.* | *I remember how it felt the first day I started school.*
2. If you **remember** to do something which you were meaning to do, you do it. *Did you remember to bring the tickets?*

The opposite is **forget**.

remind *verb*
1. If someone **reminds** you to do something, they make you remember to do it. *My mother always has to remind me to take my lunch with me.*
2. If someone or something **reminds** you of someone or something, the first person or thing makes you think about the other person or thing because they are similar in some way. *You remind me of my mother when you speak in that way.*

remote *adjective*
If something is **remote**, it is far away.

remove *verb*
If you **remove** something, you take it away from a place. *The teacher asked us to remove all the rubbish from our desks before we went to lunch.*

rent *noun*
Rent is the money someone pays for a house or a flat that they live in but do not own.

repair *verb*
If you **repair** something, you make it work again after it has been broken or has stopped working. *I have been trying to repair my old bike.*

repeat *verb*
If you **repeat** something, you say or do it again. *I didn't hear you. Could you please repeat what you said?*

replace *verb*
1. If someone **replaces** someone else, they take their place. They do the thing that the other person was doing. *We need someone to replace Kelly because she's got the measles and can't play for two weeks.*
2. If you **replace** something, you put it back in its place. *The librarian asked us to replace the books on the shelves where we found them.*

reply *verb* (**replies**, **replying**, **replied**, **has replied**)
1. When you **reply**, you give an answer. *Mum asked if we wanted to go to the beach and of course we replied that we did.*
—*noun* (*plural* **replies**) **2.** A **reply** is an answer.

report *noun*
1. A **report** is when someone tells the important facts about something, either by speaking or writing. *We were all keen to hear the reports of how the game had gone.*
2. If you write a **report**, you do a piece of writing about information you have found about something. *Our class is writing a report on the history of flying.*
3. A school **report** is a kind of letter which your teacher sends to your parents about your school work. *Mum was very pleased with my report because it said that I had been working hard.*

reporter *noun*
A **reporter** is someone whose job is to gather news for radio, television or a newspaper.

represent /*say* rep-ruh-**zent**/ *verb*
1. If you **represent** someone else or other people, you act for them. You say things that they would like to say but you say it for them. *We elected Ally to represent our class because she is a good speaker.*
2. If something **represents** something else, it stands for that thing. *She drew a circle to*

represent the sports field and some crosses to represent where the players should stand.

reptile *noun*
A **reptile** is a kind of animal which has a thick, strong skin and is cold-blooded, which means that they become hot or cold depending on the temperature around them. The babies of some **reptiles** start their life in eggs. Some examples of reptiles are snakes, lizards, crocodiles and alligators.

republic *noun*
A **republic** is a country which does not have a king or queen as its leader. Usually the leader of the country is a president who is chosen by the people.

request *verb*
1. If you **request** someone to do something, you ask them to do it, in a polite way. *At the library, there were signs up requesting people be quiet.*
–*noun* **2.** If you make a **request**, you ask in a polite way for something to be done.

require /*say* ruh-**kwuy**-uh/ *verb*
If you **require** something, you need it. *The swimming club requires a lot of money to fix up the pool.*

> ✦ *Spelling Tip:* Remember the *qu* spelling for the 'kw' sound.

rescue *verb*
If you **rescue** someone, you save them from the danger that they are in. *Tom rescued his sister by pulling her out of the path of the car as it rolled down the hill.*

research *noun*
Research is when someone studies a lot or does a lot of tests to find out more about something they are interested in. *Stephen did a lot of research for his space project on the internet. | One day, research might discover a cure for colds and no-one will ever have to use a tissue again.*

reserve *verb*
If you **reserve** something, you ask for it to be kept for you to use at a later time. *Mum rang up the library for me to reserve a book on the history of cricket.*

> *Word Building:* **reservation**, *noun* When you reserve something, you make a **reservation**.

reservoir /*say* **rez**-uh-vwah/ *noun*
A **reservoir** is a place where a lot of water is kept until it is needed.

> ✦ *Spelling Tip:* Remember the *er* spelling in the middle of this word. This will be easier to remember if you see that **reservoir** is connected with the word *reserve*. The *e* has been dropped and the word ending *oir* added. You need also to remember the spelling of this word part, which comes from French, which is why it sounds like 'wah'.

respect *noun*
1. Respect is the feeling you have about someone when you think they are good. You admire them.
–*verb* **2.** If you **respect** someone, you behave in a way which shows that you admire them. *They respected their teachers and tried to learn from them.*

> *Word Building:* **respectful**, *adjective* If you show respect for someone or something, you are **respectful**. *We have to be respectful in church.*

responsible *adjective*
1. You are **responsible** for someone or something if you must look after them. *Mum said I had to be responsible for my little sister when we went to the park.*
2. You are **responsible** for something that goes wrong if it was your fault. *We knew Andrew was responsible for breaking the window because he had been kicking the ball close to the house all morning.*
3. You are a **responsible** person if you can be trusted to do things properly. *The teacher always asks Charlotte to do the hard jobs because she is so responsible.*

rest[1] *noun*
1. Rest is when you do not have to work or be active. It is when you stop doing something or you have a sleep. *At the end of the hike up the mountain, we threw ourselves on the ground and had a rest. | I'm tired – I need some rest.*
–*verb* **2.** When you **rest**, you sleep or lie or sit quietly. *The old lady was resting in the sun.*
3. If you **rest** something somewhere, you leave it there. *Janelle rested her bike against the fence.*

rest[2] *noun*
If you have been talking about a certain number of a group, **the rest** is the other ones.

restaurant /*say* **res**-tuh-ront/ *noun*
A **restaurant** is a room or a building where you buy a meal and eat it.

> ✳ *Spelling Tip:* Remember the *au* spelling in the middle of this word. Also remember the *ant* ending (which gives the 'ont' sound). This is because the word **restaurant** comes from French.

result *noun*
A **result** is something that happens because of something else.

retire *verb*
When someone **retires**, they do not go to work any more because they are getting old. *When my grandfather retired, he and my grandmother went on a long trip.*

retreat *verb*
If you **retreat**, you go back because you see that there is danger ahead. *The soldiers retreated when they saw the enemy.*

return *verb*
1. If someone or something **returns** to a place they have been before, they go or come back there. *All the parents were waiting when the buses from the excursion returned to the school.*
2. If you **return** something, you give or send it back to where it should be or to the person who owns it, or put it back in its proper place. *Can I borrow this book and return it to you tomorrow?*

reveal *verb*
If you **reveal** something, you show or tell something which no-one knew before. *Ally promised not to reveal my secret to anyone.*

revenge /*say* ruh-**venj**/ *noun*
Revenge is something bad you do to someone because of something bad they have done to you.

reverse *noun*
1. The **reverse** of something is the opposite of it.
–*verb* 2. If someone **reverses** a car, they drive it backwards. *Mum always reverses the car into the garage so that we can drive out facing the street.*

review /*say* ruh-**vyooh**/ *noun*
1. A **review** is a piece of writing in a newspaper or magazine which describes and gives you an opinion of a book, a film, a play, or a concert. *The review in the paper was so good that we're going to see the film.*
2. If you write a **review**, you do a piece of writing to tell what is good or bad about something like a book or a film. *We had to write a review of our favourite television show.*

revise /*say* ruh-**vuyz**/ *verb*
If you **revise** something, you go back over it so that you will remember it. *At the end of each week we revise the maths we have learned.*

> *Word Building:* **revision** /*say* ruh-**vizh**-uhn/, *noun* If you revise something, you're doing **revision**.

revolution /*say* rev-uh-**looh**-shuhn/ *noun*
A **revolution** is a complete change in the way a country is governed, usually because many people have fought to change it.

reward *noun*
A **reward** is something you get for doing good work.

rhinoceros /*say* ruy-**nos**-uh-ruhs/ *noun* (*plural* **rhinoceroses**)
A **rhinoceros** is a large, heavy, African animal with a thick skin and with one or two horns at the front of its head.

> ✳ *Spelling Tip:* This animal has a hard skin and is also hard to spell. Don't forget the silent *h* following the *r* at the start. Also remember the *c* spelling for the *s* sound and the *os* (not *ous*) ending. The first part of the word, *rhino*, means 'having to do with the nose' and comes from the Greek word for 'nose'.

rhyme /*say* ruym/ *verb*
If words have the same sound at the end, they **rhyme** with each other. *'Cat' rhymes with 'bat' and 'lion' rhymes with 'iron'.*

> ✳ *Spelling Tip:* This is a difficult word to spell. Don't forget the silent *h* following the *r* at the start. The other hard part is the *y* spelling. You might think this word would be spelt *rime* and this is in fact an old spelling of the word. However the one to learn now is **rhyme**. Try thinking 'real hippopotamuses yell most evenings' as a way of remembering it.

rhythm /*say* **ridh**-uhm/ *noun*
Rhythm is the pattern of strong and weak sounds you can hear in music or when someone is reading a poem.

> ✳ *Spelling Tip:* Don't forget the silent *h* following the *r* at the start, as in *rhyme*. This is an unusual looking word because it has a *y* for the 'i' sound and the *m* follows straight after the *th* at the end. Look at the suggestion at *rhyme* and change it to 'real hippopotamuses yell to halt monsters.

ribbon *noun*
A **ribbon** is a band of material you use for tying things up or to make something look pretty.

rice *noun*
Rice is a kind of white or brown grain, used as food.

rich *adjective*
If someone is **rich**, they have a lot of money.

The opposite is **poor**.

riddle *noun*
A **riddle** is a question with the meaning cleverly hidden in it, that you ask someone for fun.

ride *verb* (**rides, riding, rode, has ridden**)
1. If you **ride** an animal, such as a horse, or **ride** a bicycle, you sit on it and control it while it is moving. *I would like to learn how to ride a horse.*
2. If you **ride** in a car or bus, you sit in it and travel in it. *My little brother loves to go for a ride on the train.*
–*noun* 3. A **ride** is any sort of trip, whether you are on a horse or a bike or in a car, bus or train.

Word Building: **rider**, *noun*: *Both the horse and the rider were hurt in the accident.*

ridge *noun*
A **ridge** is a long, narrow line of something that is higher than what is around it.

ridiculous /*say* ruh-**dik**-yuh-luhs/ *adjective*
Something or someone **ridiculous** makes people laugh at them.

❉ *Spelling Tip:* Remember the two *i*'s in this word – one after the *r* at the start and one after the *d*. Also remember that there are no double letters in this word and that there is a *c* alone for the 'k' sound. Try breaking the word up as *rid+ic+u+lous*.

rifle *noun*
A **rifle** is a long gun.

right¹ /*say* ruyt/ *adjective*
1. If you do something that is **right**, you do a good thing. It is something that should be done. *We told Chris that it was not right to take the flowers from the school garden.*
2. If something is **right**, it does not have a mistake in it. *If the man on the quiz show gets the next question right, he is going to win $100 000.*
–*noun* 3. If someone has the **right** to do or have something, the law or a rule says that they should be allowed to do or have it.

The opposite of definitions 1 and 2 is **wrong**.

right² /*say* ruyt/ *adjective*
1. Your **right** side is the side of your body opposite where your heart is. –*noun*
2. The **right** is the direction to the right side of your body.

The opposite is **left**.

rim *noun*
A **rim** is the outside edge, usually of some round thing.

rind *noun*
A **rind** is the thick, hard skin that you find on fruit, like oranges, and some other foods as well.

ring¹ *noun*
1. A **ring** is a circle of metal that you wear on your finger. *My mother's wedding ring is gold, but I think I will have a silver one.*
2. A **ring** is anything that has the shape of a circle. *At the party, we formed a ring and had to pass the parcel around until the music stopped.*

ring² *verb* (**rings, ringing, rang, has rung**)
1. If something **rings**, it makes the sound of a bell or a sound like a bell. *There is something ringing – is it your mobile?*
2. If you **ring** a bell or something similar, you make it make a sound. *Eddie was supposed to ring the bell for lunch but he forgot.*
3. If you **ring** someone, you telephone them. *I will ring you on Wednesday.*

rinse *verb*
If you **rinse** something, you run water over it to wash off the soap or dirt. *After the painting class, we all had to go outside to rinse our brushes under the tap.*

riot /*say* **ruy**-uht/ *noun*
There is a **riot** when many people shout and act noisily and angrily in a public place.

rip *verb* (**rips, ripping, ripped, has ripped**)
If you **rip** something, you tear it in a rough way. *Mum ripped a piece off an old sheet to make a bandage.*

ripe *adjective*
If fruit or a vegetable is **ripe**, it is ready to be taken off the tree or plant or ready to be eaten.

rise *verb* (**rises, rising, rose, has risen**)
1. If something **rises**, it goes upwards. *As our plane rose in the sky, the people waving to us from the airport looked smaller and smaller.*

a b c d e f g h i j k l m n o p q **r** s t u v w x y z

2. If you **rise**, you stand up. *Everybody rose from their seats to applaud the runner as she got to the finishing line.*

3. When you **rise**, you get out of bed. *We have to rise early in the morning to get to the airport on time.*

Compare **rise** with **raise**. Remember that when you **raise** something or someone, you lift them up, but that something or someone **rises** by themselves.

risk *noun*
A **risk** is the chance that something might go wrong or might hurt you.

river *noun*
A **river** is a long area of water going through the land.

road *noun*
A **road** is a track for vehicles like cars, buses and trucks to travel along.

roam *verb*
If you **roam**, you walk or travel about without really trying to get anywhere. *We roamed for hours, seeing what shells we could find on the beach.*

roar *verb*
If something or someone **roars**, they make a loud, deep sound. *The storm roared across the bay.*

roast *verb*
If you **roast** food, you cook it in an oven. *Dad's roasting a leg of lamb for dinner.*

Another word that means nearly the same is **bake**.

robbery *noun* (*plural* **robberies**)
When there is a **robbery**, a person steals something from someone else.

Word Building: **robber**, *noun* A person who steals things is a **robber**.

robot /*say* **roh**-bot / *noun*
A **robot** is a machine which does a job that is usually done by a person.

rock¹ *noun*
1. Rock is the hard material that helps make up earth. *In America we saw mountains that were all rock.*
2. A **rock** is a large piece of stone. *Kim and Sally sat on a flat rock and ate lunch.*

Word Building: **rocky**, *adjective*: *The ground was rocky and hard to walk on.*

rock² *verb*
1. If something **rocks**, it moves from side to side. *The waves made the little boat rock.*
—*noun* **2. Rock** is a kind of loud popular music with a strong beat.

rock art *noun*
Rock art is a kind of Aboriginal art in which pictures are made on rock surfaces by painting or drawing on or cutting out sections of rock.

rocket *noun*
A **rocket** is a long thin vehicle for travelling in space.

rod *noun*
A **rod** is a stick of wood or metal.

role *noun*
An actor's **role** is the part or character that they play in a film or play.

roll *verb*
1. When something **rolls**, it moves along by turning over and over as a wheel does. *The ball rolled down the hill and was soon out of sight.*
—*noun* **2.** A **roll** is something long and flat that has been turned over and over until it is has a long, round shape. *We'll need to get a few rolls of paper to wrap all the Christmas presents.*
3. A **roll** is a list of names. *The teacher called the roll to see if everyone was present.*
4. A **roll** is a small rounded piece of bread. *Do you want salad on your roll?*

rollerblade *noun*
1. A **rollerblade** is like a boot but underneath it has narrow wheels that are in a straight line from the front to the back.
—*verb* **2.** If you **rollerblade**, you move along the ground using rollerblades. *Alexis's brother can rollerblade around the block in five minutes.*

rollerskate *noun*
1. A **rollerskate** is like a boot which underneath has two wheels at the front and two wheels at the back.
—*verb* **2.** If you **rollerskate**, you move along the ground using rollerskates. *Alexis doesn't want to rollerskate any more.*

roof *noun* (*plural* **roofs**)
A **roof** is the top covering of a building or a car.

room *noun*
1. A **room** is a part of a building that is separated by walls from other parts. *There are six rooms in our house.*
2. **Room** is space. *We all moved up so there was room for Margaret to sit down.*

rooster *noun*
A **rooster** is the male bird you keep with chickens.

The female of this is a **hen**.

root *noun*
The **root** of a plant is the part of it which usually grows downwards into the soil and allows the plant to get food and water.

rope *noun*
A **rope** is a strong, thick string made of many threads wound together, which is used for tying things down or together.

rose[1] *noun*
A **rose** is a beautiful flower which often has a sweet smell.

rose[2] *verb*
Look up **rise**.

rosella /*say* roh-**zel**-uh/ *noun*
A **rosella** is an Australian bird with brightly coloured feathers.

rotten *adjective*
Something is **rotten** if it has gone bad or if it is falling apart. *We found a rotten apple that had been behind the cupboard for a month. | The wharf is not safe to walk on because the wood is rotten.*

rough /*say* ruf/ *adjective*
1. If something is **rough**, it is not even or smooth. *We had to put on a sack for the sack race and it felt rough and horrible.*
2. If something or someone is **rough**, they are wild or not calm. *The small boat was thrown about on the rough sea.*

Word Building: **roughly**, *adverb* If you are not careful when you do something, you do it **roughly**. *The house was built roughly.*

✴ *Spelling Tip:* Remember that there is no *f* in **rough** – the spelling *ough* gives the 'uf' sound, as it does in some other words like *enough* and *tough*.

round *adjective*
1. If something is **round**, it has the shape of a circle or ball. *The white mat in my room is round, and so is the orange on the table.*

–*adverb* 2. You can use **round** to mean the same as 'around'. Look up **around**.

Word Building: **rounded**, *adjective* Something that is **rounded** has curves a bit like a part of a circle. *The corners of my bed are rounded.*

route /*say* rooht/ *noun*
A **route** is the road or way that you take to get from one place to another.

✴ *Spelling Tip:* Don't confuse the spelling of **route** with **root** which has the same sound. The **root** of a plant grows under the ground.

row[1] /*rhymes with* go/ *noun*
A **row** is a line of people or things.

row[2] /*rhymes with* go/ *verb*
If you **row** a boat, you make it move by using oars. *We rowed the boat across the river.*

row[3] /*rhymes with* how/ *noun*
A **row** is a noisy fight.

royal *adjective*
Something is **royal** if it has to do with a king or queen.

✴ *Spelling Tip:* Remember that **royal** has two parts, *roy* and *al*, though you sometimes don't hear the *a* when the word is said.

rub *verb*
If you **rub** something, you move something backwards and forwards over it. *Mum rubbed the car until it was clean and shining.*

rubber *noun*
1. **Rubber** is a special kind of material that can be pulled into different, longer shapes. *Rubber is used to make things like car tyres and balls.*
2. A **rubber** is a small piece of soft rubber used to rub paper to take away pencil marks. *Everyone should bring a pencil and a rubber to the test.*

Another word for definition 2 is **eraser**.

rubbish *noun*
Rubbish is anything that you cannot use or that needs to be thrown out because you do not want it any more.

Another word for this is **garbage**.

rudder *noun*
A **rudder** is a flat piece of wood attached to the back of a boat that you move to make the boat change direction.

rude *adjective*

If someone is **rude**, they are not polite. They speak or behave in a way that shows they do not respect or want to please other people.

> **Word Building: rudely**, *adverb*: *She answered rudely.* **–rudeness**, *noun*: *He was punished because of his rudeness to the teacher.*

rug *noun*

1. A **rug** is a thick cover, made of something warm, that you put over yourself. *We took a rug in the car in case we got cold.*
2. A **rug** is something used to cover a floor. *My room looked much better with a bright blue rug beside the bed.*

Rugby League /*say* rug-bee **leeg**/ *noun*

Rugby League is a kind of football, played by two teams of 13 players each.

> You can also spell this without capital letters: **rugby league**.

Rugby Union /*say* rug-bee **yoohn**-yuhn/ *noun*

Rugby Union is a kind of football, played by two teams of 15 players each.

> You can also spell this without capital letters: **rugby union**.

ruin /*say* **rooh**-uhn/ *verb*

If something or someone **ruins** something, they destroy it or spoil it completely. *Oh no! Look at the dirt on my shirt. Now it's ruined!* | *It was going to be a secret but Bonnie ruined our plans by telling everybody.*

rule *noun*

1. A **rule** is a kind of law which says what is allowed and what is not allowed.
–verb 2. If a person or a group of people **rule** a country, they are in charge of it. *They argued about whether the government was ruling the country well or not.*

ruler *noun*

1. A **ruler** is someone in charge of a country. *The rulers met to discuss how to end the war.*

2. A **ruler** is a long, thin piece of wood or plastic with a straight edge, used for measuring and drawing straight lines. *You'll need a ruler and some pencils when you do the test.*

rumble *noun*

A **rumble** is a long, loud, deep, rolling sound. *We knew when we saw the dark clouds and heard the rumble of thunder in the distance that a storm was coming.*

rumour *noun*

A **rumour** is something that a lot of people are saying about someone or something even though it might not be true.

> Another spelling for this word is **rumor**.

run *verb* (**runs**, **running**, **ran**, **has run**)

1. If you **run**, you move quickly using your legs. *She ran to the railway station to catch the train.*
2. **run out**, If you **run out** of something, you have no more of it left. *We ran out of milk and had to buy some more.*

> **Word Building: runner**, *noun*: *Sue is a fast runner.*

rung[1] *noun*

A **rung** is one of the steps of a ladder.

rung[2] *verb*

Look up **ring**[2].

runway *noun*

A **runway** is a piece of land that a plane takes off from and lands on.

rush *verb*

If you **rush**, you do something quickly. *You don't have to rush. There's plenty of time before the bus leaves.*

rustle /*say* **rus**-uhl/ *noun*

A **rustle** is the soft sound that leaves make when something, such as wind, makes them rub together.

> ✿ *Spelling Tip:* Don't forget the *st* (not double *s*) spelling. The *t* is silent.

snake

sack *noun*
A **sack** is a large bag made out of strong material.

sacred /*say* **say**-kruhd/ *adjective*
If something is **sacred**, it is important and special because it has to do with religion.

sad *adjective* (**sadder**, **saddest**)
If you are **sad**, you are not happy or you feel sorry about something.

> **Word Building: sadly**, *adverb* If you do things in an unhappy way, you do them **sadly**. –**sadness**, *noun* If you have a feeling of not being happy or you are feeling bad, you have a feeling of **sadness**.

saddle *noun*
A **saddle** is a leather seat that you put onto the back of a horse so that you can ride it.

safari /*say* suh-**fah**-ree/ *noun* (*plural* **safaris**)
A **safari** is a long journey made by a group of people who want to watch or hunt wild animals.

safe *adjective*
1. If someone or something is **safe**, they are not in danger or at risk. *You can't fall now that I have hold of you – you are safe now.*
2. If something is **safe** to do, there is no danger in doing it. *It's not safe to swim in that part of the river.*
3. If a place is **safe**, you can leave something there without worrying and it will not be harmed. *Make sure you put your bag somewhere safe where it won't get stolen.*
–*noun* 4. A **safe** is a strong steel box in which you can keep money or other valuable things.

> **Word Building: safely**, *adverb* If you do something in such a way that you are not at risk of harm, you are doing things **safely**.

> The opposite of definition 2 is **dangerous**.

safety *noun*
Safety is when someone or something is safe.

sail *noun*
1. A **sail** is a piece of strong material on a boat which catches the wind and makes the boat move through the water.
–*verb* 2. If you **sail**, you travel in a ship or boat. *We sailed right up the east coast.*
3. If a boat or ship **sails**, it moves along on water. *There are ferries sailing from here to the city every hour.*

> ✴ *Spelling Tip:* Don't confuse the spelling of **sail** with **sale** which sounds the same.

sailor *noun*
A **sailor** is someone who sails a boat, or whose job is to work on a ship.

salad *noun*
A **salad** is a kind of food eaten cold, often made with vegetables and fruit.

> ✴ *Spelling Tip:* Remember that there is only one *l* in the middle of this word. Notice also that the letter on either side of the *l* is an *a*.

salary /*say* **sal**-uh-ree/ *noun* (*plural* **salaries**)
A **salary** is the regular money paid to someone each week or each month for the work they do in their job.

sale *noun*
1. A **sale** is the selling of something. *This house is not for sale.*
2. A **sale** is a time when things are sold at a lower price than usual. *There is a sale of computer games. Let's go and look.*

> ✴ *Spelling Tip:* Don't confuse the spelling of **sale** with **sail**.

salmon /*say* **sam**-uhn/ *noun*
A **salmon** is a silver-coloured fish with pink flesh that you can eat.

> ✴ *Spelling Tip:* Don't forget the silent *l* before the *m*. Try breaking the word up as *sal + mon*.

a
b
c
d
e
f
g
h
i
j
k
l
m
n
o
p
q
r
s
t
u
v
w
x
y
z

salt *noun*
Salt is a white powder, made from water from the sea, used to give taste to food.

> ***Word Building: salty,*** *adjective* Something that tastes of salt is **salty.**

salute *verb*
If you **salute**, you raise your right hand to the top part of your face and lower it again quickly to your side, as a way of showing respect for someone. *The soldiers stood in a line to salute the prime minister.*

same *adjective*
1. If two or more things are the **same** in some way, they are exactly like each other in that way. There is no difference. *We need two boxes the same size.*
2. You use **the same** to show that something has not changed. *She never changes the way she does her hair. It has been the same for years.*

sample *noun*
A **sample** is a small piece that shows what something is like.

sand *noun*
Sand is very, very small bits of rocks that have been broken up or worn away. You find **sand** under the sea or on the beach or in a desert.

sandal *noun*
A **sandal** is a kind of light shoe that has thin pieces of material with openings between them for holding your feet in, rather than being solid across the top. You wear **sandals** in summer.

> ⭐ ***Spelling Tip:*** Remember that the ending is *al* (not *el* or *le*). Think of other words with this ending, such as *capital* or *metal*.

sandshoe *noun*
A **sandshoe** is a soft shoe with a rubber bottom part, that you wear especially when you play sport.

sandwich /*say* **san**-wich/ *noun* (*plural* **sandwiches**)
A **sandwich** is two pieces of bread with some other food, usually cold, in between them.

> ⭐ ***Spelling Tip:*** Don't forget the silent *d* following the *n*. Think of this word in two parts – *sand* and *wich* (remember *witch* without the *t*). In fact, the word comes from the name of an English lord, the Earl of Sandwich (1718–1792) who is said to have eaten sandwiches rather than stop playing gambling games to have a full meal.

sane *adjective*
You are **sane** if you have a normal and healthy mind.

sap *noun*
Sap is the sticky liquid that carries food and water around a plant.

sapling *noun*
A **sapling** is a young tree.

sarcastic *adjective*
When you say ordinary things in a sharp way that will hurt or make fun of someone, you are being **sarcastic.**

sardine *noun*
A **sardine** is a small fish, often cooked in oil and packed into tins ready for eating.

sash *noun*
A **sash** is a length of material that you wear around your waist.

satchel *noun*
A **satchel** is a school bag that hangs on your back from your shoulders.

satellite *noun*
1. A **satellite** is something in space that goes around and around a larger thing such as a planet. *The moon is the earth's satellite.*
2. A **satellite** is a kind of spaceship that is sent into space to go around the earth or another planet. *The television pictures were sent around the world by satellite.*

> ⭐ ***Spelling Tip:*** Remember that the *t* is single both times it appears, the *l* is doubled.

satin *noun*
Satin is a smooth and shiny cloth.

satisfaction *noun*
Satisfaction is a feeling of being pleased or happy about something. It is the feeling you have when something satisfies you.

satisfactory *adjective*
1. If something is **satisfactory**, it makes you feel pleased. It is what is needed. *That was a very satisfactory meal.*
2. You can use **satisfactory** to mean that something is good enough for what is needed but it is not very, very good. *The teacher said my work was satisfactory but I could get a lot better.*

⭐ *Spelling Tip:* Can you see that there are three words in **satisfactory** – *sat*, *is* and *factory*. Although these have nothing to do with its meaning, they will help you to remember the spelling, especially the *ory* ending.

satisfy /*say* **sat**-uhs-fuy/ *verb* (**satisfies, satisfying, satisfied, has satisfied**)
If someone or something **satisfies** you, it pleases you or makes you happy. *Nothing ever seems to satisfy him. He is always complaining.*

Word Building: **satisfied**, *adjective*: *She has a satisfied look on her face.* –**satisfying**, *adjective*: *It is very satisfying to wake up and find it is Saturday.*

Saturday *noun*
Saturday is one of the days of the week. It comes between Friday and Sunday.

sauce *noun*
A **sauce** is a thick liquid that you put on food to make it taste better.

saucepan *noun*
A **saucepan** is a pot with a lid and a handle, used for cooking.

saucer *noun*
A **saucer** is a small plate that you put under a cup.

sausage /*say* **sos**-ij/ *noun*
A **sausage** is a piece of food made of meat cut into very small pieces and packed into a thin skin.

save *verb*
1. If you **save** someone, you get them out of danger. You stop them being hurt or dying. *The police managed to save all the people in the burning car.*
2. If you **save** something, such as money, you keep it and do not use it so that you can use it at a later time. *I am saving up my pocket money so I can buy some rollerblades.*

saw[1] *noun*
A **saw** is a tool with an edge like a row of sharp, pointed teeth, that you move backwards and forwards across a piece of wood to cut it.

⭐ *Spelling Tip:* Don't confuse the spelling of **saw** with **sore** which sounds the same. **Sore** means 'hurting'.

saw[2] *verb*
Look up **see**.

say *verb* (**says** /*say* sez/, **saying, said** /*say* sed/, **has said**)
If you **say** something, you tell it using spoken words. *Don't worry, I won't say anything about it.*

scab *noun*
A **scab** is the hard, dry part that forms on the surface of a sore or cut when it starts to get better.

scald /*say* skawld/ *verb*
When very hot liquid goes on someone's body, it **scalds** them. *The patient was scalded with boiling water when she knocked the kettle off the stove.*

scale *noun*
A **scale** of a fish or some other animal is one of the thin, hard, flat pieces that cover their skin.

Word Building: **scaly**, *adjective* Anything that is covered with scales is **scaly**.

scales *noun*
The machine that you use to find out how much something weighs is a set of **scales**.

scalp *noun*
Your **scalp** is the skin on your head under your hair.

scamper *verb*
If a person or animal **scampers**, they run about quickly. *Our dog loves to chase waves and scamper on the beach.*

scanner *noun*
A **scanner** is a machine that looks at written information and puts it straight into a computer so that you can use it.

scar *noun*
A **scar** is the mark left on your skin after a sore or a burn has got better.

scarce *adjective*
1. If something is **scarce**, there is not as much of it as you need. *Water is scarce during a drought.*
2. If something is **scarce**, it is not seen very often. *Koalas are becoming scarce in some areas because the trees they need to survive are being cut down.*

scare *verb*
If someone or something **scares** someone, it frightens them. *The film that we were watching scared us so much we had to cover our eyes.*

scarecrow *noun*
A **scarecrow** is a figure made to look like a person that a farmer puts in a field to frighten birds away from plants.

a
b
c
d
e
f
g
h
i
j
k
l
m
n
o
p
q
r
s
t
u
v
w
x
y
z

scarf *noun* (*plural* **scarves**)

A **scarf** is a piece of cloth that you wear around your head or neck.

scarlet *adjective*

If something is **scarlet**, it is bright red.

scatter *verb*

If you **scatter** things, you throw them carelessly so that they land in many different places. *Mum was angry because we had scattered the jigsaw pieces all over the floor.*

scene /*sounds like* seen/ *noun*

1. The **scene** of something is the place where it happened. *The police arrived at the scene of the accident.*
2. A **scene** is what you can see at a particular place. *We had to paint a scene of a farm with fields and animals.*

> ✷ *Spelling Tip:* Don't forget the silent *c* after the *s* in **scene**. Don't confuse it with **seen** which sounds the same. **Seen** is a form of **see**: *It is a long time since I have seen you.*

scenery /*say* **seen**-uh-ree/ *noun*

Scenery is the things that are around you when you are in a particular place. You often use **scenery** to describe things like trees, rivers and hills in the country.

> ✷ *Spelling Tip:* Don't forget the silent *c* after the *s*. Also remember the *ery* ending. This will be easier if you remember that **scenery** comes from the word *scene*.

scent /*sounds like* sent/ *noun*

1. A **scent** is a sweet smell that people like. *In the spring, there are lots of beautiful scents around from all the flowers.*
2. A **scent** is the smell of an animal. *The dogs followed the scent of the rabbit until they found its burrow.*

> ✷ *Spelling Tip:* Don't forget the silent *c* after the *s*. Don't confuse **scent** with **sent** or **cent**, both of which have the same sound. **Sent** is the past form of the verb *send*: *I sent the letter yesterday.* A **cent** is a unit of money.

scheme /*say* skeem/ *noun*

A **scheme** is a plan of how to do something.

> ✷ *Spelling Tip:* Remember the *sch* spelling for the opening 'sk' sound, as at the start of *school*. Also notice the *eme* spelling for the 'eem' sound.

school /*say* skool/ *noun*

1. A **school** is a place where children go to be taught and learn things. *My school is about a kilometre away from my home.*
2. **School** is the time during which classes are held in a school. *School begins at nine o'clock.*

science /*say* **suy**-uhns/ *noun*

1. **Science** is a subject where you study and find about how the world works and about the natural things in the world like animals, plants, rocks, water, air and heat. *By using science, people have been able to work out how to cure some terrible diseases.*
2. A **science** is one part of this study and knowledge. *Chemistry, physics and biology are all different sciences.*

> ***Word Building:*** **scientific** /*say* suy-uhn-**tif**-ik/, *adjective* Something which has to do with science is **scientific**. *My big sister does scientific experiments at school.*

scientist /*say* **suy**-uhn-tuhst/ *noun*

A **scientist** is someone who studies science or whose job is to do work using science.

scissors /*say* **siz**-uhz/ *noun*

Scissors are a tool for cutting, made of two pieces with sharp edges which can be moved apart from each other to go around an object and then moved together to cut it.

> You can also say **a pair of scissors**.

> ✷ *Spelling Tip:* Don't forget the silent *c* following the *s*. Also remember the double *s* in the middle – you will notice that altogether there are four *s*'s in **scissors**.

scold *verb*

If someone **scolds** you, they tell you angrily that they do not like something you have done or the way you have done it. *Mum scolded me for being careless.*

scone /*say* skon/ *noun*

A **scone** is a small, plain cake that you can break open and fill with things like jam and cream.

scooter *noun*

A **scooter** is a toy that you ride standing up. It has two wheels, a flat board in between for your feet, and a bar to control the direction with your hands.

scorch *verb*

If you **scorch** a piece of clothing, you make it too hot while you are ironing it so that it goes brown.

My dad scorched his shirt because he was too busy watching television while he was ironing.

score *noun*
A **score** is a number showing how well a person or a team is performing in a game or sport.

scout *noun*
1. A **scout** is someone sent to find out things, especially things about an enemy. *A couple of scouts had found out that enemy troops were hiding about a kilometre away.*
2. A **Scout** is a member of a club for young people in which interesting and fun activities are organised, often in the outdoors. *There were some Scouts camping near our tent.*

scowl *verb*
If you **scowl**, you have an angry look on your face. *My dad scowled when he heard his favourite team had lost again.*

scramble *verb*
1. If you **scramble**, you climb quickly using your hands to help you. *Little Sally scrambled over the rocks, trying to catch up with the others.*
2. **scrambled eggs**, **Scrambled eggs** are eggs that have been mixed together with milk, and heated. *Do you want scrambled eggs for breakfast?*

scrap *noun*
A **scrap** is a small piece of something.

scrape *verb*
If you **scrape** something, you rub it with something hard or sharp to get off dirt or paint. *We had to scrape our boots on the step to get the mud off them.*

scratch *verb*
1. If you **scratch** something, you make a mark or cut on something with anything sharp. *The kitten scratched Vijay's arm with its claws.*
2. If you **scratch**, you rub your skin with your nails because it is itching. *Mum told me not to scratch the rash or it would get worse.*

scream *verb*
1. If you **scream**, you cry out loudly because you are very frightened or you are in pain. *He screamed when someone touched his broken arm.*
–*noun* 2. A **scream** is a loud cry made because of fear or pain.

screech *noun* (*plural* **screeches**)
A **screech** is a loud, high noise.

screen *noun*
1. A **screen** is the smooth glass part of a computer or television where you can see pictures or words. *We bought a larger computer screen so it was easier to see things.*
2. A **screen** is the large flat surface where you see a film when you go to the cinema. *We were sitting too close to the screen and the picture was not clear.*
3. A **screen** is a thin wall that you use to separate things or to hide something. *The cafe had a screen separating the kitchen from the eating area.*
4. A **screen** is a net of thin wire that you put over a window to keep out insects. *No wonder mosquitoes are getting in – there's a big hole in the screen.*

screw *noun*
1. A **screw** is a kind of nail that you turn around and around until it fits tightly in a hole.
–*verb* 2. If you **screw** something, you turn it around and around. *Screw the lid back on the jar when you've finished.*

scribble *verb*
If you **scribble**, you write or draw something quickly, without trying to be neat. *My little brother was in trouble for scribbling all over the walls.*

scrub¹ *verb* (**scrubs, scrubbing, scrubbed, has scrubbed**)
If you **scrub** something, you rub it very hard with a stiff brush to clean it. *We scrubbed the bottom of the cage ready for our new pets.*

scrub² *noun*
Scrub is a lot of low trees and other plants growing together.

scurry *verb* (**scurries, scurrying, scurried, has scurried**)
If a person or animal **scurries**, you move with quick small steps. *We could hear the mice scurrying about looking for food.*

sea *noun*
1. The **sea** is the water that covers most of the earth's surface. *If you look at a map of the world, you will see that there is more sea than land.*
2. A **sea** is a particular large part of this water. *They sailed across the South China Sea.*

✪ *Spelling Tip:* Don't confuse the spelling of **sea** with **see** which has the same sound but is spelt with a double *e*. **See** means 'to know about things using your eyes'.

seafood *noun*
Seafood is food which comes from the sea.

seal¹ *verb*

If you **seal** something, you close it up in such a way that you cannot open it again without breaking a part of it. *After we sealed the parcel, we realised we had forgotten to put the card inside.*

seal² *noun*

A **seal** is a sea animal with a long, smooth body covered with short fur.

search /*say* serch/ *verb*

1. If you **search** a place, you look through it very carefully because you want to find something or someone. *We searched everywhere for our lost pet mouse.*
–*noun* (*plural* **searches**) 2. A **search** is when people look for something or someone.

> ✴ *Spelling Tip:* Remember the *a* in this word. The group of letters *ear* spells the *er* sound, as in many other words such as *earn* and *learn*.

season *noun*

1. A **season** is one of the four main divisions of the year. *The four seasons are spring, summer, autumn and winter.*
2. A **season** is a part of the year that is special in some way, because it has a particular kind of weather or because something happens then. *Drew can't wait for the football season.*

seat *noun*

1. A **seat** is something for sitting on.
–*verb* 2. If you **seat** yourself, you sit down somewhere. *He seated himself beside her and started to talk.*

seatbelt *noun*

A **seatbelt** is a narrow length of strong material which you put around you in a car or plane to hold you safely in place if there is a sudden stop or an accident.

> Another name for this is **safety belt**.

seaweed *noun*

Seaweed is a plant that grows in the sea.

second¹ *adjective, adverb*

If something or someone is **second**, they are next after the first. *The second time I saw the film, I remembered all the best bits that I had liked the first time.* | *Damien finished second in the race.*

second² *noun*

A **second** is a very small amount of time. There are 60 **seconds** in a minute.

secondary *adjective*

Something is **secondary** if it comes after something else. A **secondary** school is the school you go to after primary school.

> ✴ *Spelling Tip:* Remember that **secondary** is made up of the word *second* and the ending *ary*, although you do not usually hear the *a* in the ending. Try breaking it up as *sec+ ond+ar+y*.

secret *adjective*

1. If something is **secret**, it is done or made without other people knowing about it.
–*noun* 2. A **secret** is some information that you do not let other people know about.

> ***Word Building:*** **secretly**, *adverb* If you do something in a secret way, you do it **secretly**.

secretary /*say* **sek**-ruh-tree/ *noun* (*plural* **secretaries**)

A **secretary** is someone whose job is to type letters, keep things in order in the office and make phone calls for someone else, usually someone with an important position in an organisation.

> ✴ *Spelling Tip:* Although there is nothing secret about a **secretary**, it will help with the spelling of the word if you think of it as being made up of *secret* and the ending *ary* (although you do not usually hear the *a* in the ending). In fact, **secretary** does come from the Latin word for 'secret', and was used first in the sense of 'a person who you can trust with secrets'.

section *noun*

A **section** is a part of something.

secure *noun*

If someone or something is **secure**, they are safe.

see *verb* (**sees, seeing, saw, has seen**)

1. If you can **see**, you can take information into your mind using your eyes. *A baby can see soon after it is born.*
2. If you **see** something or someone, you know about them in your mind by using your eyes. *You can see the swimming pool from the window.*
3. You can use **see** to mean 'find out'. *Go and see who is at the door.*
4. When you **see** someone, you meet them or visit them. *I saw an old friend the other day.*

> ✴ *Spelling Tip:* Don't confuse the spelling of **see** with **sea** which has the same sound but is

spelt with *ea*. The **sea** is the water that covers most of the earth.

seed *noun*
A **seed** is the small part that comes from one plant from which another new plant of the same kind can grow.

seek *verb* (**seeks, seeking, sought, has sought**)
If you **seek** something, you try to find it or get it. *The police are seeking information from anyone who saw the accident.*

seem *verb*
If someone or something **seems** to be a certain way, they appear to be that way but it is not certain. *The bike seems to go well but I would like to try it on a few hills.*

seesaw *noun*
A **seesaw** is a length of wood balanced in the middle, so that it goes up and down when someone sits on each end.

seize /*say* seez/ *verb*
If you **seize** someone or something, you take hold of them suddenly or by using force. *When the film got to the frightening bit, she suddenly seized my arm.*

> � *Spelling Tip:* Remember that **seize** is spelt with *ei*, breaking the rule that *i* comes before *e*, except after *c*.

seldom *adverb*
If something **seldom** happens, it does not happen often. *We seldom go home by bus – we usually walk.*

select *verb*
If you **select** something or someone out of a group, you decide that is the one that you want. *It was hard to select which ice-cream to have – there were so many that I liked.*

> *Word Building:* **selection**, *noun* When you select something, you make a **selection**.

self *noun* (*plural* **selves**)
Your **self** is you, your own person.

> **Self** is usually part of another word. It makes words like **myself, yourself, himself, herself, itself, ourselves, yourselves** and **themselves**.

selfie *noun*
A **selfie** is a photograph you take of yourself using a smart phone.

selfish *adjective*
You are **selfish** if you only think about yourself.

sell *verb* (**sells, selling, sold, has sold**)
1. If you **sell** something, you give it to someone who pays you money for it. *We sold our car and bought a new one.*
2. If a shop **sells** something, they keep it for people to buy. *Does the newsagent sell computer disks?*
3. sell out, If a shop **sells out** of something, or something **sells out**, there are none left to be bought. *Sorry, we sold out of those tickets an hour ago.*

semitrailer *noun*
A **semitrailer** is a very large truck with many wheels for carrying heavy loads. The driver sits in one section which is attached to the other section that has the load.

send *verb* (**sends, sending, sent, has sent**)
1. If you **send** something or someone to a place, you make them go there. *She said she did not want to see him and sent him away.*
2. send for, If you **send for** someone or something, you ask them to come to you. *The teacher has sent for me – I wonder what I did!*
3. send up, If you **send up** someone or something, you make fun of them, usually by acting as they do but in a funny way. *She cried because they were sending up the way she talks.*

senior *adjective*
If someone is **senior**, they are older or more important than the others.

sense *noun*
1. Your **senses** are the powers your body has to taste, touch, hear, see, and smell. *Dogs have a very good sense of smell.*
2. Sense is when you are able to work out the best thing to say or do. *He had the sense to move away when he realised the danger.*
3. The **sense** of something is what it means. *I can't understand the sense of this poem.*

sensible *adjective*
If you are **sensible**, you can make a good decision about what is the best thing to do or say.

> *Word Building:* **sensibly**, *adverb* If you act in a sensible way you are acting **sensibly**.

> ✦ *Spelling Tip:* Remember that the ending is *ible* (not *able*).

sentence *noun*

1. A **sentence** is a group of words which go together to form a complete idea or question, such as *He jumped the fence* or *Do you like bananas?* A written sentence begins with a capital letter and has a special mark (either . or ? or !) at the end. *The teacher told us to make a sentence with the words 'gold', 'silver' and 'fork' in it.*

2. A **sentence** is the punishment given to someone by law when they have done something very wrong. *He was given a sentence of two years in prison.*

separate *verb* /*say* **sep**-uh-rayt/

1. If you **separate** things or people, you put or keep them away from each other. *It's hard to separate these stamps because they are stuck together.*

–*adjective* /*say* **sep**-ruht/ **2.** If things are **separate**, they are away from each other and not connected.

> **Word Building: separately** /*say* **sep**-ruht-lee/, *adverb*: *Answer each question separately.*

> ✹ *Spelling Tip:* Remember that the middle sound is spelt with an *a*. Try thinking that **separate** has 'a rat' inside it.

September *noun*

September is the ninth month of the year, with 30 days. It comes between August and October.

sergeant /*say* **sah**-juhnt/ *noun*

A **sergeant** is a soldier or a police officer with a high enough rank to be in charge of others.

serial /*say* **sear**-ree-uhl/ *noun*

A **serial** is a story in a magazine or on radio or television that you read, hear or see one part at a time.

series /*say* **sear**-reez/ *noun* (*plural* **series**)

A **series** is a number of things that are similar or are joined in some way and that happen in order.

serious /*say* **sear**-ree-uhs/ *adjective*

1. If you are **serious**, you think about things a lot and you do not laugh much. *Jack is a serious boy who is more interested in working than in playing games.*

2. If you are **serious** about something, you are telling the truth and not joking. *Are you being serious or are you trying to trick us?*

3. If something is **serious**, it makes you worried because something bad could happen if proper care is not taken. *She has a serious sickness.*

> **Word Building: seriously**, *adverb*: *She is seriously ill.*

servant *noun*

A **servant** is someone who works for someone else, usually living in their house and helping to look after it.

serve *verb*

1. If you **serve** food, you put it on the table to be eaten. *Mum served the pasta as soon as everybody sat down.*

2. If someone who works in a shop **serves** you, they help you to find what you want or they give you what you want to buy and take your payment. *The shop assistant hurried over to serve her.*

service *noun*

1. **Service** is what you do when you help someone in a useful way, especially when it is your job. *He left the army after 30 years of service.*

2. A **service** is a business which supplies something useful to a large number of people. *Dad says the telephone service is too dear.*

> **Word Building: service station**, *noun* A **service station** is a place where you buy petrol for a car.

serviette *noun*

A **serviette** is a piece of cloth or paper you use at a meal to wipe your lips and hands and to keep your clothes clean.

> ✹ *Spelling Tip:* Remember the double *t*. This is part of the ending *ette* that appears in several words that have come from French and usually means that something is small. Another word with this ending is *cigarette*.

session *noun*

A **session** is the length of time you spend doing one thing.

set *verb* (**sets, setting, set, has set**)

1. If you **set** something somewhere, you put it in that place. *Eleni set some orange juice on the table.*

2. If you **set** a table, you put things needed for eating on it. *It always seems to be my turn to set the table.*

3. If something soft **sets**, it becomes hard or solid. *Has the jelly set yet?*

4. When the sun **sets**, it sinks down from the sky and it begins to get dark. *The sun sets very early in winter.*

5. When you **set** something like a clock, you organise it so that it is at a particular time or position. *Set the alarm so we get up at six o'clock.*

6. set off, When you **set off** or **set out**, you begin a journey. *At the end of the day, we set off for home.*

7. set up, a. If you **set up** something, you build it or get it into place. *The Scouts set up their tents near the river.* **b.** If you **set up** something like an organisation, you start it. *We are going to set up a video-sharing club.*

—*noun* **8.** A **set** is a number of things that are like each other in some way or which you use together.

settle *verb*

1. If someone or something **settles** somewhere, they put themselves in a position where they are going to stay for a while. *We settled in front of the television for the night.*

2. If you **settle** a disagreement, you make an agreement to end it. *Harry and Sam have settled their argument at last.*

3. settle down, If someone or something **settles down**, they become calm. *The baby can't settle down because there is too much noise.*

settler *noun*

A **settler** is someone who goes to live in a new country or a new place where there are not many people living.

seven *noun, adjective*

Seven is a number which you can write as 7.

> *Word Building:* **seventh**, *adjective*: *This is the seventh time we have tried to climb the mountain.*

seventeen *noun, adjective*

Seventeen is a number which you can write as 17.

> *Word Building:* **seventeenth**, *adjective*: *The seventeenth person off the bus had to pick up anything the others left behind.*

seventy *noun, adjective*

Seventy is a number which you can write as 70.

> *Word Building:* **seventieth**, *adjective*: *For his seventieth birthday, we will make our grand-father a special cake in the shape of 70.*

several /*say* **sev**-ruhl / *adjective*

If there are **several** people or things, there are more than two of them, but not many of them.

> ✱ *Spelling Tip:* Remember there is an *e* in the middle of **several**, although you usually don't hear it. Also remember that the ending is *al* (with one *l* only). Try breaking the word up as *sev+ er+ al.*

severe /*say* suh-**vear** / *adjective*

Something is **severe** if it is very bad and worrying.

sew /*sounds like* so / *verb*

If you **sew**, you use a needle and thread to join pieces of cloth together or to join something on to cloth. *The sailors had to sew the boat's sail because it was torn.*

> *Word Building:* **sewing**, *noun*: *Mum is good at sewing.*

sex *noun*

A person's **sex** is what makes them be part of either a male or female group. All humans and animals belong to one of these two groups.

shabby *adjective* (**shabbier, shabbiest**)

If something is **shabby**, it looks old because it has been worn or used for such a long time.

shack *noun*

A **shack** is a roughly-made, small house.

shade *noun*

Shade is an area where the light of the sun has been blocked off and so it is a little dark.

> *Word Building:* **shady**, *adjective* (**shadier, shadiest**): *We found a shady place to sit.*

shadow *noun*

A **shadow** is a dark shape made by something or someone who is blocking out light.

shaggy *adjective* (**shaggier, shaggiest**)

Something or someone is **shaggy** if they are covered with long, rough hair.

shake *verb* (**shakes, shaking, shook, has shaken**)

1. If someone or something **shakes**, they move backwards and forwards with very quick, short movements. *Charlotte shook with fear.*

2. If you **shake** something, you make it move backwards and forwards quickly. *She shook the bottle to mix the juice and water together.*

3. shake your head, If you **shake your head**, you move your head quickly or slowly from side to side, to say no or to show disagreement. *I asked Mum if I could go out but she shook her head.*

a b c d e f g h i j k l m n o p q r **s** t u v w x y z

shall *verb*
You use **shall** with *I* or *we* to show you are clearly speaking about the future. *I shall go tomorrow but not today.*

Remember that you always use **shall** with another verb.

shallow *adjective*
Something is **shallow** if it does not go a long way down.

The opposite is **deep**.

shame *noun*
1. Shame is the unhappy feeling that you have when you know you have said or done something wrong or silly. *His face went red with shame when the teacher told the class how rude he had been.*
2. a shame, You say that something is **a shame** when you are sorry about it and wish it could be different. *It's a shame he can't come today.*

Also look up **ashamed**.

shampoo *noun*
Shampoo is a liquid for washing your hair.

shape *noun*
1. A **shape** is the form made by the outside edge of something.
–*verb* **2.** If you **shape** something, you make it into a particular shape. *The present was shaped like a large egg.*

share *noun*
1. Someone's **share** of something is the part given to them or owned by them.
–*verb* **2.** If people **share** something, it is divided into parts and they each have a part. *We all did some work so we decided to share the money equally between us.*
3. If you **share** something with others, you use it and so do the others. *We share a vegetable garden with the people next door.*

shark *noun*
A **shark** is a large fish which is dangerous to other fish and sometimes to people.

sharp *adjective*
Something that is **sharp** has a thin edge that can be used for cutting, or has a point like a needle that could hurt you if it went into you.

The opposite is **blunt**.

shave *verb*
When a man **shaves**, he cuts off the hair that grows on his face so that his skin is smooth. *Dad shaves every morning.*

she *pronoun*
You use **she** to stand for a woman, girl or female animal. *She is my mother. | Judy is my friend. She is taller than I am.*

Also look up **her** and **hers**.

shear *verb* (**shears, shearing, sheared, has sheared** *or* **has shorn**)
If someone **shears** a sheep, they cut off their wool. *On our holidays, we went into the sheds and watched the men shearing the sheep.*

Word Building: **shearer**, *noun* Someone whose job is to shear sheep is a **shearer**.

✸ *Spelling Tip:* Don't confuse the spelling of **shear** with **sheer** which has the same sound but is spelt with a double *e*.

shed *noun*
A **shed** is a small building, often simply made of wood or metal, that you use for keeping things or animals in.

sheep *noun* (*plural* **sheep**)
A **sheep** is an animal which is kept on farms for its meat and its thick wool.

A female sheep is a **ewe**. A male sheep is a **ram**.

sheer *adjective*
If something is **sheer**, it is very steep, almost going straight up and down.

✸ *Spelling Tip:* Don't confuse the spelling of **sheer** with **shear**.

sheet *noun*
1. A **sheet** is a large piece of material which is used to cover a bed and which you sleep on. *The sheets that I like the best on my bed have stars and moons on them.*
2. A **sheet** is a large thin piece of something, such as paper, glass or metal. *I started my drawing on a clean sheet of paper.*

shelf *noun* (*plural* **shelves**)
A **shelf** is a long, thin, flat piece of wood or something similar, fixed to a wall or inside a cupboard, so that you can keep things on it.

shell *noun*
A **shell** is the hard part that covers the outside of an egg or covers the outside of some animals.

shelter *noun*
A **shelter** is something that protects you from bad weather or that keeps you safe from danger.

shield /*say* sheeld / *noun*
1. A **shield** is a broad piece of metal or wood that soldiers once carried when they were fighting. *The soldiers raised their shields and ran towards the enemy.*
2. A **shield** can be anything you use to protect yourself. *We used an umbrella as a shield against the sun.*

> ✴ *Spelling Tip:* Remember the *ie* spelling for the 'ee' sound. This follows the rule that *i* comes before *e* except after *c*.

shift *verb*
If you **shift** something, you move it from one place to another. *I shifted the chair out of the way so my grandmother wouldn't fall over it.*

shine *verb* (**shines**, **shining**, **shone** /*say* shon /, **has shone**)
1. If something **shines**, it gives out light, especially bright light. *The lights of the city were shining in the distance.*
2. If a surface **shines**, it looks bright, often because it has been rubbed hard. *We cleaned Dad's car until it shone.*

> *Word Building:* **shiny**, *adjective* If a surface shines, it is **shiny**. *He rubbed his shoes until they were shiny.*

> ✴ *Spelling Tip:* Remember that **shine** loses its *e* when the adjective **shiny** is formed.

ship *noun*
A **ship** is a very large boat for carrying people or goods over the sea.

shirt *noun*
A **shirt** is a piece of clothing for the top part of your body, usually with buttons down the front.

shiver *verb*
If you **shiver**, you shake because you are cold, frightened or excited. *We were shivering from the cold so we put on some more clothes.*

shock *noun*
A **shock** is what you feel when something unpleasant or surprising happens to you.

shoe *noun* (*plural* **shoes**)
A **shoe** is a covering for your foot, often made of leather.

shoot *verb* (**shoots**, **shooting**, **shot**, **has shot**)
1. If someone **shoots** a person or animal, they hit or kill the person or animal using a gun. *In the film the murderer shot four people.*
2. If you **shoot** a photo of something or someone, you take a photo of them with a camera. *Can I shoot some photos of you while you are giving the speech?*
–*noun* 3. A **shoot** is a new growth on a plant.

shop *noun*
1. A **shop** is a building or part of a building where things are sold.
–*verb* (**shops**, **shopping**, **shopped**, **has shopped**)
2. If you **shop**, you go to a shop or to shops to look for and buy things. *Mum shops every Friday.*

> *Word Building:* **shopper**, *noun*: *The streets were full of shoppers.* –**shopkeeper**, *noun* Someone who owns or runs a shop is a **shopkeeper**.

shopping *noun*
1. **Shopping** is going to a shop or shops to look for and buy things. *Some people like shopping.*
2. **Shopping** is the things that you buy at the shops. *Sometimes, I help Mum to carry the shopping.*

shopping centre *noun*
A **shopping centre** is a place where there are many different shops all found inside a single, huge building.

> You can also call this a **shopping mall**.

shore *noun*
The **shore** is the land along the edge of the sea or a lake.

short *adjective*
1. If something is **short**, it does not measure much from one side to the other or from top to bottom. *That's a very short skirt that Margaret is wearing.*
2. If someone is **short**, they do not have much height. *He is a short man but he is strong.*
3. If something is **short**, it does not go on for much time. *It was only a short holiday – just a couple of days.*

> The opposite of definitions 1 and 3 is **long**; the opposite of definition 2 is **tall**.

a b c d e f g h i j k l m n o p q r **s** t u v w x y z

shorts *noun*
Shorts are short trousers, usually not going below your knees.

You can also say **a pair of shorts**.

shot *noun*
1. A **shot** is the shooting of a gun. *He killed the bird with his third shot.*
2. A **shot** is a photograph. *We took some shots of our house.*
–*verb* **3.** Look up **shoot**.

should /*rhymes with* wood / *verb*
1. You use **should** to show that it is important to do something because it is your duty, or because it is a kind thing to do, or because it is sensible. *We should take Mum breakfast in bed because she is sick.*
2. You use **should** to show that something will probably happen. *The bus should be here soon.*

Remember that **should** is always used with another verb.

shoulder /*rhymes with* folder / *noun*
Your **shoulder** is one of the two parts of your body where your arms join your body.

shout *verb*
1. If you **shout**, you call or cry out loudly, either to make people hear you or because you are angry. *It was so noisy in the restaurant that you had to shout when you talked.*
–*noun* **2.** A **shout** is a loud call.

shove /*say* shuv / *verb*
If you **shove**, you push something or someone in a rough way. *Lloyd shoved all the mess behind the door so the visitors wouldn't see it.*

shovel /*say* **shuv**-uhl / *noun*
A **shovel** is a tool with a long handle and a curved metal front for lifting and moving heavy things like soil or sand.

❇ *Spelling Tip:* Remember that this word comes from *shove* (meaning 'to push') where *ove* spells the 'uv' sound, the same as in *love*. **Shovel** ends with a single *l*.

show *verb* (**shows, showing, showed, has shown**)
1. If you **show** something, you place it so that people can see it. *The students showed their paintings in the school hall.*
2. If you **show** someone something, you let them to see it. *Anita showed me a photo of her house.*

3. If you **show** how to do something, you tell or explain how to do it. *I showed my little brother how to tie his laces.*
4. If something **shows** that something is true, it is a fact that makes people believe that it is true. It proves it is true. *The finger marks on the paint showed that someone had touched it while it was still wet.*
–*noun* **5.** A **show** is a showing of something that people can come and look at. *We went to an art show.*
6. A **show** is an entertainment in a theatre or on television. *We watched a good television show last night.*

shower *noun*
1. A **shower** is a fall of rain that does not last for a long time. *There were a few showers but we kept walking.*
2. A **shower** is a place where you can stand under water that is falling from above and wash your body. *The plumber came to fix the taps in the shower.*
3. A **shower** is washing your body using a shower (definition 2). *Everyone wanted a shower after swimming at the beach.*

shriek /*say* shreek / *noun*
1. A **shriek** is a short, high cry or noise which comes out suddenly and is usually loud.
–*verb* **2.** If you **shriek**, you cry out suddenly when you are excited, frightened or laughing very loudly. *We shrieked with laughter at the jokes he was telling.*

❇ *Spelling Tip:* Remember the *ie* spelling for the 'ee' sound, following the rule that *i* comes before *e* except after *c*.

shrill *adjective*
If a sound is **shrill**, it is very loud and high.

shrink *verb* (**shrinks, shrinking, shrank, has shrunk**)
If something **shrinks**, it gets smaller. *My new jumper got wet in the rain and shrank.*

shrub *noun*
A **shrub** is a small, low tree.

shrug *verb* (**shrugging, shrugged, has shrugged**)
If you **shrug**, you make your shoulders go up and then down, to show that you do not know something or you do not care. *We asked him if he wanted to come but he just shrugged, so we asked Tim instead.*

shudder *verb*
1. If you **shudder**, you shake suddenly because you feel frightened or cold. *They were shuddering as they stood in the cold wind.*
2. You also **shudder** if something unpleasant affects you so much that you shake. *She shuddered at the thought of what would have happened if the boat had sunk.*

shut *verb* (**shuts**, **shutting**, **shut**, **has shut**)
1. If you **shut** something, you move it or move parts of it so that it is not open. *Please shut the door.*
–*adjective* 2. If something is **shut**, it is not open.

shy *adjective* (**shyer**, **shyest**, **shier**, **shiest**)
If you are **shy**, you feel a bit frightened when you have to talk to other people, especially if you do not know them well.

sick *adjective*
If you are **sick**, you have a disease or you do not feel well in your body.

> *Word Building:* **sickness**, *noun* A **sickness** is a disease.

> Another word with a similar meaning is **ill**.

sick bay *noun*
A **sick bay** is the place that you go to if you are feeling sick or if you are hurt while you are at school.

side *noun*
1. A **side** of something is one of its surfaces, usually not the top, bottom, front, or back. *There is a row of trees along the side of our house.*
2. A **side** of something like a piece of paper or cloth is one of its two surfaces. *The paper in this writing pad has lines on one side only.*
3. A **side** is a sports team that plays against other teams. *No wonder we always lose – the other side has really good players.*

sigh /*say* suy/ *verb*
If you **sigh**, you let out your breath slowly and with a soft sound, often because you are tired or sad. *We sighed when we saw how much work there was to do.*

sight /*say* suyt/ *noun*
1. **Sight** is the power to see. *My grandfather has lost his sight.*
2. A **sight** is something which is seen or should be seen. *Our guide showed us the sights of the city.*

> ✴ *Spelling Tip:* Don't confuse the spelling of **sight** with **site** which has the same sound. A **site** is a place.

sightseeing /*say* **suyt**-see-ing/ *noun*
Sightseeing is travelling around looking at objects and places of interest.

sign /*say* suyn/ *noun*
1. A **sign** is anything that shows that something exists, has happened or might happen. *There were signs that someone had been there.*
2. A **sign** is something such as special mark, a special movement or a written notice that gives important information. *The sign said to go left.*
3. A **sign** is a special mark or picture used to mean a particular word, idea or mathematical value. *$ is a dollar sign.*
–*verb* 4. If you **sign** something, you write your name on it. *I finished my letter and signed it.*
5. If you **sign** your name, you write it as you usually do. *She signed her name at the end of the letter.*

> ✴ *Spelling Tip:* Remember the *g* in this word. The group of letters *ign* gives the 'uyn' sound. It comes from the Latin word *signum*. If you remember this, you will be able to spell other words which have *sign* in them, such as *design*.

signal /*say* **sig**-nuhl/ *noun*
A **signal** is a sound, light or movement that tells you something you need to know.

signature /*say* **sig**-nuh-chuh/ *noun*
Your **signature** is the way you write your own name.

> ✴ *Spelling Tip:* Remember that the middle sound is spelt *a*. Think of the word *nature* which is hidden in this word.

silence *noun*
Silence is when there is no sound or noise.

silent *adjective*
1. If someone is **silent**, they not talking or making any sound. *She asked him a question but he remained silent.*
2. If a place is **silent**, there is no sound or noise in it. *The classroom was silent during the test.*

> *Word Building:* **silently**, *adverb* If something is done in a silent way, it is done **silently**.

silk *noun*
Silk is a very fine, soft cloth.

a b c d e f g h i j k l m n o p q r **s** t u v w x y z

silkworm *noun*

A **silkworm** is one of the caterpillars that produce soft threads to cover themselves totally before they turn into moths.

silly *adjective* (**sillier**, **silliest**)

1. If someone is **silly**, they are not very sensible. *Her mother said that she was a silly girl to lose her bag.*
2. If what someone does is **silly**, it shows they do not have good sense. *It is very silly to cross the road without looking carefully first.*
3. If something is **silly**, it doesn't make any sense. *Walking backwards to school is a silly idea.*

Word Building: **silliness**, *noun*: *His silliness makes me angry.*

silo /*say* **suy**-loh/ *noun* (*plural* **silos**)

A **silo** is a tall building which is used for keeping many kinds of grain.

silver *noun*

Silver is a white shiny metal used for making things like jewellery, coins, knives and forks.

silverback *noun*

a fully mature male gorilla with white hair on its back.

similar /*say* **sim**-uh-luh/ *adjective*

If two or more things or two or more people are **similar**, they are like each other in some general way but they are not the same.

Word Building: **similarity** /*say* sim-uh-**la**-ruh-tee/, *noun* When things are similar, there is a **similarity** or there are **similarities** between them.

simple *adjective*

1. If something is **simple**, it is easy to understand, do, or use. *She gave us a simple explanation of how the earth moves around the sun.*
2. If something is **simple**, it does not have anything extra added. It is ordinary. *My mum doesn't like complicated recipes so we eat lots of simple food.*

simply *adverb*

1. If you do something **simply**, you do it in a simple, plain way. You do not add too many things. *She told her story simply and truthfully.*
2. You use **simply** to mean 'only this and nothing more'. *You simply need to fill in this form and you will receive the money.*
3. You use **simply** to make the following word stronger. *Your singing is simply wonderful.*

since *adverb*

1. You use **since** to mean 'from then until now'. *He went to another school and we haven't heard from him since.*
–*preposition* 2. You use **since** to talk about the time that has passed after an earlier time that you have mentioned. *I haven't seen him since yesterday.*
–*conjunction* 3. You use **since** to talk about the time following when something happened. *We have gone down to the oval every day since we bought the dog.*
4. You can use **since** to mean 'because'. *Since the tide was coming in, we had to hurry.*

sincere /*say* sin-**sear**/ *adjective*

If you are **sincere**, you are telling the truth or showing your true feelings.

Word Building: **sincerity** /*say* sin-**se**-ruh-tee/, *noun* If you seem to be sincere, you are showing **sincerity**.

sing *verb* (**sings**, **singing**, **sang**, **has sung**)

When you **sing**, you produce musical sounds with your voice. *I always sing when I feel happy.*

Word Building: **singer**, *noun*: *He is not a very good singer.* –**singing**, *noun*: *I like listening to singing.*

single *adjective*

1. You use **single** to mean 'one and only that one'. *Thousands of people have gone into the competition but only a single person can win.*
2. If someone is **single**, they are not married. *My uncle is still single.*

singlet *noun*

A **singlet** is something you wear on the top part of your body, usually under your other clothes. It usually has narrow pieces that go over your shoulders.

sink *verb* (**sinks**, **sinking**, **sank**, **has sunk**)

1. If something **sinks**, it goes down slowly in water. *The people swam to shore when their boat sank.*
2. If something **sinks**, it goes downwards slowly. *The sun is sinking and it will soon be dark.*
–*noun* 3. A **sink** is a place in a kitchen which you can fill with water from taps above it and use for washing dishes. There is a hole in the bottom where the water goes out.

sir *noun*

Sir is a word that someone can use when they are talking to a man and want to be polite and show respect for him.

> The word you use for a woman is **madam**.

siren *noun*

A **siren** is the loud noise you hear on vehicles like police cars, fire engines and ambulances to warn people that they are coming.

sister *noun*

Someone's **sister** is a woman or girl who has the same parents as them.

sit *verb* (**sits**, **sitting**, **sat**, **has sat**)

When you **sit**, you rest with your legs forward and your back straight up, with the bottom part of your body on something like a chair or on the ground. *Let's sit here for a while. These chairs are comfortable.*

site *noun*

1. A **site** is the land where something is built or will soon be built. *It was a fantastic site for a holiday house – right near the beach.*
2. A **site** is a place on the internet that you get to by typing in an address and where you find information on a particular subject. *My mum has found a site which has a lot of recipes for fruit cakes.*

> **Site** as in definition 2 is short for **website**.

> ✴ *Spelling Tip:* Don't confuse the spelling of **site** with **sight** which has the same sound. **Sight** is the ability to see.

situation /*say* si-chooh-**ay**-shuhn/ *noun*

A **situation** is the way things are in a particular time or place, or for a particular person.

> ✴ *Spelling Tip:* Remember that there is neither a *ch* nor a *sh* spelling in this word but there are two separate *t*'s. The first *t* with the following *u* gives a 'chooh' sound, and the second *t* forms part of the *tion* ending which gives a 'shuhn' sound. Try breaking the word up as *sit+ u + a + tion*.

six *noun*, *adjective*

Six is a number which you can write as 6.

> *Word Building:* **sixth**, *adjective*: *You are the sixth person who has wished me a happy birthday.*

sixteen *noun*, *adjective*

Sixteen is a number which you can write as 16.

> *Word Building:* **sixteenth**, *adjective*: *The sixteenth person couldn't come so there were only fifteen at my party.*

sixty *noun*, *adjective*

Sixty is a number which you can write as 60.

> *Word Building:* **sixtieth**, *adjective*: *For my grandmother's sixtieth birthday, we are giving her a pet canary.*

size *noun*

The **size** of something is how much it measures. It is how big or small something is.

sizzle *verb*

If something **sizzles** while it is cooking in oil or fat, it makes a 'sss' noise like a snake does. *John started to get really hungry when he could hear the bacon sizzling in the pan.*

skate *noun*

1. A **skate** is a special shoe with a long, sharp part underneath, which you wear to move on ice (an **ice skate**), or with wheels under it that you use to move quickly along the ground (a **rollerskate**).
–*verb* 2. If you **skate**, you move easily over ice wearing skates, or you rollerskate. *The ice is not yet strong enough to skate on.*

> *Word Building:* **skater**, *noun*: *She is a very good skater.* –**skating**, *noun*: *She is good at skating.*

skateboard *noun*

1. A **skateboard** is a narrow, wooden or plastic board, with wheels attached to the bottom, which you usually ride while standing up.
–*verb* 2. If you **skateboard**, you move along, riding a skateboard.

skeleton /*say* **skel**-uh-tuhn/ *noun*

A **skeleton** is all the bones inside the body of a person or an animal.

> ✴ *Spelling Tip:* Remember that the middle sound is spelt *e*. Don't 'let on' but there is a **skeleton** inside each one of us, just as the words *let on* are hidden inside the word **skeleton**.

ski *noun* (*plural* **skis**)

1. A **ski** is a long, thin piece of wood or other material that you attach to your shoe, that lets you move easily over the snow.
–*verb* (**skis**, **skiing**, **ski'd** *or* **skied**, **has ski'd** *or* **has skied**)

2. If you **ski**, you move quickly over the snow, wearing skis. *Bella can ski down the mountain as fast as her parents.*

> *Word Building:* **skier**, *noun* A person who skis is a **skier**.

skid *verb* (**skids**, **skidding**, **skidded**, **has skidded**)
If something or someone **skids**, they slide forward or to the side on something slippery or smooth. *Our bikes skidded on the wet grass.*

skill *noun*
If you have **skill** at something, you do it very well.

> *Word Building:* **skilful**, *adjective* If you do something with skill, you are **skilful** at it. –**skilfully**, *adverb*: *She repaired the clock very skilfully.*

> ✱ *Spelling Tip:* Remember you drop one of the *l*'s at the end of **skill** to make the word **skilful**. And, as usual, the ending *ful* (meaning 'full of') is spelt with one *l*. So be a **skilful** speller and remember that the *l* is single both times it appears in this word.

skim *verb* (**skims**, **skimming**, **skimmed**, **has skimmed**)
1. If you **skim** something that has formed on the top of a liquid, you take it off. *Dad skimmed the cream from the top of the milk.*
2. If a person or animal **skims** over the top of something, they move over it in a quick, light way. *Look how the birds skim across the lake.*

skin *noun*
1. Your **skin** is the thin, outside covering of your body or the similar covering on the body of animals. *Be careful your skin doesn't get burnt in the sun.*
2. The **skin** is the outside covering of some fruit and vegetables. *The rubbish bin was full of potato skins.*

skinny *adjective* (**skinnier**, **skinniest**)
If someone is **skinny**, they are thin and there is not much fat on their body.

skip *verb* (**skips**, **skipping**, **skipped**, **has skipped**)
1. If you **skip**, you move along lightly, putting one foot down, then the other. *Our leg muscles were sore after we skipped round the oval twice.*
2. If you **skip** something, you leave it out or do not do it. *I skipped some bits of the book because they were boring.*

skirt *noun*
A **skirt** is a piece of outer clothing, worn by women and girls, that covers the lower part of the body.

skull *noun*
A **skull** is the bony part of your head, covering your brain.

sky *noun* (*plural* **skies**)
The **sky** is the part of the air above the earth where the clouds are and where you can see the sun, moon and stars.

> The plural **skies** is mainly used when someone is talking about the weather: *At last there were clear skies again after all the rain.*

skydiving *noun*
Skydiving is the sport of jumping from a plane and falling through the air before opening a parachute.

slack *adjective*
1. If something like a rope is **slack**, it is loose. It is not stretched tight. *The rope went slack and we knew that Peter must have let go at the other end.*
2. If someone has done **slack** work, they have done it carelessly. *The teacher said that his work was slack and he must try harder.*

slam *verb* (**slams**, **slamming**, **slammed**, **has slammed**)
If you **slam** something, you shut it so hard that it makes a loud noise. *Andrew was in a bad mood and slammed his door as hard as he could.*

slap *verb* (**slaps**, **slapping**, **slapped**, **has slapped**)
If someone **slaps** you, they hit you quickly, with their hand open. *Mum slapped me on the arm to squash the mosquito on it.*

slash *verb*
If someone **slashes** something, they cut it in a violent way with a sharp cutting tool. *Someone slashed the tyres of my bike.*

slate *noun*
Slate is a rock which is easy to split into thin layers. It is used to cover roofs and floors.

slave *noun*
A **slave** is someone who works without being paid and is the prisoner of someone else.

sleep *verb* (**sleeps**, **sleeping**, **slept**, **has slept**)
When you **sleep**, you rest with your eyes closed and with your mind not knowing what is happening around you. *I couldn't sleep during the storm.*

a b c d e f g h i j k l m n o p q r **s** t u v w x y z

> *Word Building:* **sleepy**, *adjective* If you are tired and want to sleep, you are **sleepy**. –**sleepiness**, *noun* If you are tired and want to sleep, you have a feeling of **sleepiness**.

sleeve *noun*
A **sleeve** is the part of a shirt, coat or dress that covers your arm.

sleigh /*say* slay/ *noun*
A **sleigh** is a kind of vehicle people use for travelling over the snow. It has lengths of metal underneath so it slides and it is usually pulled along by horses.

> ❄ *Spelling Tip:* Remember the *eigh* spelling for the 'ay' sound. It might help if you think of other words with the same spelling for this sound, such as *eight* and *weigh*.

slender *adjective*
Someone or something is **slender** if they are thin in an attractive way.

slice *verb*
1. If you **slice** something, you cut it into pieces. *It was very hard to slice my birthday cake into even pieces.*
–*noun* **2.** A thin piece of something is a **slice**.

slide *verb* (**slides**, **sliding**, **slid**, **has slid**)
If something or someone **slides**, they move along smoothly. *The drawers of the cupboard should slide in and out easily.*

slightly /*say* **sluyt**-lee/ *adverb*
You use **slightly** to mean 'a little' or 'a bit'. *My sister is slightly taller than me but I will catch up to her one day.*

slim *adjective* (**slimmer**, **slimmest**)
If you are **slim**, you are thin and not fat.

sling *noun*
1. A **sling** is a piece of cloth tied around your neck to hold your arm steady if it is hurt.
–*verb* (**slings**, **slinging**, **slung**, **has slung**)
2. If you **sling** something, you throw it in a careless way. *Jonathon was sitting by the lake slinging pebbles across the water.*

slip *verb* (**slips**, **slipping**, **slipped**, **has slipped**)
If you **slip**, you fall over. *Be careful not to slip on the floor – it's just been washed.*

slippery *adjective*
If something is **slippery**, it is so smooth or wet that it is hard to hold or to walk on.

slit *noun*
A **slit** is a long, straight cut or opening in something.

slope *verb*
If something **slopes**, it is higher at one end than at the other. *We put the tent on a bit of a hill so everything was sloping downwards.*

slot *noun*
A **slot** is a narrow opening or hole, often for putting money in.

slow *adjective*
1. If someone or something is **slow**, they are not moving quickly. *She is a slow swimmer.*
2. If something is **slow**, it does not happen quickly or it is not done quickly. It takes a long time. *It was a slow journey.*
3. If a clock or watch is **slow**, it shows a time that is behind the real time. *The clock in my bedroom is five minutes slow.*

> *Word Building:* **slowly**, *adverb*: *The old man walked slowly.* –**slowness**, *noun*: *The slowness of the trip was annoying.*

> The opposite of definitions 1 and 2 is **quick** or **fast**; the opposite of definition 3 is **fast**.

slug *noun*
A **slug** is a small, wet and slippery animal like a snail without its shell.

slum *noun*
A **slum** is a place where many poor people live crowded together.

sly *adjective*
If someone is **sly**, they do things in a way that is not honest or truthful.

smack *verb*
If someone **smacks** a person or animal, they hit them with their hand open. *I smacked my dog for jumping up on me.*

small *adjective*
If something or someone is **small**, they are not big.

smart *adjective*
1. If someone is **smart**, they are clever. *He's pretty smart. He can do maths problems we haven't even learned about.*
2. If clothes are **smart**, they look neat and modern. *My dad looked good in his smart new trousers.*

smart phone *noun*

A **smart phone** is a mobile phone that has access to the internet.

You can also write this as **smartphone**.

smash *verb*

1. If something **smashes**, it breaks into pieces with a loud noise. *The window smashed with the force of the storm.*
2. If you **smash** something, you do something to make the thing break into pieces with a loud noise. *Annie dropped her plate onto the ground and smashed it.*

smell *noun*

1. **Smell** is the ability to know about something through the nose. *Many animals have a very good sense of smell.*
2. The **smell** of something is a special thing about it that you can notice through your nose. *I love the smell of mangoes.*
–*verb* (**smells**, **smelling**, **smelt** *or* **smelled**, **has smelt** *or* **has smelled**)
3. If you **smell** something, you know about it through your nose. *I can smell a fire burning.*
4. If something **smells**, it gives off a smell (definition 2). *These flowers smell lovely.* | *Those old shoes smell terrible.*
5. You can say something **smells** when it gives off a bad smell. *The dog smells – he needs a wash.*

Word Building: **smelly**, *adjective* (**smellier**, **smelliest**) If something has a bad smell, it is **smelly**.

smile *verb*

1. When you **smile**, you show you are happy by making your mouth wider and turning it up at the corners, often showing your teeth. *We all had to smile for the camera.*
–*noun* **2.** A **smile** is how your face looks when you smile.

smoke *noun*

1. **Smoke** is what you see going up in the air when something burns.
–*verb* **2.** If someone **smokes**, they breathe in the smoke of a cigarette, while holding it between their lips. *Not many people smoke these days.*

Word Building: **smoking**, *noun*: *Smoking is not allowed in restaurants.*

smooth *adjective*

If something is **smooth**, it is flat and does not have any rough parts or parts that are not even.

Word Building: **smoothly**, *adverb*: *Our boat moved smoothly across the lake.* –**smoothness**, *noun*: *Feel the smoothness of the baby's skin.*

smoulder /rhymes with folder/ *verb*

If something **smoulders**, it burns slowly with smoke, but without flame. *A few big logs were still smouldering at the end of the night.*

SMS message *noun*

Look up **text message**.

SMS stands for *Short Messaging Service*.

smudge *noun*

A **smudge** is a dirty mark.

smuggle *verb*

If you **smuggle** something, you take something you should not have into or out of a country without anyone finding out. *People can go to jail if they smuggle parrots out of Australia.*

Word Building: **smuggler**, *noun* A person who smuggles is a **smuggler**.

snack *noun*

A **snack** is a small amount of food you eat quickly.

snail *noun*

A **snail** is a small animal with a soft body covered by a thin shell on top. *Snails move very slowly.*

snake *noun*

A **snake** is an animal with a long thin body and no legs. Some **snake** bites can affect people in a way that can make them sick or even kill them.

snap *verb* (**snaps**, **snapping**, **snapped**, **has snapped**)

If something **snaps**, it breaks with a sudden sharp sound. *The branch snapped in two when Dad tried to hang the swing from it.*

snarl *verb*

If someone or something **snarls**, they make a low, angry, rough sound. *'Get out of here', he snarled.* | *The dog began to snarl as I walked towards it.*

snatch *verb*

If you **snatch** something, you take it suddenly. *A thief snatched Belinda's mobile phone when she wasn't looking.*

sneak *verb*

If you **sneak**, you move or take something in a way that you hope you will not be seen. You act in a quiet or secret way. *Try to sneak past without them seeing you.*

> **Word Building: sneaky**, *adjective* If you like to sneak about or sneak things, then you are **sneaky**.

sneer *verb*
If you **sneer** at someone, you speak or look at them in a mean way that shows you think they are stupid. *Don't sneer at me – you don't know the answer either.*

sneeze *verb*
If you **sneeze**, you breathe air into your nose and then suddenly blow it out again through your mouth and nose making a very big noise. *You sneeze a lot when you have a cold.*

sniff *verb*
If you **sniff**, you breathe in quickly through your nose in a way which makes a noise. *I know you've got a cold, but please don't sniff – blow your nose!*

snob *noun*
A **snob** is someone who thinks that only rich, well-known or clever people are important and is not interested in anyone else.

snore *verb*
If you **snore**, you breathe in a noisy way while you are asleep. *We were all awake in the tent because Ted snored so loudly.*

snorkel *noun*
A **snorkel** is a tube that lets you breathe fresh air as you swim with your face just under the water.

snort *verb*
If you **snort**, you breathe out hard through your nose with the loud, blowing sound a horse makes. *We could hear the pigs snorting as they ate their food.*

snow *noun*
1. **Snow** is frozen water which falls to the ground as tiny white bits (called **snowflakes**).
–*verb* 2. When it **snows**, snow falls to the ground. *It snowed for two weeks.*

snowboard *noun*
1. A **snowboard** is a board on which you can stand on and glide over the snow, with your feet strapped onto it.
–*verb* 2. If you **snowboard**, you glide over the snow on a snowboard. *When we went to the snow for our holidays, we snowboarded every day.*

> **Word Building: snowboarder**, *noun* Someone who rides a snowboard is a **snowboarder**.

snuggle *verb*
If people or animals **snuggle** up, they lie closely together for warmth or comfort. *The kittens snuggled up in their basket.*

so *adverb* You use **so** in many ways, for example:
1. when you are talking about how much, how big or how fast something is. *Do not walk so quickly.*
2. to make the following word stronger. *He is so naughty.*
3. to mean 'also'. *I am tall and so is Josh.*
–*conjunction* 4. You use **so** when you are saying a reason for something. *It is raining so we cannot go outside.*
5. **so ... that**, You use **so** with **that** when you are talking about how much or how big, something is and what the result of this is. *The mountain is so high that I cannot see the top.*
6. **so that**, You use **so that** when you giving the reason for something happening or being done. *The teacher made him go outside so that everybody else could work.*

soak *verb*
If you **soak** something, you make it very wet, often by leaving it in water for a long time. *Mum soaked our clothes in a bucket to try to get out the dirt.*

soap *noun*
Soap is something that you use for washing yourself or for washing clothes or other things.

soar /*sounds like* saw/ *verb*
If something **soars**, it flies up into the sky the way a bird does. *The kite soared higher and higher as the wind carried it away.*

soccer *noun*
Soccer is a game that two teams play with a round ball that they are not allowed to touch with their hands.

society /*say* suh-**suy**-uh-tee/ *noun* (*plural* **societies**)
1. **Society** is people as a whole. *Scientists say that people in our society eat too much.*
2. A **society** is a group of people who are interested in the same thing. *My aunt belongs to a society that is interested in rare plants.*

sock *noun*
A **sock** is a piece of clothing that you wear under a shoe, covering your foot and a bit higher and sometimes reaching up to the knee.

sofa *noun*
A **sofa** is a long, comfortable seat with sides and a back, for two or more people.

Other words that mean the same are **couch** and **lounge**.

soft *adjective*
  1. If something is **soft**, you can easily change it or press it into a different shape. *I don't like sleeping on a bed that is too soft.*
  2. If something is **soft**, it is smooth and nice to touch. *A cat has soft fur.*
  3. If a sound is **soft**, it is low and not easy to hear. *We could hardly hear her soft voice.*

  Word Building: **softly**, *adverb: She spoke so softly that we couldn't hear her.* –**softness**, *noun: Feel the softness of this material.*

  The opposite of definition 1 is **hard**; the opposite of definition 3 is **loud**.

softball *noun*
  Softball is a ball game, similar to baseball, played by two teams in which a long, thin bat is used to hit a ball.

software *noun*
  Software is the collection of programs that are put into a computer to make it do certain things.

soil *noun*
  Soil is earth of the ground, especially the kind that plants can grow in.

solar /*say* **soh**-luh/ *adjective*
  Something is **solar** if it has to do with the sun.

solar energy *noun*
  Solar energy is a type of energy that is made by the sun.

soldier /*say* **sohl**-juh/ *noun*
  A **soldier** is someone who belongs to an army and is trained to fight on land.

sole *noun*
  The **sole** is the bottom part of your foot or of a shoe.

solemn /*say* **sol**-uhm/ *adjective*
  Something that is **solemn** is very serious.

  ❇ *Spelling Tip:* Don't forget the silent *n* at the end.

solid *adjective*
  1. If something is **solid** it is hard and has a shape. It is not like liquids and gases that can change their shapes. *Wood is solid but water is not.*
  2. If something is **solid**, it has its inside full of the same material that the outside is made of. There

are no empty spaces or other kinds of material in it. *You play this game with a solid rubber ball.*

  Think about how definition 1 is different from **gas** and **liquid**.

solo *noun* (*plural* **solos**)
  A **solo** is music you play or a song you sing all by yourself.

  Word Building: **soloist**, *noun* Someone who performs a solo is a **soloist**.

solve *verb*
  If you **solve** something, you find the answer to it. *The police are trying to solve the mystery of the missing jewels.*

some *adjective*, *pronoun*
  You use **some** to talk about a number or amount when you are not saying exactly what number or amount.

someone *pronoun*
  You use **someone** to talk about a person when you do not know who the person is or when it is not important who the person is. *I can hear someone at the door.*

  You can also say **somebody**.

somersault /*say* **sum**-uh-solt/ *noun*
  A **somersault** is a way of putting your head down and rolling your body forward over your head.

  ❇ *Spelling Tip:* You may feel hot after doing **somersaults**, but this word has nothing to do with summer, nor anything to do with salt. It comes from French, and before that from two Latin words meaning 'over' and 'leap'. Try splitting it into its two parts and memorising them – *somer*, then *sault* (like *salt* but with a *u* added in).

something *pronoun*
  You use **something** when you don't know exactly what a thing is or when it is not important to say exactly what it is. *Something is making her sad but I don't know what.*

sometimes *adverb*
  If something happens **sometimes**, it happens at some times and not at other times. *Sometimes she arrives on time, and sometimes she's late.*

somewhere /*say* **sum**-wair/ *adverb*
  You use **somewhere** to say that someone or something is in, at or to some particular place which you do not know or which is not important. *I've put my bag down somewhere. I can't find it.*

son *noun*
If someone has a male child, they have a **son**. He may be a boy or he may have grown up to be a man.

song *noun*
A **song** is a short piece of music with words that you can sing.

soon *adverb*
If something will happen **soon**, it will happen after a short time only. *I'll see you soon.*

soothe /*say* soohdh/ *verb*
If you **soothe** someone who is hurt or sad, you try to make them feel happy and calm again. *The coach tried to soothe the team after they lost their final match.*

sore *adjective*
1. If part of your body is **sore**, you feel pain there.
–*noun* **2.** A **sore** is a small part on the outside of your body which hurts because the skin has been broken there.

> ✷ *Spelling Tip:* Don't confuse the spelling of **sore** with **saw** which sounds the same. A **saw** is a cutting tool. **Saw** is also a form of **see**: *I saw her yesterday.*

sorry *adjective* (**sorrier**, **sorriest**)
1. If you are **sorry**, you feel sad because you have done something wrong and you want to say that you wish you had not done it. *I am very sorry that I was so rude to you.*
2. If you are **sorry**, you feel sad because something bad has happened to someone. *We felt sorry for our neighbours because they had to move away.*
–*interjection* **3.** You can say **Sorry!** when you want to tell someone that you did not mean to do something that has hurt them in some way. *Sorry, I did not mean to put salt in your tea. I thought it was sugar.*

sort *noun*
1. A **sort** is a kind or type of something.
–*verb* **2.** If you **sort** things, you put them into groups of the same kind or type. *We need to sort the oranges. Put the large ones here and the small ones over there.*

soul /*say* sohl/ *noun*
Some people think that the **soul** is a part of a person which you cannot see but which makes them that special person. Some people also believe that a person's soul lives on after the body of the person dies.

Another word that means nearly the same is **spirit**.

sound *noun*
1. **Sound** is what you can hear with your ears. *There was no sound in the room. | My parents don't like the sound of modern music. | I think I heard a sound in the next room.*
–*verb* **2.** If something **sounds** a particular way, it seems that way when you hear it. *Her voice sounded strange.*

sound system *noun*
A **sound system** is a collection of machines that produce sound like a CD player, cassette recorder and radio.

soup *noun*
Soup is a food made mainly of a liquid with meat, fish, or vegetables in it or the taste of these things in it.

sour *adjective*
If something is **sour**, it is not sweet but has a sharp taste that some people think is unpleasant.

source /*rhymes with* horse/ *noun*
A **source** is the place or thing that something comes from.

south /*say* sowth/ *noun*
1. **South** is the direction which is to your left when you look towards where the sun goes down.
–*adjective* **2.** If something is **south**, it is in or towards the south.
–*adverb* **3.** If something goes **south**, it goes towards the south. *The boat sailed south.*

> *Word Building:* **southern** /*say* **sudh**-uhn/, *adjective* Something is **southern** when it is in or towards the south.

> The opposite direction is **north**. The other directions are **east** and **west**.

souvenir /*say* sooh-vuh-**near**/ *noun*
A **souvenir** is something you keep to remind you of a place.

> ✷ *Spelling Tip:* Remember the *ou* spelling for the 'ooh' sound, and the rather unusual *ir* ending. **Souvenir** comes from French, where it means 'to remember'.

sow[1] /rhymes with go/ *verb* (**sows**, **sowing**, **sowed**, **has sown**, **sowed**)

If you **sow**, you spread seeds in the earth so that they will grow. *The farmer will sow this field with wheat, and that one with corn.*

sow[2] /rhymes with how/ *noun*

A **sow** is a female pig.

soybean *noun*

A **soybean** is the seed of an Asian plant that can be eaten as a bean or used for oil.

> You can also use **soy** or **soya bean**.

soy sauce *noun*

Soy sauce is a dark brown sauce that tastes very salty, used in Asian cooking.

> This is also called **soya sauce**.

space *noun*

1. Space is the place outside of the world where the sun, moon and stars are. *Maybe one day someone will travel through space and land on another planet.*

2. Space is an area that is empty. *Let's move this table out so that we have more space.*

3. Space is an empty area that is big enough to be used for a particular purpose. *Is there space for me in the back of the car? | We had to write our answer in the space underneath.*

> You can also say **outer space** for definition 1.

spaceship *noun*

A **spaceship** is a vehicle which travels into outer space.

> You can also say **spacecraft**.

spade *noun*

A **spade** is a tool with a long handle and a wide, flat metal part, for digging the ground in your garden.

spaghetti /*say* spuh-**get**-ee/ *noun*

Spaghetti is a food made from flour, water and salt, cut into long, thin lengths and cooked in boiling water. It is a kind of pasta.

> ✳ *Spelling Tip:* Don't forget the silent *h* following the *g*. Also remember the *i* ending. **Spaghetti** is spelt like this because it comes from Italian.

spank *verb*

If someone **spanks** you, they hit you with their hand, usually to punish you for something.

spanner *noun*

A **spanner** is a tool for holding something tight and turning it around. You often use a **spanner** to undo a nut or make it tighter.

spare *adjective*

If something is **spare**, it is extra. You do not need it now but you might need it later.

spark *noun*

1. A **spark** is a tiny piece of burning wood or coal that shoots up from a fire. *A few sparks spat out of the fire and fell onto the carpet.*

2. A **spark** is a sudden burst of light, made by electricity. *Be careful of that plug – there were sparks coming from it.*

sparkle *verb*

If something **sparkles**, it sends out little bursts of light. *The sunlight made her diamond ring sparkle.*

sparrow *noun*

A **sparrow** is a small brown bird, common in many parts of the world.

speak *verb* (**speaks**, **speaking**, **spoke**, **has spoken**)

1. When you **speak**, you say words in your ordinary voice. *She didn't hear him speak.*

2. If you can **speak** a particular language, you know the words of that language and are able to use it. *Can you speak Italian?*

> *Word Building:* **speaker**, *noun*: *There will be three speakers at the meeting.*

spear *noun*

A **spear** is a weapon with a long handle and a sharp point at the end, used for hunting or fighting.

special /*say* **spesh**-uhl/ *adjective*

1. If something is **special**, it is of a particular kind. It is for a particular group of people or has a particular use. *We get a special bus to go the swimming carnival.*

2. If something is **special**, it is more important than usual. It is different from what is ordinary. *Today is a special day – it's my birthday.*

> *Word Building:* **specially**, *adverb*: *Mum bought a dress specially to wear to the wedding.*

specialist /*say* **spesh**-uhl-uhst/ *noun*

A **specialist** is a person who knows a lot about an area of study or work, such as a doctor who works in one particular part of medicine.

species /say **spee**-seez/ noun (plural **species**)
A **species** is one of the groups into which animals and plants are divided.

speck noun
A **speck** is a very small piece or bit of something.

> **Word Building: speckled**, adjective Something with specks on it is **speckled**.

speech noun (plural **speeches**)
1. **Speech** is the power to speak. *The sound made by some birds is almost like speech.*
2. A **speech** is when someone speaks in front of a group of people. *Our school captain made a good speech wishing all the best to the team.*

speed noun
1. **Speed** is quickness in moving, going, or doing something. *We were amazed at the speed of the trains in Japan.*
2. **Speed** is how fast or how slow something or someone moves. *He started running at a slow speed and then got faster.*

spell[1] verb (**spells, spelling, spelt** or **spelled, has spelt** or **has spelled**)
When you **spell**, you say or write the letters of a word in the correct order. *Wayang can spell very well.*

> **Word Building: spelling**, noun: *I always have trouble with the spelling of 'elephant'.* –**speller**, noun: *I wish I was a good speller.*

spell[2] noun
A **spell** is a group of words that is supposed to make things happen that do not normally happen. You read about people who have magic powers and can 'cast' **spells** in some stories.

spend verb (**spends, spending, spent, has spent**)
1. When you **spend** money, you pay it out, usually to buy things. *I spent a lot of money today buying Christmas presents for my family.*
2. When you **spend** a period of time doing something, you do that thing during that time. *Anna's family always spend their holidays at the beach.*

spice noun
A **spice** is something you use to make food taste better or to keep it from going bad. **Spices** come from plants.

> **Word Building: spicy**, adjective Food cooked with lots of spices is **spicy**.

> ✳ **Spelling Tip:** Notice that you drop the *e* from the end of **spice** to make the word **spicy**.

spider noun
A **spider** is a small creature, like an insect, but with eight legs and no wings. Some **spiders** can bite people in a way that makes them sick or kills them.

spike noun
A **spike** is a sharp, pointed bit that sticks out from something.

> **Word Building: spiky**, adjective Something with spikes is **spiky**.

spill verb (**spills, spilling, spilt, has spilt**)
If you **spill** something, you let it run or fall from the container that is holding it. *If you bump me, I'll spill the milk.*

spin verb (**spins, spinning, spun, has spun**)
1. If something **spins**, it turns around and around very fast. *The wheels of the bike were spinning around.*
2. If you **spin** something, you make it turn very fast. *Spin the coin and see whether it drops down heads or tails.*
3. If you **spin**, you pull cotton or wool into long thin lengths and wind it around to make threads. *People used to spin their own wool but now it is spun on big machines.*
4. Spiders **spin** their webs by letting out a long, sticky thread from their bodies and making something like a net with it. *It is amazing to watch a spider spin its web.*

spinach /say **spin**-ich/ noun
Spinach is a plant with large, green leaves which you can eat as a vegetable.

> ✳ **Spelling Tip:** Remember that there is only one *n* in **spinach**. Also remember that the ending is *ach*.

spine noun
1. Your **spine** is the long row of bones in your back. *Laura has hurt her spine and has to rest it to make it better.*
2. A **spine** is a stiff pointed thing on an animal or a plant. *Watch out for the spines on that fish – they can hurt you.*

> **Word Building: spiny**, adjective Anything with spines or with leaves shaped like spines is **spiny**.

spirit *noun*

1. Some people believe that a person's **spirit** is a part of them which you cannot see but which makes them that particular person. They believe that the **spirit** is like their soul and lives on after the person's body dies. *'Her spirit is in heaven,' he said.*

2. Some people believe in **spirits** who are not part of the normal world but who can change things that happen in the world. *She was afraid that she had done something wrong and made the spirits angry.*

3. If someone has **spirit**, they are brave or they keep doing things even when they are difficult. *She has plenty of spirit – she will be at the game even though her leg is injured.*

4. in good spirits, If you are **in good spirits**, you are feeling happy. *Melissa has just found out she's won a spelling competition so she's in very good spirits.*

spit *verb* (**spits**, **spitting**, **spat**, **spit**, **has spat** *or* **has spit**)

1. If you **spit**, you send liquid out from your mouth. *It is very rude to spit at someone.*

2. If you **spit** something out, you send it out from your mouth. *The meat tasted so terrible that I spat it out.*

spite *noun*

1. If you do something out of **spite**, you do it because you want to hurt someone in some way. *Sasha hit Andre out of spite.*

2. in spite of, You use **in spite of** when you are saying that something is going to happen even though something else has happened which might have stopped it. *We will play in spite of the bad weather.*

> **Word Building: spiteful**, *adjective* If you are full of spite, then you are **spiteful**.

splash *verb*

1. If you **splash** someone or something, you wet them by putting drops of liquid over them. *Tom jumped into the pool and splashed everyone who was standing on the side.*

2. If you **splash** around in water, you jump in the water or hit it so that it flies around. *The kindergarten kids were having a great time splashing in the pool.*

–*noun* **3.** A **splash** is a sound like the one the water makes when you jump in.

splendid *adjective*

If something is **splendid**, it is very beautiful to look at or very good in another way.

splint *noun*

A **splint** is a thin piece of something hard and straight, such as wood, which is fastened on both sides of a broken bone to hold it in place.

splinter *noun*

A **splinter** is a thin, sharp piece of wood, metal or glass.

split *verb* (**splits**, **splitting**, **split**)

If something **splits**, it breaks into parts, usually from one end to the other. *The peach was too ripe and had split open.*

spoil *verb* (**spoils**, **spoiling**, **spoiled** *or* **spoilt**, **has spoiled** *or* **has spoilt**)

If something or someone **spoils** something, they hurt it or change it so that it is no good any more or it cannot be used any more. *The rain spoiled our beach holiday.*

> **Word Building: spoilt**, *adjective*: *a spoilt child.*

spoken *verb*

1. Look up **speak**.

–*adjective* **2.** If something is **spoken**, it is said, not written.

sponge /*say* spunj/ *noun*

1. A **sponge** is a material with lots of holes for taking in water and other liquids. You use it for cleaning things. *We need a new sponge for the kitchen – this one is too dirty.*

2. A **sponge** is a cake that is very easy to eat because it is so light. *My grandmother made a sponge filled with jam and cream.*

> ✳ **Spelling Tip:** Remember the *o* spelling in this word, although it sounds like 'u'.

spoon *noun*

A **spoon** is a tool with an oval or round end which you use for stirring or eating soft or liquid food like soup.

sport *noun*

1. Sport is when people play games or go in races for exercise, fun or competition. *She is not interested in sport. She never watches it on television.*

2. A **sport** is a particular game. *Tennis is an exciting sport to watch.*

> **Word Building: sporting**, *adjective* A **sporting** event is one where sport is played. –**sports**, *adjective* You use **sports** to describe something that is for sport or something that

has to do with sport. *We have a sports day at school once a year.*

spot *noun*
1. A **spot** is a small, round mark. *There's a spot of gravy on your shirt.* | *Lots of teenagers have spots on their face.*
2. A **spot** is a place. *We sat in a nice, sunny spot and had a picnic.*
–*verb* (**spots, spotting, spotted, has spotted**)
3. If you **spot** someone or something, you see them. *Can you spot Yael in the photo – she's the one in the middle.*

spout *noun*
A **spout** is the specially shaped part of something like a kettle which makes it easy to pour liquid out.

sprain *verb*
If you **sprain** a part of your body, you damage it accidentally by moving it in in an unusual way. *I sprained my ankle playing soccer.*

spray *verb*
If you **spray** water or some other liquid, you spread tiny drops of it on someone or something. *It was a very hot day so Sally and Ben sprayed themselves with the hose.*

spread *verb* (**spreads, spreading, spread, has spread**)
1. If something **spreads**, it moves so that it covers more or reaches further. *The fire started in the kitchen and quickly spread to the whole house.*
2. If you **spread** something, you make it go to more places or people. *You can spread colds if you cough without covering your mouth.*
3. If you **spread** something out, you make it flat instead of folded so that it reaches as far as it can. *Dad spread out the cloth to see if it was big enough to cover the table.*
4. If you **spread** something over or on something, you make it cover that thing. *He spread some butter on his toast.*

spring[1] *noun*
1. A **spring** is a piece of wire that is rolled around and around very tightly. It jumps back into shape when you stretch it out or push it in.
–*verb* (**springs, springing, sprang, has sprung**)
2. If you **spring**, you jump up suddenly. *Lyn sprang out of bed as soon as she heard the alarm.*

spring[2] *noun*
Spring is the season of the year after winter when it starts to warm up; new leaves start to grow on trees and lots of flowers come out.

The other seasons of the year are **summer**, **autumn** and **winter**.

sprinkle *verb*
If you **sprinkle** something, you let little bits or drops of it fall. *I sprinkled too much pepper on my meal and now I can't eat it.*

sprint *verb*
If you **sprint**, you run a short way as fast as you can. *Makiko sprinted down the last 20 metres and beat everybody else.*

sprout *verb*
1. If a seed **sprouts**, it starts to grow by sending out a new growth. *The seeds on our nature table have started to sprout – little bits of green are beginning to come out of them.*
–*noun* 2. The **sprout** of a seed is the new growth that comes out of it. Some vegetable seeds have **sprouts** that you can eat.

spurt *verb*
If something **spurts**, it suddenly flows or runs out very fast. *Water spurted from the broken pipe.*

spy *noun* (*plural* **spies**)
1. A **spy** is someone who watches people without them knowing and who finds out everything about them.
–*verb* (**spies, spying, spied, has spied**)
2. If you **spy** on someone, you watch them secretly and report everything you find out about them. *Our government sent people to spy on another country to find out what secret weapons they were making.*

squabble /*rhymes with* wobble/ *verb*
If you **squabble**, you fight or argue about little things that are not important. *They always squabble about whose turn it is to set the table.*

squad /*rhymes with* rod/ *noun*
A **squad** is a small group of people who work or play together.

square *noun*
1. A **square** is a shape with four straight sides that are all the same length. *We had to draw a square and a circle.*
2. A **square** is an open place in a city or town, surrounded by buildings, where people can meet. *Some old men were sitting in the square feeding the pigeons.*

A **square** (as in definition 1) is a kind of **rectangle**.

a b c d e f g h i j k l m n o p q r **s** t u v w x y z

squash /*say* skwosh / *verb*
1. If you **squash** something, you make it flat. *She accidentally sat on the bananas and squashed them.*
–*noun* 2. **Squash** is a game that two people play by hitting a small rubber ball against the walls of a court. *Squash is a very fast game.*
3. **Squash** is a fizzy drink made with fruit juice. *Would you like some orange squash?*
4. A **squash** is a small green or yellow vegetable. *My parents make us eat all our vegetables, even the squash.*

squeak *verb*
If something **squeaks**, it makes a small, high-sounding cry. *I heard a mouse squeak.*

> **Word Building: squeaky**, *adjective* If a gate squeaks, then it is **squeaky**.

squeal *verb*
If something or someone **squeals** , they make a sudden high cry as though they are in pain. *Sandra squealed with excitement when the elephants came onto the stage.*

squeeze *verb*
If you **squeeze** something or someone, you press them hard from two sides. *Don't squeeze me so tightly – you're hurting my arms.*

squirrel *noun*
A **squirrel** is a small wild animal with a bushy tail, which lives in trees in North America and Europe.

> ✸ *Spelling Tip:* Remember that there is a double *r* in **squirrel**, but only one *l* at the end.

squirt *verb*
If you **squirt** someone or something, you wet them with a burst of water or other liquid. *We broke up the dog fight by squirting them both with water from the hose.*

stable *noun*
A **stable** is a place for keeping and feeding horses.

stadium *noun*
A **stadium** is a large place where sports are played (often inside), with seats for people to watch.

staff *noun*
The **staff** of a place is all the people who work there.

stag *noun*
A **stag** is a male deer.

> The female is a **doe**.

stage *noun*
1. A **stage** is a floor raised above the usual level, as in a theatre, where actors or other performers can be seen. *As soon as the curtains opened, the children dressed as koalas came onto the stage.*
2. A **stage** is one part of something that continues on. One stage must be finished before the next stage starts. *The second stage of the hike was the hard bit where we had to start climbing the mountain.*

stagger *verb*
If you **stagger**, you walk as if you are about to fall. Your walking does not look steady at all. *He was hit by the ball and staggered off the field.*

stain *noun*
A **stain** is a mark on something which has been made from liquid or something else and which is hard to remove.

stairs *noun*
Stairs are a number of steps that come one after another that you use to get to a higher or lower level.

stake *noun*
A **stake** is a stick with a point at one end so that you can push it easily into the ground.

> ✸ *Spelling Tip:* Don't confuse the spelling of **stake** with **steak** which has the same sound. A **steak** is a piece of meat.

stale *adjective*
Something that is **stale** was made a long time ago and is not fresh.

stalk[1] /*rhymes with* fork / *noun*
A **stalk** is the stem of a plant.

stalk[2] /*rhymes with* fork / *verb*
1. If an animal **stalks** another animal, they follow it quietly and with so much care that it does not hear a sound. *My cat stalks all the birds in the garden.*
2. If someone **stalks** another person, they follow them secretly and constantly. *She told the police she was being stalked on the internet.*

stall *noun*
1. A **stall** is a stand or a table for selling things. *At the school fete, we helped with the stall that sold the cakes.*
2. A **stall** is the small area in a building where you keep a horse or a cow. *It is time to bring the horses out of their stalls for some exercise.*

stallion /*say* **stal**-yuhn / *noun*
A **stallion** is an adult male horse.

The female is a **mare**.

stammer *verb*

If you **stammer**, you cannot stop yourself repeating the first sounds of some words. *Whenever he was nervous, he would start to stammer.*

Another word that means the same is **stutter**.

stamp *verb*

1. If you **stamp**, you push your foot down hard on the ground or onto something on the ground. *They stamped their feet in time to the music.*
–*noun* **2.** A **stamp** is a small piece of paper printed by the government for sticking to letters to show that you have paid for them to be posted.

You can also say **postage stamp** for definition 2.

stand *verb* (**stands**, **standing**, **stood**, **has stood**)

1. When you **stand**, you are on your feet with your body going straight up and you are not moving forward. *We had to stand for hours waiting for the bus.*
2. If you **stand** or **stand up**, you move into this position after you have been sitting or lying down. *Everyone should stand when the judge comes into the room.*
3. If you cannot **stand** something or someone, you do not like them at all. *I can't stand people who are cruel to animals.*
4. **stand for**, If something or someone **stands** for something, they are a sign of it. *A drawing of a heart can stand for love.*

standard *noun*

The **standard** of something is how good or bad it usually is. You can use this to make a comparison.

star *noun*

1. A **star** is a large body in space. Most **stars** look like bright points of light in the sky at night. They look small because they are very far away from the earth. The sun is also a **star**. *You can see lots of stars when you are away from the city.*
2. A **star** is someone who is excellent at doing something or who is famous, especially a film actor. *We saw the stars arriving at the ceremony on television.*

starch *noun*

Starch is a white powder or liquid that people use to make clothes stiff.

stare *verb*

If you **stare**, you look straight at someone or something or look straight ahead for a long time, especially with your eyes wide open. *He surprised us so much that we just stood and stared at him.*

start *verb*

1. If you **start** something, you do it when you have not been doing it before. *We'll start cleaning the bath as soon as this show finishes.*
2. If something **starts**, it happens when it was not happening before. *The rain started just as we were about to play.*
3. If you **start** something, you make it happen or exist when it didn't before. *We have decided to start a new chess club.*
4. If you **start** a machine, you make it work or begin to move. *Dad couldn't start the car.*
–*noun* **5.** The **start** of something is the very first part of it.

startle *verb*

If you **startle** a person or an animal, you give them a sudden fright. *Danielle startled me when she suddenly came out of the dark room.*

starve *verb*

If a person or animal **starves**, they do not have enough to eat and can even die. *The lost walker was starving when they found him. It was lucky they found him before he starved to death.*

Word Building: starvation, *noun* Someone who starves can die of **starvation**.

state *noun*

1. The **state** of someone or something is the way they are. It is the condition they are in. *The books in the library are in a very untidy state.*
2. You can use **the state** to talk about a country and its government. *In some countries, all the industries are owned by the state.*
3. A **state** is part of a country that has its own government, as well as being under the main government. *Australia's states joined together to make one country in 1901.*
–*verb* **4.** If you **state** something, you say it in a very clear way or in a serious way. *At the police station, we had to state our name and address.*

Word Building: statement, *noun* When you state something, you make a **statement**. *The principal made a statement to the whole school about why she was leaving.*

station *noun*

1. A **station** is a place at which a train stops for people to get on and off it. *We have to be at the* *station early because the train leaves at seven o'clock.*

2. A **station** is a place set up for some particular kind of work or service. *Josh ran to the police station to get help.*

3. A **station** is an organisation that makes television or radio programs. It has a number that you turn to on your television or radio to be able to watch or listen to programs made by that company. *Which station will we watch tonight?*

For definition 1, you can also say **railway station** or **train station**.

statue /*say* **stach**-ooh/ *noun*
A **statue** is something in the shape of a person or an animal, made out of stone, wood or metal.

⭐ *Spelling Tip:* Remember the *t* in this word. With the *u* following it has a 'ch' sound and you might not hear the *t*.

stay *verb*
1. If you **stay** somewhere, you are in that place and you do not go away for some time. *Anna told her dog to stay where she left him while she went into the video shop.*
2. If someone or something **stays** a certain way, they keep on being like that. *It's not a good idea to wear white because it never stays clean.*
3. stay up, If you **stay up**, you do not go to bed at the usual time. *Tomorrow is Saturday so we can stay up late.*

steady *adjective* (**steadier**, **steadiest**)
1. If something is **steady**, it is firm and not likely to move. *Make sure the ladder is steady before you go up it.*
2. Something is **steady** if it goes on in the same way, without changing. *Steady rain has been falling for three days now.*

⭐ *Spelling Tip:* Remember the *ea* spelling for the 'e' sound, as in some other words such as *ready*.

steak /*say* stayk/ *noun*
A **steak** is a thick piece of meat or fish that you can cook.

⭐ *Spelling Tip:* Don't confuse the spelling of **steak** with **stake** which has the same sound. A **stake** is a wooden post.

steal *verb* (**steals**, **stealing**, **stole**, **has stolen**)
If someone **steals** something, they take something that does not belong to them, especially in a secret way. *Someone stole my mother's purse.*

Someone who steals things is a **thief** or a **robber**.

⭐ *Spelling Tip:* Don't confuse the spelling of **steal** with **steel** which has the same sound but is spelt with a double *e*.

steam *noun*
Steam is what comes from boiling water. It can be used for making machines work and for heating.

steel *noun*
Steel is a very strong, hard material made mainly from iron. It is used in buildings and for making machines, tools and many other things.

⭐ *Spelling Tip:* Don't confuse the spelling of **steel** with **steal** which has the same sound but is spelt with *ea*. **Steal** means 'to take things that are not yours'.

steep *adjective*
Something is **steep** if it rises upwards suddenly and if it is hard to climb.

steer *verb*
If someone **steers** a vehicle or a bicycle, they make it go the right way. *We had to steer our bikes very carefully to miss all the holes in the road.*

stem *noun*
1. A **stem** is the main part of a plant that grows up from the root. *Dad cut the stem to ground level but the bush soon started growing again.*
2. A **stem** is the part which joins a flower, leaf or fruit to a plant. *You'll need a large vase as those flowers have long thick stems.*

step *noun*
1. A **step** is a movement made by lifting your foot and putting it down again in a new position. *No wonder Roger is so far ahead – he takes such long steps!*
2. A **step** is the flat area where you put your foot when you are going up or coming down stairs. *At last she reached the top step.*
–*verb* (**steps**, **stepping**, **stepped**, **has stepped**)
3. When you **step**, you lift your foot and put it down again in new position. *You almost stepped on the cat!*

stepfather *noun*
Someone's **stepfather** is a man who is married to their mother but is not their own father.

stepmother *noun*
Someone's **stepmother** is a woman who is married to their father but is not their own mother.

stern¹ *adjective*
If someone is **stern**, they are strict or firm.

stern² *noun*
The **stern** of a boat is its back section.

stew *noun*
A **stew** is food, such as meat and vegetables, that has been cooked slowly in liquid.

stick¹ *noun*
A **stick** is a long thin piece of wood.

stick² *verb* (**sticks**, **sticking**, **stuck**, **has stuck**)
1. If you **stick** something sharp into something, you make the sharp thing go into it. *He stuck a nail into the wall and hung a picture on it.*
2. If you **stick** something in a place, you fasten it into that position with a special material (glue) that makes it stay there. *He stuck a stamp onto the envelope.*
3. **stick out**, If something **sticks out**, it goes out further than the area around it, sometimes further than is usual or needed. *I bumped into the drawer because it was sticking out.*

Word Building: sticky, *adjective* (**stickier**, **stickiest**) If something is **sticky**, it has something on it that makes other things stick to it. *You wet the sticky side of a stamp before you put it on an envelope.*

sticker *noun*
A **sticker** is small piece of paper or plastic that has a printed picture or message on the front and something to make it stick on the back.

sticky tape *noun*
Sticky tape is a long, narrow piece of plastic, which is sticky on one side, and is used to join things together.

stiff *adjective*
1. If something is **stiff**, it is hard to bend. *We made a model of our school building with some stiff cardboard.*
2. If something is **stiff**, it is hard to move. *The key was so stiff in the lock that we couldn't turn it.*

still *adjective*
1. If someone or something is **still**, they are not moving.
–*adverb* 2. You use **still** to show that something has not changed up to this time. *Bella's dog was still waiting for her outside the shop.*
3. You use **still** to say that there is no movement. *She stood completely still.*

sting *verb* (**stings**, **stinging**, **stung**, **has stung**)
If something **stings**, it hurts with a short, sharp pain. *Dad was stung by a bee while he was working in the garden.*

stingy /*say* **stin**-jee/ *adjective* (**stingier**, **stingiest**)
If someone is **stingy**, they are mean about spending money.

stink *verb* (**stinks**, **stinking**, **stank**, **has stunk**)
If something **stinks**, it has a very bad smell. *We had forgotten that the meat was in our packs until it began to stink.*

stir *verb* (**stirs**, **stirring**, **stirred**, **has stirred**)
If you **stir** a liquid, you move a spoon or something like that around in it to mix the parts of it together. *We stirred the red and the yellow paints together to make orange.*

stockman *noun* (*plural* **stockmen**)
A **stockman** is someone on a farm out in the bush, whose job is to look after the cattle.

stomach /*say* **stum**-uhk/ *noun* (*plural* **stomachs**)
1. Your **stomach** is the inside part of your body where food goes after you eat it. *I have eaten too much and my stomach is hurting.*
2. Your **stomach** is the soft part of the front of your body below your chest. *He has a fat stomach.*

stone *noun*
1. **Stone** is the very hard material which rocks are made of. *They live in an old house made of stone.*
2. A **stone** is a small piece of this hard material. *Jason threw a stone into the water and watched it sink to the bottom.*
3. A **stone** is a the hard round seed in the middle of some fruits. *Julie saved the stone from her peach to see if it would grow.*

stool *noun*
A **stool** is a seat with no sides or back.

stop *verb* (**stops**, **stopping**, **stopped**, **has stopped**)
1. When something **stops**, it does not happen or go on any more. It finishes or comes to an end. *I wish the rain would stop.*
2. If something **stops**, it does not move or go any more. *This is where the bus stops for the night.*
3. If you **stop** something, you make it stop. *They asked the crowd to stop their noise.*
–*noun* 4. A **stop** is when something does not move any more. *Suddenly the train came to a stop.*
5. A **stop** is a place where a bus or a train stops to let people get off or get on. *They waited at the bus stop.*

a
b
c
d
e
f
g
h
i
j
k
l
m
n
o
p
q
r
s
t
u
v
w
x
y
z

The opposite of definition 1 is **begin** or **start**; the opposite of definition 3 is **start**.

store *verb*
1. If you **store** a thing or things, you put them somewhere until you need to use them. *Mum is storing all my old toys in the garage for my little brother to play with when he gets older.*
–*noun* 2. A **store** is a large shop that sells many different types of goods.

Another name for definition 2 is **department store**.

storey *noun* (*plural* **storeys**)
A **storey** is one level of a building and all the rooms that are on it.

Another word that means nearly the same is **floor**.

✿ *Spelling Tip:* Don't confuse the spelling of this word with **story** (something that you tell or write). Remember that **storey** has an *e* before the *y*.

storm *noun*
A **storm** is a lot of rain, usually with a strong wind and sometimes thunder and lightning.

Word Building: **stormy**, *adjective* (**stormier**, **stormiest**): *It was a stormy night.*

story *noun* (*plural* **stories**)
A **story** is something told or written which has either happened in real life or has been made up in someone's mind.

stove *noun*
A **stove** is something you cook food on. It uses gas, electricity or burning wood to give out heat.

straight /*say* strayt/ *adjective*
1. If something is **straight**, it has no bends.
–*adverb* 2. You use **straight** to say that something is done without stopping or right now. *We had to go home straight after school.*

strain *verb*
1. If you **strain** something, you separate a liquid from the solid things that are in it. *We always have to strain Mum's tea because she doesn't like tea leaves in the bottom of her cup.*
2. If you **strain** a part of your body, you hurt it by pushing, pulling or stretching it too hard. *The hike was so hard that we all strained our leg muscles.*

strange *adjective*
1. If something is **strange**, it is unusual or not what you would expect. *This meat has a strange taste.*
2. If someone or something is **strange**, you have not seen them or known them before. *The plane was forced to land and we found ourselves in a strange city.*

stranger *noun*
1. A **stranger** is someone you have not met before. *We are always taught to be careful of strangers.*
2. A **stranger** is someone who has not been in a place before. *Can you please tell me the way to the station. I'm a stranger in this town.*

strangle *noun*
If someone **strangles** a person, they kill them by holding their throat so tightly that they cannot breathe.

strap *noun*
A **strap** is a long, thin piece of leather or some other material that you use to tie or hold things in place.

straw *noun*
1. A **straw** is a thin, hollow tube that you use for drinking liquids. *Could I have a straw with my lemonade, please.*
2. **Straw** is the dry, yellow sticks left after a grain like wheat or corn has been taken off. *We put straw in the barn for the animals to sleep on.*

strawberry *noun* (*plural* **strawberries**)
A **strawberry** is a small, juicy, red fruit that has many tiny seeds on its skin.

stray *noun*
A **stray** is an animal, such as a dog or a cat, that is lost and has no home.

streak *noun*
A **streak** is a long, thin mark.

stream *noun*
A **stream** is a small amount of water that flows. It is smaller than a river.

street *noun*
A **street** is a road with buildings along the side of it.

When you are writing an address, you usually spell this with a capital letter: *20 Johnson Street*. You can also use the short form **St** in an address.

strength *noun*

Strength is what someone or something has when they are strong.

> *Word Building:* **strengthen**, *verb* When you make something stronger, you **strengthen** it.

> ⭐ *Spelling Tip:* Remember **strength** is formed from *strong* and so it has a *g* in it.

stretch *verb*

1. If you **stretch** something, you make it bigger by pulling it in different directions. *I have grown so big that I have to stretch my jumpers to get them over my head.*
2. You **stretch** when you make any part of your body long and straight. *Billy yawned and stretched.*

strict *adjective*

If someone is **strict**, they say that you have to behave well and obey the rules. They often punish you if do not behave well.

strike *verb* (**strikes**, **striking**, **struck**, **has struck**)

1. If someone or something **strikes** something, they hit it hard. *He struck the drum with his stick.*
—noun **2.** A **strike** is what happens when a group of workers stop work until changes they want are made.

string *noun*

String is a strong, thick thread used for tying things.

strip¹ *verb* (**strips**, **stripping**, **stripped**, **has stripped**)

1. If you **strip** something, you take something off or away. *Mum stripped the sheets off the bed and took them to the laundry.*
2. If you **strip**, you take off your clothes. *I am going to strip and get under the shower.*

strip² *noun*

A **strip** is a long, narrow part of something.

stripe *noun*

A **stripe** is a long, narrow part of something that is a different colour from the rest.

stroke¹ *noun*

A **stroke** is a movement where one thing hits another thing.

stroke² *verb*

If you **stroke** something, you move your hand along it in an even and soft way. *My mum loves me to stroke her hair.*

strong *adjective*

1. If something or someone is **strong**, they have a lot of power. *A strong wind blew up.*
2. If something is **strong**, it cannot be broken easily. *They built a strong fence to keep in the horses.*
3. If you have **strong** feelings or ideas, you feel or believe those things very firmly. You might use **strong** words, or words with a lot of force, to express them. *I have a strong feeling that something bad is going to happen.*

> *Word Building:* **strongly**, *adverb*: *She argued strongly against the plan.*

struggle *verb*

1. If you **struggle**, you fight hard and push your arms and legs to get away. *The prisoner struggled to escape but the rope held him tightly.*
2. If you **struggle**, you work hard to do something which is difficult. *He struggled to lift the heavy load.*

stubborn /*say* **stub**-uhn/ *adjective*

You are **stubborn** if you will not change your mind about something, even though you might be wrong.

student *noun*

A **student** is someone who is learning or is studying, especially at a school or university.

study *verb* (**studies**, **studying**, **studied**, **has studied**)

1. If you **study** a subject, you spend time learning it. *He started studying music when he was very young.*
2. When you **study**, you read or do other work to help you learn something. *My big brother studies for a few hours every night.*
3. If you **study** something, you look at it very carefully. *He studied the map but still couldn't work out where he was.*

stuff *noun*

1. **Stuff** is anything that you can touch, see, or use.
—verb **2.** If you **stuff** something, you push it firmly inside another thing. *In the morning we stuffed our sleeping bags back into their covers.*

> Definition 1 is an informal word that you might use when talking to your friends.

stuffy *adjective* (**stuffier**, **stuffiest**)

If a place is **stuffy**, it is without fresh air.

stump *noun*

A **stump** is the part of something, especially a tree, that is left after the rest has been cut or broken off.

a b c d e f g h i j k l m n o p q r s t u v w x y z

stupid *adjective*

1. If someone is **stupid**, they are not clever, or not quick to understand things. *He must be stupid – he often tries to cross the road when the light is red.*

2. If an action is **stupid**, it is not sensible. *It was stupid to leave my bag where it might get stolen.*

sturdy *adjective* (**sturdier**, **sturdiest**)

If something is **sturdy**, it is strong or not easily damaged.

stutter *verb*

If someone **stutters**, they keep repeating the first sounds of some words. *Some people stutter when they are nervous.*

sty *noun* (*plural* **sties**)

A **sty** is a place where pigs are kept.

style *noun*

Style is the special way something is made or designed. *Miss Barker said the style of my painting was very unusual.* | *He dresses in an old-fashioned style.*

subject *noun*

1. The **subject** of a conversation, a piece of writing, or film is what it is about. *We could choose whatever subject we liked for our project – so I am going to do dinosaurs.*

2. A **subject** is an area of learning at school or university. *My favourite subject is maths.*

submarine *noun*

A **submarine** is a type of ship that can travel under water.

substance *noun*

A **substance** is anything that you can see, touch or use. A **substance** could be solid, liquid or gas.

subtract *verb*

When you **subtract**, you take one number or amount away from a larger number or amount. *If you subtract 2 from 6, you get 4.*

> *Word Building:* **subtraction**, *noun* When you subtract one thing from another thing, you make a **subtraction**.

suburb *noun*

A **suburb** is any part of a city that has its own name, and its own shops, schools and parks.

succeed /*say* suhk-**seed**/ *verb*

If you **succeed**, you do something you have tried to do. *At last he succeeded in opening the box.*

> ✵ *Spelling Tip:* Remember that there is both a double *c* and double *e* in this word.

success /*say* suhk-**ses**/ *noun*

Success is when someone or something does well, often after a lot of effort. It is when someone or something succeeds. *Our parents are very proud of our success in getting to the finals.* | *The school concert was a great success.*

> *Word Building:* **successful**, *adjective* If someone succeeds or has a lot of success, they are **successful**. *She tried many times to climb the mountain and at last she was successful.* | *He is a successful actor. He appears in many films.* –**successfully**, *adverb*: *The school concert went off very successfully.*

such *adjective*

1. You use **such** when you are talking about how much or how big something is, and what the result of this is. *We decided to go to the beach because it was such a sunny day.*

2. You use **such** to make the next word stronger. *Emma reads such strange books!*

3. such as, You use **such as** when you are giving examples of a general thing. *He likes sports such as tennis and football.*

suck *verb*

If you **suck** air or liquid, you move it into your mouth through something. *The baby has always had a bottle but now she has learned to suck through a straw.*

sudden *adjective*

If something is **sudden**, it happens so quickly that it can surprise you.

> *Word Building:* **suddenly**, *adverb* Something that is sudden happens **suddenly**.

suffer *verb*

If someone **suffers**, they feel a lot of pain, sickness or sadness. *He suffered a lot of pain before he was finally rescued.*

> *Word Building:* **suffering**, *noun*: *She has had a lot of suffering in her life.*

suffocate *verb*

If someone **suffocates**, they die because there is not enough air to breathe. *Open the windows please – I feel as though I am suffocating.*

> ✵ *Spelling Tip:* Remember the double *f* spelling. Also notice that the following letter is an *o*.

sugar /*say* **shoog**-uh/ *noun*

Sugar is a sweet food that you can add to other foods or drinks to make them taste sweet.

suggest /*say* suh-**jest**/ *verb*
If you **suggest** an idea or a plan, you tell someone the idea to see if they agree with it. *We all had to suggest ways we thought we could improve our play.*

> *Word Building:* **suggestion**, *noun* When you suggest something, you make a **suggestion**.

> ✴ *Spelling Tip:* Remember the double *g* spelling for the 'j' sound.

suicide /*say* **sooh**-uh-suyd/ *noun*
Suicide is when someone kills themselves.

suit /*say* sooht/ *noun*
1. A **suit** is a set of clothes for wearing to work or for important events. A man's **suit** is made up of a coat and trousers of the same material, and a woman's **suit** is made up of a coat and either trousers or a skirt of the same material. –*verb* 2. If something **suits** you, it fits in with what you want to do. It is right for you. *It suited me to stay at home instead of going out because I had things to do.*
3. If clothes or particular colours **suit** you, you look good when you wear them. *That red shirt really suits you.*

suitable /*say* **sooht**-uh-buhl/ *adjective*
If something is **suitable**, it is right for you, or it is right for a particular event.

suitcase /*say* **sooht**-kays/ *noun*
A **suitcase** is a large bag for carrying clothes and other things when you travel.

sulk *verb*
If you **sulk**, you stop speaking to someone because you are angry and unhappy about something they have done. *Tessa sulked all day after they told her that her hair was a mess.*

sullen *adjective*
You are **sullen** if you are rude and do not talk to people because you are not happy.

sultana *noun*
A **sultana** is a grape that has been dried.

sum *noun*
1. A **sum** of money is an amount of money. *I have only a small sum of money with me.*
2. The **sum** of two or more numbers is the total that they make when added together. *The sum of 8 and 7 is 15.*
3. A **sum** is an exercise in which you work with numbers in some way. *The teacher gave us ten sums to do before lunch.*

summer *noun*
Summer is the season of the year when the weather is the hottest.

> The other seasons of the year are **autumn**, **winter** and **spring**.

summit *noun*
A **summit** of a mountain is the top.

sun *noun*
1. The **sun** is the round, bright star which you can see in the sky during the day. It gives light and warmth to the earth. *The earth goes around the sun.*
2. **Sun** is the light given by the sun. *Let's sit under the tree, not in the sun.*

Sunday *noun*
Sunday is one of the seven days of the week. It comes between Saturday and Monday.

sunny *adjective* (**sunnier**, **sunniest**)
If the weather is **sunny**, the sun is shining a lot.

sunrise *noun*
Sunrise is the time when the sun comes up in the morning. It is when the day begins.

sunscreen *noun*
Sunscreen is a cream which you put on your skin to protect it from the sun.

> This is sometimes called **sunblock**.

sunset *noun*
Sunset is the time when the sun goes down in the evening. It is the end of the day.

sunshine *noun*
Sunshine is the light of the sun.

superior /*say* suh-**pear**-ree-uh/ *adjective*
If someone or something is **superior**, they are better than someone or something else.

> The opposite is **inferior**.

supermarket *noun*
A **supermarket** is a large shop which sells mainly food and other things you need in the house. You choose what you want from the shelves and take them to a place where you pay.

supersonic *adjective*
If an aircraft is **supersonic**, it travels faster than sound travels.

supper *noun*
Supper is a small meal that some people have late in the evening.

supply /say suh-**pluy**/ verb (**supplies, supplying, supplied, has supplied**)
1. When someone or something **supplies** something, they give or provide something that is needed. *The new shop supplies camping equipment.* | *These pipes supply water to the town.*
–noun (plural **supplies**)
2. A **supply** is an amount of something that you keep and use when you need it. *I have a good supply of paper and pens.*

support verb
1. If something **supports** something else, it holds it up. *You can't take that wall down. It supports the roof.*
2. If you **support** a person, an organisation or an idea, you agree with them and want them to be successful. *We all support the plan to have more parks in our state.*
3. If you **support** a particular sports team, you like them and want them to win all the time. *We support our local football team.*
–noun **4.** A **support** is something that supports something else.

> **Word Building: supporter,** *noun* Someone who supports a person, an idea or a team is a **supporter.**

suppose verb
If you **suppose** something is true, you think it is true although you do not know definitely if it is true or not. *I suppose it was an accident but sometimes I think he meant to do it.*

sure /say shaw/ adjective
1. If you are **sure** about something, you have no doubts that it is right or true. *I'm sure I left my bag here.* | *I think the station is around the next corner, but I'm not completely sure.*
–adverb **2. make sure,**
a. If you say that you will **make sure** that you do something, you say that you will certainly remember to do it. *Peter said he would make sure that he locked the door.*
b. If you **make sure,** you check carefully that something is true. *Peter thinks he locked the door but I'll go back and make sure.*

surf noun
1. The **surf** is the big waves with a line of white bubbles of water on top, that roll onto the beach over and over.
–verb **2.** If you **surf,** you swim in the surf or ride the waves on a board. *Ben and his friends went to the beach and surfed all day.*

3. If you **surf** the internet, you use it to go to lots of different sites to find out things. *We surfed the internet for information for our spider project.*

surface /say **ser**-fuhs/ noun
1. The **surface** of something is its outside part or side. *The magician rubbed the surface of the box – and guess what jumped out?*
2. The **surface** of water or other liquid is the top of it. *We could see our ball floating on the surface of the water.*

surfboard noun
A **surfboard** is a long, narrow board that you can stand or lie on to ride waves.

surgeon /say **ser**-juhn/ noun
A **surgeon** is a doctor who is trained to cut people's bodies to fix a part of the body that is damaged or to try to cure a sickness.

> ✸ *Spelling Tip:* Remember the *g* spelling for the 'j' sound. Also notice that the ending is *eon,* although you do not hear the *e.* You could think of the sentence 'Surgeons use red gloves every other night' to remind you of the order of the letters.

surgery /say **ser**-juh-ree/ noun (plural **surgeries**)
1. A **surgery** is the room where you see your doctor or dentist. *The doctor had a sight chart in her surgery to test how well people could see.*
2. **Surgery** is any operation where a doctor cuts open your body to fix an injury or to try to cure a sickness. *My mother is having some surgery done to improve her vision.*

surname noun
Your **surname** is your last name or the name that most of the people in your family have.

> ✸ *Spelling Tip:* Remember that the first part is spelt *sur* (not *sir*). The word part *sur* comes from the French word for 'over' or 'above'.

surprise verb
1. If something or someone **surprises** you, they give you the feeling you have when something is not expected or is very unusual. *The ending of the film surprised us all.*
–noun **2.** A **surprise** is something that surprises you.

> **Word Building: surprised,** *adjective: She looked at him in a surprised way.* –**surprising,** *adjective: We have had some very surprising news.*

a
b
c
d
e
f
g
h
i
j
k
l
m
n
o
p
q
r
s
t
u
v
w
x
y
z

✱ Spelling Tip: Remember that there is an *r* in the first part of this word, so that the first part is spelt *sur*. Also note that there is no *ize* spelling choice for the last part of this word, as there is in some other words ending in *ise*. **Surprise** must always end in *ise*.

surrender *verb*
If someone **surrenders**, they stop fighting and agree to do what the other side wants. *They didn't want to surrender but they had no choice.*

surround *verb*
If you **surround** something or someone, you go all around them. *We surrounded the Christmas tree with presents for everyone.*

survive *verb*
If someone or something **survives**, they are alive or not damaged after an accident or a disaster. *Sergio was the only one to survive the bus accident. | Luckily, my coin collection survived the fire.*

Word Building: survivor, *noun* If you survive something, then you are a **survivor**. –**survival**, *noun* The act of surviving is called **survival**.

suspect /*say* suhs-**pekt**/ *verb*
If you **suspect** something, you think that something has happened or that someone has done something wrong, though you do not know for sure. *We suspect that the people down the road complained to the police about the noise from our party.*

Word Building: suspicion /*say* suhs-**pish**-uhn/, *noun* When you suspect something you have a **suspicion**. –**suspicious** /*say* suhs-**pish**-uhs/, *adjective* When you suspect something, you are **suspicious**.

sustain *verb*
1. If something **sustains** something else, it keeps it going. *The movie sustained our interest for two hours.*
2. If something **sustains** you, it gives you strength and keeps you going *We knew we would be having a late dinner so we ate a big lunch to sustain us.*

Word Building: sustainable, *adjective* If something can be sustained, it is **sustainable**. Something that is environmentally **sustainable** can keep on going while not causing a lot of harm to the environment.

swallow /*say* **swol**-oh/ *verb*
If you **swallow**, you make something go down your throat. *Mum told me if I swallowed the medicine, I would soon feel better.*

swamp /*say* swomp/ *noun*
A **swamp** is an area of wet, soft ground.

Another word that means nearly the same is **marsh**.

swan /*say* swon/ *noun*
A **swan** is a large beautiful bird with a long neck, that swims and flies. Some **swans** are white and some are black.

swap /*say* swop/ *verb* (**swaps**, **swapping**, **swapped**, **has swapped**)
If you **swap** something, you give one thing and get something else in return. *I did a very good deal – I swapped a cheese sandwich for a meat pie and sauce.*

swarm /*rhymes with* form/ *noun*
A **swarm** is a large group of insects, such as bees or ants.

swear *verb* (**swears**, **swearing**, **swore**, **has sworn**)
1. If someone **swears**, they use bad words. *He couldn't help swearing when the brick landed on his foot.*
2. If you **swear**, you make a serious promise. *She swore to me that she would never tell my secret to anybody.*

sweat /*say* swet/ *noun*
Sweat is tiny drops of salty water that come through your skin when you are very hot or sick, or when you have been working your body a lot.

sweater /*say* **swet**-uh/ *noun*
A **sweater** is a piece of warm clothing, which you wear on the top half of your body, often over other clothes.

sweep *verb*
1. If you **sweep** an area, you move dirt away from it, usually with a broom. *Toby, could you please sweep the floor. There are bits of bread on it.*
2. If you **sweep** dirt or something else, you move it away from an area with a broom. *Dad asked me to sweep the leaves from the front path.*

sweet *adjective*
1. If food or drink is **sweet**, it has the taste of sugar or a taste like sugar. *I put too much sugar in Dad's tea so it was too sweet.*

2. If you describe something as **sweet**, you mean that it is attractive or it makes you feel like loving it. *What a sweet little puppy!*

–*noun* **3.** A **sweet** is a small piece of something very sweet which is made of sugar.

> *Word Building:* **sweetly**, *adverb*: *She smiled sweetly.*

> ✤ The opposite of definition 1 is **sour**.
> ✤ Another word for definition 3 is **lolly**.

swell *verb* (**swells, swelling, swelled, has swollen**)

If something **swells**, it gets bigger. *A bee stung Jacinta and now her hand has swollen up.*

> *Word Building:* **swelling**, *noun* A part that swells is a **swelling**.

swerve *verb*

If something **swerves**, it turns suddenly and moves in a different direction. *The boy on the skateboard swerved to avoid the bin.*

swift *adjective*

If something is **swift**, it is very fast.

swim *verb* (**swims, swimming, swam, has swum**)

1. If someone or something **swims**, they move through water by moving parts of their body. People swim by moving their arms and legs. Fish swim by moving their tail and fins. *Some of the kids at school haven't learned to swim yet.*

–*noun* **2.** A **swim** is an act or time of swimming.

> *Word Building:* **swimmer**, *noun* Someone who swims is a **swimmer**. –**swimming**, *noun*: *He is not very good at swimming.*

swimming costume *noun*

A **swimming costume** is a piece of clothing that you wear for swimming.

> There are many other names for what you wear when you are swimming, such as **bathers**, **swimmers**, **swimsuit** and **togs**.

swing *verb* (**swings, swinging, swung, has swung**)

1. If something **swings**, it moves backwards and forwards or from side to side while joined to something else at the top or side. *The door swung backwards and forwards in the wind.*

–*noun* **2.** A **swing** is a seat hanging from two ropes. You can sit on it and move backwards and forwards for fun.

switch *noun* (*plural* **switches**)

1. A **switch** is a button that you press or turn to make something go on or off.

–*verb* **2.** If you **switch** something, you change one thing for another. *We switched our training time from Wednesday to Thursday so we could all go.*

sword /*say* sawd / *noun*

A **sword** is a weapon with a long, sharp, pointed edge.

> ✪ *Spelling Tip:* Don't forget the silent *w* following the *s*.

sympathy /*say* **sim**-puh-thee / *noun*

Sympathy is the feeling you have when you are sorry for someone who is sad, sick or in trouble.

> *Word Building:* **sympathetic** /*say* sim-puh-**thet**-ik /, *adjective* If you feel sympathy, then you are **sympathetic**.

> ✪ *Spelling Tip:* Remember the *y* (not *i*) spelling in the first part of the word. Like many words with a *y* spelling, **sympathy** comes from Greek. It is made up of *sym* (meaning 'together') and *pathy* (from the Greek word for 'feeling').

synagogue /*say* **sin**-uh-gog / *noun*

A **synagogue** is the building where Jews worship.

> ✪ *Spelling Tip:* Don't forget the *ue* at the end which you do not hear when you say the word. Also remember the *y* spelling in the first part of this word. **Synagogue** comes from the Greek word for 'meeting' or 'assembly'.

syrup /*say* **si**-ruhp / *noun*

Syrup is a thick, sweet, sticky liquid made by cooking sugar and water together.

> ✪ *Spelling Tip:* Remember the *y* (not *i*) spelling. Also remember that there is only one *r* and only one *p*. Try breaking the word up as *sy+ rup*.

system /*say* **sis**-tuhm / *noun*

A **system** is the way something is organised or arranged.

tap

tabby *noun* (*plural* **tabbies**)
A **tabby** is a cat that has grey or brown fur marked with dark lines of colour.

table *noun*
A **table** is a piece of furniture which has a flat top resting on one or more legs.

tablet *noun*
1. A **tablet** is a small, flat, solid piece of medicine.
2. A **tablet** is a flat piece of some hard material that you can carve or write on.
3. A **tablet** is a small, flat computer that you can carry and operate with your finger.

You can also say **tablet computer** for definition 3.

table tennis *noun*
Table tennis is a game in which two players, or two pairs of players, hit a small, light ball to each other over a net on a large table.

Another name for this game is **ping-pong**.

tabouli /*say* tuh-**booh**-lee/ *noun*
Tabouli is a salad made with parsley, mint, wheat, oil and lemon juice.

tack *noun*
1. A **tack** is a short nail with a flat head.
–*verb* 2. If you **tack** something, you sew it together, usually loosely. *Mum tacked my new dress, then sewed it properly later.*

tackle *verb*
1. If you **tackle** something that is difficult, you try to do it. *Dad told me to tackle my homework before I watched television.*
2. If you **tackle** someone, you quickly take hold of them around their body or legs to make them stop running. *The policeman tackled the man and wrestled him to the ground.*

taco /*say* **tah**-koh, **tak**-oh/ *noun* (*plural* **tacos**)
A **taco** is a kind of food, made of a flat piece of bread made of corn folded around meat, tomato and lettuce.

tadpole *noun*
A **tadpole** is a baby frog or toad. It has a round body and a tail and it lives in water. As it gets bigger it grows legs and is able to leave the water.

tai chi /*say* tuy **chee**/ *noun*
Tai chi is a set of exercises where you move smoothly from one exercise to the next while keeping your balance.

This word comes from the Chinese language and means 'fist of the Great Absolute'.

tail *noun*
An animal's **tail** is the end of its back, especially when it is a separate part of the body, as in animals like dogs and cats.

✿ *Spelling Tip:* Don't confuse the spelling of **tail** with **tale** which has the same sound. A **tale** is a story.

tailor *noun*
A **tailor** is someone who makes or fixes clothes, especially for men.

taipan /*say* **tuy**-pan/ *noun*
A **taipan** is a long, thin, brown snake whose bite can kill you.

This word comes from an Aboriginal language of Queensland called Wik-Mungkan.

take *verb* (**takes**, **taking**, **took**, **has taken**)
1. If you **take** something, you reach for it and hold it, usually with your hands. *We took the books from the teacher.*
2. If you **take** something from somewhere, you remove it without someone saying you can. *He was crying because the other children had taken his toys.*
3. If you **take** something, you carry it. *We offered to take the heavy things.*
4. If you **take** a train, bus or boat, you travel in it. *I think we'll have to take the bus – it's too far to walk.*

5. If you **take** something, like a bath or a rest, you have that thing. *My grandmother takes a rest after lunch.*

6. If you **take** medicine, you swallow it. *Take this medicine three times a day.*

7. take after, If you **take after** someone in your family, you are like them in some way. *She takes after her aunt – they both have the same nose.*

8. take away, **a.** If you **take** something **away** from someone, you remove it from them. *The teacher took away our ball because we weren't listening during class.* **b.** If you **take** one number **away** from another, you make the second number smaller by the amount of the first number. *If you take away 7 from 15 you get 8.*

9. take off, **a.** If you **take** something **off**, you remove it. *Take off your uniform and get into your pyjamas.* **b.** If an aircraft **takes off**, it leaves the ground and begins to fly. *Our plane took off just as the sun was setting.*

10. take out, **a.** If you **take** something **out**, you pull it out from where it was. *He had to have his tooth taken out.* **b.** If someone **takes** someone **out**, they bring them somewhere, such as to a restaurant or a film. *My uncle took his children out to dinner on Saturday.*

takeaway *noun*
Takeaway is a hot or cold meal that you buy at a shop, but take to a different place to eat. *We were too tired to cook, so we got takeaway.*

take-off *noun*
A **take-off** is when a plane starts its journey by leaving the land and flying into the air.

tale *noun*
1. A **tale** is a story, which may be true or made up. *He told us a tale about his life as a child in Germany. | She read us a tale about a woman who used magic to turn people into frogs.*

2. tell tales, If you **tell tales** about someone, you say things about them which may not be true. *She's always telling tales about the other children.*

> ✪ *Spelling Tip:* Don't confuse the spelling of **tale** with **tail** which has the same sound. A **tail** is the end part of the spine of an animal.

talent *noun*
Talent is what you have if you can do something very well.

talk *verb*
1. If you **talk**, you use words out loud to say what you are thinking or feeling, to give information or to ask questions. *I don't feel like talking at the moment. | We had to talk about what happened on our holidays.*

2. talk someone into doing something, If you **talk** someone **into** doing something, you get them to do it although they had not been meaning to. *She is pretty shy but we talked her into coming to the party.*

–*noun* **3.** If you have a **talk** with someone, you have a discussion or a conversation with them. *We need to have a talk about when the team is going to train.*

> *Word Building:* **talkative**, *adjective* If someone talks a lot, they are **talkative**.

tall *adjective*
1. If someone or something is **tall**, they are of more than average height. *My mother is tall, so she could see over the heads of all the other people at the football match.*

2. You use **tall** when you are talking about a person being a particular height. *That man is two metres tall.*

> The opposite of definition 1 is **short**.

tame *adjective*
An animal is **tame** if it is used to being touched and fed by humans.

tan *verb* (**tans, tanning, tanned, has tanned**)
1. If you **tan**, you let the sun make your skin turn brown. *You should not spend too long lying on the beach tanning – you should protect your skin.*

2. If someone **tans** the skin of an animal, they turn it into leather. *He works at a factory where they tan cow skins.*

> *Word Building:* **tanned**, *adjective* If you have skin that is brown from the sun, you are **tanned**. *She was very tanned after her holiday.*

tangled *adjective*
If something is **tangled**, it is all twisted up in knots or in an untidy pile.

tank *noun*
1. A **tank** is a large container for liquid, such as water. *The tank on the farm was almost empty, as it had not rained for two months.*

2. A **tank** is a heavy fighting vehicle used in war. *The tanks entered the town with their guns pointing left and right.*

tanker *noun*
A **tanker** is a ship or a truck for carrying a lot of oil or any other kind of liquid.

tap[1] *verb* (**taps**, **tapping**, **tapped**, **has tapped**)
If you **tap** something, you hit it lightly and quickly. *I turned around when she tapped me on the shoulder.*

tap[2] *noun*
A **tap** is something that you can turn on and off to control the flow of a liquid.

tape *noun*
1. A **tape** is a long, narrow piece of paper, cloth, plastic or other material. *The runners ran through the tape at the end of the race.*
2. A **tape** is a long, narrow piece of special plastic, usually in a hard case, that you use in a machine to record sound or film. *We have to buy a new tape to record the film on television tonight.*
3. Look up **sticky tape**.

A tape that you use to record film, as in definition 2, can also be called a **videotape**.

tar *noun*
Tar is a thick, black, sticky substance that comes from coal or wood. It is used for making roads.

target *noun*
A **target** is something that you aim at and try to hit or reach.

tart *noun*
A **tart** is a sweet pie that has no pastry on the top.

task *noun*
A **task** is a piece of work that you have to do, especially one that is difficult.

Tasmanian devil /*say* taz-may-nee-uhn **dev**-uhl/ *noun*
A **Tasmanian devil** is an animal that lives in Tasmania, and is about the size of a small dog. It has black fur with white marks, eats meat and can look frightening.

taste *noun*
1. The **taste** of a food or drink is the way it seems to you when you put it in your mouth.
–*verb* 2. If you **taste** something, you take a small bite or drink of it, often to see what it is like. *He tasted the soup to see if it was ready.*
3. If something **tastes** a particular way, it seems that way to you when you begin to eat or drink it. *This orange tastes beautiful!*

tax *noun*
Tax is the money people pay each year to the government to use in running the country. The money is used for schools, hospitals, roads and many other things.

taxi *noun* (*plural* **taxis**)
A **taxi** is a car with a driver who will take you where you want to go for payment of money which is worked out on the distance you travel.

Another word for this is **cab**.

✦ *Spelling Tip:* The spelling of this word is unusual but not difficult, if you remember the *x* and then the *i* at the end. It comes from *taxe*, the French word for 'an amount of money charged'.

T-ball *noun*
T-ball is a type of baseball for children in which the ball is not thrown to the person who bats, but is hit from a pole that stands at waist height.

You can also spell this **tee-ball**.

tea *noun*
1. **Tea** is a drink made by pouring boiling water onto the dried leaves from a particular plant that grows in very hot areas. *My mother offered her visitors a cup of tea.*
2. **Tea** is a meal you have in the late afternoon or evening. *We had an early tea and then went out to the movies.*

teach *verb* (**teaches**, **teaching**, **taught** /*say* tawt/, **has taught**)
1. If you **teach** someone, you give them knowledge or help them get a skill. *He teaches blind children.* | *She is teaching me to play the piano.*
2. If you **teach** something, you pass on your knowledge about it or help people learn how to do it. *She teaches dancing.*

teacher *noun*
A **teacher** is someone whose job is to pass on knowledge to people or to help them get a skill.

team *noun*
A **team** is a group of people who do something together, especially a sport or work. *Our swimming team is doing well this year.* | *A new doctor joined the team.*

tear[1] /*rhymes with* here/ *noun*
A **tear** is a drop of water that falls from your eyes when you cry.

tear[2] /*rhymes with* bare/ *verb* (**tears**, **tearing**, **tore**, **has torn**)
1. If you **tear** something or **tear** something **up**, you pull it apart or into pieces leaving rough edges. *He tore the paper.* | *He tore up the used bus ticket.*

a b c d e f g h i j k l m n o p q r s t u v w x y z

2. If you **tear** something, you pull it so that a hole appears. *She tore her skirt on a nail which was sticking out of the wall.*
3. If you **tear** somewhere, you run quickly. *She tore after the man who had stolen her bag.*

tease *verb*
If you **tease** someone, you say or do things to annoy them and make them embarrassed. *My sister teased me about needing a haircut.*

technical /*say* tek-nik-uhl / *adjective*
Something is **technical** if it has to do with machines and or the way that things like industry and communications work. *We have technical problems with the telephone service, so you can't make any calls at the moment.*

technique /*say* tek-**neek** / *noun*
A **technique** is a particular way of doing something.

> ✳ *Spelling Tip:* Remember that the end of **technique** is spelt *ique* (although it sounds like 'eek'). It might help if you think of other words which have the same spelling for this sound, such as *antique* and *unique*. These are all spelt like this because they come from French. The beginning of **technique** can also be difficult. Remember the *ch* spelling for the 'k' sound (as in *technical*).

teddy bear *noun*
A **teddy bear** is a toy in the form of a small bear.

teenager *noun*
A **teenager** is someone who is between the ages of 12 and 20.

telegram *noun*
A **telegram** is a message sent by electrical signals along wires and delivered to someone as a printed note.

> Today, people generally use a **fax** or **email** when they want to send a written message quickly.

telephone /*say* tel-uh-fohn / *noun*
1. A **telephone** is a piece of equipment which lets you talk over long distances by sending electrical signals over wires.
–*verb* **2.** If you **telephone** someone, you call them or speak to them on a telephone. *I will telephone you after dinner.*

> The short form is **phone**.

telescope *noun*
A **telescope** is something you look through, which makes things that are far away seem closer

and bigger. It is shaped like a tube and has curved glass at both ends.

television /*say* tel-uh-vizh-uhn / *noun*
1. A **television** is a piece of equipment which receives pictures and sounds sent by waves through the air.
2. **Television** is all the shows that are shown on television. *He watches too much television.*

> The short form is **TV**.

tell *verb* (**tells**, **telling**, **told**, **has told**)
1. If you **tell** someone something, you give them information about it by speaking to them. *Gareth told us his family was moving to another state.*
2. If you can **tell** something, you know it. *It's hard to tell which is the right house in the dark.*
3. If you **tell** someone to do something, you order them to do it. *Tell him to go.*

temper *noun*
1. If someone has a **temper**, they get angry very easily. *He has a terrible temper and is always shouting at people.*
2. Your **temper** is the way you are feeling at any one time. *Ellie is in a bad temper because she can't find her favourite book.*

temperature /*say* temp-ruh-chuh / *noun*
Temperature is the measure of how hot or cold someone or something is. *She was very sick, with a temperature of more than 41°. | The temperature today is 15°.*

temple *noun*
A **temple** is a special place where people worship a god or gods.

temporary /*say* temp-ree / *adjective*
Something is **temporary** if it lasts for only a short time.

> The opposite is **permanent**.

> ✳ *Spelling Tip:* You need to remember that this word has four parts (*temp* + *or* + *ar* + *y*), although you hear only two when you say it. Concentrate on the *orary* ending.

tempt *verb*
If you **tempt** someone, you try to make them do something that they should not do. *I was tempted to go to the movies, but I had a lot of work to do.*

> ***Word Building:*** **temptation**, *noun* When someone tempts you, you feel **temptation**.

ten *noun, adjective*
Ten is a number which you can write as 10.

> **Word Building: tenth**, *adjective*: *When the tenth bottle accidentally fell after the other nine, there were none left on the wall.*

tender *adjective*
1. If food is **tender**, it is soft and easy to eat and cut. *It was a tender piece of meat.*
2. If someone shows **tender** behaviour, they are kind and full of love. *My mother is always tender to me when I have hurt myself.*
3. If something is **tender**, it is sore when you touch it. *My knee felt very tender where I had fallen on it.*

> **Word Building: tenderness**, *noun* If you have tender feelings, you treat people with a lot of **tenderness**. –**tenderly**, *adverb*: *He kissed her tenderly.*

tennis *noun*
Tennis is a game in which two players, or two pairs of players, hit a small ball to each other over a net.

tense *adjective*
If you are **tense**, you are worried and nervous about something.

> **Word Building: tension**, *noun* When you are tense, you are feeling **tension**.

tent *noun*
A **tent** is a covering that you put up to protect yourself from rain while you are sleeping outdoors. It is usually made of a type of strong cloth and is held up by one or more posts.

tentacle /*say* **ten**-tuh-kuhl/ *noun*
A **tentacle** is one of the long, thin parts which some sea animals use to touch or hold things.

term *noun*
1. A **term** is one of the parts the year is divided into at places like schools and universities. *At the end of the term, we're going to spend our holidays in the country.*
2. A **term** is a period of time which has a limit. *He received a four-year prison term as punishment for stealing the money.*
3. A **term** is a word which names something. *This book explains the meanings of many scientific terms.*

termite *noun*
A **termite** is a white insect that eats wood and which can destroy houses.

Another name for this insect is **white ant**.

terrible *adjective*
If something is **terrible**, it is very bad.

> **Word Building: terribly**, *adverb*: *Her leg was aching terribly.*

terrier *noun*
A **terrier** is one of the small dogs that were once used for hunting.

terrific *adjective*
1. If something is **terrific**, it is very great. *The explosion went off with a terrific noise.*
2. If something is **terrific**, it is very good. *We had a terrific time riding our bikes along the beach.*

terrify /*say* te-ruh-fuy/ *verb* (**terrifies, terrifying, terrified, has terrified**)
If something **terrifies** someone, it frightens them very much. *I was terrified when I saw the snake.*

> **Word Building: terror**, *noun* Things that terrify you fill you with **terror**.

> ✦ **Spelling Tip:** Remember the double *r* spelling. Also remember that the following letter is an *i*. Try breaking the word up as *ter+ri+fy*.

territory /*say* te-ruh-tree/ *noun* (*plural* **territories**)
A **territory** is an area of land belonging to a particular country. *Australia has six states and two territories, as well as some territories that are separate from the main part of Australia.*

> ✦ **Spelling Tip:** Remember the double *r* spelling (as in the Latin word *terra*, meaning 'land', which is where the word **territory** comes from). Also remember the *ory* ending. Try breaking the word up as *ter+ri+tor+y*.

terrorist *noun*
A **terrorist** is someone who kills or hurts people to try to make the government of a country do what he or she wants.

test *noun*
1. A **test** is a set of questions to answer, designed to see how much you know about something. *I hate tests – they make me nervous.*
2. A **test** is an examination of something to see if it is working properly. *The car failed the safety test and so they have to fix the brakes.*
3. A **test** is a medical examination to find out if there is something wrong with part of your body. *The doctor wanted to do some more hearing tests.*

a b c d e f g h i j k l m n o p q r s t u v w x y z

text *noun*
1. **Text** is anything that is written. In a book, the **text** is the main written part of it, not including pictures or notes. *This book has 200 pages of text and 50 pages of pictures.*
2. **Text** can also be something that is written or spoken, or a picture, especially when it is about a particular subject or in a particular style. *The type of text we had to present to the class was a discussion.*
3. Look up **textbook**.
–*verb* 4. To **text** someone is to send them a text message.

texta *noun*
A **texta** is a thick, brightly coloured pen that is used like a coloured pencil.

This is sometimes called a **felt-tip pen**.

textbook *noun*
A **textbook** is a book that gives students information about a particular subject.

text message *noun*
A **text message** is a message in words or a short form of words, sent to someone's mobile phone. They can read the message on the screen of the phone.

Another term is **SMS message**.

than *conjunction, preposition*
You use **than** when you are comparing two things. It comes before the second thing you are talking about. *He's taller than I am.*

thank *verb*
If you **thank** someone, you tell them that you are pleased that they have done something kind for you. You usually say 'Thank you' or 'Thanks' to them. *I thanked my friend's mum for driving me to school last week.*

that *adjective, pronoun*
You use **that** to show a person, thing or idea that you are pointing out or mentioning. *My dad said that car is the best sports car around at the moment. | That is exactly what I want for Christmas.*

That can be the opposite of **this**: *That book is the one I want. I don't want this one.*

thaw *verb*
If something frozen **thaws**, it becomes soft or liquid. *Mum had to thaw the meat before she could cook it.*

theatre /*say* **thear**-tuh/ *noun*
A **theatre** is a building or hall for showing things like plays.

their *pronoun*
You use **their** to show that the people you are talking about own something. *A new family has moved into the street – that's their house on the corner.*

⭐ *Spelling Tip:* Don't confuse the spelling of **their** with **there** which has the same sound. **There** means 'in that place'.

theirs *pronoun*
Your use **theirs** to show that the people you are talking about own something. *Those ice-creams are theirs and these ones are ours.*

them *pronoun*
1. You use **them** for the people or things you are talking about. *'Where are the chocolate biscuits?' 'I put them in the cupboard.'*
2. You can use **them** when you are talking about a single person and you do not want to say whether they are male or female. *If anyone needs a new pen, I am happy to give them one.*

themselves *pronoun*
You use **themselves** to mean 'them and no-one else'. *Some of the kids hurt themselves when they jumped into the river.*

then *adverb*
1. You use **then** when you are talking about a time in the past. *We were in kindergarten then.*
2. You use **then** to talk about something that is next in order of time or place. *He opened the door, then walked inside. | Along this road there's a park, then a school.*

there *adverb*
If something is **there** or happens **there**, it happens in a particular place away from where you are. **There** means 'in that place' or 'to that place'. *The paper is there, on the top shelf.*

The opposite is **here**.

⭐ *Spelling Tip:* Don't confuse the spelling of **there** with **their** which has the same sound. **Their** means 'belonging to them'.

therefore *conjunction*
You use **therefore** when you are talking about something being a result of something else. *It was raining and therefore the game was called off.*

thermometer /say thuh-**mom**-uh-tuh / noun
A **thermometer** is an instrument for measuring how hot or cold someone or something is.

> ⭐ **Spelling Tip:** Although the strong sound in this word is the *mom* in the middle, the spelling will be easier if you see that it is made up of *thermo* (meaning 'heat' or 'temperature') and *meter* (a measuring instrument).

thesaurus /say thuh-**saw**-ruhs / noun (plural **thesauruses** or **thesauri** /say thuh-**saw**-ruy /)
A **thesaurus** is a kind of book in which words which have a similar meaning are put together.

> ⭐ **Spelling Tip:** Remember the spelling of the ending: *saurus*. With this ending, you might think that **thesaurus** was the word for a kind of dinosaur, rather than a book of words. In fact, it comes from the Greek word for 'a place where treasure is kept'.

these adjective, pronoun
You use **these** to show the people, things or ideas that you are pointing out or mentioning. *These socks are exactly what I want.* | *Whose books are these?*

> **These** can be the opposite of **those** when you use **these** to talk about some things that are closer than others: *These socks are a nicer colour than those.*

they pronoun
1. You use **they** when you are talking about more than one person or thing and you are not including yourself or the people you are speaking to. *They didn't have any idea where they were going.*
2. You can use **they** instead of *he* or *she*, when you are talking about a single person and you do not want to say whether they are male or female. *If anyone wants to come, they are welcome.*

> Also look up **them**, **their** and **theirs**.

thick adjective
1. If something is **thick**, it measures rather a lot from one surface or side to the other. *She cut a thick slice of bread.* | *She used a wide brush to paint three thick red lines.*
2. You use **thick** when you are saying how much something measures from one surface or side to the other. *The board was two centimetres thick.*
3. If something is **thick**, it is made up of parts packed closely together. *We had to walk though thick smoke to get away from the fire.*

4. If a liquid is **thick**, it does not flow easily. *The paint was too thick to use.*

> *Word Building:* **thickly**, adverb: *I tried not to spread the butter too thickly.* –**thicken**, verb When you make something thick, you **thicken** it. –**thickness**, noun If something is thick, you talk about its **thickness**.

> The opposite of definitions 1, 3 and 4 is **thin**.

thief /say theef / noun (plural **thieves**)
A **thief** is someone who steals something.

> ⭐ **Spelling Tip:** Remember that **thief** is spelt with *ie* (to spell the 'ee' sound). This follows the rule that *i* comes before *e* except after *c*. Think of similar words such as *brief* and *chief*.

thigh /rhymes with my / noun
Your **thigh** is the top part of your leg, above your knee.

thin adjective
1. If something is **thin**, it does not measure very much from one surface or side to the other. *The paper was so thin you could see through it.* | *The painting was full of thin red lines.*
2. If a person or animal is **thin**, they do not weigh much. *She keeps thin by dieting.* | *We found a thin, hungry cat.*
3. If something is **thin**, it is made up of parts which are spread quite far apart. *My dad is worried that his hair is starting to get thin.*

> *Word Building:* **thinness**, noun If something is thin, you talk about its **thinness**.

> The opposite of definitions 1 and 3 is **thick**; the opposite of definition 2 is **fat**.

thing noun
1. A **thing** is an object that is not alive. *My bike is the most precious thing I own.*
2. You use **thing** when you are talking about some object or idea that you cannot easily describe. *The stick had a metal thing at the end of it.* | *We had some things we had to discuss.*

think verb (**thinks**, **thinking**, **thought** /say thawt /, **has thought**)
1. If you **think**, you have ideas, words or pictures in your mind, sometimes to try and work out a problem. *We don't know if animals are able to think.* | *Keep quiet for a moment – I'm thinking.*
2. If you **think** that something is so, you have that as your opinion. *He thought the film was good.*

3. If you **think** something, you believe that it is true, but you are not completely sure. *I haven't spoken to Leah but I think she is coming to the party.*

third *adjective*
If something is **third**, it comes next after the second thing.

thirsty *adjective* (**thirstier**, **thirstiest**)
If you are **thirsty**, you have a dry feeling in your mouth and throat because you need something to drink.

> **Word Building: thirst**, *noun* When you are thirsty, you feel **thirst**.

thirteen *noun*, *adjective*
Thirteen is a number which you can write as 13.

> **Word Building: thirteenth**, *adjective*: *The thirteenth person will be the reserve player.*

thirty *noun*, *adjective*
Thirty is a number which you can write as 30.

> **Word Building: thirtieth**, *adjective*: *The thirtieth kid on the roll has a name starting with 'Z'.*

this *adjective*, *pronoun*
You use **this** to show a person, thing or idea that you are pointing out or mentioning. *This boy saved my life.* | *This is my entry for the show.*

> **This** can be the opposite of **that** when you use **this** to talk about a thing that is closer than another: *I would like to buy this video – I don't want that one.*

thorn *noun*
A **thorn** is a bit that sticks out from the stems of some plants and has a sharp point.

those *adjective*, *pronoun*
You use **those** to show the people, things or ideas that you are pointing out or mentioning. *Those shoes are exactly what I want.* | *Those are the best cakes in the whole shop.*

> **Those** can be the opposite of **these** when you use **those** to talk about some things that further away than others: *I have read those books, but I haven't read these.*

though /*say* dhoh/ *conjunction*
1. You use **though** when you are talking about something which is true, but which makes something else you are saying seem not likely. *Though we had no money, we had a good time.*

2. You can use **though** to mean 'but'. *I will go, though I think it is silly.*

> You can also say **although** for definition 1.

> ⚙ *Spelling Tip:* Remember to learn the *ough* spelling for the 'oh' sound. It can be confusing as other words with this spelling can sound quite different. It might help to think of another word with the same spelling and sound, such as *dough*.

thought /*say* thawt/ *verb*
1. Look up **think**.
–*noun* **2.** A **thought** is something that has come into your mind as a result of thinking.

> ⚙ *Spelling Tip:* Remember the *ough* spelling for the 'aw' sound. Other words like this are *bought* and *brought*.

thoughtful *adjective*
If your thoughts are often about other people and what they would like, you are **thoughtful**.

thoughtless *adjective*
If you do not think about other people and what they would like, you are **thoughtless**.

thousand *noun*, *adjective*
A **thousand** is a number which you can write as 1000.

> **Word Building: thousandth**, *adjective*: *This must be the thousandth time I've tried to do this.*

thread /*rhymes with* red/ *noun*
1. Thread is cotton, or something similar, in the form of a very thin, long piece, often used for sewing. *Mum used some black thread to fix my tunic.*
2. A **thread** is a single piece of this. *Let me cut off that loose thread.*

three *noun*, *adjective*
Three is a number which you can write as 3.

> Also look up **third**.

thrill *noun*
1. A **thrill** is a sudden, very excited feeling.
–*verb* **2.** If something **thrills** you, it makes you feel very excited. *Mum was thrilled when she won a trip to Japan.*

> **Word Building: thrilling**, *adjective* Something that thrills you is **thrilling**.

throat *noun*
1. Your **throat** is the front of your neck, under your chin. *The diamond sparkled on her throat.*
2. Your **throat** is the part of your body at the back of your mouth where food passes through on its way to your stomach, and where air travels down to your lungs. *I knew I was getting a cold because my throat was sore.*

throne *noun*
A **throne** is the special chair that a king or queen sits on at special times.

through /*say* throoh/ *preposition*
1. If something goes **through** something else, it goes in at one end or side and out the other. *He pulled the rope through the hole.*
2. If you go **through** something, you go among or between the parts of it. *She swam through the water.*

> ✸ *Spelling Tip:* Remember the *ough* spelling for the 'ooh' sound. Don't confuse **through** with **threw** which sounds the same. **Threw** is a form of **throw**: *I threw the ball to her.*

throughout /*say* throoh-**owt**/ *preposition*
1. If something is **throughout** something else, it is everywhere in it. *Police were placed throughout the crowd.*
2. If something goes on **throughout** a period of time, it goes on from the beginning to the end of that time. *They had to work throughout the night to get the leak fixed.*

> ✸ *Spelling Tip:* If you remember the spelling of *through*, you will be all right with this word. Just add *out* at the end.

throw *verb* (**throws, throwing, threw, has thrown**)
If you **throw** something, you make it move through the air. *I'm going to throw the ball to you.*

thumb /*rhymes with* sum/ *noun*
Your **thumb** is the finger that is shorter and thicker than the others.

> ✸ *Spelling Tip:* Don't forget the *b* at the end. Other words with a similar spelling are *dumb* and *crumb*.

thump *verb*
If you **thump** something or someone, you hit them strongly and loudly. *Sally thumped on the door for a long time but nobody came.*

thunder *noun*
Thunder is the loud noise that you hear in a storm.

Thursday *noun*
Thursday is a day of the week. It comes after Wednesday and before Friday.

tick[1] *noun*
1. A **tick** is the small, regular sound a clock makes. *All I could hear in the dark was the tick of the clock.*
2. A **tick** is a small mark (✓) that shows something has been done the right way. *The teacher put a tick next to all the sums we got right.*
–*verb* 3. When a clock **ticks**, it makes a small regular sound. *The clock ticked noisily in the still night.*
4. If someone **ticks** something, they put a mark next to it to say it is right. *The teacher ticked all of my answers.*

tick[2] *noun*
A **tick** is a tiny animal like an insect, that attaches itself to an animal and takes in its blood. It can kill dogs and cats.

ticket *noun*
A **ticket** is a small printed card which shows that you have paid for something.

tickle *verb*
If you **tickle** someone, you rub a particular part of their body to make them laugh. *My friends were tickling me under my arms – I couldn't stop laughing!*

tide *noun*
The **tide** is the movement of the seas and oceans towards the land and away from it. This happens twice each day. At **high tide** you can see the water is high up on the sand of a beach, and at **low tide**, it is further down the sand.

tidy *adjective* (**tidier, tidiest**)
1. If something is **tidy**, everything in it is properly arranged and in its right place.
–*verb* (**tidies, tidying, tidied, has tidied**)
2. If you **tidy** an area, you put everything in its right place. *I wish you would tidy your room!*

> *Word Building:* **tidily**, *adverb*: *I put away my clothes really tidily.*

> The opposite is **untidy**.

tie *verb* (**ties, tying, tied, has tied**)
1. If you **tie** something to something else, you fasten it with something like thread or rope. *He tied a red cloth at the back of his truck to warn other drivers that he was carrying a long load.*

2. If two people or teams **tie**, they get the same number of points in a game. *The two schools tied in the tennis game.*
–*noun* **3.** A **tie** is a narrow piece of cloth worn around your neck, usually over a shirt.

tiger *noun*
A **tiger** is a large, meat-eating wild animal of the cat family which has yellow-brown and black fur.

tight /*say* tuyt/ *adjective*
1. If clothes are **tight**, they are too close to your body, without leaving enough room to be comfortable. *My shoes are too tight and now my feet are sore.*
2. Something is **tight** if it is pulled as far as it can go. *The rope connecting the boat to the shore was stretched tight.*

Word Building: tightly: *He tied the boxes together tightly.* –**tighten**, *verb* If you make something more tight, you **tighten** it.

The opposite is **loose**.

tile *noun*
A **tile** is a thin piece of baked clay that is used for covering roofs, floors and walls.

till *preposition, conjunction*
Look up **until**.

timber *noun*
Timber is wood which has been cut into pieces so that it can be used to build things.

time *noun*
1. **Time** is the passing of the hours, days, weeks, months and years. *Time goes quickly when you're busy.*
2. You use **time** when you talk about a period between two events. *I haven't seen her for a long time.*
3. The **time** is a particular moment shown by a clock. *What's the time?*
4. A **time** is a particular moment or period. *The first time I went, there was nobody home.*
5. in time, If something happens **in time**, it happens early enough. *She arrived in time for the start of the concert.*
6. on time, If something happens **on time**, it happens when it should. *We arrived on time – dinner had just been served.*

time line *noun*
A **time line** is a line with dates marked on it to show the order in which events have happened.

timid /*say* **tim**-uhd/ *adjective*
If you are **timid**, you are easily frightened.

Word Building: timidly, *adverb* If you are timid, you do things **timidly**. –**timidity** /*say* tuh-**mid**-uh-tee/, *noun* If you are timid, you do things with **timidity**.

tin *noun*
1. **Tin** is a light silver-coloured metal. *Tin is found in the hills near our town.*
2. A **tin** is a metal container which is used to keep food fresh. *She opened a tin of apples.*

tiny *adjective* (**tinier, tiniest**)
If something is **tiny**, it is very small.

tip[1] *noun*
The **tip** of something is the pointed part at the end of it.

tip[2] *verb* (**tips, tipping, tipped, has tipped**)
1. If you **tip** something, you make it turn on its side. *If you tip the cup, the milk will spill.*
2. tip over, a. If you **tip** something over, you knock it and make it fall. *He accidentally tipped over the bottle and the milk spilt.* **b.** If something **tips over**, it turns right over. *The little boat tipped over in the storm.*
–*noun* **3.** A **tip** is a place where you go to leave your rubbish.

tip[3] *noun*
A **tip** is a piece of useful information. *She gave me a tip on where to sit for the best view.* | *There are a lot of spelling tips in this dictionary.*

tiptoe *verb* (**tiptoes, tiptoeing, tiptoed, has tiptoed**)
If you **tiptoe**, you walk softly and carefully on your toes. *We tiptoed to the kitchen to give Dad a surprise.*

tire *verb*
If something **tires** you, it makes you lose strength. *The long walk tired the children.*

Word Building: tiring, *adjective* If something tires you, it is **tiring**.

✴ **Spelling Tip:** Don't confuse the spelling of **tire** with **tyre** which has the same sound but is spelt with a *y*. A **tyre** goes round the wheel of a car or bike.

tired *adjective*
1. If you are **tired**, you are feeling weak from some kind of effort. *I was so tired after school that I fell asleep in front of the television.*

2. tired of, If you are **tired of** something, it no longer interests you. *We're tired of playing cricket – how about we go for a swim.*

tissue /*say* **tish**-ooh/ *noun*
A **tissue** is a handkerchief made of paper.

title *noun*
1. The **title** of a book, film or piece of music is the name it is known by. *I can't remember the title of the book I'm looking for.*
2. A **title** is a special name showing what job someone has, or what position they have in society. *My aunt has finished her medical studies and can now use the title 'Doctor'.*

to *preposition*
You use **to** when you are talking about movement in a certain direction: *We went from the east to the west.*; *She caught the train to the city.* This is the basic meaning of **to**, but you can use it in many ways, for example. *Give the book to me. | Show your work to the teacher. | I changed seats to be able to see better. | We tied the piece of cloth to a stick.*

> ✸ *Spelling Tip:* Don't confuse the spelling of **to** with **too** or **two** which have the same sound. **Too** means 'also' and **two** is a number.

toad *noun*
A **toad** is an animal like a big frog which lives mostly on land and has a dry skin.

toadstool *noun*
A **toadstool** is a plant that looks like a mushroom but some of them are poisonous. If you eat one of these, you could get very sick or die.

toast *noun*
Toast is bread cut into thin pieces and cooked until it is brown on both sides.

tobacco *noun*
1. **Tobacco** is a plant whose leaves are dried and used for smoking in cigarettes. *Tobacco is grown in very hot areas.*
2. You can use **tobacco** when you are talking about the dried leaves themselves. *Smoking tobacco is very bad for your health.*

> ✸ *Spelling Tip:* Remember that there is only one *b* but a double *c* in this word.

today *adverb*
1. If something is happening **today**, it is happening on this day. *I'll give it to you today.*
–*noun* 2. You use **today** when you are talking about the day that is happening now.

toe *noun*
Your **toe** is one of the five parts at the end of your foot.

> ✸ *Spelling Tip:* Don't confuse the spelling of **toe** with **tow** which has the same sound. **Tow** means to pull something.

toffee *noun*
Toffee is a sticky sweet made by boiling sugar and water together.

together *adverb*
1. If people do something **together**, they do it with each other. *They planned the party together.*
2. If several things happen **together**, they happen at the same time. *The conductor asked everybody in the school orchestra to start together.*
3. You use **together** when you are talking about things being joined, or touching each other. *Just sew the two edges together.*

toilet *noun*
A **toilet** is a bowl-like container, connected to pipes, where you sit to empty liquid or solid stuff that your body needs to get rid of.

token *noun*
A **token** is a ticket or metal disc you can use instead of money to pay for something.

tomato *noun* (*plural* **tomatoes**)
A **tomato** is a juicy red fruit which can be cooked or eaten raw.

tomorrow *adverb*
1. If something is going to happen **tomorrow**, it will happen on the day after today. *She's coming tomorrow.*
–*noun* 2. **Tomorrow** is the day after today.

ton /*say* tun/ *noun*
A **ton** is a unit of weight used in some countries, such as America, for measuring very heavy things, such as trucks.

tongue /*rhymes with* hung/ *noun*
Your **tongue** is the soft part in your mouth that moves around and helps you to taste food and to speak.

> ✸ *Spelling Tip:* Don't forget the silent *ue* at the end. Also remember the *o* spelling where you might expect a *u*.

tonight /*say* tuh-**nuyt**/ *adverb*
1. If something happens **tonight**, it happens on the night of the same day. *We're leaving for our holidays tonight.*
–*noun* 2. **Tonight** is the night of this day.

tonne /rhymes with on/ noun
A **tonne** is a unit of weight used to measure very heavy things. It is equal to 1000 kilograms.

tonsil /say **ton**-suhl/ noun
A **tonsil** is one of the two soft pieces of flesh on the sides of the back of your throat.

> **Word Building: tonsillitis** /say ton-suh-**luy**-tuhs/, noun If your tonsils are sore, then you have **tonsillitis**.

> ✷ **Spelling Tip:** Remember that there is only one *l* at the end of **tonsil**, but the *l* is doubled in the word **tonsillitis**.

too adverb
1. You use **too** to show that something is being added to what has already been said. *I hope you can come, and bring your friend too – there's plenty of room in the car.*
2. You use **too** when there is more than you want or need. *The speech was too long and people started to fall asleep.* | *Hubert ate too much cake.*

> ✷ **Spelling Tip:** Remember that **too** has a double *o*. Don't confuse the spelling with **to** or **two**.

tool noun
A **tool** is a piece of equipment you use for doing some kinds of work. You usually hold it in your hand.

tooth noun (plural **teeth**)
A **tooth** is one of the hard white parts inside your mouth that you use to eat.

toothpaste noun
Toothpaste is a special, soft substance that you brush on your teeth to clean them.

top noun
1. The **top** of something is its highest point. *We climbed almost to the top of the tree.*
2. The **top** of something is its highest surface. *The top of the table needs to be cleaned.*
–adjective 3. The **top** thing is the highest thing.

topic noun
A **topic** is the thing that you are talking about.

topple verb
If something **topples**, it falls over or drops down to the ground. *We put too many books on the pile and it toppled over.*

torch noun (plural **torches**)
A **torch** is a light which you carry around in your hand, with a battery to make it work.

tortoise /say **taw**-tuhs/ noun
A **tortoise** is a reptile with a hard shell covering its body.

> ✷ **Spelling Tip:** Remember the *oise* spelling at the end, making an 'uhs' sound. You could think of a **tortoise** making a lot of *noise* to remind you.

torture /say **taw**-chuh/ verb
If someone **tortures** a person, they cause that person very great pain, usually to find out something from them. *The man was tortured while he was held prisoner.*

toss verb
If you **toss** something, you throw it. *Toss the paper into the bin.*

total noun
1. A **total** is the result you get when you add up different amounts.
–adjective 2. **Total** describes something that is complete or whole. That is all there is of it.

> **Word Building: totally**, adverb: *The colour of her hair has totally changed.*

touch /say tuch/ verb
1. If you **touch** something, you feel it with your hand or finger. *Touch the material and feel how soft it is.*
2. If two things **touch**, they are so close that one rests against the other. *It is dangerous if those wires touch each other.*
–noun (plural **touches**) 3. A **touch** is the act of putting your hand on something. *The dog jumped up when he felt my touch.*
4. A **touch** is a small amount of something. *This soup needs a touch of salt.*

tough /say tuf/ adjective
If something is **tough**, it is hard to break or cut.

> ✷ **Spelling Tip:** Remember that there is no 'f' in **tough** – the spelling *ough* gives the 'uf' sound, as it does in some other words like *enough* and *rough*.

tour verb
1. If you **tour**, you travel through a place. *We toured the north of the country.*
–noun 2. A **tour** is an organised journey, stopping at different places along the way.

tourist noun
A **tourist** is someone who travels around a place, stopping to look at things that interest them.

tow /say toh/ verb

If you **tow** something, you pull it along using a rope or chain. *The truck towed the car to the closest garage.*

⭐ *Spelling Tip:* Don't confuse the spelling of **tow** with **toe** which has the same sound. Your **toes** are on your feet.

towards preposition

If you go **towards** something, you go in the direction of it. *We must walk towards the north.*

You can also say **toward**.

towel noun

A **towel** is a piece of cloth that you use to dry yourself after you have washed or swum.

tower noun

A **tower** is a tall narrow building, or part of a building.

town noun

A **town** is an area of houses, shops and offices where people live and work. It is smaller than a city.

toy noun

A **toy** is an object that you play with.

trace noun

1. A **trace** is a mark or sign that tells you someone or something has been somewhere.
–verb 2. If you **trace** something, you copy a drawing, plan or map by putting a piece of thin paper over it and following along its lines with a pencil. *The teacher told us to trace around the outline of the leaf.*

track noun

1. A **track** is a rough path made by humans or animals through the bush. *We followed the track along the bottom of the valley.*
2. **Tracks** are marks that people or animals leave in the ground when they walk, showing that they have been that way. *We followed their tracks across the sand towards the rocks.*
3. **Tracks** are the long metal bars that a train runs along. *Don't walk across the railway tracks.*
4. A **track** is a special path for races. *I hope I get to run on the inner track.*

tractor noun

A **tractor** is used by a farmer to pull heavy loads and large tools. It has large back wheels and a powerful motor.

trade noun

1. **Trade** is the buying and selling of things. *The prime ministers met to discuss trade between their two countries.*
2. Someone's **trade** is the kind of work they do. *Her grandfather was a carpenter by trade.*

tradition noun

If older people hand down a **tradition** to younger people, they tell them of the beliefs, customs and stories that they were taught.

Word Building: **traditional**, *adjective* If something is done according to tradition, you say it is **traditional**.

traffic noun

1. **Traffic** is the coming and going of vehicles like cars and trucks along a road. *There's too much traffic today – let's get the train.*
2. **traffic lights**, **Traffic lights** are lights on a road that change from red to orange to green, as a sign to cars to stop, slow down or go. *You have to stop when the traffic lights turn red.*

tragedy /say **traj**-uh-dee/ noun (plural **tragedies**)

A **tragedy** is a very sad or terrible thing that happens.

Word Building: **tragic** /say **traj**-ik/, *adjective* Any tragedy is **tragic** for the people it happens to.

⭐ *Spelling Tip:* Remember the *g* spelling for the 'j' sound, and the *edy* (not *idy*) ending. It might help if you realise the word *age* is hidden inside the word **tragedy**. Try breaking the word up as *tra + ge + dy*.

trail noun

1. A **trail** is a path made across any rough country. *The trail through the thick grass and trees was hard to follow.*
2. A **trail** is the set of marks left behind by an animal or person being hunted. *He was easy to follow because of the trail he left behind him.*

trailer noun

A **trailer** is something a car or truck pulls along to carry heavy loads.

train noun

1. A **train** is a vehicle that moves along railway tracks, carrying people or things from one place to another. A **train** is made up of several sections (called 'carriages') joined together. The first section has an engine and pulls the other carriages along.

–verb **2.** If you **train** a person or animal, you teach them how to do something. *She trained her dog to collect the newspaper each morning.*

training *noun*
If you are having **training** in something, you are being taught how to do it.

traitor *noun*
A **traitor** is someone who tells an enemy secrets about their country.

tramp *verb*
1. If you **tramp**, you walk with strong steps, usually for quite a long time. *They tramped all around the city looking for a post office.*
–noun **2.** A **tramp** is someone who does not have a home and lives on the streets.

trampoline /*say* tram-puh-**leen**/ *noun*
A **trampoline** is a frame with material stretched over it and joined to it by springs. You jump up and down on it for fun and for exercise.

trance *noun*
Someone is in a **trance** when they do not know what is happening around them.

transfer /*say* trans-**fer**/ *verb* (**transfers, transferring, transferred, has transferred**)
If you **transfer** someone or something, you take them from one place to another. *When we moved, my parents transferred me to another school.*

translate *verb*
If you **translate** something, you change it from one language to another. *I want to learn how to translate books from my language into other ones.*

> **Word Building: translation,** *noun* If you translate something, you do a **translation.** **–translator,** *noun* If your job is to translate things, you are a **translator.**

transparent *adjective*
Something is **transparent** if you can see through it as if it was not there.

transport *verb* /*say* trans-**pawt**/
1. If you **transport** something, you carry it from one place to another. *We'll have to transport this furniture in a truck.*
–noun /*say* **trans**-pawt/ **2. Transport** is a way of moving people or things from one place to another.

trap *noun*
A **trap** is something made for catching animals.

trapdoor *noun*
A **trapdoor** is a small door in a floor or ceiling.

trapeze /*say* truh-**peez**/ *noun*
A **trapeze** is a short bar that hangs from ropes that people swing on while they do balancing tricks.

> ✴ *Spelling Tip:* It is definitely not easy to perform on the **trapeze.** Think of this to remind you that the ending is spelt *eze* (not *ease* or *ese*).

travel *verb* (**travels, travelling, travelled, has travelled**)
If you **travel**, you go from one place to another, often over a long distance. *When I grow up, I'm going to travel around the world.*

traveller *noun*
A **traveller** is someone who travels from one place to another, usually over a long distance.

> ✴ *Spelling Tip:* This word comes from *travel* but remember that the *l* has been doubled.

tray *noun*
A **tray** is a flat piece of wood, plastic or metal used for carrying things, especially food.

tread /*rhymes with* led/ *verb* (**treads, treading, trod, has trodden**)
If you **tread**, you walk or step on something. *Be careful where you tread.*

treasure /*say* **trezh**-uh/ *noun*
1. Treasure is a large amount of things that are worth a lot, like gold, silver or money. *In my dream, I discovered heaps of treasure and became very rich.*
2. A **treasure** is anything which is very valuable. *His car is his greatest treasure.*

> ✴ *Spelling Tip:* Remember the *ea* spelling for the 'e' sound in the first part of this word. Also remember the *sure* ending which sounds like 'zhuh'. Think of other words with this spelling and sound, such as *measure* and *pleasure*.

treat *verb*
1. When you **treat** someone in a particular way, you behave towards them in that way. *They treated the boy kindly.*
2. When a doctor **treats** you or **treats** a disease, he or she tries to make you better. *The doctor has been treating her for a cough.*
–noun **3.** A **treat** is something special that you are given.

Word Building: treatment, *noun*: *Doctors are trying to find a new treatment for this terrible disease.*

tree *noun*
A **tree** is a tall plant with leaves and branches.

tremble *verb*
If you **tremble**, you shake because you are frightened, weak or cold. *When I got out of the swimming pool, my knees began to tremble.*

trespass *verb*
If you **trespass**, you go onto someone's land when you should not. *He put up a sign warning people not to trespass on his land.*

Word Building: trespasser, *noun* If you trespass, then you are a **trespasser**.

trial *noun*
1. A **trial** is the time when a person is brought into a court of law. A judge or a jury have to decide whether or not they have done something wrong. *At the trial, he admitted that he was guilty.*
2. A **trial** is a test to see if something works. *They are doing a trial to see how good this new type of tyre is.*

triangle *noun*
A **triangle** is a shape with three sides.

tribe *noun*
A **tribe** is a group of families that are related to each other. They do things the same way and they live in the same place.

trick *verb*
1. If you **trick** someone, you make them believe something that is not true, often to get something for yourself. *He tricked us into letting him come into our house and then he stole our television.*
–*noun* 2. A **trick** is something that makes people believe something that is not true. *We let him into the house because he said he was a police officer, but it was a trick.*
3. If you do a **trick**, you do something skilful or clever. *I can do a trick with five balls and a stick.*

trickle *verb*
If a liquid **trickles**, a very small amount of it flows slowly. *Tears began to trickle down his cheeks.*

tricky *adjective* (**trickier**, **trickiest**)
If something is **tricky**, it is difficult to do or deal with.

Word Building: trickiness, *noun*

tricycle /*say* **truy**-sik-uhl/ *noun*
A **tricycle** is something you ride, with one wheel at the front and two wheels at the back.

trigger *noun*
The **trigger** is the part on a gun that you press to fire it.

trim *verb* (**trims**, **trimming**, **trimmed**, **has trimmed**)
If you **trim** something, you cut it so that it is neat and tidy. *We trimmed the dog's hair because it was growing over his eyes.*

trip *noun*
1. If you go on a **trip**, you travel from one place to another.
–*verb* (**trips**, **tripping**, **tripped**, **has tripped**)
2. If you **trip**, you knock your foot against something, and sometimes fall over. *She tripped on the rock and fell, hurting her leg.*

triumph /*say* **truy**-umf/ *noun*
A **triumph** is something important that you have done well, such as winning a race.

Word Building: triumphant /*say* truy-**um**-fuhnt/, *adjective* If you have a triumph, then you are **triumphant**.

Spelling Tip: Remember the *ph* spelling for the 'f' sound at the end.

troop *noun*
A **troop** is a group of people who do things together.

tropical *adjective*
Something is **tropical** if it comes from one of the hot parts of the world near the equator.

Word Building: tropics, *plural noun* The tropical parts of the world are called **the tropics**.

trot *verb* (**trots**, **trotting**, **trotted**, **has trotted**)
If a person or animal **trots**, they move in a way that is fast and steady. *We watched the horses trot around the oval.*

trouble /*rhymes with* bubble/ *noun*
1. If you have **trouble** doing something, you find it difficult to do. *My mother had trouble getting the car started this morning.*
2. If you have **troubles**, you have problems or worries. *She has had a lot of troubles since her husband died.*
3. **in trouble**, **a.** If you are **in trouble**, you are in a difficult situation of some kind. *His boat seems to be sinking. I think he is in serious trouble.* **b.** If you are **in trouble**, you have done something

wrong and someone, such as your parent or your teacher, is punishing you. *You're late – you'll be in trouble when you get home.*
–*verb* **4.** If you **trouble** someone, you disturb or worry them. *Don't trouble him when he's tired.*

trousers *noun*
Trousers are a piece of clothing for the lower half of your body, divided into two parts for the legs.

You can also say **a pair of trousers**, but then you speak about them as though they are one thing: *This pair of trousers is getting old.*

truck *noun*
A **truck** is a vehicle which is used to carry large loads along roads. Large **trucks** often have many sets of wheels and separate parts in which the load is carried.

true *adjective*
1. Something is **true** if it is what has really happened. *It's true! I really did see a horse in the garden!*
2. If someone is a **true** friend, you can depend on them when you need them. *You're a true friend to help me today.*
3. come true, If something that you have thought about **comes true**, it actually happens. *I had always wanted to live near the beach, and now it's come true.*

trumpet *noun*
A **trumpet** is a musical instrument that you blow, made of brass.

trunk *noun*
1. A **trunk** is the main part of a tree. *We attached the rope to a strong tree trunk.*
2. A **trunk** is an elephant's long nose. *The elephant was carrying a large log with its trunk.*

trust *verb*
1. If you **trust** someone, you believe what they say, and you know that they will not hurt you in any way. *I trust him when he says he can do it.*
–*noun* **2.** If you have **trust** in someone, you are sure that they are truthful and that they will not hurt you.

truth *noun*
The **truth** is what has really happened.

Word Building: **truthful**, *adjective* If you tell the truth, you are **truthful**. –**truthfully**, *adverb*: *You must answer truthfully.*

try *verb* (**tries, trying, tried, has tried**)
1. If you **try** to do something, you make an effort to do it. *Try to read this book – I'll help you with the difficult words.*
2. To **try** something is to test it to see what happens. *Did you try it first to see if it worked?*
3. try on, If you **try on** a piece of clothing, you put it on to see if it fits or if it looks nice. *I tried on the shoes and they were perfect.*

T-shirt *noun*
A **T-shirt** is a shirt with short sleeves and no buttons.

tsunami /*say* sooh-**nah**-mee, tsooh-**nah**-mee/ *noun* A **tsunami** is an extremely large sea wave caused by an earthquake under the sea.

✳ *Spelling Tip:* Don't forget the *t* at the beginning of this word. Also remember the *i* at the end. **Tsunami** has an unusual spelling because it comes from Japanese.

tub *noun*
A **tub** is a container with a flat bottom.

tube *noun*
1. A **tube** is a long, thin, empty container, that gas or liquid can move through. *The patient was being fed through a tube until he could eat properly.*
2. A **tube** is a soft, thin container. *Once you squeeze toothpaste out of the tube, you can't put it back again.*

tuck *verb*
If you **tuck** something, you fold it and put it somewhere in a neat way. *Tuck the sheet under the mattress.*

tuckshop *noun*
A **tuckshop** is a shop in a school which sells food.

Another word for this is **canteen**.

Tuesday *noun*
Tuesday is a day of the week. It comes after Monday and before Wednesday.

tuft *noun*
A **tuft** is a bunch of things like hairs, feathers or bits of grass.

tug *verb* (**tugs, tugging, tugged, has tugged**)
1. If you **tug** something, you pull it hard. *Both teams were tugging on either end of the rope.*
–*noun* **2.** A **tug** is a small, powerful boat that is used to pull and push big ships.

You can also call definition 2 a **tugboat**.

tulip /*say* **tyooh**-luhp / *noun*
A **tulip** is a beautiful flower that is shaped like a cup.

tumble *verb*
If someone or something **tumbles**, they fall or roll over. *She tumbled off the wall and fell into the soft grass.*

tune *noun*
A **tune** is musical sounds that go together to make a pattern that sounds good for singing or playing.

tunic /*say* **tyooh**-nik / *noun*
A **tunic** is a loose dress that has straight sides and no sleeves. Girls often wear them as part of their school uniform.

tunnel *noun*
A **tunnel** is a long hole that goes through the ground. Some are big enough for trains and cars to go through.

turkey *noun* (*plural* **turkeys**)
A **turkey** is a large bird that is usually kept for food.

turn *verb*
1. If something **turns**, it goes round and round. *The wheels turned slowly.*
2. If you **turn**, you move so as to face in a particular direction. *He turned and looked at me.*
3. If you **turn**, you go in a different direction by following something, like a road or a path. *She turned the corner.*
4. You can use **turn** to mean 'become'. *He was so cold that his toes turned blue.*
5. turn down, If you **turn** something **down**, you make it quieter. *Please turn down the television so I can hear what you're saying to me.*
6. turn into, If you **turn** something **into** something else, you make it become that thing. *The witch turned the prince into a frog.*
7. turn off, If you **turn** something **off**, you make it stop flowing by moving something that controls it. *Quick! Turn off the water! The bath's too full!*
8. turn on, If you **turn** something **on**, you make it start flowing by moving something that controls it. *Now the bath is too cold – please turn on the hot water.*
9. turn out, a. If you **turn out** a light, you make it stop operating. *We turned out all the lights and told each other frightening stories.* **b.** If something **turns out** in a particular way, it is like that in the end. *I spent a lot of time on my story and I think it turned out well.*
10. turn over, a. If you **turn over**, you change your position from lying on your front to lying on your back, or the other way around. *Her back started hurting, so she turned over.* **b.** If you **turn** something **over**, you move it so that the opposite side is facing upwards. *He turned the dog over and scratched its stomach.*
–*noun* **11.** A **turn** is a movement which changes your direction. *The driver made a turn to the right.*
12. Your **turn** is your chance or time to do something or to get something. *It never seems to be my turn to watch TV!*

turtle *noun*
A **turtle** is a reptile with a hard shell covering its body, that lives in the sea.

tusk *noun*
A **tusk** is one of two long, curved teeth that some animals have at the front of their heads.

TV *noun*
A **TV** is a television.

twelve *noun, adjective*
Twelve is a number which you can write as 12.

Word Building: twelfth, *adjective*: *The twelfth person couldn't come to my party, so now there will be only eleven guests.*

twenty *noun, adjective*
Twenty is a number which you can write as 20.

Word Building: twentieth, *adjective*: *The twentieth person to come into the room won a prize.*

twice *adverb*
1. If something happens **twice**, it happens two times. *He wrote to me twice a week.* | *We had only seen him twice.*
2. If something is **twice** the amount or size of something else, it is two times as much or as big. *This test is twice as hard as the last one we did.* | *Their car is twice the size of ours.*

twig *noun*
A **twig** is a small, thin branch of a tree.

twin *noun*
A **twin** is one of two children who have the same parents and who were born at the same time.

twinkle *verb*
If something **twinkles**, it shines with many quick bursts of light. *Stars twinkle in the sky at night.*

twirl *verb*
If something **twirls**, it turns around and around quickly. *She twirled many times in her new dress.*

twist *verb*
1. If you **twist** things, you turn them around and around each other. *To make a rope, you twist many strings together.*
2. If you **twist** something, you turn or bend it. *The bottle top will come off if you twist it around.*

two *noun, adjective*
Two is a number which you can write as 2.

Also look up **second**[1].

⚑ *Spelling Tip:* Remember the silent *w* in **two**. Don't confuse it with **to** or **too**. **Too** means 'also'. Look up **to** to see the many ways in which you can use this word.

type /*say* tuyp/ *noun*
1. A **type** is a group of people, animals or things that are similar in some way.
–*verb* **2.** If you **type** something, you use a typewriter or computer to write it. *I type all my letters because my writing is so bad.*

typewriter /*say* **tuyp**-ruy-tuh/ *noun*
A **typewriter** is a machine with keys which you press to produce numbers and letters like those used in printing.

tyre /*say* **tuy**-uh/ *noun*
A **tyre** is a ring of rubber, usually filled with air, that goes around the wheel of a vehicle like a car, truck or bicycle.

⚑ *Spelling Tip:* Remember that this word is spelt with a *y*. Don't confuse it with **tire** which has the same sound. If something **tires** you, it makes you feel weak.

underwear

ugly *adjective* (**uglier**, **ugliest**)
If you say that something or someone is **ugly**, you mean that they are not pleasing in appearance.

The opposite is **beautiful** or **lovely**.

umbrella *noun*
An **umbrella** is something you use to keep dry when it is raining, and sometimes to protect you from the sun. It is a circle of material stretched over a frame which is attached to a long handle that you hold.

umpire *noun*
An **umpire** is someone who makes sure that you keep to the rules when you play games like tennis or cricket.

Another word that means nearly the same is **referee**.

uncle *noun*
Your **uncle** is the brother of your father or mother.

unconscious /*say* un-**kon**-shuhs / *adjective*
If you are **unconscious**, you look as if you are asleep, but you have fainted or have had a hard knock on the head.

under *preposition*
1. If something is **under** something, it is in a lower position than it, or on the bottom surface of it. *William hid under the table.*
2. If you use **under** before a number or amount, you mean less than that number. *Everyone in our class is under ten.*

underground *adjective*
If something is **underground**, it is under the ground.

undergrowth *noun*
Undergrowth is plants and bushes that grow under tall trees.

underline *verb*
If you **underline** words on a page, you draw a line under them. *The teacher underlines in red the words we need to learn carefully.*

underneath *preposition*, *adverb*
You use **underneath** to mean 'below' or 'under'. *Write your address underneath your name.* | *Dad pulled up the carpet and you won't believe what was underneath!*

understand *verb* (**understands, understanding, understood, has understood**)
1. If you **understand** what someone is saying to you, you know what they mean. *When they told us how hard the hike was, we understood because they described it so well.*
2. If you **understand** something, you know how it works. *I don't understand computers.*
3. If you **understand** a language, you know what the words mean. *My big sister understands French.*

Word Building: **understanding**, *noun*: *She has a good understanding of the rules of netball.*

underwear *noun*
Underwear is clothes such as singlets and small pants that you wear under your other clothes.

undo *verb* (**undoes, undoing, undid, has undone**)
If you **undo** something, you open it or make it loose. *Undo your buttons and take off your coat.* | *I can't undo this knot.*

unemployed *adjective*
Someone is **unemployed** if they do not have a job.

unfair *adjective*
1. If someone is **unfair**, they do not treat people equally. They treat some people better than others. *You are unfair giving me all this work when Jane has almost nothing to do.*
2. If you say that something is **unfair**, you mean that everyone is not being treated the same. *It's unfair that you get all the cake!*

unicorn /*say* **yooh**-nuh-kawn / *noun*
A **unicorn** is an animal in stories that looks like a horse with a long, straight horn in the middle of the front of its head.

uniform /say **yooh**-nuh-fawm / noun
A **uniform** is a set of special clothes worn by people to show they have a particular job or go to a particular school.

union /say **yoohn**-yuhn / noun
A **union** is an organisation of workers who have joined together to ask for things that affect them all like more money or safer conditions.

This is short for **trade union**.

unique /say yooh-**neek** / adjective
Something is **unique** if there is no other thing like it.

⭐ *Spelling Tip:* Remember the *ique* spelling of the 'eek' sound in this word which comes from French. The first part of this word, *un*, comes from *unus* the Latin word for 'one', just as it does in *union*. This is why it makes a 'yoohn' sound.

unit /say **yooh**-nuht / noun
1. A **unit** is something thought of as a single thing, often a group of people or things considered together. *A special police unit was asked to help find the missing child.*
2. A **unit** is an amount used when you count or measure. *A metre is a unit of length.*
3. A **unit** is one of several homes that are all in one large building. *My best friend lives in the unit next to ours.*

Unit (as in definition 3) is short for **home unit**.

unite /say yooh-**nuyt** / verb
1. If several things **unite**, they join together, becoming one thing. *The two clubs united to form one big club.*
2. If something **unites** people or things, it makes them join together. *The fight to save the forest united the people of the town.*

universe /say **yooh**-nuh-vers / noun
The **universe** is the whole of space and everything that exists in it.

university /say yooh-nuh-**ver**-suh-tee / noun
(*plural* **universities**)
A **university** is a place where you study after you have finished high school.

unknown /say un-**nohn** / adjective
If something is **unknown**, it is not familiar or known. *We were going into unknown territory and we had to use our maps.* | *The future is unknown.*

unless conjunction
You use **unless** when you are saying that something will only happen if something else

happens. *Malcolm wouldn't go unless his brother went too.*

until preposition, conjunction
You use **until** when you are talking about something happening or not happening up to a particular time or event. *We have to wait until Monday to get our tests back.* | *I will not leave the party until you do.*

You can also say **till**.

⭐ *Spelling Tip:* Remember that there is only one *l* at the end of this word. It can be confusing because the similar word *till* has a double *l*.

unusual /say un-**yooh**-zhooh-uhl / adjective
If something is **unusual**, it is not usual, common or ordinary.

up adverb
1. If someone or something moves **up**, they move to a higher place. *He climbed up the tree.*
2. If something goes **up**, it goes into the air. *He threw the ball up as high as he could.*
–preposition **3.** You use **up** to talk about going to or being at a higher part of something. *He walked up the stairs.*

upon preposition
You use **upon** to mean 'on' or 'on top of'. *The dog was lying still, his head upon his front paws.*

upper adjective
If something is **upper**, it is higher than something else.

upright /say **up**-ruyt / adjective
Something is **upright** if it goes straight up.

uproar noun
An **uproar** is a lot of noise made by a crowd of people.

upset verb (**upsets**, **upsetting**, **upset**, **has upset**)
1. If something or someone **upsets** you, it makes you feel sad or hurt. *Seeing our dog so sick upset all of us.*
2. If you **upset** something, you knock it over. *He upset his cup of tea and it spilt all over the chair.*

upstairs adverb
1. If you go **upstairs**, you go to a higher floor in a building. *She rushed upstairs to get her books.*
–adjective **2.** If something is **upstairs**, it is on a higher floor of a building.

upwards *adverb*

If something goes **upwards**, it goes to a higher place. *The TV news showed the rocket going upwards into the sky.*

You can also say **upward**.

urge /*say* erj/ *verb*

1. If you **urge** someone to do something, you try hard to make them do it. *The police urged the people to leave their houses before the fire came any closer.*
–*noun* 2. An **urge** is a strong wish to do something.

urgent /*say* **er**-juhnt/ *adjective*

Something is **urgent** if it has to be done at once.

Word Building: **urgently**, *adverb* Something urgent must be done **urgently**.

us *pronoun*

You use **us** when you are speaking about yourself together with at least one other person. *Could you please take us home?*

USB drive *noun*

A **USB drive** is a small object that you can store computer files on, carry around with you, and plug into different computers to access the information stored on it.

Other terms for this are **memory stick** and **USB stick**.

It is called a **USB drive** because you plug it into the connection part of a computer called a **USB**.

use *verb*

1. /*say* yoohz/ If you **use** something, you make it work for you. *I'll use a knife to cut the rope.* | *Do you know how to use this machine?*
2. /*say* yoohst/ **used to, a.** If you are **used to** something, you do it or see it a lot. *I'm used to getting up early so it doesn't worry me.* | *I'm used to the way she behaves so it doesn't surprise me.*
b. If you say you **used to** do something, you mean that you did it all the time in the past. *I used to like bananas, but now I think they taste horrible.*
–*noun* /*say* yoohs/ 3. The **use** of something is the act of making it work for you. *We have to clean our brushes after each use.*
4. If something has a **use**, it has a purpose. *Rope has many uses.* | *What's the use of crying? It doesn't help.*
5. If you have the **use** of something, you are able or allowed to use it. *She lost the use of her legs after the accident.* | *They offered us the use of their surfboards while we were at the beach.*

used /*say* yoohzd/ *adjective*

Something that is **used** is not new.

useful /*say* **yoohs**-fuhl/ *adjective*

If something is **useful**, it helps you do a job or solve a problem.

usual /*say* **yooh**-zhooh-uhl/ *adjective*

If something is **usual**, it is what most often happens in a particular situation.

Word Building: **usually**, *adverb* If it is usual for something to happen, then it **usually** happens.

a b c d e f g h i j k l m n o p q r s t u v w x y z

valley

---

vacant /say **vay**-kuhnt / adjective
If something is **vacant**, it is empty or not being used.

vacation noun
1. A **vacation** is a time when you do not have to go to school or university. *During the vacation I had tennis lessons.*
2. A **vacation** is a time when you go away somewhere to enjoy yourself or rest. *We're going camping for our vacation.*

> The more usual term is **holiday** or **holidays**.

vacuum /say **vak**-yoohm / noun
A **vacuum** is an empty space with no air or any other gas in it.

> ✳ *Spelling Tip:* There is only one *c* but notice that the *u* is doubled.

vacuum cleaner noun
A **vacuum cleaner** is a machine that cleans floors by drawing the dirt up into itself.

vain adjective
1. You are **vain** if you are too proud of yourself and of the way you look.
–noun 2. **in vain**, If you do something **in vain**, you do it without success.

> ✳ *Spelling Tip:* Don't confuse the spelling of **vain** with **vein** which has the same sound but is spelt with *ei*. Your **veins** carry blood in your body.

valley noun
A **valley** is the long, low piece of land between hills or mountains, usually with a river flowing through it.

valuable /say **val**-yuh-buhl / adjective
1. If something is **valuable**, it is worth a lot of money. *The painting that was stolen was very valuable.*
2. Something is **valuable** if it is of great use or importance. *Thank you for your valuable help.*

value noun
1. The **value** of something is the amount of money it is worth. *This bracelet does not have much value but I like it anyway.*
2. The **value** of something is how important or useful it is. *The principal said it was important for people to think about the value of education.*

van noun
A **van** is a covered truck that is used for carrying things, like furniture.

vanilla noun
The **vanilla** plant has a bean that is used to give a taste to food like ice-cream or milk drinks.

> ✳ *Spelling Tip:* Remember that **vanilla** has only one *n* but a double *l*. Try breaking the word up as *van + il + la*.

vanish verb
If someone or something **vanishes**, you suddenly cannot see them any more. *She was there one minute and the next minute she had vanished.*

vapour noun
A **vapour** is a cloud of steam or mist made up of tiny drops of water.

> Another spelling for this word is **vapor**.

variety /say vuh-**ruy**-uh-tee / noun (plural **varieties**)
1. **Variety** is change from what usually happens. *We got sick of our swimming lessons because there was never any variety in them.*
2. A **variety** is a number of things of different kinds. *This shop sells a variety of cakes.*
3. A **variety** is a type or sort of something. *The variety of cake I like best is chocolate.*

various /say **vair**-ree-uhs / adjective
You use **various** when you are talking about several different things.

vary /say **vair**-ree / verb (**varies**, **varying**, **varied**, **has varied**)

If you **vary** something, you make it different. *We're going to vary this cake recipe by adding more sugar.*

vase /*say* vahz/ *noun*
A **vase** is a container for flowers.

vast *adjective*
If something is **vast**, it covers a very large area.

veal *noun*
Veal is meat from a young cow.

vegetable /*say* **vej**-tuh-buhl/ *noun*
A **vegetable** is a plant with a part that you can eat. You can cook **vegetables** or eat them raw.

> ✪ *Spelling Tip:* There are three separate *e's* in **vegetable**. Don't forget the second *e* which you sometimes don't hear when people say the word. Try breaking the word up as *veg+e+ta+ble*

vegetarian /*say* vej-uh-**tair**-ree-uhn/ *noun*
A **vegetarian** is someone who does not eat meat.

> ✪ *Spelling Tip:* Remember that this word comes from *vegetable* and so has the same *vege* beginning.

vehicle /*say* **vee**-ik-uhl/ *noun*
A **vehicle** is something, like a car, truck or bus, which is used to carry people or things from one place to another.

> ✪ *Spelling Tip:* Don't forget the *h* in **vehicle**. Try breaking the word up as *ve+hic+le*.

veil /*rhymes with* pale/ *noun*
A **veil** is a piece of thin material that some women use to cover their faces or heads.

vein /*say* vayn/ *noun*
A **vein** is one of the tubes that carries blood from your body to your heart.

> The tubes that carry blood *from* your heart are called **arteries**.

> ✪ *Spelling Tip:* Don't confuse the spelling of **vein** with **vain** which has the same sound but is spelt with *ai*. **Vain** means 'too proud'.

venom /*say* **ven**-uhm/ *noun*
Venom is the poison that a spider or snake puts into the body of the person or animal that it bites.

> *Word Building:* **venomous** /*say* **ven**-uh-muhs/, *adjective* A creature that can put venom into the body of something that it bites is **venomous**.

verandah *noun*
A **verandah** is a part on the outside of a house that is covered by a roof but which does not have walls.

> Another spelling for this word is **veranda**.

verb *noun*
A **verb** is a type of word which tells you what someone or something does or feels, such as 'walks' and 'hear' in *If anyone walks past, I'll hear them*.

verdict *noun*
A **verdict** is what a judge or a jury decides about a prisoner in a court of law.

verse *noun*
A **verse** is a part of a song.

vertical *adjective*
Something is **vertical** if it stands straight up.

> Think about how this is different from **horizontal**.

very *adverb*
You use **very** to make the meaning of the following word stronger. *The bus is always slow, but today it's very slow because of the rain.*

vessel *noun*
1. A **vessel** is a ship or boat. *A rescue vessel was sent out for the survivors.*
2. A **vessel** is a container, such as a cup or bottle, that can hold liquid. *We needed a vessel to hold the water we were collecting.*

> ✪ *Spelling Tip:* Remember the double *s* and the *el* (not *le*) ending.

vet *noun*
A **vet** is someone whose job is to try to make animals that are sick or hurt well again.

> This is short for **veterinary surgeon**.

vibrate *verb*
If someone or something **vibrates**, they shake backwards and forwards quickly. *The boat began to vibrate when the captain started the engine.*

victim *noun*
A **victim** is someone who has had something bad happen to them.

victory *noun* (*plural* **victories**)
1. You have a **victory** if you win something like a race or game. *My victory in the swimming was a surprise to everyone.*

a b c d e f g h i j k l m n o p q r s t u v w x y z

2. If an army or country wins a war, they have a **victory**. *In the history of our country there have been great victories and great losses.*

video *noun (plural* **videos***)*
1. A **video** is a machine which allows you to record films and television programs onto a special tape which you can then watch on television. *Our video is being repaired – would you mind recording this show for me?*
2. A **video** is a film, television show or event which has been recorded on a special tape, and which you can watch on television. *We made a video of my aunt's wedding.*

Definition 1 is short for **video cassette recorder**. Definition 2 is short for **video recording**.

view /*say* vyooh/ *noun*
A **view** is everything you can see from one place.

village *noun*
A **village** is a small town in a country area.

villain /*say* vil-uhn/ *noun*
A **villain** is a bad person in a play or film.

⭐ *Spelling Tip:* Remember the double *l* and also the *ain* ending (which sounds like 'uhn').

vine *noun*
A **vine** is a kind of plant with long, thin branches that can climb around other plants or up walls or fences.

vinegar /*say* vin-i-guh/ *noun*
Vinegar is a strong-tasting liquid that you use in cooking.

⭐ *Spelling Tip:* Remember that the middle sound is spelt *e*. Think of it as being part of *vine* – like wine, **vinegar** come from grapes which grow on a *vine*. Also remember the *ar* ending.

violent /*say* vuy-uh-luhnt/ *adjective*
If someone or something is **violent**, they are strong and dangerous.

Word Building: **violence**, *noun* Something violent causes **violence**.

violet /*say* vuy-uh-luht/ *noun*
A **violet** is a small plant with purple flowers and a beautiful smell.

violin /*say* vuy-uh-**lin**/ *noun*
A **violin** is a musical instrument which is made of wood and has strings. You hold it against your neck and pull a special stick across the strings.

virus *noun (plural* **viruses***)*
1. A **virus** is a very tiny living thing that causes disease and is easily caught from someone else. *My mother's boss told her not to come to work because she had a virus.*
2. A **virus** is a program that causes computers to break down. *The virus was transferred to my computer by an email.*

⭐ *Spelling Tip:* Remember that the ending is *us*, as in many words coming from Latin. The meaning of *virus* in Latin was 'a thick, unpleasant liquid' or 'poison'.

visible /*say* **viz**-uh-buhl/ *adjective*
Something is **visible** if you can see it.

vision /*say* **vizh**-uhn/ *noun*
Vision is the power people and their animals have to see things with their eyes.

visit *verb*
1. If you **visit** someone, you go to their home to see and talk to them. *I'm going to visit my grandfather tonight.*
2. If you **visit** a place, you go there. *The architect visited the site to see how the building was going.*

visitor *noun*
A **visitor** is someone who comes to your home to see and talk to you, or who goes to see a place. *We have visitors coming for dinner tonight. | He was a visitor to our country and didn't know all the road rules.*

voice *noun*
Your **voice** is the sound or sounds you make with your mouth when you speak or sing.

voicemail *noun*
1. **Voicemail** is a way of recording messages over the telephone system so that you can listen to them later. *We used to have an answering machine but now we have voicemail.*
2. A **voicemail** is a telephone message that you get in this way. *There were a lot of voicemails waiting for us when we got back from holidays.*

volcano *noun (plural* **volcanoes** *or* **volcanos***)*
A **volcano** is a mountain with an opening in the top. Sometimes gases and rocks that have melted from extremely hot temperatures inside the earth come out of the opening.

volleyball *noun*
Volleyball is a team game in which you hit a large ball over a high net. The ball is not allowed to land on the ground.

volume *noun*

1. A **volume** is one book from a set. *The third volume of my encyclopedia of animals is all about reptiles.*

2. The **volume** of sound is how loud it is. *The neighbours asked us to turn down the volume of the music at the party.*

volunteer *noun*

A **volunteer** is someone who offers to do something that they do not have to do, and are not paid to do.

vote *verb*

If you **vote**, you say which person you choose to do a particular thing. *I'll vote for you to be class captain.*

vowel *noun*

A **vowel** is one of a special group of five letters of the alphabet. The vowels are *a*, *e*, *i*, *o*, *u*, and sometimes *y*, depending on how it is said.

Look up **consonant**.

voyage *noun*

A **voyage** is a journey by sea to somewhere quite far away.

vulnerable /*say* **vul**-nuh-ruh-buhl / *adjective*

Something is **vulnerable** if it is not strong or protected, and so is likely to be hurt.

❄ *Spelling Tip:* Don't forget the *l* in this word which you sometimes don't hear when people say it. **Vulnerable** comes from the Latin word *vulnus*, meaning 'wound', so the basic meaning is 'able to be wounded'.

vulture /*say* **vul**-chuh / *noun*

A **vulture** is a large bird that eats dead animals.

a b c d e f g h i j k l m n o p q r s t u **v** w x y z

whiskers

waddy /*rhymes with* body / *noun*
A **waddy** is a heavy wooden stick which Aboriginal people used to use in war.

> This word comes from an Aboriginal language of New South Wales called Dharug.

wade *verb*
If you **wade**, you walk through water. *She took off her shoes so that she could wade across the creek.*

wage *noun*
A **wage** is the money that is paid to someone for the job that they do.

wagon *noun*
1. A **wagon** is a strong vehicle with four wheels, that is pulled by horses and used for carrying things. *They put their possessions on an old wagon, ready to escape.*
2. A **wagon** is one of the sections of a train without a roof in which goods are carried. *The train was very long and had lots of wagons filled with coal.*

wail *verb*
If someone **wails**, they make a long, sad cry. *The woman whose family died wailed with grief.*

waist *noun*
Your **waist** is the part of your body which is just above your hips.

> ✳ *Spelling Tip:* Don't confuse the spelling of **waist** with **waste** which has the same sound. When you **waste** something, you don't use it well.

wait *verb*
1. If you **wait**, you stay somewhere until something happens that you think is going to. *Wait here until I come back.*
–*noun* 2. A **wait** is a time of waiting.

waiter *noun*
A **waiter** is someone, usually a man, who serves food and drink to you at your table in a restaurant or hotel.

waitress *noun*
A **waitress** is a woman who serves food and drink to you at your table in a restaurant or hotel.

wake *verb* (**wakes, waking, woke, has woken**)
1. When you **wake** or **wake up**, you stop being asleep. *When she woke up, it was time to go.*
2. If someone or something **wakes** you or **wakes** you **up**, they make you stop sleeping. *What time do you want me to wake you?*

walk *verb*
1. When you **walk**, you move by using your legs in the usual way, not as fast as when you run. *Will we walk to the train station or catch the bus?*
–*noun* 2. A **walk** is some walking done for exercise or pleasure.

> *Word Building:* **walker**, *noun* –**walking**, *noun*

wall *noun*
A **wall** is one of the sides of a building or room or a fence made of stone or bricks.

wallaby /*say* **wol**-uh-bee / *noun* (*plural* **wallabies**)
A **wallaby** is an Australian animal that is like a kangaroo but smaller. The female carries her babies in a pouch.

> This word comes from an Aboriginal language of New South Wales called Dharug.

wallaroo /*say* wol-uh-**rooh** / *noun*
A **wallaroo** is a small kind of kangaroo with a heavy, strong body and rough, dark fur that lives in rocky or hilly land.

> This word comes from an Aboriginal language of New South Wales called Dharug.

wallet /say **wol**-uht/ noun
A **wallet** is a small, folding case for paper money. You can put it in your pocket.

wand /say wond/ noun
A **wand** is a thin stick that fairies and other creatures in stories use to make spells and magic.

wander /say **won**-duh/ verb
If you **wander**, you move around without wanting to go anywhere in a hurry. *Tony loved to wander along the beach looking for shells.*

want verb
1. If you **want** something, you feel that you would like to have it or you need it. *She told her mother that she wanted some new clothes.*
2. If you **want** to do something, you feel that you would like to do it. *We wanted to go swimming.*

war noun
A **war** is a fight between two or more countries, which usually goes on for a long time.

waratah /say wo-ruh-**tah**/ noun
A **waratah** is an Australian plant that has big red flowers.

> ✵ *Spelling Tip:* Remember that there is only one *r* in this word. Also remember the *h* at the end, and the fact that there are three separate *a*'s. (After all, it is an Australian plant).

> This word comes from an Aboriginal language of New South Wales called Dharug.

wardrobe noun
A **wardrobe** is a large cupboard where you hang your clothes.

warm adjective
1. If a thing or a place is **warm**, it has some heat but not a lot. *She filled the bath with warm water.*
2. If clothes are **warm**, they keep your heat in. *It's a cold day so take a warm coat with you.*
–verb 3. If you **warm** something, you make it warm. *Sit here near the fire and warm your feet.*

> *Word Building:* **warmth**, **warmness**, noun If something gives off warm heat, you talk about its **warmth** or **warmness**.

warn verb
If you **warn** someone, you let them know that there is danger. *She warned him not to stay in the sun too long.*

> *Word Building:* **warning**, noun If you warn someone, you give them a **warning**.

warrior /say **wo**-ree-uh/ noun
A **warrior** is someone who fights in a battle.

> ✵ *Spelling Tip:* Remember the *a* spelling in the first part of this word. You will remember this by thinking of the connected word *war*. Double the *r* and add *ior* (not *ier*) and you have **warrior**.

wash verb
If you **wash** something, you wet it and rub it, usually with water and soap, to make it clean. *Make sure you wash your hands before you eat.*

wasp /say wosp/ noun
A **wasp** is an insect with wings, that can sting you.

waste verb
1. If you **waste** something, you do not get the use from it that you could do. *We don't waste the cake mixture that's left over when Mum's cooking – we eat it.*
–noun 2. If you say that something is a **waste**, you mean that it has not been used well. It has been wasted. *It's a waste of time looking for anything in his room – you'll never find it.*
3. **Waste** is something that has no use any more so people throw it away. *Waste from the factory has made the river dirty.*

> *Word Building:* **wasteful**, adjective If you waste something, you are **wasteful**. *It was wasteful to throw all that good food away.*

> ✵ *Spelling Tip:* Don't confuse the spelling of **waste** with **waist** which has the same sound. Your **waist** is the middle part of your body.

watch verb
1. If you **watch** something or someone, you look at them because you are interested or because they need to be looked at. *We watched the parade for hours. | Sarah was asked to watch the soup and make sure it didn't boil.*
–noun (plural **watches**)
2. A **watch** is a small clock which you wear on the lower part of your arm near your hand. *She looked at her watch to see how long she had left to wait before the train arrived.*

water noun
Water is the liquid which forms rivers, lakes, and seas. It has no colour and you can see through it.

watermelon noun
A **watermelon** is a large fruit with a thick green skin and a dark pink inside part that has a juice like sweet water.

a b c d e f g h i j k l m n o p q r s t u v **w** x y z

waterproof *adjective*
Something is **waterproof** if water cannot go through it.

wattle *noun*
Wattle is a plant or tree with small, soft, round, yellow flowers, that grows in Australia.

wave *noun*
1. A **wave** is one of the lines of high water that moves across the surface of the sea.
–*verb* 2. If you **wave** something, you hold it in your hand and make it move up and down or from side to side. *There were people waving flags in the parade.*
3. If you **wave**, you move your hand from side to side as a greeting or to say goodbye. *I waved at my friend across the street.*

wax *noun*
Wax is a solid material made of a kind of oil which goes soft when you heat it. It is used for making different shapes and for rubbing furniture to make it shiny.

way *noun*
1. The **way** you do something is how you do it. *Can you show me the way to open this box? I can't get it open.*
2. The **way** to somewhere is the direction. *Which way is the bus stop?*
3. **by the way**, You use **by the way** to show that you are starting to talk about something new that is not connected to what you have been talking about. *I must be going now. By the way, have you emailed Victoria yet?*

we *pronoun*
You use **we** to talk about yourself and at least one other person. *I'm ready and so are you – we can go.*

Also look up **us**, **our** and **ours**.

weak *adjective*
1. If something is **weak**, it is not strong. It could easily fall down or break. *Mum thought the supports under the old wooden bridge looked very weak and decided to go another way.*
2. If someone is **weak**, they are not healthy or strong. *She was weak for a long time after she was sick.*

Word Building: **weakness**, *noun*: *There was a weakness in the bridge supports.*

wealth /*say* welth / *noun*
Wealth is having a lot of money or owning a lot of things such as houses and land.

Word Building: **wealthy**, *adjective* (**wealthier**, **wealthiest**) If someone has wealth, they are **wealthy**.

✹ *Spelling Tip:* Remember the *ea* spelling for the 'e' sound. **Wealth** comes from an old word *weal*, meaning 'the state of being well', and has the same sound and spelling pattern as *health*.

weapon /*say* **wep**-uhn / *noun*
A **weapon** is something, like a gun, that is used in a fight to hurt someone.

✹ *Spelling Tip:* Remember the *ea* spelling for the 'e' sound in the first part of this word.

wear *verb* (**wears**, **wearing**, **wore**, **has worn**)
When you **wear** clothes or something like a ring, you have them on your body. *Have you worn your new coat yet?* | *She always wears her grandmother's wedding ring.*

✹ *Spelling Tip:* Don't confuse the spelling of **wear** with **where** which sounds the same. You use **where** to talk about the place something is in.

weary *adjective* (**wearier**, **weariest**)
If you are **weary**, you are very tired.

weather /*say* **wedh**-uh / *noun*
The **weather** is how it is outside – if it is hot or cold, wet or dry. Wind, rain, snow, sun and clouds are all part of the **weather**.

✹ *Spelling Tip:* Don't confuse the spelling of **weather** with **whether** which has the same sound. **Whether** is a word you use when you talking about two choices.

weave *verb* (**weaves**, **weaving**, **wove**, **has woven**)
If you **weave**, you make things like wool or cotton into material by passing the threads under and over each other. *She was weaving a mat.*

web *noun*
1. A **web** is the sticky net that spiders make to catch insects. *I walked into a spider web and ended up with sticky stuff through my hair.*
2. The **Web** is the system of storing information on the internet so that people all around the world can find it from their computers. *The teacher told us to use the Web for our project on rivers.*

definition 2 is short for **the World Wide Web**.

webbed *adjective*
Fingers and toes are **webbed** if they are joined together by a piece of skin.

webcam *noun*
A **webcam** is a kind of camera linked to a computer so that the pictures it takes can be sent over the internet.

web page *noun*
A **web page** is a section of a website.

website *noun*
A **website** is a place on the internet. When you type its address, you can go there to get information.

You can also spell this as two words: **web site**. You often say **site** for short.

wedding *noun*
A **wedding** is the special time when two people get married to each other.

Wednesday /*say* **wenz**-day / *noun*
Wednesday is one of the days of the week. It comes between Tuesday and Thursday.

⭐ *Spelling Tip:* Don't forget the silent *d* before the *n* in this word. It is there because **Wednesday** is named after *Woden*, the chief god believed in by the people living in England long ago. Try breaking the word up as *Wed + nes + day*.

weed *noun*
A **weed** is a plant that grows where you do not want it.

week *noun*
A **week** is a period of seven days, usually thought of as starting on Sunday and lasting until Saturday, or starting on Monday and lasting until Sunday.

weekend *noun*
The **weekend** is the two days Saturday and Sunday, sometimes also including Friday evening, when people do not have to work or go to school.

weep *verb* (**weeps, weeping, wept, has wept**)
If you **weep**, tears come out of your eyes. *They wept when they heard their grandfather had died.*

weigh /*sounds like* way / *verb*
1. If you **weigh** something, you measure how heavy it is. You find out its weight. *This machine weighs your bags before they are put on the plane.*

2. If someone or something **weighs** a certain amount, that is their weight. *Amanda found out she weighed forty kilograms.*

Word Building: **weight**, *noun* How much something weighs is its **weight**.

⭐ *Spelling Tip:* Remember to learn the *eigh* spelling for the 'ay' sound. The word *eight* has a similar spelling so you might remember these two words together.

weird /*say* weard / *adjective*
If something is **weird**, it is very strange.

⭐ *Spelling Tip:* Remember that **weird** is spelt with *ei*, breaking the rule that *i* comes before *e*, except after *c*.

welcome *verb*
1. If you **welcome** someone, you tell them that you are happy they have arrived. *The teacher welcomed the new boy into the class.*
—*noun* **2.** A **welcome** is something you say or do to tell someone you are happy they have arrived, or the time when you do it.
—*interjection* **3.** You say **Welcome!** as a way of greeting someone in a polite and friendly way. *Welcome! Please come in and take a seat.*

⭐ *Spelling Tip:* Notice that there is only one *l* in **welcome**. Though it is made up of *well* and *come*, you have to remember that one of the *l*'s in *well* has been dropped.

welcome to country *noun*
A **welcome to country** is a ceremony at the start of a public event in Australia in which someone who is a representative of the traditional Indigenous custodians of the land on which the event is taking place welcomes the people who have come to the event.

You can also spell this with capital letters: **Welcome to Country**.

well[1] *adjective*
1. If you are **well**, you are healthy.
—*adverb* **2.** If you do something **well**, you do it in a way that shows skill. *She swims well.*

well[2] *noun*
A **well** is a hole dug into the ground to get water or oil.

well-known *adjective*
If someone or something is **well-known**, a lot of people know them or have heard about them.

a b c d e f g h i j k l m n o p q r s t u v **w** x y z

You can also spell this **well known** when it does not come before a noun. *The main facts are well known.*

west *noun*

1. The **west** is the direction in which the sun goes down at night.
–*adjective* 2. If something is **west**, it is in or towards the west.
–*adverb* 3. If you go **west**, you go towards the west. *He travelled west for several days.*

Word Building: **western**, *adjective* If something is in the west, it is **western**. *America is in the western part of the world.*

The opposite direction is **east**. The other directions are **north** and **south**.

wet *adjective* (**wetter**, **wettest**)

1. If something is **wet**, it is covered with water or some other liquid or has just a bit of water on it. *That seat is wet – are there any others?*
2. If the weather is **wet**, it rains a lot. *It has been a wet summer.*

wetland *noun*

A **wetland** is a natural area of land which is usually covered by shallow water.

whale /*say* wayl/ *noun*

A **whale** is a very large animal that lives in the sea.

wharf /*say* wawf/ *noun* (*plural* **wharves**)

A **wharf** is a place built on the shore of a port where goods are put on and taken off ships.

⭐ *Spelling Tip:* Remember the *arf* spelling for the 'awf' sound. Another word with this sound and spelling pattern is *dwarf*. Also remember the silent *h* following the *w*, as in many other words.

what /*say* wot/ *pronoun, adjective*

1. You can use **what** in many ways, sometimes when you are asking a question. Here are some examples. *What's your name?*
2. You say **What?** as a way of finding out what someone said. *What? I didn't hear you.*

whatever /*say* wot-**ev**-uh/ *pronoun, adjective*

1. You use **whatever** to mean 'any' or 'every'. *Do whatever you like.*

2. You can use **whatever** to show that something is not important when you are talking about something else that is important. *Come home early, whatever your friends tell you to do.*

wheat /*say* weet/ *noun*

Wheat is the grain of a plant that is grown on farms. It is used for making flour.

wheel /*say* weel/ *noun*

1. A **wheel** is a thing in the shape of a circle, usually made of metal or wood, that goes around to make something move or to make a machine work.
–*verb* 2. If you **wheel** something that has wheels, you push it along. *I had to wheel the bike with a flat tyre up the hill.*

wheelchair /*say* **weel**-chair/ *noun*

A **wheelchair** is a special chair on wheels, for people who can't walk.

when /*say* wen/ *adverb, conjunction*

You use **when** when you are asking or talking about time. *When are you coming? | I don't know when he's leaving. | We will leave when we've packed our bags. | He gets impatient when he has to wait for a long time.*

whenever /*say* wen-**ev**-uh/ *conjunction*

You use **whenever** to say 'at any time when'. *Come whenever you like.*

where /*say* wair/ *adverb, pronoun*

You use **where** when you are asking or talking about the place someone or something is in. *Where is he? | Where did you put it? | The book is where you left it.*

⭐ *Spelling Tip:* Don't forget the silent *h* after the *w* in **where**. Don't confuse it with **wear** which sounds the same. When you **wear** clothes, you have them on your body.

wherever /*say* wair-**ev**-uh/ *conjunction*

You use **wherever** to say 'in, at, or to any place'. *She goes wherever she likes.*

⭐ *Spelling Tip:* Remember that, although **wherever** is made up of *where* and *ever*, it has only one *e* in the middle, because the *e* at the end of *where* has been dropped when the words were joined. Also remember the silent *h* following the *w*, as in *where* and many other words.

whether /*say* **wedh**-uh/ *conjunction*

You use **whether** before the first of two or more possible happenings. You can sometimes repeat **whether** before the second one. *We* *asked whether he was coming or not.* | *It doesn't matter whether we go or whether we stay.*

> ✴ *Spelling Tip:* Don't forget the silent *h* after the *w* in **whether**. Don't confuse it with **weather** which has the same sound. The **weather** is sun, rain, wind, and so on.

which /*say* wich / *pronoun, adjective*
You use **which** when you are asking or talking about a particular thing or person. *Which of these books do you want?* | *Which book do you want?* | *What colour is the car which they stole?*

> ✴ *Spelling Tip:* Don't forget the silent *h* after the *w* in **which**. Don't confuse it with **witch** which has the same sound. A **witch** is a woman who can do magic.

while /*say* wuyl / *noun*
1. A **while** is a period of time, but not a particular amount of time.
–*conjunction* 2. You use **while** to say 'during or in the time that'. *Stay here while I'm out.*

whimper /*say* **wim**-puh / *verb*
If a person or animal **whimpers**, they cry softly. *The injured dog was whimpering at the side of the road.*

whine /*say* wuyn / *verb*
If someone **whines**, they complain. *My mother was sick of my little brother whining about missing his favourite TV show.*

> ✴ *Spelling Tip:* Don't forget the silent *h* after the *w* in **whine**. Don't confuse it with **wine** which sounds the same. **Wine** is a kind of drink.

whip /*say* wip / *noun*
1. A **whip** is a long piece of rope or leather joined to a handle. It is used to make animals move.
–*verb* (**whips, whipping, whipped, has whipped**)
2. If someone **whips** an animal, they hit them with a whip. *He was whipping the horse to make it go faster.*
3. If you **whip** something like cream, you stir it quickly until it is thick. *My mother always gets me to whip the cream to go inside the cakes.*

whiskers /*say* **wis**-kuhz / *noun*
Whiskers are the long, thick hairs that grow on the faces of some animals, such as cats.

whisper /*say* **wis**-puh / *verb*
If you **whisper**, you speak very softly, using your breath more than your voice. *She whispered to her friend so that no-one else could hear.*

whistle /*say* **wis**-uhl / *verb*
1. If you **whistle**, you make a sound like a bird's call, by blowing through a round opening you make with your lips and your teeth. *My dog comes running when I whistle.*
–*noun* 2. A **whistle** is a small pipe which makes very high sounds when you blow through it.

> ✴ *Spelling Tip:* Don't forget the *st* (not double *s*) spelling. The *t* is silent. As in many other words beginning with *wh*, the *h* is also silent.

white /*say* wuyt / *adjective*
If something is **white**, it has the colour of snow or of cows' milk.

whiteboard /*say* **wuyt**-bawd / *noun*
A **whiteboard** is a large, white, plastic board used for writing or drawing on with a special felt pen.

white-out *noun*
White-out is a thin, white paint that is used to cover mistakes on paper.

> Another word for this is **liquid paper**.

who /*say* hooh / *pronoun*
1. You use **who** when you are asking what person. *Who told you to do that?*
2. You use **who** when you want to say more about someone you have already talked about. *The woman who sold the book to me isn't here.*
3. You use **who** when you want to say what particular person someone is or what particular people. *I know who did it.*

whole /*say* hohl / *adjective*
If something is **whole**, the full amount of it is there.

whose /*say* hoohz / *pronoun*
Whose is the form of **who** that you use when you are talking about someone owning something. *Whose book is this?*

why /*rhymes with* eye / *adverb, conjunction*
You use **why** when you are asking or talking about a reason or cause. *Why did you leave so early?* | *I have a lot of work to do. That's why I can't go out with you.*

wicked /*say* **wik**-uhd / *adjective*
If someone is **wicked**, they are evil or bad.

wicket *noun*

A **wicket** is a set of three sticks standing in a row with two small pieces of wood resting on top, used in the game of cricket. The person who is bowling tries to hit it with the ball.

wide *adjective*

1. If something is **wide**, it measures a lot from one side to the other. *The river is so wide that I wouldn't try to swim across it.*
2. You use **wide** when you are measuring something from side to side. *The paper is 20 centimetres wide.*

❖ Look up **width**.
❖ The opposite of definition 1 is **narrow**.

widow *noun*

A **widow** is a woman whose husband is dead.

A man whose wife dies is a **widower**.

width *noun*

The **width** of something is how wide it is from one side to the other.

❖ **Width** comes from the adjective **wide**.
❖ Another word that means the same is **breadth**.

wife *noun* (*plural* **wives**)

A man's **wife** is the woman he is married to.

The man a woman is married to is her **husband**.

wig *noun*

A **wig** is a covering of hair that is made to wear on the head and look like real hair.

wild *adjective*

1. If an animal or plant is **wild**, it is living or growing in a natural state without humans taking care of it.
–*adverb* **2.** You use **wild** to mean 'in a wild way'. *These bushes are growing wild. You can see that no-one is looking after the garden.*

will¹ *verb*

You use **will** to show you are talking about something in the future. *They will be here in the morning.*

You often join **will** to the word before it and when you do this you use the short form **'ll**. *I'll see you tomorrow.* You can use **won't** as the short form of **will not**.

will² *noun*

1. Your **will** is what you want or wish. *He was taken to the doctor against his will.*

2. A **will** is a written statement about what a person wants done with their property after they die. *She was left some jewellery in her grandmother's will.*

willing *adjective*

If you are **willing** to do something, you are happy to agree to do it.

***Word Building:* willingly**, *adverb*: *She went with him willingly.*

willy-willy *noun*

A **willy-willy** is a strong wind that moves around in circles.

This word comes from an Aboriginal language of Western Australia called Yindjibarndi.

win *verb* (**wins**, **winning**, **won** /*say* wun/, **has won**)

If you **win**, you do better than anyone else in a something like a fight or a game. You get the first prize or the first position. *Our team is happy because we won the tennis game last night.*

***Word Building:* winner**, *noun*: *The person who gets to the line first will be the winner.*

The opposite is **lose**.

wind¹ /*rhymes with* pinned/ *noun*

Wind is air that moves and blows things about.

***Word Building:* windy**, *adjective* (**windier**, **windiest**): *It is a very windy day.*

wind² /*say* wuynd/ *verb* (**winds**, **winding**, **wound**, **has wound**)

If something **winds**, it turns first one way and then another. *The path winds up the hill.*

***Word Building:* winding**, *adjective*: *We had to drive slowly on the winding road.*

window *noun*

A **window** is an opening in a wall for letting in light and air, usually covered with glass.

wine *noun*

Wine is a drink made from grapes.

✸ *Spelling Tip:* Don't confuse the spelling of **wine** with **whine** which sounds the same, but is spelt with a silent *h*. **Whine** means 'to make a complaining sound'.

wing *noun*

1. A **wing** is one of the parts of the body of a bird or insect that is used for flying. *The bird spread its wings and flew away.*

2. The **wing** of an aircraft is one of the long flat parts that go out from its sides. *I was sitting next to a window but it was near the wing so I couldn't see much.*

wink *verb*
If you **wink**, you close and open one eye very quickly, often as a signal to a friend. *He winked at me to tell me that what he was saying was really a joke.*

winter *noun*
Winter is the coldest season of the year.

Word Building: **wintry**, *adjective*: *It was a cold, wintry day.*

The other seasons of the year are **spring**, **summer** and **autumn**.

wipe *verb*
1. If you **wipe** something, you rub it lightly to clean it or make it dry. *We'd better wipe the table before we put the paintings on it.*
2. If you **wipe** something away or off or from an area, you take it away from there by removing it with a light touch. *He wiped the tears from her face.*

wire *noun*
Wire is a piece of thin metal that can be bent.

wise *adjective*
1. If someone is **wise**, they are able to decide what is true or right or the best thing to do. *My grandfather is a wise man, and can always think of a plan that keeps everybody happy.*
2. If a decision is **wise**, it is one that is the best thing to do. *Mum said that his decision not to spend the money on lollies was very wise.*

wish *verb*
1. You use **wish** when you are saying you want something very much, usually something that you don't think will happen or that has not happened. *I wish we could go swimming but I think it's going to rain.*
2. If you **wish** to do something, you want to do it. *Mum said she wished to speak to the manager immediately.*
3. When you **wish** someone 'happy birthday' or 'good luck' or something like that, you say those words and hope they have what you have said. *He wished us all good morning.*
—*noun* **4.** A **wish** is something you have wanted or asked for.

Wish as in definition 2 is a formal word which you use when you want to sound important. You usually say **want** or **would like**.

wisp *noun*
A **wisp** of something is a small piece of it.

witch *noun* (*plural* **witches**)
A **witch** is a woman in stories who makes magic.

✻ *Spelling Tip:* Don't confuse the spelling of **witch** with **which**.

with *preposition*
You use **with** to mean 'together': *I will go with you.*; *Put this book with the other ones.* This is the basic meaning of **with**, but you can use it in many ways, for example. *You can mix water with milk.* | *He talked with his friend for hours.* | *They've been fighting with each other for years.* | *I agree with you.* | *He did not agree with what I said.* | *I was very happy with my birthday presents.* | *He is an old man with white hair.* | *Can you see the woman with the baby over there?* | *Cut it with a knife.*

within *preposition*
If something is **within** something else, it is inside it. *Everyone must stand within the circle.*

without *preposition*
You use **without** to show the lack of something. *I can't do this work without help.*

witness *noun*
A **witness** is someone who sees something that happens.

wizard *noun*
A **wizard** is a man in stories who makes magic.

wobble *verb*
If something **wobbles**, it moves from side to side. *The bike began to wobble and I fell off.*

Word Building: **wobbly**, *adjective* If something wobbles, then it is **wobbly**.

wolf /*say* woolf / *noun* (*plural* **wolves**)
A **wolf** is a large animal like a dog with thick grey fur which lives in cold countries and hunts in large groups.

woman /*say* **woom**-uhn/ *noun* (*plural* **women** /*say* **wim**-uhn/)
A **woman** is an adult female human.

wombat *noun*
A **wombat** is a short, heavy, Australian animal that digs a hole under the ground for its home. The female carries her babies in a pouch.

This word comes from an Aboriginal language of New South Wales called Dharug.

wonder /say **wun**-duh/ verb
If you **wonder** you think about something with interest. Often you ask yourself a question and you do not know the answer. *I wonder why he suddenly decided to go.*

wonderful /say **wun**-duh-fuhl/ adjective
If something or someone is **wonderful**, they are very, very good.

wood noun
Wood is the hard material that makes up the main part of a tree. It is used to make things like building and furniture, and is burnt to make fires.

> *Word Building:* **wooden**, adjective If something is made of wood, it is **wooden**.

wool noun
Wool is the thick hair of sheep, used to make things like warm clothes and floor coverings.

> *Word Building:* **woollen**, adjective If something is made of wool, it is **woollen**.

woomera noun
A **woomera** is a strong piece of wood which Aboriginal people used to use to help them throw a spear further. The end of the spear fits onto the end of the **woomera** and is then thrown.

This word comes from an Aboriginal language of New South Wales called Dharug.

word noun
A **word** is a sound or group of sounds that people make as a basic part of language. A **word** means something – it stands for an idea, action, thing or person.

work noun
1. Work is something that needs you to make an effort with your body or mind to do it. *Did the teacher give you any work to do at home?*
2. Someone's **work** is the job they do for payment. *Her work is teaching.*
–verb **3.** If someone **works**, they do work. They make an effort with their body or mind to do something. *Mum's been working in the garden all day – she's having a rest now.*
4. If someone **works** in a place or in a particular job, that is how they earn money. *She works in a camera shop.*

5. If something, like a machine, **works**, it goes the way it should. *This heater isn't working. The room is still cold.*
6. work out, If you **work out** something, you think about it until you find how to do it. *I think I've worked out the answer to this problem.*

worker noun
1. A **worker** is someone who works in a job to earn money. *The factory employs hundreds of workers.*
2. A **worker** is someone who does any work. *Just about everyone in this class is a good worker.*

world noun
The **world** is the earth that we live on.

World Wide Web noun
The **World Wide Web** is the system of storing information on the internet so that people all around the world can find it from their computers.

> ❖ Most people talk about **the Web** now, instead of the full phrase.
> ❖ The **World Wide Web** can be shortened to **WWW** or **www**, which is why you see these three letters at the beginning of internet addresses.

worm /rhymes with firm/ noun
A **worm** is a small animal with a long, thin, soft body. Some kinds of **worm** live in the ground, and some kinds live in the sea.

worry /rhymes with hurry/ verb (**worries, worrying, worried, has worried**)
If you **worry**, you feel afraid of something bad happening. *We were worried that the referee would notice that our uniforms weren't quite right.*

> *Word Building:* **worried**, adjective: *You have a worried look on your face.*

worse adjective, adverb
1. If something is **worse** or is done **worse** than something else, it is not as good. *That film was worse than the one we saw last week.* | *Our team played much worse than we usually do.*
2. If you are feeling **worse**, you have been sick and now you are sicker. *'Are you feeling any better?' No, I'm a lot worse.'*

worship /say **wer**-shuhp/ verb (**worships, worshipping, worshipped, has worshipped**)
1. If someone **worships**, they act in a way that shows they feel great love for their god. *The people were meeting to worship in the mosque.*

2. If you **worship** someone, you love them very much. *He worships his wife.*

> ✳ *Spelling Tip:* Remember the *or* spelling for the 'er' sound in the first part of this word.

worst *adjective*
1. If someone or something is the **worst**, they are as bad as possible or bad to a greater degree than any other.
–*noun* **2.** The **worst** is someone or something that is the one who or which is bad to the greatest degree.

worth /*say* werth / *adjective*
If something is **worth** an amount of money, it has that value and people would pay that amount for it.

would /*sounds like* wood / *verb*
You use **would** in many ways, for example:
1. when you are describing what someone said in the past when they were talking about something in the future. *He said that he would do it the next day.*
2. when you are talking about something that is not real, to show what would happen if the situation was real. *If I had lots of money, I would buy a swimming pool.*
3. when you are saying that someone wants to have something or do something. *I would like to have a holiday.*
4. as a polite way of asking someone to do something, or of asking if someone wants to do something. *Would you please help me carry these bags.* | *Would you like to come with us?*

> You often join **would** to the word before it and when you do this you use the short form '**d**. *She asked if I'd like to come with them.* You can use **wouldn't** as the short form of **would not**. *He said he wouldn't be able to come.*

wound[1] /*say* woohnd / *noun*
A **wound** is a place on your body where you have been hurt badly, by being cut, burnt, shot with a gun or hurt in some other other way.

> ✳ *Spelling Tip:* Remember the *ou* spelling for the 'ooh' sound.

wound[2] /*say* wownd / *verb*
Look up **wind**[2].

wrap /*say* rap / *verb* (**wraps**, **wrapping**, **wrapped**, **has wrapped**)

If you **wrap** something, you fold something like paper or cloth around it. *I always get my big sister to wrap presents for me.*

wreath /*say* reeth / *noun*
A **wreath** is flowers and leaves tied together in the shape of a circle.

wreck /*say* rek / *verb*
If you **wreck** something, you spoil or break it in such a way that it cannot be used. *The car collided with the bicycle and wrecked it completely.*

wren /*say* ren / *noun*
A **wren** is a very small bird with a long tail which is almost upright.

wrestle /*say* **res**-uhl / *verb*
If you **wrestle** someone, you try to throw them to the ground. *Harry was able to wrestle John to the ground even though he was smaller.*

> *Word Building:* **wrestler**, *noun* People who wrestle in a ring are **wrestlers**. –**wrestling**, *noun* People who wrestle in a ring take part in a game of **wrestling**.

> ✳ *Spelling Tip:* Don't forget the *st* (not double *s*) spelling. The *t* is silent. As in many other words beginning with *wr*, the *w* is also silent.

wriggle /*say* **rig**-uhl / *verb*
If you **wriggle**, you turn from side to side. *The baby wriggled so much that all her blankets fell off.*

wrinkle /*say* **ring**-kuhl / *noun*
A **wrinkle** is a line or fold on something that is usually smooth. *When you frown, you get wrinkles on your forehead.* | *She ironed out the wrinkles in her shirt.*

wrist /*say* rist / *noun*
Your **wrist** is the part of your body where your hand joins onto your arm.

write /*say* ruyt / *verb* (**writes**, **writing**, **wrote** /*say* roht /, **has written** /*say* **rit**-uhn /)
1. When you **write**, you make letters or words with a pen, pencil, or something similar. *We had to write answers next to the questions in the book.*
2. When you **write** something, such as a story, a poem or a letter, you make it up in your mind and

put it down on paper. *We had to write a poem about our best friend.*

> **Word Building:** **writer**, *noun*: *She is a famous writer of children's stories.* —**writing**, *noun*: *I like her style of writing.*

wrong /*say* rong/ *adjective*

1. If something is **wrong**, it has a mistake in it. *He gave the wrong answer. He said that five and four make eight.*

2. If what someone does is **wrong**, they are doing something they should not do. *It's wrong to steal things.*

3. wrong with, If you say that something is **wrong with** someone or something, you mean that the person is not well or happy for some reason, or that the thing is not working properly. *I wonder what's wrong with James – he won't talk to us. | Something is wrong with the television. The picture's not very clear.*

> **Word Building:** **wrongly**, *adverb*: *She answered the question wrongly.*

> The opposite of definition 1 is **right** or **correct**; the opposite of definition 2 is **right**.

x-ray

X-ray *noun*

An **X-ray** is a photograph of the inside of someone's body, taken with a special machine. Doctors look at **X-rays** to see if part of the body is damaged or has a disease.

xylophone /*say* **zuy**-luh-fohn/ *noun*

A **xylophone** is a musical instrument with a row of wooden bars that get longer to make deeper sounds. You hit these with small wooden sticks (called 'hammers').

✷ *Spelling Tip:* Concentrate on remembering the *xylo* start to this word (the *x* makes a 'z' sound). Think of *x* and *y* coming next to each other in the alphabet. The last part is *phone*, a word you know well. Here it is a word part, as in several other words having to do with sound, such as *microphone* and *telephone*.

yoga

yabby *noun*
A **yabby** is an animal like a lobster with a hard shell, which lives in fresh water.

This word comes from an Aboriginal language called Wembawemba from along the Murray River in Victoria and New South Wales.

yacht /rhymes with cot/ *noun*
A **yacht** is a boat with a sail.

⭐ **Spelling Tip:** Don't forget the silent *ch* before the *t*.

yard[1] *noun*
Your **yard** is the ground around your house. It often has a fence around it.

yard[2] *noun*
A **yard** is a measurement of length used in some countries, such as America. It is equal to a little less than one metre.

yawn *verb*
If you **yawn**, you take a long deep breath through your mouth when you are bored or tired. *I couldn't stop yawning while his story about his holiday was going on and on.*

Word Building: **yawn**, *noun*: *Her yawn was so loud that everyone turned around and looked.*

year *noun*
1. A **year** is the period of 12 months from 1 January to 31 December. *It is almost the end of the year.*
2. A **year** is any period of 12 months. *I saw her a year ago when she was still at school.*
3. A **year** is a division of a school, made up of a group of classes for students of about the same age. *Which year are you in?*

Another word for definition 3 is **grade**.

yeast *noun*
Yeast is what you add to dough so that it swells up when you make bread.

yell *verb*
If you **yell**, you call out loudly. *They yelled out to us to bring some rope.*

yellow *adjective*
If something is **yellow**, it has a bright colour like the colour of the sun in the middle the day.

yes *interjection*
Yes is a word that you use when you are answering a question if you want to say that something is correct, or that you agree to something you have been asked to do, or that you want something that you have been offered. *'Did you catch a fish?' 'Yes, just a little one.'* | *'Will you sweep the floor?'. 'Yes, I'll do it now.'* | *'Would you like a drink?' 'Yes, please, I would like some lemonade.'*

The opposite is **no**.

yesterday *noun*
1. **Yesterday** is the day before today.
—*adverb* 2. If you did something **yesterday**, you did it on the day before today. *We went on a long hike yesterday and we can hardly walk today.*

yet *adverb*
1. You use **yet** to mean 'now'. It shows that you think it is early to do something. *Don't ask yet. Wait until she's in a better mood.*
2. You use **yet** to talk about the time up to now. *Have you read that book yet?*

yoghurt /say **yoh**-guht/ *noun*
Yoghurt is thick food that is made from milk and sometimes has a sour taste.

Another spelling for this word is **yogurt**.

yolk /say yohk/ *noun*
The **yolk** of an egg is the yellow part.

⭐ **Spelling Tip:** Don't forget the *l*. The *olk* spelling gives an 'ohk' sound.

you *pronoun*

1. You use **you** to talk about the person or people you are speaking or writing to. *Can you hear what I'm saying? | All of you need to work harder.*

2. You use **you** to talk about anyone or people in general. What you have just read starts with **you** used in this way. *Can you get a train to the city from here?*

Also look up **your** and **yours**.

young /*say* yung / *adjective*

If a person or an animal is **young**, they are in the early part of their life.

The opposite is **old**.

✳ *Spelling Tip:* Remember the *oung* for the 'ung' sound. In particular, don't forget the *o*. You can do this by thinking that 'you are young' and the word *you* appears in **young** with the letters *ng* following.

your *pronoun*

You use **your** in front of a noun to show that it belongs to the person or people you are talking to. *I think this is your bag.*

✳ *Spelling Tip:* Don't confuse the spelling with **you're** which is a short way of writing 'you are'.

yours *pronoun*

You use **yours** for something that belongs to the person or people you are talking to. *Is that book yours?*

yourself *pronoun*

You use **yourself** to mean 'you (the person you are talking to) and no-one else'. *Did you do it yourself?*

yourselves *pronoun*

You use **yourselves** to mean 'you (the people you are talking to) and no-one else'. *Make sure you look after yourselves on the beach – don't forget to put on some sunscreen.*

youth /*say* yoohth / *noun*

Your **youth** is the time when you are young.

a b c d e f g h i j k l m n o p q r s t u v w x y z

zigzag

zebra *noun*
A **zebra** is an animal like a horse, coloured with lines of black and white, which lives in Africa.

zero *noun* (*plural* **zeros** *or* **zeroes**)
Zero is the number you use when there is nothing to count. You can write it as 0.

zigzag *noun*
A **zigzag** is a line that goes up and down in sharp points.

zoo *noun*
A **zoo** is a place where wild animals are kept in special areas so that people can go and look at them.

zucchini /*say* zuh-**kee**-nee / *noun*
A **zucchini** is a long, thin vegetable, usually with a green skin.

> ✱ *Spelling Tip:* Don't forget the silent *h* following the double (not single) *c*. Also remember the *ini* ending. **Zucchini** has this spelling because it comes from Italian. Try breaking the word up as *zuc+chi+ni*.

APPENDIXES

WELCOME TO COUNTRY
AND ACKNOWLEDGEMENT OF COUNTRY

When you are at a ceremony or meeting, such as a school assembly or another public event, you will often hear someone open the ceremony with a **Welcome to Country** or an **Acknowledgement of Country**. This is a very important way to show respect to the Indigenous people of Australia and their culture, and to recognise their special position as the first people to live in Australia.

A **Welcome to Country** is a welcome given by someone, such as an Aboriginal elder, who is a representative of the traditional Indigenous custodians of the land on which the event is taking place. The welcome may be a speech only or it may include a performance. This depends on the region where the welcome is taking place.

An **Acknowledgement of Country** is an official recognition of the Indigenous traditional custodians of a locality and can be performed by either a non-Indigenous or an Indigenous person.

The wording may be different in different places, but here are some examples of what is commonly said in an Acknowledgement of Country:

> *I would like to acknowledge and pay respect to the traditional custodians of the land on which this meeting takes place, and to pay respect to elders both past and present.*

> *I would like to acknowledge the _____ people who are the traditional custodians of this land. I would also like to pay respect to elders both past and present of the _____ nation and extend that respect to other Aboriginal people present.*

> *(The name of the people who are the traditional custodians would be filled in.)*

You will find the meanings of the words used in relation to a **Welcome to Country** or an **Acknowledgement of Country** in the main part of the dictionary. Some of the words have a special meaning when used by Indigenous people or in relation to Indigenous people. Here is some extra information.

welcome When you **welcome** someone, you are in your own place and you are saying to the people who have come that you are pleased to have them in your place. That is why it is always an Indigenous person who performs a **Welcome to Country**. That person is welcoming the other people to his or her land.

acknowledge When you **acknowledge** someone or something, you show that you recognise them or understand something important about them. That is why **acknowledging** is a way of showing respect.

Indigenous An **Indigenous** person is either an Aboriginal person or a Torres Strait Islander. Aboriginal and Torres Strait Islander people are the earliest inhabitants of Australia.

country	In the way that Indigenous people talk about **country**, it refers to the land where they have traditionally lived, with all its features as it came to them from the **Dreaming**.
traditional custodian	A **custodian** is someone who looks after or guards something. A **traditional custodian** is an Indigenous person who is entitled to know about the secret rituals that connect his or her people to the land and to its history going back to the Dreaming.
elder	An **elder** is an important person in an Indigenous community, especially someone who knows all about the traditional language and culture.
nation	A **nation** can be a group of people who have the same customs, history and language, even though they may not have their own government.

AUSTRALIAN NATIONAL SONGS

Advance Australia Fair

'Advance Australia Fair' has been Australia's national anthem since 1984, but it has a much longer history. It was written many years ago, probably in the 1870s, and was sung at the ceremony for Australian Federation in 1901. The following two verses are the ones that are usually sung:

> *Australians all let us rejoice,*
> *For we are young and free;*
> *We've golden soil and wealth for toil;*
> *Our home is girt by sea;*
> *Our land abounds in nature's gifts*
> *Of beauty rich and rare;*
> *In history's page, let every stage*
> *Advance Australia Fair.*
> *In joyful strains then let us sing,*
> *Advance Australia Fair.*
>
> *Beneath our radiant Southern Cross*
> *We'll toil with hearts and hands;*
> *To make this Commonwealth of ours*
> *Renowned of all the lands;*
> *For those who've come across the seas*
> *We've boundless plains to share;*
> *With courage let us all combine*
> *To Advance Australia Fair.*
> *In joyful strains then let us sing,*
> *Advance Australia Fair.*

You have probably noticed that there are some words in this song are the kind that are used more in songs or writing than in normal language. For that reason, you won't find them in the dictionary. Here is what they mean:

toil	**Toil** is hard work. If someone **toils**, they work hard.
girt	To be **girt** by something is to be surrounded by it. This is an old-fashioned word.
strain	As well as having other meanings, a **strain** can be a tune.
radiant	Something or someone which is **radiant** is beautiful and bright.
renowned	If something or someone is **renowned**, they are very famous.
boundless	Something that is **boundless** is very large. It seems to go on as if it has no end.

Waltzing Matilda

The words to this song were written by a famous Australian poet, AB ('Banjo') Paterson. The words have since been changed a little and you may see the song written in slightly different ways. The music came from an old Scottish song. It was first sung in 1895 and ever since has been a special song for Australians.

Once a jolly swagman camped by a billabong,
Under the shade of a coolibah tree,
And he sang as he watched and waited till his billy boiled.
'Who'll come a-waltzing Matilda with me?'

Chorus:
Waltzing Matilda, Waltzing Matilda,
Who'll come a-waltzing Matilda with me?

Down came a jumbuck to drink at that billabong,
Up jumped the swagman and grabbed him with glee,
And he sang as he shoved that jumbuck in his tucker-bag,
'You'll come a-waltzing Matilda with me.'

Up rode a squatter, mounted on his thoroughbred;
Down came the troopers – one, two, three:
'Whose that jolly jumbuck you've got in your tucker-bag?
You'll come a-waltzing Matilda with me.'

Up jumped the swagman, jumped into the billabong,
'You'll never catch me alive,' said he.
And his ghost may be heard as you pass by that billabong
'Who'll come a-waltzing Matilda with me?'

Some of the Australian words used in this song, such as **billabong**, **billy** and **coolibah**, you will find in this dictionary. But because 'Waltzing Matilda' is about an Australian way of life that now is past, there are several words that are not used very much now, except when we sing this song. Also, as in 'Advance Australia Fair', there are some words that are used mainly in songs and writing.

The most important word for understanding the song is **swagman**. A **swagman** was a man who camped and walked through the Australian bush, carrying everything he owned in a bundle on his shoulders (a **swag**). Here are the meanings of some of the other words:

waltzing Matilda	A **matilda** was a word for a `swag' so **waltzing Matilda** meant `to travel about carrying a swag'.
jolly	Someone who is **jolly** is full of fun. This is a rather old-fashioned word.
jumbuck	A **jumbuck** is a sheep. This is an old-fashioned, informal word.
glee	A feeling of **glee** is a feeling of happiness and delight.
tucker-bag	A **tucker-bag** was a bag used for carrying food.
squatter	A **squatter** was someone in Australia in the 19th century who settled on land to farm, especially to keep sheep, at first without government permission, but later with permission. **Squatters** usually had a lot of land and became rich.
thoroughbred	A **thoroughbred** is a kind of horse of very good quality.
trooper	A **trooper** is a soldier. In Australian history, a **trooper** was also a police officer working on horseback. This is the meaning of **trooper** in this song.

ABORIGINAL LANGUAGES

Many words in this dictionary come from an Aboriginal language. The lists below show you the words in the dictionary that come from each language. The maps show you where the languages are from. These are only some of the many languages spoken by different Aboriginal peoples.

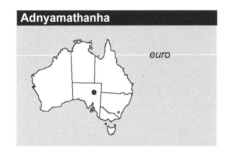

Adnyamathanha

euro

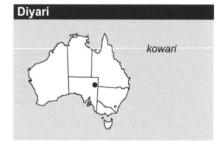

Diyari

kowari

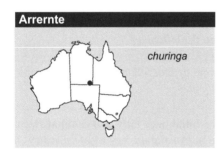

Arrernte

churinga

Guugu Yimidhirr

kangaroo
quoll

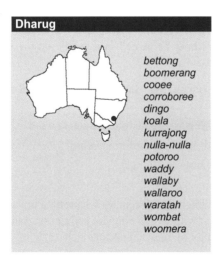

Dharug

bettong
boomerang
cooee
corroboree
dingo
koala
kurrajong
nulla-nulla
potoroo
waddy
wallaby
wallaroo
waratah
wombat
woomera

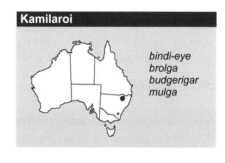

Kamilaroi

bindi-eye
brolga
budgerigar
mulga

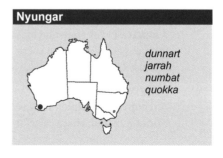

Nyungar

dunnart
jarrah
numbat
quokka

287

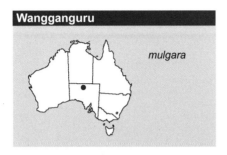

Wangganguru

mulgara

Yagara

dillybag

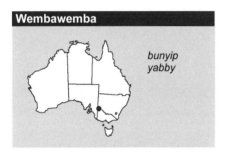

Wembawemba

bunyip
yabby

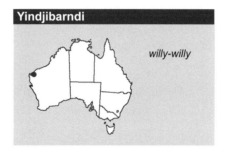

Yindjibarndi

willy-willy

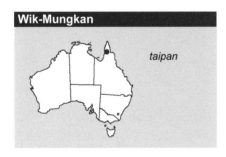

Wik-Mungkan

taipan

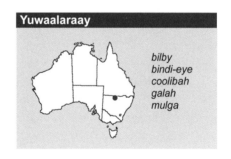

Yuwaalaraay

bilby
bindi-eye
coolibah
galah
mulga

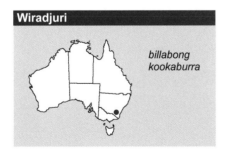

Wiradjuri

billabong
kookaburra

THEME LISTS

You will find these words in the dictionary. Use them when you are doing work on these subjects, or doing a piece of writing.

Australian animals

bandicoot	goanna	possum
bettong	joey	potoroo
bilby	kangaroo	quokka
blue-tongue	koala	quoll
crocodile	kowari	taipan
dingo	marsupial	Tasmanian devil
dunnart	monotreme	wallaby
echidna	mulgara	wallaroo
euro	numbat	wombat
glider	platypus	yabby

Australian birds

brolga	galah	magpie
budgerigar	jabiru	parrot
cockatiel	kookaburra	rosella
cockatoo	lorikeet	
emu	lyrebird	

Australian plants

banksia	eucalypt	mulga
bindi-eye	gum tree	waratah
bottlebrush	jarrah	wattle
coolibah	kurrajong	

Our world – the environment

air pollution	fog	rainbow
atmosphere	forest	rainforest
avalanche	fossil fuel	reef
beach	glacier	river
billabong	greenhouse effect	rock
boulder	ground	sand
breeze	gully	sea
bush	hail	season
bushfire	harbour	shore
canyon	hill	sky
channel	lagoon	snow
climate	lake	soil
climate change	land	stone
cloud	lava	storm
coast	lightning	stream
crater	mirage	sun
creek	mist	surf
current	mountain	tide
cyclone	mud	tsunami
desert	nature	valley
dew	ocean	volcano
drought	ozone layer	water
earthquake	plain	wave
ecosystem	pollute	weather
environment	pond	wetland
erosion	pool	willy-willy
flood	rain	wind

The human body

abdomen	foot	nostril
ankle	hair	shoulder
appendix	head	skeleton
arm	heart	skin
artery	heel	sole
back	hip	spine
blood	jaw	stomach
bone	knee	thigh
brain	knuckle	throat
calf	lap	toe
cheek	leg	tongue
chest	lip	tonsil
chin	lung	tooth
ear	mouth	vein
elbow	muscle	waist
eye	nail	wrist
face	neck	
finger	nose	

COLLECTIVE NOUNS

A collective noun is a word for a group or collection of similar things. Here is a list of collective nouns for some animals, birds, insects, reptiles and fish.

ants	**colony**
bats	**colony**
bears	**sloth**
bees	**hive; swarm**
cattle	**herd; drove** (when being driven)
crows	**murder**
cubs	**litter**
deer	**brace** (two); **leash** (three)
dogs	**brace** (two); **leash** (three); **pack**
dolphins	**herd; pod; school**
elephants	**herd**
fish	**school; shoal**
geese	**gaggle** (on the ground); **skein** (in flight)
gorillas	**band**
hens	**brood**
jellyfish	**smack**
kangaroos	**flock; mob; troop**
leopards	**leap**
lions	**pride**
monkeys	**troop**
owls	**parliament**
penguins	**colony**
sheep	**flock**
snakes	**bed**
sparrows	**host**
toads	**knot**
turkeys	**rafter**
vipers	**nest**
whales	**gam; herd; plump; pod**
wolves	**pack**

SHAPES

Flat shapes

square

rectangle

triangle

quadrilateral

pentagon

hexagon

heptagon

octagon

diamond

circle

semi-circle

oval

Solid shapes

cube

pyramid

sphere

hemisphere

prism

cylinder

cone

NUMBERS AND MEASUREMENTS

Numbers

How many

1	one
2	two
3	three
4	four
5	five
6	six
7	seven
8	eight
9	nine
10	ten
11	eleven
12	twelve
13	thirteen
14	fourteen
15	fifteen
16	sixteen
17	seventeen
18	eighteen
19	nineteen
20	twenty
30	thirty
40	forty
50	fifty
60	sixty
70	seventy
80	eighty
90	ninety
100	hundred
1000	thousand
1 000 000	million

In what order

1st	first
2nd	second
3rd	third
4th	fourth
5th	fifth
6th	sixth
7th	seventh
8th	eighth
9th	ninth
10th	tenth
11th	eleventh
12th	twelfth
13th	thirteenth
14th	fourteenth
15th	fifteenth
16th	sixteenth
17th	seventeenth
18th	eighteenth
19th	nineteenth
20th	twentieth
30th	thirtieth
40th	fortieth
50th	fiftieth
60th	sixtieth
70th	seventieth
80th	eightieth
90th	ninetieth
100th	hundredth
1000th	thousandth

Measurements

Length

1 millimetre (mm)

1 centimetre (cm) = 10 mm

1 metre (m) = 100 cm

1 kilometre (km) = 1000 m

Area

1 square metre

1 are = 100 square metres

1 hectare = 100 ares

1 square kilometre = 100 hectares

Mass

1 milligram (mg)

1 gram (g) = 1000 mg

1 kilogram (kg) = 1000 g

1 tonne (metric ton) = 1000 kg

Capacity

1 millilitre (mL or ml)

1 litre (L or l) = 1000 mL

1 kilolitre (kL) = 1000 L